T0190321

Communications in Computer and Information Science 1677

More information about this series at https://link.springer.com/bookseries/7899

Mohamed Hamlich · Ladjel Bellatreche ·
Ali Siadat · Sebastian Ventura (Eds.)

Smart Applications and Data Analysis

4th International Conference, SADASC 2022
Marrakesh, Morocco, September 22–24, 2022
Proceedings

Springer

Editors
Mohamed Hamlich ⓘ
University of Hassan II Casablanca
Casablanca, Morocco

Ladjel Bellatreche ⓘ
ISAE-ENSMA
Poitiers, France

Ali Siadat ⓘ
Arts et Metiers Institute of Technology
Paris, France

Sebastian Ventura ⓘ
University of Cordoba
Cordoba, Spain

ISSN 1865-0929   ISSN 1865-0937 (electronic)
Communications in Computer and Information Science
ISBN 978-3-031-20489-0   ISBN 978-3-031-20490-6 (eBook)
https://doi.org/10.1007/978-3-031-20490-6

This Springer imprint is published by the registered company Springer Nature Switzerland AG
The registered company address is: Gewerbestrasse 11, 6330 Cham, Switzerland

Preface

With a track record of four editions, the International Conference on Smart Applications and Data Analysis for Smart Cyber-Physical Systems (SADASC) has established itself as a high-quality forum for researchers, practitioners, and developers in the field of Cyber-Physical Systems. SADASC topics cover the different layers of the life cycle of designing data-enabled systems/applications: the source layer, network layer, data layer, learning layer, and reporting layers. This year's conference (SADASC 2022) built on this tradition, facilitating the interdisciplinary exchange of ideas, theory, techniques, experiences, and future research directions, and promoting African researchers.

Our call for papers attracted 64 papers, from which the international Program Committee finally selected 24 full papers and 11 short papers, yielding an acceptance rate of 37%. Each paper was reviewed by an average of three reviewers and in some cases up to four. Accepted papers cover a number of broad research areas on both theoretical and practical aspects. Some trends found in accepted papers include the following: Internet of Things, Industry 4.0, smart monitoring, AI-driven systems, networking, and green infrastructures.

For this edition of SADASC, we had three keynote talks by experts from Australia and Spain. The first keynote talk was given by Fadi Dornaika, from UPV/EHU, San Sebastian, Spain, on "Graph-based neural networks (GNN)". The second one was given by Athman Bouguettaya, from the University of Sydney, Australia, on "Drone-Based Service Delivery in Skyway Networks". The third one was delivered by Michael Sheng, from Macquarie University, Australia, on "Bringing Order to the Internet of Things: A Search Engine Perspective".

We would like to thank all authors for submitting their papers to SADASC 2022 and we hope they submit again in the future. In addition, we express our gratitude to all the Program Committee members who provided high-quality reviews. We want to acknowledge the ease of use and flexibility of the EasyChair system to manage papers. Finally, we would like to thank the support of the local organizers.

For conference attendants, we hope they enjoyed the technical program, informal meetings, and interaction with colleagues from all over the world. For readers of these proceedings, we hope these papers are interesting and they give you ideas for future research.

Mohamed Hamlich
Ladjel Bellatreche
Ali Siadat
Sebastian Ventura

Organization

General Chair

Mohamed Hamlich   Hassan II University of Casablanca, Morocco

Program Committee Chairs

Ladjel Bellatreche   ISAE-ENSMA, France
Ali Siadat   ENSAM-LCFC, France
Sebastián Ventura Soto   University of Cordoba, Spain

Program Committee

El Hassan Abdelwahed	Cadi Ayyad University, Morocco
Mustapha Ahlaqqach	ESITH, Morocco
Abdellah Azmani	Abdelmalek Essaâdi University, Morocco
Hassan Badir	Abdelmalek Essaâdi University, Morocco
Mostafa Baghouri	Hassan II University of Casablanca, Morocco
Khalid Bahani	Hassan II University of Casablanca, Morocco
Ladjel Bellatreche	ISAE-ENSMA, France
Soumia Benkrid	ESI, Algeria
Djamal Benslimane	Lyon 1 University, France
Alami Chaibrassou	Hassan II University of Casablanca, Morocco
Asmae Chakir	EMSI, Morocco
Imane Daoudi	Hassan II University of Casablanca, Morocco
Ibrahim Dellal	Semantic Web Consulting, France
Fadi Dornaika	University of the Basque Country, Spain
Adil El Bouziri	Hassan II University of Casablanca, Morocco
Loubna El Faquih	Mohammed V University, Morocco
Aziz Elafia	Hassan II University of Casablanca, Morocco
Omar Elbeggar	Hassan II University of Casablanca, Morocco
Bachar Elhassan	Lebanese University, Lebanon
Faycal Fedouaki	Université Hassan I, Morocco
Rachida Fissoune	Abdelmalek Essaâdi University, Morocco
Philippe Fournier-Viger	Shenzhen University, China
Dufrenois Franck	ULCO, France
Jeau Paul Gaubert	University of Poitiers, France
Ayad Habib	Hassan II University of Casablanca, Morocco

Keynote Talks

Graph Neural Networks: Principles and Models

Fadi Dornaika[1,2]

[1] University of the Basque Country UPV/EHU, San Sebastian, Spain
[2] IKERBASQUE, Basque Foundation for Science, Bilbao, Spain
fadi.dornaika@ehu.eus

Abstract. Learning with graph data, such as social networks, citation networks, has attracted increasing attention recently. Graph Neural Network (GNN) has become the most important tool for learning representations on graphs. GNNs have proven useful in modeling graph data in many scientific fields. GNN is an extension of the traditional neural network for processing graph data and other structured data. GNN processes data and their graphs together with the main goal of creating a new representation of the data and solving many machine learning problems, including clustering, node classification, graph classification, data representation, and link prediction.

This talk will include an introduction to some principles of GNN. In particular, the Graph Convolution Network (GCN), a widely used type of GNN, will be introduced from both spectral theory and spatial perspectives. Variants of GCNs and GNNs are also presented. Concepts such as graph pooling and graph attacks are briefly introduced.

Drone-Based Service Delivery in Skyway Networks

Athman Bouguettaya

School of Computer Science, The University of Sydney, Australia
athman.bouguettaya@sydney.edu.au

Abstract. Service delivery is set to experience a major paradigm shift with fast advances in drone technologies coupled with higher expectations from customers and increased competition. We focus on developing a novel service framework to effectively provision drone-based delivery services, called Drone-as-a-Service (DaaS), in a skyway network. A skyway network enables the safe and scalable deployment of drone-based delivery solutions in shared airspace. We propose a novel formal definition of a drone service as the delivery of packages between two nodes along a line segment in a skyway network. We use existing infrastructure of a city where each building rooftop may be easily and cheaply fitted with a wireless recharging pad. The objective of our proposed research is to provide fast, cost-effective, and resilient end-to-end single and swarm drone-based delivery solutions under a range of constraints and QoS properties.

Bringing Order to the Internet of Things: A Search Engine Perspective

Quan Z. Sheng

School of Computing, Macquarie University, Sydney, NSW 2109, Australia
michael.sheng@mq.edu.au

Abstract. Since the term first coined in 1999 by Kevin Ashton, the Internet of Things (IoT) has gained significant momentum and is widely regarded as an important technology to change the world in the coming decades [1, 2]. Indeed, IoT will play a critical role to improve productivity, operational effectiveness, decision making, and to identify new business service models for social and economic opportunities. While IoT-based digital strategies and innovations provide industries across the spectrum with exciting capabilities to create a competitive edge and build more value into their services, there are still significant technical gaps in making IoT services a reality, especially on effectively managing large volume of IoT devices and the big data generated from them [3, 4]. In this talk, I will first briefly discuss the IoT-related background and then report my research team's 15-year research and implementation activities on IoT search and discovery [5–7].

References

1. Sheng, Q.Z., Li, X., Zeadally, S.: Enabling next-generation RFID applications: solutions and challenges. Computer **41**(9), 21–28 (2008)
2. Sheng, Q.Z., Qin, Y., Yao, L., Benatallah, B.: Managing the Web of Things: Linking the Real World to the Web. Morgan Kaufmann (2017)
3. Zhang, W.E., et al.: The 10 research topics in the Internet of Things. In: 2020 IEEE 6th International Conference on Collaboration and Internet Computing (CIC 2020), pp. 34–43 (2020)
4. Bouguettaya, A., et al.: An Internet of Things service roadmap. Commun. ACM **64**(9), 86–95 (2021)
5. Tran, N.K., Sheng, Q.Z., Babar, M.A., Yao, L.: Searching the web of things: state of the art, challenges and solutions. ACM Comput. Surv. **50**(4), 55 (2017)
6. Tran, N.K., Sheng, Q.Z., Babar, M.A., Yao, L., Zhang, W.E., Dustdar, S.: Internet of Things search engine. Commun. ACM **62**(7), 66–73 (2019)
7. Yao, L., Sheng, Q.Z., Ngu, A.H.H., Li, X.: Things of interest recommendation by leveraging heterogeneous relations in the Internet of Things. ACM Trans. Internet Technol. **16**(2), 9 (2016)

Contents

Case Studies and Cyber-Physical Systems 3

AI-Driven Methods 1

Detection of COVID-19 in X-Ray Images Using Constrained Multi-view Spectral Clustering

Sally El Hajjar[1], Fadi Dornaika[1,2]($\boxtimes$), and Fahed Abdallah[3,4]

[1] University of the Basque Country UPV/EHU, San Sebastian, Spain
[2] IKERBASQUE, Basque Foundation for Science, Bilbao, Spain
fadi.dornaika@ehu.eus
[3] Lebanese University, Beirut, Lebanon
[4] Urban Development and Mobility Department, Luxembourg Institute
of Socio-Economic Research (LISER), 11 Porte des Sciences,
4366 Esch-sur-Alzette, Luxembourg

Abstract. Machine learning, and specifically classification algorithms, has been widely used for the diagnosis of COVID-19 cases. However, these methods require knowing the labels of the datasets, and use a single view of the dataset. Due to the widespread of the COVID-19 cases, and the presence of the huge amount of patient datasets without knowing their labels, we emphasize in this paper to study, for the first time, the diagnosis of COVID-19 cases in an unsupervised manner. Thus, we can benefit from the abundance of datasets with missing labels. Nowadays, multi-view clustering attracts many interests. Spectral clustering techniques have attracted more attention thanks to a well-developed and solid theoretical framework. One of the major drawbacks of spectral clustering approaches is that they only provide a nonlinear projection of the data, which requires an additional clustering step. Since this post-processing step depends on numerous factors such as the initialization procedure or outliers, this can affect the quality of the final clustering. This paper provides an improved version of a recent method called Multiview Spectral Clustering via integrating Nonnegative Embedding and Spectral Embedding. In addition to keeping the benefits of this method, our proposed model incorporates two types of constraints: (i) a consistent smoothness of the nonnegative embedding across all views, and (ii) an orthogonality constraint over the nonnegative embedding matrix columns. Its advantages are demonstrated using COVIDx datasets. Besides, we test it with other image datasets to prove the right choice of this method in this study.

Keywords: Multi-view clustering · Constrained nonnegative embedding · Similarity graph · Smoothness constraints · Spectral embedding

---

Supported in part by Project PID2021-126701OB-i00 of the Spanish Ministry of Science and Innovation and by Lebanese University.

1   Introduction

Due to COVID-19 spread around the world, and the large use of the RT-PCR test which is not precise especially at the initial appearance of the disease, it is imperative to run machine learning algorithms on X-ray images, in order to detect and diagnose the COVID-19 cases. Nowadays, the field of machine learning witnesses many advances, making the task of handling the datasets easier. As opposed to the RT-PCR test, the result given by the use of these images is more precise. Clustering is an important research area for dividing data into several categories, called clusters. The type of datasets and their structure have a significant impact on how well a clustering approach works. Therefore, it is crucial to find the best strategy to cluster a given dataset. Different views of the data can provide more information about the cluster distribution, leading to more meaningful clustering results. These views should be merged using a method that reduces the dissimilarity between them and shows their similarities. In recent years, many methods have been proposed for clustering with multiple views. Spectral clustering algorithms [8,9,25] are one of the most widely used clustering algorithms. These methods follow a three step procedure: (1) creating a similarity matrix between the data points; (2) computing a spectral projection matrix; (3) generating the clustering result using any extra method such as k-means, k-medoids or spectral rotation. It is worth noting that this last step has several limitations, as they depend on the initialization phase and the presence of noise and outliers. Subspace clustering algorithms [11,24,29] are used to develop a consistent graph from numerous views in the common subspace of the data to cluster them using the spectral clustering approaches. By projecting the data into a space where they are linearly separable, Multiple Kernels algorithms [6,19] are used to overcome the arbitrary shapes of clusters. The use of numerous kernels helps in selecting the best kernel for each view. Matrix factorization algorithms [3,10] are widely used to reduce the number of features and have lower computational cost compared to other approaches, but cannot handle nonlinear data.

   In this paper, a novel approach inspired by the method "Multi-view spectral clustering via integrating nonnegative embedding and spectral embedding" (NESE) in [4] was developed to address some of the shortcomings of the previous methods. This method is called one-step multi-view spectral clustering by learning Constrained Nonnegative Embedding (OCNE). This current approach retains the advantages of the NESE technique, in particular the simultaneous construction of non-negative and spectral projection matrices, which allows direct clustering results without the need for an extra step such as k-means or the use of additional parameters. Moreover, our approach imposes two types of constraints on the non-negative embedding matrix: the first is based on the smoothness of the cluster indices over the graphs, while the second is based on the orthogonality of the columns of the non-negative embedding matrix (cluster labels), which supports the separation of clusters. An efficient optimization framework is provided to optimize the given criterion. Furthermore, this method is tested on the COVIDx dataset, which is gathered from many public datasets. It consists of images of chest X-Rays formed by three classes and three views (each image has three types of deep features). The problem of diagnosing a specific disease is in general a supervised problem. However, collecting enough COVID-19 data with labels in real-world applications is expensive and time-consuming. Furthermore, learning with several views (also known as multi-view learning) is not investigated in such topics. Multi-view learning technology, can fully understand the effective aspects of many views and enhance data prediction performance. Combining different views of data is further motivated by the fact that different views have varying degrees of significance and prior information. As a result, multi-view COVIDx dataset and unsupervised learning models are implemented for the diagnosis of COVID-19. Although unsupervised clustering is a class agnostic classifier, the obtained clusters can be easily associated with a real label.

Figure 1 shows examples of lung X-Rays images with their corresponding labels.

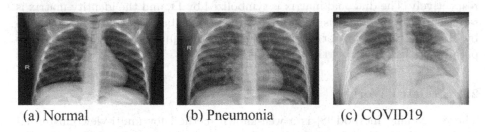

(a) Normal   (b) Pneumonia   (c) COVID19

Fig. 1. Lung X-Rays images for the three mentioned classes: Normal, Pneumonia and COVID-19.

The following is a summary of the main contributions of the paper.

1. The proposed approach retains the advantages of both graph-based and matrix factorization-based approaches.
2. Our technique includes a smoothing term for cluster indices as well as an orthogonality constraint for the nonnegative embedding matrix. The constrained nonnegative embedding matrix can lead to better clustering results than the approach NESE.
3. This is the first work where multi-view clustering algorithms are used to detect the COVID-19 cases.
4. In addition, to justify the choice of the multi-view clustering algorithm applied on this dataset, we tested it also on other datasets to prove its efficiency.

The rest of this paper is organized as follows. Section 2 presents some relevant work on multi-view clustering and reviews the approach NESE of [4]. The proposed approach and the corresponding optimization scheme are described in detail in Sect. 3. Experimental results are presented in Sect. 4 along with a comparison of our method with several state-of-the-art methods. The paper concludes with Sect. 5.

2 Related Work

2.1 Notations

In this study, matrices are shown in bold and upper case, while vectors are shown in bold and lower case. Denote by $\mathbf{X}^{(v)}$ the data matrix of view v, with $v = 1, ..., V$. $\mathbf{X}^{(v)}$ is equal to $(\mathbf{x}_1^{(v)}, \mathbf{x}_2^{(v)}, ..., \mathbf{x}_n^{(v)}) \in \mathbb{R}^{n \times d^{(v)}}$ where n is the total number of samples and d_v is the dimensionality of the data in each view v. Our goal is to cluster the data into K clusters. Moreover, $\mathbf{x}_i^{(v)}$ is the ith sample of the matrix $\mathbf{X}^{(v)}$. The trace of a matrix $\mathbf{M}$ is defined by $Tr(\mathbf{M})$, while the transpose is represented by $\mathbf{M}^T$. M_{ij} is the element of the i-th row and j-th column of the matrix $\mathbf{M}$. The Frobenius norm of this matrix is denoted as $\|\mathbf{M}\|_2$, and the l_2-norm of a vector $\mathbf{m}$ can be given by $\|\mathbf{m}\|_2$. The main matrices used in our work are: 1) The similarity matrix of each view represented by $\mathbf{S}_v$, the corresponding spectral projection matrix and the Laplacian matrix are defined by $\mathbf{P}_v$ and $\mathbf{L}_v$, respectively. The diagonal matrix is symbolized by $\mathbf{D}$, and the identity matrix is represented by $\mathbf{I}$. The cluster index matrix (non-embedding matrix) is denoted by $\mathbf{H}$. $\mathbf{1}$ is a column vector where all elements are equal to one, and the balance parameters used in the article are α and λ.

2.2 Related Work

The co-training method [8] is a well-known method for multi-view clustering. In this method, the same instance is clustered over multiple views by using the clustering result of the first view to modify the affinity matrix of the second view to make it similar to that of the first. Co-regularized spectral clustering [9], which adaptively mixes numerous similarity matrices from different views to obtain more accurate results, is another well-known method.

Another type of multiview clustering methods that takes into account the influence of each view by assigning a weight to each view is presented in [25,26]. Although these methods include a practical solution by providing a common framework for combining different graphs, this is done at the cost of additional weighting factors for each view. To address this weakness, we incorporate automatic weight learning that eliminates the need for hyperparameters, as in other approaches such as those in [5,14,15,20,38].

Recently, spectral clustering has been used for clustering in multiple views [7,21,30]. Spectral-based approaches are based on creating the similarity matrix over all views and then create the spectral projection matrix with K connected components from V graphs. The authors in [16] proposed a method called "Adaptively Weighted Procrustes" (AWP), which is a version of spectral-based clustering and uses spectral rotation to learn the cluster indicator matrix. Compared to previous graph-based approaches, this method has low computational cost and good precision. The authors proposed a Multi-View Subspace based clustering algorithm in [11,24,29] (MVSC). These approaches are used to create the most coherent representation matrix of the data.

In [12], the authors presented a Multi-view Learning with Adaptive Neighbors algorithm (MLAN) that can simultaneously learn the graph structure and perform the clustering step. Due to the matrix inversion and eigenvalue decomposition step, the main drawback of these methods is the high computational cost. By using two weighting systems, one for each view and the other for the features in each view, the study in [27] selects both the best view and the most useful features of each view based on the idea that feature selection can increase clustering quality. When the data is characterized by high dimensional features and its dimensionality needs to be reduced to achieve higher performance, this algorithm performs feature selection and multiview clustering simultaneously.

The method described in [22] can simultaneously learn three tasks: 1) the similarity matrix, 2) the unified graph matrix, and 3) the final clustering assignment using a new multiview fusion method that automatically assigns a weight to the graph of each view to obtain the unified graph matrix. This method enforces a rank constraint on the Laplacian matrix to obtain exactly K clusters. The authors of [7] have created a coherent framework for a multiview spectral clustering approach that can simultaneously provide the different learned graphs from each view, the unified fused graph, and the spectral clustering matrix. In addition, two automatically weighted clustering algorithms for multiple views are described in [5].

Recently, a method called Dual Shared-Specific Multi -view Subspace Clustering method (DSS-MSC) was presented in the work of [32]. This method uses a dual learning model to jointly explore the features of each view in the low-dimensional space, in order to exploit the meaningful and precise information of each view as well as the relationships between the shared information of different views. The authors in [18] propose a novel idea for learning a unified consistent graph by jointly computing the self-expressive coefficients and affinity matrix of different kernels. On the resulting graph, they perform the final clustering.

Two surveys on multiview clustering are given by [1,28]. They cover a wide range of multiview clustering methods, including both generative and discriminative methods.

2.3   Review of the (NESE) Method

The "Nonnegative Embedding and Spectral Embedding method" (NESE) is intoduced in [4]. By simultaneously identifying the nonnegative embedding and spectral embedding matrices, this method can provide the clustering result without the necessity for any extra-step for clustering or the need of additional parameters. The authors introduced a novel objective function in [4] to compute a coherent non-negative embedding matrix $\mathbf{H}$, which was motivated by the symmetric nonnegative matrix factorization and the relaxed continuous Ncut. NESE's primary goal is to:

$$\min_{\mathbf{H},\,\mathbf{P}_v} \sum_{v=1}^{V} \|\mathbf{S}_v - \mathbf{H}\mathbf{P}_v^T\|_2 s.t.\ \ \mathbf{H} \geq 0,\ \ \mathbf{P}_v^T \mathbf{P}_v = \mathbf{I}, \tag{1}$$

where $\mathbf{S}_v$ is the similarity matrix of the corresponding view v, $\mathbf{P}_v$ is the spectral projection matrix, and $\mathbf{H}$ is the coherent nonnegative embedding used as cluster membership matrix (each row corresponds to a sample). This matrix avoids the use of extra-parameters or extra-step to get the clustering assignment. The extra-step, like k-means for example, may be substantially influenced by the initialization.

The authors use an iterative optimization approach, to calculate the output of their approach which are: the spectral projection matrices and the unified nonnegative embedding matrix.

3   Proposed Approach

In this article, we introduce a novel approach, which is an improvement of the NESE method. This method is named "One-step multi-view spectral clustering by learning Constrained Nonnegative Embedding" (OCNE). Our proposed technique adds a constraint to the nonnegative embedding matrix $\mathbf{H}$ in order to improve clustering quality. The main difference between our method and the NESE method is that it adds two constraints on the matrix $\mathbf{H}$: the view-based label-like smoothness constraint and the orthogonality constraint.

Let n denote the total number of samples. Given V views, each view's data can be written as: $\mathbf{X}^{(v)} = (\mathbf{x}_1^{(v)}, \mathbf{x}_2^{(v)}, ..., \mathbf{x}_n^{(v)})$.

As in NESE, given the graph matrices of each view $\mathbf{S}_v \in \mathbb{R}^{n \times n}$ as input of the algorithm, we aim to compute the spectral projection matrix $\mathbf{P}_v \in \mathbb{R}^{n \times K}$ and the coherent nonnegative embedding matrix $\mathbf{H} \in \mathbb{R}^{n \times K}$.

In NESE method (see Eq. (1)), only the nonnegative condition on the matrix $\mathbf{H}$ is imposed. We suggest using a set of additional restrictions on the matrix $\mathbf{H}$ to make the clustering more precise. One of the constraints is to impose the smoothness of the cluster label across all views. This constraint indicates that, if the similarity value between two data points $\mathbf{x}_i^{(v)}$ and $\mathbf{x}_j^{(v)}$ is high, then the vector $\mathbf{H}_{i*}$ should be similar to $\mathbf{H}_{j*}$. Mathematically, this is achieved by minimizing the following term:

$$\frac{1}{2} \sum_i \sum_j \|\mathbf{H}_{i*} - \mathbf{H}_{j*}\|_2^2 \, S_{ij}^{(v)} = Tr\left(\mathbf{H}^T \mathbf{L}_v \mathbf{H}\right), \tag{2}$$

where $\mathbf{L}_v \in \mathbb{R}^{n \times n}$ is the Laplacian matrix of the similarity matrix $\mathbf{S}_v$. $\mathbf{L}_v$ is equal to $\mathbf{D}_v - \mathbf{S}_v$ where $\mathbf{D}_v$ is a diagonal matrix whose i-th diagonal element in the v-th view is given by: $D_{ii}^{(v)} = \sum_{j=1}^{n} \frac{S_{ij}^{(v)} + S_{ji}^{(v)}}{2}$.

The authors of [2] shown that adding an orthogonality restriction on the soft label matrix can enhance semi-supervised classification results. We therefore impose the orthogonality constraints over the columns of the nonnegative embedding matrix $\mathbf{H}$. This can be enforced by minimizing the following term.

$$\|\mathbf{H}^T \mathbf{H} - \mathbf{I}\|_2^2 = Tr\left((\mathbf{H}^T \mathbf{H} - \mathbf{I})^T (\mathbf{H}^T \mathbf{H} - \mathbf{I})\right). \tag{3}$$

Finally, the objective function of the OCNE method, will be :

$$\min_{\mathbf{P}_v, \mathbf{H}} \sum_{v=1}^{V} ||\mathbf{S}_v - \mathbf{H}\mathbf{P}_v^T||_2 + \lambda \sum_{v=1}^{V} \sqrt{Tr\left(\mathbf{H}^T \mathbf{L}_v \mathbf{H}\right)} +$$
$$\alpha Tr\left((\mathbf{H}^T\mathbf{H} - \mathbf{I})^T(\mathbf{H}^T\mathbf{H} - \mathbf{I})\right) \ s.t. \ \mathbf{H} \geq 0, \ \mathbf{P}_v^T\mathbf{P}_v = \mathbf{I}, \tag{4}$$

where λ is a balance parameter, and α is a positive scalar that ensures the orthogonality of the matrix $\mathbf{H}$.

In addition, our method inherits the advantages of some approaches, as in [5,14,15,20], that use an auto-weighted scheme in their objective function, to reduce the number of additional parameters. In our method, two sets of adaptive weights, corresponding to the first and second terms in our objective function (4), are used. The first set of weights is given by:

$$\delta_v = \frac{1}{2 * ||\mathbf{S}_v - \mathbf{H}\mathbf{P}_v^T||_2} \qquad v = 1, ..., V. \tag{5}$$

The second set of weights is given by:

$$w_v = \frac{1}{2 * \sqrt{Tr\left(\mathbf{H}^T \mathbf{L}_v \mathbf{H}\right)}} \qquad v = 1, ..., V. \tag{6}$$

Finally, the minimization problem, corresponding to our method, will be equivalent to minimize the following objective function.

$$\min_{\mathbf{P}_v, \mathbf{H}} \sum_{v=1}^{V} \delta_v ||\mathbf{S}_v - \mathbf{H}\mathbf{P}_v^T||_2^2 + \lambda \sum_{v=1}^{V} w_v Tr\left(\mathbf{H}^T \mathbf{L}_v \mathbf{H}\right) +$$
$$\alpha Tr\left((\mathbf{H}^T\mathbf{H} - \mathbf{I})^T(\mathbf{H}^T\mathbf{H} - \mathbf{I})\right) \ s.t. \ \mathbf{H} \geq 0, \ \mathbf{P}_v^T\mathbf{P}_v = \mathbf{I}. \tag{7}$$

Once $\mathbf{H}$ is estimated, each sample will have the cluster index given by the position of the highest value in the corresponding row in $\mathbf{H}$.

3.1 Optimization

In this section, we describe how to optimize the objective function in (7). To update the matrices $\mathbf{H}$ and $\mathbf{P}_v$, we employ an alternating minimization approach. It means updating one of these two matrices while fixing the other. This technique is repeated until convergence is achieved.

First, we set the parameters λ and α to zero, and solve the resulting minimization problem. The latter is the NESE method. As a result, the matrix $\mathbf{H}$ estimated by NESE constitutes the initial matrix for our optimization. Besides, we utilize the same schemes discussed in [17] to compute the matrices $\mathbf{S}_v$ of each view v, and to initialize $\mathbf{P}_v$.

Update $\mathbf{P}_v$: Fixing $\mathbf{H}$, w_v, and δ_v, the objective function of OCNE will be equivalent to:

$$\min_{\mathbf{P}_v} \sum_{v=1}^{V} \delta_v \, \|\mathbf{S}_v - \mathbf{H}\,\mathbf{P}_v^T\|_2^2 \tag{8}$$

Given that $\mathbf{P}_v^T\mathbf{P}_v = \mathbf{I}$, this problem is the famous orthogonal Procrustes problem, and its solution is get by using the singular value decomposition of $\mathbf{S}_v^T\mathbf{H}$. Let $\mathbf{O}\mathbf{\Sigma}\mathbf{Q}^T = \mathrm{SVD}\,(\mathbf{S}_v^T\mathbf{H})$. The solution of Eq. 8 will be obtained by:

$$\mathbf{P}_v = \mathbf{O}\,\mathbf{Q}^T \quad \text{with} \quad \mathbf{O}\mathbf{\Sigma}\mathbf{Q}^T = SVD\,(\mathbf{S}_v^T\mathbf{H}). \tag{9}$$

Update H: If we fix $\mathbf{P}_v$, w_v, and δ_v, we calculate the derivative of the function in (7) w.r.t. $\mathbf{H}$:

$$\frac{\partial f}{\partial \mathbf{H}} = 2 \sum_{v=1}^{V} \delta_v\,(\mathbf{H} - \mathbf{S}_v\,\mathbf{P}_v) + 2\lambda \sum_{v=1}^{V} w_v\,\mathbf{L}_v\,\mathbf{H} + 4\alpha\,\mathbf{H}\,(\mathbf{H}^T\mathbf{H} - \mathbf{I}).$$

Knowing that any real matrix $\mathbf{T}$ can be written as the difference of two nonnegative matrices, i.e., $\mathbf{T} = \mathbf{T}^+ - \mathbf{T}^-$ where $\mathbf{T}^+ = \frac{1}{2}\,(|\mathbf{T}| + \mathbf{T})$ and $\mathbf{T}^- = \frac{1}{2}\,(|\mathbf{T}| - \mathbf{T})$. Suppose that $\mathbf{N}_v = \mathbf{S}_v\mathbf{P}_v = \mathbf{N}_v^+ - \mathbf{N}_v^-$, and $\mathbf{L}_v = \mathbf{L}_v^+ - \mathbf{L}_v^-$.

After some algebraic manipulations, the gradient matrix will be equivalent to: $\frac{\partial f}{\partial \mathbf{H}} = 2\,(\mathbf{\Delta}^- - \mathbf{\Delta}^+)$ where:

$$\mathbf{\Delta}^- = \sum_{v=1}^{V} \delta_v\,\mathbf{H} + \sum_{v=1}^{V} \delta_v\,\mathbf{N}_v^- + \lambda \sum_{v=1}^{V} w_v\,\mathbf{L}_v^+\,\mathbf{H} + 2\alpha\,\mathbf{H}\mathbf{H}^T\,\mathbf{H}.$$

$$\mathbf{\Delta}^+ = \sum_{v=1}^{V} \delta_v\,\mathbf{N}_v^+ + \lambda \sum_{v=1}^{V} w_v\,\mathbf{L}_v^-\,\mathbf{H} + 2\alpha\,\mathbf{H}.$$

According to the nonnegative embedding matrix $\mathbf{H}$, it is updated by using the gradient descent algorithm. A step is given by:

$$H_{ij} \leftarrow H_{ij} - \mu_{ij}\,\frac{\partial f}{\partial H_{ij}} = H_{ij} - \frac{1}{2\,\Delta_{ij}^-}\,H_{ij} * 2 * (\Delta_{ij}^- - \Delta_{ij}^+)$$

$$= H_{ij} * \frac{\Delta_{ij}^+}{\Delta_{ij}^-}. \tag{10}$$

The learning parameter of the above equation μ_{ij} is set to $\frac{1}{2\,\Delta_{ij}^-}\,H_{ij}$. Therefore, the matrix $\mathbf{H}$ can be updated as follows:

$$H_{ij} \leftarrow H_{ij} * \frac{\Delta_{ij}^+}{\Delta_{ij}^-} \qquad i = 1,....,n; \quad j = 1,...,K. \tag{11}$$

Update w_v and δ_v: The weights are updated using Eqs. 5 and 6, respectively, once all the mentioned matrices have been updated.

The procedure of our OCNE method is summarized in Table 1.

Table 1. Algorithm 1 (OCNE).

Algorithm 1	(OCNE)
Input:	Data samples $\mathbf{X}^{(v)} \in \mathbb{R}^{n \times d_v}, v = 1, ..., V$
	The similarity matrix $\mathbf{S}_v$ for each view
	Parameters α and λ
Output:	The consistent non negative embedding matrix $\mathbf{H}$
	The spectral embedding matrix $\mathbf{P}_v$ for each view
Initialization:	The weights $w_v = \frac{1}{V}$ and $\delta_v = 1$
	Initialize $\mathbf{P}_v$ and $\mathbf{H}$ as mentioned in Sect. 3.1
	Repeat
	Update $\mathbf{P}_v, v = 1, ..., V$ using (9)
	Update $\mathbf{H}$ using (11)
	Update $w_v, v = 1, ..., V$ using (6)
	Update $\delta_v, v = 1, ..., V$ using (5)
	End

4   Performance Evaluation

4.1   Experimental Setup

Four image datasets were used to evaluate the effectiveness of our approach. MSRCV1[1] Caltech101-7[2], MNIST-10000[3], and COVIDx[4]. The MNIST-10000 and COVIDx datasets are relatively large for the graph-based multiview clustering approaches. The COVIDx dataset contains 13892 chest X-ray images divided into three classes, namely: COVID-19, normal and pneumonia. Although this dataset is commonly used for supervised classification, we use it to test the proposed unsupervised method. For each X-ray image, we extract three image descriptors given by three different deep CNNs. These deep descriptors are ResNet50, ResNet101 [37] and DenseNet169 [36], trained on the ImageNet dataset. The dimensions of these descriptors are 2048, 2048 and 1664 respectively.

Our method is compared with the Auto-weighted Multi-View Clustering via Kernelized graph learning (MVCSK) [5], (SC Fused) which is the famous spectral clustering algorithm applied on the average of all views' affinity matrices, Multiview spectral clustering via integrating Non-negative Embedding and Spectral Embedding approach (NESE) [4], Multi-View Spectral Clustering via Sparse graph learning (S-MVSC) [35], and Consistency-aware and Inconsistency-aware Graph-based Multi-View Clustering approach (CI-GMVC) [34].

Two hyper-parameters are used in our optimization procedure: α and λ. The value of α is set to 10^{+6} to enforce the orthogonality constraint (any value

---

[1] https://www.researchgate.net/publication/335857675.
[2] http://www.vision.caltech.edu/ImageDatasets/Caltech101/.
[3] http://yann.lecun.com/exdb/mnist/.
[4] https://github.com/lindawangg/COVID-Net/blob/master/docs/COVIDx.md.

greater or less than 10^{+6} has no significant influence on the result). In our experiments, we vary the value of the parameter λ in the range $[10, 10^{+8}]$. To test the performance of our approach, four evaluation metrics are used, namely clustering accuracy ACC, normalized mutual information (NMI), purity indicator, and adjusted rand index (ARI). The definition of these different metrics can be found in [30]. It is worth noting that the higher the value of these indicators, the better the performance, which means that the resulting clusters are similar to the real clusters.

4.2 Experimental Results

In this section, the evaluation of the experimental results is detailed. The best performances are shown in bold. The standard deviation of the indicator parameters recorded over numerous trials is indicated by the number within parentheses. This only concerns the methods that require an additional clustering step like K-means. Our approach is compared to the state-of-the-art methods: SC Fused, MVCSK, NESE, S-MVSC and CI-GMVC. Besides testing our method on the COVIDx dataset, its performance is also proved by testing other datasets: MSRCv1, Caltech101-7 and MNIST-10000. The obtained results are depicted in Tables 2 and 3. It is clear from Tables 2 and 3 that by applying OCNE, the results are higher than SC Fused, MVCSK, NESE, S-MVSC and CI-GMVC for most of the four datasets. Besides, since the MNIST-10000 and the COVIDx datasets can be considered as large datasets in graph-based clustering, our algorithm achieves higher performance for these datasets which proves the effectiveness of our method on different sizes of the datasets. To the best of our knowledge, our method is the first work that deploys clustering algorithms to detect COVID-19 cases in lung images. Although the obtained clustering on this dataset was far from perfect, the presented techniques paves the way to the use of unsupervised and semi-supervised learning algorithms on this type of data. However, using clustering algorithms in this case is a good opportunity to benefit from datasets with missing labels.

4.3 Convergence Study

Concerning the convergence of OCNE, Fig. 3 illustrates the variation of the objective function versus the number of iterations, for the MSRCv1 dataset. It is clear from this figure that our method converges very fast, even before 10 iterations.

4.4 Parameter Sensitivity

In this section, the sensitivity of the parameter λ is studied. Figure 2 depicts the obtained values of the ACC and NMI indicators by varying the parameter λ from 10 to 10^{+8} for the MSRCv1 dataset. α was fixed to 10^{+6} It is clear from this figure, that the best performance of OCNE are got for a value of the parameter λ equal to 10^{+5}.

Table 2. Clustering performance on the COVIDx dataset.

Dataset	Method	ACC	NMI	Purity	ARI
COVIDx	SC Fused	0.44 (± 0.03)	0.08 (± 0.02)	0.40 (± 0.02)	0.07 (± 0.05)
	MVCSK	0.43 (± 0.05)	0.07 (± 0.03)	0.55 (± 0.02)	0.09 (± 0.03)
	NESE	0.62 (± 0.00)	0.11 (± 0.00)	0.71 (± 0.00)	0.15 (± 0.00)
	S-MVSC	0.57 (± 0.01)	0.11 (± 0.00)	0.57 (± 0.02)	0.15 (± 0.03)
	CI-GMVC	0.63 (± 0.00)	0.10 (± 0.00)	0.63 (± 0.00)	0.08 (± 0.00)
	OCNE	**0.65** (± **0.00**)	**0.12** (± **0.00**)	**0.72** (± **0.00**)	**0.16** (± **0.00**)

Table 3. Clustering performance on the MSRCv1, Caltech101-7 and MNIST-10000 datasets.

Dataset	Method	ACC	NMI	Purity	ARI
MSRCv1	SC Fused	0.77 (± 0.00)	0.70 (± 0.00)	0.79 (± 0.00)	0.61 (± 0.00)
	MVCSK	0.70 (± 0.02)	0.59 (± 0.03)	0.70 (± 0.02)	0.50 (± 0.04)
	NESE	0.77 (± 0.00)	0.72 (± 0.00)	0.80 (± 0.03)	0.64 (± 0.00)
	S-MVSC	0.60 (± 0.00)	0.69 (± 0.02)	0.74 (± 0.02)	**0.79** (± **0.01**)
	CI-GMVC	0.74 (± 0.00)	0.72 (± 0.00)	0.77 (± 0.00)	0.59 (± 0.00)
	OCNE	**0.86** (±**0.00**)	**0.76** (±**0.00**)	**0.86** (± **0.00**)	0.72 (± 0.00)
Caltech101-7	SC Fused	0.53 (± 0.03)	0.45 (± 0.03)	0.60 (± 0.02)	0.40 (± 0.03)
	MVCSK	0.57 (± 0.02)	0.51 (± 0.02)	0.83 (± 0.01)	0.45 (± 0.03)
	NESE	0.67 (± 0.00)	0.55 (± 0.00)	0.87 (± 0.00)	0.52 (± 0.00)
	S-MVSC	0.64 (± 0.03)	0.55 (± 0.02)	0.72 (± 0.01)	0.51 (± 0.03)
	CI-GMVC	**0.74** (± **0.00**)	0.54 (± 0.00)	0.85 (± 0.00)	0.48 (± 0.00)
	OCNE	0.69 (± 0.00)	**0.58** (± **0.00**)	**0.88** (± **0.00**)	**0.56** (± **0.00**)
MNIST -10000	SC Fused	0.20 (± 0.00)	0.13 (± 0.00)	0.20 (± 0.00)	0.05 (± 0.00)
	MVCSK	0.49 (± 0.00)	0.41 (± 0.00)	0.50 (± 0.00)	0.29 (± 0.00)
	NESE	**0.81** (± **0.00**)	**0.83** (+ **0.00**)	0.85 (+ 0.00)	0.76 (+ 0.00)
	S-MVSC	0.77 (± 0.01)	0.81 (+ 0.01)	0.81 (+ 0.02)	0.76 (± 0.07)
	CI-GMVC	0.66 (± 0.00)	0.71 (± 0.00)	0.71 (± 0.00)	0.51 (± 0.00)
	OCNE	**0.81** (± **0.00**)	**0.83** (± **0.00**)	**0.86** (± **0.00**)	**0.78** (± **0.00**)

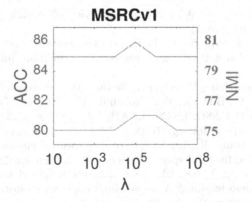

Fig. 2. Clustering performance ACC (%) and NMI (%) as a function of λ on the MSRCv1 dataset.

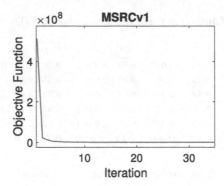

Fig. 3. Convergence of OCNE on the MSRCv1 dataset.

5   Conclusion

We proposed an improved version of Nonnegative Embedding and Spectral Embedding, a recent graph-based clustering approach. We presented a new criterion that uses two restrictions on the nonnegative embedding matrix to achieve better clustering performance. The smoothness of the cluster indices over the graphs is the first constraint, and the orthogonality of the cluster index matrix is the second constraint. The proposed method is used, for the first time, to detect COVID-19 cases. It is also validated by using other datasets with different sizes. Besides, other image datasets such as CT images can be used as additional views for each patient to improve the performance of our method. In addition, we can extend our work to diagnose the disease at an earlier stage, allowing the severity of the disease to be recognized and a treatment program adapted with the case to be implemented.

References

1. Chao, G., Sun, S., Bi, J.: A survey on multi-view clustering. IEEE Trans. Artif. Intell. **2**(2), 146–168 (2021)
2. Dornaika, F., Baradaaji, A., El Traboulsi, Y.: Semi-supervised classification via simultaneous label and discriminant embedding estimation. Inf. Sci. **546**, 146–165 (2021)
3. Greene, D., Cunningham, P.: A matrix factorization approach for integrating multiple data views. In: Buntine, W., Grobelnik, M., Mladenić, D., Shawe-Taylor, J. (eds.) ECML PKDD 2009. LNCS (LNAI), vol. 5781, pp. 423–438. Springer, Heidelberg (2009). https://doi.org/10.1007/978-3-642-04180-8_45
4. Hu, Z., Nie, F., Wang, R., Li, X.: Multi-view spectral clustering via integrating nonnegative embedding and spectral embedding. Inf. Fusion **55**, 251–259 (2020)
5. Huang, S., Kang, Z., Tsang, I.W., Xu, Z., Auto-weighted multi-view clustering via kernelized graph learning: Auto-weighted multi-view clustering via kernelized graph learning. Pattern Recogn. **88**, 174–184 (2019)
6. Kang, Z., Peng, C., Cheng, Q., Kernel-driven similarity learning: Kernel-driven similarity learning. Neurocomputing **267**, 210–219 (2017)

7. Kang, Z., et al.: Multi-graph fusion for multi-view spectral clustering. Knowl.-Based Syst. **189**, 105102 (2020)
8. Kumar, A., Daumé, H.: A co-training approach for multi-view spectral clustering. In: Proceedings of the 28th International Conference on International Conference on Machine Learning, ICML2011, pp. 393–400 Madison, WI, USA (2011)
9. Kumar, A., Rai, P., Daumé, H.: Co-regularized multi-view spectral clustering. In: Proceedings of the 24th International Conference on Neural Information Processing Systems, NIPS2011, pp. 1413–1421 Red Hook, NY, USA (2011)
10. Li, J., Wang, J. Z.: Real-time computerized annotation of pictures. IEEE Trans. pattern Anal. Mach. Intell. **30**(6), 985–1002 (2008)
11. Liu, X., et al.: Late fusion incomplete multi-view clustering. IEEE Trans. Pattern Anal. Mach. Intell. **41**(10), 2410–2423 (2018)
12. Nie, F., Cai, G., Li, J., Li, X.: Auto-weighted multi-view learning for image clustering and semi-supervised classification. IEEE Trans. Image Process. **27**(3), 1501–1511 (2017)
13. Nie, F., Cai, G., Li, X.: Multi-view clustering and semi-supervised classification with adaptive neighbours. In: Thirty-First AAAI Conference on Artificial Intelligence (2017)
14. Nie, F., Li, J., Li, X., et al.: Parameter-free auto-weighted multiple graph learning: a framework for multi-view clustering and semi-supervised classification. In: IJCAI, pp. 1881–1887 (2016)
15. Nie, F., Li, J., Li, X., et al.: Self-weighted multi-view clustering with multiple graphs. In: IJCAI, pp. 2564–2570 (2017)
16. Nie, F., Tian, L., Li, X.: Multiview clustering via adaptively weighted procrustes. In: Proceedings of the 24th ACM SIGKDD International Conference on Knowledge Discovery Data Mining, pp. 2022–2030 (2018)
17. Nie, F., Wang, X., Jordan, M. I., Huang, H.: The constrained Laplacian rank algorithm for graph-based clustering. In: AAAI, pp. 1969–1976 (2016)
18. Ren, Z., Lei, H., Sun, Q., Yang, C.: Simultaneous learning coefficient matrix and affinity graph for multiple kernel clustering. Inf. Sci. **547**, 289–306 (2021)
19. Z. Ren, H. Li, C. Yang, and Q. Sun.: Multiple kernel subspace clustering with local structural graph and low-rank consensus kernel learning. Knowl.-Based Syst. **188**, 105040 (2020)
20. Shi, S., Nie, F., Wang, R., Li, X., Auto-weighted multi-view clustering via spectral embedding: Auto-weighted multi-view clustering via spectral embedding. Neurocomputing **399**, 369–379 (2020)
21. Tang, C., et al.: Learning a joint affinity graph for multiview subspace clustering. IEEE Trans. Multimedia **21**(7), 1724–1736 (2018)
22. Wang, H., Yang, Y., Liu, B.: GMC: graph-based multi-view clustering. IEEE Trans. Knowl. Data Eng. **32**(6), 1116–1129 (2020)
23. Wang, H., Zong, L., Liu, B., Yang, Y., Zhou, W.: Spectral perturbation meets incomplete multi-view data. In: International Joint Conference on Artificial Intelligence, pp. 3677–3683 (2019)
24. White, M., Zhang, X., Schuurmans, D., Yu, Y.L.: Convex multi-view subspace learning. In: Advances in neural information processing systems, pp. 1673–1681 (2012)
25. Xia, T., Tao, D., Mei, T., Zhang, Y.: Multiview spectral embedding. IEEE Trans. Syst. Man Cybern. Part B (Cybernetics), **40**(6), 1438–1446 (2010)
26. Xu, C., Tao, D., Xu, C.: Multi-view self-paced learning for clustering. In: Proceedings of the 24th International Conference on Artificial Intelligence, IJCAI2015, pp. 3974–3980. AAAI Press (2015)

27. Xu, Y.-M., Wang, C.-D., Lai, J.-H., Weighted multi-view clustering with feature selection: Weighted multi-view clustering with feature selection. Pattern Recogn. **53**, 25–35 (2016)
28. Yang, Y., Wang, H.: Multi-view clustering: a survey. Big Data Min. Analytics **1**(2), 83–107 (2018)
29. Yin, Q., Wu, S., He, R., Wang, L., Multi-view clustering via pairwise sparse subspace representation: Multi-view clustering via pairwise sparse subspace representation. Neurocomputing **156**, 12–21 (2015)
30. Zhan, K., Nie, F., Wang, J., Yang, Y.: Multiview consensus graph clustering. IEEE Trans. Image Process. **28**(3), 1261–1270 (2019)
31. Zhan, K., Zhang, C., Guan, J., Wang, J.: Graph learning for multiview clustering. IEEE Trans. Cybern. **48**(10), 2887–2895 (2017)
32. Zhou, T., Zhang, C., Peng, X., Bhaskar, H., Yang Yang Yang, J., Dual shared-specific multiview subspace clustering: Dual shared-specific multiview subspace clustering. IEEE Trans. Cybern. **50**, 3517–3530 (2020)
33. El Hajjar, S., Dornaika, F., Abdallah, F.: Multi-view spectral clustering via constrained nonnegative embedding. Inf. Fusion **78**(6), 209–217 (2021)
34. Horie, M., Kasai, H.: Consistency-aware and inconsistency-aware graph-based multi-view clustering. In: 2020 28th European Signal Processing Conference, pp. 1472–1476 (2021)
35. Hu, Z., Nie, F., Chang, W., Hao, S., Wang, R., Li, X.: Multi-view spectral clustering via sparse graph learning. Neurocomputing **384**, 1–10 (2020)
36. Huang, G., Liu, Z., Van Der Maaten, L., Weinberger, K.: Densely connected convolutional networks. In: Proceedings Of The IEEE Conference On Computer Vision And Pattern Recognition, pp. 4700–4708 (2017)
37. He, K., Zhang, X., Ren, S. Sun, J.: Deep residual learning for image recognition. In: Proceedings of The IEEE Conference on Computer Vision and Pattern Recognition, pp. 770–778 (2016)
38. El Hajjar, S., Dornaika, F., Abdallah, F.: One-step multi-view spectral clustering with cluster label correlation graph. Inf. Sci. **592**, 97-111 (2022)

Automatic SPECT Image Processing for Parkinson's Disease Early Detection

Jihad Boucherouite$^{(\boxtimes)}$, Abdelilah Jilbab, and Atman Jbari

E2SN, ENSAM, Mohammed V University in Rabat, Rabat, Morocco
jihad_boucherouite@um5.ac.ma,
{abdelilah.jilbab,atman.jbari}@ensam.um5.ac.ma

Abstract. The absence of an effective cure to Parkinson as a neurodegenerative disease calls for early diagnosis and appropriate therapeutic process to provide patients with better quality of treatment. Therefore, to diagnose Parkinson's Disease (PD) at its early stage, clinicians rely on visual observation of dopaminergic deficit in both caudate and putamen in the striatum region of the brain. SPECT images (Single Photon Emission Computed Tomography) are among functional neuroimaging scans that can show putamen and caudate, and hence help visualizing Dopamine deficit. In this work, we developed an automatic SPECT image model to classify patients as Healthy Control (HC) or Early PD, starting from Dicom SPECT images from PPMI (Parkinson's Progression Markers Initiative) database to Machine learning classification. The approach we proposed starts with image processing of SPECT images, then extraction of boundary, radial, Striatal Binding Ratio (SBR) and threshold features, then classification using Support Vector Machine (SVM). To the best of our knowledge, no work in the literature has used this combination of the mentioned features together in the classification model. The use of this combination demonstrates promising results. We used a database of 526 images, with 130 HC and 396 PD. The results of our approach show that the Medium Gaussian SVM has a high performance with an accuracy of 97.3%, sensitivity of 95.3%, and specificity of 98%.

Keywords: Early Parkinson's Disease (PD) · Image processing · Automatic model · Support Vector Machine (SVM) classifier

1   Introduction

Parkinson's Disease is the second most common neurodegenerative disorder after Alzheimer; it is a chronic degenerative neurological disease that affects the central nervous system [4]. Parkinson is a group of movement disorders characterized by tremor, bradykinesia, and rigidity, and it causes loss of dopaminergic in both caudate and putamen in the striatum region of the brain [3]. This disease is most detected by using brain scans such as MRI, fMRI, SPECT, PET, etc. [12]. Particularly, functional neuroimaging scans like PET and SPECT can better detect it at an early stage [2]. Furthermore, the early identification of PD is a hard

M. Hamlich et al. (Eds.): SADASC 2022, CCIS 1677, pp. 17–23, 2022.
https://doi.org/10.1007/978-3-031-20490-6_2

task that can be done only by high medical experts. However, image processing techniques and machine learning algorithms enable clinicians to better diagnose the disease in its early stages and prescribe the right treatment. In this context, Martínez-Murcia et al. [6] implemented a model to classify SPECT scans based on imaging features like Haralick texture features. Later, Bhalchandra et al. [1] calculated the radial and gradient features and used them among the inputs to their classification model. Other studies like Prashanth et al. [8] and Shiiba et al. [11] implemented Striatal Binding Ratios for both caudates and putamines and used sharp features in the classification.

We aim through this work to develop an automatic SPECT image model to diagnose PD in its early stages. This process categories SPECT images whether as PD or HC; it consists of three main stages: image processing, calculation of boundary, radial, and SBR features, and classification of images using SVM classifier and cross-validation technique. The main contributions of this paper are: (1) The combination of boundary and radial features in the same SVM classifier; this combination implies a promising accuracy. (2) The total automaticity of our model which does not require any interference of any kind. (3) The use of threshold as a highly significant feature in data categorization; the threshold value is computed according to the characteristics of each image.

2   Materials and Methods

This research aims to classify early PD patients from the healthy controls. This section presents the data and methods used to carry out this study (Fig. 1).

Parkinson's Progression Markers Initiative (PPMI) [5] database includes PD subjects in early stage of the disease. We used 526 SPECT images from PPMI divided into two groups: PD (396 images) and Healthy Control (130 images).

Pre-processed PPMI images were presented as 3D volume spaces, each volume is characterised by 91 slices, and each slice is 2D image with dimensions of 109x91 pixels. Taking into account the methods of image preprocessing adopted by previous publications in this filed [9,10], the deep analysis of region of interest(ROI), and the recommendation of the Society of Nuclear Medicine (SNM) that emphasizes the use of at least 3 consecutive slices with the highest activity in the target region, we selected the slices with max aggregated surface of ROI in the range [39 - 42]. The challenge is to determine the factors deciding which slice to use for the remainder of the analysis.

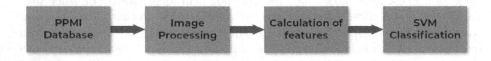

Fig. 1. Stages of the Model

3   Image Processing

We followed several steps for processing SPECT images and extracting their features:

- **Image Enhancement:** In order to remove noise, accentuate ROI and facilitate further image analysis, we converted the slice image from RGB to Gray Scale, then we applied a sharpening mask.
- **Segmentation by Thresholding:** The main challenge in using gray scale images is to determine a threshold to segment the slice and calculate both regional and boundary features. The intention of this research is to investigate a fully automated process from processing SPECT images to the elaboration of an accurate classification model. Thus, finding a suitable threshold should be also an automatic process. To this end, we applied the **Global Thresholding** algorithm.
- **Canny Edge Detection:** Following automatic thresholding and binarization of SPECT Slices using the yielding cutoff, we proceeded to extract shape descriptive features from these slices using Canny Edge Detection method [9] (defacto method used for detecting edges of surface bound objects within images based on changes of intensity levels between pixels).

4   Calculation of Features

Calculation of features is essential to accurately categorize early PD from HC. The calculated boundary features of both right and left of striatum are: area left, area right, circularity left, circularity right, major axis length left, major axis length right, equivalent diameter left, equivalent diameter right, perimeter left and perimeter right.

We also extracted a radial feature vector [13]. Radial measures are defined as the distance from the centroid to 8 peripheral points of striatum boundary. The latter points correspond to intersection of lines drawn at $45°$ angular interval starting from right as $0°$, rotating clockwise from $0°$ to $360°$, so as Rad1 corresponds to the distance to pixel at angle $45°$, Rad2 pixel at angle $90°$, and so on.

The final feature used is Striatal Binding Ratio (SBR), it is the count density measure for the four striatal regions - Caudate Left and Right, Putamen Left and Right - in reference to the occipital cortex. These values are extracted by PPMI SPECT Lab team using standardized volume of interest template.

5   Results and Discussion

Figure 2 describes the results of image processing applied to a Healthy control ((a) and (b)) and an early Parkinson's disease ((c) and (d)). We observe that the global threshold gives a high statistically significant (p-value < 0.01) in categorizing an early PD from Healthy control. It also presents a standard deviation

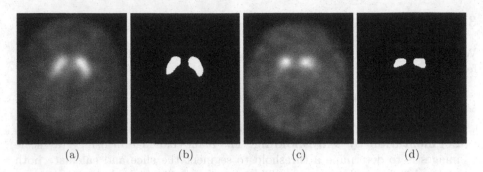

(a)   (b)   (c)   (d)

Fig. 2. Image processing result for a healthy patient (a) and (b) and PD patient (c) and (d)

(0.79 +/- 0.04 for PD and 0.71 +/- 0.12 for HC), which means that the dataset are clustered around the mean of threshold.

We observe that all boundary features (area, circularity, perimeter, major axis lengh and equivalent diameter) and radial features (except rad1 et rad5) are highly statistically significant with (p-value < 0.01), and their values decrease in PD as compared to HC. Table 1 demonstrates an example of the calculated features for Early PD and HC.

Table 1. Example of features values for a Healthy Control and an Early Parkinson's Disease

Features	Early PD	HC	Features	Early PD	HC
Area Left	38	122	Area Right	55	130
Circularity Left	17,41	43,72	Circularity Right	24,84	42,13
Major Axis Length Left	12,46	22,15	Major Axis Length Right	17,67	24,15
Equivalent Diameter Left	6,95	12,46	Equivalent Diameter Right	8,37	12,86
Perimeter Left	34,53	104,38	Perimeter Right	49,38	114,90
Rad1	13,71	19,76	Rad2	13,55	22,85
Rad3	9,96	22,05	Rad4	12,92	12,58
Rad5	13,80	17,24	Rad6	13,33	22,41
Rad7	12,04	27,95	Rad8	12,90	18,18
SBR Left Caudate	2,79	2,26	SBR Right Caudate	2,05	2,11
SBR Left Putamen	1,12	1,58	SBR Right Putamen	0,59	1,15

Concerning the classification model, we used the SVM classifier of Matlab. We adopted a 5-fold cross validation as a technique to validate our model. We divided the dataset into 5 subsets, i.e., folds and in each iteration, a unique fold is used as a validation dataset while the remaining ones are used for the training. Table 2 below shows the results of training different SVM classification models using all features including the threshold feature. We run our model on AMD Rysen processor 74700U with Radeon Graphics (4 CPUs, $\sim$ 2GHz). The accuracy, sensitivity, and specificity values are computed using the following formulas:

$$\text{Sensitivity} = \frac{TP}{TP + FN} \times 100 \tag{1}$$

$$\text{Specificity} = \frac{TN}{TN + FP} \times 100 \tag{2}$$

$$\text{Accuracy} = \frac{Tp + TN}{Tp + TN + FP + FN} \times 100 \tag{3}$$

where TP (True Positives) is the number of PD patients correctly classified, TN (True Negatives) is the number of HC subjects correctly classified , FP (False Positives) is the number of HC classified as PD, and FN (False Negatives) is the number of PD classified as HC.

Table 2. Performance obtained from different SVM classifiers

SVM classifier	Accuracy	Sensitivity	Specificity	AUC
Linear SVM	96,2 %	93 %	97,2 %	0,99
Quadratic SVM	96,2 %	93,7 %	97 %	0,99
Cubic SVM	93,9 %	90,2 %	95 %	0,97
Fine Gaussian SVM	91,1 %	92,8 %	90,7 %	0,98
Medium Gaussian SVM	97,3 %	95,3 %	98 %	0,99
Goarse Gaussian SVM	95,4 %	94,2%	95,8 %	0,99

The results indicate that Medium Gaussian SVM has offered better classification performance with an accuracy of 97.3%, sensitivity of 95.3%, specificity of 98%, and AUC of (Area Under the Curve) 0.99. Those results are significant and cover a large dataset of images (526 images). The process also is fully automatic and challenges related works in the literature.

We achieved better performance than other several works in the literature, namely [8] which reports an accuracy of 97, 29%. In their approach, they manually selected the threshold of segmentation for each patient. In a similar manner, [11] got the help of a radiological technologist to segment images. In contrast, this process is fully automatic in our work. Other existing works resort to other different techniques such as using Convolutional Neural Networks (CNN) and Feedforward Neural Networks (FNN). [14] reported an accuracy of 96, 45% using a FNN while [7] achieved 95, 1% using CNN. Moreover, we attained the above presented results (2) by combining boundary, radial, Striatal Binding Ratio (SBR) and threshold features which no previous works tried this combination as far as we know.

6 Conclusion

In this work, we developed an automatic SPECT image model to diagnose Parkinson's Disease in its early stages. This model consists of two phases: the first one is SPECT image processing and extraction of features, and the second is performing classification using SVM techniques. The two phases are fully automatic and do not need any humain interference. Our results show a promising performance of the proposed approach as we reached an accuracy of 97.3%. As a future work, We look forward to further enhance the segmentation of SPECT images and the extraction of the suitable slices in order to increase the accuracy of our model. We aim also to try other features and explore new ones.

References

1. Bhalchandra, N.A., Prashanth, R., Roy, S.D., Noronha, S.: Early detection of Parkinson's disease through shape based features from [123]i-ioflupane spect imaging. In: 2015 IEEE 12th International Symposium on Biomedical Imaging (ISBI), pp. 963–966 (2015). https://doi.org/10.1109/ISBI.2015.7164031
2. Booij, J.: [123i]fp-cit spect shows a pronounced decline of striatal dopamine transporter labelling in early and advanced parkinson's disease. J. Neurol. Neurosurg. Psychiatry 62(2), 133–140 (1997). https://doi.org/10.1136/jnnp.62.2.133
3. Booth, T.C., Nathan, M., Waldman, A.D., Quigley, A.M., Schapira, A.H., Buscombe, J.: The role of functional dopamine-transporter SPECT imaging in parkinsonian syndromes. Part 1. Am. J. Neuroradiol. 36(2), 229–235 (2014). https://doi.org/10.3174/ajnr.a3970
4. De Lau, L.M., Breteler, M.M.: Epidemiology of parkinson's disease. Lancet Neurol. 5(6), 525–535 (2006). https://doi.org/10.1016/s1474-4422(06)70471-9
5. Marek, K., et al.: The Parkinson progression marker initiative (PPMI). Prog. Neurobiol. 95(4), 629–635 (2011). https://doi.org/10.1016/j.pneurobio.2011.09.005
6. Martinez-Murcia, F.J., Górriz, J.M., Ramírez, J., Moreno-Caballero, M., Gómez-Río, M., Initiative, P.P.M.I.: Parametrization of textural patterns in [123]i-ioflupane imaging for the automatic detection of parkinsonism. Nucl. med. phys. 41, 012502 (2014). https://doi.org/10.1118/1.4845115
7. Ortiz, A., Munilla, J., Martínez-Ibañez, M., Górriz, J., Ramírez, J., Salas-Gonzalez, D.: Parkinson's disease detection using isosurfaces-based features and convolutional neural networks. Front. Neuroinform. 13, 48 (2019). https://doi.org/10.3389/fninf.2019.00048
8. Prashanth, R., Roy, S.D., Mandal, P.K., Ghosh, S.: High-accuracy classification of Parkinson's disease through shape analysis and surface fitting in [123]i-ioflupane spect imaging. IEEE J. Biomed. Health Inform. 21(3), 794–802 (2017). https://doi.org/10.1109/JBHI.2016.2547901
9. Prashanth, R., Roy, S.D., Mandal, P.K., Ghosh, S.: High-accuracy classification of parkinson's disease through shape analysis and surface fitting in 123i-ioflupane spect imaging. IEEE J. Biomed. Health Inform. 21(3), 794–802 (2017). https://doi.org/10.1109/JBHI.2016.2547901

10. Rumman, M., Tasneem, A.N., Farzana, S., Pavel, M.I., Alam, A.M.: Early detection of parkinson's disease using image processing and artificial neural network. In: 2018 Joint 7th International Conference on Informatics, Electronics Vision (ICIEV) and 2018 2nd International Conference on Imaging, Vision Pattern Recognition (icIVPR), pp. 256–261 (2018). https://doi.org/10.1109/ICIEV.2018.8641081
11. Shiiba, T., Arimura, Y., Nagano, M., Takahashi, T., Takaki, A.: Improvement of classification performance of Parkinson's disease using shape features for machine learning on dopamine transporter single photon emission computed tomography. PLoS ONE **15**(1), 1–12 (2020). https://doi.org/10.1371/journal.pone.0228289
12. Skidmore, F., et al.: Reliability analysis of the resting state can sensitively and specifically identify the presence of parkinson disease. NeuroImage **15**(75), 249–261 (2013). https://doi.org/10.1016/j.neuroimage.2011.06.056
13. Towey, D.J., Bain, P.G., Nijran, K.S.: Automatic classification of ^{123}i-fp-cit (datscan) spect images. Nucl. Med. Commun. **32**, 699–707. https://doi.org/10.1097/MNM.0b013e328347cd09
14. Wang, W., Lee, J., Harrou, F., Sun, Y.: Early detection of Parkinson's disease using deep learning and machine learning. IEEE Access **8**, 147635–147646 (2020). https://doi.org/10.1109/access.2020.3016062

Graph Convolution Networks
for Unsupervised Learning

Maria Al Jreidy[1,2]($\boxtimes$), Joseph Constantin[2], Fadi Dornaika[3,4],
and Denis Hamad[1]

[1] LISIC -ULCO, 50 rue Ferdinand Buisson, BP 699, 62228 Calais Cedex, France
[2] LaRRIS, Faculty of Sciences, Lebanese University,
Fanar, Jdeidet BP 90656, Lebanon
mariajreidy@hotmail.com
[3] University of the Basque Country UPV/EHU, San Sebastian, Spain
[4] IKERBASQUE, Basque Foundation for Science, Bilbao, Spain

Abstract. In recent years, graph convolution networks (GCN) have
been proposed as semi-supervised learning approaches. In this paper, we
introduce a new objective function to train a GCN in order to adapt it
in unsupervised learning context. More precisely, we propose a loss function composed only of unsupervised terms, the first term is the kernel
k-means objective function used to capture the shared features information between nodes, and the second is a regularization term that imposes
the smoothness of the predicted clusters of the whole data. Thanks to the
proposed objective function, we are able to keep the advantages of the
classical semi-supervised GCN, while using it in an unsupervised way.
Experiments on benchmark datasets show that our proposed unsupervised GCN achieves superior performance compared to state-of-the-art
clustering algorithms.

Keywords: Graph convolution network · Unsupervised learning ·
Kernel k-means · Spectral clustering · Regularization term

1 Introduction

Graphs are powerful forms of describing and modeling complex systems. In recent
years, the problem of graph clustering has been well studied [1–3]. Several methods have been proposed to achieve this goal, some of them rely only on the
structure of the graph in the learning process, [4,5], while others just rely on
data features.

One of the well-known methods in the clustering process is k-means clustering [6,7] where the number of clusters is initially needed to know. k-means
clusters graph by considering node features only. After that, the spectral clustering algorithm [8] was introduced where the graph clustering is done based
on the structure of the graph built from data features. Then, other methods
combining auto-encoders with the clustering algorithm [9,10] were proposed to

M. Hamlich et al. (Eds.): SADASC 2022, CCIS 1677, pp. 24–33, 2022.
https://doi.org/10.1007/978-3-031-20490-6_3

give better solutions with high-dimensional databases. For example, adversarially regularized variational graph autoencoder (ARVGE) [11], that learns node embedding by graph autoencoder and graph variational autoencoder. The spectral embedding network (SENet) [12] where the graph structure and node feature information via higher-order graph convolution are used to train the model with a spectral clustering loss function.

All these methods can be considered as unsupervised methods as they do not impose prior knowledge of the fundamental truth label in their learning phase.

However, there are other graph-based methods which require a small part of their inputs to be labelled, we can mention the Graph Convolution Network (GCN) [13] which has a very important advantage where the structure of the graph and the features of the data are convolved together in order to obtain the final outputs, namely the soft labels. In this sense, a GCN processes nodes in a graph based on their structure as well as their feature similarities. Yet, as said before a GCN usually relies on prior knowledge of some labels that are often not available for multiple databases, as data labeling is a tedious task to perform.

To keep the advantage of the GCN, and to be able to use it with unlabeled data, unsupervised graph clustering using GCN model where proposed. In [14] an unsupervised model for clustering graphs via a joint GCN has been introduced. In [15] a label sampling method was introduced and used before the GCN model. However, these methods are considered complex as they require labelling generation techniques followed by the GCN to use it in an unsupervised way.

In this paper, we propose a new unsupervised learning framework based on GCN only. The main contribution of our work is as follows: Without any prior knowledge of node labels, we propose a GCN model trained with the kernel k-means objective function where the kernel matrix K represents the data features, integrated with a regularization term reflecting the graph structure. In other words, our proposed loss has two clustering-friendly terms. In this case, if two nodes share a larger proportion of neighbors and features, they have a higher probability of belonging to the same cluster. Therefore, both network topology and data features are considered during model training to obtain consistent clustering.

The rest of this paper is organized as following. In Sect. 2, we introduce some related work. In Sect. 3, we present some preliminary notations and formulations related to this work. Section 4 gives a detailed description of the proposed method. We present experimental results on various real-world networks to validate the performance of the method proposed in Sect. 5, we also compare our approach with other state-of-the-art algorithms. Finally, in Sect. 6, we give the conclusion.

2   Related Work

Early graph clustering techniques merely grouped nodes based on the graph topology. Such as, DeepWalk [4] and node2vec [16], which produce node sequences using reduced random walks before obtaining node embeddings using the Skip-gram model [17]. Different k-order proximities between nodes are captured by GraRep [18]. Then, models based on autoencoders were created in order to capture the highly nonlinear graph structures [19]. In order to increase the model strength and generalizability, ANE [20], a clustering technique that uses adversarial learning to learn node representations, attempts to regularize the embedding learning process.

The developed node-clustering techniques that use both node properties and graph structure are referred to as the attributed methods. Some techniques employ spectral clustering [8], random walks [21], matrix factorization, and Bayesian models [22] on them to make use of both structure and feature information. Other approaches [23] develop a trade-off distance metric between them.

Graph convolutional network (GCN) is a semi-supervised approach that was recently presented for graph classification problems [13]. GCN-based algorithms help to merge network topology and attribute information, but they depend on a large number of node labels to classify unlabeled nodes, in contrast to most semi-supervised methods that concentrate on maintaining network structure. Sun et al. [24] suggested a network embedding framework for node clustering based on a graph convolutional autoencoder. Additionally, few unsupervised techniques have been recently developed. An unsupervised model for community detection using GCN embedding was proposed by Jin et al. [25]. A spectral embedding network for attributed graph clustering (SENet) was suggested in [12] and uses a spectral clustering loss with GCN to learn node embeddings while also enhancing graph structure. In this work,the GCN model formed with two loss functions commonly used in clustering problems, which manages both data structure and data attributes.

3   Preliminary

The section briefly presents the preliminary knowledge of this work, and the architecture of convolution networks of graphs.

3.1   Weighted Kernel K-Means and Spectral Clustering

Weighted kernel k-means is a k-means clustering algorithm enhanced by the use of a kernel function [26]. The kernel weighted k-means objective function is defined as follows:

$$D(\{\pi_j\}_{j=1}^k) = \sum_{j=1}^k \sum_{v_i \in \pi_j} w(x_i)\|\phi(x_i) - m_j\|^2 \tag{1}$$

with $w(x_i)$ is the weight of data x_i, π_j denote the clusters, k is the number of clusters, ϕ a non-linear function and $m_j = \frac{\sum_{x_i \in \pi_j} w(x_i)\phi(x_i)}{\sum_{x_i \in \pi_j} w(x_i)}$ the i-th cluster center.

According to [26], there is a direct relationship between the trace maximization of the normalized cut in spectral clustering and the kernel k-means problems. Therefore, the objective function represented in (1) can be written as follows:

$$D(\{\pi_j\}_{j=1}^k) = trace(W^{\frac{1}{2}}\phi^T\phi W^{\frac{1}{2}}) - trace(Y^TW^{\frac{1}{2}}\phi^T\phi W^{\frac{1}{2}}Y) \qquad (2)$$

where, W is the diagonal matrix of all the weights. Y is the $N * k$ orthonormal cluster assignment matrix, i.e., $Y^TY = I$.

Considering that $\phi^T\phi$ is simply the kernel matrix K of the data, and $trace(W^{\frac{1}{2}}\phi^T\phi W^{\frac{1}{2}})$ is a constant term, the minimization of the objective function in (2) is equivalent to the minimization of $- trace(Y^TW^{\frac{1}{2}}KW^{\frac{1}{2}}Y)$.

In situations where computing the spectral clustering algorithm is difficult, the weighted-kernel k-means algorithm is particularly useful as an alternative algorithm.

3.2   Graph Convolution Network Overview

A graph is represented by G = (V, E, X) where V is a set of N nodes, and E a set of edges such as an edge (v_i, v_j) is a link connecting the nodes v_i and v_j. $X = [x_1; x_2; ...; x_N]$, $\in R^{N*d}$ is a node feature matrix, where $x_i \in R^d$ denotes a feature vector of node v_i [12]. The structure of a graph G can be represented by two principal matrices: the adjacency matrix $A \in R^{N*N}$ where $a_{ij} = 1$ if there is an edge between nodes v_i, v_j , and $a_{ij} = 0$ otherwise, and the similarity matrix S which is a square matrix of $N * N$ and symmetric ($s_{ij} = s_{ji}$), s_{ij} represents the weight of the edge (v_i, v_j).

The GCN presented in [13] uses a semi-supervised learning approach on data structured in graphs. It handles the challenge of labeling nodes in a network where labels are only known for a limited portion of nodes by estimating labels for unlabeled data, for that it is referred to as semi-supervised learning technique. A GCN model learns hidden layer representations that encode both local graph structure and node characteristics.

The layer-wise propagation rule of the GCN for semi-supervised learning is:

$$H^i = \sigma(\widehat{A}H^{i-1}W^i) \qquad (3)$$

H^i: output matrix of the i-th inner layer of the GCN, $H^i \in R^{N*h_i}$ with h_i the number of features of the inner-layer i. H^{i-1}: the input of the i-th inner layer of the GCN, $H^{i-1} \in R^{N*h_{i-1}}$. For the first layer, H^{i-1} is the features matrix X of the graph. A: indicates the adjacency matrix of the graph. $\widehat{A}$ its normalized matrix calculated as follows: $\widehat{A} = \widehat{D}^{\frac{-1}{2}}(A + I)\widehat{D}^{\frac{-1}{2}}$ where, $D = \sum_i(A + I)_{ij}$, and I the identity matrix. W^i: the weight of the layer i, $W^i \in R^{d_{i-1}*d_i}$. σ is an activation function of internal layers such as rectified linear unit (ReLu) [13].

Then, the Softmax activation function, defined in [13] is applied in order to obtain the predicted label matrix $F \in R^{N*k}$ where k is the number of classes.

The GCN network is usually trained with the cross-entropy loss function which is typically used in classification problems. In Kejani, Dornaika & Talebi

(2020) [27], multiple regularization loss was added to the cross-entropy loss function to give better clustering results. The loss equation then becomes:

$$Loss = -\sum_{i=1}^{l}\sum_{c=1}^{k} y_{ic}\, log(F_{ic}) + \lambda\, trace(F^{T}LF) \tag{4}$$

where y_{ic} represents the true label of the dataset, F_{ic} is the estimated probability of the i-th sample to be in class c. l denotes the total number of labels samples, λ is a hyper-parameter, and L denotes the Laplacian matrix of the graph. The model parameters W^{i} of GCN can be trained by minimizing Eq. (4) with gradient descent.

4   The Proposed Method

Given a graph G(V, E, X), and its adjacency matrix A, our goal is to partition the nodes of this graph into k different clusters using GCN in an unsupervised way.

4.1   Model Architecture

To achieve our goal, we design a three-layer GCN as shown in Fig. 1. We first feed the node feature matrix $X \in R^{N*d}$ into the network, then learn the first propagation layer output $H^{1} \in R^{N*h_{1}}$, and $H^{2} \in R^{N*h_{2}}$ for the second layer by:

$$H^{1} = ReLu(\widehat{A}XW^{1}) \tag{5}$$

$$H^{2} = ReLu(\widehat{A}H^{1}W^{2}) \tag{6}$$

where ReLu() is an activation function, $\widehat{A}$ the normalized adjacency matrix of the graph, $W^{1} \in R^{d*h_{1}}$, and $W^{2} \in R^{h_{1}*h_{2}}$ are the trainable weight matrices of the inner layers and h_{1}, h_{2} the number of features in the hidden layers.

In the output layer H^{3}, we map H^{2} to a k-dimensional space, where k indicates the number of clusters:

$$H^{3} = H^{2}W^{3} \tag{7}$$

$W^{3} \in R^{h_{2}*k}$ is a learnable model parameter matrix. Then, to be able to use the output of the GCN in an unsupervised learning strategy, we perform a cholesky decomposition [12] on $(H^{3})^{T}H^{3}$, i.e. $(H^{3})^{T}H^{3}=Q^{T}Q$, where $Q \in R^{k*k}$ is a lower triangular matrix. Finally, we obtain the orthogonal form of the GCN output which also represents the soft clustering assignment matrix output of the model:

$$H = H^{3}(Q^{-1})^{T} \tag{8}$$

After getting the orthogonalized output, our clustering loss function will be applied to it in order to train the model parameters.

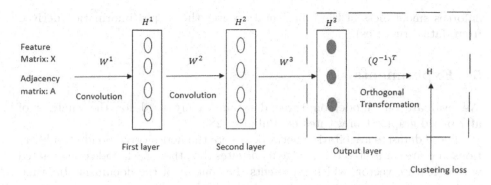

Fig. 1. The model architecture of the graph convolution neural network.

4.2 Model Loss Function and Clustering

As mentioned before, our main goal is to train the GCN in an unsupervised manner, i.e. the training process does not include any prior information about the ground truth labels. To achieve it, we have merged the rectified version of the kernel k-means objective function given by $-trace(Y^T W^{\frac{1}{2}} K W^{\frac{1}{2}} Y)$ with the classic spectral loss that use the graph. IN the rectified version of the kernel k-means loss we replace W by I (Identity matrix) and Y by H the model output. the model output. In this case, our proposed model is trained by minimizing the following loss function:

$$Loss = - \ trace(H^T K H) + \lambda \ trace(H^T L H) \tag{9}$$

where H is the model orthogonalized output, L the Laplacian graph matrix, λ is a hyper-parameter used to balance between the two terms, usely $\lambda \in [0,1]$. K is the kernel matrix, in our case, we choose K the Gaussian kernel matrix given by: $K = exp(\frac{-\|x_i - x_j\|^2}{s^2})$, $x_i, x_j \in X$ and s^2 is equal to the average value of the distance between the data points. Using this loss function, the main advantage is that no prior knowledge is needed to train the parameters of our model. Therefore, our GCN model is an unsupervised model. Moreover, the use of kernel k-means loss function allows us also to acquire the advantages of spectral clustering as already mentioned in paragraph Sect. 3.1. The objective function of spectral clustering and kernel k-means are similar. Furthermore, during the feature propagation phase and the learning phase, the model adapts both the structure and the features of the graph.

The parameters of the model W^1, W^2, W^3 are trained by minimizing equation (9) with gradient descent. After finishing the model training process, we perform k-means on its output H to obtain the partitions of nodes.

With the proposed loss function (9), two interesting and friendly clustering types of constraints are imposed on the unknown representation matrix H: (i) the kernel K-means loss enforces compactness in the space induced by the kernel matrix (information derived from features) and (ii) the spectral clustering term enforces smoothness of the representation over the graph (information derived from data structures).

5 Experiments

We evaluate our model on three datasets widely used for the analysis of attributed graphs: Cora, Citeseer, Pubmed [28].

These datasets are citation networks where the nodes correspond to publications and are connected by an edge if one cites the other. Each node is associated with a feature vector, which represents the content of the document. Informations of these datasets are summarized in Table 1.

Table 1. Datasets Information

Datasets	Nodes	Edges	Features	Clusters
Cora	2708	5429	1433	7
Citeseer	3327	4732	3703	6
Pubmed	19717	44338	500	3

5.1 Baselines

We compare our methods with two different types of baselines:

The first type is methods that use only node features or graph structure: k-means partition nodes using the graph features matrix [7], spectral clustering [8] which takes the adjacency matrix of nodes hence the structure of graph.

The second type is methods adopting both node characteristics and graph structure: such as variational graph autoencoder (ARVGE) [11], and SENet [12] method which improves graph structure by leveraging the information of shared neighbors, and learns node embedding with the help of a spectral clustering loss.

5.2 Evaluation Metrics and Experimental Setups

To assess the clustering performance of our method, we use three performance measures [29]: clustering accuracy (Acc), normalized mutual information (NMI), and adjusted rand index (ARI). Acc is the ratio of correctly predicted data. NMI assesses cluster quality by measuring the match between true and predicted labels. ARI measures the separation ability between clusters and the recognition ability for each cluster.

For our model, we build the network with randomly initialized weights with 16 hidden units and two internal layers as in [12]. We adopt the Adam optimizer [30] with a 0.001 learning rate and run experiments on Pytorch. The λ hyperparameter in the proposed loss function is fixed to 0.5.

5.3   Result Analysis

Tables 2, 3, and 4 show the clustering and standard deviation results obtained after running each method 10 times on each dataset. The best results are in bold. The interpretations are as follows: U-GCN, the algorithm proposed in this paper, outperforms clustering approaches that just use node attributes or graph structure such as k-means and spectral clustering, as it effectively incorporates and captures both kinds of information.

Furthermore, U-GNC improves the results of methods that use the attributes and structure of the graph at the same time, since U-GCN adapts the structure and attributes of the graph in the propagation of features in the model and in the training process not as ARVGE as it only uses them both during the propagation phase. In addition, the use of the weighted kernel k-means objective loss function which is similar to the spectral clustering objective loss function facilitates the transmission of information about the cluster structure at each layer.

Table 2. Clustering results on Cora

Methods	ACC	NMI	ARI
k-means	0.3465 ± 0.0136	0.1673 ± 0.0154	0.0958 ± 0.0107
Spectral	0.3419 ± 0.0203	0.1949 ± 0.0194	0.0181 ± 0.0186
ARVGE [11]	0.6380 ± 0.0096	0.4500 ± 0.0083	0.3740 ± 0.0071
SENet [12]	0.7192 ± 0.0066	0.5508 ± 0.0065	0.4896 ± 0.0109
U-GCN(this paper)	$\mathbf{0.73 \pm 0.00872}$	$\mathbf{0.56 \pm 0.00569}$	$\mathbf{0.495 \pm 0.00859}$

Table 3. Clustering results on Citeseer

Methods	ACC	NMI	ARI
k-means	0.3849 ± 0.0237	0.1702 ± 0.0206	0.1243 ± 0.0192
Spectral	0.2591 ± 0.0109	0.1184 ± 0.0168	0.0012 ± 0.0137
ARVGE [11]	0.5440 ± 0.0139	0.2610 ± 0.0172	0.2450 ± 0.0164
SENet [12]	0.6752 ± 0.0075	$\mathbf{0.417 \pm 0.0082}$	0.4237 ± 0.0097
U-GCN(this paper)	$\mathbf{0.68 \pm 0.00617}$	$\mathbf{0.417 \pm 0.00632}$	$\mathbf{0.43 \pm 0.00859}$

Table 4. Clustering results on Pubmed

Methods	ACC	NMI	ARI
k-means	0.5732 ± 0.0381	0.2912 ± 0.0352	0.2505 ± 0.0346
Spectral	0.3974 ± 0.0267	$0.0346 \pm \pm 0.0309$	0.0018 ± 0.0291
ARVGE [11]	0.5822 ± 0.0100	0.2062 ± 0.0057	0.2045 ± 0.0065
SENet [12]	0.6759 ± 0.0062	0.3061 ± 0.0145	0.2966 ± 0.0113
U-GCN(this paper)	$\mathbf{0.68 \pm 0.00527}$	$\mathbf{0.3105 \pm 0.0102}$	$\mathbf{0.31 \pm 0.0010}$

6   Conclusion

In this work, we proposed an unsupervised method based on GCN for the partitioning problem in graphs without prior knowledge. Inspired by the mechanism of GCN and the relationship between kernel weighted k-means and spectral clustering, we integrated two objective functions to achieve clustering of nodes by merging structural and feature information. The proposed loss function is suitable for training the GCN model when there is no information available on the labels. This approach is also a new solution for clustering graphs in an unsupervised way. The experimental results demonstrate that the proposed method achieves better performance on three citation networks, compared to state-of-the-art algorithms. In future work, we aim to study the effect of changing the trade-off hyper-parameter λ.

References

1. Shah, S.A., Koltun, V.: Deep continuous clustering. arXiv:1803.01449 (2018)
2. Aljalbout, E., Golkov, V., Siddiqui, Y., Strobel M., Cremers D.: Clustering with deep learning: taxonomy and new methods. arXiv:1801.07648 (2018)
3. Wang, X., Li, J., Yang, L., Mi, H.: Unsupervised learning for community detection in attributed networks based on graph convolutional network, Neurocomputing **456**, 147–155 (2021)
4. Perozzi, B., Al-Rfou, R., Skiena, S.: Deepwalk: online learning of social representations. In: Proceedings of the 20th ACM SIGKDD International Conference on Knowledge Discovery and Data Mining (KDD) (2014)
5. Cao, S., Lu, W., Xu, Q.: Deep neural networks for learning graph representations. In: Proceedings of the Thirtieth AAAI Conference on Artificial Intelligence (AAAI) (2016)
6. Moradi Fard, M., Thonet, T.: Gaussier E. Jointly clustering with k-means and learning representations, pattern recognition letters, deep k-means (2020)
7. Gao, B., Yang, Y., Gouk, H., Hospedales, T.M.: Deep Clustering with Concrete k-means. University of Edinburgh, United Kingdom Samsung AI Centre, Cambridge, United Kingdom (2020)
8. von Luxburg, U.: A tutorial on spectral clustering. Stat. Comput. **17**, 395–416 (2007).https://doi.org/10.1007/s11222-007-9033-z
9. Yang, X., Deng, C., Zheng, F., Yan, J., Liu, W.: Deep spectral clustering using dual autoencoder network. In: Proceedings of the IEEE Computer Society Conference on Computer Vision and Pattern Recognition (2019)
10. Affeldt, S., Labiod, L., Nadif, M.: Spectral clustering via ensemble deep autoencoder learning (SC-EDAE). Pattern Recogn. **108**, 107522 (2020)
11. Pan, S., Hu, R., Long, G., Jiang, J., Yao, L., Zhang, C.: Adversarially regularized graph autoencoder for graph embedding. In: Proceedings of the Twenty-Seventh International Joint Conference on Artificial Intelligence (IJCAI) (2018)
12. Zhang, X., Liu, H., Xiao-Ming, W., Zhang, X., Liu, X.: Spectral embedding network for attributed graph clustering. Neural Netw. 142, 388–396 (2021)
13. Kipf, T.N., Welling, M.: Semi-supervised classification with convolutional networks. In: 5th International Conference on Learning Representations (2017)

14. Jin, D., Li, B., Jiao, P., He, D., Shan, H.: Community detection via joint graph convolutional network embedding in attribute network. In: Proceedings of ICANN, pp. 594–606 (2019)
15. Wang, X., Li, J., Yang, L., Mi, H.: Unsupervised learning for community detection in attributed networks based on graph convolutional network. Neurocomputing **456**, 147–155 (2021)
16. Grover, A., Leskovec, J.: Node2vec: scalable feature learning for networks. In: Proceedings of the 22nd ACM SIGKDD International Conference on Knowledge Discovery and Data Mining (KDD), pp. 855–864 (2016)
17. Mikolov, T., Sutskever, I., Chen, K., Corrado, G. S., Dean, J.: Distributed representations of words and phrases and their compositionality. In: Proceedings of 27th Annual Conference on Neural Information Processing Systems (NeurIPS), pp. 3111–3119 (2013)
18. Cao, S., Lu, W., Xu, Q.: Grarep: learning graph representations with global structural information. In: Proceedings of the 2015 ACM on Conference on Information and Knowledge Management (CIKM), pp. 891–900 (2015)
19. Wang, D., Cui, P., Zhu, W.: Structural deep network embedding. In: Proceedings of the 22nd ACM SIGKDD International Conference on Knowledge Discovery and Data Mining (KDD), pp. 1225–1234 (2016)
20. Dai, Q., Li, Q., Tang, J., Wang, D.: Adversarial network embedding. In: Proceedings of the Thirty-Second AAAI Conference on Artificial Intelligence (AAAI), pp. 2167–2174 (2018)
21. Zhou, Y., Cheng, H., Yu, J.X.: Clustering large attributed graphs: an efficient incremental approach. In: Proceedings of the 10th IEEE International Conference on Data Mining, Sydney, Australia (ICDM), pp. 689–698 (2010)
22. Xu, Z., Ke, Y., Wang, Y., Cheng, H., Cheng, J.: A model-based approach to attributed graph clustering. In: Proceedings of the ACM SIGMOD International Conference on Management of Data (SIGMOD), pp. 505–516 (2012)
23. Zhou, Y., Cheng, H., Yu, J.X.: Graph clustering based on structural/attribute similarities. VLDB Endowment **2**(1), 718–729 (2009)
24. Sun, H., He, F., Huang, J., Sun, Y., Li, Y., Wang, C., et al.: Network embedding for community detection in attributed networks. ACM Trans. Knowl. Discov. Data **14**, 1–25 (2020)
25. Jin, D., Li, B., Jiao, P., He, D., Shan, H.: Community detection via joint graph convolutional network embedding in attribute network. In: Proceedings of ICANN, pp. 594–606 (2019)
26. Dhillon, I. S., Guan, Y., Kulis, B: Kernel k-means, spectral clustering and normalized cuts. In: Proceedings of the Tenth ACM SIGKDD International Conference on Knowledge Discovery and Data Mining (2004)
27. Kejani, M.T., Dornaika, F., Talebi, H.: Graph Convolution Networks with manifold regularization for semi-supervised learning. Neural Network **127**, 160–167 (2020)
28. Kipf, T.N., Welling, M.: Variational graph auto-encoders (2016)
29. Aggarwal, C.C., Reddy, C.K.: Data clustering: algorithms and applications. The CRC Press, Boca Raton (2014)
30. Kingma, D. P., Ba, J.: Adam: a method for stochastic optimization. In: Proceedings of the 3rd International Conference on Learning Representations (ICLR) (2015)

Collaborative Kernel Discriminant Analysis for Large Scale Multi Class Problems

Amine Khatib[1,2,3]([✉]), Franck Dufrenois[1], Mohamed Hamlich[2],
and Denis Hamad[1]

[1] Univ. Littoral Cote d'Opale, UR 4491, LISIC, Laboratoire d'Informatique
Signal et Image de la Cote d'Opale, 62100 Calais, France
`amine.khatib@etu.univ-littoral.fr`,
`{franck.dufrenois,denis.hamad}@univ-littoral.fr`
[2] CCPS Laboratory, ENSAM, University of Hassan II, Casablanca, Morocco
`MOHAMED.HAMLICH@univh2c.ma`
[3] Study and Research Center for Engineering and Management(CERIM), HESTIM,
Casablanca, Morocco

Abstract. The use of kernel learning methods in large-scale contexts is
still today rather limited. Indeed in this case, the memory and computing footprint of the kernel matrix can be a constraining factor. Among
these methods, Kernel Discriminant Analysis (KDA) is no exception to
this rule. In this paper, we present a new learning strategy to solve this
issue. Instead of entrusting the entire learning task to a single classifier,
we propose to share it with an ensemble of classifiers with a limited storage capacity. Our contribution relies on several points: firstly, our ensemble learning algorithm is "dynamic", i.e. a new classifier is initialized when
the previous one has an overflow of its rated capacity. Secondly, a compression strategy is proposed after each learning step in order to minimize
the number of classifiers generated during the learning process. based on
the overall classification cost of the network allows to reduce the size of
the kernel matrix build in the last layer. To our knowledge, this strategy
of collaboration between classifiers is new and allows to share the computational and storage burden between several classifiers while insuring the
compression of the kernel matrix. In our study, our network will be based
on the spectral regression kernel discriminant analysis (SRKDA) which is
an efficient multi-class classifier. Extensive experiments on several large-
scale data sets show the effectiveness of the proposed algorithm.

Keywords: Large scale problem · Multi-class learning · KLDA ·
Compression

1 Introduction

Kernel Discriminant Analysis (KDA), a nonlinear extension of the Linear Discriminant Analysis, is a cutting edge method for dimension reduction and class separation. It is used in numerous domains such as speech and music classification [1],

M. Hamlich et al. (Eds.): SADASC 2022, CCIS 1677, pp. 34–50, 2022.
https://doi.org/10.1007/978-3-031-20490-6_4

video classification [2], outlier detection [3], supervised novelty detection [4], etc. Its popularity relies on several points: a consistent criterion for one or multi-class separation, a problem solving based on standard algebraic tools and the possibility to handle complex data by using the kernel trick. If KDA has all the ingredients to be a popular tool of the data mining community, its attractiveness darkens when we have to process large-scale data sets. In big data era, the size and the dimensionality of the data bases grow exponentialy and kernel methods fail to scale up. The main reason is that KDA must maintain in memory a kernel Gram matrix whose the dimension grows with the number of training data and the KDA's solution results from the eigendecomposition of this kernel matrix.

The first attempt to make KDA scalable to large data sets is due to Mika et al. in [5]. Considering that KDA can be also formulated as a convex quadratic optimization problem, they propose a sparse greedy approximation to solve this problem. Although their algorithm improves the KDA's performance, it is limited to solve a two class problem. With the same goal, Cai et al. in [6] show that KDA can be equivalently solved by a set of regularized kernel regression problems. Called Spectral Regression Kernel Discriminant Analysis (SRKDA). Other works propose to accelerate kernel methods by finding a compressed, often low-rank approximation to the kernel matrix. Among low-rank approximation methods, the *Nyström method* is certainly the most popular. The accuracy of this approximation mainly depend on how is selected the landmark points to build the sketch of the kernel Gram matrix. Several sampling strategies such as uniform, random or informed based on leverage scores can be found in the literature. For instance, recently, Musco et al. in [7] proposed a fast algorithm based on recursive leverage score which achieves both accurate approximation of the kernel matrix and efficiency. Leverage scores capture how important an individual data point is in composing the span of the kernel matrix. However, the problem is that you have to fix the number of landmarks at the beginning, and for large scale data sets, we still get large size matrices, and more we learn, harder is to compute them, which can impact the accuracy of the classification. Other strategies introduce a compression mechanism during the learning process to reduce the size of the kernel matrix. For instance, Dufrenois presents in [8] an incremental version of the null KDA so as to deal with large streaming data sets. The principle of the method is to maintain a set of thresholds during the learning in order to identify redundant data in the new data chunk. Redundancy, i.e. data points having similar characteristics (in some sense) that the already processed data, is *measured* by using some properties of the null space of KDA. Consequently, the size of the kernel Gram matrix no longer grows linearly with data but stabilizes since the redundancy of the data increases over time. The compression rate of the proposed method is monitored by an user-defined compression factor. Following the same goal, WonHei et al. propose in [9] an online sketch LDA based on the frequent direction algorithm [10]. The principle of sketch LDA consists in maintaining a low rank sketch matrix of principal components which captures main data variations. However, this method assumes that the data distribution is Gaussian making it potentially inefficient for nonlinear data sets.

Instead of putting all the computational load on a single classifier, another strategy is to share the load between several classifiers. These methods, grouped under the name *ensemble learning*, combine the output of several individual learners or *weak* learners for better predictive performance. They use a simple majority voting, weighted majority voting as combination rules [11,12]. Boosting and Bagging are two major types of ensemble learning that use this combination principle [13]. Boosting ensembles are based on the idea of correcting prediction errors. The models are fit and added to the ensemble sequentially such that the second model attempts to correct the predictions of the first model, the third corrects the second model, and so on [14]. Bagging ensembles is a learning ensemble based on decision trees, each of them fitting on different samples of a dataset [15,16].

In the context of multi-class classification tasks, the error-correcting output coding (ECOC) is an interesting strategy for dealing with this problem by decomposing the original multi-class problem into a series of binary sub-problems. In going from two-class to multi-class classification, most boosting algorithms have been restricted to reducing the multi-class classification problem to multiple binary classification problems for example Friedman et al. who propose a multi class generalization version of Adaboost [17]. In the same context but with other type of methods called Support Vector Machine [18–20], Allwein et al. developed a multi-class extension of the SVM method [21]. We need to clarify that there is two main strategies for reducing the problem of multiclass classification to multiple binary classification problems. It can be categorized into One versus One and One versus All which is the most commonly used strategy. The strategy of one vs all consists in fitting one classifier per class. For each classifier, the class is fitted against all the other classes. In addition to its computational efficiency, one of the advantages of this approach is its ease of interpretation. The One vs One strategy constructs one classifier per pair of classes and the class that received the most votes will be selected. Since it requires fitting $(nb * (nb - 1)/2)$ classifiers with nb is the number of classes. This method is generally slower than One vs All. However, this strategy can be advantageous for the kernel methods because each learning task problem involves only a small subset of data, whereas with One vs All, the entire data set is used [22–24].

We propose in this article a method which covers these two aspects discussed before which are, a compression of the kernel matrix and a combination of classifiers. The goal of this paper is to answer to all these issues by proposing a new compression strategy based on a principle of collaboration between classifiers, this approach is new and different from that of boosting, it allows to share the computational and storage burden between several classifiers while insuring the compression of the kernel matrix. The rest of the article is organised as follows: Sect. 2 presents the general learning framework while Sect. 3 focuses on the properties of the studied classifier. In Sect. 4, we introduce our collaborative kernel discriminant analysis (CKDA) and develop its main properties. Section 5 details the experimental results and Sect. 6 finally concludes the paper.

2   General Learning Framework

Let $\mathcal{X}$ and $\mathcal{Y}$ be the space of pattern or data (typically, $\mathcal{X} = \mathbb{R}^d$) and the space of responses (*regression* problem) or labels (*classification* problem), respectively. The goal of many supervised learning approaches is to learn a function $h : \mathcal{X} \rightarrow \mathcal{Y}$ (often called *hypothesis*) which predicts an output $\hat{y} = h(x)$, given $x \in \mathcal{X}$ with minimum error. To learn h, we consider a training set composed of n instances $(x_1, y_1), (x_2, y_2), ..., (x_n, y_n)$ which are drawn i.i.d from a joint probability distribution $P(x, y)$ over $\mathcal{X}$ and $\mathcal{Y}$. The *risk* associated whith hypothesis $h(x)$ is then defined by

$$\mathcal{R}_n(h) = \mathop{\mathbb{E}}_{(x,y)\sim P}[\mathcal{L}(h(x), y)] \tag{1}$$

where $\mathcal{L}(h(x), y)$ is a non negative loss function which measures the difference between the prediction $\hat{y} = h(x)$ and the true label y. A commonly used loss function is the 0–1 loss function $\mathcal{L}(\hat{y}, y) = \begin{cases} 1 \text{ if } & \hat{y} \neq y \\ 0 \text{ if } & \hat{y} = y \end{cases}$. Then supervised learning amounts to find the hypothesis h^* for which the risk $\mathcal{R}(h)$ is minimal, i.e.

$$h^* = \operatorname*{argmin}_{h \in \mathcal{H}} \mathcal{R}_n(h) \tag{2}$$

Kernel methods are subjected to the same learning framework where most of the time h^* is the result of the inversion of a kernel matrix K or the eigenvalue decomposition of K. When dealing with large scale data sets, the size of K significantly increases involving very rapidly unsurmontable storage and computational efforts. This is the major limit of kernel methods.

In this paper, we present a new alternative to solve this issue. We propose to distribute the computational load between a set of homogeneous classifiers $\{h_1, h_2, ..., h_M\}$ which collaborate in order to minimize the empirical risk. Each classifier will have a limited storage capacity, noticed C. To make it easier to read, consider that it is possible to share the large training data set into MC equal data chunks, the empirical risk can be formulated as the sum of M empirical risks such as

$$\mathcal{R}_n(h_1, h_2, ..., h_M) = \frac{1}{n} \sum_{k=1}^{M} \sum_{i=(k-1)C+1}^{kC} \mathcal{L}(h_k(x_i), y_i)$$

$$= \frac{1}{n} \sum_{k=1}^{M} C\mathcal{R}_C(h_k) \tag{3}$$

Then minimizing $\mathcal{R}_n(h_1, h_2, ..., h_M)$ amounts to minimize each risk independently, i.e. finding the set of classifiers $\{h_1^*, h_2^*, ..., h_M^*\}$ such that

$$h_k^* = \operatorname*{argmin}_{h_k \in \mathcal{H}} \mathcal{R}_C(h_k) \quad k = 1...M \tag{4}$$

Of course, there is no question of building a network of M classifiers where the entire training data will be considered but rather to generate a network that minimizes the number of classifiers by considering a minimal subset of the training data set. Our learning strategy which will be detailed in Sect. 4 consists in generating a set of $\widetilde{M}$ classifiers $(\widetilde{M} < M)$ corresponding to a minimal subset of n_1 $(n_1 \ll n)$ samples *large enough* to satisfy

$$\begin{aligned}
\mathcal{R}_{n_1}(h_1^*, h_2^*, ..., h_{\widetilde{M}}^*) &= 0 \\
\mathcal{R}_{n_2}(h_1^*, h_2^*, ..., h_{\widetilde{M}}^*) &= 0
\end{aligned} \tag{5}$$

where $n_2 = n - n_1$ is the remaining data in the training set and the set of classifiers $\left\{ h_1^*, h_2^*, ..., h_{\widetilde{M}}^* \right\}$ solves independently

$$h_k^* = \underset{h_k \in \mathcal{H}}{\operatorname{argmin}} \, \mathcal{R}_{C_k}(h_k) \quad k = 1...\widetilde{M} \tag{6}$$

with $\sum_{k=1}^{\widetilde{M}} C_k = n_1$ and $C_k \leq C$.

In order to study the compression rate of a given method, we will define the following measure

$$\tau = log(\frac{n}{n_1}) \tag{7}$$

Thus the highest positive value of τ will correspond to a high level of compression while a negative value of τ will mean that the method uses more data than the training data size. This situation may appear when the method is based on data sampling with replacement.

3   Multi-class Kernel Learning

Recently in [6], it has been shown that Kernel Discriminant Analysis can be formulated as $L-1$ regularized regression problems which facilitate both efficient computation and the use of regularization techniques. More formally, consider a training set composed of n instances $((\boldsymbol{x}_1, y_1), (\boldsymbol{x}_2, y_2), ..., (\boldsymbol{x}_n, y_n))$ belonging to L classes and define n_l the number of samples in the $l - th$ class. Moreover, let $k : \mathcal{X} \times \mathcal{X} \to \mathbb{R}$ be a Mercer kernel with φ being the associated feature map, i.e., $k(x, x') = \langle \varphi(x), \varphi(x') \rangle$. From [6], solving KDA amounts to find $L-1$ projective functions $\{f_1, f_2, ..., f_{L-1}\}$ defining a linear combination of the mapped data

$$f_l(\boldsymbol{x}) = \langle \boldsymbol{\alpha}_l, \varphi(\boldsymbol{x}) \rangle = \sum_{i=1}^{n} \alpha_{il} k(\boldsymbol{x}, \boldsymbol{x}_i) \quad \text{for } l = 1...L-1, \tag{8}$$

each of them minimizing the regularized empirical risk, i.e.

$$\underset{f_l \in \mathcal{F}}{min} \sum_{i=1}^{n} \mathcal{L}(f_l(\boldsymbol{x}_i), z_{il}) + \delta \Omega(f_l) \quad \text{for } l = 1...L-1 \tag{9}$$

where z_{il} is the response associated to the data x_i for the $l - th$ projective function, $\mathcal{L}(u, v) = (u - v)^2$ is the standard squared error loss and $\Omega(f_l)$ is the regularization term weighted by a positive constant δ. In our study, we will consider only the L_2-norm regularizer, i.e. $\Omega(f_l) = \alpha_l^\top \alpha_l$. Then, it is easy to show that solving the set of problems (Eq. 9) amounts to find the projective matrix $A = [\alpha_1, \alpha_2, ..., \alpha_{L-1}]$ which is the solution of the linear equations system:

$$(K + \delta I)^{-1} A = Z \tag{10}$$

where $K = [k(x_i, x_j)]_{(i,j)=(1...n)^2}$ is the kernel Gram matrix build from the training data set, I is the identity matrix and $Z = [z_{il}]_{(i,l)=(1..n,1..L-1)}$ is $n \times (L-1)$ matrix of responses associated to the n data samples. Then, KDA can be seen as a multiple regression problem. From [], it can be show that Z corresponds to find $L - 1$ eigenvectors solution of the following eigen-problem

$$WZ = Z\Lambda \tag{11}$$

with Λ is the corresponding matrix of eigenvalues and $W = [w_{ij}]_{(i,j)=(1...n)^2}$ is the class-centering matrix where $w_{ij} = \frac{1}{n_l}$ if x_i and x_j both belongs to the $l - th$ class and $w_{ij} = 0$ otherwise. It is noticed that W has a block-diagonal structure and consequently it can be built from the sum of L outer products, then the rank of W is L or in other words W has exactly L eigenvectors with the same eigenvalue 1. Moreover, it can be shown that the vector of all ones, e is one solution of Eq. 11 and represents the sum of the other $L - 1$ eigenvectors of W. Of course this solution is useless and only the other $L - 1$ eigenvectors are kept.

Now consider a test data (x, y) with y is its true class number and define $\{z_l\}_{l=1...L}$ the set of response vectors associated to the L classes, where $z_l \in \mathbb{R}^{1 \times (L-1)}$. The classification of x will be determinated by the following rule

$$h(x) = \hat{y} = \underset{l=1...L}{argmin} \; \|z(x) - z_l\|^2 \tag{12}$$

where $z(x) = [k(x, x_1), ..., k(x, x_n)]A$ with $A = [\alpha_1, \alpha_2, ..., \alpha_{L-1}]$ is the KDA transformation matrix where each components are obtained from Eq. 10.

4   Collaborative Kernel Discriminant Analysis

The main goal of our collaborative KDA (CKDA) is to build a learning ensemble based on a set of kernel discriminant analysis classifiers which together minimizes the empirical risk. By limiting their storage capacity and combining their outputs, we propose to learn a large-scale training data set which will be computationally expensive for a single classifier, mainly due to the size of the kernel Gram matrix generated by the training data.

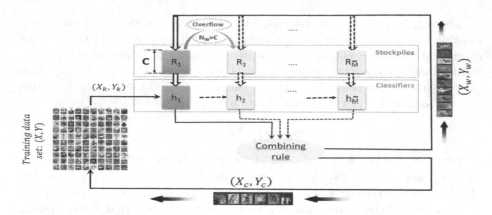

Fig. 1. Collaborative KDA: synoptic

4.1 General Framework

The general principle of our *collaborative* kernel discriminant analysis (CKDA) is illustrated on Fig. 1. Our CKDA consists in building a ensemble of M KDA learners $(h_1, h_2, ..., h_M)$ fed by M stockpiles $(R_1, R_2, ..., R_M)$ of limited storage capacity, noticed C. Each stockpile is used to build the kernel Gram matrix of the corresponding learner. Thus, this learning ensemble collaborates by *combining* their outputs following a given *decision rule* (see Sect. 4.2). The training data set (X, Y) iteratively feeds the learning ensemble by data chunks, noticed (X_k, Y_k) of size n_k and a third-order tensor of scores $\left(\mathbb{R}^{n_k \times L \times M}\right)$ is generated from the learners. Next, the chosen combining rule converts the tensor of scores into a decision vector which classifies each data as *correctly classified data* or *wrongly classified data,* represented by the data matrices X_c and X_w, respectively (see Fig. 1). If X_w is not empty, it is used to update the last generated learner and X_c is replaced at the end of the training data base. One important point of our learning strategy is that a new learner is initialized when the stockpile of the last learner exceeds its storage capacity C (see Sect. 4.3). Thus, by this way the generation of our learning ensemble will be dynamic and its final size will depend on two parameters : the value of C and the complexity of the data. Indeed, if the training data set is composed of classes with high variability, the number of learners will have to be "sufficient" to capture the complexity of each class. We consider that the learning ensemble will have completed one *learning cycle* when the training data set will have been entirely classified. The learning process will stop when the empirical risk will be below a given threshold. All the studied experiments show that the proposed strategy decreases the empirical risk at each learning cycle and finally converges. When the learning stops, the ratio between the remaining training data set and the total size of the stockpiles will provide the compression rate of the learning ensemble.

4.2   The Combining Rules of the Network

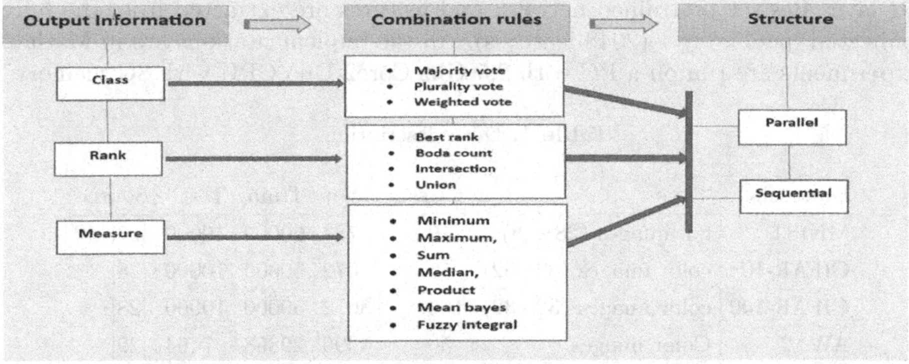

Fig. 2. Combination rules

Figure 2 shows the different types of classifier outputs which are either class, rank or a measure of score, distance, likelihood...etc. it also shows the combination rules for each type and finally the structure of this combination, that mean how classifiers are organized as a network and connected to the process. In our study we have a measure of score as output of classifiers, then we chose a minimum as rule of decision, the other rules will be implemented in the future works.

4.3   Capacity of the Classifiers and Overflow Management

Consider that $C = 2C_m$ where C_m is the minimal capacity of the classifier and let us define $C^{(l)}$, the current capacity associated to the lth class which of course must verify $\lfloor \frac{C_m}{L} \rfloor \leq C^{(l)} \leq \lfloor \frac{C}{L} \rfloor$, where the operator $\lfloor a \rfloor$ denotes the bottom integer part of a. Then, when the capacity of a class exceeds $\lfloor \frac{C}{L} \rfloor$, the corresponding class is no longer supplied and the training of the classifier continues until the capacity of the last class not having reached this threshold reaches it in turn. When it is the case, a new classifier is initialized. The previous classifier shares its final stockpile with the new classifier so that the stockpile of each class is initialized with a least $\lfloor \frac{C_m}{L} \rfloor$ data samples for each classifier. In this way, we maintain a balanced sample size per class in the network.

5   Experimental Evaluation

5.1   Data Sets

In this section we study the efficiency of the proposed method on several large scale training data sets: MNIST, CIFAR-10, CIFAR-100 and AWA2. Table 1 summarizes the main features of these data sets. Moreover, images from all data sets have been preprocessed. For MNIST, we use the image pixels as features. Features are normalized in $[0, 1]$. For CIFAR-10, CIFAR-100 and AWA2, we follow the experimental setup used in the literature [25, 26]. We extract learned image features from a pretrained convolutional neural network and use those features to train the studied classifiers. In this experiment, we choose the deep 101-layer ResNet pretrained network and features are extracted from the fully connected 'pool5' layer (2048 features). All the implementations are in Matlab. Experiments are run on a PC with 2.5 Ghz Core2 Duo CPU with 8G memory.

Table 1. Data description

Data sets	Types	Classes	Dim	Train	Test	Source
MNIST	g.l. images (28×28)	10	784	60000	10000	[27]
CIFAR-10	color images (32×32)	10	3072	50000	10000	[28]
CIFAR-100	color images (32×32)	100	3072	50000	10000	[28]
AWA2	Color images	50	4096	29858	7464	[29]

5.2 Competitors

The proposed approach is compared to several cutting-edge multi-class classifiers. In front of a large litterature on this subject, our study focuses on two points: the ability to compress the information and/or the capacity of combining classifiers. Our selection focuses on the following methods (Table 2) presented previously (see Sect. 1).

Table 2. Algorithm description

Algorithms	Authors	Free-parameters	Compression
CKDA	Proposed method	σ and C	yes
ICNKDA	Dufrenois [8]	σ and ν	yes
SoDA	Hong et al. [30]	s	yes
Nys-KDA	Musco et al. [7]	σ and m	yes
MC-SVM	Allwein et al. [21]	σ	no
MC-AdaBoost	Friedman et al. [17]	n_{tree}	no
MC-BagTree	Breiman et al. [15]	n_{tree}	no

Concerning kernel learning methods, the kernel width σ will be selected beforehand by cross-validation. Otherwise, some critical parameters will be specifically set by the user during the experimental evaluations.

5.3 Influence of the Capacity C

In this part, we will study the influence of changing the value of the capacity C on the evolution of the accuracy, the training time, the compression rate as well as on the number of classifiers created and collaborated. We will do this study

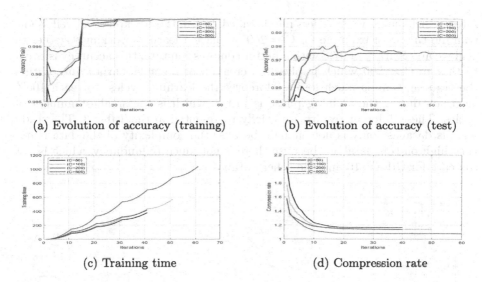

(a) Evolution of accuracy (training)   (b) Evolution of accuracy (test)

(c) Training time   (d) Compression rate

Fig. 3. Influence of the capacity C on MNIST dataset. (a) Evolution of accuracy (training) -(b) Evolution of accuracy (test) -(c) Training time -(d) Compression rate

Table 3. Influence of C on MNIST (train:50000/test:1000)

C	Lear.Cycle	Acc.	τ	t(sec)	# learners
50	4	95.00	1.1661	9.2177	10
100	5	96.30	1.1411	11.1621	6
200	4	97.50	1.1404	10.2053	4
500	6	97.50	1.0804	17.0169	1

only on the MNIST and CIFAR-10 databases by taking all the training data set (5000 samples per class) and 1000 test data randomly extracted from the test data. This study will be done with a fixed value of the kernel width parameter σ which is already set after a cross validation step to 4 for the MNIST database and 20 for the CIFAR-10 database.

Figures 3a and b shows the evolution of the accuracy during the training and testing phase respectively for different values of C. We can see that the performance indicators are better for large values of C, but it is also clear that to reach the maximum accuracy during the training phase, a different training cycle and training time are needed, which is illustrated in Fig. 3c. It shows the evolution of the training time for different values of C. In general, the time is high for large values of the capacity, because CKDA requires several learning cycles and that leads to an increase in computation time. The compression rate is also an important parameter that needs to be considered when choosing the appropriate value of C. The best compression rate is that of C = 50 with 10 collaborative learners created. For small values of C, we have high compression rates, which means we have less misclassified data in the stockpiles, as well as low training times, for example for C = 200, we have 4 learners working together to achieve an accuracy of 97.5 with a better compression rate, this accuracy is equal to that of C = 500 which implies the creation of a single learner, in addition the training time is much lower. Moreover the learning cycles, to reach 100% accuracy during the training phase is just 4, which is the smallest number of cycles. These different results are briefly represented in the Table 3. The study on this database only is not enough. because the complexity of the data is not very high on this database because there is not much redundancy, which is not the case for CIFAR-10 and the other databases.

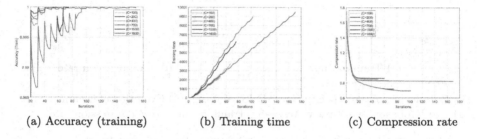

(a) Accuracy (training)   (b) Training time   (c) Compression rate

Fig. 4. Influence of the capacity C on CIFAR-10. (a) Accuracy (training) -(b) Training time – (c) Compression rate

Table 4. Influence of C on CIFAR-10 (train:50000/test:1000)

C	Lear.Cycle	Acc.	τ	t(sec)	# learners
100	7	90.10	0.8328	56.5444	12
200	6	89.80	0.8612	52.2519	6
400	5	91.10	0.8489	47.1593	4
700	17	90.60	0.8229	55.7184	2
1500	8	89.80	0.7193	81.8287	2
1600	11	89.30	0.6949	87.0162	1

Table 4 summarize the evaluation results of CKDA on the CIFAR-10 database for different values of C {100,200,400,700,1500,1600}. For large values of C, low compression rates and high learning times are observed. In addition, the learning cycle is also very high. But unlike the analysis performed on the MNIST database, for large values of C we have low test accuracies. For example, for C = 1600, which involves the creation of a single classifier, we have the lowest test accuracy in 11 learning cycles, with the highest learning time and the lowest compression rate. In contrast, for C = 400, which involves the creation of 4 collaborative classifiers, we have the best test accuracy in only 5 learning cycles, with the lowest learning time and high compression rate. These results demonstrate the effectiveness of this approach as well as the usefulness of this collaborative strategy among multiple capacity constrained classifiers. The performance also depends on the kernel width parameter. It is therefore important to choose a good combination of these two parameters to obtain good performance. The curves of Figs. 4a, b and c show that the indicators of performance of CKDA for low values of C are better than the high values.

5.4 Evaluation on Moderately Size Datasets

Since not all competitors are equipped with a compression strategy, we limited the training sample size. More precisely, 10000 training data are randomly drawn from the MNIST (1000/class), CIFAR10 (1000/class), CIFAR100 (100/class) data sets and 1000 unseen test data are randomly extracted from these data base. AWA2, being a smaller data set compared to the previous ones, we have randomly selected 4000 training data (80/class) and 1000 test data (20/class).

Tables 5-8 summarize the results recorded by the different methods. Several indicators of performances are analyzed: accuracy (acc. in $[0, 1]$) , the number of layers (# learners), the final compression rate ($\tau \in \mathbb{R}$) and the training time (t in sec).

From Tables 5-8, Several comments can be deduced from theses tables: 1) First, CKDA records better results when the maximal capacity of each learner is increased. This trend is clearly observed in each experiment. Moreover, if the value of the capacity obviously influences the number of layers, it has also an impact on the compression rate τ . Indeed, we note that the smaller the capacity, the larger the number of learners and the larger the compression rate. In other words, this means that the larger the learning ensemble, the less data it needs to minimize the empirical risk but at the expense of the generalization error. 2) Second, CKDA is a good alternative to existing methods and records most of the time better accuracy when the capacity C is correctly selected. However, minimizing the empirical risk with CKDA requires several learning cycles and consequently leads to an increase in computation time.

Table 5. MNIST (train:10000/test:1000)

Methods	acc.	# learners	τ	Time (sec)
$CKDA_{50}$	93.40	4	0.9412	2.0703
$CKDA_{200}$	96.10	1	0.9872	2.4449
$ICNKDA_{0.30}$	94.80	6	0.3486	1.4582
SoDa	88.64	6	–	6.5891
$Nys\text{-}KDA_{200}$	84.37	1	–	17.52
$Nys\text{-}KDA_{600}$	84.66	1	–	19.25
$Nys\text{-}KDA_{1000}$	84.74	1	–	20.06
MC-SVM	94.8	45	–	3.95
MC-AdaBoost	83.5	200	–	4.61
MC-BagTree	86.2	200	–	2.78

Table 6. CIFAR-10 (train:10000/test:1000)

Methods	acc.	# learners	τ	Time (sec)
$CKDA_{50}$	86.20	7	0.6897	12.6355
$CKDA_{200}$	88.70	2	0.7194	10.2709
$ICNKDA_{0.30}$	87.30	5	0.2259	2.7763
$ICNKDA_{0.35}$	86.10	7	0.3259	2.8863
SoDa	85.20	5	–	9.7510
$Nys\text{-}KDA_{200}$	83.08	1	–	18.11
$Nys\text{-}KDA_{600}$	84.29	1	–	20.49
$Nys\text{-}KDA_{1000}$	84.58	1	–	23.38
MC-SVM	87.7	45	–	12.24
MC-AdaBoost	81.3	200	–	44.31
MC-BagTree	85.4	200	–	23.53

Table 7. CIFAR-100 (train:10000/test:1000)

Methods	acc.	# learners	τ	Time (sec)
$CKDA_{30}$	66.38	3	0.4244	90.52
$CKDA_{50}$	66.34	3	0.2445	131.6757
$ICNKDA_{0.20}$	65.98	10	0.0400	20.4422
$ICNKDA_{0.25}$	54.41	10	0.1500	21.5179
$ICNKDA_{0.30}$	54.41	10	0.2198	25.0154
SoDa	65.38	5	–	75.01
$Nys\text{-}KDA_{200}$	47.44	1	–	220.45
$Nys\text{-}KDA_{600}$	51.31	1	–	200.59
$Nys\text{-}KDA_{1000}$	52.32	1	–	250.56
MC-SVM	58.85	4950	–	160.2
MC-AdaBoost	52.3	200	–	$2.36 \ 10^3$
MC-BagTree	62.56	200	–	266.5

Table 8. AWA2 (train:4000/test:1000)

Methods	acc.	# learners	τ	Time (sec)
$CKDA_{30}$	75.10	3	0.3752	28.2460
$CKDA_{50}$	75.40	2	0.3454	31.2804
$ICNKDA_{0.30}$	69.90	5	0.3300	9.2567
SoDa	75.37	3	–	29.0597
$Nys\text{-}KDA_{200}$	58.13	1	–	51.49
$Nys\text{-}KDA_{600}$	61.81	1	–	51.68
$Nys\text{-}KDA_{1000}$	63.08	1	–	51.92
MC-SVM	71.4	1225	–	25.88
MC-AdaBoost	52.3	200	–	536.3
MC-BagTree	75.7	200	–	48.18

5.5   Comparative Study with Large Size Datasets

In this part, the comparison is made only with the methods equipped with a compression mechanism. We used all the training data, precisely,50000 training data from MNIST and CIFAR10 (1000 per class) datasets, and 1000 unseen test data are randomly extracted from these databases. Tables 9-10 summarizes the results recoded by the different methods CKDA, ICNKDA, SoDA. Several indicators of performances are analyzed : accuracy (acc.) , the number of layers (# learners), the final compression rate ($\tau \in \mathbb{R}$), the training time (t in sec).The curves of the test accuracy of the multi-class MNIST and CIFAR-10 data sets are shown in Fig. 5.

Table 9. MNIST (train:50000/test:1000)

Methods	acc.	# learners	τ	t (sec)
$CKDA_{50}$	95.00	10	1.1662	9.2177
$CKDA_{200}$	97.50	4	1.1404	10.2053
$ICNKDA_{0.30}$	94.36	11	0.2218	3.2726
SoDa	90.48	6	–	6.8035

Table 10. CIFAR-10 (train:50000/test:1000)

Methods	acc.	# learners	τ	t (sec)
$CKDA_{200}$	89.80	6	0.8612	52.2519
$CKDA_{400}$	91.10	4	0.8489	47.1593
$ICNKDA_{0.30}$	90.30	5	0.1518	24.3783
SoDa	90.00	5	–	48.0350

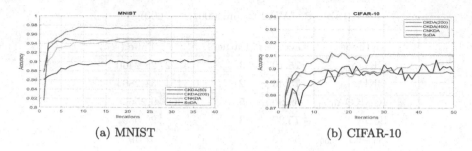

(a) MNIST   (b) CIFAR-10

Fig. 5. Evolution of the accuracy. (a) MNIST dataset - (b) CIFAR-10 dataset

From Tables 9-10 taking into account the whole training dataset, we observe the same findings on moderate datasets, that CKDA has higher test accuracies on all datasets which is clearly illustrated in Fig. 5. On the other hand the training time is high compared to other methods since we have to calculate the response for each classifier output and if the number of classifiers increases therefore the training time will increase. But it remains much better in term of compression.

6   Conclusion and Future Work

We have seen that the computation and storage of the kernel matrix are the two main limitations to solve large-scale kernel problems. In this paper, we proposed a new collaborative and dynamic learning strategy to solve this problem in which the whole learning task will be shared with a ensemble of classifiers with limited storage capacity. In addition, a compression strategy is proposed after each learning step to minimize the number of classifiers generated during the learning process which allows to reduce the size of the kernel matrix. The experimental results of the proposed CKDA method on MNIST CIFAR-10, CIFAR-100 and AWA2 datasets and in comparison with other methods, show that the proposed method has comparative and better performances in terms of accuracy and compression rate. However its training time is a bit high compared to the other algorithms, but this can be surpassed in future works by using parallel computation.Moreover, We will address the problem of novelty detection in multi-class scenarios.

Acknowlegment. The authors would like to thank the University of the Littoral Opal Coast (Calais-France) and HESTIM Engineering and Business School (Casablanca-Morocco) for their support to this work.

References

1. Alexandre-Cortizo, E., Rosa-Zurera, M., Lopez-Ferreras, F.: Application of fisher linear discriminant analysisto speech/music classification. In: EUROCON 2005 - The International Conference on Computer as a Tool, vol. 2, pp. 1666–1669 (2005)
2. Pang, S., Ozawa, S., Kasabov, N.: Incremental linear discriminant analysis for classification of data streams. In: IEEE Trans. Syst. Man Cybern. Part B (Cybern.) **35**(5), 905–914 (2005)
3. Roth, V.: Kernel fisher discriminant for outlier detection. Neural Comput. **18**, 942–960 (2006)
4. Bodesheim, P., Freytag, A., Rodner, E., Kemmler, M., Denzler, J.: Kernel null space methods for novelty detection. In: Computer Vision and Pattern Recognition, pp. 3374–3381 (2013)
5. Mika, S., Smola, A.J., Schölkopf, B.: An improved training algorithm for kernel fisher discriminants. In: International Workshop on Artificial Intelligence and Statistics, pp. 209–215 PMLR (2001)
6. Cai, D., He, X., Han, J.: Speed up kernel discriminant analysis. VLDB J. **20**, 21–33 (2011)
7. Musco, C., Musco, C.: Recursive sampling for the nyström method. In: NIPS, pp. 3834–3846 (2017)
8. Dufrenois, F.: Incremental and compressible kernel null discriminant analysis. Pattern Recogn. **127**, 108642 (2022)
9. Li, W.-H., Zhong, Z., Zheng, W.-S.: One-pass person re-identification by sketch online discriminant analysis. Pattern Recogn. **93**, 11 (2017)
10. Liberty, E.: Simple and deterministic matrix sketching. In: The 19th ACM SIGKDD International Conference on Knowledge Discovery and Data Mining, Chicago, USA, pp. 581–588 (2013)
11. Sagi, O., Rokach, L.: Ensemble learning: a survey. Wiley Interdisc. Rev. Data Min. Knowl. Discovery **8**(4), e1249 (2018)
12. Kumar, G., Thakur, K., Ayyagari, M.R.: Mlesidss: machine learning-based ensembles for intrusion detection systems-a review. J. Supercomput. **76**(11), 8938–8971 (2020)
13. Gomes, H.M., Barddal, J.P., Enembreck, F., Bifet, A.: A survey on ensemble learning for data stream classification. ACM Comput. Surv. (CSUR) **50**(2), 1–36 (2017)
14. Tanha, J., Abdi, Y., Samadi, N., Razzaghi, N., Asadpour, M.: Boosting methods for multi-class imbalanced data classification: an experimental review. J. Big Data **7**(1), 1–47 (2020)
15. Breiman, L.: Random forests. Mach. Learn. **45**, 5–32 (2001)
16. Ho. T.K.: Random decision forests. In: Proceedings of 3rd International Conference on Document Analysis and Recognition, vol. 1, pp. 278–282 IEEE (1995)
17. Friedman, J., Hastie, T., Tibshirani, R.: Additive logistic regression: a statistical view of boosting. Ann. Stat. **28**, 337–407 (2000)
18. Hamlich, M., Belbounaguia, N.E., et al.: Short-term load forecasting using machine learning and periodicity decomposition. AIMS Energy **7**(3), 382–394 (2019)
19. Khatib, A., Hamlich, M., Hamad, D.: Machine learning based intrusion detection for cyber-security in IoT networks. In: E3S Web of Conferences, vol. 297. EDP Sciences (2021)
20. Hamlich, M., El Khantach, A., Belbounaguia, N.: Machine learning methods against false data injection in smart grid. Int. J. Reasoning-based Intell. Syst. **12**(1), 51–59 (2020)

21. Allwein, E.L., Schapire, R.E., Singer, Y.: Reducing multiclass to binary: a unifying approach for margin classifiers. J. Mach. Learn. Res. **1**, 113–141 (2000)
22. Weston, J., Watkins, C.: Multi-Class Support Vector Machines. Technical report, CiteSeer (1998)
23. Liu, Y., Zheng, Y.F.: One-against-all multi-class SVM classification using reliability measures. In: Proceedings 2005 IEEE International Joint Conference on Neural Networks, 2005, vol. 2, pp. 849–854. IEEE (2005)
24. Debnath, R., Takahide, N., Takahashi, H.: A decision based one-against-one method for multi-class support vector machine. Pattern Anal. Appl. **7**(2), 164–175 (2004)
25. Liu, J., Lian, Z., Wang, Y., Xiao, J.: Incremental kernel null space discriminant analysis for novelty detection. In: CVPR, pp. 4123–4131 (2017)
26. Wang, Y., et al.: Novelty detection and online learning for chunk data streams. IEEE Trans. Pattern Anal. Mach. Intell. **43**(7), 2400–2412 (2021)
27. Lecun, Y., Bottou, L., Bengio, Y., Haffner, P.: Gradient-based learning applied to document recognition. **86**, 2278–2324 (1998)
28. Krizhevsky, A., Hinton, G.: Learning multiple layers of features from tiny images. (2009)
29. Lampert, C.H., Nickisch, H., Harmeling, S.: Attribute-based classification for zero-shot visual object categorization. IEEE Trans. Pattern Anal. Mach. Intell. **36**(3), 453–465 (2014)
30. Wei-Hong, L., Zhuowei, Z., Wei-Shi, Z.: One-passe person re-identification by sketch online discriminant analysis. Pattern Recogn. **93**, 122–132 (2017)

Spectral Clustering Based on a Graph Model for Airspace Sectorization

Zineb Hidila[1,2]($\boxtimes$), Attoumane Loukmane[1], Naoufal Rahali[1],
and Mohammed Mestari[1]

[1] University Hassan II-Casablanca-ENSET Mohammedia-Morocco Computer
Science, Artificial Intelligence and Cyber Security Laboratory (2IACS),
Mohammedia, Morocco
zineb.hidila@gmail.com, mestari@enset-media.ac.ma
[2] Pluridisciplinary Research and Innovation Laboratory (LPRI), EMSI Casablanca,
Casablanca, Morocco

Abstract. This paper focuses on exploring the usage of clustering techniques to form new sector designs conforming to the constraints imposed
by the problem. As an initial step we generate DBSCAN clusters based
on the sector's geographical points for analyzing the structural design
of the airspace. As a second step, we form a graph model through the
Voronoi Diagram to generate sites for each sector. Next, we transform the
diagram into a Delaunay Triangulation. For the weighted graph model,
we use two main metrics: the traffic flow and the number of intersections
on each link. For the final step, we analyze spectral clustering on sectors
to test how suitable the results are via convex bounding.

Keywords: DBSCAN · Spectral clustering · Sectorization ·
Optimization · Airspace · Graph

1 Introduction

Air traffic management is a complex system containing many interconnected components. The increased workflow in air traffic represents a big challenge for Air
traffic management, knowing that the sector's geometry had remained static in
the composition without considering the demographic growth of the worldwide
population. Presenting a new partition of the airspace remains a complex problem
in formulation and application due to the sensitivity and the daily fluctuations.

Many projects have known light like the NEXTGEN that first came in 2007
(still ongoing) by the United States National Airspace System (NAS) and the US
Federal aviation administration [6]. The main goal of this project is to use tools
and procedures that follow the new technologies and advancements in industries.
On the other side of the globe, we have the Single European Sky ATM Research
Joint Undertaking [5] established in the same year. The philosophy behind those
projects is to seek and implement a unified sky model to increase safety, efficiency
and capacity.

We see from both projects that any research must aim for flexible, realistic and optimized models while respecting the constraints.

Since we are dealing with the airspace structure, it is necessary to outline the different aspects of the traffic management system to display the complexity. We first define the Air Traffic Management(ATM) as a group of three main components : air traffic services, airspace management and air traffic flow management [9].

1. Air traffic services: Ensure safety and order of the traffic flow under the air traffic control (ATC) service), those services supply crucial information to flight crews (flight information service, FIS) and alerting services for emergency case. Those tasks are performed mainly by air traffic controllers. Their primary functions are to prevent collisions by applying proper separation standards and administering real-time clearances and instructions.
2. Airspace traffic flow management: The basic goal of airspace management is to monitor the movement and the flow of aircraft as accurately as possible to be able to minimize congestion in specific control sectors. The methods and techniques employed does aim at guaranteeing the best available match between the supply and demand.
3. Airspace management: The primary objective is how to manage airspace in accordance with the other resources including the civil and military. Specifically this service encapsulate the many components such as the network of routes, flying zones and the levels of flying.

Going through the components of the air traffic management, it presents how the airspace should be adequately formed so both the air traffic controllers and the aircraft have a safe exchange process of navigation and a rapid conflict resolution. Based on [4], we have the following air traffic control tasks:

. Flight data management: Contains loading, computer updates notifications and the disposal progress of flights.
. Conflict search: Where for any separation, the controller have to make sure the separation action does not jeopardize safety.
. Coordination: Logs the coordination between the internal and external sectors , in other words the controller keep monitoring the aircraft entering and exiting the sector
. Radar tasks : Characterizes the tasks of preserving the separation of aircraft by radar actions and,for crucial scenarios, radar-related coordination with adjacent sectors is required.
. Routine R/T: Exchange of routinely information via radio communication (weather report, first call, last call, new clearance, route's opening and so on)

Apart from the controller's tasks workload, we also have geometrical constraints. Our objective is to create a new design to improve the controllers experience therefore, we must not bypass the geometric restrictions and the flow conformance requirements. We have the following constraints:

- Boundary constraint: Airplanes should pass far enough from a sector boundary and intersection angles should be nearly orthogonal.
- Dwell time constraint: Each airplane should stay for a minimum amount of time in each sector.
- Convexity constraint: The sector shapes should be convex and not fragmented.
- Location constraint: Airports and conjunction/intersection of major flows should be inside sectors.

The first, second and fourth constraints are for managing and dealing with conflicts. Figure 1 illustrates the shape of sectors.

Fig. 1. The shape of French sectors

To optimize an airspace we see that we have to juggle and incorporate many constraints either geometrically and operationally. For this work we are going to focus on the coordination workload generated via route's intersections while maintaining the geometrical structure which is the convexity. For the case studied we are going to consider a weighted undirected graph generated via Voronoi Diagram and Delaunay Tessellation.

The structure of the paper is as follow: we start by describing the related work associated with the problem, then we explore the use of DBSCAN clustering by generating clusters via the geographical points. Afterward, we generate once again sub-graphs based on the spectral clustering starting with a weighted graph model.

2 Related Work

Many researchers have addressed the sectorization problem via multiple approaches. We have [3] who proposed a Voronoi diagram to generate convex shapes which were converted to a network model. The same model was optimized with meta-heuristics.

In the same direction [8] used the same two methods described above as a metamorphic Voronoi Diagram to accommodate the changes in the workflow. Also, [13] carried the same approach via a Voronoi Diagram to a graph model by the delaunay triangulation as a constraint graph problem.

The same work of using the Voronoi diagram was use by [15] by mixing the Voronoi diagram and the genetic algorithm by an iterative deepening approach.

For to minimizing the coordination workload and cost functions [10] proposed a graph constraint partitioning problem for satisfying the capacity constraint via a spectral clustering to adjust the partitions generated by the graph.

Moving to the cell based method we have [17] who proposed a sectorization process based on three different layers: low, high and ultra high altitude. Those layers were converted to a hexagonal-cell mesh and implementing a clustering algorithm for balancing the distribution of the workload.

The extensive use of meta-heuristics is seen in [11], the author partitioned the sectors using the Voronoi diagram with the k-mean clustering, adding a stochastic optimization with the genetic algorithm for complexity reduction purposes. The second work once again used a genetic algorithm to minimize controller workload. The author concluded that more metrics should be added to conform with the complexity.

[16] created an extensive framework to automate the sectors in order to delete the irregularities found in sector shapes by using graph cutting techniques such as Monte Carlo and the radius one. As a conclusion, the framework can be a useful design tool for airspace planners.

Last but not least [7] suggested free routing where each flight uses a direct path between the origin and the destination, this system generates a traffic distribution making intersections between the trajectories. The intersections of the trajectories are then clustered into center point that creates new networks. From these papers we can undeniably see that meta-heuristics, computational geometry and clustering are the main methods for the airspace sectorization.

3   Spatial Clustering

Clustering is defined as grouping objects based on their similarities. In other words, segregating groups with similar traits and assign them into clusters. Since we are dealing with geographical coordinates as our dataset, using spacial clustering will permit exploring the distribution our data. Spacial clustering enters in the category of density models, for this purposes we applied the DBSCAN (Density-based spatial clustering of applications with noise) as a first clustering method. We first perform the algorithm on our five sectors separately and then for the whole dataset.

> Note: the one cluster in the figure is due to having columns of the x-axis with zero standard deviation plus using the Standardized Euclidean distance. Each coordinate difference between observations is scaled by dividing the corresponding element of the standard deviation.

We observe that there's a recurrent pattern of two main clusters, either the separate sector clusters or the whole dataset, which can be explained as the following:

– The first group of clusters with higher density represents the airspace geographical borders.

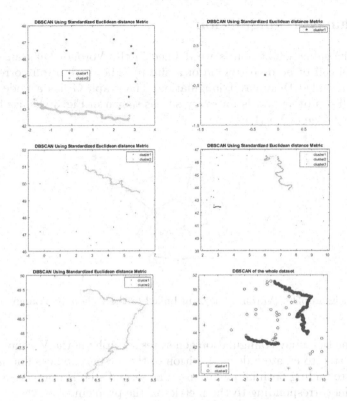

Fig. 2. Sector clustering using DBSCAN

- The second group of clusters are those none constricted to the borders.

To conclude, creating sectors based on political border restrictions is a conflicting point to optimize the distribution of the space. To simplify, we are going to represent the airspace by computational geometry.

4 Voronoi Diagram

To discretize our problem, we are going to convert our from a polygonal geometric shape to a graph structure by using the Voronoi diagram and the Delaunay Tessellations. We define the Voronoi diagram and the Delaunay Triangulation from [1] by:

let P be a set of n points in the euclidean plane where :
$$P := \{p_1, p_2....p_n\} \quad \forall p_i, pj \in P, \quad p_i \neq pj \quad with \quad i, j \in \{1, 2, ..., n\}.$$
A Voronoi Diagram of P is the subdivision of the plane into n cells one for each site in P forming a group of convex non overlapping polygons.

5   Delaunay Triangulation

let P be the same set of points we defined in the Voronoi Diagram and $\nu(p)$ the Voronoi cell of point p (region of a site p). The dual graph corresponding to Vor(P) is called Delaunay triangulation. The graph G has a node for every Voronoi cell - in other words for every site as shown in Fig. 3 besides having an arc for every edge of Vor(P).

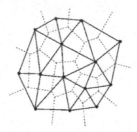

Fig. 3. Example of Voronoi Diagram linked to the Delaunay Triangulation

Since the Delaunay triangulation generates a graph via the Voronoi Diagram, it is a first step to create a decomposition of the airspace, where finding optima is reduced to finding optimal partitions. The second step is to create a weighted graph model corresponding to the metrics of the problem.

6   Airspace Graph Model

The structure of the airspace we proposed is based on creating a graph model that preserves the airspace information. We used the air routes and the traffic counts on each French airport. Described on the previous sections , using the Voronoi diagram along with the Delaunay triangulation is going to generate the first primary graph.

6.1   Sub-graphs

Let us consider the graph G generated by the Delaunay triangulation, any subgraph T of G can be modeled by the set of tuples represented by the total number of edges where:

$X = (x_1, x_2, ...xn)$

such that:

$$\begin{cases} x_i = 1 \; if \; ei \in T \\ x_i = 0 \; otherwise. \end{cases}$$

From this formula, we can generate our vector space associated with the graph G of the Delaunay Triangulation associated with Fig. 4b

6.2   Weighted Graph Model

To have a weighted graph model from the Delaunay triangulation we use the following conditions:

1. For the vertex weights, we attribute values representing the workload based on the following scenario described in Figs. 4 and 5: if a route is crossing an edge and the node associated with that edge is too near , it is considered having a higher probability. This probability is calculated via the inverse of the euclidean distance.
2. For the edge weight, the measures are based on the number of times a route crosses a certain link.

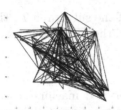

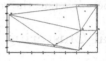

(b) Partitions of the Delaunay graph

(a) The network of french routes

Fig. 4. Route's net used for calculating intersections with DT

The property we used consist of computing the number of times a flight route intersects with the links corresponding to our Graph based on the traffic flow as a way to estimate a weight for the edges. The resulting values were then normalized based on the min-max formula.

(b) the weight of the edge

(a) Vertex weight's calculation

Fig. 5. Weight's calculation on vertices and edges

6.3   Objective Function

The graph model discussed have the following notations: $G = G(V, W)$ where: $V = \{v_1, v_2...v_n\}$ is the set of vertices and W is the weight matrix associated with each edge. The generation of the sub-graphs was done directly via the Delaunay triangulation to minimize the workloads associated, respecting the constraints.

In terms of workloads, the degree of the sub-graph can be seen as the monitoring workload associated with the triangulation and the cut cost of the graph as the coordination. Thus, the problem can be seen as a normalized cut problem [2,10] with the following equation:

$$min = \left\{ J = cut(G) \sum_{i=1}^{k} \frac{1}{W(T_i)} \right\} \tag{1}$$

where the cut function is the cost of the graph G with respect to a given partition of G into $T_1, T_2, T_3...T_k$ where:

$$G = \cup_{i=1}^{k} T_i T_i \cap T_j = \emptyset; \quad i \neq j; \quad i, j = (1, 2, 3, ...k) \tag{2}$$

$$cut(G) = cut(T_i, \bar{T}_i) \tag{3}$$

It is observed that the the larger the weight of the sub-graph T_i, the smaller the cost function J, versus the smaller the cut cost, the smaller the cost function.

7   Spectral Clustering

Spectral clustering can be defined as an unsupervised machine learning technique. Like the DBSCAN, this method determines what points fall under which cluster. For our case, the minimum cut problem (normalized cut) is relaxed to an Eigenvalue problem which is solved using the spectral clustering [12,14].

7.1   Graph Laplacian

The first step is to apply a data transformation to have a weighted graph representation. Afterward, we construct a square similarity matrix. The next step, is to calculate the Adjacency matrix based on the formula:

$$A[i][j] = \begin{cases} w_{i,j}, & \text{the weight of the edge between node i and node j ,} \\ 0, & \text{otherwise.} \end{cases} \tag{4}$$

To calculate the Laplacian matrix, we must calculate the degree Matrix which is filled by summing the element corresponding to the adjacency Matrix on each row. We have the following property for the degree Matrix:

$d[i][i] = $ The number of adjacent edges in node i or the degree of node i
$d[i][j] = 0$ Lastly we compute the Laplacian:

$$L = D - A \tag{5}$$

The Laplacian Matrix permits to classify the data based on the eigenvectors: if the graph G has k connected components then L has K eigenvectors with an Eigen value of 0.

The final step is to generate the clusters, we chose the value of five for the cluster to be compared with the actual design of the airspace, but usually an estimation of the optimal number of clusters is crucial for better results. Below in Fig. 6 are the results obtained from each cluster.

Fig. 6. Spectral clustering results

8 Conclusion

Spectral clustering is a technique known to perform well particularly in the case of non-Gaussian clusters, where the most common clustering algorithms such as K-Means fails to give good results. The first phase of this research focuses on exploring the impact of clustering in generating defined shaped conforming to the sectors design. From the results, we applied a convex bounding to the subgraphs to outline the figures. From the Airspace sectors designs we can say that same convex shapes were irregular and need further improvements to flatten the irregularities. Next, we will determine the optimal number of clusters via the knows methods such us:elbow method or adding more features to the graph and exploring the use of the graph neural network respecting the constraints and the metrics. As a conclusion, the overall results showed how the airspace system is complex when we generated the network associated with the triangulation and how many links overlapped in the output.

References

1. de Berg, M., Cheong, O., van Kreveld, M., Overmars, M.: Computational Geometry–Algorithms and Applications, 3rd Ed. Springer, Heidelberg (2008). https://doi.org/10.1007/978-3-540-77974-2
2. Chen, Y., Zhang, D.: Dynamic airspace configuration method based on a weighted graph model. Chin. J. Aeronaut **27**(4), 903–912 (2014). https://doi.org/10.1016/J.CJA.2014.06.009
3. Delahaye, D., Schoenauer, M., Alliot, J.M.: Airspace sectoring by evolutionary computation. In: 1998 IEEE International Conference on Evolutionary Computation Proceedings. IEEE World Congress on Computational Intelligence (Cat. No. 98TH8360), pp. 218–223 IEEE (1998)
4. Eurocontrol: workload calculation and Determination of Capacity with RAMS 1 ATC TASKS. Tech. rep. Eurocontrol (2006)
5. Eurocontrol: SESAR (2022). http://www.sesar.eu/
6. Federal Aviation Administration: NextGen Annual Report. Tech. rep. FAA (2020). https://www.faa.gov/nextgen/media/NextGenAnnualReport-FiscalYear2020.pdf
7. Gerdes, I., Temme, A., Schultz, M.: From free-route air traffic to an adapted dynamic main-flow system. Transp. Res. Part C: Emerg. Technol. **115**, 102633 (2020)
8. Han, S.C., Zhang, M.: The optimization method of the sector partition based on metamorphic voronoi polygon. Chin. J. Aeronaut. **17**(1), 7–12 (2004)

9. ICAO: Doc 4444, Air Traffic Management. Tech. rep. ICAO (2016). https://
   ops.group/blog/wp-content/uploads/2017/03/ICAO-Doc4444-Pans-Atm-
   16thEdition-2016-OPSGROUP.pdf
10. Li, J., Wang, T., Savai, M., Hwang, I.: Graph-Based Algorithm for Dynamic
    Airspace Configuration. J. Guidance Control Dyn. **33**(4), 1082–1094 (2010).
    https://doi.org/10.2514/1.47720
11. Sergeeva, M.: Automated airspace sectorization by genetic algorithm, Ph. D. thesis,
    Université Paul Sabatier (Toulouse 3) (2017)
12. Shi, J., Malik, J.: Normalized cuts and image segmentation. IEEE Trans. Pattern
    Anal. Mach. Intell. **22**(8), 888–905 (2000). https://doi.org/10.1109/34.868688
13. Trandac, H., Baptiste, P., Duong, V.: Airspace Sectorization Constraints. RAIRO-
    Oper. Res. **39**(2), 105–122 (2005)
14. Von Luxburg, U.: A tutorial on spectral clustering. Stat. Comput. **17**(4), 395–416
    (2007). https://doi.org/10.1007/s11222-007-9033-z. https://arxiv.org/abs/0711.
    0189v1
15. Xue, M.: Airspace sector redesign based on voronoi diagrams. In: AIAA Guidance,
    Navigation and Control Conference and Exhibit 18–21 August 2008, Honolulu,
    Hawaii AIAA AIAA, pp. 2008–7223 (2008)
16. Ye, Z., Kong, F., Zhang, B., Gao, W., Mao, J.: A method framework for auto-
    matic airspace reconfiguration-monte Carlo method for eliminating irregular sector
    shapes generated by region growth method. Sensors **19**(18), 3934 (2019)
17. Yousefi, A., Donohue, G.: Temporal and spatial distribution of airspace complex-
    ity for air traffic controller workload-based sectorization. In: AIAA 4th Aviation
    Technology, Integration and Operations (ATIO) forum, p. 6455 (2004)

Networking Technologies and IoT

Solar Charging Station for Electric Vehicles with IoT Solution for Monitoring Energy Production

Younes Ledmaoui[1(✉)], Adila El Maghraoui[1,2], and Ahmed Chebak[1]

[1] Green Tech Institute (GTI), Mohammed VI Polytechnic University (UM6P), Benguerir, Morocco
Younes.ledmaoui@um6p.ma
[2] Institute of Science, Technology and Innovation (IST&I), Mohammed VI Polytechnic University (UM6P), Benguerir, Morocco

Abstract. After exposing our planet to high levels of pollution and carbon emissions, climate change has become one of the most important issues facing our generation, the combination of solar power and electric vehicle (EV) is the key to dramatically reducing our reliance on fossil fuels. This work presents the design, sizing, and modeling of a solar charging station of 7.4 kW of AC type, for charging electric vehicles in the public area with monitoring daily energy production. The method includes an analysis of the solar resource available at the location in Paris (France), as well as analysis, evaluation, and selection of the components of the solar station using simulation software such as PVSOL, in addition, the development of a datalogger with the print circuit board (PCB) used for monitoring energy production by solar panels, and the storage of data in a cloud with the display of results on a web interface, Finally, the use of blender software, to create the installation's final 3D design.

Keywords: Solar chargers · Smart Grid · Smart Meter · Monitoring · Internet of Things · Electrical vehicle

1 Introduction

Energy deficiency and degradation of ecosystems have emerged as two of the most pressing global concerns in the latest two decades, Forasmuch the transportation sector is among the top contributors to greenhouse gas (GHG) emissions. Du to the fact that conventional vehicles are driven by an internal combustion engine (ICE) using fossil fuels; emitting carbon monoxide, nitrogen oxides, hydrocarbons, and carbon dioxide, causing a greenhouse effect on the climate and a toxic effect on human health.

According to the statistical data, transportation stands for over half of the global oil consumption, more precisely 64% of our final oil consumption, furthermore, the population continues growing throughout the 21st century until it reaches 9.5 billion or 10 billion people, therefore energy consumption will continue to grow throughout the century. Lastly, to produce this energy, there are many different possible energy sources,

M. Hamlich et al. (Eds.): SADASC 2022, CCIS 1677, pp. 63–77, 2022.
https://doi.org/10.1007/978-3-031-20490-6_6

in this context, renewable energy sources become competitive and available worldwide. Solar energy has become one of the most demanded sources of energy [1]. Indeed, many domestic, industrial, or commercial applications use solar energy [2]. Moreover, sustainable energy [3] is a key source to meet the reduction of carbon emissions and especially if it is paired with electric vehicles (EV) which are a promising solution [4]. In fact, electric vehicles can be tied to major macroeconomic challenges with regard to energy [5], especially for oil importers, it can help to improve the energy supply security by reducing imported oil dependence. There are real upsides, especially to the geopolitical balance of power, which are hard to quantify. Electric vehicles can also help reduce the oil bill thanks to concrete short-term economic gains and benefit from the upsides for the economy of being less exposed to oil price volatility [6]. 78% of car drivers travel less than 50 km per day, in the city, the average distance is about 25–30 km, which corresponds to a reasonable EV range allowing an average charging time of one hour. In France, the electric fleet is highly developed, and mobility has become highly electric, and this can be associated with several factors: Environmental since thermal cars reject up to 14% of greenhouse gas emissions, besides, an economical factor, especially since the state makes subsidies to encourage the transformation of mobility, political factor, with the rise in oil prices during the wars and Technological factor, with the birth of smart grids and real-time consumption supervision. Moreover, solar energy is widely available [7], so it is better to use solar energy to charge electric cars, which is the basic idea of this work. It consists of using solar energy for charging stations, considering this idea; we propose a study and a simulation for a 7.4 kW AC solar charging station, with the two options connected to the network and autonomous, for electric vehicles with a solution of supervision of the energy production. Charging an EV is typically done at three levels of voltage and current: Level 1 AC requires 8–14 h to fully charge a vehicle, depending on EV, battery, and control dump. Level 2 requires 4–6 h to fully charge and Level 3 direct current for fast charging EVs in minutes instead of hours.

This paper is organized into four sections. In the first section, we present the related works on this topic. The second section gives the manual sizing steps and the design considerations of the charging station under study, and we validate the study by a simulation with the PVSOL software and an overview of the structure of the smart meter. In the third section, we shed light on the result of the datalogger supervising energy production in the web application, and the last section provides a conclusion of our work with projections of future perspective.

2   Related Works

Many types of research on the solar charging station for electric vehicles have been conducted, and many successful ways have proved the value in areas such as The Integrated Systems for Recharging Electric Vehicles project (SIRVE) [8]. The SIRVE project was developed in Spain to desaturate the LV electrical network if the aggregate demand for fast charging and moderate charging systems exceeds the line's or transformation mall's capacity. A 1kWp photovoltaic system powers the SIRVE project, which feeds the 30 kWh lithium batteries. Shanghai became the first city in the world to open a solar-powered electric vehicle charging station in 2017. It consists of 40 solar panels on the roof of the building. It was also powered by backup batteries and connected to the power grid. The quick charge took half an hour to fully charge the battery.

The authors deal with solar charging stations for electric vehicles in India [9], they used the direct current (DC) charging type from the photovoltaic panels to the vehicle's battery, this solution doesn't need inverters between the sources and the load, however, it is limited to small loads.

Tarun et al. [10] made a prototype of a datalogger based on Arduino UNO and facilitated the data logging on an SD card which represents a limitation in terms of storage, moreover, ELWATI et al. [11] proposed a Bluetooth-based wireless system is developed in an optimal way for real-time data logging of energy production, and it requires an inverter with Bluetooth communication.

The integration of wind power, photovoltaic (PV) solar power, and Li-Ion battery energy storage into a DC microgrid-based charging station for electric vehicles is investigated in the work made by Ahmad Hamidi [12]. The goal is to have as much charging energy as feasible come from renewable energy sources. Furthermore, the work made by M.Longo et al. [13] which evaluates a solar roof with an electric vehicle charging station, in this study, various situations were examined, taking into account various EV models and charging states. The findings show that PV systems can effectively power electric vehicles and reduce pollution. Most of these studies focus on the sizing of the panels according to the type of terminal and the required needs and the location is generally in private places.

In this context, not too many papers have treated solar stations with monitoring of energy production in public places. Our work provides a solution to this issue using theoretical methodology with simulation to evaluate the obtained results.

3 Materials and Methods

3.1 Description of the Study Area

When designing and choosing the charging station, the needs and lifestyle of the customer as well as the place of installation play a major role in choosing all the specifications. In our case, the project will be installed in a public residence to test the contribution of solar panels, The coordinates for the place in France are 48° 54′ 55″S, 02° 22′ 58″W, and the elevation is 294 m.

Figure 1 shows in detail the approach to follow to design a photovoltaic system for our study, and Table 1 shows vehicles used to determine energy demand [14].

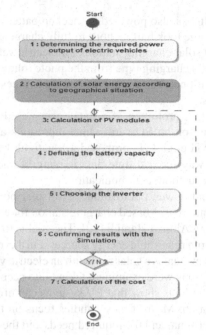

Fig. 1. Flowchart of the optimal sizing design PV for EV

Table 1. Technical data of electric vehicles

Make and Model of the Car	Hyundai Ioniq Eléctrico	Kia eSoul Standard	Kia eSoul Autonomía Extendida	Nissan Leaf S	Dacia Spring	Renault New ZOE
Type	EV	EV	EV	EV	EV	EV
Year of production	2019	2019	2019	2019	2019	2019
Maximum speed (km/h)	165	155	167	144	157	160
Battery capacity (kWh)	38.3	39.2	64	40	26.8	52
Autonomy (km)	293	277	452	270	230	390
Motor power (kW)	100	100	150	110	33	100

(*continued*)

Table 1. (*continued*)

Make and Model of the Car	Hyundai Ioniq Eléctrico	Kia eSoul Standard	Kia eSoul Autonomía Extendida	Nissan Leaf S	Dacia Spring	Renault New ZOE
Internal charger power (kW)	7.2	7.2	7.2	6.6	6.6	7.4
Price (USD.)	38639.00	40121.0	47320.00	29990.00	19100.00	32300.00

3.2 Calculation of Energy Consumption by Charging Electric Vehicles

To calculate the energy consumed, we took into consideration the elements: A 7.4 kW AC charging station is considered for charging electric vehicles and the charging stations will be available from 09:00 am until 9 pm, generally 9 h of charging supported by the panels and the rest either by the network or the batteries depending on the solution chosen.

According to Table 2, the average battery capacity for 1 h of charging is equivalent to 7.4 kWh. In addition to that, the energy consumed from 9:00 a.m. to 6:00 p.m. is 66.6 kWh, while the energy consumed from 6:00 p.m. until 9 p.m. is 22.2 kWh.

Furthermore, The installation connected to the network will be sized to supply 50% of the energy consumed between 9:00 am and 6:00 pm, which is equivalent to 33.3 kWh. Finally, considering a night load of 3 h, the evening production required is 22.2 kWh. The normal 7.4 kW charger can feed the vehicle in 01h30 to 04h30 [15]. The accelerated charge will last about 1 h at 22 kW. As for fast charging, it will charge the vehicle in 20 to 30 min at over 43 kW. On a daily basis, the normal charge is the most common charge mode. The vehicle can thus be charged when it is parked at home, at the office, or on the street. Cars are idle 80% of the time. Thus, the 7.4 kW charge speed is enough to charge a vehicle when not in use. Public space charging is often an opportunity or booster charge for a complement on the place of activity.

In general, for the need for suitable infrastructure, we have opted for an AC-type charging station with a power of 7.4 kW, with charging mode 2 and ocpp protocol which allows communication between the charger and the application [16]. Thus, Fig. 2 gives a view of the connection between the terminal and the electric vehicle.

Table 2. Battery capacity and autonomy for one hour of charge

Brand and model of the car	Battery capacity for one hour of charge (kWh)	Autonomy for one hour of charge (km)
Hyundai Ioniq Eléctrico	7.2	55.08
Kia eSoul Standard	7.2	50.88

(*continued*)

Table 2. (*continued*)

Brand and model of the car	Battery capacity for one hour of charge (kWh)	Autonomy for one hour of charge (km)
Kia eSoul Autonomía Extendida	7.2	50.85
Nissan Leaf S	6.6	44.55
Nissan Leaf S Plus	6.6	40.98
ByD E5–400	7.0	46.28
Porsche Taycan 4S	9.6	49.33
Dacia Spring	6.7	66.00
Renault ZOE	7.4	58.00
Average	7.3	52.00

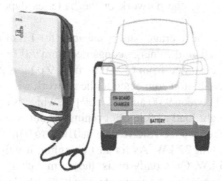

Fig. 2. A type 2 level AC electric vehicle charging station

3.3 Calculation of the Photovoltaic GEnerator's Power

Table 5 summarizes the technical parameters derived using the Global Solar Atlas website and the geographical coordinates of our site: To be certain of having energy in all seasons, the calculations are made under the least favorable sunshine conditions during the period of use:

$$P = \frac{Wdd}{Id} \tag{1}$$

$$Id = 5.6 \text{kWh/day Irradiation value.} \tag{2}$$

Wdd: Energy consumed.

It will take 12 photovoltaic panels with 500 Wp, the current and voltage at the maximum power point are respectively 12.81A and the 39.03V. Thus, the power of the real photovoltaic generator is 6000 Wp.

Since the system is a 39.03V and uses a charge controller, the voltage will be regulated and each string requires 6 panels and will provide, given 9 h of sunshine per day, a total of capacity 115.29Ah/day.

3.4 Calculation of the Battery Capacity

To determine the required battery capacity, the following calculations are necessary:
Using 95% inverter efficiency

$$DCload = \frac{ACload}{Inverterefficiency} \tag{3}$$

With a system voltage of 39 V, the batteries must supply the load.
Thus, the relationship to determine the capacity of the battery is as follows:

$$C = \frac{Ec \times N}{D \times U} \tag{4}$$

With:

- Ec: Energy consumed;
- U: Battery voltage in volts;
- D: Depth of discharge ~ 0.8;
- N: Desired autonomy in days equal to 1.

3.5 Calculation of the Inverter

The inverter's nominal power must be between 80% and 90% of the power generated by the solar generator. So the inverter chosen has a power range of 6.6–12.7 kW, a voltage range of 270V–480V, a maximum continuous current of 34.2 A, and a 97 percent efficiency.

3.6 Monitoring of Energy Production

Figure 3 represents the main components of our system, solar panels convert the sun into electricity, while the inverter converts the direct current into an alternating current which could supply the charging station, The smart meter counts the energy produced by the solar panels and the cloud to store data.

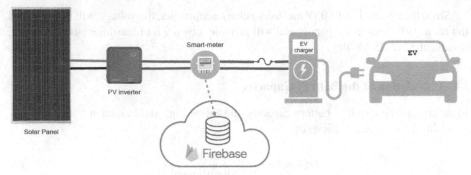

Fig. 3. Main components of the system

Figure 5 depicts the smart meter's structure, which is based on a controller (ESP-32) that receives energy consumption data from the sub-meter as a pulse count. Then calculates the energy production in kWh the cost as shown in Fig. 4. The controller sends the calculated data to the cloud (Firebase database) via the GSM module. The communication between the ESP-32 and GSM module is a (9600 baud rate)serial communication.

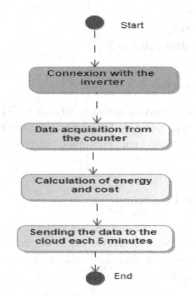

Fig. 4. Flow Diagram of the Datalogger

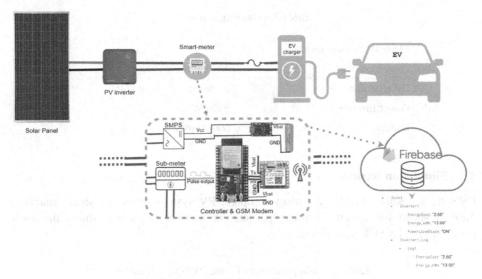

Fig. 5. Structure of the monitoring system

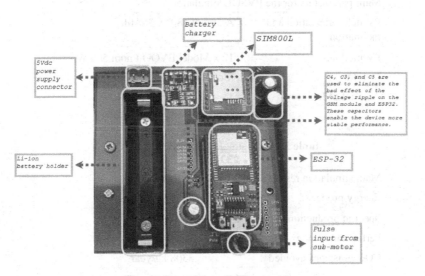

Fig. 6. Smart Meter PCB prototype

4 Results and Discussion

4.1 Theoretical Results

Table 3 summarizes the obtained results after the theoretical calculation based on the aforementioned equations. The total solar panels' voltage is 234 V within the voltage range of the inverter selected and the current delivered equals 26 A less than 34.2 A. which gives power, voltage, and current compatibility.

Table 3. Theoretical results

Main Theoretical results	
Power required	5946.4 W
PV modules	12 panels
Power Inverter	5400 W
Battery	600 Ah/day

4.2 Simulation Results

PVSOL Software provides the most complete PV system setup and shade analysis. Table 4 shows the system's primary parameters, as well as Table 5, shows the main results of the PVSOL simulation:

Table 4. Main parameters for the PVSOL simulation

Main parameters for the PVSOL simulation	
PV field orientation and inclination	Azimuth 180° y 36° tilt
PV modules	12 x Model EVOO Pnom.500 Wp
Invertor	Model Fronius 8.2–1 (v3)
Amount of Investors	1

Table 5. Main simulation results in PVSOL

Main simulation results in PVSOL 2021 (R8)	
Energy produced	7050 kWh/year
Specific production	1 kWh/kWp/year
Performance index (PR)	77.2%
CO_2 emissions avoided	3308 kg/year

4.3 Economic Study

This project concerns the study and design of a charging station powered by photovoltaic panels, it is economically viable for the solution connected to the network, because the return-on-investment time is approximately 8 years. The economic study of the system is represented in Table 6:

We can conclude that the simulation with the PVSOL software confirms the study carried out, so for our solar station, and in order to fulfill the required points, we will

Table 6. Economic study of the system

Parameter	Installation with Battery	Installation with Battery
Price of battery(€)	9050	-
Price of installation (€)	6200	6200
Return on investment (year)	15	8

need twelve (12) solar panels, an inverter and in case of storage, we will add a battery pack of 24.3 kWh.

4.4 Design with Blender Software

We chose 3D modeling to illustrate the results of our effort after completing the theoretical analysis and the simulation validation. In addition, as indicated in Fig. 6, we attempted to put a location slightly below the solar panels to house all of the components of our systems, particularly the inverter and batteries (Fig. 7).

Fig. 7. Modeling of the solar station with the blender software

4.5 Firebase Database as Cloud

Firebase is a Google-backed app development platform that was originally developed by James Tamplin and Andrew Lee in 2011. Firebase Realtime Database allows apps to access cross-platform data in real-time after joining storage in the NoSQL cloud. Another attractive advantage of Firebase is its secure and fast hosting service. Firebase hosting supports all types of content including web apps, and dynamic and static content [17].

For our project, we designed a three tiers architecture as in Fig. 8, we created a firebase database as shown in Fig. 9, and we connected it with the ESP32 card.The data arriving from the server via the SIM card with a send interval of 5 min. The energy produced is stored in the capacity attribute, while the corresponding production price in the srno attribute, with the price per kWh considered in this study, is 0.2 €.

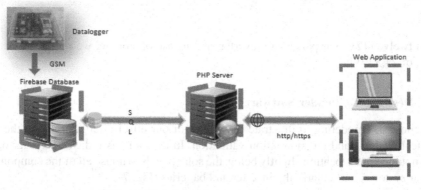

Fig. 8. Global Architecture of the system

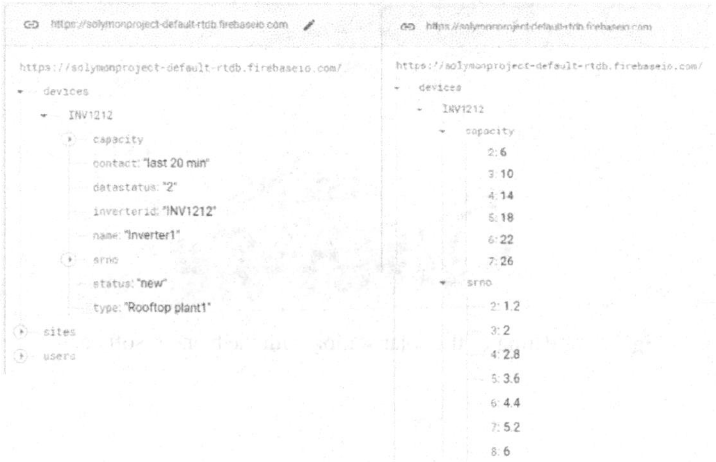

Fig. 9. Data Storage in Firebase Database

4.6 Software for Monitoring

We created an IT solution for this study using the free PHP language version 7.1, which we connected to the Firebase database with. Our application's web interface is depicted in Fig. 10 where we put an email address and a password to authenticate.

Fig. 10. Authentification interface

In the web application, we have created three linked tables which will contain the data of the user or the owner of the solar site, also another called site which contains the data of the site as well as the location, the number of panels installed and the type of installation, and the last called device which contains the inverters and the results of storage in the database. Figure 11 shows the performance of our site connected to a single inverter.

Fig. 11. Data visualization on the web application

5 Conclusion and Future Works

This project concerns the study and design of a charging station powered by photovoltaic panels, it is economically realizable for the solution connected to the network, because the return-on-investment time is approximately 8 years.

Indeed, this project makes it possible to eliminate 3308 kg of CO_2/year contributing to the preservation of the environment and demonstrating that the use of renewable energies is the solution to the pollution of the environment.

Furthermore, The proposed energy monitoring system gives accurate values of energy production and cost each 5 min.

In addition, The software developed using PHP language, which gets the data from the datalogger using GSM protocols and sends it to the Firebase database.The monitoring of photovoltaic panels production can connect to this solution as many inverters in order to have a global follow-up.

Our top objective for future work is to confirm the accuracy of this work through implementation in real project, and then to test the system's capacity to guarantee good performance for numerous loading terminals and adding in the same software a machine learning algorithm to predict future energy production.

References

1. Hu, A., et al.: Impact of solar panels on global climate. Nat. Clim. Change **6**(3), 3 (2016). https://doi.org/10.1038/nclimate2843
2. Saleem, A., Liu, N., Junjie, H., Iqbal, A., Hayyat, M. A., Mateen, M.: An electric vehicle using on-board maximum utilization of renewable energy for a green and clean environment. In 2020 3rd International Conference on Computing, Mathematics and Engineering Technologies (iCoMET), pp. 1–5 (2020). doi:https://doi.org/10.1109/iCoMET48670.2020.9074114
3. Kotilainen, K., Mäkinen, S. J., Valta, J.: Sustainable electric vehicle-prosumer framework and policy mix. In 2017 IEEE Innovative Smart Grid Technologies—Asia (ISGT-Asia), pp. 1–6 (2017). doi:https://doi.org/10.1109/ISGT-Asia.2017.8378406
4. Iqbal, F., Siddiqui, A., Deb, T.: Study of xEV charging infrastructure and the role of microgrid and smart grid in its development (2017). https://doi.org/10.1080/23080477.2017.1317197
5. Zhou, X. *et al.*: The current research on electric vehicle. In 2016 Chinese Control and Decision Conference (CCDC), pp. 5190–5194 (2016). doi:https://doi.org/10.1109/CCDC.2016.7531925
6. Electric Vehicles—IEEE Transportation Electrification Community: https://tec.ieee.org/newsletter/june-2021/electric-vehicles
7. Kurniawan, D., Priharta, A., Putri, N. S. F.: Solar panel modeling and simulation with MPPT technique on micro grid. In: 2021 7th International Conference on Electrical, Electronics and Information Engineering (ICEEIE), pp. 1–6 (2021). doi:https://doi.org/10.1109/ICEEIE52663.2021.9616834
8. Fig. 1. SIRVE EV Charging Station: https://www.researchgate.net/figure/SIRVE-EV-charging-station_fig1_327727586
9. Pinjari, T.S., Shinde, S., Salunkhe, R., Gadhave, S., Bansode, S.: Solar charging station for electric vehicles. **2**(1), 7 (2016)
10. Singh, T., Thakur, R.: Design and development of PV solar panel data logger. Int J Comput Sci Eng **7**, 364–369 (2019). https://doi.org/10.26438/ijcse/v7i4.364369
11. Elwati, J., Khalid, E. M., Hartiti, B.: PV monitoring system : Data logger based on PcDuino a single board computer (2021)
12. Hamidi, A., Weber, L., Nasiri, A.: EV charging station integrating renewable energy and second-life battery. In 2013 International Conference on Renewable Energy Research and Applications (ICRERA), pp. 1217–1221 (2013). doi:https://doi.org/10.1109/ICRERA.2013.6749937
13. Longo, M., Yaïci, W., Foiadelli, F.: Electric vehicles charged with residential's roof solar photovoltaic system: A case study in Ottawa. In 2017 IEEE 6th International Conference on Renewable Energy Research Appllication, ICRERA (2017). doi: https://doi.org/10.1109/ICRERA.2017.8191252

14. Global Solar Atlas: https://globalsolaratlas.info/map.
15. Electric Car Charge Time Calculator: (2020). https://www.nimblefins.co.uk/electric-car-cha
    rge-time-calculator
16. Table 1 : Technical data of the investigated electric vehicles: https://www.researchgate.net/
    figure/Technical-data-of-the-investigated-electric-vehicles_tbl1_238042729
17. Firebase Realtime Database|Firebase Documentation: https://firebase.google.com/docs/dat
    abase

Low-Cost Smart Irrigation System Based on Internet of Things and Fuzzy Logic

Ali Mhaned[(✉)], Salma Mouatassim, Mounia El Haji, and Jamal Benhra

Laboratory of Advanced Research in Industrial and Logistic Engineering, Superior National School of Electricity and Mechanic (ENSEM), University Hassan II, Casablanca, Morocco
ali.mhaned.doc21@ensem.ac.ma

Abstract. The world's needs for water, energy and food are constantly increasing. This pattern which only seems to be growing creates global challenges which are critical for our survival as a species, mainly the need to provide enough food while conserving the limited water sources that are still available. Irrigation is one of the most resource hungry processes in this global chain, accentuated most by the use of traditional methods. New systems based on the technologies of the Internet of Things (IoT) and Wireless Sensor Networks (WSN) are available to automate the irrigation process. In this paper we present a low-cost system that aims at reducing both human intervention and water consumption. This system acquires data about soil moisture, ambient temperature and humidity as well as rain presence parameters. MQTT protocol is used to transmit data between nodes and the Raspberry Pi device, data is then sent to ThingSpeak in order to be checked by the user in real time. The latter can then decide either to automate the irrigation scheduling based on sensed parameters, or to manually control the wireless solenoid valves through a mobile application. Fuzzy logic was implemented to assure proper functioning of the system at the operational stage, through defining the rules that govern the flow of the right quantities of water.

Keywords: Low-cost · Smart irrigation systems · Internet of Things (IoT) · Wireless Sensor Networks (WSN) · Fuzzy logic

1 Introduction

The world population has been continuously growing, the global needs for water and food following suit. To be able to provide, agriculture at its current level consumes about 70% of water compared to other sectors [1]. Traditional systems present relatively large volumes irrigation water, their main fault being that the dispensed quantities of water are often more than what the plantation actually needs. Automated irrigation systems are used to limit human intervention, which often requires muscle labor, and to control the quantities of applied water.

Intelligent irrigation systems are able to define the right quantities used in irrigation. Creating intelligent irrigation strategies from the acquired physical parameters related to the plant and its environment. Most systems are based on: soil temperature and humidity, ambient temperature and humidity, luminosity, wind speed and even compounds of the preceding parameters such as evapotranspiration.

Technological advances in the fields of electronics, communication and data monitoring have allowed systems such as wireless sensor networks to present their applicability. WSN are often used in agriculture to monitor physical-chemical parameters from the field, as well as to facilitate real-time access to the acquired values.

The aim being to develop a reliable system for smart irrigation of greenhouses using artificial neural networks, and an IoT architecture. The solution agreed upon was to employ a Raspberry Pi which would be responsible for communicating with the cloud server and the end points. The Raspberry Pi communicates with endpoint devices using a ZigBee device [2]. MQTT-SN which is a version of MQTT more adapted to wireless sensor networks was used as the communication protocol for the network. Each end point consists of moisture sensors embedded in different depths of the soil that provide sensory data, and solenoid valves as actuators. At the end point's heart is a low-power and low-cost microcontroller.

An IoT platform based on ThingSpeak and NodeMCU is demonstrated, which will help the end user to control the irrigation by using a PC or smartphone from anywhere at any time. The system also provides access to moisture and temperature parameters in order to reduce user effort and to optimize the use of water [3]. A PIR sensor is used to sense the motion of a warm body. Sensor's value is sent to the IoT platform and if a value is below the threshold a notification will be sent to the user through e-mail to take appropriate action. A ThingSpeak cloud platform is used to store the data and apply MATLAB analysis to take action.

In [4], the analysis covers the design and construction of an intelligent irrigation system based on fuzzy logic applied in vegetable crops. The fundamental mechanism of this system was to realize the control of irrigation through a scheme consisting of two modules, the data acquisition module, and the decision-making module. Meteorological variables such as precipitation, temperature, the humidity of the environment and soil moisture were evaluated, they are considered as input variables for the diffuse system. Fuzzy logic was used as a control mechanism, the operation of the prototype is crystallized in a functional graphical interface and tested in two scenarios, where its efficiency in the proper use of the water supply is demonstrated.

The main system in [5] consists of the three sensors i.e., temperature and humidity sensor, soil moisture sensor, and PIR sensor. All these sensors are interfaced with NodeMCU which has inbuilt WIFI. By using wireless communication, the data is uploaded to the ThingSpeak cloud platform at a regular interval of 15 s. There is a threshold value assigned to each sensor as the sensor value crosses threshold value an e-mail notification is sent to the user.

After flying over some works related to the subject, in what follows we will present the proposed system, the results obtained and the conclusions.

2   Methodology

2.1   Smart Irrigation System Architecture

The proposed system, as shown in Fig. 1, is based on NodeMCU 32S boards functioning to acquire ambient temperature and humidity, soil moisture and temperature, luminance and rain presence. Node MCU boards are connected to a wireless network and sensed parameters are sent over MQTT protocol. To control irrigation pumps, NodeMCU boards receive command from the system implanted in the Raspberry Pi. When the order of irrigation is received, the relay module operates on a solenoid valve. The farmer can at any time check real time values of sensed data by using a mobile application. ThingSpeak is used to monitor parameters.

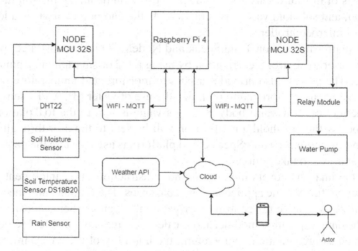

Fig. 1. Smart irrigation system design

Table 1 includes the hardware price list of boards and sensors used in the system presented in Fig. 1. The nodes are based on Node MCU 32S which act as an IoT board, the board includes a wireless module that grants easy connection to a wireless network. For sensing nodes, the DHT22 module is used to sense ambient temperature & humidity. A capacitive soil moisture sensor has been chosen to avoid corrosion which is the main problem in resistive soil moisture sensors. The DS18B20 sensor is used to acquire soil temperature values. A rain sensor is used to detect rain presence. Control nodes are connected to a relay module responsible for actuating the solenoid valve. Sensing and control node material cost respectively about 29 and 22$ per node. A Raspberry Pi 4 costs approximately 40$ depending on the board characteristics.

Table 1. Smart irrigation system list of materials

	Material	Description	Price
Sensing Node	Node MCU 32 S	IoT Board	8$
	DHT 22	Ambient Temperature & Humidity	8$
	Capacitive Soil Moisture Sensor	Soil Moisture Sensor	6$
	DS18B20	Soil Temperature	4$
	Rain Sensor	Rain Presence	3$
	Total price/ per node		29$
Control Node	Node MCU 32 S	IoT Board	8$
	Relay Module	Relay Module	3$
	Solenoid Valve	Solenoid Valve	11$
	Total price/ per node		22$

2.2 Fuzzy Logic System

The fuzzy logic control system strurcture is illustrated in Fig. 2 [10, 11]. The system consists of four blocks that are Fuzzification, Inference engine, if-then rules and Defuzzification similar to [6]. The inputs to the system will be analog values. However, the Fuzzificaiton will allocate the crisp inputs into fuzzy sets. The if-Then rules are applied to the inference engine together with the fuzzified sets. The fuzzified inputs are then put into different sets according to the membership functions. The output from the controller is the defuzzified form in the crisp form.

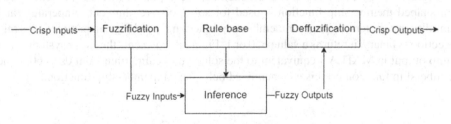

Fig. 2. Fuzzy Logic structure

In Table 2, a linguistic description of each fuzzy parameter is given. The soil moisture input is divided into three intervals "Dry, Medium, Wet" corresponding to a value between 0% and 100%. Ambient humidity values between 0% and 100% are divided into three intervals "Low, Medium, High". Ambient Temperature values between −10 °C and 50 °C correspond to three intervals "Low, Medium, High". Rain presence is a binary input: if 0 no rain is present, 1 means rain presence.

Table 2. Linguistic description of Fuzzy parameters

Fuzzy parameters [Range]	Linguistic description
Soil Moisture [0% 100%]	Dry Medium Wet
Ambient Temperature [-10 °C 50 °C]	Low Medium High
Ambient Humidity [0% 100%]	Low Medium High
Rainfall [0 1]	No_Rain Rainy
Water Pump [0min 60min]	Off Short Medium Long

In Fig. 3, the proposed fuzzy system is represented. The system is created in MAT-LAB using Fuzzy Logic Designer extension [6–9, 12, 13]. Four inputs are considered: Soil Moisture, Ambient Temperature, Ambient Humidity and Rain. The output is the water quantity to be delivered to the plant, equivalent to the operating time of the water pump between 0 and 60 min.

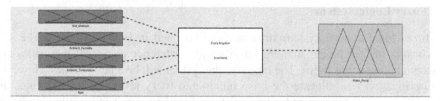

Fig. 3. Fuzzy irrigation system inputs/outputs in MATLAB

Figures 4, 5, 6 and 7 represents the membership inputs in MATLAB. Generalized bell-shaped membership function is used for soil moisture, ambient temperature and humidity parameters. Triangular membership function is used for rain parameter, as rain detection is binary, it returns a value of 0 or 1. Figure 8 represents the fuzzy system water pump output in MATLAB equivalent to the solenoid opening time from 0s to 60s. The membership function used is a Generalized bell-shaped membership function.

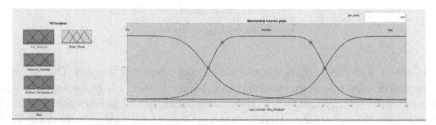

Fig. 4. Input Membership Function of Soil Moisture

There are 54 rules proposed based on farmer experience. The format of the fuzzy rules takes on an aspect as specified in Tables 3, 4, 5 and 6. The rules have been established

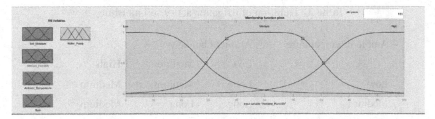

Fig. 5. Input Membership Function of Ambient humidity

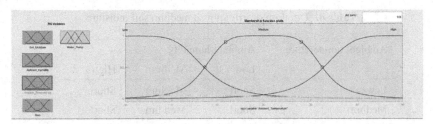

Fig. 6. Input Membership Function of Ambient temperature

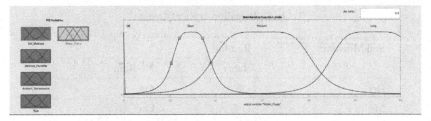

Fig. 7. Input Membership Function of rain

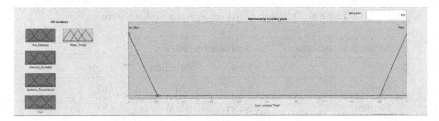

Fig. 8. Output Membership Function of Water pump

corresponding to the soil moisture in relation to the ambient temperature and humidity. The ruler system is designed to stop irrigation when it rains to avoid overirrigation. Tables 3, 4, 5 and 6 introduces the rule system on MATLAB fuzzy logic designer, it's based similar to [6–8] adding in consideration rain presence. Rules can be modified later according to the customer's experience or in case of lack of water resources.

Table 3. Duration of irrigation at dry soil moisture

Ambient temperature	Ambient humidity		
	Low	Medium	High
Low	Long	Medium	Medium
Medium	Long	Long	Medium
High	Long	Long	Long

Table 4. Duration of irrigation at medium soil moisture

Ambient temperature	Ambient humidity		
	Low	Medium	High
Low	Short	Medium	Short
Medium	Short	Medium	Short
High	Medium	Medium	Medium

Table 5. Duration of irrigation at wet soil moisture

Ambient temperature	Ambient humidity		
	Low	Medium	High
Low	Off	Off	Off
Medium	Short	Short	Off
High	Short	Short	Short

Table 6. Irrigation at Rainfall state

Soil Moisture	Rainfall	
	Rainy	No Rain
Dry	Off	On
Medium	Off	On
Wet	Off	On

After establishing the different rules of the fuzzy irrigation controller, they were used to create the fuzzy ruler, as shown in Fig. 9. Using If-Then formulas. The weight of each rule has been set to 1, it could be modified later.

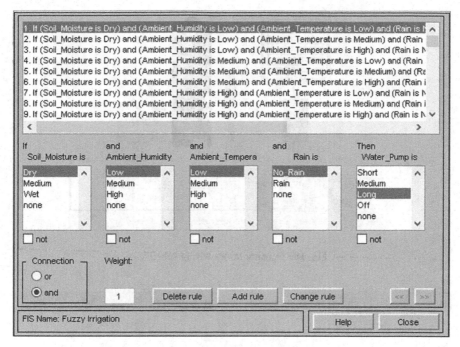

Fig. 9. Fuzzy rules on MATLAB

3 Results

The sensing node is wired as in Fig. 10, the NodeMCU 32S node is embedded in a waterproof box to prevent water damage. Soil moisture and soil temperature sensors will be planted in the ground, rain presence sensor will face upwards. Visible electronic parts must be kept out and away from water to avoid parts damage.

Figure 11 represents the ThingSpeak dashboard, each chart contains real time data visualization, each field contains a graph of the relevant value in real time. A backup history of sensed data is available in ThingSpeak platform.

The serial communication through the Arduino IDE, Fig. 12, allows to visualize in real time the execution of the algorithm implemented on the node. A node can be either a sensing node or a control node. When turned on, the node connects to the WIFI network. The network credentials are defined in the program implemented. The node IP address, ID and type (sensing or control node). In case of a sensing node, the system reads values from sensors, displays the reading on the serial monitor and sends variables values to ThingSpeak server. In case of a control node, the system acts when an instruction is received, an instruction contains the solenoid opening time.

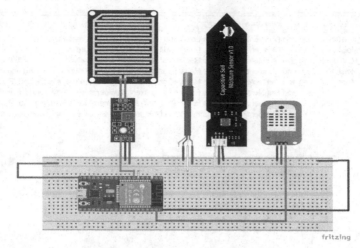

Fig. 10. Sensing nodes wiring schema

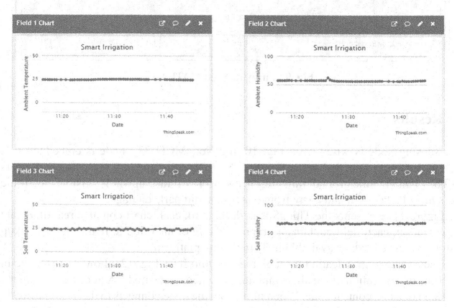

Fig. 11. Ambient temperature, Ambient humidity, Soil temperature and Soil humidity monitoring from node 1 viaThingSpeak

The designed fuzzy logic controller for smart irrigation permit to calculate the solenoid opening time. Figure 13, the output value of solenoid opening time corresponding to the input values according to the established rules.

In most works that use fuzzy logic, the number of inputs generally varies between 3 and 6 variables among these parameters: ambient temperature, ambient humidity, soil humidity, luminance, soil temperature and precipitation. The number of inputs and the number and type of membership function affects the number of rules established. For that it is necessary to define the characteristics of the system so as not to have a large number of rules.

```
12:01:56.983 -> Connecting to WiFi .....
12:02:00.003 -> WiFi connected
12:02:00.003 -> IP ADDRESS: 192.168.2.129
12:02:00.003 -> Node ID: Node 1
12:02:00.003 -> Node Type: Sensing Node
12:02:05.741 -> Ambient Humidity: 64.80 %,  Ambient Temperature: 25.80 C ,  Soil Temperature: 23.00 C ,  Soil Humidity: 70.00 % , Rain: No_Rain
12:02:17.321 -> Channel updated successful. Data is uploaded to ThingSpeak channel
12:02:28.099 -> Ambient Humidity: 64.90 %,  Ambient Temperature: 25.80 C ,  Soil Temperature: 23.00 C ,  Soil Humidity: 70.00 % , Rain: No_Rain
12:02:39.777 -> Channel updated successful. Data is uploaded to ThingSpeak channel
12:02:50.533 -> Ambient Humidity: 65.00 %,  Ambient Temperature: 25.80 C ,  Soil Temperature: 23.00 C ,  Soil Humidity: 70.00 % , Rain: No_Rain
12:03:02.136 -> Channel updated successful. Data is uploaded to ThingSpeak channel
12:03:12.901 -> Ambient Humidity: 64.80 %,  Ambient Temperature: 25.70 C ,  Soil Temperature: 23.00 C ,  Soil Humidity: 70.00 % , Rain: No_Rain
12:03:24.640 -> Channel updated successful. Data is uploaded to ThingSpeak channel
12:03:35.440 -> Ambient Humidity: 65.00 %,  Ambient Temperature: 25.80 C ,  Soil Temperature: 23.00 C ,  Soil Humidity: 70.00 % , Rain: No_Rain
12:03:47.021 -> Channel updated successful. Data is uploaded to ThingSpeak channel
12:03:57.822 -> Ambient Humidity: 65.00 %,  Ambient Temperature: 25.80 C ,  Soil Temperature: 23.00 C ,  Soil Humidity: 70.00 % , Rain: No_Rain
```

Fig. 12. Arduino serial communication

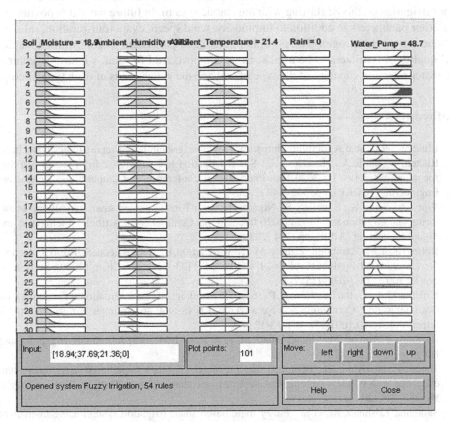

Fig. 13. Fuzzy system Output simulation

4 Conclusion

In this work, we were able to construct a data acquisition system that transmits in real time the values of monitored parameters such as soil moisture, ambient temperature and humidity, luminosity and the presence of rain. These parameters are necessary to define the right quantities of irrigation water. The design of the acquisition and control system is inspired by wireless sensor networks, the acquisition and control nodes are based on the NODE MCU32S cards, these cards are equipped with a WIFI module which helps avoid connection problems when using microcontroller cards with a separate WIFI module. The MQTT protocol was used to transmit the data via WIFI connection since it offers lightness and ease of integration. Fuzzy logic was used to set the valve opening time, the predefined opening time corresponds to the plants water needs based on the environmental conditions of the plant. By that rounding up the system achieving the goals set of minimizing human labor, optimizing the use of resources in the irrigation network and assuring correct assumptions about ambient conditions. To prove the effectiveness of this system, the work that will follow will focus on the comparison with other irrigation methods: starting with the classic system. In future work it is possible to use other parameters in addition to luminosity, wind speed, evapotranspiration, salinity, conductivity, pH, nitrogen (N), phosphorus (P), and potassium to control the quantity and quality of fertilizers to be used such as compost. And for that, we have to control the water retention capacity of the type of soil and the water needs of each type of crop.

References

1. Link: Water-Global Agriculture: https://www.globalagriculture.org/report-topics/water.html
2. Risheh, A., Jalili A., Nazerfard, E.: Smart irrigation IoT solution using transfer learning for neural networks. In: 2020 10th International Conference on Computer and Knowledge Engineering (ICCKE), pp. 342–349 (2020)
3. Vijay, A., Saini, K., Banerjee, S., Nigam, H.: An IoT instrumented smart agricultural monitoring and irrigation system. In: 2020 International Conference on Artificial Intelligence and Signal Processing (AISP), pp. 1–4 (2020)
4. Botto-Tobar, M., Zambrano Vizuete, M., Torres-Carrión, P., Montes León, S., Pizarro Vásquez, G., Durakovic, B. (eds.): ICAT 2019. CCIS, vol. 1193. Springer, Cham (2020). https://doi.org/10.1007/978-3-030-42517-3
5. Krishna, C.R., Dutta, M., Kumar, R. (eds.): Proceedings of 2nd International Conference on Communication, Computing and Networking. LNNS, vol. 46. Springer, Singapore (2019). https://doi.org/10.1007/978-981-13-1217-5
6. Izzuddin, T. Ahmad, M. Ahmad Johari, M. Z. A. Rashid, M. Hafiz Jali: Smart irrigation using fuzzy logic method (2018)
7. Touati, F., Al-Hitmi, M., Benhmed, K., Tabish, R.: A fuzzy logic based irrigation system enhanced with wireless data logging applied to the state of Qatar. Comput. Electron. Agric. **98**, 233–241 (2013)
8. Santhana Krishnan, R., et al.: Fuzzy logic based smart irrigation system using internet of things. J. Clean. Prod. **252**, 119902 (2020)
9. Ibrahim, F.S., Dominic, K., Musyoki, S.: Smart irrigation system using a fuzzy logic method. Int. J. Eng. Res. Technol. **11**, 1417–1436 (2018)

10. Zhang, Q. X., Wu, C. H., Tilt, K.: Application of fuzzy logic in an irrigation control system. In: Proceedings of the IEEE International Conference on Industrial Technology (ICIT'96), 2–6 December, Shanghai, China, pp. 593–597 (1996)
11. Mirabbasi, R., Mazloumzadeh, S.M., Rahnama, M.B.: Evaluation of irrigation water quality using fuzzy logic. Res. J. Environ. Sci. **2**(5), 340–352 (2008)
12. Ben Ali, R., Bouadila, S., Mami, A.: Development of a fuzzy logic controller applied to an agricultural greenhouse experimentally validated. Appl. Therm. Eng. **141**, 798–810 (2018)
13. Martínez, S.L., Tarifa, E.E., Domínguez, S.F.J.D.: Algoritmo para linealización de controladores fuzzy. **11**, 11 (2017)

AI-Driven Methods 2

autoTimeSVD++: A Temporal Hybrid Recommender System Based on Contractive Autoencoder and Matrix Factorization

Abdelghani Azri[1]([✉])([iD]), Adil Haddi[2], and Hakim Allali[1]

[1] Hassan First University of Settat, FST, LAVETE Laboratory,
Settat 26000, Morocco
{a.azri,a.haddi,hakim.allali}@uhp.ac.ma

[2] Hassan First University of Settat, ENSA, LAVETE Laboratory,
Berrechid 26100, Morocco

Abstract. Matrix factorization is one of the successful approaches used largely in Recommender systems to provide recommendations to users based on their historical preferences. In recent years, many approaches based on deep learning, such as autoencoders, were used alone or combined with other methods to extract non-linear relationships between items. But most of these models are static and do not capture dynamic changes regarding the rating process which is dynamic and may change over time. In this paper, we propose a new hybrid model **autoTimeSVD++** which combines timeSVD++ and autoencoder to extract item side information including time effect. The experimental results show that the proposed model achieves competitive results compared to many baselines models.

Keywords: Recommender system · Collaborative filtering · Deep learning · TimeSVD++ · Contractive autoencoder

1 Problem Formulation

Let's define S_I a set of items i of size $n \in \mathbb{N}$: $S_I = \{i_1, i_2, ..., i_n\}$ and S_U a set of users u of size $m \in \mathbb{N}$: $S_U = \{u_1, u_2, ..., u_m\}$. The matrix representing the interaction between users and items is called the rating matrix R. It's defined as a sparse matrix with n lines and m columns: $R \in \mathbb{R}^{m \times n}$. The rating value $r_{ui}(t)$ is the rating given by a user u for an item i in a day t. Let's also define an item features vector $f_i = \{f_1, .., f_X\}$ of size X.

2 Introduction

Nowadays, it's hard to avoid Recommender Systems. At many companies, recommendations are used to help customers to find relevant products and businesses

© The Author(s), under exclusive license to Springer Nature Switzerland AG 2022
M. Hamlich et al. (Eds.): SADASC 2022, CCIS 1677, pp. 93–103, 2022.
https://doi.org/10.1007/978-3-031-20490-6_8

sell more items or products. In general, A Recommender System (RS) is a platform used to provide adequate items to Users such as products, books, movies and music.

Collaborative Filtering (CF) is one of the successful approaches especially after the success of the Netflix context. CF approach uses user's historical preferences over items to propose new items that can interest this user. Many notable methods used in the CF are those based on Matrix Factorization [4], Other methods use probabilistic techniques such as PMF [9] and BPR [11] which uses ranking personalization in prediction and Bayesian Probability.

Recently, some other methods use the Deep Learning techniques such as the Autoencoder (AE) techniques [13,15]. But most of these approaches are static. Most of them are widely used to capture the interaction between users and items. However, the recommendation process is dynamic and may change over time. In this article, we first present some successful approaches that use matrix factorization techniques [6,14] and an approach based on Autoencoder: autoSVD++ that used the item features in addition to the rating information. Then, we will present our approach which is a combination of the autoSVD++ and timeSVD++. Our approach is based on the timeSVD++ model and uses a Contractive Autoencoder applied on item features. Finally, we present the results of our experiments and the future work.

3   Related Work

Matrix factorization(MF) [2,6,7,10] is a solution for sparse data problems based on latent factors, it has become widely known since the Netflix Prize Challenge. We assume that we have k latent factors where $k \in \mathbf{K}$ ($\mathbf{K}$ is the latent factors space). The MF technique is based on Single Value Decomposition (SVD) aims to transform items and users to the same latent factor space, thus making them directly comparable. The principle of the MF consists to approximate the rating matrix $R \in \mathbb{R}^{m \times n}$ using k latent factors, so we look to find two matrices: $Q \in \mathbb{R}^{m \times k}$ and $P \in \mathbb{R}^{k \times n}$. So R is approximately the product of two matrices: Q and P.

Many variants of MF are largely studied by the researchers:

3.1   SVD

The basic version of matrix factorization using SVD [6] is given by the Eq. 1 without any bias:

$$\hat{r}_{ui} = q_i^{\mathsf{T}} p_u = \sum_{k=1}^{k} q_{ki} p_{uk} \tag{1}$$

3.2   Biased-SVD

It's a variant of SVD model built by adding an item bias b_i and a user bias b_u. The model's equation is given in the Eq. 2:

$$\hat{r}_{ui} = q_i^{\mathsf{T}} p_u + \mu + b_i + b_u \tag{2}$$

3.3 SVD++

The SVD++ [6,7] is an extension version of Biased-SVD built by adding a term representing the user's implicit feedback. This feedback represents the tendencies of the user regarding some items, it can be represented by binary values, so if the user rates an item, we give the value 1, otherwise the value 0 is taken. SVD++ is given in Eq. 3:

$$\hat{r}_{ui} = \mu + b_i + b_u + q_i^{\mathsf{T}}(p_u + \frac{\sum_{j \in N(u)} y_j}{\sqrt{|N(u)|}}) \tag{3}$$

In recent years, many extensions of matrix factorization have been developed using deep learning techniques such as Autoencoder (AE) or Convolution Neural Network (CNN).

3.4 autoSVD++

autoSVD++ is a hybrid model proposed in [15], it extends the SVD++ model by adding item features extracted based on the Contractive Autoencoder (CAE) model proposed by [12]. The idea of CAE is to make the learned representation to be robust towards small changes around the training examples.

$$\hat{r}_{ui} = \mu + b_i + b_u + (\beta \cdot CAE(c_i) + q_i)^{\mathsf{T}}(p_u + \frac{\sum_{j \in N(u)} y_j}{\sqrt{|N(u)|}}) \tag{4}$$

where $CAE(f_i)$ is mentioned in Eq. 10 and f_i is the item features vector.

4 Our Model

The discussed models are static and don't include the factor of time in the rating process. It's known that Users preferences may change over time, for example, A user who preferred "action movies" some years ago, may now like "fiction movies". In this section we propose a new hybrid model called **auto-TimeSVD++** which extends the autoSVD++ model proposed in [1,15] by adding a temporal aspect based on timeSVD++ cited in [5]. It includes the implicit feedback, the temporal aspect and the item side information. Let us first introduce the components of our model as follows:

4.1 Contractive Autoencoder (CAE)

Definition 1 (Autoencoder). *An Autoencoder [3] is a type of Artificial Neural Network composed of two parts: An encoder and a decoder. The encoder is used to encode an input using a hidden layer into a compressed representation and the decoder is used to decode it to a reconstruction of this input.*

Definition 2 (Contractive Autoencoder (CAE)). *The CAE [12] is a variant of the Autoencoders that aims to make the input robust regarding the small changes around the training points level, by adding a penalty term to the usual reconstruction error function.*

CAE Computation. The CAE is computed as follows:

– We project the input in a hidden latent space h via the Eq. 5:

$$h = f(x) = \sigma(Wx + b_h) \tag{5}$$

where $x \in \mathbb{R}^{d_x}$ is the input, $h(x) \in \mathbb{R}^{d_h}$ is the hidden layer, $b_h \in \mathbb{R}^{d_h}$ is bias vector and W is a weight matrix corresponding to the encoder.
– Then, the CAE reconstructs the output by computing the reconstruction of the given input via the Eq. 6:

$$y = g(h) = \sigma(W'h + b_y) \tag{6}$$

where $b_y \in \mathbb{R}^{d_x}$ is the bias vector and W is a weight matrix of the decoder.

As proposed by the authors in [12], we assume that $W^{\top} = W'$ where $\{W, W'\} \in \mathbb{R}^{d_y \times d_x} \times \mathbb{R}^{d_y \times d_x}$
– Finally, we use an objective function to learn the CAE parameters $\{W, W', b_h, b_y\}$. The objective function formula is given by the Eq. 7:

$$Loss_{CAE}(\theta) = \sum_{x \in D_n} (L(x, g(f(x)))) + \lambda \|J_h(x)\|_F^2 \tag{7}$$

L is the reconstruction error. In our case, we use the cross-entropy loss:

$$L(x, y) = \sum_{i=1}^{d_x} x_i log(y_i) + (1 - x)log(1 - y_i) \tag{8}$$

same as chosen in the CAE paper [12]. $J_h(x)$ is the regulation term corresponds to the Jacobian matrix in Frobenius norm $\| \|_F^2$ is given by the Eq. 9:

$$\|J_h(x)\|_F^2 = \sum_{ij} \left(\frac{\partial h_j(x)}{\partial x_i} \right)^2 \tag{9}$$

where σ is the *sigmoid* activation function : $\sigma(z) = \frac{1}{1+\exp(-z)}$.

This regulation term is computed by summing the squares of all partial derivatives corresponding to the extracted features of the input dimensions.

We summarise these operations in Fig. (1):

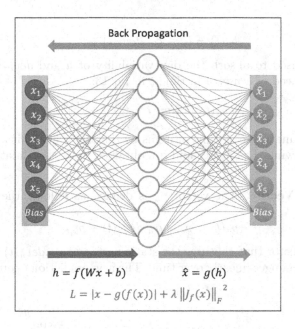

Fig. 1. Contractive Autoencoder (CAE)

Features Extraction with CAE. The CAE model is applied to extract compressed features from the One-Hot encoding features.

The feature vector is generated using the Eq. 10:

$$CAE(f_i) = \sigma(W.f_i + b_h) \qquad (10)$$

where σ is the *sigmoid* activation function.

4.2 TimeSVD++

timeSVD++ introduced for the first time in [5] is an extension of the SVD++. The authors have introduced many changes in the existing parameters of SVD++ in order to express user's preferences over time. The change impacts the following levels:

Item Bias: The item bias b_i is transformed to a new parameter $b_i(t)$ which contains both the static part and dynamic part. The time range is split into time-based bins (30 bins) as defined in the original paper [1,5]. Each bin presents a period of time. The new expression of the item bias is given in Eq. 11:

$$b_i(t) = b_i + b_{i,Bin(t)} \qquad (11)$$

User Bias:
$$b_u(t) = b_u + \alpha_u.dev_u(t) + b_{u,t} \tag{12}$$

Where $b_{u,t}$ is used to absorb the day variability of u and $dev_u(t)$ is the drift concept introduced of a user u in time t in Eq. 13:

$$dev_u(t) = sign(t - t_u).|t - t_u|^\beta \tag{13}$$

where t_u is the mean rating time of items by the user u and β is a parameter to be defined following the dataset and it's obtained by cross-validation.

User Latent Vector: The vector p_u is defined as follows, the same way in [1,5]:
$$p_u(t) = p_u + \alpha_u.dev_u(t) + p_{u,t} \tag{14}$$

where p_u is a vector that captures the static part, and $\alpha_u.dev_u(t)$ approximates a portion that changes linearly over time. The new prediction expression is given by the Eq. 15:

$$\hat{r}_{ui}(t) = \mu + b_u(t) + b_i(t) + q_i^\mathsf{T}(p_u(t) + \frac{\sum\limits_{j \in N(u)} y_j}{\sqrt{|N(u)|}}) \tag{15}$$

.

4.3 AutoTimeSVD++

By combining equations (10) and (15) we obtain the prediction rating formula of the **autoTimeSVD++** model given in Eq. 16:

$$\hat{r}_{ui}(t) = \mu + b_i(t) + b_u(t) + (\theta.CAE(f_i) + q_i)^\mathsf{T}(p_u + \alpha_u.dev_u(t) + p_{u,t} + \frac{\sum\limits_{j \in N(u)} y_j}{\sqrt{|N(u)|}}) \tag{16}$$

θ is a parameter used to normalize $CAE(f_i)$.
In order to implement the model:

- First, we extract and encode features from each item using One-Shot encoding (values are 1 if the feature is present or otherwise, the value of 0 is used).
- Then, we use CAE to extract compressed features in order to capture more significant relationships
- We apply a linear transformation to reduce the dimension of each feature vector to the latent factor space dimension k
- Finally, the timeSVD++ model is combined with CAE to compute the rating for each user r_{ui}.

The architecture of our model is described in Fig. (2):

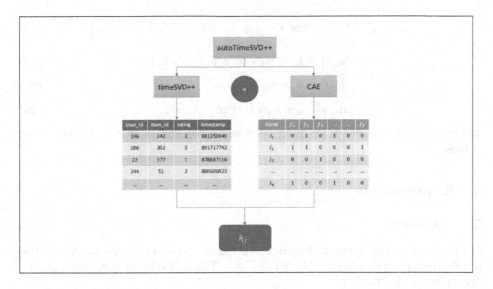

Fig. 2. autoTimeSVD++ model architecture

4.4 Optimization

The loss function of our model is given in Eq. 17:

$$
\mathcal{J} = \min \sum_{u,i \in K} \left[r_{ui}(t) - (\theta.CAE(f_i) + q_i)^\mathsf{T} (p_u(t) + \frac{\sum\limits_{j \in N(u)} y_j}{\sqrt{|N(u)|}}) \right.
$$
$$
- \mu - b_u - b_i]^2 +
$$
$$
\lambda(b_u^2 + b_i^2 + b_u(t)^2 + b_i(t)^2 + \alpha_u^2 + \|p_u\|^2 + \|q_i\|^2 + \sum_{j \in N(u)} \|y_j\|^2) \quad (17)
$$

In order to learn the parameters corresponding to the model, we use the Stochastic Gradient Descent (SGD) algorithm using 20 epochs. The SGD calculates a single prediction $r_{ui}(t)$ and it's error, in Eq. 18:

$$
error_{ui} = r_{ui}(t) - \hat{r}_{ui}(t) \quad (18)
$$

The update rules for the autoTimeSVD++ are as follows:

$$
b_u = b_u + \gamma_1 * (error - \lambda_1 * b_u) \quad (19)
$$

$$
b_i = b_i + \gamma_1 * (error - \lambda_1 * b_i) \quad (20)
$$

$$
q_i = q_i + \gamma_2 * (error * p_u - \lambda_2 * q_i) \quad (21)
$$

$$
p_u = p_u + \gamma_2 * (error * (q_i + \theta.CAE(f_i)) - \lambda_2 * p_u) \quad (22)
$$

$$y_j = y_j + \gamma_2 * (error * \frac{1}{\sqrt{|N(u)|}}(\theta.CAE(f_i)) - \lambda_2 * q_i) \tag{23}$$

$$b_u(t) = b_u + \gamma_3 * (error - \lambda_3 * b_u) \tag{24}$$

$$b_i(t) = b_i + \gamma_3 * (error - \lambda_3 * b_i) \tag{25}$$

$$\alpha_u = \alpha_u + \gamma_\alpha * (error - \lambda_\alpha * \alpha_u) \tag{26}$$

where γ_1, γ_2 and γ_3 are the learning rates and λ_1, λ_2 and λ_3 are the regularization values.

5 Experiments

5.1 Datasets

For training and evaluation of models, we conducted several experiments on two public datasets provided by MovieLens site. The statistics of both datasets are presented in the Table (1):

Table 1. Movielens Datasets

dataset	#items	#users	#ratings	sparsity(%)
MovieLens 100k	1682	943	100000	93.7
MovieLens 1M	3706	6040	1000209	95.54

5.2 Evaluation

For evaluation, we use the Root Mean Square Error (RMSE) metric given by the Eq. 27:

$$\mathbf{RMSE} = \sqrt{\frac{1}{|T|} \sum_{(u,i)\in T} (\hat{r}_{ui} - r_{ui})^2} \tag{27}$$

where T is the test set, $\hat{r}_{ui}$ is the score predicted by the model and r_{ui} is the actual score of the test set.

5.3 Results and Discussions

We use the following parameter configuration for training the timeAutoSVD++ model. in this experiment, $\gamma_1 = \gamma_2 = 0.007$, $\gamma_3 = 0.001$, $\gamma_\alpha = 0.00001$, $\lambda_1 = 0.005$, $\lambda_2 = 0.015$, $\lambda_3 = 0.015$, $\lambda_\alpha = 0.0004$, $\theta = 0.1$, $\beta = 0.015$. We set the dimension of latent factors $k = 10$

We have compared our model with the following baselines models:

1. SVD [6]: A basic version of Matrix Factorization with user and item bias.
2. NMF [8]: A collaborative filtering algorithm based on Non-negative Matrix Factorization. The idea of the NMF model is to keep user and item factors positive.
3. PMF [9]: A CF model using probabilistic approach.
4. timeSVD++ [5]: An extension of the SVD++ model using the time factor.
5. autoSVD++ [15] : An extension of the SVD++ model by adding item features.

The experimental results are presented in Table (2):

Table 2. Experimental results

Model	ML-100K (RMSE)	ML-1M(RMSE)
PMF	0.952	0.883
NMF	0.963	0.916
SVD	0.934	0.873
SVD++	0.924	0.862
timeSVD++	0.924	0.861
autoSVD++	0.924	0.855
autoTimeSVD++	**0.919**	**0.847**

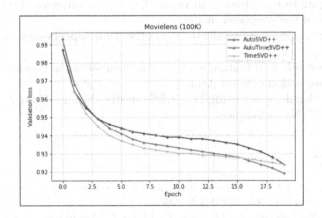

Fig. 3. Validation loss (Movielens 100K)

The analysis of both Fig. (3) and (4) shows that: All three models decrease and don't overfit. The autoTimeSVD++ is slightly better than autoSVD++ and timeSVD++ for the $100K$ dataset. In the case of the dataset $1M$, the auto-TimeSVD++ converges better than the other models with significant improvement over the compared models. This proves that adding the factor time has significantly improved the accuracy of the autoSVD++ model.

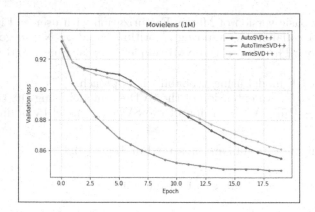

Fig. 4. Validation loss (Movielens 1M)

6   Conclusion

We proposed a new hybrid model **autoTimeSVD++** by adding the temporal aspects inspired from timeSVD++ and item side information using the Contractive Autoencoder inspired from autoSVD++ model. The experimental results show that our model outperforms the compared baselines models. Many extensions of this model are possible in future:

- Executing more experiments in other datasets to improve and increase the robustness of the proposed model.
- Extending the proposed model to cover other time aspects such as user session or time sequence.
- Adding user-side information such as age, occupation, and gender may influence the prediction over an item.
- Adding a visual aspect using the item's media through Convolution Neural Network (CNN) techniques.

References

1. Aggarwal, C.C.: Recommender Systems: the Textbook. Springer, Cham (2016). https://doi.org/10.1007/978-3-319-29659-3
2. Anelli, V.W., Bellogin, A., Di Noia, T., Pomo, C.: Reenvisioning the comparison between neural collaborative filtering and matrix factorization. In: RecSys 21: Fifteenth ACM Conference on Recommender Systems, Amsterdam, The Netherlands (2021). https://sisinflab.poliba.it/Publications/2021/ABDP21
3. Bank, D., Koenigstein, N., Giryes, R.: Autoencoders. arXiv: 2003.05991 (2021)
4. Koren, Y.: Factorization meets the neighborhood: a multifaceted collaborative filtering model. In: Li, Y., Liu, B., Sarawagi, S. (eds.) Proceedings of the 14th ACM SIGKDD International Conference on Knowledge Discovery and Data Mining, Las Vegas, Nevada, USA, August 24–27, pp. 426–434. ACM (2008). https://doi.org/10.1145/1401890.1401944

5. Koren, Y.: Collaborative filtering with temporal dynamics. In: Proceedings of KDD 2009, pp. 447–456 (2009)
6. Koren, Y., Bell, R., Volinsky, C.: Matrix factorization techniques for recommender systems. Computer **42**(8), 30–37 (2009)
7. Koren, Y., Labs, T.: Factorization meets the neighborhood: a multifaceted collaborative filtering model, p. 24
8. Lee, D., Seung, H.S.: Algorithms for non-negative matrix factorization. In: Leen, T., Dietterich, T., Tresp, V. (eds.) Advances in Neural Information Processing Systems 13. MIT Press (2001). https://proceedings.neurips.cc/paper/2000/file/f9d1152547c0bde01830b7e8bd60024c-Paper.pdf
9. Mnih, A., Salakhutdinov, R.R.: Probabilistic matrix factorization. In: Platt, J.C., Koller, D., Singer, Y., Roweis, S.T. (eds.) Advances in Neural Information Processing Systems 20, pp. 1257–1264. Curran Associates, Inc. (2008). https://papers.nips.cc/paper/3208-probabilistic-matrix-factorization.pdf
10. Rendle, S., Krichene, W., Zhang, L., Anderson, J.: Neural collaborative filtering vs. matrix factorization revisited. In: 14th ACM Conference on Recommender Systems (RecSys) (2020)
11. Rendle, S., Freudenthaler, C., Gantner, Z., Schmidt-Thieme, L.: BPR: Bayesian personalized ranking from implicit feedback . In: Appears in Proceedings of the Twenty-Fifth Conference on Uncertainty in Artificial Intelligence (UAI2009) (2012). https://arxiv.org/abs/1205.2618
12. Rifai, S., Vincent, P., Muller, X., Glorot, X., Bengio, Y.: Contractive auto-encoders: explicit invariance during feature extraction, pp. 833–840. https://dblp.uni-trier.de/db/conf/icml/icml2011.html#RifaiVMGB11
13. Sedhain, S., Menon, A.K., Sanner, S., Xie, L.: AutoRec: autoencoders meet collaborative filtering. In: Proceedings of the 24th International Conference on World Wide Web, pp. 111–112. ACM (2015)
14. Wang, S., Sun, G., Li, Y.: SVD++ recommendation algorithm based on backtracking. Information **11**(7), 369 (2020) https://doi.org/10.3390/info11070369
15. Zhang, S., Yao, L., Xu, X.: AutoSVD++: an efficient hybrid collaborative filtering model via contractive auto-encoders. In: Proceedings of the 40th International ACM SIGIR Conference on Research and Development in Information Retrieval, pp. 957–960. https://doi.org/10.1145/3077136.3080689 arXiv: 1704.00551 (2017)

Toward a Holistic Public Procurement 4.0. Case Study: Moroccan Public Procurement

Amina Oussaleh Taoufik[✉] and Abdellah Azmani

Intelligent Automation Laboratory, Faculty of Sciences and Techniques of Tangier,
Abdelmalek Essaadi University of Tetouan, Tetouan, Morocco
oussalehtaoufik.amina@etu.uae.ac.ma, a.azmani@uae.ac.ma

Abstract. Public procurement is of tremendous significance in the global economy due to the huge volume of investments and expenditure involved. In Morocco, it accounts for about 17% of Gross Domestic Product (GDP). It is a strategic governance tool for governments to promote economic growth and provide sustainable social development, if conducted efficiently and transparently. However, many studies report that public procurement is one of the government fields that is highly vulnerable to corruption, fraud, mismanagement and lack of performance. To address these issues and other challenges, innovative digital tools have proven their significance efficiency in delivering a citizen-centric public procurement. The main objective of our paper is to review the cutting-edge technologies that can enhance the procurement process so as to present an integrated frame- work for public procurement 4.0 based on a holistic approach that aims to satisfy all stakeholders and leverage Morocco to become a digital African hub.

Keywords: Public procurement · E-Procurement · Procurement 4.0 · E-democracy · Artificial Intelligence · Block chain · Big Data

1 Introduction

Nowadays, the world is encountering unprecedented changes, brought about by science and new technologies. The emergence of the web 4.0, has led to the industrial revolution 4.0. Striving to survive, private organizations had to rethink their management and leadership process especially in the supply chain field [1]. Unlike the private sector, governments are way behind in this frantic race and still struggle to build successful e-government projects [2]. Enabling trust and integrity and putting citizen at the core of the governments' priorities are fundamental factors to consider when building an e-government project [3]. Disparities are also very noticeable between developed and developing countries, when exploiting the numerous opportunities offered today by cutting-edge technologies, to thrive [4]. Smart cities [5], intelligent transportation systems [6], smart contracts [7], to name a few, exemplify the opportunities offered nowadays by the revolutionary technologies of Internet of Things, Big Data Analytics, Artificial Intelligence, Blockchain, Cloud Computing and Multi Agent systems [8].

© The Author(s), under exclusive license to Springer Nature Switzerland AG 2022
M. Hamlich et al. (Eds.): SADASC 2022, CCIS 1677, pp. 104–114, 2022.
https://doi.org/10.1007/978-3-031-20490-6_9

Amidst the fields impacted by the digital large scale and pervasive wave, we are interested in our work on public procurement. The aim of this paper is to exploit the innovative technologies in improving the current public e-procurement system and promoting trust and integrity in government as well as serving as a springboard for e-democracy implementation.

This paper is structured as follows. The Sect. 2 draws up a contextual overview of the digital transformation in Morocco. Then it defines public procurement and its keys integrity issues. In Sect. 3, we review the cutting-edge technologies that have been implemented in procurement. Finally, we present our holistic public procurement framework 4.0.

2 Context of the Study

2.1 Digital Transformation in Morocco

Digital transformation is one of the strategic axes of the Moroccan New Development Model. The Moroccan digital transformation began since the early 2005 with an arsenal of reforms and plans, in particular the 'Digital Morocco 2010', the 'Digital Morocco 2020' plans, the 'Open Data strategy', to name a few. To accompany his steading strategy of becoming a leading economic power and a digital hub in the region, great emphasis was placed on creating an appropriate regulatory framework and organizational and institutional structures (ex. The creation of the Digital Development Agency, the National Commission for the Control of Personal Data Protection).

The Covid 19 Pandemic, which led to a global economic disruption, has urged Morocco to accelerate his digital transformation by encouraging Small and Medium Sized Enterprises and startups to invest in developing digital services to curb the pandemic effects and prevent future outbreaks. Nonetheless, despite the manifest efforts in the digital movement, many shortcomings are still to be addressed especially in the public sector. According to the United Nations survey of 2020, Morocco is still under the world average index related to E-Government Development Index (EGDI) and its sub-components indexes like E-Participation Index (EPI), Online Service Index (OSI), Telecommunication Infrastructure Index (TII) and Human Capital Index (HCI).

2.2 Public Procurement

Public procurement refers to the acquisition and purchase of goods, works and services by public authorities. Its main goal is to award effective contracts to qualified contractors in order to provide public services or support government operations.

Public procurement is bound by a set of ethical conduct such as *transparency, openness, fairness, competition and governance* that represent the basic principles of public procurement. However, that does not rule out the fact that many public procurement contracts are not awarded with respects to these basics. The financial interests at stake pose integrity issues [12]. Public procurement still suffers from corruption, fraud and anti-competitive behavior, which impedes social and economic growth.

Public procurement can be conducted through either an open procedure or a restricted one and the contract characteristics may change from one contract to another. The choice of the appropriate procedure, pricing method (unit/lump, fixed/reviewed prices) or even the suppliers/ bidders selection method (the lowest price or the most economically advantageous) depends on the size of the contract, the technicity evolved and sometimes the urgency imposed. However, it is important to highlight that the choice of an open procedure does not indicate a more transparent process. Counterbalancing integrity may happen even in open procedures and in every stage of the process.

Morocco has taken major strides in his public procurement strategy. The budget reform on 2001 allowed the launch of three main public procurement systems: the Moroccan Public Procurement Portal (PMP), the Integrated Expenditure Management System (GID) and Barid E-Sign.

2.3 Integrity Issues in Public Procurement

Public procurement is a strategic governance tool for governments to promote economic growth and provide sustainable social development. However, many studies conducted by global organizations such as Organization for Economic Co-operation and Development [13],Word Bank[14] and Transparency International [15] reported that public procurement is one of the government fields that is highly vulnerable to corruption and fraud. This problem has been reported to lead 10 up to 30% of the investments to failure [12]. Hence, citizen trust in their government policy has decreased tremendously [16]. The critical risks to integrity exist in every stage of the procurement process. Table 1 summarizes the most common risks reported by [17].

Table 1. Integrity risks in public procurement

Stage	Risks
Pre-tendering / Pre-purchasing	Lack of appropriate/thorough needs assessment, planning and budgeting
	Inappropriate or overestimation of the contract size and price
	Inadequate choice of the procedure and subjective selection criteria of suppliers
	Lack of knowledge both in the process and in the preparation of the tender/bid
	Absence of sourcing for new qualified competitors in the restricted procedures
	Insufficient or incompatible timeframe for the preparation of the bids

(*continued*)

Table 1. (*continued*)

Stage	Risks
Tendering / Purchasing	Inconsistent access to information about tenders for bidders Collusive bidding resulting in poor competition and high prices Conflict-of-interest and bribes resulting in corruption in the evaluation stage Absence of details related to the evaluation process, restraining the bidders to call the award decision into question Unjustified delays during the evaluation sessions
Post-tendering/Post-purchasing	Insufficient monitoring and poor follow up Non-respect to the specifications and clauses of the contract Non-transparent choice of subcontractors Delays in payment, which affect badly the suppliers

3 State of the Art

3.1 Procurement and Artificial Intelligence

Artificial Intelligence (AI) triggered the interests of academics since 1956 at the Dartmouth conference [15] promising revolutionary solutions for complex problems and smart tools for enhanced performance and efficiency. Hence, there was an exponential growth of academic researches as well as governments [18], non-profit organization [19] and firms initiatives to explore the wide-reaching applications of AI [11]. AI can be defined as an intelligent agent that has the ability to imitate the intelligence of human behavior (cognitive functions and attributes) and to improve its performance by continual learning. AI has been hugely empowered in the last decades by computational powers and big data [20]. However, there is still a dearth in its implementation in e-government projects in general and in public procurement in particular although, it can be embedded into a number of processes from budgeting to contract management (Audit [21, 22], Budgeting [23, 24], Planification [25]), strategic sourcing [26, 27], or evaluation of bids [28–30] and collaboration [31].

3.2 Procurement and Blockchain

Procurement is a complex process that is structured into internal and external sub processes and it involves the exchange of many confidential documents. The many issues of integrity that characterize the public procurement in particular, impose looking for solutions to curb them. Since Blockchain technology has been designed to hold decentralized and highly secured transactions of data and information without a need of a third party intervening [32], it has therefore the potential to offer enhanced secured solutions for public e-procurement [33]. Blockchain has been adopted in smart contracts [34, 10] as well as in securing e-voting [35] and other applications.

3.3 Procurement and Data

Data is a great asset of every organization. It can be collected through multiple sources and cannels and vary in form, in size and in nature. Businesses pay great attention to the analyses of their data as it can provide them with significant insights about the markets trends [36]. Even politicians use data to influence public votes [37]. However, data governance might be challenging as it relies on many factors. Holistic digital leadership, regulatory and organizational framework, qualified human capital and adequate IT infrastructures are important pillars to data governance. Moreover, the exponential grow of data imposes the use of cutting-edge IT solutions to gather, process, analyze and exploit the information hold in that data. The synergy of Big Data Technologies, Internet of Things, Geographic Information System and Machine Learning has proved its efficiency in data exploitation. Hence, promising to revolutionize the public sector as well if used properly. The best application to exemplify it is smart cities [38].

4 Proposed Approach

4.1 General View

4.1.1 From E-Public Procurement Toward Procurement 4.0

The emergence of Information and Communication Technology (ICT) has disrupted the traditional way of managing the procurement system. E-Procurement refers to the use of ICT in procurement process. It has evolved in many countries from being just an online portal to a more mature stage offering a full package of electronic services like e-Sourcing, e-Tendering, e-Reverse auctioning, e-Ordering, e-Markets, to name a few.

Procurement 4.0 is a widespread transition process of e-procurement, introduced by the web 4.0, the industry 4.0 and even the government 4.0. Nonetheless, the success of the procurement digital reform is not limited to the implementation of ICT [34] or even to the numerous legislative reforms [35]. Instead, more focused should be placed on building hyper integrated evolutionary systems that aim at empowering citizenship, reducing digital divide and leading to social, political and economic growth as described by [36] in his integrated conceptual framework for a future e-government.

- *From E-Voting to I-Voting.* E-Voting is an E-Democracy instrument. Despite the controversy around the use of the e-voting especially in political goals, e-voting remains an incentive tool for citizen to approve public investments or orient them in order to optimize costs and public service performance especially when based on cutting- edge technologies as Blockchain [30, 37]. E-Voting consists on providing an interface to allow citizen to vote for the projects they need the most. Data analysis and Machine learning can be used later to analyze the registered votes and therefore predict future social trends in a more developed I-Voting system.
- *From E-Participation to I-Participation.* [38] highlights the differences between e-Participation and other e-democracy tools and defines it, as an online consultation and dialogue between government and citizens. The success of e-participation is not evident not even in Estonia, the world leader in e-participation index. [39] relates the failure of the Estonian e-participation platform Osale.ee to the common ICT projects

constraints, to the characteristics of public sector organization and finally to the complexity of the implementation of democracy and satisfying the expectations of all stakeholders. E-Participation allows citizens to share their needs with the government's entities. It is an important process in our framework. This process can be upgraded with the use of advanced AI tools that enable to analyze citizens' tweets and social media posts.

- *From E-Budgeting to I-Budgeting.* Budgeting is a dynamic financial activity of governments, which is very sensitive to economic events like crises, pandemics, inflation, to exemplify. Monitoring and optimizing public expenditures induce sustainable socio-economic growth and enable citizens regain trust in their governments. [40] tries to fill the gap in the literature related to the optimization of public budgeting. He is using the multilayer perceptron and multi objective genetic algorithms to optimize budget allocations. In our proposed framework, E-Budgeting, consists, at a first stage, in generating contracts' estimation based on a smart price referential implemented with the previous contracts' prices and enhanced with different socio, geopolitical and economic metrics to predict contracts' prices.
- *From E-Planning to I-Planning.* E-Budgeting implies E-Planning, which is a manifestation of transparency. Publishing the Government National Strategy and action plans as well as annual operation plan like annual local procurement plans offer a sufficient timeframe for suppliers to optimize their load plan, source for smart joint collaboration and allocate the appropriate resources to enhance their chances to win contracts.
- *From E-Assistance to I-Assistance.* Preparing a tender or a bid is an important stage of the procurement process. Many public officers and even suppliers lack of appropriate skills to prepare the necessary documents needed. This may result on the cancelation of the contract because of procedural defects. Offering an assisting tool for both buyers and sellers for the preparation of the bid will save them time and resources and enhance the chances of delivering a more accurate tender/bid. Today, chat bots are widely used in many fields and relays on artificial intelligence technologies [42]. Chat bots can be used to answer and assist companies during the preparation of their bids or offers.
- *From E-Signature to I-Signature.* E-Signature is a fundamental key to e-procurement success. It can be either digital cipher, electronic Identity Documents 'eID' or stamp. Regardless of how it is presented, the adoption of E-signature either in business or in public procurement implies a legal framework to counter the risks of digital attacks or fraudulent misuse. Curbing the security issues in smart contracts are refraining the acceleration of the digital signature. However, Blockchain technology is promising to present a disruptive base for smart contract despite the numerous challenges [43].
- *From E-Submission to I-Submission.* The success of E-Submission relies on the success of E-Signature and advanced security technologies. Many public procurement projects allow the supplier to submit their bids through online portals. Smart submission, though, implies a more integrated and secured process. For example, the procurement system should verify the accuracy of the information forming the bids by interacting with other public entities or partners like banks, insurances, and social security agencies. The qualified bids are then encrypted using disruptive security technologies like Blockchain to ensure the confidentiality of the submitted documents.

- *From E-Evaluation to I-Evaluation.* E-Evaluation is often a three stages process. At the beginning, a qualification evaluation is considered to pre-select the suppliers that are legally and technically eligible to participate. This E-Qualification is usually followed by a financial evaluation but it can be sometimes preceded by a deeper technical evaluation. E-evaluation consists on opening the bids, evaluating and validating the three stages online. However, even if the bids are opened online, and registered in the procurement database, this that does not rule out the fact that the evaluation is not always objective. Hence, I-Evaluation, triggered the interests of many researches who explore different approaches to computing [44, 45] and artificial intelligence algorithms [46] or a combination of the two [47] to offer a more subjective selection output.
- *From E-Monitoring to I-Monitoring/I-Audit.* E-Monitoring is already implemented in the Moroccan GID system. It registers the progress of the contract, work and payments. However, the electronic tool still relies on the data entered by public procurement officers and therefore lacks of integrity. [48] uses a full suite of sensing technologies (drones, sensors environmental factors, point cloud motion detection, mixed vision glasses, automated machines…) to monitor craft workers productivity. Same technologies can be used to monitor the progress of work and detect any non-respect to the specifications and clauses of the contract or even predict delays to prevent them.

4.2 Proposed Framework

The implementation of AI and other cutting-edge technologies in public sectors, especially in developing countries, entails to overcome a set of challenges including, but not limited to, the lack of qualified resources able to develop trustworthy AI applications, the absence or insufficient regulatory framework for data security and privacy, the citizen and other stakeholders lack of trust in their governments, the poor IT investments and the digital divide.

Many studies report that a holistic approach is fundamental to the success of any e-government project. Firstly, developing a digital leadership is important to define the right digital strategy based on the analysis of accurate metrics. Secondly, reinforcing the institutional and reviewing the legal framework enable to benefit surely and securely from the digital offered opportunities. Thirdly, a digital transformation cannot be reached if the digital divide persists. Investing in IT infrastructures as well as in forming qualified resources and popularizing digital culture is important to enable social inclusiveness. Finally, yet importantly, data governance cannot be seized if the data ecosystem is not well managed. The proposed framework (see. Fig. 1) gives a holistic approach to the public procurement process, taking into consideration the different stakeholders, the different canals to access the system as well as main pillars that determines the success of the implementation of the system. The framework covers also the gradual transition from E-procurement to a procurement 4.0 that relies mainly on data governance and aims at promoting e-democracy, performance and integrity through the use of intelligent technologies.

Fig. 1. Holistic public procurement 4.0 framework (Author)

5 Conclusion and Future Works

Going digital is not a frantic race, although the global trends are imposing the use of advanced technologies. The real goal of leveraging public procurement from a traditional process with distorted outcomes, to a transformational process, is to improve government accountability and enable social inclusiveness and economic growth. To ensure the success of any IT project and e-government in particular, it is mandatory to adopt a holistic approach and take measured and tempered steps to reach the goals. Despite the great strides made by the revolutionary technologies described in the review, there are still challenges to be addressed. Morocco has already taken steady steps toward the digitalization of its public procurement. Yet, there are still challenges to face and opportunities to seize to reach a maturity in digital transformation.

In this paper, we presented a holistic framework that can be adopted progressively in Morocco, to elevate the current public procurement to a higher level of integrity and performance. The literature review conducted allowed us to highlights the great opportunities to be seized from the integration of smart technologies. We are currently working on a holistic model based on the Multi-Agent System paradigm and the HADOOP Distributed File System to conceptualize our framework using a set of intelligent agents as well as experts. The model intends to be integrated, intelligent and holistic.

References

1. Matzler, K., Friedrich von den Eichen, S., Anschober, M., Kohler, T.: The crusade of digital disruption. J. Bus. Strat. **39** (2018). https://doi.org/10.1108/JBS-12-2017-0187
2. Ndou, D.: E-Government for developing countries: opportunities and challenges. EJISDC Electron. J. Inf. Syst. Develop. Countr. **18**, 1–24 (2004). https://doi.org/10.1002/j.1681-4835.2004.tb00117.x
3. Suarez, D. and Abdallah, E.: Public sector readiness in the age of disruption your journey to readiness answering tomorrow's questions today (2019). https://www.pwc.com/m1/en/world-government-summit/documents/wgs-age-of disruption.pdf
4. United Nations: E-Government Survey 2020—digital government in the decade of action for sustainable development: With ADDENDUM ON COVID-19 response. https://publicadmini stration.un.org/egovkb/en-us/Reports/UN-E-Government-Survey-2020
5. Allam, Z., Dhunny, Z.A.: On big data, artificial intelligence and smart cities. Cities **89**, 80–91 (2019). https://doi.org/10.1016/j.cities.2019.01.032
6. Guerrero-Ibáñez, J., Zeadally, S., Contreras-Castillo, J.: Sensor technologies for intelligent transportation systems. Sensors **18**, 1212 (2018). https://doi.org/10.3390/s18041212
7. Mohanta, B. K., Panda, S. S., Jena, D.: An overview of smart contract and use cases in blockchain technology. In: 9th International Conference on Computing, Communication and Networking Technologies (ICCCNT) pp. 1–4 (2018). https://doi.org/10.1109/ICCCNT.2018.8494045
8. Akter, S., Michael, K., Uddin, M.R., McCarthy, G., Rahman, M.: Transforming business using digital innovations: the application of AI, blockchain, cloud and data analytics. Ann. Oper. Res. **308**(1–2), 7–39 (2020). https://doi.org/10.1007/s10479-020-03620-w
9. OECD: Preventing corruption in public procurement (2016). http://www.oecd.org/gov/ethics/Corruption-Public-Procurement-Brochure.pdf
10. OECD: Compendium of good practices for integrity in public procurement (2014). https://www.oecd.org/gov/public-procurement/compendium-for-good-practices-forintegrity-in-pub lic-procurement.pdf
11. The World Bank: Fraud and corruption awareness handbook: A handbook for civil servants involved in public procurement, pp. 1–84 (2013). http://documents.worldbank.org/curated/en/309511468156866119/Fraud-and-corruption-awareness-handbook-a-handbook-for-civil-servants-involved-in-public-procurement
12. Transparency International: Public procurement planning and corruption (2015). https://www.transparency.org/files/content/corruptionqas/Public_procurement_planning_and_cor ruption_2015.pdf
13. Transparency International: Transparency in budget execution (2014). https://knowledgehub.transparency.org/helpdesk/transparency-in-budget-execution

14. OECD: Integrity in public procurement: good practice from a to z (2007). https://doi.org/10.1787/9789264027510-en. https://www.oecd-ilibrary.org/governance/integrity-in-public-procurement_9789264027510-en

15. OECD: State of the art in the use of emerging technologies in the public sector (2019). https://www.oecd-ilibrary.org/governance/state-of-the-art-in-the-use-of-emerging-technologies-in-the-public-sector_932780bc-en

16. Berryhill, J, Kok Heang, K., Clogher, R., McBride, K.: Hello, World: Artificial intelligence and its use in the public sector. OECD Working Papers on Public Governance No. 36 (2019). https://doi.org/10.1787/726fd39d-en

17. Al-mushayt, O.S.: Automating E-government services with artificial intelligence. IEEE Access 7(146821–146829), 2019 (2019). https://doi.org/10.1109/ACCESS.2019.2946204

18. Ovsyannikova, A., Domashova, J.: Identification of public procurement contracts with a high risk of non-performance based on neural networks. Proc. Comput. Sci. **169**, 795–799 (2020). https://doi.org/10.1016/j.procs.2020.02.161

19. Rabuzin, K., Modrušan, N.: Prediction of public procurement corruption indices using machine learning methods. In: IC3K 2019—R Fraudulent Misuse 11th International Jt. Conference Knowledge Discovery, Knowledge Engineering and Knowledge Management, Vol. 3, no. Ic3k, pp. 333–340 (2019), https://doi.org/10.5220/0008353603330340 (2019)

20. Leśniak, A., Zima, K.: Cost calculation of construction projects including sustainability factors using the case based reasoning (CBR) method. Sustain **10**(5), 2018 (2018). https://doi.org/10.3390/su10051608

21. Wang, H., Lin, Q.: Risk cost measurement of value for money evaluation based on case-based reasoning and ontology: A case study of the urban rail transit public-private partnership projects in China. Sustainability **14**(9) (2022). https://doi.org/10.3390/su14095547

22. Choi, Y., Lee, H., Irani, Z.: Big data-driven fuzzy cognitive map for prioritising IT service procurement in the public sector. Ann. Oper. Res. **270**(1–2), 75–104 (2016). https://doi.org/10.1007/s10479-016-2281-6

23. Amadou, D., Azmani, A., Harzli, M.: Tendering process: Improvement of analysis and evaluation of tenders based on the use of fuzzy logic and rule of proportion. Int. J. Comput. Appl. **101**, 44–51 (2014). https://doi.org/10.5120/17759-8892

24. García Rodríguez, M.J., Montequín, V.R., Fernández, F.O., Villanueva Balsera, J.M.: Bidders recommender for public procurement auctions using machine learning: Data analysis, algorithm, and case study with tenders from Spain. Complexity (2020). https://doi.org/10.1155/2020/8858258

25. García Rodríguez, M.J., Rodríguez Montequín, V., Ortega Fernández, F., Villanueva Balsera, J.M.: Public procurement announcements in spain: regulations, data analysis, and award price estimator using machine learning. Complexity (2019). https://doi.org/10.1155/2019/2360610

26. Yuyang, T., Wenchao, Z., Chunxiang, G.: The joint procurement model and algorithm for small and medium enterprise., Comput. Ind. Eng. **155** (2021). https://doi.org/10.1016/j.cie.2021.107179

27. Lykidis, I., Drosatos, G.: The use of blockchain technology in e-government services. Computers **10**(12), 168 (2021). https://doi.org/10.3390/computers10120168

28. Ghadimi, P., Ghassemi Toosi, F., Heavey, C.: A multi-agent systems approach for sustainable supplier selection and order allocation in a partnership supply chain. Eur. J. Oper. Res. **269**(1), 286–301 (2018). https://doi.org/10.1016/j.ejor.2017.07.014

29. Wang, H., Qin, H., Zhao, M., Wei, X., Shen, H., Susilo, W.: Blockchain-based fair payment smart contract for public cloud storage auditing. Inf. Sci. (Ny) **519**(88), 348–362 (2020). https://doi.org/10.1016/j.ins.2020.01.051

30. Bellini, E., Ceravolo, P., Damiani, E.: Blockchain-based e-vote-as-a-service. IEEE Int. Conf. Cloud Comput. Cloud 484–486 (2019). https://doi.org/10.1109/CLOUD.2019.00085

31. Hajli, N., Tajvidi, M., Gbadamosi, A., Nadeem, W.: Understanding market agility for new product success with big data analytics. Ind. Mark. Manag. **86**, 135–143 (2018). https://doi.org/10.1016/j.indmarman.2019.09.010

32. Jungherr, A.: Twitter use in election campaigns: A systematic literature review. J. Inf. Technol. Polit. **13**(1), 72–91 (2016). https://doi.org/10.1080/19331681.2015.1132401

33. Hashem, I.A.T., et al.: The role of big data in smart city. Int. J. Inf. Manag. **36**(5), 748–758 (2016). https://doi.org/10.1016/j.ijinfomgt.2016.05.002

34. European Bank for Reconstruction and Development: Are you ready for eProcurement? Guide to electronic procurement reform. https://www.ebrd.com/documents/legalreform/guide-to-eprocurement-reform.pdf

35. Bosio, E., Djankov, S., Glaeser, E., Shleifer, A.: Public procurement in law and practice. Am. Econ. Rev. **112**(4), 1091–1117 (2022). https://doi.org/10.1257/aer.20200738

36. Malodia, S., Dhir, A., Mishra, M., Bhatti, Z.A.: Future of e-Government: An integrated conceptual framework. Technol. Forecast. Soc. Change **173**, 121102 (2021). https://doi.org/10.1016/j.techfore.2021.121102

37. Gibson, J.P., Krimmer, R., Teague, V., Pomares, J.: A review of E-voting: the past, present and future. Ann. Telecommun. **71**(7–8), 279–286 (2016). https://doi.org/10.1007/s12243-016-0525-8

38. Macintosh, A.: Characterizing e-participation in policy-making. Proc. Hawaii Int. Conf. Syst. Sci. **37**(C) 1843–1852 (2004). https://doi.org/10.1109/hicss.2004.1265300

39. Toots, M.: Why E-participation systems fail: The case of Estonia's Osale.ee. Gov. Inf. Q. **36**(3), 546–559 (2019). https://doi.org/10.1016/j.giq.2019.02.002

40. Valle-Cruz, D., Fernandez-Cortez, V., Gil-Garcia, J.R.: From E-budgeting to smart budgeting: Exploring the potential of artificial intelligence in government decision-making for resource allocation. Gov. Inf. Q. **39**(2), 101644 (2022). https://doi.org/10.1016/j.giq.2021.101644

41. Gamayuni, R.R., Agusta, E.: E-Planning and e-budgeting implementation: a qualitative study in lampung province. Int. J. Econ. Bus. Entrep. **2**(2), 105–122 (2019). https://doi.org/10.23960/ijebe.v2i2.54

42. Lokman, A.S., Ameedeen, M.A.: Modern chatbot systems: A technical review. In: Arai, K., Bhatia, R., Kapoor, S. (eds.) FTC 2018. AISC, vol. 881, pp. 1012–1023. Springer, Cham (2019). https://doi.org/10.1007/978-3-030-02683-7_75

43. Hewa, T., Ylianttila, M., Liyanage, M.: Survey on blockchain based smart contracts: Applications, opportunities and challenges, J. Netw. Comput. Appl. **177**, 102857 (2021). https://doi.org/10.1016/j.jnca.2020.102857

44. Pani, M., Verma, R., Sahoo, G.: A heuristic method for supplier selection using AHP, entropy and TOPSIS. Int. J. of Procurement Management. **5**, 784–796 (2012). https://doi.org/10.1504/IJPM.2012.049715

45. Adewole, S., Rafiu, I., Ronke, B.: A fuzzy logic approach for evaluation of government performance in ICT projects implementation. J. Emerg. Trends Comput. Inf. Sci. **3**, 1487–1494 (2012)

46. Asthana, N., Gupta, M.: Supplier selection using artificial neural network and genetic algorithm. Int. J. Indian Cult. Bus. Manag. **11**(4), 457 (2015). https://doi.org/10.1504/ijicbm.2015.072428

47. Gegovska, T., Koker, R., Cakar, T.: Green supplier selection using fuzzy multiple-criteria decision-making methods and artificial neural networks. Comput. Intell.. Neurosci. (2020). https://doi.org/10.1155/2020/8811834

48. Calvetti, D., Mêda, P., Chichorro Gonçalves, M., Sousa, H. Worker 4.0: The future of sensored construction sites. Buildings **10**, 169. (2020). https://doi.org/10.3390/buildings10100169

Classifiers-Based Personality Disorders Detection

Fatemeh Sajadi Ansari[1,2]($\boxtimes$), Djamal Benslimane[2], Aymen Khelifi[1],
and Mahmoud Barhamgi[2]

[1] Kaisens Data, 9/11 Allee de l'Arche, 92400 Courbevoie, France
fansari@kaisensdata.fr
[2] Claude Bernard Lyon 1 University, Lyon, France

Abstract. Internet technologies including social networks allow users
to easily communicate with each other. This provides us an interesting
resources space to early detection of abnormal behavior such as mental disorders. Important mental factors were initially proposed in some
psychological solutions. Recently, machine learning-based approaches are
proposed and tend to exploit the large data that social networks can
provide to detect abnormal behavior in its early stage. In this paper,
we propose a set of classifiers-based troubles detection in the context of
social media. Diverse unit classifiers are used including messages toxicity detection, gender classifier, age estimation, and personality estimation. Outputs of these classifiers can be combined to intercept abnormal
behavior of profiles that can represent a risk. Our different classifiers are
trained by using different datasets in the context of twitter and instagram
platforms.

Keywords: Abnormal behavior · Personality features · Social media ·
Big fives · Classifiers

1 Introduction

Advances in mobile and Internet technologies such as smart phones, and social
media have truly transformed our lives and reshaped the way we interact with
each other and socialize. The arrival of fast 5G networks and the Internet of
Multimedia Things (IoMT) is even expected to take this transformation to an
advanced level where people can communicate and exchange multimedia content with each other through a multitude of smart interfaces embedded in their
surrounding physical objects (e.g., cars, fridges, etc.). However, while these technologies promise to ease our lives, they also come with a wide range of undesirable
side effects such as Nomophobia, mental disorders [1], network addictions and
cyberbullying [2].

Psychological solutions were initially proposed to mainly identify important
mental factors. Recently, new machine-learning based approaches were proposed
to exploit the large data available on social media to detect mental disorders at
its early stage.

M. Hamlich et al. (Eds.): SADASC 2022, CCIS 1677, pp. 115–125, 2022.
https://doi.org/10.1007/978-3-031-20490-6_10

In this paper we present a machine learning-based approach for personal troubles detection. Different unit classifiers are proposed and combined together. We think that messages content is not necessary sufficient by itself to detect personality troubles cases. It should be assisted by analysing the potential personality troubles case from other perspectives. In this work, four unit classifiers are combined: toxicity detection of exchanged messages, gender prediction, age estimation, and big five model-based personality estimation.

The rest of this paper is organized as follows. Section 2 describes related work. Section 3 presents an overview of the proposed approach, and describes its different components. Section 4 gives a general view of a prototype, presents experiments and discusses some results. Section 5 concludes the paper.

2 Related Work

A considerable work has been devoted to mental disorders and cyberbullying detection in teh context of social media.

In [1], authors argue that mining behaviors from social media is one way to identify some social network mental disorders such as net compulsion and cyber-relationship addiction. They propose a machine-learning based approach to identify potential cases of mental disorders. Mental Disorder Detection is considered as a semi-supervised classification problem and three types of disorders are detected with a binary tranductive SVM: Cyber-Relationship Addiction, Net Compulsion, and Information Overload. The proposed approach is mainly based on extracting and exploiting different features of users including social structure, online and offline interaction ratio, and social diversity. Tensor techniques are also exploited to better infer teh user behavior from logs of differents social media platforms. In [3], authors consider that mental disorders occur often in combination and are then related to each other. Several online mental health communities are studied to extract topics and psycho-linguistic features with an interest on depression from a large number of posts (620K) initiated by a huge number of users (80K). These features are used as an input of a join modelling framework to classify mental health-related communities. The efficacy of the proposed framework was evaluated against both single-task logistic regression and a multi-task learning model.

In [4], authors explore social media usage and statistical classifier technique to detect and diagnose at eraly stage depressive disorder on Twitter platform. They rely on crowdsourcing technique to compile a set of Twitter users who reported being diagnosed with clinical depression. Different behavioral attributes are extracted from posts over a year preceding teh onset of depression. These attribute are related to social engagement (number of posts, Proportion of reply posts, etc.), emotion measures (positive affect, negative affect, activation, and dominance), and Depression Language (Depression lexicon and Antidepressant usage) The authors in [5,6] introduced the use of the victim behavior as an indicator of cyberbullying. The immediate reactions of victims such as their posts and statuses on social networks could constitute a warning signal of their emotional and psychological state when cyberbullied. Along the same lines, the authors of [7] demonstrated the benefits of exploiting the personal features of users such as their demographics and social dynamics, in addition to the content of their communications, to detect cyber bullies with a Decision Tree classifier.

Dadvar et al. in [8] explored the use of deep learning models to cyberbullying detection. A compassion study showed that deep learning based models outperform the conventional machine learning models when both are applied to the same dataset. In [9], the authors proposed an expert solution to detect bully users on social platforms. The solution combines the expertise of cyberbullying (human) experts and the results from supervised machine learning models to improve the detection precision of bully users. The experiments showcased the superiority of this expert system relative supervised machine learning models.

3 Our Approach

3.1 Approach Overview

We present in Fig. 1 an overview of our approach. Our approach exploits data mining and machine learning models to determine whether or not the profile has abnormal trends called "unconventional", and this in order to detect any weak signal of cyberbullying threats.

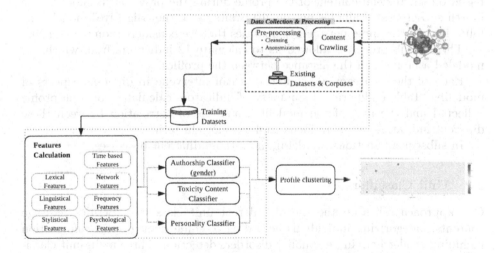

Fig. 1. An overview of the proposed approach for profile clustering

In our approach 4 different sub-processes interact together to prepare dataset of social network profiles clustering. First sub-process aims to prepare the indicators related to the content emitted by the profile. Since we plan to detect abnormal behavior in order to define whether a profile represents a risk, we have trained models for classifying toxic content. This process calculates also psychological content features in order to detect linguistical patterns representing personality disorder signals such as paranoid, borderline and narcissistic. To do this we have built the relevant datasets that can be used to train and sharpen our different classifiers. To build our training datasets, as shown in the Data Collection and Processing module in Fig. 1, we avail ourselves of existing datasets and corpuses that are used by the scientific community[1],[2], but also collect real data from social medias including Twitter and instagram. All collected data (Tweets and instagram posts) are cleaned and anonymized to remove personal identifying information in compliance with existing data protection regulations (e.g., GDPR).

The second sub-process calculates frequency indicators such as the average publication per day or the publication rates by time slots. These frequencies may be representative of addictive practices, stress or sleep disorders.

The third sub-process works out profile's network indicators such as number of subscribers and number of subscriptions. A demographic indicator is calculated on the basis of a gender classification. According to some psychological studies, gender correlates with certain user behavior on social networks. Finally, based on the textual content of the profile during the previous six months, the fourth sub-process evaluates personality traits using the "Big Five" model. The following are the three personality qualities that we considered: omn/ext/neu.

These 4 sub-processes allowed us to calculate 12 indicators from which, we modeled a profile and the distance between the profiles.

Each of these categories of indicators can intervene in different aspects of modeling. Table 1 illustrate a summary of indicators calculated for each profile collected and the axis of the modeling. analysis of correlation between these different indicators led us to focus on 4 axes for clustering.

In subsequent sections, we detail more those different processes.

3.2   Unit Classifiers

Our approach relies on the use of different unit classifiers. Besides message contents, categorizing individuals according to some demographic information including gender help in personality disorders detection. Three main unit classifiers are introduced: content classifier, gender classifier estimation, and personality estimation.

---

[1] https://www.kaggle.com/c/jigsaw-toxic-comment-classification-challenge/data.
[2] https://www.chatcoder.com.

Table 1. indicator interpretations

Indicator	Interpretation
Number Of Subscribers	Allows Us To Verify The Legitimacy Of The Profile.
Number Of Subscriptions	Detects Bots.
Biography - Description	Intervenes In Toxicity And Personality.
Average Daily Publication	Helps Detect Addictive Behavior.
Average Publication By Time Slot	Detects Addictions And Abnormal Behaviors.
Average Reactions Per Publication	Helps To Detect Spam.
Average Toxic Comments Per Post	Detects The Toxicity Of The Profile.
Age	Determines Trends By Age.
Gender	Determines Trends By Gender.
Shared Texts	Intervenes In The Calculation Of Toxicity And Personality.
Overall Toxicity Rate	Determines Toxic Trends.
Personality Traits	Helps Identify Mental Disorders Specially Neuroticism.

Content Classification: The content classifier is configured according to the cyberbullying semantic domain which may be that of harassment, sexual predators, insulting, racist or sexist contents. To this end, specific dictionaries and lexicons combined with a set of textual or extra-textual indicators (Sect. 4.2) are calculated and used to detect textual toxic content within the exchanges between two or more individuals. This classification is based on annotated datasets according to an ontology of cyberbullying and it characterizes a finer level of toxicity that is the category of the harassment. This fine categorization of toxicity will allow us to attribute a more precise level of risk to a detected toxic content.

Gender Classification: Its goal is to determine whether a set of data is male or female. A task like this is known to be simple and straightforward for humans but difficult for machines. Gender can be deduced from a variety of sources, including face image traits, voices, clinical measurements (electroencephalograph, etc.) and social data (handwriting, blog, ...). Our method uses information taken from several social networks to achieve automatic gender classification. When face photos are available, face-based gender categorization is employed first; otherwise, text-based gender classification is used.

Personality Classifier: we use this classifier to estimate the basic traits of a social network user profile. In this work, we use the big five model [10], which is one of the most used modles in the literature. Human differences in thought, emotion, and behavior models are referred to as "personality." A person's general traits, such as mood, attitude, and personality, are combined to form their personality. Personality traits and qualities have a big influence on our lives; they determine our lifestyle, health, and other aspirations. Consequently, the personality of each individual could influence his behaviors including his activities on social networks. We focused on 3 personality traits that According to Power RA. [11] are defined as follows: Neuroticism :Sadness, irritability, and emotional instability are all symptoms of neuroticism. Mood fluctuations, anxiety, impatience, and sorrow are common in those who score high on this attribute. Extraversion : Excitability, friendliness, talkativeness, assertiveness, and high levels of emotional expressiveness are all characteristics of extraversion (or extroversion). People with a high level of extraversion are gregarious and thrive in social circumstances. Openess: This trait features characteristics such as imagination and insight. People who are high in this trait tend to be more adventurous and creative. People low in this trait are often much more traditional and may struggle with abstract thinking.

4   Prototype, Experiments and Results

4.1   Datasets

In this section we will briefly describe the different datasets used for clustering profiles, toxicity, gender and personality classifying.

Clustering Dataset: Based on the list of Instagram profiles in the Askfm dataset[3], we collected posts and comments from over 100 Instagram profiles. we were only interested in textual publications, not Reels or Stories, which are in the field of computer vision. Then using a keyword list we built a Twitter profile list from which we collected all the associated posts and comments of 150 profiles. To be able to build a datast containing the profiles of the two social networks of Twitter and Instagram, we took that the common information of the two social networks while applying a mapping between the two types of attributes. Table 1 summarizes the final list of information common to Instagram and Twitter.

Toxicity Classification Dataset: To build a rich dataset with the toxicity classes we have defined, we concatenated several existing datasets. Then to balance our dataset, we proceeded to the data augmentation but also to the collection of data on social networks. The list of existing datasets used to train the toxicity classification is illustrated in Table 2.

4.2   Implemented Classifiers and Conducted Experiments

Five classifiers were implemented as depicted in Table 3. Some of them are multi classifiers (toxic comments detection, and age detection) when others are binary classifiers (toxic tweets detection, and gender prediction). Table 4 illustrates the personality analysis obtained from a given text. The performance, in terms of balanced accuracy for our gender classifier from first name using BERT is of 84%.

---

[3] https://sites.google.com/site/cucybersafety/home/cyberbullying-detection-project/dataset.

Table 2. Existing datasets for toxicity classification

Class of toxicity	Link to data sources
Insulting remarks	https://www.kaggle.com/c/detecting-insults-in-social-commentary/data?select=train.csvhttps://www.kaggle.com/mrmorj/hate-speech-and-offensive-language-dataset
Threatening remarks	https://www.kaggle.com/c/jigsaw-toxic-comment-classification-challenge
Defamatory remarks	https://competitions.codalab.org/competitions/26654#learn_the_details\discretionary-dataset
Obsene remarks	https://github.com/abhilashabhagat/Obscene-detection/
Racial remarks	https://github.com/HannahKirk/Hatemoji
	https://zenodo.org/record/3520152#.YjsulefMJPZ

The performance of our Camembert multiclasses classifier-based toxicity detection is 83% of accuracy and 85% of F-score. The evolution of accuracy of toxicity multiclasifier and gender prediction are illustrated in Fig. 5. Our dataset is vectorized by using either TF-IDF (Term Frequency-Inverse Document Frequency) which give us the importance of a word in the dataset, or word embedding technique via the bidirectional BERT model.

4.3   Clustering and Feature Selection

Implementation of the unitaries classifiers allowed the calculation of the indicators that we identified as the important dimensions as social networks user profile modeling. We have presented a mapping of the latter in order to determine which indications are associated with clusters forming. To better visualize the structure of the two clusters, we presented the indicators one by one and created correlation pairs between them. We were able to see which signs the two clusters emerged from using this mapping. This step will intervene in the definition of key dimensions for social network profile modeling.

On the one hand, the two clusters are formed at the intersection of publication habits according to time slots and the axis of toxicity, as shown in the Fig. 2. They are, on the other hand, made up of the two personality qualities of extravagance and neuroticism, as well as publishing habits based on time slots. We were able to establish the factors that had the strongest correlation with each other after multiple tests . The following factors are identified as most significant: (a) Average number of posts each day, (b) Average number of posts per time slot, (c) Personality profile, (d) Toxicity rate on a global scale.

Using the K-means technique, we were able to confirm the existence of two (2) separate clusters, which were, nevertheless, difficult to visualize due to the large number of criteria considered.

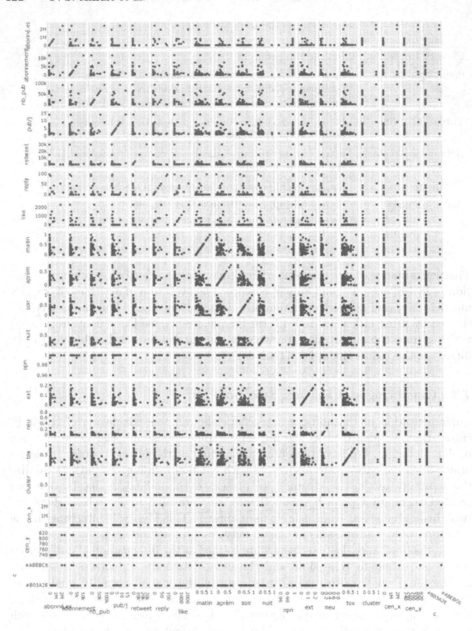

Fig. 2. Feature correlations

Table 3. Main implemented classifiers

Natural Language	Model Objective	Class Labels	ML models
english	toxic comments detection	toxic, severe toxic, insult, obscene, identity hate	Bert
english	gender prediction from text	male, female	SVM, Bert
english	gender prediction from name	male, female	LSTM, CNN
english	personality analysis	Big 5 labels	SVM, Bert
french	toxic tweets classification	Toxic, non toxic	CamemBERT

4.4   Clusters Interpretation

Visualization of Fig. 3 enables us to make a first observation. The y-axis depicts the rate of publication throughout the night, the X axis depicts the overall toxicity rate, and the size of the bubbles depicts the profiles' neuroticism. We can see two clusters in this graph: the first is distinguished by a large number of users profiles belonging to it and a low rate of publication at night and a very low rate of anxiousness. The second, on the other hand, is defined by the small number of people who belong to it, and is characterized by a high rate of publication at night and a strong neurotic attitude.

We can have a better understanding of the phenomenon by means of a second Visualization. The association between anxiousness, toxicity, and publishing behaviors. Two groups can be seen forming along the axis of toxicity, as illustrated in the Fig. 4. We notice a tiny number of people whose publishing habits are considerably more focused on the night and whose toxicity is much more than their level of anxiousness, which appears to be nonexistent or very near to nil. According to the results from these visualizations of profile's activities collected,we were able to establish some assumptions and arrive to the following conclusions: There is a substantial link between late-night posting behaviors and neuroticism. The majority of the population studied has a weak tendency for nocturnal publication and a weak neuroticism tendency, while a small portion of the population has a mixed nightly posting pattern and high level neuroticism. The second group identified has a strong tendency for toxicity in exchange for

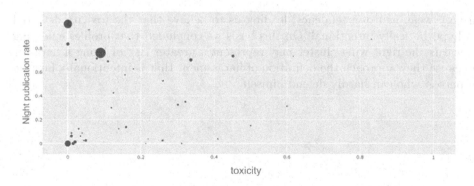

Fig. 3. Relationship between night publication habits and toxicity

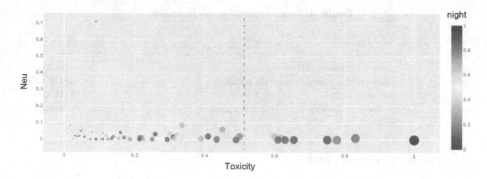

Fig. 4. Relationship between publication habits, toxicity and profile neuroticism

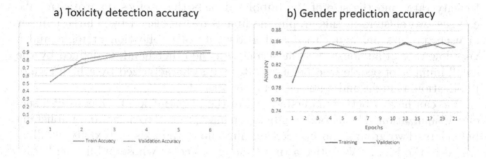

Fig. 5. Toxicity and Gender detection Accuracy

Table 4. Personality analysis from text

Big 5 / Value	Op	Co	Ag	Ex	Ne
boolean value	true	true	true	false	false
probability	0.65	0.56	0.66	0.56	0.29

a very weak neurotic tendency, leading us to believe that the toxicity detected is hypothetically intentional. On this basis we concluded that profiles emerging towards the right-wing cluster may represent a greater risk of being a harasser because they approach the definition of harassment that is intentionally hurting a person who can hardly defend himself.

5   Conclusion

In this paper, we proposed an approach to automatically detect potential users with abnormal behavior. Our approach relies on machine learning techniques and is based on combining diverse classifiers. It can works for different social networks but separately. For now, we only exploited textual posts. As for the next step, and to not miss some abnormal behaviors cases, we expect to study the effect of social network features on our models. Such features could be extracted from the graph representation of users interactions. we also intend to extend our solution to include multimedia posts by using advanced techniques of computer vision and embedding techniques. We finally project to study the user behavior by integrating the posts and the metadata that can be extracted not only from one social media but from different social media.

References

1. Shuai, H., et al.: A comprehensive study on social network mental disorders detection via online social media mining. IEEE Trans. Knowl. Data Eng. **30**(7), 1212–1225 (2018)
2. Mediacorp: 3 in 4 youngsters say they have been bullied online (2018)
3. Saha, B., Nguyen, T., Phung, D.Q., Venkatesh, S.: A framework for classifying online mental health-related communities with an interest in depression. IEEE J. Biomed. Health Inf. **20**(4), 1008–1015 (2016)
4. Choudhury, M.D., Gamon, M., Counts, S., Horvitz, E.: Predicting depression via social media. In: Kiciman, E., Ellison, N.B., Hogan, B., Resnick, P., Soboroff, I. (eds.) Proceedings of the Seventh International Conference on Weblogs and Social Media, ICWSM 2013, Cambridge, Massachusetts, USA, 8–11 July 2013. The AAAI Press (2013)
5. Choudhury, M.D., Counts, S., Horvitz, E.: Social media as a measurement tool of depression in populations. In: The Web Science Conference, pp. 47–56 (2013)
6. Dadvar, M., Ordelman, R., de Jong, F., Trieschnigg, D.: Towards user modelling in the combat against cyberbullying. In: 17th International Conference on Applications of Natural Language to Information Systems, pp. 277–283 (2012)
7. Squicciarini, A.C., Rajtmajer, S.M., Liu, Y., Griffin, C.: Identification and characterization of cyberbullying dynamics in an online social network. In: The IEEE/ACM International Conference on Advances in Social Networks Analysis and Mining, ASONAM, pp. 280–285 (2015)
8. Dadvar, M., Eckert, K.: Cyberbullying detection in social networks using deep learning based models. In: Big Data Analytics and Knowledge Discovery - 22nd International Conference. DaWaK 2020, pp. 245–255 (2020)
9. Dadvar, M., Trieschnigg, R., de Jong, F.: Experts and machines against bullies: a hybrid approach to detect cyberbullies. In: 27th Canadian Conference on Artificial Intelligence, pp. 275–281 (2014)
10. The big five trait taxonomy: history, measurement, and theoretical perspectives. In: Handbook of personality: theory and research, vol. 2, pp. 102–138 (1999)
11. Power, R., Pluess, M.: Heritability estimates of the big five personality traits based on common genetic variants. Transl. Psychiatry **5**(7), e604 (2015)

Green Energy, Computing and Technologies 1

Investigation of Different Speed Controllers to Improve the Performance of Vector-Controlled Synchronous Reluctance Motor

Yassine Zahraoui[1]([✉]), Mohamed Moutchou[1], Souad Tayane[1], and Sara Elbadaoui[2]

[1] Hassan II University, Higher National School of Arts and Crafts (ENSAM), Electrical Engineering Department, Complex Cyber -Physical Systems Laboratory, Casablanca, Morocco
yassine.zahraoui1-etu@etu.univh2c.ma
[2] Mohammed V University, Mohammadia School of Engineering (EMI), Electrical Engineering Department, Rabat, Morocco

Abstract. This research presents an investigation of different speed controller structures; the main objective is to improve the dynamic operation of vector-controlled synchronous reluctance motor (SynRM). Three controller strategies are designed and their operation is discussed in detail. The self-tuning PI-based anti-windup action (AW), the fuzzy logic (FL), and the classical PI controllers are proposed. The obtained results show the good performance and limitations of these three controllers. In fact, the self-tuning anti-windup controller is superior in terms of rapidity; its response time is very quick. The fuzzy logic controller is characterized by a high resistance against load torque perturbation and external uncertainties. While the classical PI controller presents less performance compared to the proposed controllers. Besides, the PI strategy is very sensitive to load torque, and its response time is the slowest. All simulations have been realized in MATLAB/Simulink environment.

Keywords: Vector control · Synchronous reluctance motor · Self-tuning PI-based anti-windup action · Fuzzy logic controller · Robust control

1 Introduction

The synchronous reluctance machine (SynRM) has received much attention for many applications in industry, especially for electrical vehicles, in recent years due to its simple structure and low manufacturing cost. The SynRM is also functionally robust; it is relatively inexpensive as it has no associated permanent magnets, which is also an advantage for high-temperature applications [1]. Therefore, SynRM has no demagnetization problems or associated losses. It has a clear advantage compared to an induction machine due to its natural salience,

© The Author(s), under exclusive license to Springer Nature Switzerland AG 2022
M. Hamlich et al. (Eds.): SADASC 2022, CCIS 1677, pp. 129–143, 2022.
https://doi.org/10.1007/978-3-031-20490-6_11

particularly for the sensorless control. In addition, there are no rotor losses, which allows a higher mass torque than that of an induction machine [2]. These different advantages seem to give SynRM chances for new developments [3,4].

However, SynRM has also significant drawbacks. The salience of the rotor causes high ripples in the electromagnetic torque. The origin of this salience is the torque itself. That can result in vibrations and acoustic noise. The power factor of these types of machines is generally low, leading to over-sizing of the inverter [5]. In addition, it is very sensitive to magnetic saturation, which has a strong impact on the developed average torque [6].

In order to overcome these drawbacks, many robust controller structures have been mentioned in the literature, such as sliding mode (SM) [7], anti-windup (AW) [8], fuzzy logic (FL) [9], etc. These techniques have received much attention in recent years. The fuzzy logic controller presents the high performance of speed tracking. However, this controller is insufficient to deal with systems subjected to brutal perturbation because its gains are fixed. So, to improve the limited performance of the fuzzy logic controller in case of disturbance parameters, the self-tuning anti-windup controller was developed.

2 State-Space Mathematical Model of the SynRM

In this part, we present the classical model based on the Park transformation. The following assumptions are considered [10,11]:

- Magnetic materials are isotropic and non-saturated, (there is no need to distinguish apparent inductance from incremental inductance);
- The phenomenon of hysteresis as well as iron losses are neglected;
- The inductance varies in a sinusoidal way (hypothesis of the first harmonic);
- Capacitive coupling between the windings is ignored.

In the absence of a zero-sequence current component, the electrical equations in the d-q reference frame are [12]:

$$\begin{bmatrix} v_{ds} \\ v_{qs} \end{bmatrix} = R_s \begin{bmatrix} i_{ds} \\ i_{qs} \end{bmatrix} + \begin{bmatrix} L_d \\ L_q \end{bmatrix} \frac{d}{dt} \begin{bmatrix} i_{ds} \\ i_{qs} \end{bmatrix} + p\omega_m \begin{bmatrix} 0 & -L_q \\ L_d & 0 \end{bmatrix} \begin{bmatrix} i_{ds} \\ i_{qs} \end{bmatrix} \tag{1}$$

The torque is expressed as:

$$T_{em} = p(L_d - L_q)i_{ds}i_{qs} \tag{2}$$

L_d and L_q are the inductance of the direct and the quadrature axis. In the frame related to the rotor, the total flux through the windings d and q is expressed by:

$$\begin{cases} \phi_{ds} = L_d i_{ds} \\ \phi_{qs} = L_q i_{qs} \end{cases} \tag{3}$$

hence

$$\begin{bmatrix} v_{ds} \\ v_{qs} \end{bmatrix} = R_s \begin{bmatrix} i_{ds} \\ i_{qs} \end{bmatrix} + \frac{d}{dt} \begin{bmatrix} \phi_{ds} \\ \phi_{qs} \end{bmatrix} + p\omega_m \begin{bmatrix} 0 & -1 \\ 1 & 0 \end{bmatrix} \begin{bmatrix} \phi_{ds} \\ \phi_{qs} \end{bmatrix} \tag{4}$$

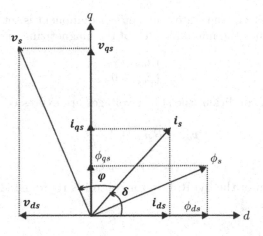

Fig. 1. Steady-state vector diagram of the SynRM

Table 1. Rated power and parameters of the machine used in the simulation

Parameter	Unit
Rated power	1.1 kW
Rated speed	1500 tr/min
Rated voltage	220/380 V
Rated torque	7 N.m
Frequency	50 Hz
Pole pair	2
Stator resistance	6.2 Ω
Apparent stator inductance L_d	0.34 H
Apparent stator inductance L_q	0.105 H
Inertia moment	0.008 N.m.s^2
Viscous friction coefficient	0.0001 N N.m.s/rad

and

$$\phi_s = \sqrt{\phi_{ds}^2 + \phi_{qs}^2} \tag{5}$$

Figure 1 shows the vector diagram of the SynRM in the steady-state. Table 1 lists the rated parameters of the machine used in the simulation.

3 Basis of SynRM Vector Control

The vector-controlled SynRM is a very accepted method for high-performance drive system response. This technique is essentially based on decoupling the flux and the torque in order to produce stator current components [13]. As a result of this condition, the stator current's q-component is set to zero while the d-component reaches the nominal value of the magnetizing current [14, 15]:

$$\begin{cases} i_{ds} = i_d \\ i_{qs} = 0 \end{cases} \tag{6}$$

As a result of this condition, the stator voltages are expressed as:

$$v_{ds} = R_s i_{ds} + L_d \frac{d}{dt} i_{ds} \tag{7}$$

$$v_{qs} = p L_d \omega_m i_{ds} \tag{8}$$

The block diagram of the SynRM vector control is represented in Fig. 2.

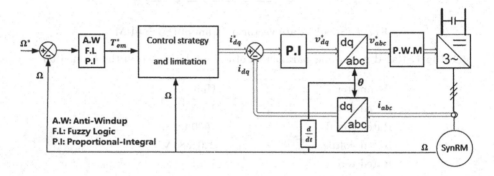

Fig. 2. Block diagram of the proposed vector control scheme

4   PI Control Design

In order to achieve good performance for both the servo (response compared to the reference) and the speed control (response compared to the disturbance), we consider the functional diagram of the speed control loop shown schematically in Fig. 3.

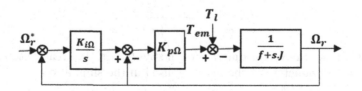

Fig. 3. PI speed loop regulation

According to the block diagram of the speed regulation, we have:

$$\Omega(s) = \frac{1}{Js + f}(T_{em} - T_l) \tag{9}$$

The transfer function of the closed-loop, after calculation, is expressed by:

$$G_{f\Omega}(s) = \cfrac{1}{\frac{J}{K_{i\Omega}K_{p\Omega}}s^2 + \frac{K_{p\Omega}+f}{K_{i\Omega}K_{p\Omega}}s + 1} \tag{10}$$

The transfer function in (10) can be identified as a second-order system in the form:

$$F(s) = \cfrac{1}{\frac{1}{\omega_n^2}s^2 + \frac{2\zeta}{\omega_n}s + 1} \tag{11}$$

This implies the following identities:

$$\begin{cases} \frac{J}{K_{i\Omega}K_{p\Omega}} = \frac{1}{\omega_n^2} \\ \frac{K_{p\Omega}+f}{K_{i\Omega}K_{p\Omega}} = \frac{2\zeta}{\omega_n} \end{cases} \tag{12}$$

If we choose $\zeta=1$, we will get a relationship between ω_n and the wanted speed response time τ_Ω, which allows us to freely set the system dynamic. This relation is written as $\omega_n\tau_\Omega=4.75$. Having properly selected the damping coefficient $\zeta=1$ and response time $\tau_\Omega=0.1s$ and next ω_n, we can calculate the controller parameters from Eq. 12, by simple identification; then we get:

$$\begin{cases} K_{p\Omega} = 2J\zeta\omega_n - f \\ K_{i\Omega} = J\frac{\omega_n^2}{K_{p\Omega}} \end{cases} \tag{13}$$

5   Fuzzy Logic Control Design

The fuzzy control system is an intelligent one that is based on fuzzy logic; it is a mathematical system, which examines the analog input values in terms of logical variables taken on continuous values between 0 and 1. Error ε_ω and error variation $\Delta\varepsilon_\omega$ are then considered as fuzzy input variables of the fuzzy controller, whose fuzzy output will generate the variation of the controlled speed $\Delta\hat{\omega}_r=\hat{\omega}_k-\hat{\omega}_{k-1}$ [16]. Fig. 4 illustrates the structure of the speed loop fuzzy controller.

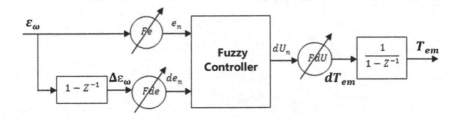

Fig. 4. Block diagram of the fuzzy speed controller

5.1   Fuzzification

The input variables are converted into fuzzy ones and are translated to linguistic labels. The membership functions linked to each label are chosen with triangular shapes. The input and the controlled output linguistic variables fuzzification is achieved by symmetric triangular membership functions normalized on [-1,+1] for each variable, as shown in Fig. 5.

The letter **N** means Negative, and **P** means Positive. **B** is Big, **M** is Medium, **S** is Small, and **Z** is Zero. **NB** means Negative Big. The triangular membership functions type led to a good linguistic classification that has positive effects on operational and control decisions [17].

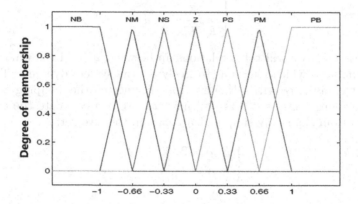

Fig. 5. Input and output membership functions of the fuzzy controller

5.2   Knowledge Base and Inference Engine

The rule base states the control goal actions by the middle course of the linguistic control rules set. The inference engine assesses the IF-THEN set and carries out 7×7 rules. The following example shows a linguistic rule form: **IF** ε_ω **is NB and** $\Delta\varepsilon_\omega$ **is NB then** T_e **is NB**. Moreover, the inference rules used to determine the output variables based on the input ones are summarized in Table 2.

Table 2. Inference matrix of the fuzzy controller

$\Delta\varepsilon_\omega$ \ ε_ω	NB	NM	NS	Z	PS	PM	PB
PB	Z	PS	PM	PB	PB	PB	PB
PM	NS	Z	PS	PM	PB	PB	PB
PS	NM	NS	Z	PS	PM	PB	PB
Z	NB	NM	NS	Z	PS	PM	PB
NS	NB	NB	NM	NS	Z	PS	PM
NM	NB	NB	NB	NM	NS	Z	PS
NB	NB	NB	NB	NB	NM	NS	Z

5.3 Defuzzification

In this phase, fuzzy variables are transformed into crisp variables. In this paper, the center of gravity defuzzification method is used. In this case, the center of gravity abscissa corresponding to the fuzzy regulator output of the Mamdani type is given by the following relation:

$$dT_e = \frac{\int x\mu_R(x)dx}{\int \mu_R dx} \tag{14}$$

Each fuzzy controller has three tuning gains; their values are determined by test, and error. This technique consists of doing repetitive tests and tuning each gain separately from the others to view its effect.

6 Self-Tuning Anti-Windup Control Design

Generally, proportional-integral (PI) controllers are used for regulation. This is done by comparing the speed reference signal to the actual measured speed value. Then the comparison error becomes the input of the PI controller. The PI controller usually ignores the physical limitations of the system, such as maximum current and voltage. The PI controller used in this research in the speed loop is the self-tuning anti-windup controller. This makes it possible to improve the performance of the speed control by canceling the **windup** phenomenon caused by saturation of the pure integrator [18]. Figure 6 shows the block diagram of the proposed self-tuning anti-windup PI controller.

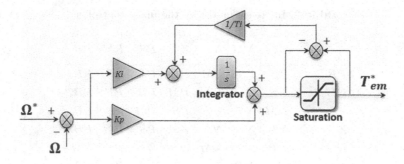

Fig. 6. Structure of the proposed self-tuning anti-windup PI controller

This strategy consists of correcting the integral action according to the difference between the control signal and the saturation limit. The difference value is transmitted to a gain block (tracking time constant Ti) before arriving back at the integrator. Each self-tuning anti-windup controller has three tuning gains; their values are also found by test and error.

7   Results and Discussion

Figure 7 shows the speed response at a step of 100 rad/s and at its reverse. To demonstrate the robustness of these controller structures throughout the steady-state phase, a load torque of 5 $N.m$ was introduced at t_1=0.6s and removed at t_2=1.6s. Figure 8 displays the speed error between the different controller structures. Figure 9 shows the electromagnetic torque waveform of the Fuzzy and self-tuning anti-windup strategies. Figure 10 shows the phase current waveform, while Fig. 11 highlights the current components in the d-q reference frame.

The response time of the self-tuning anti-windup strategy is very quick. The PI strategy is more affected by load torque application. Fuzzy and PI strategies have almost the same response time, with less speed error between them, except at the moment when the load was applied and removed. Their speed waveform is almost identical. Even at reverse speed, the three strategies self-tuning, anti-windup, fuzzy logic, and the classical PI kept the fast response time.

The fuzzy logic and the self-tuning anti-windup controllers are robust; they are insensitive to the load application. The static error of all techniques in the steady-state is null, which shows the effectiveness of these control strategies.

The torque waveforms of self-tuning, anti-windup and fuzzy logic have a reduced ripples level. The applied load value is 5 $N.m$, it's introduced at $t_1 = 0.6s$ and removed at $t_2 = 1.6s$. It can be clearly seen in the torque waveform.

The phase current waveforms of self-tuning, anti-windup and fuzzy logic have also a reduced ripples level. The PI strategy has the highest ripples level among all the three strategies.

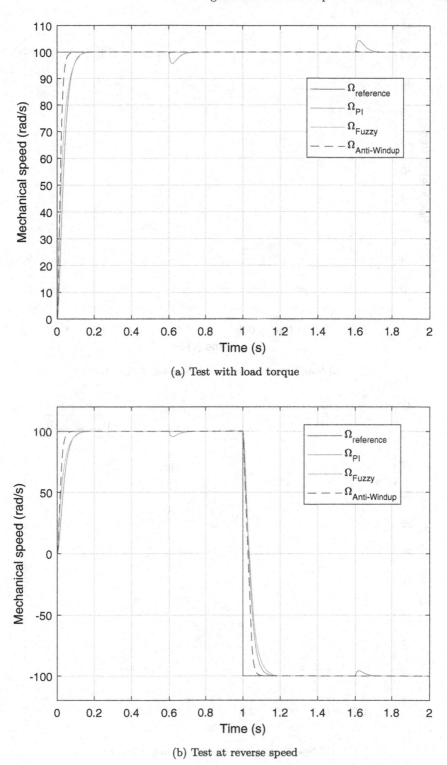

(a) Test with load torque

(b) Test at reverse speed

Fig. 7. Test of performance comparison under load torque disturbance

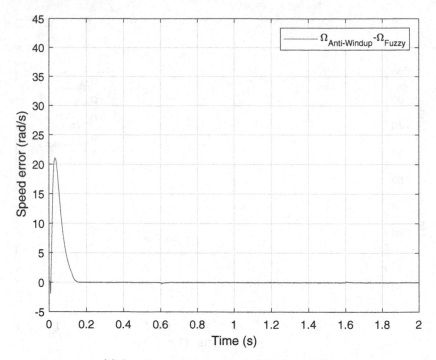

(a) Speed error between Anti-Windup and Fuzzy

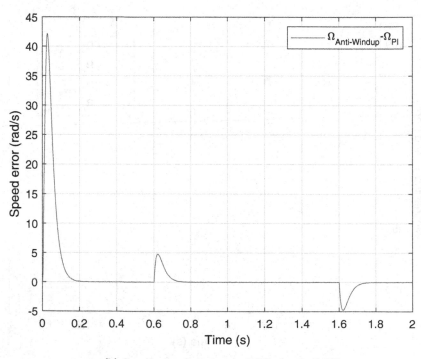

(b) Speed error between Anti-Windup and PI

Fig. 8. Speed error

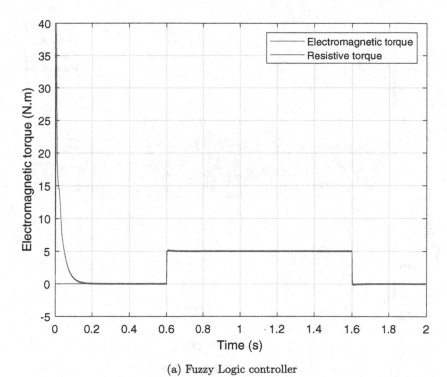

(a) Fuzzy Logic controller

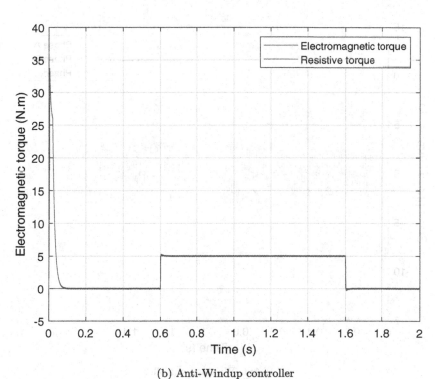

(b) Anti-Windup controller

Fig. 9. Electromagnetic torque waveform

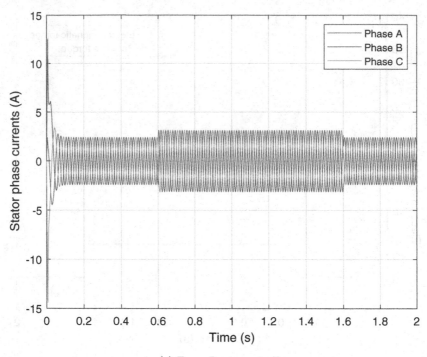

(a) Fuzzy Logic controller

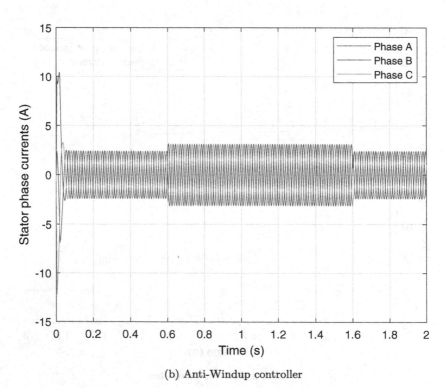

(b) Anti-Windup controller

Fig. 10. Stator phase current waveform

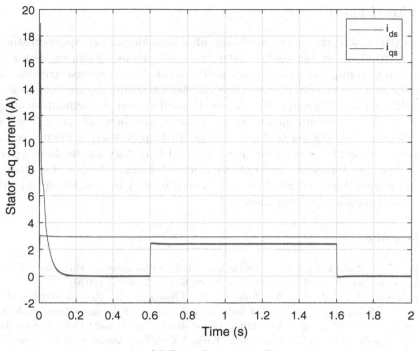

(a) Fuzzy Logic controller

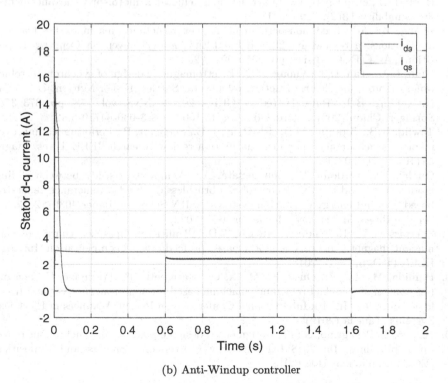

(b) Anti-Windup controller

Fig. 11. d-q current components waveform

8 Conclusion

In this paper, we present the modeling, identification, and comparison study of many controllers for the vector-controlled synchronous reluctance motor. The main goal is to improve its operating performance. The proposed strategies offer good dynamics, even at reverse speed. Different strategies are then possible, depending on the targeted performance. The self-tuning anti-windup strategy is generally used to obtain maximum acceleration and best efficiency. The fuzzy logic strategy is designed to resist instant load application, without requiring knowing the machine's exact parameters. The PI strategy has the lowest performance because it is sensitive to external uncertainties. These vector controller strategies have been adjusted, tested, and validated in simulation, and their operation is highlighted and discussed.

References

1. Wang, S., et al.: Design and performance analysis of a novel synchronous reluctance machine. Int. J. Appl. Electromagn. Mech **63**(2), 249–265 (2020)
2. Zahraoui, Y., Akherraz, M., Fahassa, C., Elbadaoui, S.: Robust control of sensorless sliding mode controlled induction motor drive facing a large scale rotor resistance variation. In: Proceedings of the 4th International Conference on Smart City Applications. SCA 2019, New York, NY, USA. Association for Computing Machinery, pp. 1–6 (2019)
3. Heidari, H., et al.: A review of synchronous reluctance motor-drive advancements. Sustainability **13**(2), 729 (2021)
4. Zhang, Z.: Advanced non-permanent-magnet reluctance machines for traction applications: a review. In: 2021 IEEE 12th Energy Conversion Congress Exposition - Asia (ECCE-Asia), pp. 2052–2058 (2021)
5. Dinh, B.M., Tan, D.T., Vuong, D.Q.: Electromagnetic design of synchronous reluctances motors for electric traction vehicle. In: Sattler, K.-U., Nguyen, D.C., Vu, N.P., Long, B.T., Puta, H. (eds.) ICERA 2020. LNNS, vol. 178, pp. 373–378. Springer, Cham (2021). https://doi.org/10.1007/978-3-030-64719-3_42
6. Tawfiq, K.B., Ibrahim, M.N., El-Kholy, E.E., Sergeant, P.: Performance improvement of synchronous reluctance machines-a review research. IEEE Trans. Magn. **57**(10), 1–11 (2021)
7. Oualah, O., Kerdoun, D., Boumassata, A.: Comparative study between sliding mode control and the vector control of a brushless doubly fed reluctance generator based on wind energy conversion systems. SSRN Scholarly Paper 4039782, Social Science Research Network, Rochester, NY (2022)
8. Zhetpissov, Y., Kaibaldiyev, A., Do, T.D.: PI anti-windup speed control of permanent magnet synchronous motor based on feedforward compensation. In: 2018 ELEKTRO, pp. 1–8 (2018)
9. Hamida, M., Tir, Z., Oued, E., Malik, O., Marignetti, F., Frosinone, C.: Sensorless control of switched reluctance machine based on nonlinear observer and fuzzy logic controller. In: 4th International Conference on Recent Advances in Electrical Systems, Tunisia (2019)
10. Ferrari, S., Pellegrino, G.: FEA-augmented design equations for synchronous reluctance machines. In: 2018 IEEE Energy Conversion Congress and Exposition (ECCE), pp. 5395–5402 (2018)

11. Boztas, G., Aydogmus, O., Guldemir, H.: Design and implementation of a high-efficiency low-voltage synchronous reluctance motor. Electr. Eng. **104**(2), 717–725 (2021)
12. Lenin, N.C., Sanjeevikumar, P., Iqbal, A., Mbohwa, C.: Linear synchronous reluctance motor—a comprehensive review. In: Konkani, A., Bera, R., Paul, S. (eds.) Advances in Systems, Control and Automation. LNEE, vol. 442, pp. 45–70. Springer, Singapore (2018). https://doi.org/10.1007/978-981-10-4762-6_5
13. Zahraoui, Y., Akherraz, M., Fahassa, C., Elbadaoui, S.: Induction motor harmonic reduction using space vector modulation algorithm. Bull. Electr. Eng. Inf. **9**(2), 452–465 (2020)
14. Babetto, C., Bacco, G., Bianchi, N.: Synchronous reluctance machine optimization for high-speed applications. IEEE Trans. Energy Convers. **33**(3), 1266–1273 (2018)
15. Zahraoui, Y., Fahassa, C., Akherraz, M., Bennassar, A.: Sensorless vector control of induction motor using an EKF and SVPWM algorithm. In: 2016 5th International Conference on Multimedia Computing and Systems (ICMCS), pp. 588–593 (2016)
16. Rajendran, A., Karthik, B.: Design and analysis of fuzzy and PI controllers for switched reluctance motor drive. Mater. Today Proc. **37**, 1608–1612 (2021)
17. Zahraoui, Y., Bennassar, A., Akherraz, M., Essalmi, A.: Indirect vector control of induction motor using an extended kalman observer and fuzzy logic controllers. In: 2015 3rd International Renewable and Sustainable Energy Conference (IRSEC), pp. 1–6 (2015)
18. Laoufi, C., Abbou, A., Akherraz, M.: Comparative study between several strategies speed controllers in an indirect field-oriented control of an induction machine. In: 2014 International Renewable and Sustainable Energy Conference (IRSEC), pp. 866–872 (2014)

Performing Energy-Efficient Motions for Wheeled Mobile Robots by Designing an Orientation Controller

Said Fadlo$^{(\boxtimes)}$, Abdelhafid Ait Elmahjoub, and Nabila Rabbah

Ensam, Hassan II University, Casablanca, Morocco
said.fadlo-etu@etu.univh2c.ma

Abstract. Wheeled mobile robots are a good candidate for a wide range of missions as exploration, search, rescue, logistics, and leisure. Many of these missions require the robot to perform long-running time and complex tasks. This article describes the design of an energy-efficient orientation controller for wheeled mobile robots. Specifically, this work compares two models and examines how they influence the mode of mobile robot locomotion. Then, the simulation results demonstrate how this approach provides a good trade-off combination of energy efficiency and the requirement of a fast convergence criterion.

Keywords: Differential wheeled mobile robot · Energy-saving · Motion controller

1 Introduction

After being massively used in industrial, logistic, and military applications. Mobile robots are now invested in human daily lives such as medicine [8,14], leisure [12], and education [4,7]. According to Research and Markets, the global autonomous mobile robot market accounted for $4.98 million in 2017 and is expected to reach $14.79 million by 2026, at a compound annual growth rate of 12.9% [2]. This growth does not come without a negative impact on the environment. So, the designers should have models and tools helping them to take into account Energy-efficient as an important. Furthermore, they must have a methodology to make mobile robots accomplish their task with accuracy, and operate over a long period of time with a minimum power.

Energy-saving for mobile robots can be achieved using two families' methods, depending on how these methods are relevant to the systems described. The first one is by optimizing the hardware. Indeed, replacement, adding components for storing, and recovering energy are common methods used for this purpose. The advantages are more emphasis when the change is easier, faster, and cheaper, or when new systems are designed. The second family focuses on enhancing the embedded software by making them able to schedule the movements of the mobile robot and estimate energy to perform needed tasks. An overview of these methods was provided by Carabin in [1]. It is evident that any

© The Author(s), under exclusive license to Springer Nature Switzerland AG 2022
M. Hamlich et al. (Eds.): SADASC 2022, CCIS 1677, pp. 144–157, 2022.
https://doi.org/10.1007/978-3-031-20490-6_12

improvement of the mobile robot capacities is conditioned by the performances of their constituent.

In this context, Control set theory is a mathematical method that allows designers to achieve a lot of advances. Combining those strategies with the optimization of the mobile robot movements lead to design systems globally efficient. Many researchers have been focused on designing models that can reduce energy consumption of mobile robots. Most of these works are based on the optimization of robot movement. Carabin et al. [1], presented a survey of existing techniques based on Richiedei et al. [9] classification. A. Štefek et al. [15] concluded, after reviewing many pieces of research, that these studies refer only to continuous or smooth curves, where the energy consumption of the robot is not mentioned. These works made the assumption that the mobile robot has a sufficient amount of energy to perform designed motion control strategies.

Few recent works modeled and estimated the mobile robot energy based on motion control strategies. Jaiem et al. [3], presented the first work that takes into account the mission level energy consumption in addition to compound level one and investigated different scenarios of motion. The main idea of this work is modeling the power behavior with a second or sixth-degree polynomial equation whose coefficients are estimated from experimental curves. one can remark that this approach is limited for a specific mobile robot. A. Štefek et al. [16] proposed an optimized controller based on fuzzy logic with 110% reduction of the energy consumption and provided a comparison with six commonly used controllers.

In this work, we adopted a comparison approach to investigate the energy consumption for different controllers in a mobile robot. In this case, the losses contributions of DC motors, and motion strategies are taken into account to perform an accurate model.

The rest of this paper is categorized as follows. In Sect. 2, the kinematic model of the WDMR is presented, Backstepping controller design is described, and two kinds of orientation models are introduced. Then, to illustrate our approach the model implementation, Simulation results are given in Sect. 3. Finally, Sect. 4 outlines the main conclusion.

2   Methodology

2.1   Total Energy Model

The total Energy consumption of the mobile robot is generally the sum of four parts and is represented by equation

$$E_{Tot} = E_{DC} + E_G + E_K + E_f \tag{1}$$

where E_{DC} term symbolize the energy losses in DC Motors, E_G the energy losses in gear-head, E_K the kinetic losses, and E_f the energy losses due to friction.

In this work we considered the kinematic energy to study the influence of the orientation motion control on power consumption.

2.2   Mobile Robot Kinematic Energy

To develop an energy model, the kinematic model of the robot is needed. In this work, a Wheeled Differential Drive Mobile Robot (WDDMR) is considered. This mobile robot has two driven wheels that are attached to DC motors and a rear castor which is added for balancing. The rotation of the wheels produces linear and angular motions of the robot. The kinematic model is illustrated in Fig. 1. Where r is drive wheel radius, b symbolize the axle length, x and y denote the position of the center of axle, θ is the angle between the robot axle and X- axis, $\dot{\varphi}_L$ and $\dot{\varphi}_R$ are the angular velocities of the wheels, which are related to the linear v and angular ω velocities of the robot by the following equations:

$$v = \frac{r\left(\dot{\varphi}_R + \dot{\varphi}_L\right)}{2} \tag{2}$$

$$\omega = \frac{r\left(\dot{\varphi}_R - \dot{\varphi}_L\right)}{2b} \tag{3}$$

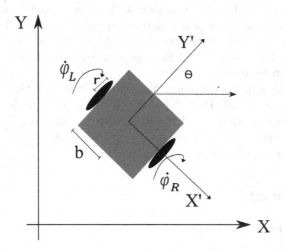

Fig. 1. Schematic Diagram of the Wheeled Mobile Robot.

Then the kinematics model can be described as follows [10]

$$\begin{cases} \dot{x} = v\cos\theta \\ \dot{y} = v\sin\theta \\ \dot{\theta} = \omega \end{cases} \tag{4}$$

and formulated by:

$$\begin{bmatrix} \dot{x} \\ \dot{y} \\ \dot{\theta} \end{bmatrix} = \begin{bmatrix} \cos\theta & 0 \\ \sin\theta & 0 \\ 0 & 1 \end{bmatrix} \begin{bmatrix} v \\ \omega \end{bmatrix} \tag{5}$$

So the kinetic energy loss equation, can be expressed as same as in [13]

$$E_k = \tfrac{1}{2}\left(mv\left(t\right)^2 + I\omega\left(t\right)^2\right) \tag{6}$$

where m is the mass, and I is the moment of inertia of the robot.

2.3 Controller Design

The proposed controller for the mobile robot is based on Backstepping technique, the diagram of this control is depicted in Fig. 2.

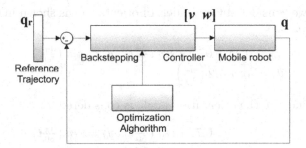

Fig. 2. The controller block diagram.

The main objective of the controller is to drive the system asymptotically to the desired position and orientation [5]. Let $\mathbf{q}_d = \begin{bmatrix} x_d\ y_d\ \theta_d \end{bmatrix}^T$ be the desired pose and orientation of the mobile robot, then as Eq. (4) we deduce

$$\begin{bmatrix} \dot{x}_d \\ \dot{y}_d \\ \dot{\theta}_d \end{bmatrix} = \begin{bmatrix} \cos\theta_d & 0 \\ \sin\theta_d & 0 \\ 0 & 1 \end{bmatrix} \begin{bmatrix} v_d \\ \omega_d \end{bmatrix} \tag{7}$$

where v_d and ω_d are the desired linear and the angular velocities respectively. The controller receives the references linear and angular velocities, and generates another pair of linear and angular velocities to be delivered to the robot DC Motors. The configuration error can be presented by

$$S_e = \begin{bmatrix} x_e \\ y_e \\ \theta_e \end{bmatrix} = \begin{bmatrix} \cos\theta & \sin\theta & 0 \\ -\sin\theta & \cos\theta & 0 \\ 0 & 0 & 1 \end{bmatrix} \begin{bmatrix} x_d - x \\ y_d - y \\ \theta_d - \theta \end{bmatrix} \tag{8}$$

Differential Eq. 8 and rearranging with Eqs. 4 and 7. Now the configuration error becomes

$$\dot{S}_e = \begin{bmatrix} \dot{x}_e \\ \dot{y}_e \\ \dot{\theta}_e \end{bmatrix} = \begin{bmatrix} v_d \cos\theta_e + y_e\omega - v \\ v_d \sin\theta_e + x_e\omega \\ \omega_d - \omega \end{bmatrix} \tag{9}$$

Finally, the proposed nonlinear kinematic trajectory tracking control law can be described by

$$\begin{bmatrix} v \\ \omega \end{bmatrix} = \begin{bmatrix} v_d \cos\theta_e + K_x x_e \\ \omega_d + K_y v_d y_e + K_\theta v_d \sin\theta_e \end{bmatrix} \tag{10}$$

where K_x, K_y, K_θ are positive control gains.

2.4   Orientation Models

In This work we considered two models of orientation as shown in Figs. 3 and 4. The fist on is as flow:

$$x_d = 0.75 + 0.75 * sin\left(\frac{2\pi}{50}t\right), y_d = sin\left(\frac{4\pi}{50}t\right),$$
$$\theta_d = arctan2\left(\frac{\dot{y}_d}{\dot{x}_d}\right) \tag{11}$$

In the second one the orientation angle is considered as

$$x_d = 0.75 + 0.75 * sin\left(\frac{2\pi}{50}t\right), y_d = sin\left(\frac{4\pi}{50}t\right),$$
$$\theta_d = \begin{cases} g(t), & 0 \le t < 12.5 \ sec \\ -\pi - g(t), & 12.5 \le t < 37.5 \ sec \\ g(t), & 37.5 < t \ sec \end{cases} \tag{12}$$

where

$$g(t) = \tan^{-1}\left(\frac{8\cos\left(2\sin^{-1}\left(\frac{4x_d}{3} - 1\right)\right)}{\sqrt[3]{1 - \left(\frac{4x_d}{3} - 1\right)^{-2}}}\right)$$

3   Model Implementation and Results

In this section, we present the simulation that was performed with Simulink and MATLAB. The parameters of the mobile robot presented in [6,11] were used. These parameters are shown in the Table 1. Table 2 report the optimized parameters of the controller.

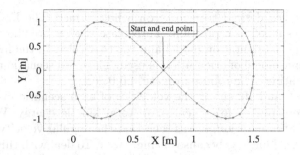

Fig. 3. Path desired for the wheeled mobile robot.

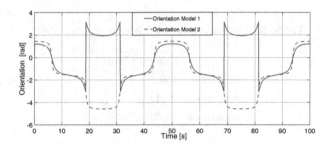

Fig. 4. Orientation models for the mobile robot.

Table 1. parameters of the wheeled mobile robot.

Parameters	Values	Parameters	Values
r	0.095 m	m_c	6.04 Kg
b	0.165 m	m_ω	1.48 Kg

Table 2. Controller parameter.

K_x	K_y	K_θ
2.52	100.00	11.15

The robot track desired trajectory on a flat surface. The Fig. 6, 11 and 15 illustrate the result of X-Y position. Three case studies are shown to examine the influence of the orientation model and the controller. In the first and second scenarios the first model of orientation is used. The third scenario use the second model of orientation. The robot start at: [0 0 0.75].

Figures 9, 14, and 19, shows the velocities of each scenario obtained by the model, that were put in (6) to calculate total kinetic energy. When we used the first model of orientation, it was seen that the angular velocity exceeded the robot limitations. That was because of singularity. To deal with this inconvenient a limiter was added to take into account the saturation of the angular velocities that can be provided by DC Motors. In Table 3, The energy of the mobile robot in each scenario is reported.

Table 3. The energy of the wheeled mobile robot.

	Energy [joule]
Scenario 1	450,1
Scenario 2	27.42
Scenario 3	28,42

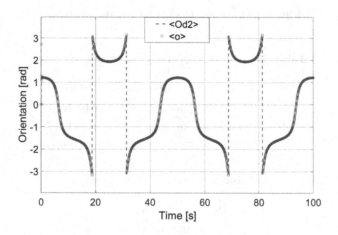

Fig. 5. Orientation of path desired of the Mobile robot.

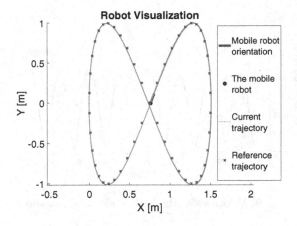

Fig. 6. X-Y path of the Mobile robot in scenario 1.

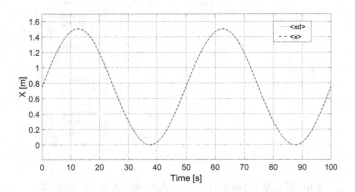

Fig. 7. X position of the Mobile robot in scenario 1.

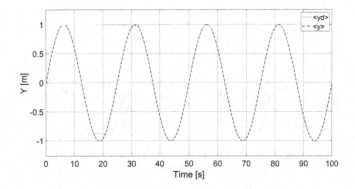

Fig. 8. Y position of the Mobile robot in scenario 1.

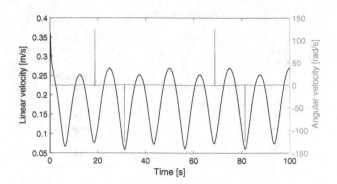

Fig. 9. Velocities of the Mobile robot in scenario 1.

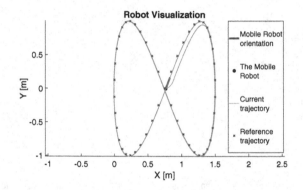

Fig. 10. X-Y path of the Mobile robot in scenario 2.

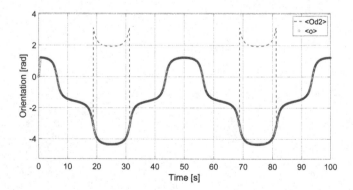

Fig. 11. Orientation of the Mobile robot in scenario 2.

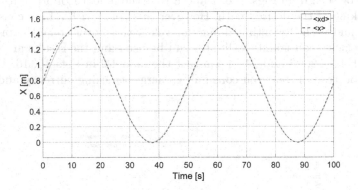

Fig. 12. X position of the Mobile robot in scenario 2.

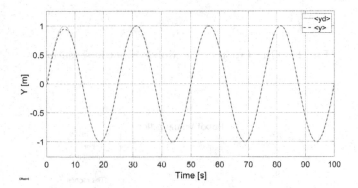

Fig. 13. Y position of the Mobile robot in scenario 2.

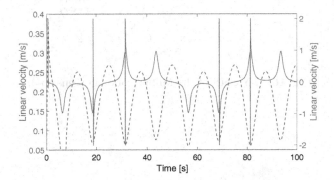

Fig. 14. Velocities of the Mobile robot in scenario 2.

It can be seen from Figs. 5, 6, 7 and 8 that the model 1 of orientation offer a good tracking of the desired path. However this come with a high consumption of energy and with discontinued angular velocity. To over come the problem of angular velocity constraints, a limiter can be used and the results are shown in Figs. 9, 10, 11, 12, 13 and 14 In contrast the model 2 in Figs. 15, 16, 17 and 18 offer a good trad-off between consuming energy, tracking currency and smooth motion.

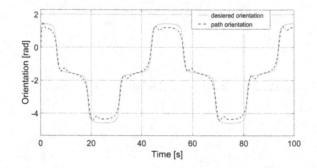

Fig. 15. Orientation of the Mobile robot in scenario 3.

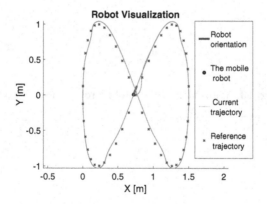

Fig. 16. X-Y path of the Mobile robot in scenario 3.

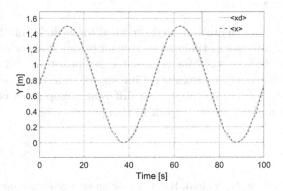

Fig. 17. X position of the Mobile robot in scenario 3.

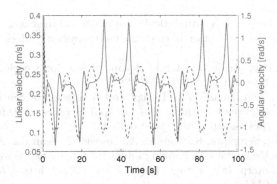

Fig. 18. Y position of the Mobile robot in scenario 3.

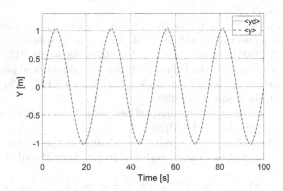

Fig. 19. Velocities of the Mobile robot in scenario 3.

4   Conclusion

A comparison of two orientation angle models for a differential wheeled drive mobile robot that influences the energy consumption, was performed. The simulation results provide a basis for parameter optimization and motion control taking into account energy constraints. Our approach in this work is still applying for a large type of mobile robot with different panoplies of controllers. This encourages us to undertake more work in this perspective.

References

1. Carabin, G., Wehrle, E., Vidoni, R.: A review on energy-saving optimization methods for robotic and automatic systems. Robotics **196**, 39 (2017)
2. Himanshu, J.: Autonomous mobile robot market by type, by application, and by end user global opportunity analysis and industry forecast. https://www.alliedmarketresearch.com/press-release/autonomous-mobile-robot-market.html. Accessed 03 Dec 2022
3. Jaïem, L., Crestani, D., Lapierre, L., Druon, S.: Energy consumption of control schemes for the pioneer 3Dx mobile robot: models and evaluation. J. Intell. Robot. Syst. **102**, 1–15 (2021). https://doi.org/10.1007/s10846-021-01374-6
4. Kassawat, M., Cervera, E., del Pobil, A.P.: An omnidirectional platform for education and research in cooperative robotics. Electronics **11**(3), 499 (2022). https://doi.org/10.3390/electronics11030499
5. kumar, D.N., et al.: Position and orientation control of a mobile robot using neural networks. vol. 32, pp. 123–131 (2015)
6. Brossog, M., Bornschlegl, M., Franke, J.: Reducing the energy consumption of industrial robots in manufacturing systems. Int. J. Adv. Manuf. Technol **78**, 1315–1328 (2015)
7. Mondada, F., et al.: The e-puck, a robot designed for education in engineering. vol. 1, pp. 59–65. IPCB: Instituto Politécnico de Castelo Branco, Portugal (2009)
8. Prakash, O.: A robot maker for health sector. In: Chandani, A., Divekar, R., Nayak, J.K. (eds) Achieving $5 Trillion Economy of India. Springer Proceedings in Business and Economics. Springer, Singapore (2020). https://doi.org/10.1007/978-981-16-7818-9_15
9. Richiedei, D., Trevisani, A.: Analytical computation of the energy-efficient optimal planning in rest-to-rest motion of constant inertia systems. Mechatronics **39**, 147–159 (2016)
10. Blazic, S.: A novel trajectory-tracking control law for wheeled mobile robots. Robot. Auton. Syst. **59**(11), 1001–1007 (2011)
11. Shamshiri, R., Wan Ismail, W.I.: Design and simulation of control systems for a field survey mobile robot platform. Res. J. Appl. Sci. Eng. Technol. **6**, 2307–2315 (2013). https://doi.org/10.19026/rjaset.6.3701
12. Srivastava, P.R., Sengupta, K., Kumar, A., Biswas, B., Ishizaka, A.: Post-epidemic factors influencing customer's booking intent for a hotel or leisure spot: an empirical study. J. Enterp. Inf. Manage. **35**(1), 78–99 (2022). https://doi.org/10.1108/JEIM-03-2021-0137
13. Trzynadlowski, A.: Energy optimization of a certain class of incremental motion DC drives industrial electronics. IEEE Trans. **35**(1), 60–66 (1988)

14. Yogiswara, Riskiawan, H.Y., Anwar, S., Ardiansyah, R.: Differential-drive wheeled robot controller using pulse-width modulation in disinfectant sprayer robot. Food Agric. Sci. Polije Proc. Ser. **3**(1), 151–157 (2020)
15. Štefek, A., Pham, T.V., Krivanek, V., Pham, K.L.: Energy comparison of controllers used for a differential drive wheeled mobile robot. IEEE Access **8**, 170915–170927 (2020). https://doi.org/10.1109/ACCESS.2020.3023345
16. Štefek, A., Pham, V.T., Krivanek, V., Pham, K.L.: Optimization of fuzzy logic controller used for a differential drive wheeled mobile robot. Appl. Sci. **11**(13), 6023 (2021). https://doi.org/10.3390/app11136023

Study of Path Optimization of an Electric Vehicle: Case of Morocco

Meryem Abid[1,2(✉)], Mohammed Tabaa[1], and Hanaa Hachimi[2]

[1] Pluridisciplinary Laboratory of Research and Innovation (LPRI), EMSI, Casablanca, Morocco
m.abid@emsi.ma
[2] Systems Engineering Laboratory (LGS), FST Beni Mellal, Beni Mellal, Morocco

Abstract. The vehicle manufacturers are racing to develop the ideal electric vehicle. These electric vehicles are often evaluated based on one factor: their driving range. Several countries started decades ago preparing for the switch towards electric vehicle by installing more and more charging stations, amongst other preparations. However, in Morocco, the electric vehicle market is still fertile. The number of charging stations available requires the use of vehicles with a more than basic driving range. Until the infrastructure for electric vehicles in Morocco is strong enough, we must find an optimal way to plan trips around the kingdom without the risk of draining the vehicles batteries. To this end, we will study the case of a trip between Tangier and Agadir using a Renault's ZOE. The path planning will be done using Dijkstra algorithm along with a cost analysis. Results prove that the trip between the two cities is feasible with the least costs possible. Our study will be a base for further studies aiming to improve the electric vehicles' infrastructure in Morocco and help encourage the switch towards electric vehicles.

Keywords: Electric vehicle · Routing · Optimization · Dijkstra · Shortest path

1 Introduction

Aware of the eminent threat we face because of global warming [1], and the receding amounts of natural resources [2], the world was driven towards seeking cleaner, renewable sources of energy. One of the cleanest sources of energy is electricity, therefore, a new era of electrification began [3]. The aim was to substitute natural resources with electricity to reduce greenhouse gases emissions and help stop the depletion of natural resources. Each sector imposed a set of rules to go by. Seeing as transportation sector accounts for almost 16% of the total greenhouse gases emissions [4], efforts were directed towards e-mobility as well.

Several manufacturers started investing in electric cars as an eco-friendly alternative for combustion vehicles [5] Although Electric vehicles were first introduced in the early 90s, they were overtaken by internal combustion vehicles for several decades due to their limited range. However, when the need for cleaner energy sources (and its applications) arose, electric vehicles returned to the stage. Several countries have taken serious steps to ensure a smooth transition towards e-mobility and to encourage drivers to switch to electric vehicles [6]. The Moroccan kingdom, also, has been investing more and more in e-mobility. A fact that can be proved by the increasing number of charging stations in the territory. Additionally, many big vehicle manufacturers have taken interest in the kingdom such as Stellantis's Kenitra implant that is set to produce both the Opel Rocks-e and the Citroën Ami [7].

However, one main barrier facing the full switch to electric vehicles is their limited range [8]. While an internal combustion vehicle can stop at any gas station to refuel, an electric vehicle requires a specific technology to recharge which might not be available at all stations. Besides, the time it takes to recharge is significantly longer than that of internal combustion vehicles, and the charging stations aren't as available as gas stations yet.

In a world where time is of the essence, along with the environmental need for eco-friendly transportation, the path planning of electric vehicles is a key solution to adopt electric vehicles. The optimal solution, certainly, would be to increase the vehicle range and set up more charging stations, but, until that is possible, we must make do with what we have. Meaning that, to avoid depleting the vehicles battery, we need to be able to foreplan the trip to know exactly when, where, and how much to recharge the vehicle. All things considered, the path planning of electric vehicles becomes considerably complicated when the constraint of charging is included. To this end, we study the path optimization of an electric vehicle in Morocco, more specifically between the two cities of Tangier and Agadir using a Renault's ZOE. Further travelling is not possible because the distance between the charging stations of Agadir and their nearest charging stations in Laayoune is of approx. 638 km [9], almost double the range of the vehicle used in our study [10]. Moreover, the Renault's ZOE is our vehicle of choice to conduct this study seeing as Renault vehicles are the most affordable vehicles in the Moroccan market.

Our paper aims to improve the path planning of electric vehicles in Morocco. This can inspire further research in this field both nationally and internationally, especially in countries where electric vehicles are yet to be sought. Moreover, the good path planning will attract more investors to the kingdom which can only be beneficial to our economy.

This paper is organized as follows: Sect. 1 presentation of electric vehicles in general, followed by Sect. 2 in which we formulate our problem. Section 3 will detail our approach to solve the described problem. Finally, in Sect. 4 we will discuss the achieved results before we wrap up with a conclusion.

2 Background

Since their first appearance in the early 1800s [11], electric vehicles represented an - eventually- ultimate replacement for internal combustion vehicles. However, due to their limited range, they were temporarily put on a shelf. Later on, when the environmental need became urgent, the interest in electric vehicles was restored.

If electric vehicles were to ever wipe out other types of vehicles (combustion, or hybrid), they will have to overcome one major issue, and that is their limited range.

Several algorithms were used throughout literature to find the shortest path, each using a different technique. Some works focused on the charging stations layout to tackle the limited range problem such as in [12] where genetic algorithm was deployed to find the perfect layout of charging stations. It was proven that the best distribution of charging stations in the studied city was provided by the genetic algorithm while taking into consideration the actual demand. However, this work only considers the case of urban areas and is yet to prove its effectiveness in interurban context. In [13], the genetic algorithm was deployed again with the intentions of finding the optimal distribution of 670 charging stations in Ireland. While the number might be important and beneficial to the routing of EVs, it is only relevant in Ireland. Further studies need to be conducted for different demographics. In another work [14], authors relied on machine learning to find the optimal path [15] with energy consumption uncertainties. Their solution is weakened by travel speeds which, unlike what they proposed in their model, is variable is real life. Sometimes, to avoid charging time which increases travel time, authors resort to battery swapping techniques [16–18] or partial recharge [19–22]. While these techniques save up on charging costs (time and energy); they increase the number of trips to charging

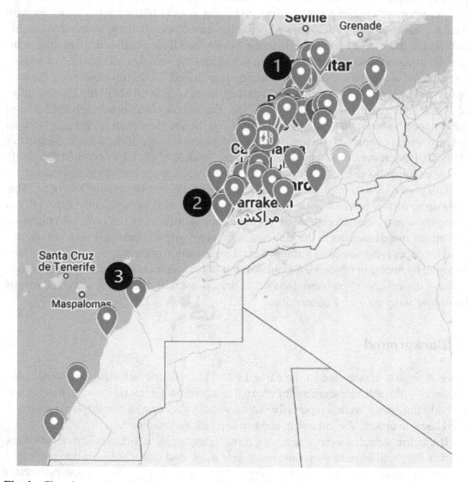

Fig. 1. Charging stations in Morocco as of May 2022 [9] (1 is Tangier, 2 is Agadir and 3 is Laayoune)

stations, thus, increasing the overall travel distance. Although these techniques were applied to routing of fleet of electric vehicles, they are a great source of inspiration and a solid base to start from.

3   Problem Formulation

3.1   Electric Vehicles in Morocco

Nowadays, vehicles manufacturers are racing to develop the ultimate electric vehicle, one that has enough range, that is. The issue here is that the ideal range is relative since range if affected by the availability of charging stations. For example, a vehicle with 300 km range is ideal in countries like Norway, Netherlands, or France [23, 24].

Meanwhile, in Morocco, which is the case of our study, a vehicle with this range will not be able to do a trip between the cities of Agadir and Laayoune. The reason is simple, the distance between the two cities is 638.2 km, with no charging stations in between (see Fig. 1), which is almost twice the range of the vehicle used. Of course, this trip can be done using another vehicle with a wider range, but for the time being, we stick to the Renault ZOE since it is the most likely to be bought by Moroccan customers, for financial and logistic reasons. Until more charging stations are installed, and other brands of electric vehicles are more commercialized in the Moroccan market, we will have to stick to trips that are possible using the Renault's ZOE. Therefore, in our paper, we will study the optimization of a trip from Tangiers to Agadir using a Renault's ZOE.

Despite the reluctant purchase of electric vehicles, the kingdom has been investing in optimizing the infrastructure for electric vehicles through the Green Mile project [25]. This project is endorsed by the Institute for Research in Solar Energy and New Energies (IRESEN) with the aim of having a charging station every 60km in the region between Tangier and Agadir (passing by Casablanca).

3.2   Data Description

So far, we count 62 charging stations [26], most of which are in the northern half of the kingdom. These stations use different charging techniques with Type 2 being the dominant [27].

Table 1 portrays the distance between different charging stations and the time it takes to travel between them. Although every city has several charging stations, for simplification purposes, we chose one random charging station per city. The chosen charging stations are portrayed by Fig. 2 and are considered nodes for adjacency matrix later.

The satellite coordinates of these charging stations were obtained using google maps, from which we obtained the distances between nodes as well.

For our study, we labelled each charging station with a number going from 1 to 31 as shown in Fig. 2 the objective is to organize all stations according to possible and logical routes. For example, to go from Tangiers (node 1) to Rabat (node 9) it wouldn't make sense to jump to node 13 through node 10.

Table 1. Distance between charging stations in Morocco [26]

From		To		Distance (km)	Time
Node	Name	Node	Name		
1	Tangiers	4	M'diq	98.8	1 h 51min
		3	Melloussa	31.9	33 min
		2	Asilah	44.5	45 min
2	Asilah	5	Larach	48.5	38 min
5	Larach	6	Moulay-bousselham	43.4	34 min
6	Moulay-bousselham	7	Lamhamid ben mansour	68.9	59 min
7	Lamhamid ben mansour	8	Kenitra	59.2	1 h 9 min
8	Kenitra	10	Khemisset	87	1 h 11 min
10	Khemisset	11	Fes	125	1 h 27 min
11	Fes	12	Taza	119	1 h 33 min
12	Taza	13	Taourirt	126	1 h 29 min
8	Kenitra	9	Rabat	50.8	40 min
9	Rabat	10	Khemisset	91.5	1 h 11 min
		14	Casablanca	86.8	1 h 5 min
14	Casablanca	15	Berrechid	49.3	43 min
		16	El jadida	102	1 h 19 min
15	Berrchid	17	Settat	40.1	30 min
16	El jadida	15	Berrchid	103	1 h 23 min
		18	Ouled bourass	40.2	48 min
18	Ouled bourass	17	Settat	175	2 h 32 min
		19	Oum rabii	128	2 h 9 min
17	Settat		Oum rabii	55.8	52 min
19	Oum Rabii	20	Ben-guerir	61.6	49 min
20	Ben guerir	21	Marrakech	74	1 h 4 min
21	Marrakech	22	Chichawa	76.2	1 h 19 min
		27	Tichka	66.6	1 h 13 min
		29	Bin el ouidan	187	3 h 2 min
22	Chichawa	23	Essaouira	102	1 h 23 min
		24	Imintanoute	54.7	43 min
24	Imintanoute	25	Ameskroud	128	1 h 25 min
25	Ameskroud	26	Agadir	38.6	43 min
27	Tichka	28	Ouarzazate	156	3 h 3 min
28	Ouarzazate	30	Tinghir	173	2 h 27 min
30	Tinghir	31	Errachidia	136	1 h 54 min

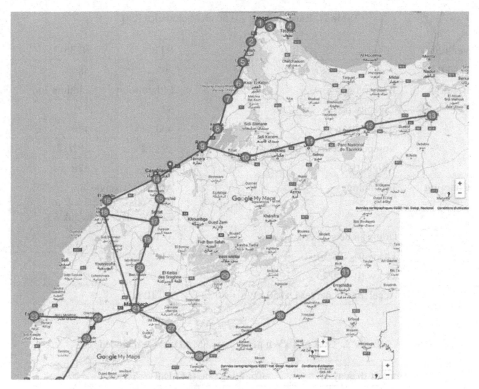

Fig. 2. Possible routes following charging stations

3.3 Vehicle Characteristics

Seeing as Renault is the most popular vehicle manufacturer in Morocco, a Moroccan customer is more likely to go for a Renault's electric vehicle. The reason behind this choice comes from the fact that Renault vehicle are locally produced, thus, they are cheaper compared to other brands. Renault ZOE ZE 50 comes in two versions: R110 and R135. The difference between the two is portrayed by Table 2.

3.4 Charging Cost

To estimate the cost of travel, we should calculate the cost of each recharge (full or partial) of the electric vehicle throughout the trip. To this end, we need to have a clear view of the charging rates.

The cost of charging an electric vehicle is fixed by the government depending on the time of the day and the season. Table 2. Portrays these charging rates whereas Table 3 describes the hour of day classification depending on the season.

Table 2. Renault ZOE ZE 50 characteristics [28]

Version		R110	R135
WLTP		395	386
Battery	Technology	Lithium-ion	Lithium-ion
	Capacity (kwh)	52	52
	Total tension (v)	400	400
	Number of cells/modules	192/12	192/12
	Weight (kg)	326	326
Charging	Technology	Adjustable single and three-phase (AC: 2 kW to 22 kW—DC: up to 50kW)	
	Domestique socket 2.3 kw	32 h	
	11 kw (0–100%)	6 h	
	22 kw (0–100%)	3 h	
	Accelerated charger DC 50 kW (0–80%)	1 h 10 min	

Table 3. Cost of 1 kWh per hour (in MAD) taxes included

Hour of the day	Charging rate (MAD/kWh)
Rush hour	1.4157
Peak hour	1.0101
Off peak	0.7398

Table 4. Time of the day schedule depending on the season

Season	Winter	Summer
Duration	01/10 to 31/03	01/04 to 30/09
Rush hour	7 h to 17 h	7 h to 18 h
Peak hour	17 h to 22 h	18 h to 23 h
Off peak	22 h to 7 h	23 h to 7 h

4   Proposed Model and Simulation

4.1   Phase 1: Finding the Shortest Path

To find the shortest path, we referred to Dijkstra algorithm since all vertices are positively weighted. We represented Table 1 as a matrix illustrating the weight of all edges. Table 4 explains the pseudocode of the algorithm used.

As in input, the algorithm takes the matrix representing the roads connecting all charging stations. As an output, the algorithm returns the shortest path connecting all nodes to node 1. Figure 3 Portrays the result of running the proposed algorithm using Jupiter notebook (Tables 5, 6).

Table 5. Dijkstra algorithm pseudocode

Algorithm 1: Dijkstra Algorithm
Input: a weighted directed graph G = (X, A, W) and a $s \in X$
Output: the shortest path from s to all nodes of G
// V: Array storing the labels of nodes of G
Initialize V at $+\infty$
V[s]=0
// P: array allowing to find path composition
Initialize P at 0
repeat
// Search for a non-fixed node x with smaller label
$V_{min} = +\infty$
for $y = 0$ *to* n **do**
If y is not marked **and** V[y] $< V_{min}$ **then**
$x \leftarrow y$
$V_{min} \leftarrow V[y]$
end
end
//Update non fixed successors of x
if $V_{min} < +\infty$ *then*
for every successor y of x
If y is not marked **and** V[x] + W[x, y] $< V[y]$ **then**
$V[y] = V[x] + W[x, y]$
P[y] = x
end
end
end
until $V_{min} = +\infty$

As portrayed by Fig. 3, the path generated by our model accounts for 940.40 km total. Since this distance is almost four times the vehicle's fixed range, the vehicle is expected to stop at least 4 times to recharge.

4.2 Phase 2: Cost of Travel

The cost of travel is equivalent to the cost of recharging the vehicle throughout the trip and to the overall travel time. The vehicle starts the trip with a full battery thus it is

Table 6. Defining the points of recharging

From	To	Distance (km)	Remaining driving range (km)	Driving range needed for the next node (km)	Driving range deficit (km)	Kilometers required to reach full driving range[a] (km)
Initial charge		–	250	44.5	205.5	0
1	2	44.5	205.5	48.5	157	0
2	5	48.5	157.0	43.4	113.6	0
5	6	43.4	113.6	68.9	44.7	0
6	7	68.9	**44.7**	59.2	− 14.5	205.3 (=250–44.7)
7	8	59.2	190.8	50.8	140	0
8	9	50.8	140	86.8	53.2	0
9	14	86.8	53.2	49.3	3.9	0
14	15	49.3	**3.9**	40.1	− 36.2	246.1 (=250–3.9)
15	17	40.1	209.9	55.8	154.1	0
17	19	55.8	154.1	61.6	92.5	0
19	20	61.6	92.5	74	18.5	0
20	21	74	**18.5**	76.2	− 57.7	231.5 (=250–18.5)
21	22	76.2	173.8	54.7	119.1	0
22	24	54.7	**119.1**	128	− 8.9	130.9 (=250–119.1)
24	25	128	122	38.6	83.4	0
25	26	38.6	83.4	–	–	0
Total		917				

[a] If the driving range deficit is positive, no recharge is required. However, whenever the driving range is negative, we calculate the number of kilometers needed to reach full driving range by subtracting the actual remaining driving range from the fixed driving range (250 km)

expected to drive for almost 250 km before running out of energy. However, the point at which the battery runs out might occur before it reaches the next node (the next charging station). To avoid this, we must plan the points of recharge in advance by recharging the battery to its full capacity before it is drained.

By using the path generated by the Dijkstra algorithm, we predict the points of recharge which correspond to the node before which the battery level goes below 0.

The amount of energy to recharge was calculated according to Eq. 1:

$$E_r = \frac{D_r \times E_v}{D_v} \tag{1}$$

```
Distance : 940.4000000000002  km
 path :
tangiers
 -> assilah
 -> larach
 -> moulay-bousselham
 -> lamhamid ben mansour
 -> kenitra
 -> rabat
 -> casablanca
 -> berrchid
 -> settat
 -> oum rabii
 -> ben-guerir
 -> marrakech
 -> chichawa
 -> imintanoute
 -> ameskroud
 -> agadir
```

Fig. 3. Path generated by Dijkstra algorithm connecting Tangiers to Agadir

where E_r is the amount of energy to be recharged (expressed in kWh), E_v is the vehicle's energy (fixed at 52 kWh as shown in Table 2), D_r is the driving range to be recharged (number of km needed), D_v is the fixed driving range of the vehicle which is 250 km.

As for the time to recharge, it changes depending on the amount of energy needed. It is calculated using Eq. 2:

$$t = \frac{E_r}{P} \tag{2}$$

where P is the power of the charging station. We fix it at 22 KW.

The cost of 1Kwh is also fixed at 1.24 MAD seeing as the hour of the day in which we travel isn't specified.

Using Eqs. (1) and (2), we were able to calculate the total cost of travel which are detailed in Table 7. The vehicles are expected to start the trip with a full battery.

Table 7. Total travel cost (charging cost and time to recharge)

Node	Energy to be recharged (kWh)	Cost (MAD)	Autonomy needed (km)	Time
1	52.00	64.48	250	2 h 22 min
7	48.88	52.95	158	2 h 56 min
15	51.19	63.47	239	2 h 20 min
21	48.15	59.71	174	2 h 11 min
24	27.23	33.76	194	1 h 14 min
Total cost of travel (+ initial cost)		274.38	Total time	10 h 4 min

The cost was calculated using Eq. 1 where the driving range to be charged was 250km. Since we didn't specify the season in which the travel takes places, we fixed the driving range at 250 km to keep the model within a realistic context.

As previously expressed, the number of constraints imposed complicates the problem even further. However, when trying to apply path planning to Moroccan infrastructure, employing charging-stations-related constraints can be delicate due to lack of data in that area. For the time being, we chose a simple yet effective model that uses available data to preplan the travel path using an electric vehicle.

5 Results Discussion

Our work consists of a basic study of routing of electric vehicles in Morocco. While results might seem rewarding, they still need several enhancements. For instance, works like [29], real-time traveler statistics were integrated into a bi-objective path finding model. Their work was simulated in Hong Kong, and it proved that the variation of speed affects the energy consumption and time of travel. It also outperforms our model in the context where the model calculates the cost of travel as it goes. Other factors were considered in [30] Using 5 different vehicles to test their non-linear model, and taking into account the temperature and charging stations technologies, their work proves effective but in Germany only.

The lack of constraints in our model compared to those of literature [8] makes it easily outperformed by other works, but the importance of our work is in attracting attention to the improvement needed in our infrastructure. Besides, existing model are hard to implement in Morocco since data isn't as available, and we have no idea of charging stations' status before reaching them.

The complexity of the routing of electric vehicles derives from its unpredictability face to different scenarios, this means that if a model is relevant in a certain country, it might not perform well in another country since the infrastructure is different. Thus, we can't project other works on the Moroccan case seeing as the available infrastructure isn't prepared yet.

6 Conclusion

In our work, we studied the case of path planning using an electric vehicle to travel between two Moroccan cities. Dijkstra was our algorithm of choice due to its simplicity compared to other complicated methods. Since no constraints were imposed it wasn't necessary to go for a complex model. However, since the batteries' capacity is evidently limited, we calculated the points of recharge post simulation.

Our method resulted in a satisfactory solution given the small amount of data available. Besides, our work came to stress the importance of increasing the number of charging stations and to incite on strengthening the actual e-mobility infrastructure if we were ever going to switch fully to EVs.

As an afterthought, we will aim to fortify our model to include more constraints. Our next work will focus on developing a tool that preplans trips of electric vehicles of different brands, with different charging capacities and technologies, and will cover a much broader range of nodes.

References

1. Callendar, G.S.: The artificial production of carbon dioxide and its influence on temperature. Quart. J. R. Meteorol. Soc. **64**, 223–240 (1938). https://doi.org/10.1002/QJ.49706427503
2. Human Consumption of Earth's Natural Resources Has Tripled in 40 Years—EcoWatch, https://www.ecowatch.com/humans-consumption-of-earths-natural-resources-tripled-in-40-years-1943126747.html
3. Al-Ghussain, L.: Global warming: review on driving forces and mitigation. Environ. Prog. Sustain. Energy. **38**, 13–21 (2019). https://doi.org/10.1002/EP.13041
4. World Greenhouse Gas Emissions: 2016|World Resources Institute, https://www.wri.org/data/world-greenhouse-gas-emissions-2016
5. Kopelias, P., Demiridi, E., Vogiatzis, K., Skabardonis, A., Zafiropoulou, V.: Connected and autonomous vehicles—environmental impacts—a review. Sci. Total Environ. **712**, 135237 (2020). https://doi.org/10.1016/j.scitotenv.2019.135237
6. Held, T., Gerrits, L.: On the road to electrification—a qualitative comparative analysis of urban e-mobility policies in 15 European cities. Transp. Policy. **81**, 12–23 (2019). https://doi.org/10.1016/J.TRANPOL.2019.05.014
7. Morocco, Stellantis sign amendment to reactivate cooperation in automotive industry, https://www.moroccoworldnews.com/2021/09/344235/morocco-stellantis-sign-amendment-to-reactivate-cooperation-in-automotive-industry
8. Abid, M., Tabaa, M., Chakir, A., Hachimi, H.: Routing and charging of electric vehicles: Literature review. Energy Rep. **8**, 556–578 (2022). https://doi.org/10.1016/J.EGYR.2022.07.089
9. Voiture électrique et hybride au Maroc. www.voitureelectrique.ma, https://www.voitureelectrique.ma/
10. The range of the Renault ZOE—Renault Group. https://www.renaultgroup.com/en/news-on-air/news/the-range-of-renault-zoe/
11. The History of the Electric Car|Department of Energy. https://www.energy.gov/articles/history-electric-car
12. Jordán, J., Palanca, J., Martí, P., Julian, V.: Electric vehicle charging stations emplacement using genetic algorithms and agent-based simulation. Expert Syst. Appl. **197**, 116739 (2022). https://doi.org/10.1016/J.ESWA.2022.116739
13. Zhou, G., Zhu, Z., Luo, S.: Location optimization of electric vehicle charging stations: Based on cost model and genetic algorithm. Energy **247**, 123437 (2022). https://doi.org/10.1016/J.ENERGY.2022.123437
14. Liu, X.H., Zhang, D.G., Yan, H.R., Cui, Y.Y., Chen, L.: A New algorithm of the best path selection based on machine learning. IEEE Access. **7**, 126913–126928 (2019). https://doi.org/10.1109/ACCESS.2019.2939423
15. Chen, X.W., Chen, B.Y., Lam, W.H.K., Tam, M.L., Ma, W.: A bi-objective reliable path-finding algorithm for battery electric vehicle routing. Expert Syst. Appl. **182**, 115228 (2021). https://doi.org/10.1016/j.eswa.2021.115228
16. Ban, M., Zhang, Z., Li, C., Li, Z., Liu, Y.: Optimal scheduling for electric vehicle battery swapping-charging system based on nanogrids. Int. J. Electr. Power Energy Syst. **130**, 106967 (2021). https://doi.org/10.1016/j.ijepes.2021.106967
17. Wang, H., Ma, H., Liu, C., Wang, W.: Optimal scheduling of electric vehicles charging in battery swapping station considering wind- photovoltaic accommodation. Electr. Power Syst. Res. **199**, 107451 (2021). https://doi.org/10.1016/j.epsr.2021.107451
18. Jie, W., Yang, J., Zhang, M., Huang, Y.: The two-echelon capacitated electric vehicle routing problem with battery swapping stations: formulation and efficient methodology. Eur. J. Oper. Res. **272**, 879–904 (2019). https://doi.org/10.1016/j.ejor.2018.07.002

19. Zhou, Y., Huang, J., Shi, J., Wang, R., Huang, K.: The electric vehicle routing problem with partial recharge and vehicle recycling. Complex & Intelligent Systems 7(3), 1445–1458 (2021). https://doi.org/10.1007/s40747-021-00291-3
20. Cortés-Murcia, D.L., Prodhon, C., Murat Afsar, H.: The electric vehicle routing problem with time windows, partial recharges and satellite customers. Transp. Res. E: Log. Transp. Rev. 130, 184–206 (2019). https://doi.org/10.1016/j.tre.2019.08.015
21. Felipe, Á., Ortuño, M.T., Righini, G., Tirado, G.: A heuristic approach for the green vehicle routing problem with multiple technologies and partial recharges. Transp. Res. E: Log. Transp. Rev. 71, 111–128 (2014). https://doi.org/10.1016/j.tre.2014.09.003
22. Macrina, G., Laporte, G., Guerriero, F., di Puglia Pugliese, L.: An energy-efficient green-vehicle routing problem with mixed vehicle fleet, partial battery recharging and time windows. Eur. J. Oper. Res. 276, 971–982 (2019). https://doi.org/10.1016/j.ejor.2019.01.067
23. Schulz, F., Rode, J.: Public charging infrastructure and electric vehicles in Norway. Energy Policy 160, 112660 (2022). https://doi.org/10.1016/J.ENPOL.2021.112660
24. Plug-In Electric Vehicles: A case study of seven markets. https://escholarship.org/uc/item/5ps3z0f5
25. GREEN MILES—IRESEN, https://iresen.org/green-miles/
26. Map des bornes de recharge au Maroc. www.voitureelectrique.ma, https://www.voitureelectrique.ma/borne-de-recharge-maroc/
27. Charging stations in Morocco. https://www.electromaps.com/en/charging-stations/morocco
28. ZOE redessine la mobilité !
29. Chen, X.W., Chen, B.Y., Lam, W.H.K., Tam, M.L., Ma, W.: A bi-objective reliable path-finding algorithm for battery electric vehicle routing. Exp. Syst. Appl. 182, 115228 (2021). https://doi.org/10.1016/J.ESWA.2021.115228
30. Hecht, C., Victor, K., Zurmühlen, S., Sauer, D.U.: Electric vehicle route planning using real-world charging infrastructure in Germany. eTransportation 10, 100143 (2021). https://doi.org/10.1016/J.ETRAN.2021.100143

AI-Driven Methods 3

Scalable Meta-Bayesian Based Hyperparameters Optimization for Machine Learning

Moncef Garouani[1,2,3]([✉]), Adeel Ahmad[1], Mourad Bouneffa[1],
and Mohamed Hamlich[2]

[1] LISIC, Laboratoire d'Informatique Signal et Image de la Côte d'Opale,
Univ. Littoral Côte d'Opale, UR 4491, 62100 Calais, France
`moncef.garouani@etu.univ-littoral.fr`,
`{adeel.ahmad,mourad.bouneffa}@univ-littoral.fr`
[2] CCPS Laboratory, ENSAM, University of Hassan II, Casablanca, Morocco
[3] Study and Research Center for Engineering and Management, HESTIM,
Casablanca, Morocco

Abstract. It is a known fact that the selection of one or more optimized algorithms and the configuration of significant hyperparameters, is among the major problems for the advanced data analytics using Machine Learning (ML) methodologies. However, it is one of the essential tasks in order to apply the ML based solutions to deal with the real-world problems. In this regard, Bayesian Optimization (BO) is a popular method for optimizing black-box functions. But, yet it is deficient for large-scale problems because it fails to leverage the knowledge from historical applications. The major challenge in this aspect is due to the BO waste function evaluations on bad design choices (such that the ML hyperparameters). To address this issue, we propose to integrate Bayesian Optimization via Meta-Guidance. Consequently, Meta-Guided Bayesian Optimization (MGBO) provide means to use the knowledge from previous optimization cycles on similar tasks. This capability takes the form of pre-requisite to decide the specific parts of the input space to be evaluated next; in this regard, we intend to guide the BO with a functional ANOVA of configurations as suggested by a meta-learning process. In this paper, we demonstrate, with the help of a large collection of hyperparameters optimization benchmark problems, that MGBO is about 3 times faster than the vanilla Bayesian optimization. Thence, it achieves a new state-of-the-art performance as proved by the experiments on 09 classification datasets.

Keywords: Hyperparameters optimization · Bayesian optimization · Meta-learning · Meta-Guided Bayesian Optimization · fANOVA

1 Introduction

The selection of appropriate algorithms and the optimization of related Hyperparameters (HPs) are ubiquitous tasks in machine learning contexts that

M. Hamlich et al. (Eds.): SADASC 2022, CCIS 1677, pp. 173–186, 2022.
https://doi.org/10.1007/978-3-031-20490-6_14

usually have to be performed with in particular context of an individual research space and real-world application [1]. The configuration of hyperparameters is an important design choice to obtain the desired performance of ML algorithms. Whereas, the correct configuration of hyperparameters might be appeased at the cost of precious resource consummations, as it requires high technical expertise in ML and mathematics along with many *ad-hoc* choices [2]. As a result, a lot of the recent research work in machine learning has been focused on the development of better hyperparameters optimization methods [1,3–8].

It is generally observed that the sequential model-based optimization (also known as Bayesian Optimization) is among the most efficient techniques of machine learning algorithms optimization [4]. For example, it has conclusively yielded better instances of convolutional network hyperparameters than domain experts and it consistently improve the top score, in a repeated manner, on the CIFAR-10 benchmark [9]. However, Bayesian Optimization is defined as a generic function optimization framework, and —like any other generic optimization method— it requires a substantial number of function evaluations to detect high performance regions whenever started on a new optimization problem.

While the same ML algorithm with the same hyperparameters space is systematically optimized for different tasks (datasets). The human experts rather often study the performance of the given algorithm on previously seen tasks, to familiarize themselves with its behaviors regarding the HPs space before tuning the algorithm for the new task, iteratively. This approach can still outperform contemporary BO methods [1,10]. By following this methodology, we argue that it is more advantageous to perform transfer learning for global black-box optimization in the framework of BO to retain the proven generalization capabilities of its underlying surrogate model.

To pursue this goal, we take the benefit of meta-learning approaches [1], which initially borrow the best performing configurations of hyperparameters from the similar tasks [10–12]. Later on, these approaches integrate the gained knowledge as a meta-guidance of the acquisition function to discover good solutions, which can be faster than vanilla BO [4].

The rest of the paper is structured as follows: The Sect. 2 formally defines the problem of hyperparameters optimization, gives the background information on BO, and introduces the functional Analysis of Variance. The Sect. 3, introduces the proposed new Meta-Guided Bayesian Optimization method for hyperparameters optimization. In Sect. 4, a broad range of experiments with 08 machine learning algorithms show that the MGBO often identifies good hyperparameters settings 2 to 3 times faster than the state-of-the-art BO methods. Finally, the Sect. 5 concludes the paper and outlines future perspectives.

2   Theoretical Background and Related Work

In this section, we discuss the theoretical background and two closely research areas: (1) the Bayesian optimization for ML hyperparameters optimization , and (2) the functional analysis of variance to assess the HPs importance. Likewise, we go through the limitations of classical BO to motivate the proposed approach.

2.1   Hyperparameters Optimization

The selection of an algorithm or a family of algorithms that are more likely to better perform on a given combination of datasets and evaluation measures is an important task [11,13–16]. The machine learning algorithms generally have two kinds of parameters, given as below:

- The ordinary parameters that the model learns and optimizes automatically based on its regular behavior during the learning phase.
- The hyperparameters (categorical, continuous and conditional) which are usually manually set before the training of the model.

From a theoretical point of view, the selection of the ideal HPs values requires an exhaustive search over all possible subsets of HPs. This task highly risk to become impractical due to the conceivable combinations of the number and types of the HPs [17].

For the sake of further clarification, let us consider, $\mathcal{H}$ represents a population of HPs and $A(H)$ represents the algorithm(s) configured with H hyperparamters configuration such that $H \in \mathcal{H}$. In order to argue that in the traditional settings, the loss function $(\mathcal{L})$ of a machine learning algorithm with a particular configuration of hyperparameters H is treated as a "black-box" problem on a given dataset $\mathcal{D}$ to find the H minimizing $\mathcal{L}(A(H), \mathcal{D})$, as follows:

$$\mathcal{L}(A(H), \mathcal{D}) \equiv \{\mathcal{L}(A(H), \mathcal{D}) \mid \exists H \in \mathcal{H} \sqsubseteq \perp\} \qquad (1)$$

where, the only mode of interaction with the objective $\mathcal{L}$ is to evaluate it for inputs $H \in \mathcal{H}$. As individual evaluations of $\mathcal{L}$ on real-world datasets may require multiple days, or even weeks, to find the only very few evaluations that are possible thus it limits the quality of the best-found value [5,6].

For the last decade, different hyperparameters tuning techniques have been applied to optimize ML algorithms [10,12,18,19]. Some of these techniques build, in an iterative manner, a population $\mathcal{H}$ of HPs settings, where the loss function $\mathcal{L}(A(H), \mathcal{D})$ is computed, for each hyperparameters configuration of algorithm(s) A on the dataset D. The different regions of the search space can be simultaneously explored by this method. There are various population-based HPs tuning strategies, which differ in respect to the evolution of the $\mathcal{H}$, at each iteration [4].

In our context, we aim to find out the HPs with optimal configuration H^+ that maximizes the loss function of a machine learning algorithm(s) A over a dataset $\mathcal{D}$ given its hyperparameters space $\mathcal{H}$, as follows:

$$\mathcal{L}(A(H^+), \mathcal{D}) \equiv \{\mathcal{L}(A(H^+), \mathcal{D}) \mid \exists H^+ \in \mathcal{L}(A(H), \mathcal{D}) \sqcap H \in \mathcal{H})\} \qquad (2)$$

Similarly, the HPs with best configuration H^- that minimizes the loss function of a machine learning algorithm(s) A over a dataset $\mathcal{D}$ given its hyperparameters space $\mathcal{H}$, as follows:

$$\mathcal{L}(A(H^-), \mathcal{D}) \equiv \{\mathcal{L}(A(H^-), \mathcal{D}) \mid \exists H^- \in \mathcal{L}(A(H), \mathcal{D}) \sqcap H \in \mathcal{H})\} \qquad (3)$$

In order to cope with this challenge, the most simple, and often used, are Grid Search and Random Search. The former is more suitable for low dimensional problems, such as, when there are few HPs to be configured. For more complex scenarios, GS is unable to explore finer promising regions due to the large hyperspace [20]. The later is able to explore any possible solution of the hyperspace, but also does not perform an informed search, which may lead to a high computational cost [2]. Meta-heuristics have also been used for HPs tuning with prominent advantage of performing informed searches. Population-based methods, such as Genetic Algorithms [21], Estimation of Distribution Algorithms [17], and Sequential Model-based Optimization [4], have been also largely explored in the literature due to their probabilistic nature. However, there still exists the configuration of HPs to be configured in order to eliminate the shortcoming of the iterative need to evaluate the function to be optimized. All these techniques are valuable alternatives to GS and RS, but they might have high computational cost and therefore they might emerge to have lower performance to convergence, since a large number of candidate configurations are usually required to be evaluated [22].

2.2 Bayesian Optimization

Bayesian Optimization [23], also known as sequential model-based optimization, is an approach for optimizing black-box functions, such as: $f : X \to \mathbb{R}$ that are expensive to evaluate over a given input space $\mathcal{X}$. Bayesian Optimization approximates H^+ by iterative fittings of a so called *surrogate model*, henceforth denoted by Ψ, on the set of observed values denoted as Γ, of loss function $\mathcal{L}$ depending on the previous function values represented as $y_1, y_2, \ldots, y_n$ with respect to $H_1, H_2, \ldots, H_n$. The set of observed values can be formally shown as follows:

$$\Gamma \equiv \{(H_1, \mathcal{L}(A(H_1), \mathcal{D})), \ldots, (H_n, \mathcal{L}(A(H_n), \mathcal{D}))\} \qquad (4)$$

The BO model requires two building blocks, given as follows:

- Bayesian prior that prescribes a prior belief over the possible objective functions, and
- Bayesian posterior that provides a mechanism to sequentially update the belief by learning from new observations.

BO achieves this objective by building a Bayesian posterior on $\mathcal{L}$ based on the set of evaluated hyperparameters. At each iteration, a new configuration is selected and evaluated based on the Bayesian posterior. The later is updated to include the new HP (H_{t+1}), using a probabilistic surrogate model conditioned on the current optimization history H_t. Typically, a Gaussian Process (GP) is employed as a surrogate model in which case the resulting posterior belief about $f(x)$ [1] follows a Gaussian distribution with mean $\mu_t(x)$ and variance $\sigma_t^2(x)$, as follows:

$$\mu_t(x) = \mathbb{E}\{f(x)|H_t \in \mathcal{H}\} \tag{5}$$

$$\sigma_t^2(x) = \mathbb{V}\{f(x)|H_t \in \mathcal{H}\} \tag{6}$$

The points explored by BO are dictated by the *Acquisition Function* (AF), which attributes a utility to each $H \in \mathcal{H}$ by balancing the predicted value and uncertainty of the prediction for each H. This process is repeated until either a certain number of trials (budget) has been conducted or the cross-validation performance has achieved an adequate level. Algorithm 1 illustrate this process.

Algorithm 1. Pseudo-code of the Sequential Model-based Optimization.

1: **Input**: Hyperparameters space $\mathcal{H}$, observation history Γ, number of iterations T, acquisition function AF, surrogate model Ψ.
2: **Output**: Best hyperparameters configuration found.
3: $\mathcal{L}^+ \leftarrow \varnothing$ ▷ the best value found so far
4: **for** t =1 to T **do**
5:     Fit Ψ on Γ
6:     $H \leftarrow \text{argmax}_{x \in \chi} AF\left((\Psi(H_t), \mathcal{L}^+\right)$
7:     Evaluate f(H)
8:     $\Gamma \leftarrow \Gamma \cup \{(H, f(H))\}$
9:     **If** $f(H) < \mathcal{L}^+$ **Then**
10:       $H^+, \mathcal{L}^+ \leftarrow H, f(H)$
11: **return** H^+

The strength of the resulting optimizer is largely based upon carefully designing the AF [18]. In this work, we used the Expected Improvement (EI) [24] as the acquisition function which quantifies the expected improvement over the best function value found so far (Eq. (7)). Alternatives to EI would be Probability of Improvement [25], Upper-Confidence Bounds [26], entropy-based methods [27], and knowledge gradient [28].

$$EI_t(x) \equiv \int_{-\infty}^{+\infty} max(y^+ - y_t), 0)p(y|x)\, dy \tag{7}$$

where y^+ is the incumbent loss value, i.e., the best Root-Mean-Square Error (RMSE) value found so far, and $p(y|x)$ is given by a probabilistic model, e.g., a GP.

2.3 Functional ANOVA for Assessing Hyperparameters Importance

The functional Analysis Of Variance (fANOVA) [29] is an efficient technique for assessing the importance of hyperparameters of a machine learning algorithm based on the efficient computations of marginal performance. More specifically,

---

[1] For the sake of simplicity, we denote H as x and $\mathcal{L}(A(H_n), \mathcal{D})$ as $f(x)$ or y.

functional ANOVA specifies the contribution of each hyperparameter to the variance of the ML algorithm performance. In the following, we give an overview of using the fANOVA to efficiently compute the importance of a set of ML algorithms hyperparameters. Given:

- an algorithm $\mathcal{A}$ with n hyperparameters in the hyperparameters space $\mathcal{H}$.
- a large number of datasets $\mathcal{D}_1, \ldots, \mathcal{D}_m$, with m being the number of datasets (in our study, $m = 400$).
- for each of the datasets, a set of empirical performance measurements $\langle H_n, y_i \rangle_{i=1}^k$ for different hyperparameter settings $H_n \in \mathcal{H}$, where y_i is the performance of the algorithm A measured by the considered performance measures (i.e., Accuracy, Precision, Recall, F1 score).
- the *marginal performance* $\hat{a}_n(H_n)$ is defined to be the average performance of the algorithm A for all complete configurations H_n that have in its common HPs space $\mathcal{H}$.

We apply the functional ANOVA on each of the considered algorithms as follows. First we collect performance data $\langle H_n, y_i \rangle_{i=1}^k$ for each of the considered algorithms with $k = 1000$ different HPs configurations (see Table 1). Next, we fit a random forest model to the performance data and then use the functional ANOVA to decompose the variance in performance of the random forest $\hat{y} : H_1 \times H_2 \ldots H_n \to \mathbb{R}$ into additive components that depends on subsets of the hyperparameters H_n:

$$\hat{y}(H) = \sum_{u \in n} \hat{f}_u(H_u) \tag{8}$$

where the components $\hat{f}_u(H_u)$ are defined as follows:

$$\hat{f}_u(H_u) = \begin{cases} \hat{f}_\emptyset & if u = \emptyset \\ \hat{a}_u(H_u) - \sum_{w \in u} \hat{f}_w(H_w) & \text{otherwise} \end{cases} \tag{9}$$

where $\hat{f}_\emptyset$ is the mean value of the function $\hat{y}$ over its domain. The unary function $\hat{f}_j(H_j)$ captures the importance of hyperparameter H_j average over all possible values for the rest of the hyperparameters, while $\hat{f}_u(H_u)$ captures the interaction effects between all hyperparameters in $\mathcal{H}$. Functional ANOVA decomposes the variance V in the $\hat{y}$ into the contributions V_u of all possible subsets of hyperparameters H_u of the algorithm $\mathcal{A}$.

$$V = \sum_{u \in n} V_u, \quad Where \quad V_u = \frac{1}{||H_u||} \int \hat{f}_u(H_u)^2 dH_u \tag{10}$$

The importance of an hyperparameter or a set of hyperparameters is captured by the fraction of the variance of the responsibility of the hyperparameter, or the set of hyperparameters. *The higher the fraction, the more important the hyperparameter or the set of hyperparameters are to the model.* Thus, such a hyperparameter should be tuned further in order to achieve a good performance.

Table 1. Hyperparameters tuned in the experiments.

Algorithm	Hyperparameter	Values
SVM	complexity (or: 'C')	$[1e^{-10}, 500]$ (log-scale)
	Kernel	{'poly','rbf'}
	coef0	[0., 10]
	gamma	$[1e^{-3}, 1.01]$ (log-scale)
	Degree	[2, 3]
Random Forest & Extra Trees	bootstrap	{true, false}
	Max_features	[0.1, 0.9]
	Min_samples_leaf	[1, 20]
	Min_samples_split	[2, 20]
	imputation	mean, median, mode
	split criterion	{entropy, gini}
Adaboost	algorithm	{SAMME, SAMME.R}
	N_estimators	[50, 501]
	learning rate	[0.01, 2.0] (log-scale)
	Max_depth	[1, 11]
Decision Trees	max features	[0.1, 0.9]
	min_samples_leaf	[1, 21]
	Min_samples_split	[2, 21]
	criterion	{'entropy','gini' }
Logistic Regression	C	$[1e^{-10}, 10.]$ (log-scale)
	penalty	{'l2','l1' }
	Fit_intercept	True, False
SGD	loss	{'hinge','perceptron','log'}
	penalty	{'l2','l1','elasticnet' }
	learning rate	{'constant','optimal','invscaling' }
	eta0	[0., 5.]
	Power_t	[0., 5.]
Gradient Boosting	Learning_rate	[0.01, 1]
	criterion	{'friedman_mse','msc' }
	N_estimators	[50, 501]
	max depth	[1, 11]
	Min_samples_split	[2, 21]

3   Meta-guided Bayesian Optimization

Figure 1 gives a global illustration of the workflow of tuning process. The configuration space used during optimization comes from the algorithms HPs listed in
Table 1. We first describe the BO model used in our framework before outlining
the process of selecting the next probed configuration.

GP [30] is a popular choice because of its salient features such as support for
noisy observations and ability to use gradient-based methods [31]. The standard

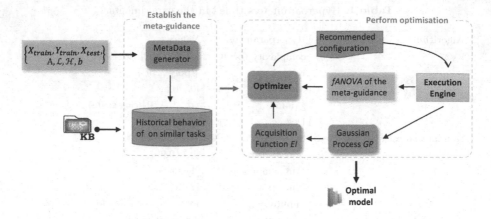

Fig. 1. Workflow of the Meta-Guided Bayesian Optimization (MGBO).

GP in Bayesian optimization directly models $p(y|x)$ to estimate the expected improvement (Eq. 7). However, technically, the model does not parameterize $p(y)$, since it is computed based on the observed data points, which are heavily biased towards low values due to the optimization process. In this paper, following the Tree-structured Parzen Estimator introduced by Bergstra *et al.* [13], we propose the formal modelling of $p(x|y)$ and $p_t(y)$ instead. This is done by constructing two parametric densities, $g(x)$ and $b(x)$, which are computed using the observations with function value below and above a given threshold, respectively. The separating threshold ν is defined as a quantile of the observed function values. We use the densities $g(x)$ and $b(x)$ to define $p(x|y)$ as:

$$p(x|y) = g(x)I(y < \nu) + b(x)(1 - I(y < \nu)) \tag{11}$$

where:

$$I = \begin{cases} 1 & \text{if } importance(x) < importance(x_{t+1}) \;\; refer\;to\;section\;2.3 \\ 0 & \text{otherwise} \end{cases} \tag{12}$$

We adopt the EI formulation used in [13] by replacing their Adaptive Parzen Estimators with our pseudo-posterior from Eq. 11, i.e.:

$$
\begin{aligned}
EI_{y_t}(x) &\equiv \int_{-\infty}^{+\infty} max(y^+ - y_t), 0) p(y|x)\, dy \\
&= \int_{-\infty}^{y^+} (y^+ - y_t), 0) \frac{p(x|y)p(y)}{p(x)}\, dy
\end{aligned}
\tag{13}
$$

In reference to the Tree-structured Parzen Estimator, we define configurations as *"bad"* if their observed importance is below a certain quantile of the observed function values (so that $p(y < f_\gamma) = \gamma$). As γ is a quantile of the correlation objective values $\{y^{(i)}\}$ therefore, $p(x)$ can be represented as follows:

$$p(x) = \int_{\mathbb{R}} p(x|y)p(y)\,dy = \gamma g(x) + (1-\gamma)b(x) \tag{14}$$

moreover,

$$\int_{-\infty}^{y^+} (y^+ - y_t)p(x|y)p(y)\,dy = g(x) \int_{-\infty}^{y^+} (y^+ - y_t)p(y)\,dy$$
$$= \gamma y^+ g(x) - g(x) \int_{-\infty}^{y^+} yp(y)\,dy \tag{15}$$

$$EI_{y^+}(x) = \frac{\gamma y^+ g(x) - g(x) \int_{-\infty}^{y^+} yp(y)\,dy}{\gamma g(x) + (1-\gamma)b(x)}$$
$$\alpha \left(\frac{1}{\gamma} + \frac{g(x)}{b(x)}(1-\gamma) \right) \tag{16}$$

The expression $EI_{y^+}(x)$ shows that in order to maximize improvement we would like HPs configurations H with high probability under $g(x)$ and low probability under $b(x)$. This formulation makes it easy to draw many candidates according to γ and evaluate them according to $g(x)/b(x)$. On each iteration, we launch the operation argmax that seeks if the algorithm returns the candidate H^* (either H^- or H^+ depending respectively on the minimization or maximization of loss function) with the greatest EI, and, thus:

$$\underset{H \in \mathcal{H}}{\text{argmax}}\, EI_{H^*}(H) = \underset{H \in \mathcal{H}}{\text{argmax}}\, \frac{g(H)}{b(H)} \tag{17}$$

Typically, the minimal set of inputs to AFs in BO is given by the GP posterior prediction μ_t and σ_t. To perform the guidance, the AF has to be able to identify relevant structure shared by the objective functions in $\mathcal{L}$. In our setting, this is achieved via extending this basic set of inputs by additional features which enable the AF to evaluate sample locations. Therefore, in addition to the mean μ_t and variance σ_t at potential sample locations, the AF also receives the input importance given by the fANOVA.

It might be useful to note that the Bayesian Optimization is an efficient approach for finding the optimal solution to the time-bounded optimization problem from Eq. (3), however, in its vanilla form new problems are tackled from scratch. A better alternative is to warm start BO with ML pipelines that are expected to work well, as done in the k-nearest datasets (KND) approach [1,32]. Furthermore, we made use of the knowledge base constructed in our previous work [1] to exploit the KND and transfer knowledge across the tasks. It consists of *4 Millions* evaluated ML pipeline on 400 real world datasets. An overview on the KB construction process is shown in Algorithm 2. Later on the analysis of the candidate algorithm(s) behaviour on the KND is used to bootstrap the optimizer as a meta-guidance.

Algorithm 2. Establish the knowledge base.

1: **Input:** $ClassificationAlgs[..]$,   ▷ available classification algorithms
   $HpSpace[..]$,   ▷ set of HPs configurations to be applied
   $PerfMeasures[..]$ ▷ set of performance measures to acquire
2: **Output:** KB[#measure][#metadata]   ▷ meta-knowledge base
3: **function** CREATEMETAKB(datasets[])
4:     $metadata[] = \varnothing$
5:     **for each** $measure$ *in* $PerfMeasures$ **do**
6:         **for each** $dataset$ DS *in* $datasets$ **do**
7:             $ds\_mf = ComputeMetaFeatures(\mathtt{DS})$;
8:             **for each** $algorithm$ Alg *in* $ClassAlgs$ **do**
9:                 **for each** $hyperparameters\_configuration$ Hp *in* $HpSpace$ **do**
10:                    $ds\_pm = GetPerformanceWith5FoldCV(\mathtt{Alg}, \mathtt{Hp}, \mathtt{DS})$;
11:                    $metadata[] \leftarrow ds\_mf \cup ds\_pm$;
12:            $meta\_ds[measure] \leftarrow metadata[]$;
13:    **return** KB

---

4   Evaluation

In this section, we briefly discuss the evaluation strategy of the proposed approach.

4.1   Experimental Setup

We empirically evaluate our MGBO approach to optimize 08 relevant Scikit-Learn machine learning algorithms. These algorithms are *Random Forest, SVM, Extra Trees, Logistic Regression, AdaBoost, Decision Tree, Gradient Boosting, and Stochastic Gradient Descent* classifiers. The exhaustive list of the optimized hyperparameters is shown in Table 1. The HPs search space is reduced to keep the computations manageable and the results interpretable.

For our experiments, we used the 09 datasets listed in Table 2 from the OpenML[2] platform. Validation performance for Bayesian Optimization is then computed by a stratified 10-fold cross-validation fashion on the training dataset.

4.2   Experimental Results

For our empirical evaluation of MGBO, we compared it to the classical Bayesian Optimization (using EI as acquisition function). For each dataset, we tracked wall clock time. Figure 2 shows the improvement obtained by our meta-guided optimization approach.

As shown in Fig. 2, on all benchmark datasets, MGBO with the prior guidance produces more efficient results than classical BO. Importantly, in all experiments, MGBO has significant speed up in the early phases of the optimization process, requiring an average of only 13 iterations to attain the performance that

---

[2] https://www.openml.org/.

Table 2. List of the datasets used for the experiments; the names refer to the names on the OpenML platform.

Dataset	Number of instances	Number of classes
splice	3190	3
numerai28.6	96320	2
haberman	306	2
eucalyptus	736	2
abalone	4177	3
scene	2407	2
haberman	306	2
phoneme	5404	2
bank8FM	8192	2

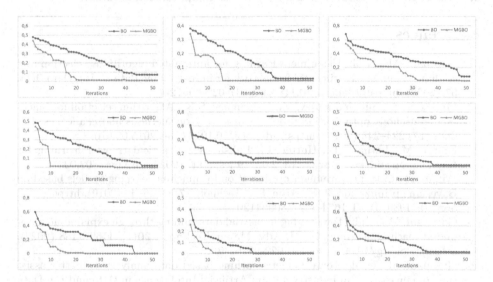

Fig. 2. Validation error between the best found hyperparameters at iteration t.

the classical BO may achieve after 20 to 40 iterations (hence, approximately three times faster).

5   Conclusion

By transferring prior knowledge about which parts of the input space can yield the best performance from previous optimization runs, we have design a simple, yet efficient, method for improving Sequential Model-Based Bayesian Optimization of hyperparameters. The proposed method combines ideas from both the meta-learning and the functional analysis of variance by initializing and guiding BO with configurations suggested by a meta-guidance procedure. We, in this work, show how black-box optimizer can be sped up by using simple meta-knowledge to guide the search space exploration. The experiments, on a total of 09 datasets using 08 ML algorithms, demonstrate the efficiency of MGBO, identifying good HPs configurations which are 2 to 3 times faster than the standard Bayesian optimization. In future work, we plan to study how our approach can be used to leverage more knowledge and guidance from meta-learning. Bringing these two domains together may likely boost the performance of BO, even further. Our code would be available at https://github.com/LeMGarouani/MGBO along with scripts for reproducing our experiments.

Acknowledgements. The authors would like to thank the University of the Littoral Cote d'Opale, School of engineering's and business sciences and technics (HESTIM) Morocco, and CNRST Morocco for the financial support, and the CALCULCO computing platform, supported by SCOSI/ULCO (Service COmmun du Système d'Information de l'Université du Littoral Côte d'Opale) for the computational facilities.

References

1. Garouani, M., et al.: Using meta-learning for automated algorithms selection and configuration: an experimental framework for industrial big data. J. Big Data **9**(1), 57 (2022). https://doi.org/10.1186/s40537-022-00612-4
2. Muñoz, M.A., Sun, Y., Kirley, M., Halgamuge, S.K.: Algorithm selection for black-box continuous optimization problems: a survey on methods and challenges. Inf. Sci. **317**, 224–245 (2015). https://doi.org/10.1016/j.ins.2015.05.010
3. Feurer, M., Letham, B., Hutter, F., Bakshy, E.: Practical transfer learning for Bayesian optimization. arXiv:1802.02219 [cs, stat] (2022). arXiv: 1802.02219
4. Wu, J., et al.: Hyperparameter optimization for machine learning models based on Bayesian optimization. J. Electron. Sci. Technol. **17**(1), 26–40 (2019). https://doi.org/10.11989/JEST.1674-862X.80904120
5. Garouani, M., et al.: Towards big industrial data mining through explainable automated machine learning. Int. J. Adv. Manuf. Technol. **120**(1), 1169–1188 (2022). https://doi.org/10.1007/s00170-022-08761-9
6. Garouani, M., et al.: Towards meta-learning based data analytics to better assist the domain experts in industry 4.0. In: Artificial Intelligence in Data and Big Data Processing. Springer International Publishing, 2022, pp. 265–277 (2022). https://doi.org/10.1007/978-3-030-97610-1_22
7. Garouani, M., et al.: Toward an automatic assistance framework for the selection and configuration of machine learning based data analytics solutions in Industry 4.0. In: Proceedings of the 5th International Conference on Big Data and Internet of Things. Springer International Publishing 2022, pp. 3–15 (2022). https://doi.org/10.1007/978-3-031-07969-6_1
8. Hamed, O., Hamlich, M.: Improvised multi-robot cooperation strategy for hunting a dynamic target. In: 2020 International Symposium on Advanced Electrical and Communication Technologies (ISAECT). IEEE (2020). https://doi.org/10.1109/isaect50560.2020.9523684
9. Domhan, T., Springenberg, J.T., Hutter, F.: Speeding up automatic hyperparameter optimization of deep neural networks by extrapolation of learning curves. In: Proceedings of the 24th International Conference on Artificial Intelligence. IJCAI 2015, pp. 3460–3468. AAAI Press, 25 (2015)

10. Volpp, M., et al.: Meta-learning acquisition functions for transfer learning in Bayesian optimization. arXiv (2020). arXiv: 1904.02642
11. Garouani, M., et al.: Towards the automation of industrial data science: a meta-learning based approach. In: 23rd International Conference on Enterprise Information Systems, pp. 709–716, 11 (2022). https://doi.org/10.5220/0010457107090716
12. Garouani, M., Ahmad, A., Bouneffa, M., Hamlich, M.: AMLBID: an auto-explained automated machine learning tool for big industrial data. SoftwareX **17**, 100919 (2022). https://doi.org/10.1016/j.softx.2021.100919
13. Bergstra, J., Bardenet, R., Bengio, Y., Kégl, B.: Algorithms for hyperparameter optimization. In: Advances in Neural Information Processing Systems, vol. 24. Curran Associates Inc, (2011)
14. Garouani, M., Kharroubi, J.: Towards a new lexicon-based features vector for sentiment analysis: application to Moroccan Arabic tweets. In: Advances in Information, Communication and Cybersecurity. Springer International Publishing, pp. 67–76 (2022). https://doi.org/10.1007/978-3-030-91738-8_7
15. Garouani, M., Chrita, H., Kharroubi, J.: Sentiment analysis of moroccan tweets using text mining. In: Digital Technologies and Applications. Springer International Publishing, pp. 597–608 (2021). https://doi.org/10.1007/978-3-030-73882-2_54
16. Hamlich, M., Ramdani, M.: Applying the SAC algorithm to extract the cardiologic indicators of an Athlete's Leve. Int. J. Intell. Inf. Syst. **5**, 23–27 (2016). https://doi.org/10.11648/j.ijiis.s.2016050301.13
17. Padierna, L.C., et al.: Hyper-parameter tuning for support vector machines by estimation of distribution algorithms. In: Nature-Inspired Design of Hybrid Intelligent Systems. Springer International Publishing, pp. 787–800 (2017). https://doi.org/10.1007/978-3-319-47054-2_53
18. Souza, A., et al.: Bayesian optimization with a prior for the optimum. In: Machine Learning and Knowledge Discovery in Databases. Lecture Notes in Computer Science. Springer International Publishing, pp. 265–296 (2021). https://doi.org/10.1007/978-3-030-86523-8_17
19. Kunjir, M.: Guided Bayesian optimization to AutoTune memory-based analytics. In: 2019 IEEE 35th International Conference on Data Engineering Workshops, pp. 125–132 (2019). https://doi.org/10.1109/ICDEW.2019.00-22
20. Garouani, M., Zaysa, K.: Leveraging the automated machine learning for Arabic opinion mining: a preliminary study on AutoML tools and comparison to human performance. In: Digital Technologies and Applications. Springer International Publishing, pp. 163 171 (2022). https://doi.org/10.1007/978-3-031-02447-4_17
21. Priya, R., de Souza, B.F., Rossi, A.L.D., de Carvalho, A.C.: Using genetic algorithms to improve prediction of execution times of ML tasks. In: Hybrid Artificial Intelligent Systems. Springer 2012, pp. 196–207 (2012). https://doi.org/10.1007/978-3-642-28942-2_18
22. Makarova, A., et al.: Automatic termination for hyperparameter optimization. arXiv:2104.08166 (21, 2021)
23. Frazier, P.I.: Bayesian optimization. In: Recent Advances in Optimization and Modeling of Contemporary Problems. INFORMS 2018, pp. 255–278 (2018). https://doi.org/10.1287/educ.2018.0188
24. Mockus, J., Tiesis, V., Zilinskas, A.: The application of Bayesian methods for seeking the extremum. J. Abbr. Towards Glob. Optim. **2**(25), 117–129 (2014)
25. Jones, D.R.: A taxonomy of global optimization methods based on response surfaces. J. Global Optim. **21**(4), 345–383 (2001). https://doi.org/10.1023/A:1012771025575

26. Srinivas, N., Krause, A., Kakade, S., Seeger, M.: Gaussian process optimization in the bandit setting: no regret and experimental design. In: Proceedings of the 27th International Conference on International Conference on Machine Learning. Omni Press 2010, pp. 1015–1022 (2010)
27. Hernández-Lobato, J.M., Hoffman, M.W., Ghahramani, Z.: Predictive entropy search for efficient global optimization of black-box functions. arXiv:1406.2541 [cs, stat] (10, 2014)
28. Wu, J., Poloczek, M., Wilson, A.G., Frazier, P.I.: Bayesian optimization with gradients. arXiv:1703.04389 (6, 2018)
29. Hutter, F., Hoos, H., Leyton-Brown, K.: An efficient approach for assessing hyperparameter importance. In: ICML (2014)
30. Rasmussen, C.E.: Gaussian processes in machine learning. In: Lecture Notes in Computer Science. Springer 2004, pp. 63–71 (2004). https://doi.org/10.1007/978-3-540-28650-9_4
31. Wistuba, M., Schilling, N., Schmidt-Thieme, L.: Scalable Gaussian process-based transfer surrogates for hyperparameter optimization. Mach. Learn. 107(1), 43–78 (2017). https://doi.org/10.1007/s10994-017-5684-y
32. Feurer, M., Eggensperger, K., Falkner, S., Lindauer, M., Hutter, F.: Auto-Sklearn 2.0: Hands-free AutoML via Meta-Learning (2020). https://doi.org/10.48550/ARXIV.2007.04074

A Novel Graded Multi-label Approach to Music Emotion Recognition

Wissal Farsal(✉)📵, Mohammed Ramdani📵, and Samir Anter📵

Computing Laboratory of Mohammedia (LIM), FSTM,
Hassan II University of Casablanca, Casablanca, Morocco
farsalwissal@gmail.com

Abstract. Music Emotion Recognition (MER) has become one of the key researched axes in Music Information Retrieval. Its main objective is to automatically recognize the effective content of music pieces. In this paper, we are interested in the task of Music Emotion Classification which success has plateaued in recent years. We wish to offer a new perspective by approaching the problem as a graded multi-label learning problem and therefore bridging the existing limitations presented by the categorical taxonomy in Music Emotion Recognition. In order to assess the suitability of this setting, we adapted a state of the art MER dataset by annotating it according to a graded multi-label format. Our initial studies conclude the promising potential of this approach.

Keywords: Music emotion recognition · Music information retrieval · Graded multi-label classification

1 Introduction

Emotion is considered an essential part of music [1–4], expressing emotions is intrinsic to the art of music and it has even been defined as its purpose [5]. An area of research in psychology was dedicated to exploring the musical emotions, and the key concepts of emotion perception and emotion induction [1,6]. Moreover, understanding the relation between music and emotion figured in many disciplines beyond psychology. This subject interested musicologists, neuroscientists, philosophers, sociologists, and even computational scientists. In fact, in computational science, automatic recognition of emotions in music is one of the key challenges of Music Information Retrieval research (MIR), an interdisciplinary area focused on providing further understanding of music via computational systems. The subfield of MIR dedicated to developing machine learning models to automatically identify the musical emotions is called Music Emotion Recognition (MER).

The field of Music Emotion Recognition received a lot of attention in the last two decades, especially with the successful implementation of models for the Music Emotion Classification task (MEC), which is a task that has been the

M. Hamlich et al. (Eds.): SADASC 2022, CCIS 1677, pp. 187–197, 2022.
https://doi.org/10.1007/978-3-031-20490-6_15

focus of many researchers since its first integration in 2007 in the Music Information Retrieval Evaluation eXchange challenge (MIREX), an annual challenge devoted to advancing the research in Music Information Retrieval and audio classification.

MER models were utilized in a variety of MIR applications, i.e. music organization, music management, search, and playlist generation [7–9]. Beyond these applications, MER models are very valuable in music recommendation and allow users to find music based on its emotional content, a fact that is appreciated by users in music websites since emotion and mood are very important in their listening experience [10]. Additionally, MER was also applied in music therapy [11], healthcare [12], marketing, film music, and the gaming industry [6].

In order to build Music Emotion Recognition models, appropriate emotional music datasets are needed. These datasets consist of a number of music excerpts annotated according to their affective content. There are two approaches for dataset annotation: a categorical approach and a dimensional approach. The former describes the emotional content in the form of discrete distinct classes i.e. happiness, sadness, anger, and fear [13,14]. The latter represents emotions in a dimensional space usually based on Russel's model [15], where an emotion is mapped in a two-dimensional plane with valence and arousal as axes. This representation was first introduced as part of a psychology study to build a circumplex model of affect and was adopted in MER. The valence axis maps emotions from displeasure to pleasure and the arousal axis ranges from calm to excited.

Both these approaches have limitations, discrete categories do not translate the variance in intensity and the dimensional representation does not depict the qualitative differences of the emotions [16]. However, it was demonstrated that in theory emotions are rather discrete [17,18]. Furthermore, some studies supported that emotions share both dimensional and categorical tendencies [1,19].

In this study, we consider the categorical taxonomy because it offers an advantage in providing clear boundaries and therefore allows for decision-making and rule deduction [1]. The potential of MER in modeling such subjective information is greater in data-driven decisions and would be valuable in a variety of emotion regulation applications [16]. Hence the need for more explainable and interpretable models for the Music Emotion Classification task.

In this paper, we propose a new approach to Music Emotion Recognition based on Graded Multi-label Learning to bridge the limitations of the existing categorical and dimensional methods. Moreover, we apply an adapted graded multi-label decision tree algorithm to deduce interpretable and useful decision rules.

The remainder of this paper is structured as follows: Sect. 2 briefly discusses related work. In Sect. 3, we present the adapted graded multi-label dataset. Section 4 introduces graded multi-label learning and the adapted decision tree used in the classification. Section 5 reports the results of the experimental study and finally, we conclude our work in Sect. 6.

2   Music Emotion Classification

Despite the conducted studies to improve the performance in the classification task of music emotions [20,21] the accuracy plateaued in the MIREX challenge since 2011 [6,7]. This was essentially attributed to the limitations of the standard categorical classification [7].

Therefore, different approaches were proposed to alleviate this limitation such as multi-label classification, fuzzy-set theory, and rough-set theory. In [22], the authors introduced a multi-label approach to MER for the first time. The experimental results showed lower performance in terms of precision and recall compared to single-label classification using SVMs. This preliminary study was based on a single annotation source and is comprised of 13 adjective groups and 6 supergroups. Further studies with more annotations concluded that the accuracy improves when the number of categories is reduced. Although these initial studies were underwhelming, further research was carried out to prove the merit of multi-label classification in MER.

In [23], the authors shed more light on the use of the multi-label paradigm in MER. This study assessed the accuracy of the multi-label classification task using k-NN and concluded that the results of multi-label classification are more accurate than those of single-label classification.

A more in-depth comparison of different multi-label algorithms was proposed to evaluate their performance in MER [24]. The comparison focused on three approaches: Binary relevance (BR), Powerset Label (LP), and Random k-label sets (RAkEL). The study showed that the performance is related to whether the algorithms take label interdependencies into account or not. Therefore, RAkEL outperforms LP which in turn outperforms BR. Further research with other models showed the improvement of the accuracy by considering the label dependencies [26,27].

3   A Graded Multi-label MER Dataset

Musical features can be categorized into eight groups; rhythm, dynamics, expressive techniques, melody, harmony, tone color, musical texture, and musical form [28]. Many studies were conducted to determine the most relevant features for Music Emotion Recognition since the first attempt to build a predictive model for MER that only used two features to describe the data: tempo and articulation. They uncovered the relations and associations between emotions and musical attributes [28] e.g. major modes are associated with the emotions of happiness whilst minor modes correspond to sadness [29]. Furthermore, other research studies revealed various musical attributes such as timing, tonality, rhythm, mode, loudness, and vibrato [30–33].

Despite these studies, MER research was still using features created for other audio information retrieval problems and therefore do not capture the emotional component in music. This is because some of these features are still researched and that others are difficult to extract from audio [28]. Hundreds of features can be extracted using audio frameworks such as Marsyas [34], MIR toolbox [35], and PsySound [36]. However, they remain insufficient or irrelevant to solve the MER problem [28].

Panda et al. [28] tackled the problem of finding which features best capture the emotional content of music. They proposed a novel set of high-level features to overcome the limitations of the standard existing features. The authors used features that were associated with musical emotions such as rhythm, harmony, melody lines, expressive techniques regarding vibrato, tremolo, glissando, and articulation, instead of the baseline low-level features. Further comparisons with state-of-the-art musical attributes used in the leading music streaming service Spotify proved the efficacy of the new set of features [37].

The authors also created a new public dataset with 900 30-second audio clips annotated in terms of Russell's four emotion model quadrants. These clips were first obtained from the AllMusic API with their metadata including the mood tags and then assigned to the quadrant with the highest corresponding number of tags. Considering the demonstrated effectiveness of this corpus, we chose this dataset as a base for our experiments.

We started by selecting the first 120 excerpts from the dataset. Since this dataset is evenly distributed between quadrants and music genres, we have a quite mixed and representative corpus. Then we proceed to the annotation of this subset according to a graded multi-label format.

We used three class-labels to depict three of the basic emotions i.e. happiness, sadness, and anger. We allowed for a gradual annotation to represent the level of the perceived emotion. These levels range from 0 to 4, and correspond to linguistic gradual descriptions of the level of relevance of the musical emotion for an excerpt i.e. not at all present and fully relevant. We initially conducted an experiment using the four basic emotions: happiness, sadness, anger, and fear. After the reported confusion caused by the class label fear by our annotators, we chose to limit this initial study to three classes. Our group of annotators comprises of 10 volunteers and includes undergraduate students and graduates.

4   Graded Multi-label Classification

In graded multi-label classification, given a d-dimensional input space $A_1, ..., A_d$ of numerical or categorical attributes and $L = \{\lambda_1, ..., \lambda_k\}$ a set of predefined labels or classes. An instance $x \in X$ can belong to each class $\lambda \in L$ to a certain degree from a finite and predefined set $M = \{\mu_1, ..., \mu_m\}$. This set of membership degrees is ordinal, i.e. the degrees μ_i, $i = 1, ..., m$ follow an ordered scale $\mu_1 < \mu_2 < ... < \mu_m$. The same scale is then respected for all labels to describe their level of relevance.

Furthermore, the degree of membership μ_1 represents the complete absence or irrelevance of a label and μ_m its full presence or relevance. Hence, a Multi-label problem is a special case of a graded multi-label learning where $M = \{0, 1\}$ i.e. each label is either relevant or not [38].

In a graded multi-label classification task, we have a training set of N labeled samples $S = \{(x^{(i)}, y^{(i)})\}_{i=1}^{N}$, where $y^{(i)}$ is the vector of membership degrees assigned to $x^{(i)}$ i.e. $y_j^{(i)}$ is the membership degree or level of relevance of the jth label assigned to the ith data instance.

The purpose is to build a classifier H that assigns each data instance x a vector y of membership degrees of the labels:

$$H \colon A_1, ..., A_d \to M^k$$
$$x \mapsto y$$

Therefore the output for a test instance $\tilde{x}$ is the prediction vector $\hat{y}$ defined as follows:

$$H(\tilde{x}) = \hat{y} = [\hat{y}_1, ..., \hat{y}_k]$$

where $\hat{y}_i$, $i = 1, ..., k$ represents the predicted grade corresponding to the ith class label for the test instance $\tilde{x}$.

We should also mention that the classifier H can be one single adapted classifier for the GMLC setting. Or a combination of standard classifiers i.e. k classifiers H_i, $i = 1, ..., k$ where each

$$H_i \colon A_1, ..., A_d \to M$$

is an independent classifier that predicts the degree of membership of the label λ_i.

4.1 GML_DT

In previous work, we introduced an adapted graded multi-label decision tree classifier [39]. We modified the formula of the entropy to handle GMLC tasks. The adapted graded multi-label heuristic generalizes the standard entropy for a single label classification:

$$Entropy(S) = - \sum_{i=1}^{n} p(c_i) \log p(c_i) \tag{1}$$

where $p(c_i)$ is the probability of the class c_i.

In GMLC, we need to compute the entropy of a set according to all class labels simultaneously. The proposed heuristic achieves that by calculating the entropy of a set as the averaged sum of the entropies of class labels:

$$Entropy(S) = -\frac{1}{k} \sum_{i=1}^{k} \sum_{j=1}^{m} p(\mu_{ij}) \log p(\mu_{ij}) \tag{2}$$

where $\mu_{ij} \in M$ and $p(\mu_{ij})$ is the probability of the grade μ_{ij} for the label λ_i, $i = 1, ..., k$.

The new formula allows the leaves of the constructed tree to be a set of grades that correspond to the predefined set of labels. Moreover, GML_DT follows a binary induction that is capable of handling both categorical and numerical features. The algorithm constructs a classification tree top-down in a greedy manner. For each node, the algorithm searches for the best attribute-value test for partitioning the remaining training samples. Therefore, splitting the samples in the node to create two children nodes based on the selected test, one for which the test succeeds and one for which the test fails. The best attribute-value test is chosen by considering all possible split values or points for each attribute and selecting the one with the smallest overall entropy. Considering an attribute-valued training set S, the overall entropy for an attribute-value test (A,v) is calculated as follows:

$$Overall\ Entropy = - \sum_{i \in \{1,2\}} \frac{|S_i|}{|S|} Entropy(S_i) \qquad (3)$$

where $S_1 and S_2$ are induced partitions from splitting S based on (A,v). If the attribute A is categorical, S is partitioned into a subset S_1 for which $A = v$ and a subset S_2 for which $A \neq v$. (Similarly, if A is numerical, S is partitioned into a subset S_1 corresponding to $A \leq v$ and a subset S_2 for which $A > v$)

After creating a node in the constructed tree with the best test point and partitioning the data, the algorithm proceeds to call itself recursively on each child node until a stopping criterion is met. The stopping conditions are:

- The number of samples remaining in a node is less than a predefined threshold.
- The samples in the node belong to the same degree class per label.
- The tree reaches a maximum predefined depth.

In addition to being very competitive with state-of-the-art approaches, GML_DT has the advantage of interpretability. It produces a single decision tree that identifies the attribute-value conditions relevant for the prediction of the complete set of degrees associated with the label set [39]. Which induces simple and intelligible rules.

5   Experiments

We conducted an experimental study using 10-fold cross-validation and the collected graded multi-label dataset, comparing our method with three standard classifiers: Support Vector Machines, a Decision Tree classifier, and k-Nearest Neighbours. The GML_DT algorithm was developed from scratch using Python. The baseline classifiers are implemented using the Scikit-learn library [41].

5.1   Evaluation Metrics

The evaluation metrics for the graded multi-label problem were first introduced by Cheng et al. in [38], where the authors generalized common multi-label loss functions. In this experimental study, we evaluated the predictive performances of GML_DT using three measures.

The Hamming Loss, which represents the mean deviation of the predicted label grades to the actual ones, is defined as follows:

$$HAMMING\ LOSS = \frac{\sum_{i=1}^{k} AE(\hat{y}_i, y_i)}{(m-1)k}$$

where AE stands for the absolute error of the predicted grades:

$$AE: M \times M \to \mathbb{N},\ AE(\mu_i, \mu_j) = |i - j|$$

The Vertical 0–1 Loss considers the percentage of class labels that were assigned the wrong degree or grade. This measure does not take into account the distance or differences between the predicted label grades.

$$VERTICAL\ 0-1\ LOSS = \frac{1}{k} \sum_{i=1}^{k} I(\hat{y}_i \neq y_i)$$

where I is the indicator function.

The C-Index measures the pairwise ranking errors of the labels. It is defined in [38] as follows:

$$C-INDEX = \frac{\sum_{i<j} \sum_{(\lambda, \lambda') \in M_i \times M_j} S([H]_\lambda, [H]'_\lambda)}{\sum_{i<j} |M_i| \times |M_j|}$$

where $M_i = \{\lambda \in L | L_x(\lambda) = \mu_i\}$
$L_x(\lambda)$ is a function returning the degree of membership of the label for an instance x and

$$S(u, v) = I(u > v) + \frac{1}{2} I(u = v)$$

5.2   Results

We started our experiments by evaluating GML_DT on our MER dataset using 10-fold cross-validation. We then averaged the scores for each graded multi-label performance measure and calculated the standard deviation across the 10 folds. The average Hamming Loss is 19.86% with a standard deviation of 4.48%, the Vertical 0–1 Loss reached 48.33% with a standard deviation of 10.49%, and finally the computed C-Index is 19.58% with a standard deviation of 8.18%. Considering that these results would be seen as good in the state-of-the-art research on GMLC [38–40], we can conclude the initial suitability of the graded multi-label setting in Music Emotion Recognition awaiting further studies.

Moreover, GML_DT possesses a clear advantage over the state-of-the-art MER methods. By implementing this adaptation-based decision tree classifier, we can generate a single tree that can be translated into a set of simple rules. These rules can provide valuable insights into which MER features are directly relevant in the prediction of the levels of a set of different emotions (see Fig. 1).

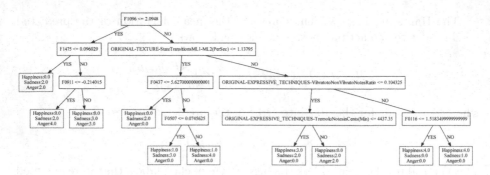

Fig. 1. A Graded Multi-label Decision Tree Constructed using GML_DT on the MER dataset.

Table 1. Label-wise performance comparison in terms of Precision, Recall, and F_1 Score.

Model	Label	Precision	Recall	F_1 score
GML_DT	Happiness	**49.42 %**	**43.33 %**	**42.18 %**
	Sadness	**49.05 %**	**45.83 %**	**42.34 %**
	Anger	59.24 %	**65.83 %**	**61.24 %**
SVM	Happiness	11.11 %	30.00 %	15.89 %
	Sadness	13.26 %	34.16 %	18.70 %
	Anger	40.90 %	62.50 %	49.12 %
Decision Tree	Happiness	29.37 %	25.00 %	25.22 %
	Sadness	37.48 %	28.33 %	28.89 %
	Anger	**64.62 %**	58.33 %	59.21 %
K-NN	Happiness	11.11 %	30.00 %	15.89 %
	Sadness	12.54 %	29.16 %	16.00 %
	Anger	05.20 %	12.50 %	06.67 %

To gain further understanding of the effect of the graded multi-label setting on Music Emotion Recognition, we carried out single-label experiments. We evaluated the classification performance of GML_DT for each label. To do so, we computed the mean of the label-wise precision, recall, and F_1 score. Furthermore, we proceeded to the comparison of our model against standard classifiers in the absence of a graded multi-label framework. Table 1 reports the obtained results of each model for each label according to the three evaluation metrics. These metrics were calculated for each of the 10-folds of the cross-validation procedure as a weighted average to account for class prevalence.

The experimental study shows that GML_DT achieves higher results overall. In fact, for both the Happiness and Sadness labels, GML_DT significantly outperformed the baseline classifiers according to all three performance measures. For the Anger label, the baseline decision tree learner achieved a higher Precision than the graded multi-label classifier (64.62% against 59.24%). However, GML-DT performed better in terms of Recall and F_1 score.

We can also observe a label-based disparity in the performance of the models. For three of these learners i.e. GML-DT, SVM, and Decision Tree , we can notice the considerably higher scores attained for the label Anger compared to the Happiness and Sadness labels. As a matter of fact, the maximal scores were attained for this label using GML-DT in the cross-validation process i.e. a precision of 91.66%, a recall of 83.33%, and an F_1 score of 80.55%. This may indicate a better discernment of the annotators of the presence of the anger emotions or its association with certain music genres.

6 Conclusion

This article presents a preliminary study to test the suitability of graded multi-label classification for Music Emotion Recognition. We started by adapting the first 120 excerpts from a state-of-the-art dataset. We modified the annotations from a multi-class quadrant-based classification into a graded multi-label one that is composed of three labels classified in a graded manner into five levels. In view of obtaining interpretable results, we chose to work with an adapted graded multi-label decision tree classifier capable of predicting the grades of all class labels simultaneously. We evaluated our model using performance measures from the GMLC literature. In addition, we conducted label-wise experiments using standard classifiers and concluded the viability of the graded multi-label approach for MER. Needless to say, the problem is still yet to be investigated furthermore, with a larger corpus, different taxonomies and more annotations.

References

1. Juslin, P.N.: Musical Emotions Explained: Unlocking the Secrets of Musical Affect. Oxford University Press, Oxford, USA (2019)
2. Budd, M.: Music and the Emotions: The Philosophical Theories. Routledge, London (2002)
3. Davies, S.: Musical meaning and expression. In: Musical Meaning and Expression. Cornell University Press, Ithaca (2019)
4. Gabrielsson, A., Juslin, P.N.: Emotional Expression in Music. Oxford University Press, Oxford (2003)
5. Cochrane, T.: On the resistance of the instrument. The Emotional Power of Music: Multidisciplinary Perspectives on Musical Arousal, Expression and Social Control, pp. 75–84 (2013)
6. Yang, Y.-H., Chen, H.H.: Music Emotion Recognition. CRC Press, Boca Raton (2011)
7. Yang, X., Dong, Y., Li, J.: Review of data features-based music emotion recognition methods. Multimedia Syst. **24**(4), 365–389 (2018)
8. Wang, J.-C., Yang, Y.-H., Wang, H.-M., et al.: The acoustic emotion Gaussians model for emotion-based music annotation and retrieval. In: Proceedings of the 20th ACM International Conference on Multimedia, pp. 89–98 (2012)

9. Yang, Y.-H., Chen, H.H.: Ranking-based emotion recognition for music organization and retrieval. IEEE Trans. Audio Speech Lang. Process. **19**(4), 762–774 (2010)
10. Hu, X., Chen, J., Wang, Y.: University students' use of music for learning and well-being: a qualitative study and design implications. Inf. Process. Manag. **58**(1), 102409 (2021)
11. Dingle, G.A., Kelly, P.J., Flynn, L.M., et al.: The influence of music on emotions and cravings in clients in addiction treatment: a study of two clinical samples. Arts Psychother. **45**, 18–25 (2015)
12. Bernatzky, G., Presch, M., Anderson, M., et al.: Emotional foundations of music as a non-pharmacological pain management tool in modern medicine. Neurosci. Biobehav. Rev. 35(9), 1989–1999 (2011)
13. Chowdhury, S., Vall, A., Haunschmid, V., et al.: Towards explainable music emotion recognition: the route via mid-level features. arXiv preprint arXiv:1907.03572 (2019)
14. Izard, C.E.: The psychology of emotions. Springer Science & Business Media (1991)
15. Hutto, D.D., Robertson, I., Kirchhoff, M.D.: A new, better BET: rescuing and revising basic emotion theory. Front. Psychol. **9**, 1217 (2018)
16. Russell, J.A.: A circumplex model of affect. J. Personal. Soc. Psychol. **39**(6), 1161 (1980)
17. Haslam, N.: The discreteness of emotion concepts: categorical structure in the affective circumplex. Personal. Soc. Psychol. Bull. **21**(10), 1012–1019 (1995)
18. Laukka, P.: Categorical perception of vocal emotion expressions. Emotion **5**(3), 277 (2005)
19. Damasio, A.R.: Descartes error revisited. J. History Neurosci. 10(2), 192–194 (2001)
20. Feng, Y., Zhuang, Y., Pan, Y.: Music information retrieval by detecting mood via computational media aesthetics. In: Proceedings IEEE/WIC International Conference on Web Intelligence (WI 2003), pp. 235–241. IEEE (2003)
21. Xu, J., Li, X., Hao, Y., et al.: Source separation improves music emotion recognition. In: Proceedings of International Conference on Multimedia Retrieval, pp. 423–426 (2014)
22. Yang, Y.-H., Chen, H.H.: Machine recognition of music emotion: a review. ACM Trans. Intell. Syst. Technol. (TIST) **3**(3), 1–30 (2012)
23. Li, T., Ogihara, M.: Detecting emotion in music (2003)
24. Wieczorkowska, A., Synak, P., Raś, Z.W.: Multi-label classification of emotions in music. In: Intelligent Information Processing and Web Mining, pp. 307–315. Springer, Berlin, Heidelberg (2006). https://doi.org/10.1007/3-540-33521-8_30
25. Trohidis, K., Tsoumakas, G., Kalliris, G., et al.: Multi-label classification of music into emotions. In: ISMIR. pp. 325–330 (2008)
26. Wu, B., Zhong, E., Horner, A., et al.: Music emotion recognition by multi-label multi-layer multi-instance multi-view learning. In: Proceedings of the 22nd ACM International Conference on Multimedia, pp. 117–126 (2014)
27. Nguyen, C.-T., Zhan, D.-C., Zhou, Z.-H.: Multi-modal image annotation with multi-instance multi-label LDA. In: Proceedings of the Twenty-Third International Joint Conference on Artificial Intelligence, pp. 1558–1564 (2013)
28. Panda, R., Malheiro, R., Paiva, R.P.: Novel audio features for music emotion recognition. IEEE Trans. Affective Comput. **11**(4), 614–626 (2018)
29. Gabrielsson, A., Lindström, E.: The influence of musical structure on emotional expression (2001)

30. Laurier, C.F., et al.: Automatic classification of musical mood by content-based analysis. Universitat Pompeu Fabra (2011)
31. Laurier, C., Lartillot, O., Eerola, T., et al.: Exploring relationships between audio features and emotion in music. In: ESCOM 2009: 7th Triennial Conference of European Society for the Cognitive Sciences of Music (2009)
32. Friberg, A.: Digital audio emotions-an overview of computer analysis and synthesis of emotional expression in music (2008)
33. Meyers, O.C.: A mood-based music classification and exploration system. Thèse de doctorat. Massachusetts Institute of Technology (2007)
34. Tzanetakis, G., Cook, P.: Marsyas: a framework for audio analysis. Organ. Sound 4(3), 169–175 (2000)
35. Lartillot, O., Toiviainen, P.: A MatLab toolbox for musical feature extraction from audio. In: International Conference on Digital Audio Effects, p. 244 (2007)
36. Cabrera, D., Ferguson, S., Schubert, E.: 'Psysound3': software for acoustical and psychoacoustical analysis of sound recordings. In: Proceedings of the 13th International Conference on Auditory Display, 26–29 June 2007, Montréal, Canada (2007)
37. Panda, R., Redinho, H., Gonçalves, C., et al.: How does the spotify API compare to the music emotion recognition state-of-the-Art?. In: Proceedings of the 18th Sound and Music Computing Conference (SMC 2021). Axea sas/SMC Network, pp. 238–245 (2021)
38. Cheng, W., Dembczynski, K., Hüllermeier, E.: Graded multilabel classification: the ordinal case. In: ICML (2010)
39. Farsal, W., Ramdani, M., Anter, S.: GML_DT: a novel graded multi-label decision tree classifier. Int. J. Adv. Comput. Sci. Appl. 12(12) (2021)
40. Brinker, C., Mencía, E.L., Fürnkranz, J.: Graded multilabel classification by pairwise comparisons. In: 2014 IEEE International Conference on Data Mining, pp. 731–736. IEEE (2014)
41. Pedregosa, F., Varoquaux, G., Gramfort, A., et al.: Scikit-Learn: machine learning in Python. J. Mach. Learn. Res. 12, 2825–2830 (2011)

Data-Driven Solutions for Electricity Price Forecasting: The Case of EU Improvement Project

Khadija Elmoukhtafi[1,3]([✉]), Ladjel Bellatreche[2], Mohamed Hamlich[1],
and Carlos Augusto Santos Silva[4]

[1] CCPS Laboratory-ENSAM, Hassan II University, Casablanca, Morocco
khadija.elmoukhtafi1-etu@etu.univh2c.ma
[2] LIAS/ISAE-ENSMA, Poitiers University, Poitiers, France
[3] CERIM/HESTIM, Casablanca, Morocco
[4] Technical University of Lisbon, Lisbon, Portugal

Abstract. Electricity is a necessity in all areas, which is why electricity consumption is increasing. With the renewable energy revolution, the variability of electricity prices has also increased. Knowing the price of electricity becomes essential to balance electricity production and consumption. In particular, for energy management systems (EMS) integrated into smart grids, long short-term electricity price forecasting is an endeavor to help control battery operators and energy demand response aggregators. In this study, we use both ordinary machine learning regression algorithms, namely Random Forest, Support vector machine, and XGBoost regressors, and a long short-term memory-based deep learning model (LSTM), which is known to solve nonlinear regression and time series problems. In several studies on electricity price prediction, LSTM has been used to solve a univariate time series problem, in this study, we use LSTM for a multivariate time series problem. Where the data on the hourly aggregated renewable and non-renewable energies, is used to predict the electricity prices. The results show that LSTM gives outstanding predictions compared to machine learning algorithms where time is not considered an important factor for electricity price prediction.

Keywords: Electricity price prediction · Long short-term memory · LSTM multivariate

1 Introduction

The price of electricity varies irregularly depending on several factors, such as demand, fuel prices, and renewable energy. Demand is one of the most important

K. Elmoukhtafi—Supported by organization Hassan II University, Casablanca Morocco.

L. Bellatreche—This work has been carried out with the financial support of the European Regional Development Fund (ERDF) under the program Interreg SUDOE SOE3/P3/E0901 (Project IMPROVEMENT).

factors. The price of electricity increases when demand increases. The variability in demand is depending on the date, time, season, and even the year. The increasing share of renewable energy sources in the electricity supply also has a greater impact on electricity prices [19]. Under favorable weather conditions, high levels of output from wind and solar facilities can reduce electricity prices to near zero, while under less favorable conditions, prices can rise to levels reflecting supply scarcity. Managing electricity demand and generation is one of the primary goals of smart renewable energy grids, where buildings are becoming net-zero energy by balancing electricity generation with its consumption. Net zero energy buildings (NZEBs) are an innovative concept in the energy field. NZEB has become not only a requirement but also an obligation thanks to the adaptation of national standards to the European directives that require transforming public buildings to be NZEBs, ensuring energy independence and synergy with the grid [5]. The energy management systems integrated in these smart grids are based on predictive models, which can forecast electricity prices in order to balance energy production and consumption.

1.1 Net-Zero Energy Buildings

According to the U.S. Department of Energy (DoE), a net-zero energy building (NZEB) is defined as a building that produces enough renewable energy to meet its own annual energy consumption needs (DoE 2015). The Energy Performance of Buildings Directive (EPBD) established by the EU, provides the following definition, "a net-zero energy building is a building with a high energy efficiency, where the required amount of energy is covered by energy from renewable sources, including energy produced on-site or in nearby" [20].

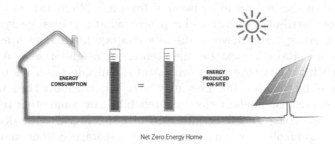

Net Zero Energy Home

Fig. 1. Net Zero Energy Building representation. Source: gmisolar.com/net-zero-energy-home-connecticut.

At the beginning of the EU Improvement project, our aim consists in predicting the energy consumption of Buildings [5]. After that, we realize a strong dependency between energy consumption and its price. This motivates us to tackle the issue of forecasting energy prices.

1.2   Concepts Related to NZEBs

Smart Electric Grids. According to [18] a smart electric grid or SG is a concept that combines New Technologies of Information and Communication (NTIC) and electric networks. Its main characteristic is to establish bi-directional communication between all the nodes of the network using advanced metering techniques. The SGs allow the circulation of information in real time between producer and consumer, in order to act on demand and optimize the production of energy. An SG associated with a decentralized energy distribution system with multiple Microgrids represents one of the 5 pillars of the famous "third industrial revolution" advocated by Jeremy Rifkin [21].

Decentralized Production. Distributed generation offers a new opportunity for renewable energy sources by placing them in new locations, especially near points of consumption. It relies on low-power generation technologies that are located close to the end users who consume them. Systems using distributed generation use multiple small power plants and provide energy to their immediate environment [14].

Energy Storage Systems. Energy storage systems, or ESS, allow energy to be stored when production exceeds demand, and to be released when demand increases, in order to minimize energy losses and waste. With the intermittent nature of renewable energy production, storage is used to meet a constant demand.

Micro Grids. A definition of a Microgrid given by [2] is the following: "a Microgrid is a system formed by generation sources, connected storage equipment that can be linked to the main grid or isolated from it." Microgrids include one or more types of distributed energy (solar panels, wind turbines, generators) that produce their energy, and power a discrete geographic area, such as a university campus, hospital complex, business center, or neighborhood. A microgrid is intelligent with a controller that orchestrates multiple resources to meet the energy goals set by the user [13]. They may be trying to achieve the lowest prices, the cleanest energy, the highest electrical reliability, or some other result.

Figure 2 shows the global architecture of a microgrid with decentralized energy production (solar and wind production), a storage system, and an energy management system. The microgrid is also linked to the main grid and is not completely autonomous.

Energy Management System. These are the micro-grid controllers described above. An Energy Management System (EMS) is expected to reduce the energy consumption of the micro-grid by up to 20–30%. According to [7], it is a set of connected hardware and software that have the following tasks: Collecting information about energy consumption to predict changes from the target. Then implementing control algorithms to correct any deviation from the target.

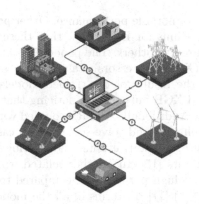

Fig. 2. Architecture of a micro-grid. Source: greensystemes.com/actualites-du-monde-de-lenergie/tout-savoir-sur-le-microgrid/.

1.3 Predictive Control of NZEBs

Forecasting energy consumption as well as the price of electricity allows decisions to be made to control and optimize the operation of the NZEB, while ensuring the user's comfort. In our article, we focus on the price prediction inside of the regional hospital of Axarquia in Spain using the data on renewable energies aggregated hourly and the energy consumption inside of the hospital grid.

2 Literature Review

In the literature, electricity price forecasting (EPF) has become a fundamental part of the decision-making mechanisms of energy companies [23] and smart grid energy management systems. A generator, utility, or large industrial consumer that can forecast volatile wholesale prices with a reasonable level of accuracy can adjust its supply strategy and generation or consumption schedule to reduce risk or maximize profits from trading ahead of time [23]. Which was the case for the smart grids. These decisions are highly dependent on the dynamics of electricity prices, so the customer will reduce consumption if a higher price is expected. Machine Learning (ML) based data analytics provide methods to cope with the massive data amounts, generated by the various manufacturing processes [12]. Among the papers deploying ML algorithms, the use of a support vector machine regressor was very common. We begin with a comparative study using deep learning (DL) and support vector regression (SVR) for electricity price forecasting in Smart Grids [3], where both approaches are effective for the EPF, but the DL approach performs better than the SVR model.

In Intelligent techniques for forecasting electricity consumption of buildings [1], five methods were used namely Multiple Regression (MR), Genetic Programming (GP), Artificial Neural Network (ANN), Deep Neural Network (DNN), and Support Vector Machine (SVM). However, ANN was the best of them, and SVM also had a notable performance. Other papers, which have used decision tree-based algorithms for EPF, show that these algorithms are robust and perform well compared to others. The paper [22] deploys the Random Forest (RF) and XGBoost (XGB) regressors as a machine learning approach for the EPF. To contextualize the results of the trained models, two baseline models were used, where RF and XGB outperform, noticing that XGBoost gives better results compared to RF. Additionally, the RF coupled with expert selection can capture complex load behavior and solve some special cases that are specific to culture, high temperature, religious events, and moving holidays thanks to an appropriate choice of inputs [15]. In another related work, regression decision trees in particular achieve high performance compared to ARIMA and a recurrent neural network (RNN) [11]. In terms of all the models mentioned, namely SVR, RF, and XGBoost, time was not retained as a distinguishing factor for the prediction task, hence the need to try another approach where time is highly considered. The electricity price data is of time series type. In several pieces of literature, the treatment of time series problems uses some statistical methods or deep learning models. Where AutoRegressive Integrated Moving Average (ARIMA) was the most common statistical model to be used for time series forecasting, which incorporates auto-correlation measures to model temporal structures within the time series data to predict future values [11,16]. ANN, DNN, RNN, and LSTM are the most commonly used deep learning models. Several studies have compared ML and DL algorithms in terms of prediction performance, with the DL approach generally giving better performance. Specifically, for time series prediction, RNN and LSTM have been the most popular among all. However, in our study, we focus on LSTM, which is known to be a model that captures long-term dependencies and sequential data modeling.

3 Methodology

In this section, we will describe the methodology that we follow for our data-driven solutions for energy price forecasting. Then, we present the performance evaluation metrics, and a description of the dataset used for training and testing, so as the predictive models.

3.1 Accuracy Metrics

Performance measures (error measures) are essential components of evaluation frameworks in various domains. The same is true for machine learning algorithms, where the evaluation of model performance is crucial to identify whether it is a good model or not and thus to compare models with each other on the level of performance. This latter is calculated based on the error between the actual and predicted values. In this section, we present the known metrics for evaluating regression models.

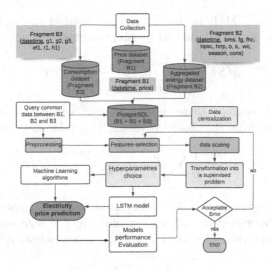

Fig. 3. Methodological process.

First, we introduce the basic of all most metrics that are the absolute error and the absolute percentage error at a time i defined respectively as

$$\left| y_i^{predict} - y_i^{observe} \right|$$

and

$$\left| \frac{y_i^{predict} - y_i^{observe}}{y_i^{observe}} \right|.$$

The Mean Absolute Error (MAE) and the Root Mean Squared Error (RMSE) are two metrics considering the accuracy of the model over a time horizon with n predictions.

Mean Absolute Error is the arithmetic mean of the absolute values of the differences between the model's predictions and its observations.

$$MAE = \frac{1}{n} \sum_{i=1}^{n} \left| y_i^{predict} - y_i^{observe} \right| \qquad (1)$$

Root Mean Squared Error. It is an extension of the mean squared error (MSE), it represents the square root of the MSE. While the RMSE uses the square operation to remove the sign of each error value and punish large errors. The square root of RMSE reverses this operation while ensuring that the result remains positive.

$$RMSE = \sqrt{\frac{\sum_{i=1}^{n}(y_i^{predict} - y_i^{observe})^2}{n}} \qquad (2)$$

Mean Squared Error. MSE is the arithmetic mean of the squared deviations between the model's predictions and its observations.

$$MSE = \frac{1}{n} \sum_{i=1}^{n} (y_i^{predict} - y_i^{observe})^2 \qquad (3)$$

Mean Absolute Percentage Error noted MAPE, which is the average of the absolute deviations from the observed values, this value must be minimized.

$$MAPE = \frac{1}{n} \sum \left| \frac{y_i^{predict} - y_i^{observe}}{y_i^{observe}} \right| \times 100 \qquad (4)$$

Determination Coefficient is called (R-squared score) and noted as R^2, it represents the ratio between the variance explained by the regression and the total variance. It is worth values between 0 and 1, a model whose R^2 is equal to 1 is perfect.

$$R^2 = 1 - \frac{\sum_{i=1}^{n} (y_i^{predict} - y_i^{observe})^2}{\sum_{i=1}^{n} (y_i^{observe} - \bar{y}_i^{observe})^2} \qquad (5)$$

MAE is the most widely used metric in the literature due to the high variance in electricity prices. However, we chose to use MAE and R^2 for the predictive model's evaluation.

3.2 Dataset

The datasets used in our research are all time series data, indexed with a time variable, We can say that these datasets are vertical fragments of an overall database including:

- Dataset containing the electricity prices in intervals of 1 h (Dataset1, 4).
- Dataset containing the aggregated renewable and nonrenewable energy in intervals of 1 h (Dataset2, 4).
- Data set containing the electricity consumption, the energy consumption inside of the Axarquia Hospital in intervals of 15 min, the outside humidity, and the solar radiations (Dataset3, 4).

Vertical fragmentation of a relational table consists in partitioning it into several fragments based on its columns [6]. The primary key of the table has to be duplicated among various fragments. In our case, it is the <u>datetime</u> plays the role of the primary key (Fig. 5). Our fragments are stocked in a PostgreSQL database.

The prediction of electricity price will be based on these three fragments, after a discovery of the variables, data cleaning, a correlation study, and a Granger causality[1] test are also applied, and a selection of features has been made for

---

[1] Granger causality is a statistical test of causality that relies on prediction. It gives if a signal **A** "causes" (or "caused by") a signal **B**, then the past values of **A** should contain information that helps predict **B** beyond the information contained in the past values of **B** alone.

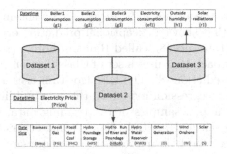

Fig. 4. Vertical fragments.

the variables that may be able to predict the price variable. Also, we have added some extra variables to the data (season, hour of the day). Down below, the figure shows the variables selected to predict the price variable.

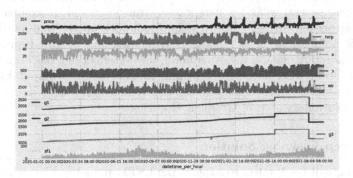

Fig. 5. Predictive variables of the electricity price.

3.3 Machine Learning Solutions

In this section, the Machine Learning algorithms used to predict the electricity price will be presented briefly.

Support Vector Regression (SVR). According to [4], SVR is formulated as an optimization problem by first defining a convex *epsilon*-insensitive loss function to be minimized and finding the flattest tube that contains most of the training instances. Therefore, a multi-objective function is constructed from the loss function and the geometric properties of the tube. Then, the convex optimization, which has a unique solution, is solved using appropriate numerical optimization algorithms. The hyperplane is represented in terms of support vectors, which are training samples located outside the tube boundary.

Random Forest (RF). the author in [8] developed an ensemble classification and regression approach that showed exceptional prediction error performance on a series of Benchmark Datasets [8], called Random Forest (RF).

The RF is an approach that uses a set of Classification And Regression Trees (CART) to make a prediction [8]. The RF algorithm uses a set of weak decision trees to build a strong regression model. In the tree building process, each tree is trained on Bootstrapped samples of the training data, this means that the same sample may be selected multiple times, while others may not be selected at all. The split of each node is selected on a random subset of input features. The final prediction is the average of the individual predictions of all trees [22].

XGBoost (XGB) Tree Boosting (TB), is a highly effective and widely used machine learning method. XGBoost is an evolutionary ML system for TB tree boosting. The Extreme gradient boosting algorithm was first introduced by (Chen and Guestrin, 2016) [9]. It is a parallel tree-based boosting designed to be "efficient, flexible, and portable" [22]. In general, the algorithm is based on the Gradient Boosting algorithm which is similar to RF, an ensemble method that combines several weak learners into a stronger model. In comparison, the XGBoost algorithm further improves the framework on the one hand from an algorithmic point of view, by enhancing regularization, weighted quantile, and sparsity-aware splitting. On the other hand, the system design has been improved by parallelization, distributed tree learning, and out-of-core computation. Thus, with the combined improvements in the algorithm and system design, XGB is the next evolutionary step in Gradient Boosting.

3.4   A Deep Learning Solution

This section, will be devoted to explain the LSTM model.

According to [17], Long-term memory is a modified RNN[2] (Recurrent Neural Network) architecture that addresses the problem of evanescent and explosive gradients and solves the problem of training over long sequences and memory retention. All RNNs have feedback loops in the recurrent layer. These feedback loops keep the information in "memory" over time. But it can be difficult to train standard RNNs to solve problems that require learning long-term temporal dependencies. Because the gradient of the loss function decays exponentially with time (a phenomenon known as the evanescent gradient problem), it is difficult to train standard RNNs. For this reason, an RNN is modified to include a memory cell capable of holding information in memory for long periods of time. The

---

[2] A recurrent neural network is a type of artificial neural network that is best suited for recognizing patterns in data sequences, such as text, video, audio, language, genomes, and time series data. An RNN is an extremely powerful algorithm that can classify, cluster, and make predictions on data, especially time series and text. The RNN can be thought of as an MLP (Multi Layer Perceptron) network with the addition of loops to the architecture. The difference is that the hidden layer nodes are interconnected. The hidden layer node is decided by the previously hidden layer node.

modified RNN is better known as an LSTM. In LSTM, a set of gates is used to control when information enters memory, which solves the problem of the gradient disappearing or exploding. Recurrent connections add state or memory to the network and allow it to learn and exploit the gradient. Internal memory means that the network's outputs are conditioned by the recent context of the input sequence, not by what was just presented to the network.

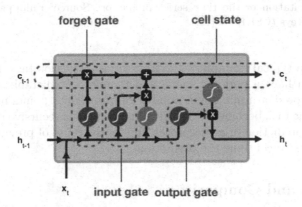

Fig. 6. The Architecture of an LSTM layer. Source: penseeartificielle.fr/comprendre-lstm-gru-fonctionnement-schema/.

An LSTM network has a memory cell, usually a layer of neurons, as well as three gates: an input gate, an output gate, and a forgetting gate. These three gates will allow the modulation of the input, output, and memorize information flow in an analog way thanks to a sigmoid activation function. Figure 6 is an unfolded representation of the functioning of an LSTM network with its three main gates.

3.5 Time Series Data

Definition. A time series T is an ordered sequence of n real-valued variables [10]:

$$T = (t_1, ..., t_n), t_i \in \mathbb{R}. \tag{6}$$

A time series is often the result of observing an underlying process in which values are collected from measurements made at uniformly spaced times (e.g., annually, monthly, weekly, daily, and hourly) and at a given sampling rate.

Time Series Prediction

Definition. Given a time series $T = (t_1, ...t_n)$, predict T is predicting the following k values $(t_{n+1}, ..., t_{n+k})$, that are most likely to occur.

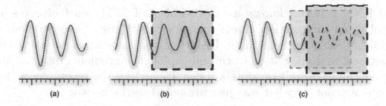

Fig. 7. Representation of the time series prediction. Source: Philippe Esling, ACM Computing Surveys (CSUR), 2012.

Figure 8 is a typical example of the time series prediction task. (a) The input time series can have a periodic shape and therefore predictable structure. (b) The goal is to predict a maximum number of future data points in a prediction window. (c) The task becomes really difficult when it is a recursive prediction, i.e. the long-term prediction of a time series implies the reuse of previous prediction values as inputs to continue the prediction.

4   Results and Comparison

The application of the machine learning algorithms had giving remarkable results, as we can see in the table below 1.

Table 1. Machine learning algorithms results.

Model	MAE	R^2		Model	MAE	R^2
SVM	20.01	0.610		SVM	17.542	0.619
RF	18.112	0.709		RF	14.230	0.701
XGB	18.703	0.685		XGB	15.816	0.683

Arguably, the RF was the best of them, but it seems that the results are not very satisfactory. It is obvious that these algorithms do not take into account the time factor to make predictions, we can see that after adding the time of day and the season to the predictive variables, the results were improved. As we can see in the right Table 1.

When applying the LSTM model the results were so improved which is obvious in Table 2, and we did notice that augmenting the size of the window of the prediction improves the results. As we can see that the LSTM gives outstanding results in terms of predicting the electricity prices of the test set.

Table 2. LSTM results.

Model	Window length	MAE	R^2
LSTM	120	11.410	0.880
	240	9.720	0.899
	720	7.007	0.938

The results of LSTM compared to ML algorithms are impressive, we can notice the high efficiency of LSTM predictions compared to the real electricity price in the Fig. 8.

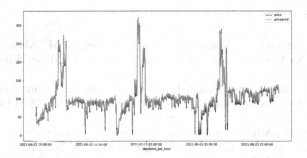

Fig. 8. The Actual price and the LSTM predicted values.

Table 3. Comparison between the two approaches.

ML approach	Time series approach
Easy to implement	Requires additional processing including a study of the time series characteristics, differentiation, and construction of the data set, including conversion of the data into a supervised problem
The prediction is made at a time t	The ability to predict electricity prices over a time interval $[t, t + k]$, or what is called multi-step forecasting
Does not take into account the temporal aspect, and therefore does not understand the sequential relationship between data	Learns long-term temporal dependencies and solves the problem of learning long sequences

5   Conclusion

In this paper, we tackled a crucial problem for making Net zero energy buildings that concerns electricity price forecasting. To do so, we proposed data-driven solutions using machine and deep learning techniques. This piece of work is a part of the EU project IMPROVEMENT[3] – is an international project co-financed in 2019 by the European Regional Development Fund (ERDF) through the Interreg Sudoe Cooperation Programme[4]. In the Machine Learning approach solutions, three methods were applied: SVR, Random Forest, and XGB. The random forest offers good results with the lowest MAE value. Concerning the deep learning solution, the LSTM was chosen. The obtained results were remarkable with minimization of more than 50% of the MAE value obtained by the machine learning algorithms.

Currently, we are exploring federated deep learning to simultaneously predict energy consumption and its price

References

1. Amber, K., Ahmad, R., Aslam, M., Kousar, A., Usman, M., Khan, M.: Intelligent techniques for forecasting electricity consumption of buildings. Energy **157**, 886–893 (2018)
2. Anduaga, J., Boyra, M., Cobelo, I., García, E., Gil, A.: La microrred, una alternativa de futuro para un suministro energético integral. TECNALIA, Corporacion Tecnológica (2008)
3. Atef, S., Eltawil, A.B.: A comparative study using deep learning and support vector regression for electricity price forecasting in smart grids. In: IEEE 6th International Conference on Industrial Engineering and Applications (ICIEA). IEEE (2019)
4. Awad, M., Khanna, R.: Support vector regression. In: Efficient Learning Machines, pp. 67–80. Springer (2015). https://doi.org/10.1007/978-1-4302-5990-9
5. Bellatreche, L., Garcia, F., Pham, D.N., Jiménez, P.Q.: SONDER: a data-driven methodology for designing net-zero energy public buildings. In: 22nd International Conference on Big Data Analytics and Knowledge Discovery (DaWaK), pp. 48–59 (2020)
6. Bellatreche, L., Simonet, A., Simonet, M.: Vertical fragmentation in distributed object database systems with complex attributes and methods. In: Seventh International Workshop on Database and Expert Systems Applications, DEXA, pp. 15–21 (1996)
7. Bourhnane, S., Abid, M.R., Lghoul, R., Zine-Dine, K., Elkamoun, N., Benhaddou, D.: Machine learning for energy consumption prediction and scheduling in smart buildings. SN Appl. Sci. **2** (2020). https://doi.org/10.1007/s42452-020-2024-9
8. Breiman, L.: Random forests. Mach. Learn. **45**(1), 5–32 (2001)
9. Chen, T., Guestrin, C.: XGBoost: a scalable tree boosting system. In: Proceedings of the 22nd ACM SIGKDD International Conference on Knowledge Discovery and Data Mining, pp. 785–794 (2016)
10. Esling, P., Agon, C.: Time-series data mining. ACM Comput. Surv. (CSUR) **45**(1), 1–34 (2012)
11. Fata, E., Kadota, I., Schneider, I.: Comparison of classical and nonlinear models for short-term electricity price prediction. arXiv preprint arXiv:1805.05431 (2018)

---

[3] Integration of Combined Cooling, Heating and Power Microgrids in Zero-Energy Public Buildings Under High Power Quality and Continuity of Service Requirements.
[4] https://www.interreg-sudoe.eu/.

12. Garouani, M., Hamlich, M., Ahmad, A., Bouneffa, M., Bourguin, G., Lewandowski, A.: Toward an automatic assistance framework for the selection and configuration of machine learning based data analytics solutions in industry 4.0. In: International Conference On Big Data and Internet of Things, pp. 3–15. Springer (2022). https://doi.org/10.1007/978-3-031-07969-6_1

13. Hamlich, M., Khantach, A.E., Belbounaguia, N.: Machine learning methods against false data injection in smart grid. Int. J. Reason.-Based Intell. Syst. **12**(1), 51–59 (2020)

14. Hernandez, L., et al.: A survey on electric power demand forecasting: future trends in smart grids, microgrids and smart buildings. IEEE Commun. Surv. Tutorials **16**(3), 1460–1495 (2014)

15. Lahouar, A., Slama, J.B.H.: Day-ahead load forecast using random forest and expert input selection. Energy Convers. Manage. **103**, 1040–1051 (2015)

16. Lee, C.M., Ko, C.N.: Short-term load forecasting using lifting scheme and Arima models. Expert Syst. Appl. **38**(5), 5902–5911 (2011)

17. Manaswi, N.K.: RNN and LSTM. In: Deep Learning with Applications Using Python, pp. 115–126. Springer (2018). https://doi.org/10.1007/978-1-4842-3516-4_9

18. Morvaj, B., Lugaric, L., Krajcar, S.: Demonstrating smart buildings and smart grid features in a smart energy city. In: 3rd International Youth Conference on Energetics (IYCE), pp. 1–8 (2011)

19. Mulder, M., Scholtens, B.: The impact of renewable energy on electricity prices in the Netherlands. Renew. Energy **57**, 94–100 (2013)

20. Recast, E.: Directive 2010/31/eu of the European Parliament and of the Council of 19 May 2010 on the Energy Performance of Buildings (recast). Official Journal of the European Union (2010)

21. Rifkin, J.: The third industrial revolution: how lateral power is transforming energy, the economy, and the world. Macmillan (2011)

22. Scholz, C., Lehna, M., Brauns, K., Baier, A.: Towards the prediction of electricity prices at the intraday market using shallow and deep-learning methods. In: Workshop on Mining Data for Financial Applications. Springer (2020). https://doi.org/10.1007/978-3-030-66981-2_9

23. Weron, R.: Electricity price forecasting: A review of the state-of-the-art with a look into the future. Int. J. Forecast. **30**(4), 1030–1081 (2014)

Determination of the Probability of Factors Occurrence Impacting Warehouse Planning by Bayesian Networks

Abdelilah Kerouich, Azmani Monir, Mouna Atik El Fetouh, and Abdellah Azmani[✉]

Intelligente Automation Laboratory, Faculty of Sciences and Technique of Tangier, Abdelmalek ESSAADI University Tetouan, Tétouan, Morocco
abdelilah.kerouich@etu.uae.ac.ma, {m.azmani,a.azmani}@uae.ac.ma, mouna.ftouh@gmail.com

Abstract. Good warehouse governance is considered one of the main components of supply chain management (SCM) and its profitability. To do this successfully, it is crucial to frame and study the major issues that affect the efficiency of a warehouse. In this context, this article aims to propose an approach which allows to identify the factors which can jeopardize the planning of a warehouse's activities, thus affecting its proper functioning. This approach is based on a causality graph highlighting the relationships between the factors that can disrupt the operations carried out within a warehouse. The exploitation of such a graph is done by applying Bayesian networks in order to calculate the probability of occurrence of problems or factors impacting the planning and the smooth running of the activities of a warehouse.

Keywords: Warehouse planning · Disruptive factors · Bayesian Networks

1 Introduction

The architecture of the warehouse and the nature of the activity carried out within its entities (reception, unloading, storage and preparation of orders, packaging and shipping of goods [2], influence the duration and the pre-established planning for freight processing. This is all the more so since several disturbances can occur within these units, thus contributing to the malfunction of the freight processing system and non-compliance with pre-established schedules. As a result, this prolongs the time a commodity spends in the warehouse and increases the risk factor. To optimize the transit time of a product in a warehouse, it is necessary to identify the problems encountered by the activities of the warehouse and to anticipate them like the approach presented here. This allows to calculate the probability of occurrence of problems or factors impacting warehouse planning by using the principle of Bayesian networks.

This paper is structured as follows. The first section exposes the various potential risks that can influence the planning of a warehouse. Subsequently, the article presents and explains the causal graph which highlights the nodes at the origin of potential

M. Hamlich et al. (Eds.): SADASC 2022, CCIS 1677, pp. 212–221, 2022.
https://doi.org/10.1007/978-3-031-20490-6_17

disturbances, as well as the nodes, called intermediate or output, which characterize the principle of cause and effect. The article presents how to exploit this graph by applying the principle of conditional probabilities of a Bayesian network. Thereafter, a section focuses on the generation of conditional probabilities based on a subjective method which relies on an analysis resulting from the indications expressed by logistics experts through a short questionnaire. The last section shows an example to get an idea of the result obtained and presents various situations that indicate the probability of a disturbance according to a combination of its causes in order to draw the consequences to program preventive actions.

2 Related Work

In general, operations planning in supply chains has been studied widely, and has attracted the interest of several researchers.

The distributed planning of logistic chains in a context of strong disruption was studied [10], where the management of the risks in relation to the sector of electronics and telecommunication was examined, by the identification, the modeling and the simulation of various business processes relating to the planning, which results in the proposal of an approach of assistance to the cooperation and in the use of the theory of the plays to evaluate the risks and to formalize the interactions between the actors who intervene at the time of the choice of the policies of cooperation. Techniques from operations research, have been widely used in the planning context. The planning and scheduling problem in a production environment has been studied by [11], where two approaches related to the context of constraint programming have been proposed with the aim of solving the planning and scheduling problem of lumber planing operations. The solution of a planning problem in a multi-echelon distribution network was proposed by [12], through the modeling of the concerned problem by a mixed linear program, while the solution was exercised by a constructive and another randomized reactive heuristic.

The approach, initiated through this first article, presents a predictive and generic vision, based on one of the AI methods, which aims to prevent various risks that can alter the proper functioning of a warehouse.

3 Issue

The course of a warehouse's activities frequently faces unforeseen events that seriously disrupt its space-time planning. This section focuses primarily on factors that can seriously impact the proper functioning of a warehouse.

3.1 Diagram of Planning Disruption

The components of the warehouse mainly are: *goods, staff, equipment, packaging and warehouse management information system* [6] are linked to each other. Thus, many problems occur when these constituents interact with each other, leading to direct and indirect problems that prevent smooth operation of goods handling operations in the warehouse. Consequently, that influences the space-time aspect, which results in a disturbance of the goods processing planning, as represented (see Fig. 1). This disruption is reflected in: delayed unloading, unloading cancelled, delayed loading, loading cancelled, internal and external incidents.

As shown in Fig. 1, warehouse planning can be disrupted by several factors:

- Order not ready: problem related to the goods (lost [1], stolen [2], non-conforming), problem in relation to handling equipment/Staff, problem in relation to packaging supplies [3].
- Unprepared delivery: problem related to handling material/Staff [8], problem with the order registration system.
- Door/vehicle blockage: problem caused by lack of regular maintenance.
- Unprepared delivery: delay in the release of goods (orders), delayed departure of the vehicle concerned, late arrival of the order to the customer.
- Door blocking: can affect the time (delay) of loading/unloading, may impact delivery time (delay).

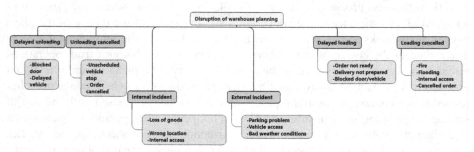

Fig. 1. Representative diagram of planning disruption

Indeed, each of the other factors influences the proper functioning of the other entities. Hence the interest in developing and applying simulation models for each freight handling operation (loading, unloading, etc.), which leads to minimizing the time involved [5].

4   Determination of Probability Factors Affecting a Warehouse Planning Using Bayesian Networks

This section contains an application of Bayesian approach in order to evaluate factors impacting a warehouse planning.

4.1   Principle of Bayesian Networks

To manage the disturbance of a planned process, the use of artificial intelligence is desired, like in our case Bayesian networks for its ability to model probabilistic events with a causal intuitive representation. A Bayesian network is a graphical probabilistic model that combines artificial intelligence with statistics to represent information that is uncertain and reason from data that is incomplete [7]. A Bayesian network consists of two components [4]: A causal acyclic oriented graph, (see Fig. 2), whose nodes are variable and whose arcs characterize the dependency relations between these variables. It is a form of qualitative representation of knowledge. The probability entity contains three branches [9], conditional probability, total probability and static independence.

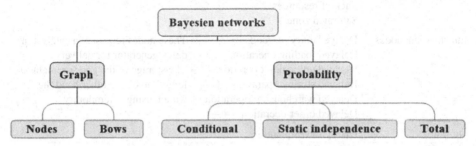

Fig. 2. Bayesian network components

The conditional probability is the degree of occurrence of an event knowing the probability of the second event that corresponds to it, and the total probability, each event of the set of possible events corresponds to a single degree of occurrence, on the other hand the static independence is the appearance of an event is dependent or independent to another event.

4.2 The Developed Bayesian Network

Figure 3 represents the developed Bayesian network modeling the amplifiers of the planning disturbance of a warehouse.

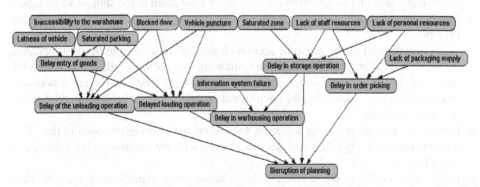

Fig. 3. Bayesian network modeling the amplifiers of the planning disturbance

Table 1, shows the nodes of this graph as Parent nodes, Intermediate nodes and Output node. This late indicates de probability of the planning disruption.

Table 1. Representation of parent and intermediate nodes

	Nodes	Description
Parent nodes	Inaccessibility to the warehouse Vehicle arrived late Parking saturated Blocked door Vehicle puncture Lack of resources Saturated zone	These nodes represent an exciter of planning disruption
Intermediate nodes	Delayed entry of goods Delayed loading operation Delayed unloading operation Delayed storing operation Delayed warehousing operation Delayed order operation	These nodes represent a catalyst or delay generator for delivery The storage of the goods remains a long time on the other hand the warehousing is temporary
Output	Disruption of planning	

4.3 Conditional Probability Generation

As mentioned in the previous section, Bayesian networks are used to represent the knowledge of a system through the simulation of its behavior, this is done through data analysis. It is therefore necessary to have data to feed our Bayesian network. These data or more generally, the conditional probabilities can be generated from two different methods:

- Objective method: By using a database for automatic learning of probabilities. The latter requires a large data size, and that the database contains exactly the parameters considered in our case study. As a result, we did not find a database that was complete enough and that met these criteria. Therefore, we returned to the subjective methods.
- Subjective methods: by extracting knowledge from experts in the field of warehouse logistics.

  As mentioned in the previous section, Bayesian networks are used to represent the knowledge of a system through the simulation of its behavior, this is done through data analysis. It is therefore necessary to have data to feed our Bayesian network. These data or more generally, the conditional probabilities can be generated from two different methods:

- Objective method: By using a dataset for automatic learning of probabilities. This dataset requires a large data size and must match with the parameters considered in a study case.
- Subjective methods: By extracting knowledge from experts in a specific field (warehouse logistics for example).

The work presented in this paper use a subjective method, this is explained by the impossibility of finding a sufficiently relevant dataset for the analysis of the planning

First name: ....   Date: DD/MM/YYYY
Last name: ....   Number of years of experience: ....
Function: □ warehouseman □ handler □ Other: ......   Society name: ....

The degree of delay in goods entry depends on lateness of vehicle, inaccessibility to the warehouse and the degree of parking saturation. Given that each variable can have two possible states "Absent" and "Present", please, thick the interval of probability occurrence of delay in goods entry according to your knowledge.

Lateness of vehicle	Inaccessibility to the warehouse	Parking saturation	Presence degree of delay in goods entry
Absent	Present	Present	□ [1-3] □ [4-6] □ [7-9]
Absent	Present	Absent	□ [1-3] □ [4-6] □ [7-9]
Absent	Absent	Present	□ [1-3] □ [4-6] □ [7-9]
Absent	Absent	Absent	□ [1-3] □ [4-6] □ [7-9]
Present	Present	Present	□ [1-3] □ [4-6] □ [7-9]
Present	Present	Absent	□ [1-3] □ [4-6] □ [7-9]
Present	Absent	Present	□ [1-3] □ [4-6] □ [7-9]
Present	Absent	Absent	□ [1-3] □ [4-6] □ [7-9]

Fig. 4. Example of questionnaire

disturbance of a warehouse. In order to consolidate the proposed work, a questionnaire was sent to 50 experts operating in the field of logistics (see Fig. 4). This questionnaire concerns a qualitative classification of the absence or presence of the various problems directly impacting the smooth running of warehouse schedules. Decimal scales from 1 to 9 are used in order to simplify the knowledge acquisition from the experts, which indicate the following meaning:

- [1–3] → as a low probability.
- [4–6] → as a moderate probability.
- [7–9] → as a high probability.

An analysis of the answers obtained, 40/50, made it possible to initialize the graph in order to apply the principle of the Bayesian network by determining the conditional probabilities for the intermediate nodes of the elaborate network (see Fig. 3).

5   Implementation and Results

According to the graph presented in Fig. 3, the entries have been classified into three groups, as shown in Table 4.

Table 5 shows the results obtained for the situations considered for each unit, such that we have two possible cases:

- Either the problem related to the unit is present, indicated by P, having as probabilities: for Present state 0.98 (98%) and for Absent state 0.02 (2%).
- Either the problem related to the unit is absent, indicated by A, having as probabilities: for Absent state 0.98 (98%) and for Present state 0.02 (2%).

Table 2. Correspondence between qualitative intervals and probability percentage

Response interval for a node probability	Associated percentage
[1–3]	20%
[3–6]	50%
[7–9]	80%

Note that the sum of Absent and Present probabilities for each case must be equal to 1. In other words, for "Delay in goods entry" node, if the chosen interval is [1–3] for Presence degree of delay in goods entry, automatically [7–9] interval is assigned to Absence degree of delay in goods entry. Furthermore, for [4–6] chosen interval for Absent probability, automatically [4–6] interval will be assigned for Present probability. The final retained response (interval) for each node consists of the interval which was the most selected. Percentage for nodes probability is generated by converting, according to responses obtained from the aforementioned questionnaire, ticked interval as shown in Table 2. The obtained results by this questionnaire are presented in Table 3 for "Delayed entry goods" as an example. Other probabilities for the rest of intermediate and final nodes of our network are obtained by the same manner.

Table 3. Conditional probabilities for 'Delay in goods entry' node

Inaccessibility to the warehouse	Lateness of vehicle	Parking saturation	Delay in goods entry	
			Absent	Present
Absent	Absent	Absent	80%	20%
Absent	Absent	Present	80%	20%
Absent	Present	Absent	80%	20%
Absent	Present	Present	50%	50%
Present	Absent	Absent	50%	50%
Present	Absent	Present	80%	20%
Present	Present	Absent	20%	80%
Present	Present	Present	20%	80%

Table 4. Classification of entries

Space	Material resources	Personal resources
Saturated zone Saturated parking Inaccessibility to the warehouse	Blocked door Lateness of vehicle Vehicle puncture Lack of equipment Information system failure Lack of packaging supply	Lack of staff resources

Table 5. Simulation result of the studied scenario

Space	Material resources	Personal resources	Disruption	
			A	P
A	A	A	0.807	0.193
A	A	P	0.564	0.436
A	P	A	0.392	**0.608**
A	P	P	0.247	**0.753**
P	A	A	0.728	0.272
P	A	P	0.513	0.487
P	P	A	0.218	**0.782**
P	P	P	0.156	**0.844**

From the analysis of the obtained results, it can be deduced that the existence of the planning disturbance is higher when faced with:

- Situation 1: Concerns the presence of the disruption only at the level of Material Resources This situation presents a disruption of the planning of 60%,
- Situation 2: Concerns the presence of disruption in Material Resources and Personal Resources This situation presents a disruption in planning of 75%,
- Situation 3: Concerns the presence of a disturbance in the Material Resources and Space class this situation presents a disturbance in planning of 78%,
- Situation 4: Concerns the presence of the disturbance at the level of the three classes this situation presents a disturbance of the planning of 84%.

  According to the conducted analysis, the most dominant factor in terms of impact on disturbance is the material resources, which involves:
- Blocked door, lateness and puncture of vehicle.
- Lack of equipment.

To Sum up, according to the above analysis, it is necessary to proceed to the implementation of a system of regular or periodic maintenance in order to avoid and eradicate to the maximum these types of unforeseen breakdown. In fact, this is with respect to the main objective of this research, which is the exclusion of the disruption of the planning in order to optimize the time of treatment and passage of goods by the warehouse.

6 Conclusion and Outlook

This article presents the different disturbances that can influence the proper functioning of a warehouse and determines their probability of occurrence through a cause and effect graph. The presented approach uses a Bayesian network to determine such a probability which makes it possible to prevent any possible risk. The perspectives of the work presented here are of several kinds. Firstly, a broadening of the parameters making it possible to explain the causes of the initial nodes presented in Fig. 3, as well as an organization by layers forming a cascading causal graph. As a second track, the implementation of a rule-based system to accentuate the diagnosis and help decision-making. Finally, the consolidation of the approach by a learning algorithm that can help predict the initial causes and determine their value dynamically in order to apply an objective approach.

Acknowledgments. This research is supported by the Ministry of Higher Education, Scientific Research and Innovation, the Digital Development Agency (DDA) and the National Center for Scientific and Technical Research (CNRST) of Morocco (Smart DLSP Project - AL KHAWARIZMI IA-PROGRAM).

References

1. Atikelftouh, M.: Modeling of a smart digital ecosystem for optimized and collaborative management of urban freight transport, aggregating several artificial intelligence methods and techniques for decision support. Faculty of Science and Technology of Tangier, Abdelmalek ESSAADI University-Tetouan Morocco, PhD (2020)
2. Bakkali, H.: Modeling of a decision support tool for improving profitability in warehouses and logistics platforms. Faculty of Science and Technology of Tangier, Abdelmalek ESSAADI University-Tetouan Morocco, PhD (2016)
3. Cherrett, T., Allen, J., McLeod, F., Maynard, S., Hickford, A., Browne, M.: Understanding urban freight activity: key issues for freight planning. J. Transp. Geogr. **24**, 22–32 (2012). https://doi.org/10.1016/j.jtrangeo.2012.05.008
4. Choi, A., Zheng, L., Darwiche, A., Mengshoel, O.J.: A tutorial on Bayesian networks for system health management. Mach. Learn. Know. Discov. Eng. Syst. Health Manag. **10**, 1–29 (2011)
5. Lee, C., Huang, H.C., Liu, B., Xu, Z.: Development of timed Colour Petri net simulation models for air cargo terminal operations. Comput. Indus. Eng. **51**(1), 102–110 (2006). https://doi.org/10.1016/j.cie.2006.07.002
6. Primor, Y., Fender, M.: LOGISTIQUE—production—distribution—soutien, 5th edn. DUNOD, France (2008)
7. Starr, C., & Shi, P. (2004). An Introduction to Bayesian Belief Networks and their Applications to Land Operations, Vol. 27. Defence Science and Technology Organisation, Victoria
8. Vieira, J.G.V., Fransoo, J.C., Carvalho, C.D.: Freight distribution in megacities: Perspectives of shippers, logistics service providers and carriers. J. Transp. Geogr. **46**, 46–54 (2015). https://doi.org/10.1016/j.jtrangeo.2015.05.007
9. Méléard Sylvie Probabilités—Concepts fondamentaux [En ligne]//Techniques de l'ingénieur—10 Avril 2001—2014. http://www.techniques-ingenieur.fr/base-documenta ire/sciences-fondamentales-th8/probabilites-et-statistique-42101210/probabilites-af166/
10. Mahmoudi, J. Simulation and risk management in distributed planning of supply chains: application to the electronics and telecommunications sector. Phd, National Higher School Of Aeronautics And Space

11. Moisan, T. Disruption minimization and parallelization for planning and scheduling. Phd, LAVAL University Quebec, Canada
12. Kand, S. Study and resolution of planning problems in multi-echelon logistics networks. Phd University of Technology of Troyes

Green Energy, Computing and Technologies 2

Smart Grid Production Cost Optimization by Bellman Algorithm

Youness Atifi$^{(\boxtimes)}$, Abdelhadi Raihani , and Mohammed Kissaoui

Electrical Engineering and Intelligent Systems Laboratory (EEIS), ENSET Mohammedia,
Hassan II University of Casablanca, Casablanca, Morocco
atifi.youness@gmail.com

Abstract. This study focuses on the application of the Bellman algorithm, one of the algorithms of dynamic programming for energy management in a microgrid with five distributed energy sources.

The management strategy of the microgrid is based on long-term planning. The latter requires that each of the distributed sources follow an optimal active power profile established the day before for the next day (D-1). Thus, the optimization strategy proposed in this study belongs to the deterministic optimization strategies, whose objective is to find the optimal control of power flows in the multi-sources micro grid. The optimal control means how to distribute the power flows among the different components of the microgrid in order to ensure the balance between production to demand with the lowest cost. The performance of dynamic programming is relative to the refinement of the discretization of the planning trajectory and reference signals. Therefore, the quality of the optimum found is sufficiently guaranteed at the expense of a consequent demand on computing and memory capacity.

The aim of this study is to establish a management by the application of the Bellman algorithm (dynamic programming) and to compare it with the strategy of the rules-based management to open later on other meta-heuristic techniques such as the genetic algorithm. The obtained results showed that the implementation of the proposed energy management strategy resulted in a 40% saving on the electricity bill.

Keywords: Optimization · Smart grid · Genetic algorithm · Bellman · Dynamic programming · Python · Cost

Nomenclature and Abbreviations

T	Planning trajectory (24h).
t	The Hourly Step (1 h).
Cgrid	The electricity purchase tariff (consumption bands) in €/Kwh.
Creseau	The cost of electricity in €/hour.
Pinjct	The power injected into the network in KW.
Pbatmax	Maximum power that can be exchanged by batteries in charge/discharge in W.
Cgridi	The injection rate (injection tranches) in €/Kwh.

© The Author(s), under exclusive license to Springer Nature Switzerland AG 2022
M. Hamlich et al. (Eds.): SADASC 2022, CCIS 1677, pp. 225–234, 2022.
https://doi.org/10.1007/978-3-031-20490-6_18

SOC	State of charge of batteries in %.
SOH	Battery health status in %.
ΔSOC	Change in battery state of charge in %.
SOCmin, SOCmax	Minimum and maximum stop of state of load in %.
SOHmin	Minimum battery health limit in %.
$\Delta SOCmax$	Maximum limit of the variation of the state of charge in %.
Cess	Operating cost of batteries (cost of wear) in €/hour.
Cinv	Investment cost of batteries in €/kWh.
η	Efficiency of the micro-gas turbine in %.
Ptgn	Rated active power of the micro-gas turbine in kW.
Ptg	Active power exchanged by the micro-gas turbine in kW.
Mg	Mass of natural gas consumed by the micro-gas turbine in kg.
MNOx, MCO, MC02	Mass of gases emitted by the micro-turbine: NOX, CO and C02 in g.
MC02eq	Mass of C02 emissions equivalent in kg.
Cexptg	Cost of production of active power by the micro-gas turbine (Fuel cost) in €/hour.
CC02eq	Environmental sustainability due to C02 emissions equivalent in €/hour.
CON/OFF	Penalty for stopping/running the micro-gas turbine in €/hour.
Pgrid	Main network power in W.

1 Introduction

All over the world, electricity consumption is growing very strongly. It seems that, under the effect of economic growth on the one hand, and the increase in electricity consumption per capita on the other hand, whatever the scenarios envisaged. We talk about various technical solutions to keep this rhythm of life, like the use and development of renewable energies.

In its new structure, the electrical installation of the building corresponds to a residential micro-grid, composed of a set of generators based on renewable energies accompanied by support systems connected to the grid at a single point of connection to promote injection. The management problem associated with this type of system is based on the monitoring of the load and the economic optimization of energy flows. In the world, this concept of a positive energy building is still at an embryonic stage. To face the challenges created by these new structures, several changes must be considered on the classic composition of a distribution network. The researchers and industrialists involved in this project are led to imagine innovative intelligent solutions based on information and communication, because conventional solutions and especially at the level of energy management have shown many limits in terms of the reliability and flexibility of the network and in terms of energy bill and environmental, among the solutions envisaged: the computerization of energy management, this application ensures an optimal distribution of the required powers of each source connected to the smart grid. This generates savings (optimization of the energy bill) while complying with regulatory and environmental requirements [1–5].

In this study we propose a deterministic optimization strategy whose objective is to find the optimal control of power flows in a multi-source microgrid, and which contains renewable energy sources (a wind turbine and a photovoltaic system), this type of management is already addressed by researchers such as [6], the novelty in this work is that we have increased the number of renewable sources.

The paper is organized as follows: energy management strategies in a microgrid are described in Sect. 2; the Microgrid cost model is developed in Sect. 3; The application of the optimization strategy is analyzed in Sect. 4; Results and comparisons are checked in Sect. 5.

2 Energy Management Strategies in a Microgrid

Many studies have contributed to defining how to manage or control energy in a network integrating distributed generation sources with a storage system. Optimization algorithms consist of finding the right combination of the input values of a function that minimizes or maximizes its output value under constraints. Indeed, the use of an optimization algorithm does not necessarily mean finding the most suitable solution to a specific problem, but this solution must also be feasible and must meet the characteristics of the problem.

According to [1, 7, 8] and other researchers, energy management strategies can be summarized into four strategies: (a) Rules-based strategies are defined in advance based on expertise or knowledge of the specificities of the system components. These strategies are simple to implement, but they do not guarantee the best degree of the solution optimality [1, 7]. (b) Strategies based on deterministic optimization methods: that make a system evolve to minimize (or maximize) a performance criterion. Various optimization techniques are based on this principle such as optimal control, dynamic programming, and linear programming. Two categories are possible: offline optimization and real-time optimization [8]. (c) Strategies based on stochastic optimization methods such as machine learning (ML): The ML offers the ability to learn to achieve the optimization goal (maximization /minimization of a criterion) without being explicitly programmed with training cycles [1, 7, 8]. (d) Strategies based on hybrid optimization techniques combining the strategies mentioned above [1].

The microgrid proposed in this study is a small-scale low-voltage urban network, composed of five distributed energy sources, namely photovoltaic (PV) generator and a wind turbine as sources of renewable generation, an electrochemical battery bank as an energy storage system (ESS), and finally, a micro-natural gas turbine (Fig. 1).

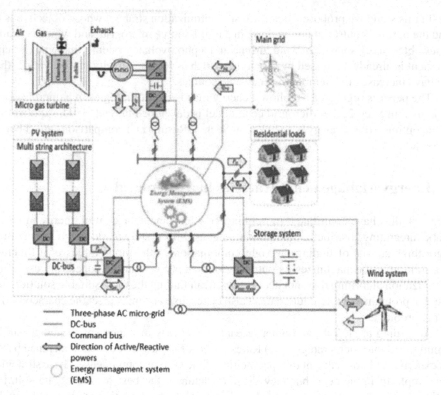

Fig. 1. Architecture of the micro smart grid

3 Microgrid Cost Model

3.1 Cost of the Grid

The cost of electricity corresponds to the price of active energy drawn from the grid (in €/kWh). This price generally varies according to the hours of consumption [9]. In this management work, we consider a pricing in two hourly shifts: peak hours (0.18 €/kWh between 11pm and 5am) / off-peak hours (0.09 €/kWh between 6am and 10pm) [9]. Thus, the purchase cost (C_p in €/hour) for a Δt time slot will be:

$$C_p = P_{grid}(t) \times C_{grid} \times \Delta t - P_{inj}(t) \times C_{inj} \times \Delta t \tag{1}$$

where $P_{grid}(t)$ is the instantaneous power drawn from the main grid, C_{grid} is the electricity purchase tariff, however $P_{inj}(t)$ is the instantaneous power injected into the grid with C_{inj} and the electricity sale tariff.

3.2 Cost of the PV and Wind System

The energies produced by the PV and Wind turbine system are considered at no cost, the surplus production will be purchased by the distribution network according to the selling tariff [9, 10]. In this work our PV system is composed of 340 panels, each with a peak power of 240 W, the wind turbine at a nominal power of 10 KW.

3.3 Cost of Micro-gas Turbine

In this work we will use a micro-gas turbine as an auxiliary source. With a nominal power: Ptgn = 30 Kw, the operating cost of the micro-gas turbine is perhaps divided into three costs.

3.3.1 Cost of Production

$$\text{Cexptg}(t) = \text{Ctg} * \frac{\text{Ptg}(t) * dt}{\eta(t) * dg} \tag{2}$$

where $\text{Ptg}(t)$ is the instantaneous power drawn from the micro gas turbine, $\text{Ctg} = 0.55$ €/Kg is the cost of one kilogram of gas, however η is the efficiency of the gas turbine and dg is energy density $dg = 13.5$ Kwh/kg [11].

3.3.2 Cost of Start and Stop

In this management work, the stop/run penalties applied are equivalent to 5 minutes of operation under full load (Ptgn = 30 Kw) during start-up and 2.5 minutes of operation under full load in case of shutdown [11].

$$C_{ON} = \frac{1}{12} \times C_{tg} \frac{Ptgn}{\eta n * dg} \tag{3}$$

$$C_{OFF} = \frac{1}{24} \times C_{tg} \frac{Ptgn}{\eta n * dg} \tag{4}$$

3.3.3 Cost of CO2 Emissions

The estimation of greenhouse gas emissions is limited to the most polluting and toxic gases, namely: NOx, CO and CO2 gas [11].

$$C_{CO2eq}(t) = M_{CO2eq}(t) \times C_{p-CO2} \tag{5}$$

where $M_{CO2eq}(t)$ is the instantaneous mass of CO2 emissions equivalent in kg and C_{p_CO2} represents the environmental penalty price.

3.4 Cost of Storage System

In this work we tried to develop a model of the cost of energy provided by the storage system that considers the state of health of the battery and the cost of investment [12].

$$\text{Cess(t)} = \frac{\text{Cinvx}\Delta\text{SOH(t)}}{1 - \text{SOHmin}} \tag{6}$$

where $\Delta\text{SOH(t)}$ is the instantaneous variation of the state of health of the battery and Cinvisthecostofinvestment, SOHmin represent the Minimum batterie health limit in %. Pbatmax $= 100\text{KW}$.

3.4.1 Constraints of Storage System
$$\Delta\text{SOC}_{\text{max}} = 30\%\text{SOC}_{\text{min}} = 20\text{SOC}_{\text{max}} = 90\%\text{SOH}_{\text{min}} = 65\%$$

3.5 Objective Function

The objective function developed in this work is to find a 24-hours schedule with an hourly step of one hour, planning means the best combination between the different sources of production, and which corresponds to the lowest production cost.

$$\min \text{f(cost)} = \sum_{t=1}^{T} \left\{ \begin{array}{l} \left[(\textbf{Pgrid(t)} \times \textbf{dt}) \times \textbf{Cgrid(t)}\right] - \left[(\textbf{Pinjct(t)} \times \textbf{dt}) \times \textbf{Cgridi(t)}\right] + \\ \left[(\textbf{Cexptg(t)} + \textbf{A(t).Con} + \textbf{B(t).Coff} + \textbf{Mco2eq(t)} \times \textbf{Cp}_{\textbf{co2}})\right] + \textbf{Cess(t)} \end{array} \right\}$$

With: A(t) and B(t): Boolean values indicating the start/stop state of the turbine.

4 Application of the Optimization Strategy

4.1 Bellman Algorithm

The Bellman algorithm is an algorithm that calculates the shortest paths from a given source vertex in a weighted oriented graph, it contains four phases as described in the following pseudo code:

Data: A weighted oriented graph G = (S, A, C) and an initial vertex s $\in$S.
Result: the shortest path of s to the other vertices of G.
    // d(s),......, d(n): the shortest path of s to any other vertex of G, Here the vertices represent the hourly steps and the arcs A represent the combinations, the weighting C of the arcs represents the cost.

Result: the shortest path of s to the other vertices of G.

// d(s), ..., d(n): the shortest path of s to any other vertex of G, Here the vertices represent the hourly steps and the arcs A represent the combinations, the weighting C of the arcs represents the cost.

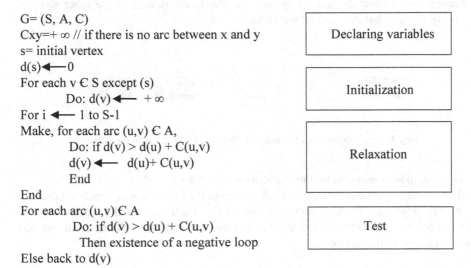

G= (S, A, C)

Cxy=+ ∞ // if there is no arc between x and y

s= initial vertex

d(s)◄—0

For each v ∈ S except (s)

    Do: d(v)◄— + ∞

For i ◄— 1 to S-1

Make, for each arc (u,v) ∈ A,

    Do: if d(v) > d(u) + C(u,v)

    d(v)◄— d(u)+ C(u,v)

    End

End

For each arc (u,v) ∈ A

    Do: if d(v) > d(u) + C(u,v)

      Then existence of a negative loop

Else back to d(v)

Declaring variables

Initialization

Relaxation

Test

4.2 Adaptation of the Strategy

The manager must consider the equality type constraint: Production (t) = demand (t). The algorithm of the proposed management is explained in Fig. 2.

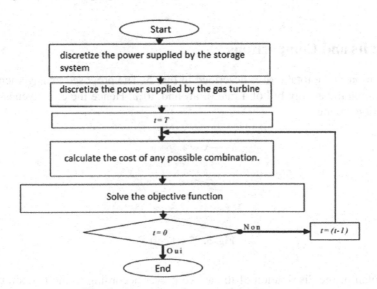

Fig. 2. Algorithm of proposed management

In each hour step a set of discrete states of the power provided by the micro-gas turbine and the storage system (See Fig. 3) will be processed by the manager, the manager and based on the objective function and on all the constraints, he will decide which iteration will be chosen. This trajectory corresponds not only to the active power levels exchanged by the gas turbine and the storage system but also to the powers of the other sources satisfying the load balance and all the constraints.

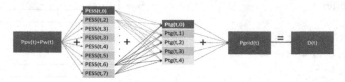

Fig. 3. Discretization of the micro turbine and storage systeme power

D(t): the power required by the loads in an hourly step.

The problem can be summarized by the graph of the Fig. 4, whose vertices represent the hourly steps, and the arcs represent the cost of each combination respecting the constraints, over a horizon of 24 hours the manager looks for the arcs (the combination) that correspond to the lowest cost.

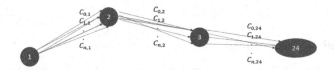

Fig. 4. Cost graph associated with possible combinations over the planning period

5   Results and Comparisons

The evolution of the total cost is described in Fig. 5. The proposed management offers a reduction in the energy bill of a rate of around 40%. Hence the effectiveness of this optimization strategy.

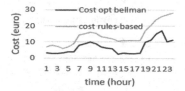

Fig. 5. Total cost

The plan of the distribution of the active power according to the two strategies is displayed on Fig. 6 and Fig. 7, the latter also shows you the respect of the constraints.

The proposed management allows an injection of the surplus power into the main grid on the contrary to the rules-based strategy.

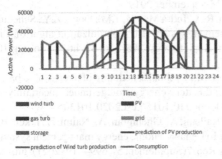 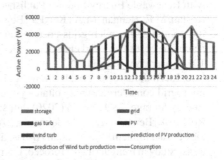

Fig. 6. Rules-based power management   **Fig. 7.** Bellman optimal power management

The choice of the bellman algorithm is justified by the quality of the optimum found which is sufficiently guaranteed with a reduced calculation time. While rules-based strategy or linear optimization strategies cannot guarantee a good optimum because of the linearization of a problem that is by default non-linear or because of the inflexibility of the strategy with unexpected changes.

Among the limitations of the bellman algorithm is that the quality of the optimum has a strong dependence on the number of discrete states and the discretization step, whose calculation time increases with the increase in the number of stretches.

In this work the consumption corresponds to a residential building, The hourly data of these two renewable sources is estimated from the weather forecast for the city of Rabat (23-05-2022).

As an indication the programming language with which we developed our algorithm is the Python language.

6   Conclusion

Where control and management in a distribution network is not based on good strategies result in an inefficient and unstable power supply to charges and entails high operating costs for consumers However, energy management in a micro grid requires an intelligent optimized controller to organize and manage the operation optimally and efficiently.

This study shows you the effectiveness of determinist optimization strategies compared to other strategies based on rules in a micro grid with five sources under different charging conditions.

The main objective of the optimized controller is to minimize the total cost of operation.

The aim is soon and in new research work to develop a controller based on stochastic optimization strategies such as the genetic algorithm.

We chose to treat the genetic algorithm in our next work because we want to make at the end a kind of comparison between heuristic and metaheuristic strategies, and we want to treat the advantages and limitations of this algorithm to open to other techniques.

References

1. García Vera, Y.E., Dufo-López, R., Bernal-Agustín, J.L.: Energy Management in Microgrids with Renewable Energy Sources Published: 13 September 2019
2. Roslan, M.F., Hannan, M.A., Ker, P.J., Begum, R.A., Indra Mahlia, T.M., Dong, Z.Y.: Scheduling controller for microgrids energy management system using optimization algorithm in achieving cost saving and emission reduction. Appl. Energy. **295**, 116883. https://doi.org/10.1016/j.apenergy.2021.116883
3. Luo, L., Abdulkareem, S.S., Rezvani, A., Reza, M.: Optimal scheduling of a renewable based microgrid considering photovoltaic system and battery energy storage under uncertainty. J. Energy Storage. **28**(January) (2020). https://doi.org/10.1016/j.est.2020.101306
4. Rochd, A., Benazzouz, A., Abdelmoula, I.A., Raihani, A., Ghennioui, A., Naimi, Z., Ikken, B.: Design and implementation of an AI-based & IoT-enabled home energy management system: a case study in Benguerir — Morocco. Energy Rep. **7**(Supplement 5), 699–719 (2021). https://doi.org/10.1016/j.egyr.2021.07.084
5. Raihani, A., Khalili, T., Rafik, M., Zaggaf, M.H., Bouattane, O.: Towards a real time energy management strategy for hybrid wind-PV power system based on hierarchical distribution of loads. Int. J. Adv. Comput. Sci. Appl. **10**(5) (2019). https://doi.org/10.14569/IJACSA.2019.0100549
6. Zahraoui, F., Eddine Chakir, H., Et-Taoussi, M., Ouadi, H. Smart grid cost optimization: comparing bellman and genetic algorithms. In: Proceedings of 2021 9th International Renewable and Sustainable Energy Conference, IRSEC 2021 (2021)
7. Castaings, A., Lhomme, W., Trigui, R., Bouscayrol, A.: Comparison of energy management strategies of a battery/supercapacitors system for electric vehicle under realtimeconstraints. Appl. Energy **163**, 190–200 (2016)
8. Hamidi, M., Raihani, A., Youssfi, M., Bouattane, O.: A new modular nanogrid energy management system based on multi-agent architecture. Int. J. Power Electron. Drive Syst. **13**(1), 178–190 (March 2022). https://doi.org/10.11591/ijpeds.v13.i1.pp178-190
9. Rigo-Mariani, R.: Méthodes De Conception Intégrée "Dimensionnement-Gestion" par Optimisation d'un Micro-Réseau avec Stockage. Thèse, Toulouse University, INP Toulouse (2014)
10. Jai Andaloussi, Z., Raihani, A., El Magri, A., Lajouad, R., El Fadili, A.: Novel nonlinear control and optimization strategies for hybrid renewable energy conversion system. Model. Simul. Eng. **2021**, Article ID 3519490, 20 pages (2021). https://doi.org/10.1155/2021/3519490
11. Kanchev, H.: Gestion des flux énergétiques dans un système hybride de sources d'énergierenouvelable: Optimisation de la planification opérationnelle et ajustement d'un micro réseau électrique urbain. Thèse, Ecole centrale de Lille, Université Lille Nord- deFrance (2014)
12. Watil, A., El Magri, A., Lajouad, R., Raihani, A., Giri, F.: Multi-mode control strategy for a stand-alone wind energy conversion system with battery energy storage. J. Energy Storage. **51**, 104481 (2022). https://doi.org/10.1016/j.est.2022.104481

Sliding Mode Control of Six-Switch Five-Level Active Neutral Point Clamped (6S-5L-ANPC)

Adnane El-Alami[1]($\boxtimes$), Mohamed Amine Kazi[1], Ibrahim Baraka[2],
Radouane Majdoul[1], and Abdelhafid AitElmahjoub[1]

[1] Complex Cyber-Physical Systems Laboratory, University Hassan II ENSAM Casablanca,
Casablanca, Morocco
adnane.elalami-etu@etu.univh2c.ma
[2] Advanced Sciences and Technologies Team, University of ABDELMALEK ESSAÄDI,
(ENSATe), Tetouan, Morocco
ibrahim.baraka@etu.uae.ac.ma

Abstract. Due to their numerous advantages, multilevel inverters are commonly employed in high and medium-voltage applications. Six-Switch Five-Level Active Neutral Point Clamped Inverter (6S-5L-ANPC) associated with LC filter can produce pure sinusoidal voltage, the proposed modulation can satisfy the regulation of the flying capacitor voltage, the behavior of the 6S-5L-ANPC inverter is validated through simulation. a Sliding Mode Controller based on voltage control is proposed which is suitable for multilevel power converters as they are inherently variable structure systems, this controller has the advantage of robustness in the presence of load or parametric variations. In addition, the use of a low-pass filter to decrease oscillation (chattering) around the sliding surface caused by rapid changes in current and voltage of the load is presented. The controller is tested under high reference change and in a strong perturbation of the output current. The validity of this strategy is demonstrated using simulation results.

Keywords: Six-Switch Five-Level Active Neutral Point Clamped Inverter (6S-5L-ANPC) · Flying Capacitor (FC) · Voltage balancing · Sliding Mode control

1   Introduction

For many years, the evolution of power electronics has been very important in a world where energy aspects have become an essential issue. The appearance of multilevel converters is one of the results of this evolution, they are used for medium and high voltage applications.

There are several topologies of multilevel inverters that are used in industry, two categories are currently listed. The first category groups the main inverters into three topologies: Cascade H-Bridge (CHB), Neutral-Point-Clamped (NPC) and Flying capacitor (FC), they are named classic topologies [1]. The second category of multilevel inverters includes the hybrid assemblies of the first category inverters these converters include the ANPC inverter which is an assembly between the FC and the NPC inverters [1].

M. Hamlich et al. (Eds.): SADASC 2022, CCIS 1677, pp. 235–244, 2022.
https://doi.org/10.1007/978-3-031-20490-6_19

The Cascade H-Bridge (CHB) is the first multilevel conversion structure to be discussed in the literature [1]. As a matter of fact, a multilevel voltage waveform can be generated at the output by cascading multiple 2-level H-bridge modules. However, because each module needs its own DC power source, only higher output voltage levels can be used [2].

The NPC-type multilevel inverters produce voltage levels from the neutral point voltage by utilizing clamping diodes. As voltage levels increase, more clamping diodes, active semiconductor switches, and DC-link capacitors are required. When too many clamping diodes are connected in series to block the higher voltage, the reverse recovery currents and conduction losses increase, which affects the switching losses of other devices. The DC-link voltage balancing issue with higher-level NPC inverters is another issue.

Capacitor Clamped Multilevel Inverter is another name for a flying capacitor multilevel inverter. Similar in structure to a diode clamped inverter, multilevel inverters use capacitors in place of the diodes (Fig. 1). The voltage levels in this situation are determined by the charging and discharging of the flying capacitors connected to the neutral point [3].

Active Neutral Point Clamped inverters (ANPC) Combining NPC and FC inverters, can produce a staircase output voltage waveform with the same number of switches and without the addition of additional clamping diodes. The ANPC structure replaces the clamp diodes of the NPC topology with active switches, and as the flying capacitor has more stages, the number of levels increases. As a result, neutral clamping switches can resolve voltage balance and the unequal sharing of losses between switching devices in NPC converters.

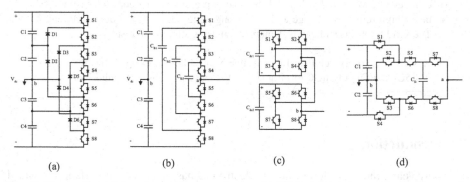

| (a) | (b) | (c) | (d) |

Fig. 1. Conventional 5-Level multilevel topologies, (a) NPC; (b) flying capacitors; (c) cascade H-bridge, (d) ANPC

5-level inverters Active Neutral Point Clamped (5L-ANPC) is one of the most popular topologies among five-level inverters. A Five-Level Active Neutral Point Clamped is proposed with a reduced number of components, which reduces the size, weight, and cost of the inverter. Since the output current and grid voltage are typically in phase for PV applications, several reactive current routes can be eliminated. Six-Switch Five-Level ANPC (6S-5L-ANPC) inverter topology is suggested as a result [4]. However, this construction has a problem with Flying Capacitor (FC) voltage unbalance, which can raise THD in the output voltage [10–15]. Numerous approaches, including carrier-based PWM [5], modified triangular carrier-based PWM [6], optimized pulse pattern [7], and selective harmonic elimination PWM (SHE-PWM) [8, 9], have been presented to produce the output voltage with reduced harmonics while also controlling the FC voltage. In this article, the proposed modulation enables the 6S-5L-ANPC inverter to balance the Flying Capacitor (FC) voltage.

This paper proposes the design of sliding mode control for the 6S-5L-ANPC inverter in order to regulate FC voltage based on voltage control, the essential feature of the control method is the robustness in relation to parameter fluctuations of the load. Section 2 presents circuit analysis of the 6S-5L-ANPC, topology description, and modulation strategy used to ensure the self-balancing of the FC capacitor. Section 3 deals with the design of the proposed sliding mode control. And Sect. 4 is the conclusion based on the simulation results.

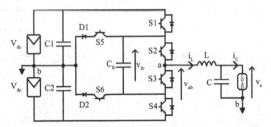

Fig. 2. Proposed circuit of 6S-5L-ANPC inverter

2 Circuit Analysis

2.1 Topology Description

The proposed 6S-5L-ANPC inverter with an output LC filter is shown in Fig. 2. The inverter is made up of six active switches (S1–S6) that may generate five different voltage levels at the output dependent on capacitor voltages (0, 0.5Vdc, Vdc, −0.5Vdc, −Vdc). (S1–S4) commutate at line frequency, while (S5, S6) operate at switching frequency. The DC-link is made up of two distinct DC sources connected in parallel by two self-balanced DC–link capacitors C1 and C2, which help to reduce leakage current and capacitor size., on the other hand, C_{fc} is a flying capacitor that achieves voltage balancing by using redundant switching states. The eight switching states of the inverter are summarized in Table 1.

2.2 Modulation Strategy

For multilevel converter applications, several modulation techniques are available [16–20]. Figure 3 depicts a PWM modulation method for the proposed inverter operation, which uses two carriers and one reference signal to generate the appropriate gating signals. The six switch pulses are obtained by comparing carrier signals to a sinusoidal waveform.

Table 1. Switching states of the 6S-5L-ANPC inverter

Switches States	S1	S2	S3	S4	S5	S6	Output voltage
a	1	1	0	0	0	1	0.5Vdc
b	1	0	1	0	0	1	0.25Vdc
c	0	1	0	0	0	1	0.25Vdc
d	0	0	1	0	0	1	0
e	0	1	0	0	1	0	0
f	0	0	1	0	1	0	−0.25Vdc
g	0	1	0	1	1	0	−0.25Vdc
h	0	0	1	1	1	0	−0.5Vdc

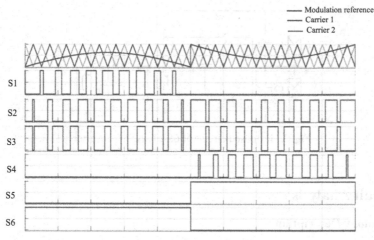

Fig. 3. Modulation strategy

3 Controller Design

3.1 Sliding Mode Control

When the structure of the system used takes two or more expressions, the concept of variable structure system comes into play, such system whose structure changes during its operation is characterized by the choice of a structure and switching logic. This choice allows the system to switch from one structure to another at any time. To control systems with variable structures by sliding mode, the state trajectory is brought to a surface, then due to the switching law, it is obliged to remain in the vicinity of this surface.

The rule of sliding mode control is to bring the state trajectory of a system towards the sliding surface and to switch it using a suitable switching logic around it up to the equilibrium point.

3.2 Mathematical Modeling

A single-phase converter connected to an LC output filter can be modeled by differential equations. Using standard Kirchhof voltage and current laws of the circuit depicted in Fig. 2, the mathematical model of the converter is derived as:

$$L\frac{di_L}{dt} = v_{ab} - v_s \tag{1}$$

$$C\frac{dv_s}{dt} = i_L - i_s \tag{2}$$

With L and C are the inductance and the capacity of the filter, i_L and v_{ab} are the output current and the output voltage, i_s and v_s are the voltage and current through the load.

As shown in Table 1, depending on the state of the switches, the inverter's output voltage v_{ab} can take one of five values: Vdc, 0.5Vdc, 0, −0.5Vdc, Vdc. So, we can deduce:

$$v_{ab} = \mu\, Vdc \tag{3}$$

With $\mu \in \{-1, -\frac{1}{2}, 0, \frac{1}{2}, 1\}$

The converter's output signal is discrete and may take five different values, which is not suitable for the design of continuous control law. To overcome this difficulty and be able to control the system under investigation, the average model of the suggested topology can be written as follows:

$$L\frac{di_L}{dt} = u.Vdc - v_s \tag{4}$$

$$C\frac{dv_s}{dt} = i_L - i_s \tag{5}$$

where u is the average value of the switching function μ

3.3 Control Law

The controller must always allow the inverter to provide purely sinusoidal voltage with fixed amplitude and frequency regardless of the load. The output voltage must follow the reference signal.

Figure 4 shows a Sliding Mode Control scheme with a low pass filter to reduce the influence of the sliding surface slip phenomenon.

The rule sliding mode control is given by:

$$u_c(t) = \frac{1}{Vdc}[-K\,sign(\sigma) + \lambda.L.C(I_L - I_S - \frac{dVref}{dt} + Vs + \frac{dis(t)}{dt} + L.C.\frac{d^2Vref(t)}{dt^2}]$$

(6)

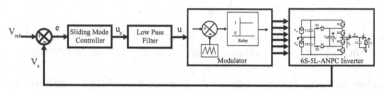

Fig. 4. Proposed Sliding Mode Controller scheme

4 Simulation Results and Discussions

The parameters and component values used for simulations are listed in Table 2. The simulation for the 6S-5L-ANPC is carried out using Matlab/Simulink. We test the performance of the closed-loop system, we evaluate the output voltage and the flying capacitor voltage behavior at a high reference change. The output voltage must follow a sinusoidal reference and the flying capacitor voltage must be balanced.

With a modulation index of 0.5 as shown in Fig. 5, the output voltage is entirely sinusoidal. In the suggested circuit, the self-balancing carries the balanced FC voltage.

Under modulation index (m = 0.62), the output voltage and current rise, the FC voltage diverges, and balance is not maintained confirming that the proposed 6S-5L-ANPC inverter is not appropriate for variable reference voltage and requires control.

Figure 6 depicts the closed-loop performance of the proposed 6S-5L-ANPC inverter controlled by a Sliding Mode controller. The output voltage is tested to follow a sinusoidal reference that suddenly undergoes a sharp increase; the peak value increases from 160V to 220V.

Table 2. Simulation parameters

Load resistance	6 Ω	Switching Frequency	20 kHz
Output inductance	15 mH	Output Capacitance	1.5 mH
DC link voltage	350 V	Fundamental frequency	50Hz
FC Capacitance	600 μF	DC Capacitance	1000 μF
λ	900	K	200000

As we can see in Fig. 7, the output voltage follows the voltage reference. The change in reference voltage from 160V to 220V causes a sharp increase in the output current. The FC voltage balance is achieved, which confirms that the proposed control strategy can ensure the FC voltage balance under reference voltage variation.

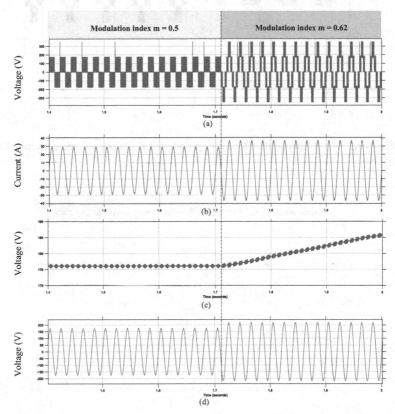

Fig. 5. Simulated waveforms of the open-loop system (modulation index m = 0.5 and m = 0.62): (a) Output voltage converter Vab, (b) Output current I_S, (c) FC Voltage, (d) Output voltage Vs

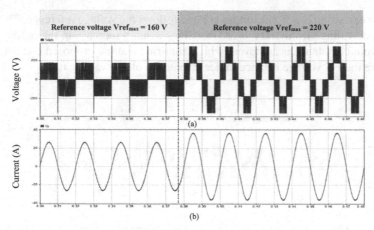

Fig. 6. Simulated waveforms of the closed-loop system: (a) Output voltage converter Vab, (b) Output current I_S

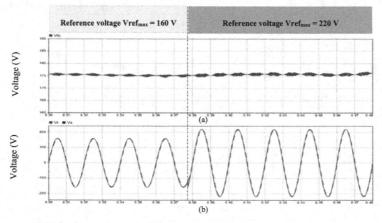

Fig. 7. Simulated waveforms of the closed-loop system: (a) FC Voltage Vfc (b) Output and reference voltage Vs, Vref.

5   Conclusion

This paper presents the Six-Switch Five-Level Active Neutral Point Clamped Inverter topology. The application of the proposed modulation based on a simple comparison between carrier signals and sinusoidal waveform to get the appropriate gate signals has been investigated, Sliding Mode control approach has been developed. The effectiveness of the proposed control strategy was validated by the simulation results, demonstrating the ability of the system to operate under different voltage references. The output voltage provides good tracking of the reference and the FC capacitor is balanced.

References

1. Vijeh, M., Rezanejad, M., Samadaei, E., Bertilsson, K.: A general review of multilevel inverters based on main submodules: structural point of view. IEEE Trans. Power Electron. **34**(10), 9479–9502 (2018)
2. Malinowski, M., Gopakumar, K., Rodriguez, J., Perez, M.A.: A survey on cascaded mutilevel inverters. IEEE Trans. Ind. Electron (July 2010). https://doi.org/10.1109/TIE.2009.2030767
3. Brückner, T., Bernet, S.: Loss balancing in three-level voltage source inverters applying active NPC switches. In: Proc IEEE. PESC 01 Vancouver, BC, Canada (2001). https://doi.org/10.1109/PESC.2001.954272
4. Wang, H., Kou, L., Liu, Y., Sen, P.C.: New low-cost five-level active neutral-point clamped converter. In: Proceeding IEEE Applied Power Electronics Conference, pp. 1489–1496 (2016)
5. Gonzalez, S.A., Valla, M.I., Christiansen, C.F.: Five-level cascade asymmetric multilevel converter. IET Power Electron. **3**, 120–128 (2010)
6. Kashihara, Y., Itoh, J.: Parameter design of a five-level inverter for PV systems. In: IEEE 8th International Conference on Power Electronics and ECCE Asia (ICPE & ECCE), pp. 1886–1893 (2011)
7. Meili, J., Ponnaluri, S., Serpa, L., et al.: Optimized pulse patterns for the 5-level ANPC converter for high speed high power applications. In: 32nd Annual Conference on IEEE Industrial Electronics, IECON, pp. 2587–2592 (2006)
8. Pulikanti, S.R., Agelidis, V.G.: Control of neutral point and flying capacitor voltages in five-level SHE-PWM controlled ANPC converter. In: 4th IEEE Conference on Industrial Electronics and Applications, ICIEA, pp. 172–177 (2009)
9. Pulikanti, S.R., Agelidis, V.G.: Hybrid flying-capacitor-based activeneutral- point-clamped five-level converter operated with SHE-PWM. IEEE Trans. Industr. Electron. **58**(10), 4643–4653 (2011)
10. Teymour, H.R., Sutanto, D., Muttaqi, K.M., Ciufo, P.: A novel modulation technique and a new balancing control strategy for a single-phase five-level ANPC converter. IEEE Trans. Ind. Appl. **51**(2), 1215–1227 (2015)
11. Siwakoti, Y.P., Mahajan, A., Rogers, D., Blaabjerg, F.: A novel seven-level active neutral point clamped converter with reduced active switching devices and DC-link voltage. IEEE Trans. Power Electron (2018). https://doi.org/10.1109/TPEL.2019.2897061
12. Jagabar Sathik, M., Tang, Z., Yang, Y., Vijayakumar, K., Blaabjerg, F.: A new 5-level ANPC switched-capacitor inverter topology for photovoltaic applications. In: IECON 2019 - 45th Annual Conference of the IEEE Industrial Electronics Society. https://doi.org/10.1109/IECON.2019.8926832
13. Chen, H.-C., Lu, C.-Y., Lien, W.-H., Chen, T.-H.: Active capacitor voltage balancing control for three-level flying capacitor boost converter based on average-behavior circuit model. IEEE Trans. Ind. Appl. **55**(2) (March–April 2019). https://doi.org/10.1109/TIA.2018.2876031
14. Siwakoti, Y.P.: A new six-switch five-level boost-active neutral point clamped (5L-Boost-ANPC) inverter. In: 2018 IEEE Applied Power Electronics Conference and Exposition (APEC). https://doi.org/10.1109/APEC.2018.8341356
15. Kasim, M.Q., Hassan, R.F.: Active voltage balancing strategy of asymmetric stacked multilevel inverter. Indones. J. Electr. Eng. Comput. Sci. **23**(2), 665–674 (August 2021). ISSN: 2502–4752. https://doi.org/10.11591/ijeecs.v23.i2.pp665-674
16. Chokkalingham, B., Padmanaban, S., Blaabjerg, F.: Investigation and comparative analysis of advanced PWM techniques for three-phase three-level NPC-MLI drives. Electr. Power Comp. Syst. (2018). https://doi.org/10.1080/15325008.2018.1445142

17. Bharatiraja, C., Sanjeevikumar, P., Munda, J.L., Norum, L., Raghu, S.: Mitigation of circulating current in diode clamped MLI fed induction motor drive using carrier shifting PWM techniques. In: Lecture Notes in Electrical Engineering (December 2017). https://doi.org/10.1007/978-981-10-4762-6_6

18. Chokkalingam, B., Bhaskar, M.S., Padmanaban, S., Ramachandaramurthy, V.K., Iqbal, A.: Investigations of multi-carrier pulse width modulation schemes for diode free neutral point clamped multilevel inverters. J. Power Electron. **19**(3), 702–713 (2019). https://doi.org/10.6113/JPE.2019.19.3.702

19. Yang, J., Yang, S., Li, R.: A novel and reliable modulation strategy for active neutral-point clamped five-level converter. In: 2017 IEEE. https://doi.org/10.1109/IFEEC.2017.7992205

20. Majdoul, R., Touati, A., Aitelmahjoub, A., Zegrari, M., Taouni. A., Ouchatti, A.: A nine-switch nine-level voltage inverter new topology with optimal modulation technique. In: 2020 International Conference on Electrical and Information Technologies (ICEIT). https://doi.org/10.1109/ICEIT48248.2020.9113170

Statistical Analysis of PV-Wind-Battery Hybrid System Energy Efficiency for Green Buildings Power Supply

Asmae Chakir[✉], Mohamed Tabaa, and Yassine Chakir

Pluridisciplinary Laboratory of Research and Innovation (LPRI), EMSI, Casablanca, Morocco
{a.chakir,m.tabaa,y.chakir}@emsi.ma

Abstract. The increased greenhouse gas emissions due to conventional power generation has driven governments to think of environment-friendly alternatives. Among these options we find renewable energies that provide green electricity production. However, they represent a major disadvantage of intermittency. They are strongly related to their renewable potential. Hence the usefulness of energy hybridization, where two or more complementary renewable sources operate in a single system to smooth its production profile. In this sense, we study the efficiency of a PV-wind-battery hybrid system supplying a residential building. The study is based on a statistical analysis of the hybrid system production following a proposed energy management strategy in this context. The corresponding renewable potential was derived from METEONORM, the power estimation was performed using MATLAB and the statistical analysis of the results was conducted using MINITAB software for four Moroccan regions, namely: Casablanca, Marrakech, Dakhla and Tetouan. The analysis results showed different grid dependencies by changing the regions, namely: 80%, 73%, 78% and 88.2% for Marrakech, Casablanca, Dakhla and Tetouan respectively.

Keywords: Hybrid renewable system · Energy management strategy · Statistical analysis

1 Introduction

The residential sector around the world is well known for being the second most energy consuming sector [1]. Since this energy is produced through conventional sources, the residence area will be indirectly the second largest greenhouse gas contributor after the transportation area [2]. Therefore, finding an alternative to produce clean electricity is becoming increasingly a necessity [2, 3]. Therefore, the use of renewable energies has started to take a great importance due to the advantages they represent. These energies are very efficient in terms of greenhouse gas reduction against the use of fossil fuels that adversely affect the global climate. Alongside the advantages, renewable sources are always intermittent and very dependent on its corresponding potential. Accordingly, researchers have thought about the hybridization to take benefit of renewable sources

M. Hamlich et al. (Eds.): SADASC 2022, CCIS 1677, pp. 245–258, 2022.
https://doi.org/10.1007/978-3-031-20490-6_20

[4, 5]. The hybrid solution concerns just complementary sources that can produce electricity in a coordinated way and keep the production profile as smooth as possible. Various hybridizations are possible and depend mainly on the implementation site [6]. For instance, PV-Wind-Battery is a suitable complementary hybrid system for a small scale local implementation.

This hybrid system can be associated with a small distributed generation strategy by coupling it to a residential building in order to facilitate renewable energy integration in the residential electric sector. Several researchers are interested in this topic following several research axis, namely: the hybrid renewable system sizing and design, its power management [7] and the extraction of its maximum energy. In fact, following a rule-based management, authors in [8, 9] proposed an energy management strategy for the hybrid PV-Battery system while studying its reliability. Also based on rule-based algorithm the authors of [10] have developed a management system for a Hybrid storage system side. A rule-based system was experimentally tested for a PV-wind-battery based system in its autonomous mode [11], the results showed the flexibility of the system to control the different variations of the renewable hybridization. Optimization systems have also been used to meet objective management functions. Indeed, the authors [12] proposed a multi-objective optimization system in order to reduce the cost of electricity and increase the users' comfort based on the antlion optimization algorithm.

Based on artificial intelligence authors in [13] proposed and energy management based on the price of time of use using swarm intelligence. Otherwise, authors in [14] used the multi-agent system to propose an effective energy management system for a PV, fuel cell, supercapacitor and home to vehicle hybrid system. In fact, electric vehicles have been widely used recently to help in smart energy management, in [15] authors used the three mode of vehicle energy share to manage energy, namely: vehicle to home, home to vehicle and grid to vehicle. The management of energy could focus in the energy storage system and not on the renewable source, which was discussed by authors in [16] by reducing the total electricity price.

Reviewing the literature, we can deduce that the majority of the studies are dedicated to the optimization of the hybrid system. This optimization affects the sizing area as a starting point to design a hybrid system [17]. Otherwise, the energy management section remains a key aspect to take benefit of a renewable hybrid system [18]. This energy management can be developed according to several models. From a rule based algorithm, through meta-heuristic approaches, or even the use of linear or non-linear programming combined or not with artificial intelligence [19]. Nevertheless, the key element to make the difference between choosing one system or another is the implementation simplicity and especially the reliability of the system. For this reason, we study in this paper the utility grid power independency of our proposed hybrid system to supply a future household and its deficit level that can be noticed during one power supply year.

The paper is organized as follows. The second section is dedicated to the hybrid system presentation and the modeling of its components. Section 3 is devoted to the description of the power management system adopted for this study. The 4th section is dedicated to the analysis of the system reliability. Finally, the conclusion and the perspectives are drawn.

2   Renewable System Hybridization

We consider for this study a hybrid architecture of the PV-Wind-Battery system powering a modern household. This building has intelligent electrical loads. Simple to estimate its consumption and to manage its energy demands. The hybrid architecture held is presented by the Fig. 1. The hybrid system is based on a photovoltaic installation, a permanent magnet synchronous generator (PMSG) and storage batteries for overnight energy production profile adjustment. These sources are grouped in a DC bus. The matching of the type of production is done through the power electronics with DC/DC, AC/DC and bidirectional DC/DC converters for solar panels, wind turbine and battery, respectively.

To facilitate the management we use electrical switches, which will be activated according to the source availability of energy and the demand of the loads installed inside the house. We have S1, S2, S3, and S4 for the collaboration of PV, wind turbine, battery or grid, respectively. The S5 and S6 are dedicated to the injection of the renewable sources excess production, solar or wind, respectively.

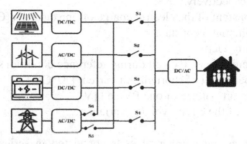

Fig. 1. Proposed grid connected PV-Wind-Battery hybrid architecture

2.1   Photovoltaic System

The photovoltaic installation consists of grouping solar panels in series or in parallel according to the necessary size and to meet the threshold voltage of the DC/DC converter to stabilize the DC bus voltage. The modeling consists in holding in count the unit PV panel [20]. Indeed, several models can be considered to do so. For our case, we consider the single diode model. Subsequently, we could estimate the solar production according to the voltage and current corresponding to the point of maximum power [8]. Equation (1) represent the maximum of energy that could be produced by the PV installation. Equations (2–5) represent constant in faction of the temperature and irradiation used to simplify the PV power expression.

$$P_{pv} = \left\{ N_p.\delta(G, T) - \frac{N_p.\text{B(T)}}{\exp\left(\frac{q.C(T)}{nN_sK_BT}\right) - 1} \cdot \left(\exp\left(\frac{q(Lambertw(0, \text{A(G, T)}) - 1)}{nN_{ss}N_sK_BT} \right) - 1 \right) \right\} \times \frac{nN}{}$$

$$(1)$$

$$\delta(G, T) = \left(\frac{G}{G_{ref}}\left(I_{scn} + \mu_i\left(T - T_{ref}\right)\right)\right) \tag{2}$$

$$A(G, T) = \frac{\delta(G, T).N_p\left(\exp\left(\frac{C(T).N_{ss}}{v_t}\right) - 1\right)\exp(1)}{B(T).N_p} \tag{3}$$

$$B(T) = I_{scn} + \mu_i\left(T - T_{ref}\right) \tag{4}$$

$$C(T) = V_{ocn} + \mu_v\left(T - T_{ref}\right) \tag{5}$$

where:

- $\eta_{DC/DC}$ is the efficiency of the converter linked to the solar system.
- G is the ambient irradiation [W/m^2]
- T is the ambient temperature estimated by °C
- Gref and Tref are the referenced of the irradiation and temperature equivalent to 1000 W/m^2 and 25 °C, respectively.
- q is the physical constant of the electric charge of one electron [C].
- K_B(J/°K) is the Boltzmann constant
- n is the diode ideality factor
- I_{scn} is the short circuit of one PV cell during reference conditions [A].
- k_i considered as coefficient of short circuit current [A/°C].
- V_{ocn} is the open circuit voltage of one PV cell [V].
- k_v is the coefficient of the circuit voltage variation.

Else, we note N_s as the number of cells connected in series in one single PV. Otherwise, N_{ss}, N_p are the numbers of panels connected in series and in parallel, respectively.

2.2 Permanent Magnet Synchronous Generator

The alternative source considered in this study is the permanent magnet synchronous generator -based wind turbine [21]. This is a subsidiary source in this study. It is responsible for exploiting the wind speed and converting it into mechanical energy and then into electrical energy [22]. Equation (6) represents the amount of maximum power that could be produced by the wind turbine according to the power coefficient represents by Eq. (7), which depends to the aerodynamic shape of the turbine.

$$P_{WT} = \frac{1}{2} \times \rho \times S \times C_p(\beta, \Omega) + 0.0068 \times R\Omega \times V_{wind}^2 \times \eta_{AC/DC} \tag{6}$$

where, V_{wind} is the wind speed at the studied area and ρ is the air density. S considered as the swept area with the wind turbine regarded for the study. R the wind turbine

$$C_p(\beta, \Omega) = 0.517\left(\frac{116}{\frac{R\Omega}{V_{wind}} + 0.08\beta} - \frac{4.06}{1 + \beta^3} - 0.8\beta - 5\right)e^{\left(-21\times\left(\frac{1}{\frac{R\Omega}{V_{wind}} + 0.08\beta} - \frac{0.035}{\beta^3 + 1}\right)\right)} \tag{7}$$

radius, Ω the wind turbine angular speed. Else, the pitch angle is noted as β. Finally, $\eta_{AC/DC}$ is the efficiency of the AC/DC converter linked to the wind turbine.

2.3 Storage System

As the renewable system is very intermittent, so combining it with a storage system seems reasonable. To do this, we adopt lead-acid batteries [23]. Their dynamics is done according to the study of the energy exchanged during the charge and the discharge [24].

For the modeling, we consider the performances of the battery during the charge and the discharge as well as the efficiency of bidirectional converter assisting it during DC voltage adaptation. The energy can be matched to power if a simulation step of one hour is kept as it's presented by Eq. (8).

$$P_{batt} \times \Delta t = E_{batt} \qquad (8)$$

where, E_{batt} is the energy of the battery, P_{batt} is the power and t is the time step. The energy variation could be estimated as follows, by Eq. (9):

$$\Delta E_{batt} = E_{batt}(t) - E_{batt}(t-1) \qquad (9)$$

where, ΔE_{batt} is the amount of energy added or subtracted during charge or discharge phases, which is clarified by the system (10). Noting that, P is the excess of energy available on the DC bus. $\eta_{DC/DC}$ is the bidirectional DC/DC convertor performance associated to the battery. η_{dis} and η_{ch} are efficiencies during discharge and battery charge periods, respectively.

$$\Delta E_{batt} = \begin{cases} P\eta_{ch}\eta_{DC/DC} & \text{if } P > 0 \\ \frac{P}{\eta_{DC/DC}\eta_{dis}} & \text{if } P < 0 \\ 0 & \text{if } P = 0 \end{cases} \qquad (10)$$

3 Energy Management System

Due to the intermittency of the renewable sources, the hybridization of the complementary sources has been considered to be a solution to overcome this drawback. However, as a consequence, we are dealing with a further limitation, which is the energy flow management. Therefore, algorithms of energy control have been proposed to remedy this issue. In this sense, we propose a management algorithm that is characterized by the hardware implementation simplicity and that will manage in total flexibility the system (Fig. 2) and the pseudo-algorithm presented in Fig. 3. This algorithm takes into account the solar system as the primary source and the wind turbine as the secondary one. The availability of the photovoltaic energy is automatically checked before the wind turbine. This choice was made following the study of the renewable potential of the implementation site. The solar potential in this location is significantly greater than the wind speed according to a comparative analysis.

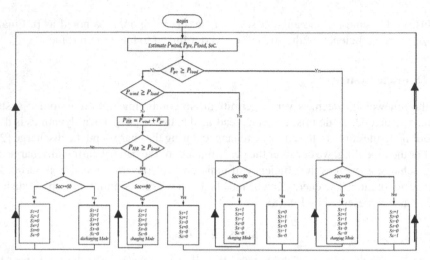

Fig. 2. Proposed grid connected PV-Wind-Battery energy management algorithm

In fact, the system starts by estimating the energy that can be produced by the renewable system and the storage system's state of charge. This estimation is done through the modeling established in Sect. 2.

Then the system starts to make the comparison before any decision. The first comparison concerns the solar production and the power demanded by all the loads installed at the house. If this comparison is true, the corresponding switch is activated and the wind energy will be totally injected into the utility grid after making sure that the battery is on its maximum state of charge.

If the solar system is not able to satisfy the demand of the loads in totality, it resorts to the wind system. In fact, if the wind system produces more energy than the house demands, its switch will be activated and the total energy produced by the solar system will be injected to the grid after making sure that the storage system is on its maximum power state.

Otherwise, if the renewable sources are not capable to satisfy the house alone in this case we count the hybridization. The comparison power output now is the sum of the solar and wind power. If the hybridization is in the capacity to cover the loads then the two switches S1 and S2 are activated. If not, the system uses its storage system or it resorts to the national grid to cover its energy deficit.

The simulation was carried out following a real database of a typical day of the year for a residential building according to four climates change, namely: Casablanca, Marrakech, Dakhla and Tetouan (Figs. 4, 5, 6 and 7). The meteorological databases are from METEONORM by means of the TRNSYS software. The simulation has been conducted following a MATLAB programming with a simulation step of one hour. The results show the flexibility of the system to manage its energy. The solar system produces during the day and the wind production continues even after sunset. The surplus is efficiently injected during the day and the system consumes just 5 hours from the utility grid at night to feed the critical electrical loads. This negative consumption from the grid can be considered as a delocalization of the surplus injection done during the day.

Algorithm 1: Energy Management Algorithm for PV-Wind-Battery- system

Estimate $P_{PV}, P_{Wind}, P_{Load}, SoC$

while *True* **do**

    if $P_{PV} \geqslant P_{Load}$ **then**

        if $SoC == 90$ **then**

            | $S_1 = 1, S_2 = 0, S_3 = 0, S_4 = 0, S_5 = 0, S_6 = 1$

        else

            Charging mode

            $S_1 = 1, S_2 = 1, S_3 = 1, S_4 = 0, S_5 = 0, S_6 = 0$

        end

    else

        if $P_{wind} \geqslant P_{Load}$ **then**

            if $SoC == 90$ **then**

                | $S_1 = 0, S_2 = 1, S_3 = 0, S_4 = 0, S_5 = 1, S_6 = 1$

            else

                Charging mode

                $S_1 = 1, S_2 = 1, S_3 = 1, S_4 = 0, S_5 = 0, S_6 = 0$

            end

        else

            $P_{HR} = P_{PV} + P_{Wind}$

            if $P_{HR} \geqslant P_{Load}$ **then**

                if $SoC == 90$ **then**

                    | $S_1 = 1, S_2 = 1, S_3 = 0, S_4 = 0, S_5 = 0, S_6 = 1$

                else

                  Charging mode

                  $S_1 = 1, S_2 = 1, S_3 = 1, S_4 = 0, S_5 = 0, S_6 = 0$

                end

            else

                if $SoC \geqslant= 50$ **then**

                  Disharging mode

                  $S_1 = 1, S_2 = 1, S_3 = 1, S_4 = 0, S_5 = 0, S_6 = 0$

                else

                  | $S_1 = 1, S_2 = 1, S_3 = 0, S_4 = 1, S_5 = 0, S_6 = 0$

                end

            end

        end

    end

end

Fig. 3. Pseudo- algorithm of proposed the grid connected PV-Wind-Battery energy management

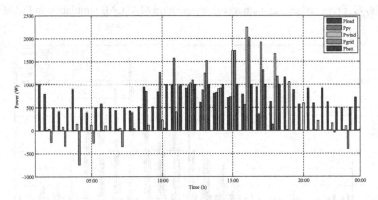

Fig. 4. Proposed energy management algorithm MATLAB simulation in Marrakech

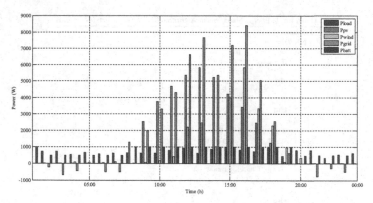

Fig. 5. Proposed energy management algorithm MATLAB simulation in Casablanca

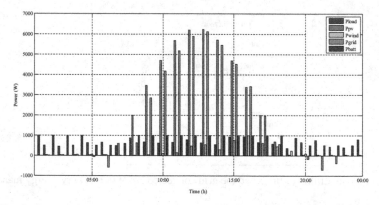

Fig. 6. Proposed energy management algorithm MATLAB simulation in Dakhla

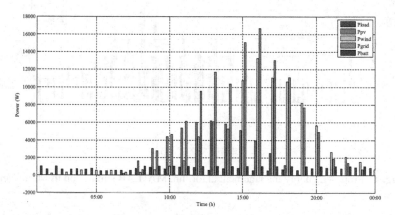

Fig. 7. Proposed energy management algorithm MATLAB simulation in Tetouan

4 System Reliability Analysis

The system consists in satisfying for each instant a balance state between the loads that consume electricity from the installed hybrid system and the renewable generation sources that constitute this system. More specifically, the interaction between the national electricity grid noted by P_{grid} must be positive or near to zero. Meaning that the system inject energy to the grid rather than consumes from it.

The study of this proposed energy management and architecture reliability consists in studying to what a certain extent the household loads consume from the grid. The variation of power vector consumed from the grid following a given energy management system was carried out by MATLAB simulation and stocked in the P_{grid} vector. So following the MINITAB software that can perform a statistical study to identify the probability that our system is during or not energy deficit period following a the database of energy management results.

To do this, we aimed to graphically study the probability and frequency histogram of the vector resulting from the transmission of the household combined to its hybrid renewable system with the national electricity grid. We conducted four studies according to four Moroccan regions, namely: Casablanca, Marrakech, Tetouan and Dakhla. The study is essentially based on a typical Moroccan household that hosts 4 people. The consumption of the inhabitants was estimated according to the statistics carried out by the High Commission for Planning of Morocco. Accordingly, a house of this size consumes 13kWh of energy per day, spread over the hours of the day following a precise consumption profile.

So on a database consisting of 8761 values the simulations have been performed. Indeed, Figs. 8 and 9 represents the cumulative probability of the equilibrium state of our system when implemented in Marrakech and its frequency histogram of values on the same location, respectively. We note that the cumulative probability that the system will consume energy from the grid is about 20%. This energy is obviously consumed from the grid. However, we notice that the system in the majority of cases is on a state of balance near to zero with a frequency of 1972. This allows us to deduce that the cumulative probability of 20% represents a large part of the null values and that the system achieves its objective in the majority of cases which is injecting energy to grid

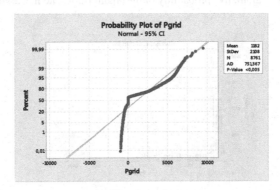

Fig. 8. Cumulative probability of the equilibrium state in Marrakech

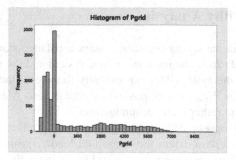

Fig. 9. Distribution probability of the equilibrium state in Marrakech

rather than consuming from it. Mean is the average of the data. StDev is the standard deviation. N is the size of the population or the size of the vector Pgrid. Pgrid is the interaction vector between the hybrid architecture and the grid in Marrakech. PgridM, PgridD and PgridT are the same vector but according to the meteorological conditions of Casablanca, Dakhla and Tetouan, respectively. AD is the Anderson Darling coefficient which is a data analysis method. The smaller the number, the more the data distribution follows the normal distribution. P-value is a parameter that must be greater than 0.05 for the data distribution to follow a normal distribution, so the larger the coefficient, the more the data follows a Gaussian curve.

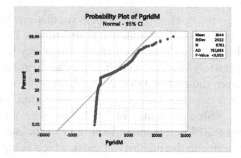

Fig. 10. Cumulative probability of the equilibrium state in Casablanca

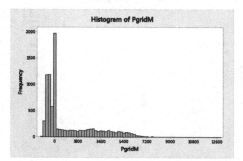

Fig. 11. Distribution probability of the equilibrium state in Casablanca

In Casablanca, simulated by Figs. 10 and 11, the system has 73% of time where it injects energy to the grid. Because we notice that the system is in energy deficit with a cumulative probability of 27%. Against a frequency of zero almost stable at the order of 1972. Therefore the states of energy deficit that has increased its utility grid dependence.

For the site of Dakhla presented by Figs. 12 and 13, the frequency of the state close to zero is about 1753 against a cumulative probability of deficit of around 22%. This proves that the cumulative probability has been increased with deficit states and not with ideal equilibrium states. Besides, we notice a very good performance of our system as well as the proposed architecture in Tetouan, Figs. 14 and 15. Indeed, the system is on a deficit following a cumulative probability of about 11.8%. Therefore, it represents the most suitable region for this proposal for a utility grid independency close to 90%. Table 1 represents a comparison between results obtained for each regions.

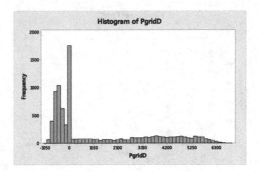

Fig. 12. Distribution probability of the equilibrium state in Dakhla

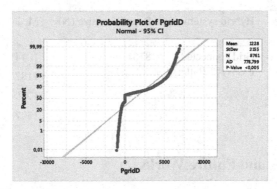

Fig. 13. Cumulative probability of the equilibrium state in Dakhla

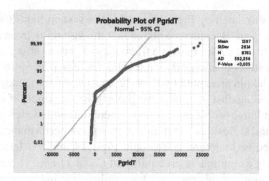

Fig. 14. Cumulative probability of the equilibrium state in Tetouan

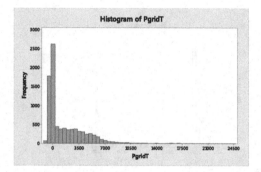

Fig. 15. Distribution probability of the equilibrium state in Tetouan

Table 1. Comparative table between MINITAB results

Implementation site	Hybrid system	Population size (N)	Mean	Utility grid independency
Casablanca	Grid connected PV-Wind-Battery	8761	1044	73%
Marrakech			1182	80%
Dakhla			1228	78%
Tetouan			1597	88,2%

5 Conclusions and Future Works

In this paper we proposed a statistical study of the energy management system reliability. We proposed a hybridization architecture for a hybrid grid connected system which is the PV-wind-Battery. The energy management strategy has also been suggested following a rule-based algorithm. The results of the control system showed the flexibility of the system to manage its energy productions according to all the scenarios spread over a typical year and according to several regions of Morocco, namely: Casablanca, Marrakech,

Dakhla and Tetouan. The results of the vector that reflects the grid collaboration was then analyzed using MINITAB for each region. The results of the statistical analysis showed different reliabilities by changing the regions, namely: 80%, 73%, 78% and 88.2% for Marrakech, Casablanca, Dakhla and Tetouan respectively. Following this analysis, the system is more reliable to be implemented in Tetouan than in Casablanca. While doing statistical analysis of data from management systems in MATLAB we noticed that these data do not follow a normal law and in MINITAB we could not find laws that can be adapted to the statistical behavior of these data, since they contain negative values that reflect the consumption of electricity from the grid during an energetic deficit of the household. For this reason, we would like to eliminate these negative values by making a variable change and find the right distribution that will fit the frequency histograms of each value in the database. Furthermore, a study of correlation and influence of the management algorithm as well as the size of the hybrid system will be conducted to try to physically eliminate the negative values of the histograms.

References

1. Ghezloun, A., Saidane, A., Oucher, N.: Energy policy in the context of sustainable development: case of Morocco and Algeria. Energy Procedia (2014). https://doi.org/10.1016/j.egy pro.2014.06.065
2. Dincer, I., Bicer, Y.: Integration of renewable energy systems for multigeneration. In: Integrated Energy Systems for Multigeneration. pp. 287–402. Elsevier (2020). https://doi.org/10.1016/b978-0-12-809943-8.00006-6
3. Scholten, D., Bazilian, M., Overland, I., Westphal, K.: The geopolitics of renewables: new board, new game. Energy Policy. **138**, 111059 (2020). https://doi.org/10.1016/j.enpol.2019.111059
4. Dileep, G.: A survey on smart grid technologies and applications. Renew. Energy. **146**, 2589–2625 (2020). https://doi.org/10.1016/j.renene.2019.08.092
5. Sinha, S., Chandel, S.S.: Review of software tools for hybrid renewable energy systems. Renewable Sustainable Energy Rev. **32**, 192–205 (2014). https://doi.org/10.1016/j.rser.2014.01.035
6. Siddaiah, R., Saini, R.P.: A review on planning, configurations, modeling and optimization techniques of hybrid renewable energy systems for off grid applications. . Renewable Sustainable Energy Rev. **58**, 376 (2016). https://doi.org/10.1016/j.rser.2015.12.281
7. Rathor, S.K., Saxena, D.: Energy management system for smart grid: An overview and key issues. Int. J. Energy Res. 44(6), 4067–4109 (2020). https://doi.org/10.1002/er.4883
8. Chakir, A., Tabaa, M., Moutaouakkil, F., Medromi, H., Julien-Salame, M., Dandache, A., Alami, K.: Optimal energy management for a grid connected PV-battery system. In: Energy Reports. **6**, 218–231 (2020). Elsevier Ltd. https://doi.org/10.1016/j.egyr.2019.10.040
9. Chakir, A., Tabaa, M., Moutaouakkil, F., Medromi, H., Alami, K.: Architecture and methodology for a grid connected PV-battery hybrid system. In: Proceedings of 2019 7th International Renewable and Sustainable Energy Conference, IRSEC 2019. pp. 1–6. Institute of Electrical and Electronics Engineers Inc. (2019). https://doi.org/10.1109/IRSEC48032.2019.9078174
10. Wang, Y., Sun, Z., Chen, Z.: Development of energy management system based on a rule-based power distribution strategy for hybrid power sources. Energy **175**, 1055–1066 (2019). https://doi.org/10.1016/J.ENERGY.2019.03.155
11. Kumar, P.S., Chandrasena, R.P.S., Ramu, V., Srinivas, G.N., Babu, K.V.S.M.: Energy management system for small scale hybrid wind solar battery based microgrid. IEEE Access. **8**, 8336–8345 (2020). https://doi.org/10.1109/ACCESS.2020.2964052

12. Ramezani, M., Bahmanyar, D., Razmjooy, N.: A new optimal energy management strategy based on improved multi-objective antlion optimization algorithm: applications in smart home. SN Appl. Sci. **2**, 1–17 (2020). https://doi.org/10.1007/S42452-020-03885-7/FIGURES/12

13. Yelisetti, S., Saini, V.K., Kumar, R., Lamba, R., Saxena, A.: Optimal energy management system for residential buildings considering the time of use price with swarm intelligence algorithms. J. Build. Eng. **59**, 105062 (2022). https://doi.org/10.1016/J.JOBE.2022.105062

14. Gherairi, S.: Design and implementation of an intelligent energy management system for smart home utilizing a multi-agent system. Ain Shams Eng. J. 101897 (2022). https://doi.org/10.1016/J.ASEJ.2022.101897

15. Chakir, A., Abid, M., Tabaa, M., Hachimi, H.: Demand-side management strategy in a smart home using electric vehicle and hybrid renewable energy system. Energy Rep. **8**, 383–393 (2022). https://doi.org/10.1016/J.EGYR.2022.07.018

16. Sarda, J.S., Lee, K., Patel, H., Patel, N., Patel, D.: Energy management system of microgrid using optimization approach. IFAC-PapersOnLine. **55**, 280–284 (2022). https://doi.org/10.1016/J.IFACOL.2022.07.049

17. Lian, J., Zhang, Y., Ma, C., Yang, Y., Chaima, E.: A review on recent sizing methodologies of hybrid renewable energy systems. Energy Convers. Manag. **199**, 112027 (2019). https://doi.org/10.1016/j.enconman.2019.112027

18. Alam, M.S., Arefifar, S.A.: Energy management in power distribution systems: review, classification limitations and challenges. IEEE Access. **7**, 92979–93001 (2019). https://doi.org/10.1109/ACCESS.2019.2927303

19. Bhandari, B., Lee, K.-T., Lee, G.-Y., Cho, Y.-M., Ahn, S.-H.: Optimization of hybrid renewable energy power systems: A review. Int. J. Precis. Eng. Manuf. - Green Technol. **2**(1), 99–112 (2015). https://doi.org/10.1007/s40684-015-0013-z

20. Yang, Y., Kim, K.A., Ding, T.: Modeling and control of PV systems. In: Control of Power Electronic Converters and Systems, pp. 243–268. Elsevier (2018). https://doi.org/10.1016/b978-0-12-805245-7.00009-3

21. Chen, J., Yao, W., Zhang, C.K., Ren, Y., Jiang, L.: Design of robust MPPT controller for grid-connected PMSG-based wind turbine via perturbation observation based nonlinear adaptive control. Renew. Energy. **134**, 478–495 (2019). https://doi.org/10.1016/j.renene.2018.11.048

22. Chakir, A., Tabaa, M., Moutaouakkil, F., Medromi, H., Alami, K., Chakir, A., Tabaa, M., Moutaouakkil, F., Medromi, H., Alami, K.: Control system for a permanent magnet wind turbine using particle swarm optimization and proportional integral controller. Int. Rev. Autom. Control. **13**, 231–243 (2020). https://doi.org/10.15866/IREACO.V13I5.18482

23. Siczek, K.J.: Modeling of batteries. In: Next-Generation Batteries with Sulfur Cathodes, pp. 201–218. Elsevier (2019). https://doi.org/10.1016/b978-0-12-816392-4.00016-5

24. Breeze, P.: Power system energy storage technologies. In: Power Generation Technologies, pp. 219–249. Elsevier (2019). https://doi.org/10.1016/b978-0-08-102631-1.00010-9

Energy Management in a Connected DC Microgrid Using Fuzzy Controller

Wassim Chouaf[(✉)], Ahmed Abbou, and Ali Agga

1RTEEC Team, Mohammadia School of Engineers (EMI), Mohammed V University in Rabat, Rabat, Morocco
wassim.chouaf.emi@gmail.com

Abstract. This paper presents an energy management strategy of a HES microgrid between the different elements of connected microgrids in an optimal way. It develops a new Fuzzy Logic Control method (FLC) of Hybrid Energy System (HES: PV/Wind turbine/battery/grid), that aims at minimizing the power fluctuation between the microgrid and the main grid (the utility grid) to cope with the power demands, reduce the troubles caused by the distributed renewable energy sources, decrease the deep discharges of the battery and preserve its lifetime. Indeed, many management scenarios can be proposed according to the available energy sources, the energy consumption, the energy exchanged with the main grid and the battery's charge state in order to ensure the algorithm's well-functioning. Rule-based and Fuzzy Logic Control systems are simulated using MATLAB/Simulink.

Keywords: Energy management of microgrid · Energy storage system · Fuzzy control · Main grid · Hybrid energy system (HES)

1 Introduction

The increase in population and the advancement in the industrial sectors calls for the need of a higher generation of power. Using renewable source as an alternative can address these issues [1]. This paves the way for distributed generation (DG) since a large-scale integration of distributed generators can change the grid's traditional structure [2]. In fact, the microgrid concept is introduced as a solution to this problem. A micro-grid refers to low voltage power grid containing various loads and DGs. The microgrid can operate in two modes namely grid connected mode and islanded mode. In island mode, the microgrid is not connected to the main grid, so no power is exchanged with the grid. While, in grid connected mode, the DC grid is connected to the main grid and can exchange power with it.

An energy management system is necessary when there are different resources in a hybrid system, renewable sources are intermittent and dependent on non-controllable conditions, such as solar irradiation and wind sources, in order to:

• Find the power's best distribution among the different elements that make up the HES.

© The Author(s), under exclusive license to Springer Nature Switzerland AG 2022
M. Hamlich et al. (Eds.): SADASC 2022, CCIS 1677, pp. 259–270, 2022.
https://doi.org/10.1007/978-3-031-20490-6_21

- Improve the stability of the microgrid system.
- Ensure, in spite of the strong variations of the produced energy, the need of the load in energy.
- Supply the load demand permanently.
- Reduce the use of storage elements to a minimum.
- Prolong the life of the HES.

Energy storage equipment is one of the most effective ways to suppress power fluctuations and improve the stability of the microgrid system, impacted by those intermittent sources. Energy storage systems are characterized by absorbing or releasing electrical energy in a short period of time, overcoming the fluctuations and volatility caused by those intermittent sources (Photovoltaic panels and wind turbines) [3].

Several management strategies have been discussed in the literature and differ depending on the composition of the multi-source system and its objectives. In particular, energy management systems have been developed on three bases, namely mathematical models, human expertise or simulations [11]. However, the references: [6–10] present the main energy management strategies applied to electric vehicles. Nevertheless, that can be easily adapted to the case of a HES. Energy management strategies can be classified into two main families which are energy-based strategies and optimization-based strategies [8].

Therefore, the purpose of this paper is to project and simulate an energy management system (EMS) for a hybrid energy generation microgrid using Fuzzy Logic Control. It takes into account the non-linearity of photovoltaic and wind turbine power's generation and the state of the battery's charge limits. The simulation results show that the proposed method does not only allows optimal energy management but also can effectively balance the peak load, reduce the power fluctuation between the microgrid and the main grid and allows to manage the battery state of charge in an optimal way.

In this paper, the energy management strategy is described is in Sect. 2. Control and simulation of a Hybrid Energy System is presented in Sect. 3. Results and discussion are shown in Sect. 4. The paper is concluded in the last section.

2 Energy Management System (Control Strategies)

An energy management strategy is required in order to improve the efficiency of the multi-source system, it is necessary to ensure the requirement of uninterrupted charging and protect the storage system (the key element in the HES) against overloads and deep loads. Thus, in order to extend its lifetime, to optimize the power distribution between the different elements that constitute the HES and also to reduce the cost of the system.

2.1 Rule-Based Management Strategies

These can be easily implemented with real-time supervisory control. Rule-based energy management laws do not have any knowledge about the prioritization of a consumer's energy needs or about the climatic conditions, which are defined beforehand, based on an estimation or on the analysis of the behavior of the system's components. These can be established by deterministic rules or by fuzzy rules.

Deterministic Rules

The rules are fixed directly to the objective. We can mention in this category the method of the "On/Off" strategy which is known for its effectiveness, its robustness and its real-time operation.

Smart Methods

These techniques should be used when the modeling of the system is difficult or when it is very complex to apply. In this category, the control by fuzzy logic allows a better understanding of the energy management. Indeed, these are considered as an improvement of deterministic rules, the fuzzy logic controller does not deal with mathematical relations but rather uses inferences with several rules [11]. There are two ways to develop these rules, either based on human expertise and profile knowledge, or based on data generated by the genetic algorithm or by using the values of dynamic programming.

2.2 Optimization-Based Strategies

In this case, the worry of energy management of a HES is to find the best way to distribute, store and consume energy in order to satisfy the demand in such a way to minimize the cost of the system. In these strategies, we distinguish two categories:

Global Optimization

The use of global or off-line optimization algorithms are intended for the solution of difficult and constrained optimization problems. Energy management strategies based on offline optimization require a prior knowledge of the load profile to find the best power distribution between the energy sources. This makes the implementation of these global optimization strategies in real time impractical.

Real-Time Optimization

In order to overcome the drawbacks of global optimization methods, researchers propose real-time optimization strategies that provide real-time control of energy flows and do not require knowledge of the load profile in advance. As previously mentioned, there are several energy management strategies for a HES. These methods vary in complexity, topology and hardware implementation. Nevertheless, the main goal of these energy management techniques concerns the exchange and distribution of electrical power flow between the energy sources and the consumer while optimizing the system [11]. In summary, Table 1 presents a recap of the different families of methods according to different criteria [10].

The system has been adapted to the deterministic fuzzy rule-based management strategy (Fuzzy Logic Control).

Table 1. Summary of energy management methods

Comparison criterion		Simplicity	Unknown profile	Calculation time	Robustness
Rule-based strategies	Smart methods	▭	✔	✔	▭
	Rules deterministic	✔	✔	✔	▭
Optimization-based strategies	Real time optimization	✖	✖	✖	✔
	Global Optimization	✖	✔	✖	✔

3 Control and Simulation of a Hybrid Energy System (HES)

3.1 Energy Management Method

The proposed multi-source system (microgrid), connected to the main grid (ON GRID-DC), includes a photovoltaic generator with a power of 1.5 kW, a wind generator with a nominal power of 1.7 kW and a battery with a capacity of 58 Ah, the HES is designed to supply a DC load.

Before proposing the supervision technique, it is considered that:

- PV and wind turbine as main sources.
- The battery is used both as a source in the case of generation deficit and as a load in the case of overproduction.
- The main DC load is always connected.
- The main grid is considered as a secondary source of energy which feeds our HES in case of under production (discharged battery) and which absorbs energy (injection) in case of over production (charged battery).

The energy management between the different sources constituting our hybrid system is ensured by a management technique based on fuzzy deterministic rules. It has been designed taking into account all the operating scenarios of the HES system. The operating principle of the proposed power management strategy is represented by the flowchart in Fig. 1.

We start with the parameter's initialization of the different subsystems and climatic data (temperature, illuminance and wind speed). Then, we estimate the total power produced by the main available sources (PV and wind turbine) and the load demand evaluated at each instant, in order to calculate the difference of the power P_{Diff} using the Eq. (1):

$$P_{Diff} = (P_{PV} + P_W) - P_{Load} \tag{1}$$

If the difference in power is equal to zero, in this case there is equality between the total power produced by the sources and the power required by the main load. As a result, the battery's charge state remains constant (battery at rest), provided that the phenomenon of self-discharge is neglected.

If the power difference is greater than zero (P_{Diff} is positive), it means that the power generated by the available main sources (PV and wind turbine) is greater than the demand of the load and there is enough energy to feed the load and store the excess energy in the battery until the maximum State Of Charge (SOC_{max}).

If the power difference is less than zero (P_{Diff} is negative), it indicates that the energy produced by the renewable sources is not sufficient to feed the load. In this case, the battery steps in to provide the energy needed to cover the load's demand up to its lower limit SOC_{min}.

The synthesis of the proposed management method is summarized in the following

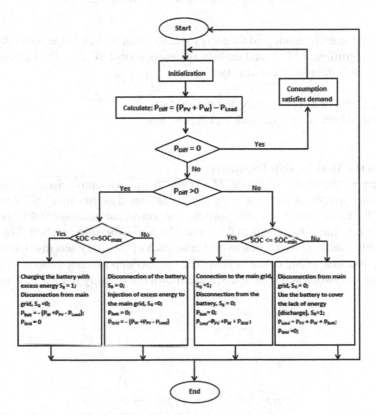

Fig. 1. Flowchart of the energy management

3.2 Control of HES - Management Strategy Based on Fuzzy Rules

Fuzzy logic is very similar to human logic and is better than other controllers. In non-linear systems, fuzzy control is more adaptable, more flexible and has shorter settling times than other traditional controllers [4, 5]. By simulating uncertainty judgment and reasoning, FLC is used to cope with optimization problems that are difficult to solve with traditional control methods. The FLC structure developed in this paper is shown in Fig. 2.

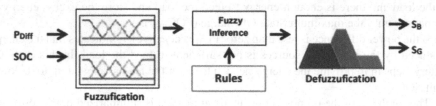

Fig. 2. Supervision system with fuzzy logic

The fuzzy controller adopted for energy management uses two input variables which are the power difference P_{Diff} and the battery state of charge SOC(t). The output variable of the system is the switch control signals.

- S_B: located between the battery and the DC bus.
- S_G: located between the network and the DC bus.

Choice of the Membership Functions

The battery's state of charge can be: Minimum "S_{Min}", Medium "S_{Med}" or Maximum "S_{Max}". Similarly, the power difference can be considered as: Negative "N", Zero "Z" or Positive "P". Finally, the states of the switches S_B and S_G can be closed "OFF" or opened "ON". Each of these fuzzy sets is designated by a membership function. Trapezoidal membership functions are chosen to designate each of the fuzzy sets distributed on the variables discourse group of our system. The membership functions chosen for battery SOC, P_{Diff} and switch state (S_B and S_G) are shown respectively in Figs. 3, 4 and 5.

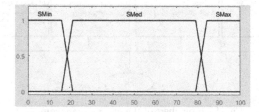

Fig. 3. SOC membership function of fuzzy logic controller

Choice of Inference Rules

The tuning strategy depends essentially on the adopted inferences, which associate the input variables with the output linguistic variable using a set of rules. The linguistic description of the inference adopted in our system is as follows:

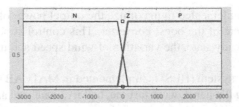

Fig. 4. P_{Diff} membership function of fuzzy logic controller

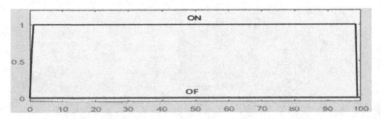

Fig. 5. SB and SG membership function of fuzzy logic controller (The state of the switches)

If P_{Diff} is N **and** SOC is S_{Min} **then** S_B is OFF and S_G is ON;
If P_{Diff} is N **and** SOC is S_{Med} **then** S_B is ON and S_G is OFF;
If P_{Diff} is N **and** SOC is S_{Max} **then** S_b is ON and S_G is OFF;
If P_{Diff} is Z **then** S_B is OFF and S_G is ON;
If P_{Diff} is P **and** SOC is S_{Min} **then** SB is ON and S_G is OFF;
If P_{Diff} is P **and** SOC is S_{Med} **then** S_B is ON and S_G is OFF;
If P_{Diff} is P **and** SOC is S_{Max} **then** S_B is OF and S_G is ON;

3.3   Control of PV Panel, Wind Turbine and DC Bus Voltage

Control of PV Pane
The PV panel is connected to the DC bus through the boost converter. To extract maximum power from the PV panel, it works under maximum power point tracking (MPPT) mode. Perturb and Observe algorithm is used for the MPPT tracking.

Control of the DC vs Voltage
The various sources of the system are interconnected via a DC bus with fixed voltage equal to 48 V. The control of the DC bus voltage will be carried out in a firstly thanks to the storage element which is the battery. This control is implemented by a reversible chopper in current through a classic PI (Proportional-Integral) regulator. If the battery reaches its lower limit SOC_{min}, it will be unable to control the DC bus voltage to its reference value. For this reason, the regulation of the DC bus voltage will be ensured by the external network which will impose its constant voltage.

Control of the Wind Turbine
The wind power system used in this work is composed formed by a turbine, a permanent magnet synchronous machine (PMSM), a three-phase rectifier and a boost chopper. An

MPPT controller is implemented to maximize the output power of the wind turbine by adjusting the duty cycle of the boost converter. This control structure is based on the assumption that, in steady state, the variation of wind speed and turbine rotation speed can be neglected [12].

The hybrid energy system (HES) is implemented in MATLAB software in an underconnected mode using PV panel, wind turbine, battery, main grid and resistive DC load, as shown in Fig. 6:

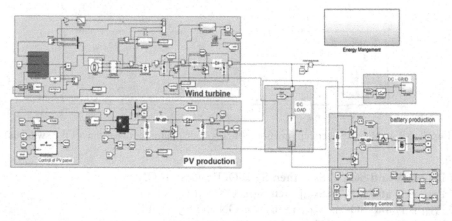

Fig. 6. Simulink model

The component values for each system (PV panels, Wind turbine and Battery) are shown respectively in Tables 2, 3 and 4.

Table 2. PV panel's components parameters

Parameters	Value
Maximum power (P_{max})	213.50 W
Open circuit voltage (V_{oc})	36.30 V
Short-circuit curent (I_{sc})	7.35 A
Number of PV cells connected in series (N_s)	7
Diode Ideality factor (α)	0.98
Resistance series (R_s)	0.39 Ω
Parallel resistor (R_{sh})	313.39 Ω
Diode saturation current (I_o)	2.9259 10^{-10} A

Table 3. Battery component parameters

Parameters	Value
Voltage	48 V
Nominal capacity	58 Ah
Resistance	0.048 Ω

Table 4. Wind turbine components parameters

Parameters	Value
Power rating (Pn)	1.7 kW
Effective flow (Ø)	0.44 Wb
Stator resistance (Rs)	0.43 Ω
Nominal speed (Ω)	153.4 rad/s
Stator inductance (Ls)	8.42 mH
Pairs of poles (P)	10
Density of the air (ρ)	1.225 kg/m^3
Swept area (S)	1.02 m^2
Optimal coefficient (Kopt)	1.67*10^{-3} Nm/(rad/s)^2
Nominal wind speed (V)	12 m/s

4 Results and Discussion

We differentiated between two cases to test the response and effectiveness of the said proposed management strategy:

$SOC = SOC_{min}$

- In the interval [0–1]: $P_{Diff} - 0$ (see Fig. 7). In this case, there is an equality between the power delivered by the two generators (PV and wind turbine) and the power requested by the load (see Fig. 9). As a consequence, the current becomes zero at the battery terminals (see Fig. 8).
- In the interval [1–3], there is an excess of energy. The battery is charged with this excess until the state $SOC = S_{Max} = 0.8$ (see Fig. 8). The main grid remains disconnected from the microgrid (see Fig. 9).
- In the interval [3–3.5]: $P_{Diff} < 0$. The produced power is zero, so it does not ensure the demand of the load anymore. The SOC of the battery is 22% > 20%, the battery feeds the load (discharge) until SOC = 20% (at t = 3.5) (see Fig. 8). The main grid remains therefore disconnected (see Fig. 9).
- In the interval [3.5–5]: $P_{Diff} < 0$ since the energy produced by the photovoltaic generators is zero, the $SOC = S_{Min} = 20\%$ so the battery disconnects (the current

becomes zero at the terminals of the battery), (see Fig. 8). The main grid connects to the microgrid to provide the load demand (see Fig. 9).

- At the beginning of the simulation, we assumed that the state of charge of the batteries was well below 0.2, as this was the first time we applied this strategy with a battery whose SOC is below SOC_{min}. This was done on purpose in order to test our strategy on the fact that it guarantees to maintain the state of charge between 0.2 and 0.8. After charging the battery, in the interval [1–3], (SOC>0.2) and discharging it, in the interval [3–3.5] (in discharge mode), we noticed that when the SOC of the battery reaches the value of 0.2, the battery stops discharging (see Fig. 8).

SOC min < SOC < = SOC_{max}

- In the interval [0–1]: $P_{Diff} = 0$ (see Fig. 7). In this case and like the previous one, the battery and the main grid are disconnected from the microgrid (see Figs. 10 and 11).
- In the interval [1–2]: $P_{Diff}>0$. There is an excess of energy, the battery is recharged by this excess provided that the SOC does not exceed S_{max} (Fig. 10). The main grid remains disconnected from the microgrid (see Fig. 11).
- In the interval [2–3]: $P_{Diff} > 0$ (excess energy). The battery is charged, SOC = $S_{Max} = 80\%$ (see Fig. 10). In this case, the external network connects to the grid so that the excess energy can be injected into the main grid (see Fig. 11).
- In the interval [3–5]: $P_{Diff} < 0$. There is a lack of energy ($P_{pv} + P_w < P_{Load}$) and since the SOC> S_{Min}, in this case, the battery assures the demand of the load (provided that SOC > S_{Min}) (see Fig. 10). The main grid is disconnected from the micro grid (see Fig. 11).
- The state of charge of the battery is always between the minimum and maximum threshold limits (0.2≤SOC≤0.8).

We conclude that the management supervision has been successfully validated.

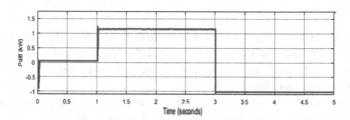

Fig. 7. Evolution of P_{Diff} power

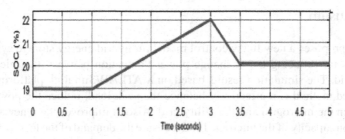

Fig. 8. Evolution of the battery's SOC

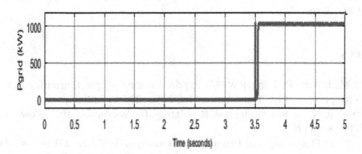

Fig. 9. Evolution of the power exchanged with the main grid

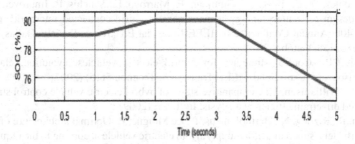

Fig. 10. Evolution of the battery's SOC

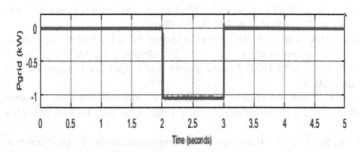

Fig. 11. Evolution of the power exchanged with the main grid

5 Conclusion

This paper proposes a new fuzzy control model for hybrid energy storage systems. The model aims for reducing the exchange power fluctuation between the microgrid and the main grid. The simulation results based on MATLAB/Simulink platform show that the proposed method can effectively balance the peak load, reduce the power fluctuation between the microgrid and the utility grid. Also, it improves the renewable energy consumption capacity of the microgrid and it ensure the demand of the load without interruption. Furthermore, it minimizes the imported or injected energy from or to the main grid and protect the batteries from overcharging and deep discharging which prolong the service life of the HES.

References

1. Katiraei, M., Iravani, R., Lehn, P.W.: Micro grid autonomous operation during and subsequent to islanding process. IEEE Trans. Power Del. **22**(1), 248–257 (2005)
2. Hatziargyriou, N., Asano, H., Iravani, R., Marnay, C.: Microgrids. IEEE Power and Energy Mag. **5**(4), 78–94 (2007)
3. Ribeiro, P.J.S.: Optimização de Estratégias de Operação de Sistemas Híbridos (2009)
4. Kanakasabapathy, P., Gopal, V.K., Abhijith, V., Mohan, A.: E H S Reddy, energy management and control of solar aided UPS. Tap Energy **2015**, 363–368 (2015)
5. Arcos-Aviles, D., Espinosa, N., Guinjoan, F., Marroyo, L., Sanchis, P.: Improved fuzzy controller design for battery energy management in a grid connected microgrid. In: IECON 2014 - 40th Annual Conference on IEEE Industrial Electronics Society, Dallas, TX, USA, pp. 2128–2133, October 2014
6. Salamsi, F.R.: Control strategies for hybrid electric vehicles: evolution, classification, comparison and future trends, IEEE Trans. Veh. Technol. **56**(5) (2007)
7. Desai, S., Williamson, S.: Comparative study of hybrid electric vehicle control strategies for improved drivetrain efficiency analysis. In: IEEE (2009)
8. Sadoun, R., Rizoug, N., Bartholomeus, P., Le Moigne, P.: Optimal architecture of the hybrid source (battery/supercapacitor) supplying an electric vehicle according to the required autonomy. In: 2013 15th European Conference on Power Electronics and Applications, EPE 2013 (2013)
9. Neffati, A., Guemri, M., Caux, S., Fadel, M.: Energy management strategies for multi-source systems. Electr. Power Syst. Res. **102**, 42–49 (2013)
10. Tedjani, M.: Design of a DC/DC power converter for li-ion battery/supercapacitor hybrid energy storage system in electric vehicles. In: Mamouri, L., Mesbahi, T., Bartholomeus, P., Paul, T. (eds.) 2020 IEEE Vehicle Power and Propulsion Conference, VPPC 2020 - Proceedings (2020)
11. Ngueveu, S.U., Caux, S., Messine, F., Guemri, M.: Heuristics and lower bounds for minimizing fuel consumption in hybrid-electrical vehicles. 4OR-Q J. Oper. Res. **15**(4), 407–430 (2017)
12. Mirecki, A., Roboam, X., Richardeau, F.: Comparative study of maximum power strategy in wind turbines. In: IEEE International Symposium on Industrial Electronics, 2004, vol. 2, pp. 993–998 (2004)

Case Studies and Cyber-Physical Systems 1

Approach for Optimisation Warehouse Storage Areas Based on the Container Storage Problem

Manal Ayad[1,2,3]($\boxtimes$) and Ali Siadat[2]

[1] Laboratoire Complex Cyber Physical Systems, École Nationale Supérieure d'Arts et Métiers, University of Hassan II, Casablanca, Morocco
manalayad1998@gmail.com
[2] Laboratoire de Conception Fabrication Commande, École Nationale Supérieure d'Arts et Métiers, University of Lorraine, Metz, France
[3] Centre d'Étude et de Recherche pour l'Ingénierie et le Management, Haute Étude Supérieure de l'Ingénierie et de Management HESTIM, Casablanca, Morocco

Abstract. Warehousing, is a pillar of logistics and a link in the entire Supply Chain. Thus, warehousing's quality is dependent on the effectiveness of its multiple missions that meets several challenges (safety, security, handling equipment, design...). Sizing warehouses & Optimization of surfaces is the research focus on this paper that mainly aims and contributes to standardize the estimation of the storage area surface to be used and optimizing it. This study arises from the fact that some companies must store different equipment (with distinct dimensions and different dates of entry and exit) on the same storage area, what makes these companies fall into the warehousing hazard trap. The proposed solution of this research results from the Benchmarking study carried out on the Container Storage Problem in port terminals. In this paper, we propose a Branch and Cut algorithm which is supported by some specific storage strategies, highlighting the Operational Research as an efficient problem-solving tool. To meet the objectives and make the work a reality, a project under construction at JESA company is taken as a reference to apply the solution and implemented it through CPLEX optimization software using the Optimization Programming Language OPL.

Keywords: Supply chain · Warehousing · Operational research · Branch and cut algorithm · Benchmarking

1 Introduction

The Supply Chain is a complex and sometimes fragile business that depends on a network of independent but interconnected moving parts through a well-planned information-, physical-, distribution- and money-flow [22]. Suppliers supply raw

---

Supported by JESA company.

materials, producers convert these raw materials into products, warehouses store this product until it is needed, distribution centers collect and deliver this product, retailers, in online and in store, bring this product to the customer [6]. Thus, striving for a best supply chain management's SCM quality has been the research focus to reach an optimized supply chain proposing methods that always being improved in many aspects. To this end, researchers resorted to the Operational Research by using different mathematical models to attain the optimized solution: Technology-Driven Supply Chains in the Industry 4.0 [10,12,16,19], Optimal inventory allocation [25], optimization of sustainable supply chain uncertainty [18]. One of the biggest challenges of the SCM in physical flow is Warehousing activities [21], since warehouses can at once store both finished and in-process products namely Work In Process products [14], and thus by extension, given the diversity of uses of warehouses, they can simultaneously store equipment with different entry and exit dates.

In this paper, we focus on warehousing challenges for large warehouses that store different equipment of different sizes, and this by benchmarking the solutions to the Container Storage Problem CSP. To generalize the solution and make it applicable to a larger number of warehouses, we will try to standardize the sizes of these equipment by converting them into 20'container units [8]. On, as in the CSP the only constraint that will be taken into account in this search to store these container equivalent equipment is their entry and exit dates [11,13,20] as Inbound and Outbound containers [9].

In the remainder of this paper, a related work of the container storage problem is given by Sect. 2, based on this, the proposed methodology and its application on a real case are the subject of Sects. 3 and 4 respectively.

2   Related Work

A container port terminal is part of the port where containers are unloaded by cranes and stored in **storage areas** by handling vehicles. The port terminal provides both transfer and temporary storage of containers [8]. Here we will focus on the processes of unloading and loading of containers, which between them is the sub-process of storage of containers. The management efficiency of these processes depends on the productivity of the port [20]. The containers, given their principle of standardization in a unit of Twenty-foot Equivalent Unit TEU, have allowed a saving of time in handling operations [8]. This particularity of standardization of containers also allowed researchers to take advantage of it and opt for the superposition of these containers as a stack [20] in order to optimize space in the port terminal.

In fact, this superposition of containers, despite of being effective in minimizing storage space, with a random arrangement of these containers, creates another phenomenon called *rehandling* [15] which refers to the operations of rearranging containers before their scheduled departure times. This operation is carried out in the case of extraction of the containers which are at the bottom of the stack.

For a guaranteed efficiency, the superposition must take into account the dates of exit of the containers [20], for that several solutions have been proposed to locate the most appropriate storage location for, generally, Inbound IB and Outbound OB containers [13]. According to [20], the solution to rehandling movements is spread over two major parts: efficient storage strategies supported by decision support algorithms.

According to [23], container storage strategies in port terminals are divided into four main categories: *Storage by Segregation and Non-segregation* [17] based on the distinction of containers by type of containers (import/export), *Storage by Grouping and Dispersion* [7] based on the distinction of containers by group of containers, *Direct and Indirect Storage* [3,4,24] based on pre-storing containers in an area called the layout area before being placed in the storage yard, and finally *Unloading Priority and Loading Priority Storage* [2,7,9] based on the date of entry/exit of the containers.

In the frame of the operational research, Container Storage Problem is considered as generalized assignment problem [1], is formulated as Mixed Integer Linear Problem *MIP* [13] or as Integer Linear Problem *ILP* [11,20], and by analogy with the *CSP* and *SSAP*, belongs thus to *NP-hard* and *NP-complete* problem category [1,11,13,20]. In the aim of minimizing the container total rehandling operations, the researchers have treated the problem with exact *Branch and Cut* algorithm considering large surfaces [20], metaheuristic *Bee Colony* algorithm in the case of a normal size warehouse [20], and in [11] the metaheuristics *Genetic* and *Harmony search* algorithms were compared in the case of one and several types of containers in the same storage area, other researchers have opted for evolutionary heuristic [5] to meet the objective.

The processes of loading and unloading of containers are diagrammed in the Fig. 1, highlighting the storage strategies and the sub-process in case of rehandling. The process is considered in the perfect case in which we neglect the verification and control sub-processes.

3 Proposed Methodology

As above-mentioned, the idea of this research is to take advantage of the standardization of the containers to provide a standard solution of estimation and optimization of large surface of warehouses in several fields considering only equipment entry and exit dates. The research carried out in this sense is summarized in the 6 steps described below:

Step 1: Choice of the Storage Case Considered
In this paper, we distinguish two storage cases, the *static* and the *dynamic* case [20]. The difference lies in the fact that, in the dynamic case, we consider that not all the containers have yet arrived in the terminal at the start of the storage operations, even if the departure and arrival dates of the containers are known, in other words the containers that will arrive after the start of storage operations are taken into account. Whereas, in the static case, it is considered

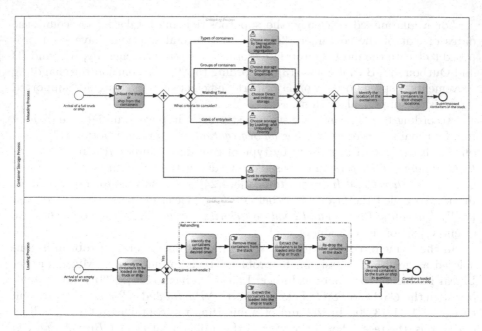

Fig. 1. Container storage process.

that all the containers have already arrived at the port before the start of storage operations. Before going into details, it should be noted that the storage case considered during the rest of the paper is the *static case*, where it considered that all the containers have already arrived before the start of storage operations.

Step 2: Calculation of the Equivalence of Equipment in Containers
The first step to facilitate the storage of equipment is to standardize it. Equipment, large or small, will be treated in a standard way. As with container storage, equipment will be handled in units of *20' containers*, because this is more economical way in terms of surface area than *40' containers*.

To do this, it is essential to follow the steps shown in the algorithm below:

1. Sort the equipment received in ascending order of date of receipt (date of entry).
2. Calculate the total surface area of the equipment having the same date of reception (date of entry) and date of exit (date of departure).
3. Divide this surface obtained by the surface of a 20' container to get the equivalence of these equipment in number of containers.
4. X = Unit Container
5. If the result X is greater than 1, we consider X containers with same input and output of these equipment.

Algorithm 1.1. *Standardization of the surface unit*

```
1 #1 : initialization :
2 Container Surface = 14,884
3 Surface = 0
4 N = Number of containers
5 ED = Entry Date
6 EXD = EXit Date
7
8 #2 : Loop :
9 For k = 1...N
10    For k'= k+1...N-1
11       If ED(k) = ED(k') and EXD(k) = EXD(k')
12          Surface = Surface(k) + Surface(k')
13          Container Unit = ⌈  Surface  /  Container surface  ⌉
14       EndIf
15    EndFor
16 EndFor
```

Step 3: Choice of the Storage Strategy

Having chosen the *20' containers* as the surface unit for the equipment, it is now time to adopt a storage strategy to give the storage of this equipment a special modality to consider: *storage with Segregation* and *Loading Priority storage*. The details of these two strategies will be revealed in Sect. 4 of the case study.

Step 4: Choice of the Distribution of the Container-Equivalent Equipment

To standardize this method, and make it valid for almost all warehouses, we will consider that there is no superposition, and we will consider the forklift as material handling equipment. On this basis, we set the maximum number of container-equivalent equipment along the Z-axis *(stack)* to 1 and 2 for X-axis *(bay)* with only one open access (see Fig. 2). Still considering the forklift as the handling equipment, the distance that will separate the chosen areas in segregated storage from the equipment will be $d = 8$ m.

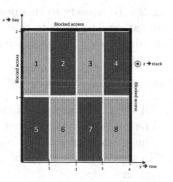

Fig. 2. Cartesian coordinate system (x, y, z).

Step 5: Calculation of the Storage Area Parameters

- **Index:**
    - x - Location along bay-axis
    - i - Location index
- **20' container dimension:**
    - L_c - Length of 20' container
    - l_c - Width of 20' container

- **Data for areas:**
  N - Number of containers
  N_A - Number of areas

Surface Storage Yard- The standard formula for calculating storage area for equipment equivalent to 20' containers is:

$$\text{Total surface area} = \sum_{i=1}^{N_A} \sum_{x=1}^{2} N_x(i) \times l_c \times (L_c + d(i))$$

$$\text{Such as} \begin{cases} \begin{cases} d(i) = 0 \text{ if } i \text{ is in the last row of the storage area or } x = 1; \\ d(i) = 8 \text{ otherwise} \end{cases} \\ N_1 = \left\lceil \dfrac{N}{2} \right\rceil \\ N_2 = N - \left\lceil \dfrac{N}{2} \right\rceil \end{cases} \quad (1)$$

Step 6: Minimization of Container-Equivalent Equipment Rehandles
As the above-mentioned Container Storage Problem, the solution proposed in this paper also causes a need for container rehandling along the X-axis since access is blocked for containers that are at the back in case of unthinking storage (Fig. 2). To remedy to this problem, the following is a proposed *Branch and Cut* exact algorithm used to find the best location for these containers in order to minimize their rehandles during their storage based solely on their entry and exit dates.

Assumptions- Below are all the assumptions considered in this paper:

1. All the containers are of the same size (20');
2. The problem is considered in the static case;
3. The storage modality is segregated (according to areas);
4. No superposition of containers: Containers are stored horizontally in bays and not in stacks;
5. Locations will be in 2D along the X and Y axis;
6. The number of containers along the X-axis is equal to 2. This is because forklift cannot remove containers too far to the back;
7. Containers are numbered in order of receipt;
8. Containers will be placed according to their date of departure;

Parameters - The parameters of this program are the following (Table 1):

Table 1. Parameters.

Indices	i	Container index
	x	X coordinate index
	y	Y coordinate index
Data for containers	N_c	Total number of container i
	$date_i(i)$	Inbound date of container i
	$date_o(i)$	Outbound date of container i
Data for bays	N	number of locations along the X-axis
	M	number of locations along the Y-axis
General Data	Z	Large Integer

Variable Decision - For this problem, there is a boolean decision variable:

$$C_i(x,y) \in \mathbb{Z} = \begin{cases} 1 \text{ if the container } i \text{ is assigned to the location (x,y)} \\ 0 \text{ otherwise} \end{cases} \tag{2}$$

Objective Function - The proposed mathematical model for this problem is as follows:

$$\underset{reh_i}{\text{Minimize}} \sum_{i=1}^{N_C} reh_i C_i(x,y) \quad (\forall x = 1..N; \; y = 1..M)$$

$$\text{s.t.} \quad (\forall i = 1..N_C) \sum_{x=1}^{N} \sum_{y=1}^{M} C_i(x,y) = 1$$

$$(\forall x = 1..N; \; \forall y = 1..M) \sum_{i=1}^{N_C} C_i(x,y) <= 1$$

$$(\forall x = 1..N \; \forall y = 1..M) \sum_{i=1}^{N_C} \sum_{j=1}^{N_c} (date_o(j) - date_o(i)) C_i(x,y) <= Z(reh_i C_i(x,y))$$

$$(\forall x = 1..N \; \forall y = 1..M) \sum_{i=1}^{N_C} \sum_{j=1}^{N_c} (date_o(i) - date_o(j)) C_j(x,y) <= Z(reh_j C_j(x,y)) \tag{3}$$

Such as:

reh_i: The number of rehandles to remove the container i

Remark 1. (**Constraints definition**).

The first constraint ensures that each container i is assigned to one and only one location (x, y).

The second constraint guarantees that each location (x, y) has at most one container i assigned.

The last two constraints force $reh = 1$ under specific entry and exit conditions of containers i and j.

Branch and Cut Algorithm - is an integer programming method which generate at the end, a tree called *branch and cut tree* whose sub-problems are named *nodes*.

The general approach of *Branch and Cut* is summarized according to [20] in the following pseudo-code:

Algorithm 1.2. *Branch & Cut algorithm [20]*

```
 1  #1 : initialization :
 2  Let P⁰ be the initial integer problem.
 3  Initialize the list of active nodes of the search tree,
 4  T = {P⁰}.
 5  Search for an upper bound UB. If it does not find a solution, then put UB=
       +∞.
 6  #2 : Stop condition :
 7  If T = ∅ , then the optimal solution is the one whose value is equal to UB
       .
 8  If UB=+∞, then there is no solution.
 9  #3 : Node selection :
10  Choose in T a Pˡ node to explore, which will then be deleted.
11  #4 : Relaxation :
12  Solve the relaxation of Pˡ.
13  If there is no solution, then set lower born LBₗ =+∞and go to step 6.
14  Otherwise, note Sᴿˡ the optimal solution of Pˡ, and use its value to update
       LBₗ .
15  #5 : Add valid inequalities :
16  Look for valid inequalities that are violated by Sᴿˡ.
17  If there are any, then add them to the relaxation of Pˡ and return to step
       4.
18  #6 : Pruning :
19  If LBₗ ≥ UB then return to step 2.
20  If LBₗ < UB and Sᴿˡ is a feasible integer solution, then update UB=LBₗ ,
       then delete from T any element j whose lower bound verifies LBⱼ ≥ BS,
       and return to step 2.
21  #7 : Branching :
22  If Sᴿˡ is fractional, then branch to the most fractional variable. We thus
       obtain two sub-problems, Pʲ,¹ and Pʲ,², which we add in T.
```

4 Case Study

The efficiency of the proposed solution is evaluated by a numerical example from a concrete case of equipment storage in warehouses before their assembly for projects conducted by *JESA* company responsible of engineering, project delivery and asset management services for their customers. The delivery of the projects resides in the fact of carrying out a whole project since the order, the control and the transport of the equipment and its storage, until its assembly. If we project this onto a simplified supply chain we can say that the physical flows at *JESA* are the equipment to be assembled, and the mission of warehouse logistics is to protect the equipment until it is assembled at the construction sites. JESA's challenge in terms of warehousing is to estimate a storage area for the equipment while optimizing it.

Assume that the project studied in this paper is divided into assembly *areas* (Area 1, Area 2, Area 2.1, Area 4, Area 5, Area 6), and the data on *the dates of receipt and assembly* of the equipment is known. The equipment is stored for a *maximum of 3 months* before assembly in an empty stockyard.

4.1   Numerical Example

Step 1: Choice of the storage case considered: static case.

The storage case adopted is the *static case* considering a duration of 3 months. Remember that this duration is the maximum time that an equipment can wait before being assembled during the project. By doing this, the economy of the storage area will be guaranteed, because the storage area will be adapted to the storage period of the equipment.

For the remainder of the paper, we consider the first 3-month storage period from 03/16/2018 to 06/16/2018, of which the areas considered are: Area 1, Area 2 and Area 5.

Step 2: Calculation of the equivalence of equipment in containers.

Based on what was previously reported and considering the first 3-month period, the results of the equivalence of the equipment in containers i in each area are shown in Table 2.

Remark 2. $date_i(i)$ and $date_o(i)$ are calculated in number of days to simplify their compilation by CPLEX.

Step 3: Choice of storage strategy: Segregated & Loading Priority storage.

Storage with segregation is about storing equipment according to their assembly areas. Therefore, the storage yard will be divided into assembly areas, which shows the advantage of having a large storage yard that offers flexibility in dividing the equipment, and *Loading Priority Storage* comes to minimize the rehandles since it acts on the outbound dates.

Step 4: Choice of the distribution of the container-equivalent equipment.

In view of the above, the distribution will be as follows (see Fig. 3). The access will be opened for Area 2 to eradicate its rehandling.

Step 5 : Calculation of the storage area.

$$\text{Total Surface} = 5 \times 2,44 \times (6,09+0) + 4 \times 2,44 \times (6,09+8)$$
$$+ 7 \times 2,44 \times (6,09+0) + 6 \times (6,09+8) + 1 \times 2,44 \times (6,09+0)$$
$$+ 1 \times 2,44 \times (6,09+8) = 551,8304\,\text{m}^2$$

Step 6: Minimization of container-equivalent equipment rehandles for Area 1.

Table 2. Container-equivalence equipment.

Area 1				
i	*Inbound date*	*Outbound date*	*date$_i$(i)*	*date$_o$(i)*
1	03/16/2018	05/04/2018	1	50
2	03/16/2018	04/19/2018	1	35
3	03/16/2018	03/23/2018	1	8
4	03/16/2018	05/20/2018	1	66
5	03/16/2018	05/13/2018	1	59
6	06/05/2018	08/22/2018	82	160
7	06/11/2018	07/24/2018	88	131
8	06/11/2018	08/17/2018	88	155
9	06/11/2018	07/24/2018	88	131

Area 2				
i	*Inbound date*	*Outbound date*	*date$_i$(i)*	*date$_o$(i)*
1	06/09/2018	06/13/2018	1	5
2	06/09/2018	06/27/2018	1	19
3	06/09/2018	08/23/2018	1	76
4	06/09/2018	06/21/2018	1	13
5	06/11/2018	12/07/2018	3	34
6	06/11/2018	27/07/2018	3	49
7	06/11/2018	08/08/2018	3	61
8	06/11/2018	08/29/2018	3	82
9	06/11/2018	09/03/2018	3	87
10	06/11/2018	07/26/2018	3	48
11	06/11/2018	08/25/2018	3	78
12	06/11/2018	06/11/2018	3	3
13	06/11/2018	07/29/2018	3	51

Area 5				
i	*Inbound date*	*Outbound date*	*date$_i$(i)*	*date$_o$(i)*
1	04/12/2018	05/15/2018	1	34
2	06/12/2018	08/13/2018	62	124

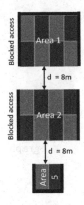

Fig. 3. First 3-month period distribution.

After compilation of equipment location decision using *Branch and Cut* algorithm, the results are displayed in Table 3 as *Location = 1* if container i is at location (x, y), and *Location = 0* otherwise.

Discussion

Looking at this, we can say that the algorithm has **eradicated rehandles**, such that (Table 4; Fig. 4):

- *Container 1* enters on *day 1* and exits on *day 50* and therefore it will not cause a rehandling of *container 6* which enters much later after the exit of *container 1* on *day 82*.
- For the case of *containers 9 and 4*, it is the same principle as containers 1 and 6, so that *container 9* enters later than the exit of *container 4*.
- *Containers 2 and 3* enter on the same *day 1* but *container 2* leaves later than *container 3*, and so *container 2* is placed at the bottom of the storage area so that *container 3* is taken out first on *day 8* without rehandling *container 2* which leaves on *day 35*.
- Between *container 7 and 8*, it is the same principle as containers 2 and 3, so that *container 8* is placed at the bottom of the storage area since it comes out last.

Table 3. Results of container location.

Index i	X-coordinate	Y-coordinate	Location
1	2	2	1
2	2	5	1
3	1	5	1
4	1	1	1
5	1	4	1
6	1	2	1
7	1	3	1
8	2	3	1
9	2	1	1

Table 4. Summary of data for Area 1.

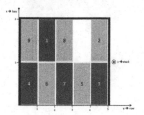

Fig. 4. Interpretation of the results on a graph (x, y).

i	$date_i$	$date_o$
	Area 1	
1	1	50
2	1	35
3	1	8
4	1	66
5	1	59
6	82	160
7	88	131
8	88	155
9	88	131

5 Conclusion

This paper proposes a standard method for sizing warehouses by optimizing their surfaces, applicable to a wide range of warehouse types based on a particular case of the Container Storage Problem PSC.

Benchmarking focused on the analysis of the storage strategies of port containers, as well as the different exact algorithms and metaheuristics that accompany these strategies in order to combine them and, in the end, give a satisfactory result that meets the needs behind the use of operational research: minimizing or even eradicating rehandles.

The biggest challenge was to project what has just been analyzed in Benchmarking on available storage data far from those of the port terminals.

In order to optimize the storage area, it was proposed to consider the equipment in container units and to place the maximum number of equipment side by side and one in front of the other in the form of a bay, so that a good storage area will be saved.

The problem behind this solution is that it requires a well thought-out storage of container-equivalent equipment, otherwise we will fall into the trap of rehandling considered unproductive movements.

In this impetus, and following in the footsteps of other researchers, we have opted for the Branch and Cut algorithm which implements by CPLEX this mathematically modeled problem.

This is just a startup for studying the standardization of warehouse sizing and their optimization based on the proposed solutions to remedy the Container Storage Problems CSP. Many open issues offer possibilities for future study. To save even more storage space, we aim to work with integer and non-integer container units in case the equipment does not form a complete container *(0,4 container; 1,2 container...)*. For a more efficient solution in terms of speed, we have to question the search of the nodes of the Branch and Cut or even the choice of the algorithm, since the exact algorithms act efficiently on a small number of data and take a lot of time for a too big number of data.

References

1. Bazzazi, M., Safaei, N., Javadian, N.: A genetic algorithm to solve the storage space allocation problem in a container terminal. Comput. Ind. Eng. **56**, 44–52 (2009). https://doi.org/10.1016/j.cie.2008.03.012
2. Borgman, B., Asperen, E.V., Dekker, R., Borgman, B., Dekker, R., Asperen, E.V.: Online rules for container stacking. OR Spectrum **32**, 687–716 (2010). https://doi.org/10.1007/S00291-010-0205-4
3. de Castillo, B., Daganzo, C.F.: Handling strategies for import containers at marine terminals. Transp. Res. Part B: Methodol. **27**, 151–166 (1993). https://doi.org/10.1016/0191-2615(93)90005-U
4. Chen, T.: Yard operations in the container terminal-a study in the 'unproductive moves. Marit. Policy Manag. **26**, 27–38 (1999). https://doi.org/10.1080/030888399287041
5. Cordeau, J.F., Gaudioso, M., Laporte, G., Moccia, L.: The service allocation problem at the Gioia Tauro maritime terminal. Eur. J. Oper. Res. **176**, 1167–1184 (2007). https://doi.org/10.1016/j.ejor.2005.09.004
6. Daroudi, S., Kazemipoor, H., Najafi, E., Fallah, M.: The minimum latency in location routing fuzzy inventory problem for perishable multi-product materials. Appl. Soft Comput. **110** (2021). https://doi.org/10.1016/j.asoc.2021.107543
7. Dekker, R., Voogd, P., Asperen, E.V.: Advanced methods for container stacking. undefined 28, October 2006. DOI:https://doi.org/10.1007/S00291-006-0038-3
8. Dubreuil, J.: La logistique des terminaux portuaires de conteneurs (2007)
9. Duinkerken, M.B., Evers, J.J.M., Ottjes, J.A.: A simulation model for integrating quay transport and stacking policies on automated container terminals (2001)
10. Garouani, M., Ahmad, A., Bouneffa, M., Hamlich, M., Bourguin, G., Lewandowski, A.: Towards big industrial data mining through explainable automated machine learning. Int. J. Adv. Manuf. Technol. **120**(1–2), 1169–1188 (2022). https://doi.org/10.1007/s00170-022-08761-9, https://www.scopus.com/inward/record.uri?eid=2-s2.0-85124533422&doi=10.1007%2fs00170-022-08761-9&partnerID=40&md5=6f8acb109c7fd98e61501acf73a737a8
11. Hajjem, I.A.: Techniques avancées d'optimisation pour la résolution du problème de stockage de conteneurs dans un port. Ph.D. thesis, https://tel.archives-ouvertes.fr/tel-01266169
12. Hamlich, M., Ramdani, M.: Data classification by sac "scout ants for clustering" algorithm. J. Theoret. Appl. Inf. Technol. **55**(1), 66–73 (2013). https://www.scopus.com/inward/record.uri?eid=2-s2.0-84883869002&partnerID=40&md5=9ed20bcce68fa42017efbb142170865a
13. Kefi, M.: Optimisation Heuristique Distribuée du Problème de Stockage de Conteneurs dans un Port. Ph.D. thesis. https://tel.archives-ouvertes.fr/tel-00366467
14. Kekana, P., Bakama, E.M., Mukwakungu, S.C., Sukdeo, N.: The impact of smart-warehousing on a local foodservice equipment-company's external customers, vol. 2020-December, pp. 771–775. IEEE Computer Society, December 2020. https://doi.org/10.1109/IEEM45057.2020.9309751

15. Khaoula, C.: Optimisation des mouvements des conteneurs dans un terminal maritime. Ph.D. thesis (12). https://publications.polymtl.ca/737/1/2011_KhaoulaChebil.pdf

16. Luo, S., Choi, T.M.: Operational research for technology-driven supply chains in the industry 4.0 era: recent development and future studies. Asia-Pacific J. Oper. Res. (2020). https://doi.org/10.1142/S0217595920400217

17. Ma, Y., Kim, K.H.: A comparative analysis: various storage rules in container yards and their performances. Ind. Eng. Manage. Syst. **11**, 276–287 (2012). https://doi.org/10.7232/iems.2012.11.3.276

18. Mirghaderi, S.D., Modiri, M.: Application of meta-heuristic algorithm for multi-objective optimization of sustainable supply chain uncertainty. https://doi.org/10.1007/s12046-020-01554-4S

19. Moncef, G., Adeel, A., Mourad, B., Mohamed, H.: Amlbid: An auto-explained automated machine learning tool for big industrial data. SoftwareX 17 (2022). https://doi.org/10.1016/j.softx.2021.100919, https://www.scopus.com/inward/record.uri?eid=2-s2.0-85121265920&doi=10.1016%2fj.softx.2021.100919&partnerID=40&md5=7f168872e6185c17a3079221d35a7d14

20. Ndiaye, N.F.: Algorithmes d'optimisation pour la résolution du problème de stockage de conteneurs dans un terminal portuaire. Ph.D. thesis. https://tel.archives-ouvertes.fr/tel-01255365/document

21. Pandian, D.A.P.: Artificial intelligence application in smart warehousing environment for automated logistics. J. Artif. Intell. Capsule Networks **2019**, 63–72 (2019). https://doi.org/10.36548/jaicn.2019.2.002

22. Singh, S., Kumar, P., Bhandari, M., Soni, G.: Risk management for e-commerce supply chain network using robust optimization approach: a case study. In: Natarajan, S.K., Prakash, R., Sankaranarayanasamy, K. (eds.) Recent Advances in Manufacturing, Automation, Design and Energy Technologies. LNME, pp. 35–46. Springer, Singapore (2022). https://doi.org/10.1007/978-981-16-4222-7_5 https://shortest.link/1-4O

23. Saanen, Y.A., Dekker, R.: Intelligent stacking as way out of congested yards? part 1. Port Technology (2007). https://www.porttechnology.org/technical-papers/intelligent_stacking_as_way_out_of_congested_yards_part_1/

24. Taleb-Ibrahimi, M., de Castilho, B., Daganzo, C.F.: Storage space vs handling work in container terminals. Transportation Research Part B: Methodological **27**(1), 13–32 (1993). https://EconPapers.repec.org/RePEc:eee:transb:v:27:y:1993:i:1:p:13–32

25. Zheng, M., Du, N., Zhao, H., Huang, E., Wu, K.: A study on the optimal inventory allocation for clinical trial supply chains. Appl. Math. Modelling **98**, 161–184 (2021). https://doi.org/10.1016/j.apm.2021.04.029

Roadmap to Implement Industry 5.0 and the Impact of This Approach on TQM

Meryem Chaabi(✉)

CCPS Laboratory, ENSAM, University of Hassan II, Casablanca, Morocco
meryem.chaabi-etu@etu.univh2c.ma

Abstract. The fifth Industrial Revolution (Industry 5.0) encompasses the transition from a digital-driven to a sustainable, human-centric, and resilient industry. Industry 5.0 recognize and value the role of workers in the production system. Therefore, it sets the health and safety of employees as a priority. Workers will be empowered and aided by robots and advanced technologies in order to improve work processes and work areas, hence improving companies' productivity and efficiency. However, the shift from Industry 4.0 to Industry 5.0 will de- pend on how employees will embrace the new vision and on how prepared they are to work alongside machines, especially since advanced technologies have developed the fear of loss of jobs among employees. In this context, we propose a roadmap to implement the industry 5.0 vision and build interest among workers for change by merging two concepts ADKAR and Quality Circles. Furthermore, we discussed the impact of industry 5.0 on Total Quality Management.

Keywords: Industry 5.0 · Human-centric manufacturing · Empowerment · Total Quality management

1 Introduction

The fourth industrial revolution often referred to as Industry 4.0, had its origins at the Hannover Fair in 2011. It describes the digital transformation of the manufacturing system and it is based on several technologies to support this transition [1, 2]. These technologies include artificial intelligence, Cyber-Physical Systems, additive manufacturing, the Internet of Things, and robotics. Industry 4.0 aims to create a highly integrated value chain to improve industrial productivity, efficiency, and competitiveness [3]. However, despite the benefits that Industry 4.0 brought to the manufacturing sector, an important element of the industrial scene was missing. Industry 4.0 has focused more heavily on the automation approach, while the human workforce was sorely neglected.

Recently, several researchers have brought the issue of the value of human operators in the manufacturing process to the forefront. In the light of the increasing complexity of the manufacturing industry [4], industrial companies are starting to place greater emphasis on the importance of human workers in the production system.

The changing customer demand and mass personalization have reshaped the manufacturing sector [5]. The salient features of modern production systems are shorter life

M. Hamlich et al. (Eds.): SADASC 2022, CCIS 1677, pp. 287–293, 2022.
https://doi.org/10.1007/978-3-031-20490-6_23

cycles of products and technologies, shorter lead times, and intense competition [6]. To fulfill these requirements, the human workforce remains indispensable, the creativity, intuition, critical thinking, and cognitive skills of humans are important in the production line [7]. Besides leveraging the industry 4.0 technologies, industrial companies need to invest in their employees.

In this context, The European Commission has defined "Industry 5.0" as a human-centric, sustainable, and resilient industry [8]. Industry 5.0 is about revaluing the human's role in the manufacturing system. This new concept considers technologies as tools provided to workers to support them in their daily activities to create a safer, healthier, and more efficient work environment. One of the main objectives of Industry 5.0 is to promote efficient human-machine collaboration [9]. Cobots (collaborative robots) will assist the workers on their tasks taking into account the conditions of the surrounding environment and the worker's intention [10], as this allows technology to be adapted to human needs.

The shift from technology-driven to a human-centric approach is not as simple as it seems. Industry 4.0 has solidified among workers the idea that new technologies and automation are a threat to the workforce [11]. Automation has destroyed many jobs and decreased the participation of operators in added value, which has lead to decreased job satisfaction and job burnout among a number of employees [12].

2   Related Works

The human-centric approach has been discussed from different perspectives by some researchers. Pinzone et al. [13] stressed the importance of the touch of human in modern production systems and investigated the impact of industry 4.0 technologies on the health and job performance of workers. Mattsson et al. [14] provided a study on ways used by companies to empower their employees in order to handle the complexity of the production system. Empowering is about adapting the workplace to the needs of the worker and supporting him to improve his competencies. The work [15] proposed a human-in-the-loop model, which is an artificial intelligence architecture based on a human-centric approach. Rowlands et al. [16] assumed that focusing only on technologies is not enough to reach expected results, so in order to get the full benefit of industry 4.0, they suggested the transition to a quality 4.0-driven strategy.

Romero et al. [17] introduced the operator of the future "operator 4.0". They presented a typology in which workers are reintegrated back into the production process. The role of operator 4.0 is vital, he is empowered, skilled, and has decision-making power. Operator 4.0 will be supported by robots and smart tools when needed. They determined a framework with eight characteristics: Super-Strength Operator, Augmented Operator, Virtual Operator, Healthy Operator, Smarter Operator, Collaborative Operator; Social Operator; and Analytical Operator. Kaasinen et al. [5] presented their vision of Operator 4.0 and they interviewed 44 workers to analyze their expectations related to the worker of future, thus they concluded that operators should be involved in the process of developing technical solutions.

3   Roadmap for Human-Centric Approach Implementation

In Industry 5.0 scenario, cobot and advanced technologies will provide assistance to the worker in order to improve safety and health. Thus, industrial companies could make the most of the skills and creativity of their employees. From a worker's point of view, advanced technologies and robots could be seen as threats of losing their jobs and as result, maybe they would not be interested in adopting these technologies [5]. To manage this resistance to change and to avoid the misconception that advanced technologies are competitors to workers, the first step is to build worker trust in digital tools. In this context, we propose a roadmap to implement the process of bringing back operators to the production line alongside machines, by merging two tools: ADKAR and quality circles.

3.1   Quality Circle

A quality circle (QC) is a tool to improve quality. It consists of a group of workers who often share the same workplace, they regularly meet in order to determine, discuss and solve issues negatively affecting their working environment [18]. Quality circle involves the following steps:

1. Identification of related work-related problems.
2. Selection of problem.
3. Analyzing the problem.
4. Develop solutions.
5. Communicate the findings to the top management.
6. Implement approved solutions.

3.2   ADKAR

ADKAR is an acronym for a change management model [19]; it enables gradual implementation of the desired change through five sequential phases:

a. Awareness of the need for change.
b. Desire to make the change.
c. Knowledge of how to change.
d. Ability to implement the change
e. Reinforcement until this change takes root.

3.3   Proposed Framework

Figure 1 depicts the steps involved in the proposed framework and the importance of each step.

Develop awareness of the need for change among the members of quality circles.	Introduce the importance of the human-centric approach to the workers.
Create the desire to perform the new roles of "operator of future".	Explain that the technologies no longer constitute a competitor to the employees.
Build knowledge.	Provide employees with the necessary knowledge to perform cooperative work with robots and to use advanced technologies to support them and improve their well-being.
QC define well-being-related problems.	Allow the workers to have an active role to adapt technologies to their needs.
QC analyze the problems.	Get a better understanding of the identified problems.
QC develop solutions based on acquired knowledge.	Create the ability for change and improve problem-solving capability among workers.
Communicate the proposed solutions to the management.	Promote mutual trust between employees and the management.
Implement approved solutions.	Improve the working environment, job satisfaction and build trust in digital tools.
Reinforce new roles of workers.	Sustain the change.

Fig. 1. Steps of proposed framework and importance of each step

As an example, we consider a quality circle consisting of 7 members with a line executive as a facilitator. The facilitator communicates with all levels of management and provides training to QC members. This QC aims to reduce ergonomic risk factors. The latter represents working conditions such as repetition, work stress, extreme heat, and vibration. Generally, all situations that can cause injuries or lead to musculoskeletal disorders (MSDs).

The proposed framework is used in this case to build and maintain worker trust in monitoring technologies, because, for example, wearing health monitoring devices such as wearable sensors could be considered uncomfortable. Furthermore, these devices may create psychological pressure or risk of privacy invasion [8].

The following steps are adopted to make use of the proposed framework:

- Develop awareness of the need for monitoring technologies.
- Highlight the benefits of monitoring technologies: these technologies will aid in ensuring workers' safety, and keeping a close eye on workers' health and the conditions of the surrounding environment.
- Provide the members of QC with the necessary knowledge to adopt and take full advantage of monitoring technologies, by delivering training and facilitating access to information.
- QC members define ergonomic risk factors in their workplace.
- QC members analyze the identified risks.
- QC members develop solutions using monitoring technologies based on their needs. The wearable sensors will generate real-time alerts (e.g., high-stress levels, extreme temperature, toxic gases...), and so the worker takes the necessary measures to handle the situation.
- The facilitator communicates the proposed solutions to the management.
- Implementation of the approved solutions by the management.
- Reinforcement of role of Healthy Operator.

This framework enables members of quality circles to embrace their new roles in the production system and participate to adapt technologies to their needs. And therefore, the proposed framework will improve participative management. Since the members work in the same functional area, it would be easier to implement the change among a group who have almost the same concerns and face similar problems. Non members also benefit from applying this framework, they help in implementing the solutions proposed by quality circle members. so, they will show interest and enthusiasm to work alongside robots and use digital tools to participate in the development of their work environment.

4   Impact of Industry 5.0 on Total Quality Management

Total Quality Management (TQM) is a management quality approach. It was first introduced by the quality guru "Deming". TQM is an approach that gives companies a competitive edge and improves their profits, by ensuring a better quality of products and services that satisfy customers and meet their expectations [20].

TQM consists of seven key principles:

1) customer focus, 2) leadership, 3) engagement of people, 4) process approach, 5) improvement, 6) evidence-based decision making, 7) relationship management.

The human-centric approach of Industry 5.0 may serve to implement and promote the TQM principles listed above, especially customer focus, engagement of people, and improvement, as explained in Table 1.

Table 1. Impact of industry 5.0 on TQM principals

TQM principal	Industry 5.0 contributions
Customer focus	Industry 5.0 has a clear focus on mass customization and it will enable employees to devote more time and energy to tasks that require creativity and critical thinking skills, in order to adapt to the changing customer demands
Engagement of people	Industry 5.0 will empower its workers with cobots and advanced technologies. The human role will be more valuable. Operators will have a say in the production line, and empowerment of workers is positively related to job involvement
Improvement	The synergy between humans and machines, and the focus on creativity will enable to develop new products and services and manage the challenge of complexity

5   Conclusion

The main concern of Industry 4.0 is to automate manufacturing and leverage new technologies. To remedy this situation, Industry 5.0 adopts a human-centric approach to bring back workers to the center of the production line. In this paper, we proposed a roadmap to implement this vision and build trust in digital tools to get rid of any technology anxiety that was associated with industry 4.0. As a result, workers will be more involved in their jobs and companies could reap the benefits of the human-centric approach. Furthermore, we presented the impact of Industry 5.0 on TQM and how Industry 5.0 can serve to promote TQM principles.

Since Industry 5.0 is a new concept, more discussions need to be held to explore this approach from a different point of view. We are planning in the future to implement this framework in various cases, furthermore, we are planning to explore the relation between the state of a worker's health and job assignment.

References

1. Garouani, M., Ahmad, A., Bouneffa, M., Hamlich, M.: AMLBID: an auto-explained automated machine learning tool for big industrial data. SoftwareX **17**, 100919 (2022)
2. Hamlich, M., Ramdani, M.: Data classification by SAC "Scout Ants for Clustering" algorithm. J. Theor. Appl. Inf. Technol. **55**(1), 66–73 (2013)

3. Chaabi, M., Hamlich, M.: A sight on defect detection methods for imbalanced industrial data. In: ITM Web of Conferences, vol. 43, p. 01012 (2022)

4. Govindarajan, U.H., Trappey, A.J., Trappey, C.V.: Immersive technology for human-centric cyberphysical systems in complex manufacturing processes: a comprehensive overview of the global patent profile using collective intelligence. Complexity. **2018** (2018)

5. Kaasinen, E., et al.: Empowering and engaging industrial workers with operator 4.0 solutions. Comput. Ind. Eng. **139**, 105678 (2020)

6. Yu, K., Luo, B.N., Feng, X., Liu, J.: Supply chain information integration, flexibility, and operational performance: an archival search and content analysis. Int. J. Logist. Manag. **29** (2018)

7. Garouani, M., Ahmad, A., Bouneffa, M., Hamlich, M., Bourguin, G., Lewandowski, A.: Towards big industrial data mining through explainable automated machine learning (2021). https://doi.org/10.21203/rs.3.rs755783/v1

8. Xu, X., Lu, Y., Vogel-Heuser, B., Wang, L.: Industry 4.0 and industry 5.0—inception, conception and perception. J. Manuf. Syst. **61**, 530–535 (2021)

9. Maddikunta, P.K.R., et al.: Industry 5.0: a survey on enabling technologies and potential applications. J. Ind. Inf. Integr. **26**, 100257 (2022)

10. Sundelin, N.: Guidelines for implementing collaborative robots in industrial application (2021)

11. Vu, H.T., Lim, J.: Effects of country and individual factors on public acceptance of artificial intelligence and robotics technologies: a multilevel SEM analysis of 28-country survey data. Behav. Inf. Technol. **41**, 1–14 (2021)

12. Cheng, W.-J., Pien, L.-C., Cheng, Y.: Occupation-level automation probability is associated with psychosocial work conditions and workers' health: a multilevel study. Am. J. Ind. Med. **64**(2), 108–117 (2021)

13. Pinzone, M., et al.: A framework for operative and social sustainability functionalities in Human-Centric Cyber-Physical Production Systems. Comput. Ind. Eng. **139**, 105132 (2020)

14. Mattsson, S., Ekstrand, E., Tarrar, M.: Understanding disturbance handling in complex assembly: analysis of complexity index method results. Procedia Manuf. **25**, 213–222 (2018)

15. Rožanec, J.M., et al.: Human-Centric Artificial Intelligence Architecture for Industry 5.0 Applications. arXiv preprint arXiv:2203.10794 (2022)

16. Rowlands, H., Milligan, S.: 'Quality-driven industry 4.0', in key challenges and opportunities for quality, sustainability and innovation in the fourth industrial revolution: quality and service management in the fourth industrial revolution—sustainability and value co-creation. In: World Scientific, pp. 3–30 (2021)

17. Romero, D., et al.: Towards an operator 4.0 typology: a human-centric perspective on the fourth industrial revolution technologies. In: 46th International Conference on Computers & Industrial Engineering, pp. 1–11 (2016), ISSN 2164-8670 CD-ROM, ISSN 2164-8689

18. Anand Jayakumar, A., Krishnaraj, C.: Quality circle–formation and implementation. Int. J. Emer. Res. Eng. Sci. Technol. **2**(2) (2015)

19. Boca, G.D.: Adkar model vs. quality management change (2013)

20. Charantimath, P.M.: Total Quality Management. Pearson Education India (2011)

Artificial Intelligence Based Plastic Injection Process for Initial Parameters Setting and Process Monitoring-Review

Faouzi Tayalati[✉], Monir Azmani, and Abdelah Azmani

FST of Tangier, Abdelmalik Essaidi University, Tetouan, Morocco
{Faouzi.tayalati,m.azmani,a.azmani}@etu.uae.ac.ma

Abstract. The thermoplastic injection process is an industrial technique that allows getting a high precision plastics part with high production rate. This process is considered one of the most complexes in the plastic industry due to its complexity and variability. The main problems in this technique can occur during two phases: first, during the initial setting when we try to identify the initial parameters for a new plastic part; and second, during mass production when there is a deviation in the production process. The purpose of this article is divided on three parts: first, is to make a basic review and to present overview of the main issues faced in this process, second part, is to present the contribution of the artificial intelligence methods to resolve this issues and finally to present a general guidelines for future researchers to resolve or reduce the process issues.

Keywords: Injection process · Initial setting · Artificial intelligence

1 Introduction

The injection molding process is a polymer processing technique that produces plastic parts from the raw material, which is often in granulated form. It is considered the most widely used process in the plastic industry due to its ability to produce medium and large quantities from simple to very complicated geometries at controlled costs. Nowadays, the qualitative requirements become more and more high and the market competitiveness becomes more demanding in terms of cost control and profit margin. However, the injection process is not a perfect process and represents some points of improvement that could be addressed separately or globally in order to master them. Through the literature review, the operation of the initial parameters setting remains the most complicated task because each injected part is considered as a particular case and has its own setting. The goal of the technician is to determine the best initial setting for each part and to maintain it over time during mass production. The objective of this article is to provide a review of the problems in the injection process and to present the contribution of artificial intelligence to improve or control the production process, and finally to suggest some general guidelines for future work to reduce or eliminate these problems.

M. Hamlich et al. (Eds.): SADASC 2022, CCIS 1677, pp. 294–307, 2022.
https://doi.org/10.1007/978-3-031-20490-6_24

1.1 The Principle of the Injection Molding Process

The plastic injection process is based on the principle of polymer's transformation from a solid state to a pasty state by using the combination of an injection machine and tooling. The injection machine consists of two main parts: the injection unit and the closing unit. The injection unit brings the plastic from the solid state to the plasticized state and injects it into the mold. The closing unit ensures the role of closing the tooling, the locking and the cooling of the plastic [1, 2]. The injection process is a cyclic production technique as opposed to a continuous process such as extrusion [3]. Each injection cycle allows having of a number of parts. The main steps of an injection cycle are the dosing phase, the plasticizing phase, the filling phase, the holding phase, and the cooling phase. The standard cycle can be schematized by sequences as indicated in Fig. 1.

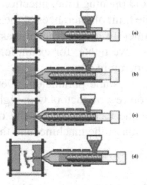

Fig. 1. The main steps of the injection process cycle. [4]

Dosing and plasticizing phase (a): the plastic material falls down from the hopper to the injection screw by gravity effect. Then the polymer is transformed into the molten state due to a double effect: the effect of shearing caused by the screw and the effect of heating caused by heating resistances surrounding the screw. The molten polymer is brought back in front of the screw by dosing the total volume of a plastic part cycle. **Filling phase (b)**: also called injection phase, the plastic is injected inside the mold via filling channels by the screw. This operation can take only a few seconds. The duration depends on the viscosity of the material and the value of the injection flow desired. The injection pressure is able to go from a few hundred to thousands of bars. **Packing phase (c)**: In this stage, the screw continues to apply pressure on the plastic to compensate for some problems that may be generated due to the shrinkage of the material as it begins to be cooled. **Cooling phase (c)**: it consists of solidifying the whole part until the desired rigidity is reached due to the thermal transfer applied by the mold. **Ejection phase (d)**: once the part is solid enough, the mold opens and the part is evacuated through an ejection mechanism.

1.2 The Key Parameters of the Injection Molding Process

Injection parameters are the variables used in the process, and that allows getting repetitive production over time. They are defined according to the geometry of the part (weight, dimension, etc.), the technical characteristics of the press (diameter of the screw, injection pressure of the press, etc.), the characteristics of the material (density, crystalline or amorphous type, etc.), and finally, according to the characteristics of the mold (size, hot or cold runner, etc.). We can classify the parameters by three major families [5, 6], setting, feedback, and control parameters.

Setting parameters are the parameters that we can act directly on as set points and that can be modified through the machine. They represent the parameters that allow the transformation of the plastic into a finished product. For example, the temperature of the screw, the rotation speed of the screw, the injection speeds, the holding pressure, etc.

Feedback parameters are the values measured by the machine during the production cycle. They are not directly adjustable, but rather indirectly by action on the set parameters. They reflect the stability of the process. We find mainly the following parameters: dosing time, injection time, mold opening time, injection pressure, etc..

Control parameters are the limit of tolerances of the set parameters. Their role is to control the process and consequently, consider any measurement outside the tolerance range as an abnormal situation. We quote, for example, the exceeding of cycle time, injection time, plasticizing temperature, etc.

Table 1 presents examples of some parameters. Defining their values remains a complex process that depends on several factors with high variability. On the one hand, it depends on the expertise of the technicians, on the other hand, it depends on the geometry of the part, the precision of the machine, and the specifications of the tooling [7, 8].

Table 1. Example of injection molding parameters

Unit	Function	Parameter	Measure unit
Closing unit	Close the mold	Closing force	[KN]: Kilo-Newton
		Closing speed	[mm/s]: Millimeter/second
		Closing stroke	[mm]: Millimeter
		Safety force	[KN]: Kilo-Newton
		Safety stroke	[mm]: Millimeter
	Clamp mold	Clamping force	[KN]: Kilo-Newton
		Clamping speed	[mm/s]: Millimeters/second
		Clamping stroke	[mm]: Millimeter
Injection unit	Dosing Clamping	Dosing stroke	[mm]: Millimeter or [cm^3]
		Screw speed	[Tr/min]: Round/ min
		Back pressure	[Bar]: Bar
		Packing pressure	[Bar]: Bar
		Packing time	[s]: second

2   Literature Review

The approach taken in our review is based on the work of [Pierre Nagorny et al. 2017] [9] from 1970 to 2015, and it is completed with the review of [Senthil Kumaran Selvaraj et al. 2022] [10] from 2000 to 2021, with a high focus on the application of artificial intelligence in the injection molding process.

2.1   Monitoring of the Injection Process: Period Between 1970 to 2015

Injection process monitoring is the application of approaches to adjust the process parameters in order to achieve the quality requirements of the injected part. It is indeed a question of correcting the difference between a given situation and the targeted situation. The target situation is to have good quality injected parts with the appropriate production rate. According to the literature review of the methods used to control the process published by [Pierre Nagorny et al. 2017] [9] which was based on a bibliography of more than 400 publications between 1970 and 2015. Their synthesis led to dividing the approaches into three levels: process modeling level, initial setup level, and control level.

2.1.1   Modeling Level

The plastic injection process is considered a complex non-linear model with linked parameters. To model it with precise mathematical representation remains difficult. The complexity of the representation is due to the different physical phenomena that come into, in particular, the characteristics of the material and the phenomena of heat transfer as well as the phenomena of the flow of the material in dynamic and static phase. In order to define the modeling of the process, several approaches have been based often on mathematics by finite elements and physics such as flow and fluid mechanics. The models developed are usually theoretical mathematical nonlinear models, as example the nonlinear modeling of [D. Mathivanan et al. 2009] [11] which propose a model based on process variables to predict the appearance defect of sink mark, the same for [béreaux et al. 2004] [12] which propose a theoretical model of plasticizing in extrusion process treating the viscosity and the velocity of the screws and in 2012 [13] present the various nonlinear models applicable to the process of the plastic industry including the plastic injection based on approaches based on numerical, thermal and mechanical models, as well as [Chiu et al. 1991] [14] which propose a model based on the analysis of the pressure in the cavity. From a practical point of view, mathematical models are often integrated into numerical simulation software and used by development departments during the mold validation phase in order to simulate the different phases of material flow and to anticipate the predictive management of part quality. The use of these models in production workshops remains limited due to their need for enormous resources in terms of calculation time and interpretation of results, which is still not practical during mass production. Several other more or less practical methods have been developed. The most used is modeling based on the design of experiments that leads to modeling the process in the polynomial equation. The purpose of the design of experiments remains the realization of a minimum number of experiments in order to reach a practical modeling. The advantages of these approaches are displayed in their practical and industrial aspects that make their implementation easier, based on predefined five tables and statistical studies. [S. M. Mohamed Yusoff et al. 2012] [15] illustrate the use of experimental designs to identify critical factors that impact the injection process, [M. Packianather et al. 2013] [16] applied experimental designs on the optimization of plastic micro injection parameters. On the artificial intelligence side, the approaches based on neural networks are the most used in modeling, according to the same review [Pierre Nagorny et al. 2017]. The appearance of recurrent neural network RNN applied to the injection process was born in the 80s. The most used algorithms are BPNN based on iterations of learning the input data based on output values. The learning of the algorithms depends on huge databases from real production. The most frequent use is the prediction of part quality from process data [Schnerr-Haselbarch et al. 2000] [17], the input data of the RNNs are usually the process data such as holding pressure, holding time, mold temperature and the part weight or quality defect as the output.

2.1.2 Initial Setting Level

Practically, the initial adjustment is based on the tests by incomplete or the tests by errors. In fact, it consists of adjusting the machine according to the error observed on the injected part. This technique is most often used by technicians to determine the initial setting, it involves skills and know-how, and is sometimes empirical to correct the setting. Studies have been conducted to show the techniques used by adjusters to fill the errors of setting [Pastré et al. 2009] [18]. Expert systems are also used to determine the initial parameters, [Jan, 1992] [19] which propose expert systems that propose settings comparable to technicians of medium level of knowledge, [Shelesh and Siores, 1997] [20] suggest intelligent systems that propose parameter settings by applying two rules: rule-based and Case-Based Reasoning.

2.1.3 Monitoring Level

The monitoring of the processes involves readjustment. We mean by readjustment, the fact of putting the process under control and restoring it once a deviation or abnormal situation has occurred. In the literature, the main methods used are based on statistics, including the SPC (Statistical Process Control), which is based on the study of the dispersion of the process around a characteristic of the process or product. The method tries to eliminate the special causes that are accidental and identifiable and reduce the effect of the common causes that are considered random phenomena that disturb the process. [D. O. Kazmer et al. 2008] [21] have applied SPC to the plastic injection molding process with a comparison of the results of the statistical control of the variability of the machine and the mold separately. Another statistical approach that is used is PCA (principal component analysis), which consists of transforming related variables (called "correlated" in statistics) into new variables that are not correlated with each other. These new variables are called "principal components." It allows reducing the number of variables and making the information less redundant. One of the uses of this method is the prediction of defects in parts, [Songtao Zhang et al. 2014] [22] used the method of principal component analysis in the prediction of warpage defects in injection molded parts. Technically, the process monitoring is based on the measurable characteristics of the part, such as the dimensional specifications or other significant characteristics of the part. The weight of the injected part remains the most commonly used data to make a generic control. Any deviation of the weight means the instability of the process. Other characteristics can be taken as an indicator of control is the part aspect. Artificial intelligence is also used to monitor the injection process, [Lau et al. 2001] [23] propose the application of neural networks via a multi-input and output model to readjust the input parameters of the control according to the dimensions of the part produced.

2.2 Complexity F the Injection Molding Process

The setting of the initial parameters is a complicated process [S.L.MOK_ C. K. KNOW. 1999] [24]. Because this setting is the result of several linked factors that are not stable and consequently influence the final result of the quality of the part and also the production cycle time. These factors can be categorized into several types: human factors, machine factors, material factors, environmental factors, measurement factors, and method factors [8]. To determine the problems that confront the setting of the presses, especially the initial one, we synthesize the main ones as follows:

2.2.1 Process Stability

The difficulty of controlling the parameters has prompted several research studies and the application of several approaches over the years. [Satadru Kashyap et al. 2014] [25] in their review of the evolution of the methods applied to the injection process, they specify that the injection process remains a process with high variability and fluctuation, which are due to the non-stability of the plastic itself and the different stress points of the process. Furthermore, they describe the multiple approaches applied for the determination of injection molding set parameters, such as design of experiments approaches and artificial neural networks as [Hasan Oktem et al. 2005] [26] and [Yarlagadda PK (2002)] [27]. Like the majority of industrial processes, the high variability of the process can be related to the machine, environment, methods, materials, measurement, and labor [8].

2.2.2 Adjuster Experience: The Know-How

The experience and skill of the technician is a real factor that impacts the determination of the parameter values. The impact of the expertise is directly linked to the performance and the quality rate of the production. The expertise of the technician adjuster is measured on the one hand by the number of years of experience acquired in the field, and on the other hand by the ability to solve the problems related to the defects of the parts according to their nature (complex, simple, technical part, etc.). [Pierre Pastré et al. 2009] [18] In their work, they conducted research on the evaluation of professional competence and its impact on the resolution of problems in the injection process. They differentiated between the skills developed by the technician in the situation of daily activities called "professional activities of reference or ergonomic" and "unusual activities", which is the image of the situation addressed by the adjuster during the confrontation of critical problems, including quality defects. He managed to model by simulator, based on a set of knowledge rules, the strategy chosen by the adjusters during complex situations, and his work has led to the distinction of several strategies, the decision strategy based on the control of injection pressure curves, the decision strategy based on the control of injection defects; and finally the decision strategy based on the combined control of curves and defects. The strategy of problem solving in the injection process necessarily implies a prior knowledge of the machine control, the handling of the molds, the types of qualitative defects, the understanding of the phenomena of the flow of the material, and the phenomena of thermal transfers. The plastic injection molding process remains a system with very complex technical problems and requires very specific know-how [S. L. MOK and al, 1999] [24].

2.2.3 Material Behavior

Thermoplastic polymers are characterized by different mechanical and chemical properties that define the final structure of the material. Its behavior should be stable during the injection processing. The variability of the material impacts the structure, the dimension, and the aspect of the part [Daniele Annicchiarico et al. 2014] [28] have shown, for example, the influence of the microscopic structure of the thermoplastic on the defects of the part, especially the shrinkage. Their conclusion shows that parts based on semi-crystalline materials shrink more than parts based on amorphous materials. [Babur Ozcelik et al. 2010] [29] present the influence of the parameters of the process on the mechanical properties of the parts based on the plastic material of the type ABS (Acronylitrine - Butadiene - Styrene), theyconclude that the temperature of the mixture of the plastic during the phase of plasticization has a significant impact on the mechanical properties such as the tensile stress and the limit of elasticity. Furthermore, moreover the parameter of the pressure of injection influences directly the modulus of flexion. [Daniele Annicchiarico et al., 2014] [28] in their review regarding the factors influencing the phenomenon of shrinkage, the authors present the relationship between the main causes and their factors. The behavior of the material varies during the filling and injection phase according to the thermodynamic aspects PVT (Pressure, Volume and Temperature), also the shrinkage is linked to the morphology of the internal crystalline structure and the process parameters (filling volume, holding time, holding pressure, etc.). [Thuy Linh Pham, 2013] [4] in his thesis on "Plasticization in injection of functional and filled polymers" has managed to model the behavior of the plasticization phase of filled plastics and has highlighted the few defects that can appear in this phase like the defect of solid mattress.

2.3 The Contribution of the Artificial Intelligence in the Injection Process

Artificial intelligence has continued to be used in the injection process over the years at all levels, from modeling to optimization and through the adjustment of qualitative defects. At the level of the process modeling [Shen Changyuel et al. 2006] [30] suggest an optimization model based on the combination of artificial neural networks with a genetic algorithm GA. The network used is a neural network by BPNN back propagation of 5 parameters and an output to determine the complex non-linear relationship between the process parameters and the qualitative aspect. The process parameters studied were defined by the design of experiment DOE (Design of Experiment) by using the Taguchi table, including the temperature of the melt, the temperature of the mold, the injection time, the holding time, and the holding pressure. So for the studied defect, it is the volumetric shrinkage. The numerical simulation based on software of CAE computer-aided engineering was used to determine the range variation of each parameter, and thereafter the genetic algorithm was used to realize the optimization of the parameters. The experimentation based on 252 trials to perform the training and the performance of the networks showed good results, so the optimization based on GA was based on a population size of 30 and a number of generations of 250 to achieve the goal of minimizing the shrinkage defect [Mohammad Reza Khosravani et al. 2019] [31] in his review of AI methods focused on Case-Based Reasoning, CBR methods remain applicable in the phase of parameterization definition as well as on the part of part quality control as well as on the part of solving the problems of non-conformity[Mikos et al. 2010] [32].

At the level of the production shop floor, [H Lee et al. 2018] [33] proposed a model of an intelligent workshop "Smart Injection Molding System Framework" capable of making decisions and self-control as well as predictions based on intelligence methods and data generated in real time production. The model is based on the application of the BPNN- back-propagation neural network at the SCADA Supervisory Control And Data Acquisition level of the workshop with six inputs, namely the mold temperature, the holding pressure, the back pressure, the mixture temperature, the cooling time, and the holding time. As output, shrinkage and deformation were considered output data of the network. [Christoph Wunck. 2016] [34] proposes a concept of intelligent workshop by applying multi-agent systems at the level of production workshop control. At the level of qualitative problem solving, especially the treatment of shrinkage, [Rafa Abdul. et al. 2019] [35] proposed a neural network model ANN to achieve two objectives: first, predict the quality defect of linear shrinkage and warpage, second to facilitate the definition of the initial adjustment parameters. The model of ANN proposed is represented by 3 inputs and 2 outputs, The input data was based on the optimum parameters defined beforehand by the designs of experiments based on the table of Taguchi. The parameters taken into account are the speed of injection, the time of maintenance, and the time of cooling. The results of the prediction of shrinkage defects have been validated by experimentation on a machine ENGEL EVECTORY 30 tons and a plastic material of high density polyethylene HDPE of 0.953 g/cm^3 and a grade of 18 g/10 min. The prediction results based on ANNs were almost similar to the results defined by Taguchi tables, and the model proposed in the study shows that the combination of experimental design and artificial neural network has high performance in predicting shrinkage and warpage defects. [PIERRE Nagorny et al. 2019] [36] has applied the methods of machine learning, including neural networks, for quality control based on vision cameras. [Julian Heinisch et al. 2021] [37] studied the application of neural networks for the prediction of the best model of the design of experiment used for the determination of the best combination of parameters. The network used consists of six input parameters, namely injection time, cooling time, holding pressure, holding time, mixing temperature, mold temperature, and three outputs, namely the weight, thickness, and length of the part. The types of DOE studied are full design, fractional design, central component design,

Taguchi tables, D-Optimum design, and space-filling design. The result with numerical simulation shows good results in the fractional plane of resolution III. [B.H.M. Sadeghi. 2000] [38] proposes a model of quality prediction based on neural networks and 9 numerical simulations based on the BPNN type model of 4-2-3 with 4 inputs and 2 outputs, the selected inputs are: grade of material, injection pressure, mold temperature, temperature of the mixture, and the defects used: incomplete and welding lines. [Hassan Tercan. et al. 2018] [39], propose a machine learning model based on transfer learning based on neural networks to predict the weight of parts from 6 machines parameters, the parameters are: injection time, holding pressure, holding time, mold temperature, cooling time, and melt temperature. The proposed neural network model was confirmed by experimentation, the first approach was based on the direct application of real process data, and the second approach was based on the application of transfer learning based on data, firstly from the numerical simulation to train the RNN and, secondly, to refine the RNN. The comparison result is satisfactory and leads to an almost similar prediction between the two approaches, with less data for the numerical simulation [Olga Ogorodnyk et al. 2019] [40] studied the application of artificial intelligence methods including RNN algorithms as well as the decision tree algorithm to predict the quality of produced parts and distinguish between good and bad parts. The proposed model is based on the Multilayered Perceptron MLP algorithm and the J48 decision tree. The parameters used are: holding pressure, holding time, back pressure, cooling time, injection speed, screw temperature, and mold temperature. At the level of online control and adjustment of process parameters, [Meaghan Charest. et al. 2018] [41] studied the application of various methods of artificial intelligence, including machine learning algorithms, and their profitability within the production workshops. In his research, 6 algorithms were studied, namely decision tree ID3, the algorithm of Ada Boost, the random forest. Naive Bayes, K-nearestneighbors (KNN) and finally the ANN. The implementation of these algorithms was applied on 150 ton press instrumented with different pressure, temperature and other sensors, so two types of parts were studied and the data were monitored online during the production [Hong Seok Park. et al. 2019] [42] studied the implementation of an autonomous intelligent system to control the injection process in real time during production based on artificial intelligence methods. With a mold equipped with pressure and temperature sensors, he was able to collect millions of data points in real time and propose a system approach based on machine learning to control and compensate for production errors and control the quality of parts produced. At the level of optimization, artificial intelligence has given rise to several works also, [Yannik Lockner 2021] [43], studied the "Transfer Learning" to minimize the need for data during the learning phase of artificial data networks, the proposed model takes the weight as a qualitative output parameter of the part and the input parameters studied are: Injection flow rate, Holding time, Holding pressure, Cooling time, Mixing temperature, Cavity temperature. The article deals with the similarity study between 59 injected parts and the impact of the model of transfer learning on the learning of ANN networks. The result was found with a reduction of 33% of the dataset. [Mohammad Saleh Meiabadi et al. 2013] [44] proposes a combined model between neural networks and genetic algorithms to obtain the optimal process parameters to get the best prediction of part weight, minimum cycle time, and minimum injection pressure. The influencing parameters studied in this app-roach were based on the DOE. They concerned the temperature of the melt, the holding pressure, the temperature of the mold and the injection time. The network used is based on 4 inputs and 3 outputs. The results of the optimization algorithm were satisfactory and confirmed by experimentation on a KRAUSS MAFAEI press of 150 tons. Finally, another use of artificial intelligence is the selection and multicriteria choices, [L. Nyanga et al. 2018] [45] proposes a model of selection and choice to multi-criteria assignments of presses by the application of multi-agent systems and the application of the method AHP- Analytical Hierarchy Process, with a choice of selection that considers the aspects of quality, cost, and time.

3 Discussions and Perspectives

According to the literature, the main problems in the injection process can be divided into two aspects, general problems and specific problems. Quality, cost, and delay can be considered as general problems, and the specific problems can be considered more technical and are related to the machine, to the mold, to the know-how of the adjusters, to the stability of the process, and to the stability of the material. Through the literature, research works typically focused on treating only a subset of the parameters rather than the entire set, with the majority of works focusing on those of the injection unit. For those related to the closing unit parameters, they are not treated or they are only treated partially, and that can open many fields of research. The process of determining the initial setting values as well as the monitoring is still a subject of research at the level of the accuracy of the setting parameters and the reduction of the effects of quality issues. As for the use of artificial intelligence, it is gaining more and more places in the injection plastic process. The fields covered by artificial intelligence cover the modeling of the process, the optimization, and finally the prediction and problem solving. Regarding the smart solutions that were suggested by the majority of the researchers to be implemented on the shop floor, they are based basically on big data treatment and the acquisition of data from the machine and from the mold. The future work and researchers can be basically based on the below recommendations to assist with the research activities.

Reducing the number of trial: the initial adjustment is considered a source of generating additional costs, especially the consumption of material and the immobilization of the machine. It would therefore be appropriate to think of solutions to be applied in the hidden phase before starting the real tests to simulate and get closer to the parameterization values without making as many test sequences and thus avoiding the cost and time losses. In fact, in order to reduce the number of tests, we should first think of solutions to reduce the number of iterations per phase: trials without and with material consumption.

Reducing the number of trial without material consumption: it consists of defin-ing the parameters that do not require plastic consumption during the trial. In fact, to minimize the number of iterations, the future solution should take as an approach the similarity of the molds and the similarity of the machines to reduce as much as possible the need to redo the test to determine the values of the kinematics mold-machine. It should be based on the feedback of the previous settings.

Reducing the number of trials with material consumption: the future solutions have to develop calculation files based on the experience of the adjusters as well as the capitalization of all the adjustments available within the workshop to build simplified and approximate calculation models customized by the workshop. In addition, it would be very appropriate to use simple mathematical models on an industrial scale, such as the model from the design of an experiment combined with artificial intelligence algorithms to select and reduce the number of tests.

Optimization of the part weight: the weight is the most targeted objective; it represents more than 70% of the cost of the injected part. For future researches, it will be interesting to focus on the following parameters: the holding phase, the dosing phase, and the switching point. It would be very appropriate to make predictions of the values and apply the most advanced approaches as well as the AI methods.

Optimization of the cycle time: The most significant parameter is the cooling time, which represents more than 60% of the standard cycle time. Future works should make focus on the prediction of the cooling time by applying AI methods.

Reduce the independence of the adjuster expertise: Another topic that future researches could lead to is reducing the reliance on the technician's expertise. In reality, the technician cannot solve all problems related to process deviation, especially with complicated geometry. It will be necessary to consider solutions that require fewer technician interventions, such as an autonomous adjustment based on AI and big data.

General smart concept: Fig. 2 shows a suggestion for a general smart concept which can be followed by future researches. It can be divided into 3 main levels, 1. Definition of the initial setting, 2. Process monitoring based on real-time data acquisition 3. Level of stability check based on Smart Statistical Process Control. The intelligent treatment is based on AI methods and especially ANN which needs a big data provided in real time from machines and molds. As indicated in this paper, each new plastic part is considered new case for the treatment; in fact the trained treatment on specific machines will be dedicated to those machines, so it will be appropriate to uses transfer learning methods to generalize the predication of the injection parameters based on similarity of the machines, molds and parts.

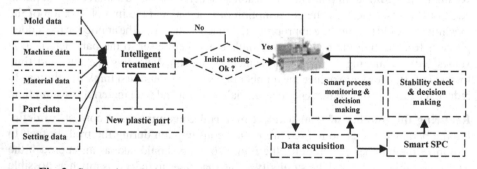

Fig. 2. Suggestion of general smart concept for initial setting & process monitoring

4   Conclusion

In this paper, we presented the main difficulties that can face the injection molding process during the initial setting and during mass production. In conclusion, injection molding is still a complex process with high variability of material, mold, machine, and human resources, and to master their parameters demands the mastering of the whole data related to the material, machine, and mold. Additionally, the initial parameter setting remains the most complicated task in this process because each injected part is considered as a particular case and has its own setting. This paper also presents the application of the method of artificial intelligence. Their scope covers the majority of processes at different levels, starting with the initial setting until the quality prediction. The interest of this paper is to make a general review of the problems in the molding process and also the application of the AI method to support the future work.

Acknowledgments. This research is supported by the Ministry of Higher Education, Scientific Research and Innovation, the Digital Development Agency and the National Center for Scientific and Technical Research of Morocco (Smart DLSP Project - AL KHAWARIZMI IA-PROGRAM).

References

1. Presses à injecter - Fonctions et solutions constructives : Dossier complet | Techniques de l'Ingénieur. https://www.techniques-ingenieur.fr/base-documentaire/materiaux-th11/procedes-d-injection-des-thermoplastiques-42151210/presses-a-injecter-am3671/. Last Accessed 24 June 2021
2. Presses à injecter - Caractéristiques et architecture : Dossier complet | Techniques de l'Ingénieur. https://www.techniques-ingenieur.fr/base-documentaire/materiaux-th11/procedes-d-injection-des-thermoplastiques-42151210/presses-a-injecter-am3672/. Last Accessed 24 June 2021
3. Extrusion - Extrusion monovis (partie 1) : Dossier complet | Techniques de l'Ingénieur. https://www.techniques-ingenieur.fr/base-documentaire/materiaux-th11/plasturgie-procedes-d-extrusion-42150210/extrusion-am3650. Last Accessed 24 June 2021
4. Pham, T.L.: Plastification en injection des polymères fonctionnels et chargés. Matériaux. INSA de Lyon. Français (2013). NNT: 2013ISAL0093. tel-01015839
5. Pichon, J.-F., Guichou, C.: Aide-mémoire-injection-des-matières-plastiques/. L'Usine Nouvelle, Dunod, Paris (2015)
6. Biron, M.: Aide-mémoire - Transformation des matières plastiques. Dunod, Paris (2010)
7. Bharti, P.K., Khan, M.I.: Recent methods for optimization of plastic injection molding process – a retrospective and literature review. Int. J. Eng. Sci. Technol. **2** (2010)
8. F. Tayalati, M. Azmani, A. Azmani, Problème de réglage initial dans le procédé de l'injection des matières thermoplastiques. In: 9ème Edition du Congrès Scientifique International en management et ingenierie des systèmes, École des mines, Rabat, Maroc (2021)
9. Nagorny, P., Pairel, E., Pillet, M.: Pilotage en Injection Plastique – Etat de l'Art. In: 12ème-Congrès International de Génie Industriel (CIGI 2017). Compiègne, France (May 2017). hal-01551840
10. Selvaraj, S.K., Raj, A., Rishikesh Mahadevan, R., Chadha, U., Paramasivam, V.: A review on machine learning models in injection molding machines. Hindawi. Adv. Mater. Sci. Eng. **2022**, 28. Article ID 1949061 (2022)

11. Mathivanan, D., Parthasarathy, N.S.: Prediction of sink depths using nonlinear modeling of injection molding variables. Int. J. Adv. Manuf. Technol. **43**(7–8) (août 2009). https://doi.org/10.1007/s00170-008-1749-1

12. Béreaux, Y., Moguedet, M., Raoul, X., Charmeau, J.Y., Balcaen, J., Graebling, D.: Series solutions for viscous and viscoelastic fluids flow in the helical rectangular channel of an extruder screw. J. Non-Newton. Fluid Mech. **123**(2–3), 237–257 (November 2004). https://doi.org/10.1016/j.jnnfm.2004.08.011

13. Bereaux, Y.: Procédés de Plasturgie: Approche par des modèles numériques, thermiques et mécaniques. Mécanique des matériaux [physics.class-ph]. INSA de Lyon (2012)

14. Chiu, C.-P., Shih, L.-C., Wei, J.-H.: Dynamic modeling of the mold filling process in an injection molding machine. Polym. Eng. Sci. **31**(19), 1417–1425 (October 1991)

15. Mohamed Yusoff, S.M., Rohani, J.M., Hamid, W.H.W., Ramly, E.: A plastic injection molding process characterization using experimental design technique: a case study. J. Teknol., févr. **41** (2012)

16. Packianather, M., Chan, F., Griffiths, C., Dimov, S., Pham, D.T.: Optimisation of micro injection moulding process through design of experiments. Procedia CIRP. **12** (2013)

17. Schnerr-Haselbarth, O., Michaeli, W.: Automation of online quality control in injection moulding. Macromol. Mater. Eng.. **284/285**, 81 (2000)

18. Pastré, P., Parage, P., Richard, J.-F., Sander, E., Labat, J.-M., Futtersack, M.: La résolution de problèmes professionnels sur simulateur. Activites. **06**(1) (avr. 2009)

19. Jan, T.-C.: Expert system for the injection molding of engineering thermoplastics, A Dissertation Submitted to the Faculty of New Jersey Institute of Technology in Partial Fulfillment of the Requirements for the Degree of Doctor of Philosophy Department of Mechanical and Industrial Engineering (October 1992)

20. Shelesh-Nezhada, K., Sioresb, E.: An intelligent system for plastic injection molding process design. J. Mater. Process. Technol. **63**(1–3) (January 1997)

21. Kazmer, D., Westerdale, S., Hazen, D.: A comparison of statistical process control (SPC) and on-line multivariate analyses (MVA) for injection molding. Business Int. Polym. Process. **23** (November 2008)

22. Zhang, S., Dubay, R., Charest, M.: A principal component analysis model-based predictive controller for controlling part warpage in plastic injection molding. Exp. Syst. Appl. **42**(6) (15 April 2015)

23. Lau, H.C.W., Ning, A., Pun, K.F., Chin, K.S.: Neural networks for the dimensional control of molded parts based on reverse process model. J. Mater. Process. Technol. **117**(1/2) (November 2001)

24. Mok, S.L., Kwong, C.K., Lau, W.S.: An intelligent hybrid system for initial process parameter setting of injection moulding. Int. J. Prod. Res. **38**(17), 4565–4576 (2000)

25. Kashyap, S., Datta, D.: Process parameter optimization of plastic injection molding: a review. Int. J. Plast. Technol. **19**(1), 1–18 (2015). https://doi.org/10.1007/s12588-015-9115-2

26. Oktem, H., Erzurumlu, T., Uzman, I.: Application of Taguchi optimization technique in determining plastic injection molding process parameters for a thin-shell part. Mater. Des. **28**(4), 1271–1278 (January 2007)

27. Yarlagadda, P.K.D.V., Teck Khong, C.A.: Development of a hybrid neural network system for prediction of process parameters in injection moulding. J. Mater. Process. Technol. **118**(1–3), 109–115 (Décember 2001)

28. Annicchiarico, D., Alcock. J.R.: Review of factors that affect shrinkage of molded part in injection molding. Mater. Manufact. Process. **2** (June 2014)

29. Ozcelik, B., Ozbay, A., Demirbas, E.: Influence of injection parameters and mold materials on mechanical properties of ABS in plastic injection molding. Int. Commun. Heat Mass Transf. **37**(9), 1359–1365 (November 2010)

30. Shen, C., Wang, L., Li, Q.: Optimization of injection molding process parameters using combination of artificial neural network and genetic algorithm method. J. Mater. Process. Technol. **183**(2–3), 412–418 (Mars 2007)

31. Khosravani, M.R., Nasiri, S.: Injection molding manufacturing process: review of case-based reasoning applications. J. Intell. Manuf. **31**(4), 847–864 (avr. 2020)

32. Mikos, W.L., Ferreira, J.C.E., Gomes, F.G.C.: A distributed system for rapid determination of nonconformance causes and solutions for the thermoplastic injection molding process: a case-based reasoning agents approach. In: IEEE International Conference on Automation Science and Engineering (2011)

33. Lee, H., Liau, Y., Ryu, K.: Real-time parameter optimization based on neural network for smart injection molding. In: IOP Conference Series: Materials Science and Engineering, Volume 324, 2017 the 5th International Conference on Mechanical Engineering, Materials Science and Civil Engineering 15–16 December 2017, Kuala Lumpur, Malaysia

34. Wunck, C.: Implementation of mobile event monitoring agents for manufacturing execution and intelligence systems using a domain specific language. In: Proceedings - International Conference on Industrial Engineering and Operations Management, Kuala Lumpur, Malaysia, March 8–10, 2016

35. Abdul, R., Guo, G., Chen, J.C., Yoo, J.-W.: Shrinkage prediction of injection molded high density polyethylene parts with taguchi/artificial neural network hybrid experimental design. Int. J. Interact. Design Manuf. **14**(2), 345–357 (2019). https://doi.org/10.1007/s12008-019-00593-4

36. Nagorny, P., Pillet, M., Pairel, E.: Contrôle Qualité 2.0: Apprentissage supervisé de la notion de Qualité, application à l'injection plastique. CIGI-QUALITA 2019, École de Technologie Supérieure de Montréal, Montréal, Canada, June 2019. ⟨hal-02142331⟩

37. Heinisch, J., Hopmann, C.: Comparison of design of experiment methods for modeling injection molding experiments using artificial neural networks. J. Manuf. Process. **61**, 357–368 (January 2021)

38. Sadeghi, B.H.M.: A BP-neural network predictor model for plastic injection molding process. J. Mater. Process. Technol. **103**(3), 411–416 (juill. 2000)

39. Tercan, H., Guajardo, A., Heinisch, J., Thiele, T., Hopmann, C., Meisen, T.: Transfer-learning: bridging the gap between real and simulation data for machine learning in injection molding. Procedia CIRP **72**, 185–190 (2018)

40. Ogorodnyk, O., Lyngstad, O.V., Larsen, M., Wang, K., Martinsen, K.: Application of machine learning methods for prediction of parts quality in thermoplastics injection molding. In: Wang, K., Wang, Y., Strandhagen, J.O., Yu, T. (eds.) Advanced Manufacturing and Automation VIII, vol. 484. Springer Singapore, Singapore (2019)

41. Charest, M., Finn, R., Dubay, R.: Integration of artificial intelligence in an injection molding process for on-line process parameter adjustment. In: 2018 Annual IEEE International Systems Conference (SysCon), Vancouver, BC (avr. 2018)

42. Park, H.S., Phuong, D.X., Kumar, S.: AI based injection molding process for consistent product quality. Procedia Manuf. **28**, 102–106 (2019)

43. Lockner, Y., Hopmann, C.: Induced network-based transfer learning in injection molding for process modelling and optimization with artificial neural networks. Int. J. Adv. Manuf. Technol. **112**(11–12), 3501–3513 (févr. 2021)

44. Meiabadia, M.S., Vafaeesefatb, A., Sharifi, F.: Optimization of plastic injection molding process by combination of artificial neural network and genetic algorithm. J. Optimiz. Ind. Eng. **13** (2013)

45. Nyanga, L., et al.: Design of a multi agent system for machine selection. In: Competitive Manufacturing, International Conference on Competitive Manufacturing (COMA '16), 27–29 January 2016, Stellenbosch, Stellenbosch University, South Africa (2016)

The Benefits of Combining Digitalization with Quality Tools: Application in the Field of Wiring Systems Manufacturing for the Automotive Industry

Karima Azzaoui[✉], Samia Yousfi, and Mouna Latifa Bouamrani

LCAM Laboratory, FSBM University Hassan II, Casablanca, Morocco
karima.azzaoui-etu@etu.univh2c.ma

Abstract. In an economic context of increasing pressure, manufacturing companies acting in the automotive field are struggling to maintain their margins and market share. To maintain consistently high-quality products at low cost, it's increasingly crucial to remain competitive. The automation of production systems has emerged as an answer to competitiveness in this age of accelerated industrial expansion within the 4.0 era. In this context, is anchored the main objective of this paper: The benefits of combining digitalization with quality tools: application in the field of wiring systems manufacturing for the automotive industry. This combination is used for the first time in the wiring systems manufacturing in the automotive field. The novelty of this research is the proposal of a new methodical framework which we will call "CRAFTER" using seven steps including the reverse failure mode and effect analysis (reverse-FMEA) in addition to several traditional quality tools, and combining this new methodology with the Digitalization. This approach contributes, in our case of study, to increasing competitiveness through the improvement of the plant cost rate by 7%, reducing non-quality costs by 30%, and improving the quality of products and services. This particular contribution in our activity area can be applied to all companies with manual manufacturing processes.

Keywords: CRAFTER · Digitalization · Manufacturing · Wiring systems

1 Introduction

The automotive manufacturers are currently facing a big pressure to reduce the overall manufacturing conversion cost to be more competitive in the global market [1]. This pressure has driven the industrial world to seek innovative technological solutions over the last few years to improve the quality of direct and indirect services and to generate savings to remain competitive. Industry 4.0

M. Hamlich et al. (Eds.): SADASC 2022, CCIS 1677, pp. 308–322, 2022.
https://doi.org/10.1007/978-3-031-20490-6_25

appears after the three industrial revolutions which are the result of several technological advances in the last centuries and which were focused on productivity and efficiency increase [2]. Industry 4.0 is the overlapping of several technological developments covering products and processes [3]. The vision of Industry 4.0 refers to networks of autonomous, sensor-equipped, and self-configuring manufacturing resources through the integration of many different digital technologies [4]. The focus of I4.0 is to combine production, information technology, and the Internet [5,6]. In addition; it promotes flexibility. While some literature has recently considered the performance impacts of Industry 4.0, there is some dispute in the academic literature regarding how Lean Manufacturing and Industry 4.0 interplay to impact business performance [4]. Many researchers find that it is still unclear how Industry 4.0 will impact manufacturing industries, for example, The vision of G.Reischauer posits that Industry 4.0 is a manufacturing policy innovation debate that aims to institutionalize innovation systems that embrace the industry, academia, and the policy [7]. In this paper, we aim to develop a methodology to prove that the combination of lean tools and digitalization impact both quality performance and cost-effectiveness. The paper proposes in Sect. 2 the scope of the research and highlights the problematic, in Sect. 3 a complete description of the research method. In Sect. 4, implementation and analysis. Section 5 is dedicated to the result, and lastly, Sect. 6 wraps up the paper by outlining its findings and introducing new insights.

2 Background and Objectives

Due to its geographical position and its socio-economic situation, Morocco presents several characteristics which provide interesting advantages for multinational companies in the automotive sector. The automotive industry has been part of the kingdom's vision [8]. Indeed, many multinationals in this field relocate a large part of their production to Morocco to benefit from the various characteristics of the eco-system.

2.1 Scope of the Research

This research is carried out in a multinational company based in Morocco, (we will call it the case study company). It is specialized in the production of manual automotive wiring also called harnesses. It is a worldwide supplier of the automotive industry whose culture is customer-centric and where operational excellence and quality policy are set to even exceed customer expectations.

2.2 Problematic

The rigors and strict quality requirements on a global scale are increasingly more challenging [9]. The continuous improvement of the case study manufacturing processes and product quality are the only way to achieve industrial excellence and stand out from competitors. In addition, it is not obvious to position the company in the international market and to keep its position with manual production, while other suppliers take great advantage of the digitalization in the industry 4.0 expansion. Most customers, today, use the same KPI (Key Process Indicator) to rank and classify their suppliers without taking into account the fact that some suppliers have manual processes and others have automated processes. The real challenge is how to use digitalization to improve the efficiency of direct and indirect processes and thus achieve sustainable competitiveness and customer satisfaction for such a company acting in manual Manufacturing of automotive wiring systems? To compensate for the errors inherent in human activities which lead to manufacturing defects and dangers linked to the handling of the product, it is necessary to equip the production tool and in certain cases the product itself with an "anti-error" or " error-proofing" system. In Japanese industry, the error-proofing system known as "Poka-Yoke" was invented by the engineer Shigeo Shingo (1909–1990), who also created the SMED method (Single Minute Exchange of Dies). Poka-Yoke is derived from the words "Poka" which means mistake and error, and "Yoke" which means to avoid and to prevent [10]. The digitalization of the effectiveness of the Poka-Yoke can provide the solution to our problematic. There are significant advantages to be gained from digitalization; costs can be reduced by up to 90% and cycle times can be significantly improved [11]. Moreover, the substitution of manual processes and paper with software enables companies to automate data collection and analysis for a deeper knowledge of process and cost drivers as well as potential sources of risk [11].

3   Description of the Research Methodology

We decided to implement the CRAFTER methodology, which integrates the reverse-FMEA and several quality tools for solving complex problems, and then combine it with digitization in this research work. This combination will be used for the first time in the manufacturing of automotive wiring.

3.1   CRAFTER

CRAFTER is a 7-step problem-solving method, its name originates from the first letter of each of the basic steps in this approach, which must be performed in consecutive order:

- Characterization of a problem: the identification of a problem using the PARETO diagram, 5W2H (What, Who, Where, Why, When, How, How much) and SIPOC (Suppliers, Inputs, Process, Outputs and Customers).
- Root causes Analysis: The analysis of the problem using the ISHIKAWA diagram and the 5Why for occurrence and non-detection.
- Action plan implementation of PDCA (Plan, Do, Check, Act) in link with digitalization of poka-yoke check and Brainstorming based on previous steps.
- Follow up on the implementation of the solutions: very important step to experiment the solutions and test their robustness.

- Tracking of the main KPIs: Daily tracking of quality and productivity KPIs.
- Effectiveness of the action plan: like DMAIC (Define, Measure, Analyze, Improve and Control), this step is to control the effectiveness of the action plan after the KPI tracking.
- Reverse failure mode and effect analysis (reverse-FMEA): This step offers a significant added value to CRAFTER that will be continuously implemented throughout the company's processes. This was the reason for illustrating CRAFTER as a continuous improvement cycle, unlike the DMAIC method which ends at the control stage.

"CRAFTER", as shown in Fig. 1, is a relevant and effective method, it complements DMAIC and PDCA by adding important axes for the success of the research project which is the introduction of the reverse-FMEA to reduce the risks and costs of non-quality as highlighted by the SNECI website (www.sneci.com). The choice of its steps is made in the logic of the implementation in the field.

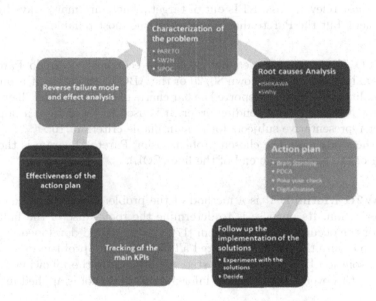

Fig. 1. CRAFTER problems solving framework.

3.2 Digitalization

The potential gains from digitization are significant [11]. Many papers are calling for digital transformation, but there has been insufficient empirical research to comprehend how digitalization impacts and defies quality management (QM) practice today [12]. Ponsignon, Kleinhans, and Bressolles confirm in 2019 that QM activities and digitalization are not limited to one specific process of activity in an organization, they are both wide-spread throughout the organization and its value-added processes [13]. From a quality management perspective, the key to customer satisfaction is to achieve good quality results competitively. Moreover, S. Markovitch and P. Willmott stated in their work that Real-time reports and dashboards on digital process performance allow managers to intervene before critical thresholds are reached [14]. In this perspective we will use the opportunity to improve competitiveness through implementing digitalization in several steps of the CRAFTER methodology, we will proceed by creating a macro to enhance onetime collection data for manufacturing processes, automatic generating of PARETO diagram, Poka Yoke automatization to prevent failure and creating an interface between semi-automatic machine and operator.

4 Implementation and Analysis

4.1 Characterization of a Problem

It is the identification of a problem, to be dealt with, based on difficulties experienced, most relevant loss, KPIs out of target...There are many ways to choose the problem, but the Pareto diagram remains the most reliable.

PARETO Diagram: Named by the Italian economist Vilfredo Pareto, the Pareto analysis is the well-known 80/20 or the ABC method [15], it is one of the seven quality tools which is reported as bar charts of attributes and their relative frequency, presented in descending order. It is used to select from a population the most representative subjects for a quantifiable criterion [16].

For the study case, the chosen problem using Pareto Diagram is the waterproofing of the wires at the end of the line (EOL).

The 5W2H Method: It is a method of the problem (error, non-conformity) characterization. Its purpose is to determine the root cause of the failure of a system or the occurrence of a problem [17], it is a method developed by Sakichi Toyoda to ensure that we have covered all the bases of a problem before setting out on a solution [17]. It involves systematically asking the following questions in order not to overlook any known information. This tool is applied in Table 1:

Table 1. T5W2H: problem characterization.

5W2H	Question	Response
What	What is the problem?	The process of testing the water-proofing of the wires is not fully effective
Why	Why it is a problem?	Risk of water infiltration into the electrical system and generating major dysfunction
Where	Where does the problem occur?	In the assembly process
Who	Who is impacted by the problem?	The EOL process and the final customer
When	When does the problem occur?	During the harness assembly

SIPOC Model is the acronym for: "Supplier Input Process Output Customer". The SIPOC model was developed by Deming to manage and improve processes [18]. The model is a detailed visualization tool that will allow us to describe the process from input integration to output generation towards the customer.

4.2 Root Causes Analysis

To analyse the problem, we will use the ISHIKAWA diagram and the 5Why.

The ISHIKAWA Diagram was introduced in the 1960s by Kaoru Ishikawa. It is a simple graphical tool for analysing all possible causes. Every category of causes starts with the letter M (machines, methods, man, materials, measurement, mother nature - environment, management) for the production areas. An interesting model of the Ishikawa diagram was developed in the case of some automotive defects [19]. Accordingly, we have developed an ISHIKAWA diagram for the potential factors of occurrence and potential factors for non-detection.

5WHY is an investigative technique developed by Sakichi Toyoda in the 1930s. It aims to identify the root cause of a defect or problem by reiterating the question "Why? Every answer constitutes the basis for the next question [20]. We have integrated the 5 why into the ISHIKAWA diagram in Fig. 2 to find the root causes of occurrence and non-detection.

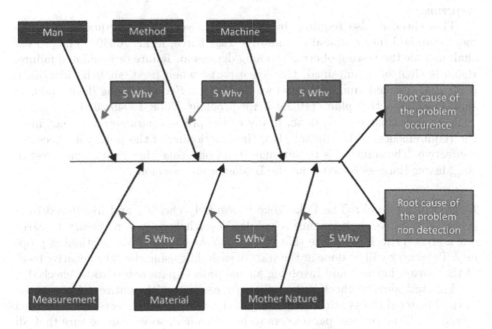

Fig. 2. 5why integrated to ISHIKAWA diagram.

4.3   Action Plan

We are convinced that identifying the root cause is about %80 of the solution. When the root cause is identified, corrective action should be immediately undertaken. If the problem reappears, the identified cause is most likely not the root cause, therefore the solutions must be tested and checked to ensure their effectiveness. These solutions can be the result of the Creativity/Brainstorming Tool or the PDCA Tool.

The Creativity Tool or Brainstorming: "Creativity", as defined by Pelz and Andrews (1966), occurs when an idea is considered both novel and beneficial [21]. The technique of creativity is known as "brain-storming", it strengthens the working group's capacity for innovation. [22]. all ideas, even unusual ones, are retained without criticism, to encourage the gathering of the greatest number of ideas to constitute the reservoir of potential solutions [23].

PDCA Tool (Plan-Do-Check-Act): it's a quality management tool for solving qualitative and quantitative issues. It is applied in the manufacturing industry for continuous improvement [24]. In our PDCA, to ensure the efficacy of the poka-yoke of water-proofing control, we will use the "Master Harness".

In the study case, for each shift, the first harness tested electrically is a so-called "Master Harness", which is a perfect harness produced for each function in the vehicle. A set of defects selected according to customer complaints is created in it to ensure that the poka-yoke detects it and prevent the defect from recurring.

This check is also required by the automotive industry's quality management standard International Automotive Task Force, IATF 16949: "The process shall include the testing of error-proofing devices for failure or simulated failure. Records shall be maintained. Challenge parts, when used, shall be identified, controlled, verified, and calibrated where feasible. Error-proofing device failures shall have a reaction plan" (10.2.4 Error-proofing, IATF 16949:2016).

Although this check is done, if any of the process parameters do not meet the requirements of the control plan, the functioning of the poka-yoke becomes ineffective. The solution is to automate the Poka-Yoke check with a new test of the Master Harness issued from the Brainstorming sessions.

Poka-Yoke Check: The Poka-Yoke is regularly checked and monitored by a special preventive maintenance schedule. Nevertheless, it is necessary to carry out a second check to ensure that the Poka-Yoke systems are functioning properly. This check will be done at the start of each shift using the "the negative test" of the Master harness and involving all the process parameters to be checked.

This test aims to check if the poka-yoke can detect the entire defect created in the Master Harness at the beginning of the shift. These defects will be chosen to reflect all the process parameters to be controlled, so we can be sure that all the poka-yoke of water-proofing is working properly.

Digitalization: To ensure that the Poka-Yoke check will be performed at the startup of each shift, we had to automate the startup process. The working group developed a graphical interface for the user with a checklist to fill in. This checklist will be linked to a database to provide traceability using a computer program language. The possible solutions to be applied based on a brainstorming session are the following:

- Create our graphical interface on PyQT which is based on QT and link it to a database on MySQL using a program edited in python.
- Create the PHP language to link a graphical interface designed in Xataface to a database created in MySQL.
- Create the database in Excel and link it with an interface in Visual Basic and then program this link in VBA.

4.4   Follow up on the Implementation of the Solutions

Decide: To evaluate the above solutions, the decision matrix is an effective tool that can be documented and enriched according to the complexity of the choices. In our case, the decision was trivial after testing the proposed solutions.

Experiment with the Solutions: Based on a risk analysis study, we did not develop the first two solutions under MySQL, because the operators may find problems to master this program. So the solution we tried is the last one based on Excel, which is simple software, easy for the operator to understand and handle, and easy for the working group to program and design the graphical interface.

Apply and Solution Track: To apply our solution in an efficient way we decided to detail this step according to the following algorithm:

- Perform the Negative Test of the MASTER harness using the HETOS software
- Create the Excel database for the startup of the control process
- Create the graphical interfaces needed in Visual Basic
- Link by VBA code
- Create a new standard and validate it by the quality manager

The MASTER Harness Negative Test: The first step is to modify the MASTER harness program in HETOS Software; this stage involves creating water-proofing defects on the Master harness which already contains other defects, then declaring the errors in the program editor as being control points. If the program detects all the defects, then the control with the poka-yoke is effective, so a label is printed to launch the production start. We call this validation: OK startup.

In order to ensure that the operator performs this test at the beginning of each shift, the label is created with two barcodes to be automatically generated at each test, these barcodes contain the current time and data to allow the launch of the OK startup.

Creation of the Excel Database for the Startup of the Control Process: It is an Excel database containing the various checklist items, the operator will fill in all the necessary data to be archived and exploited according to a well-made checklist requesting the following information: operator's ID number, shift number, process parameters such as air pressure, validity date of preventive maintenance, validity date of work and control tools, operator's level.

Create the Graphical Interfaces Needed in Visual Basic for Applications VBA: The VBA allows the creation of user-defined functions, process automation, access to the Windows application programming interface (API)and access to other functionality via dynamic link libraries. It replaces and extends the capabilities of previous application-specific macro programming languages. We have created three graphical interfaces in VBA that are integrated in Excel: The Home interface, the Interface to include the operator's data, and the OK Startup interface.

The Home Interface: The first interface we designed in Visual Studio is the Home interface in Fig. 3. It includes four buttons to be clicked: the first one helps the operator to access the interface of the OK Startup to be filled in, the second one allows us to access the archive (database), the third one allows us to search the database by date and the last one is a simple button to exit the program. The date and time are automatically inserted in this interface.

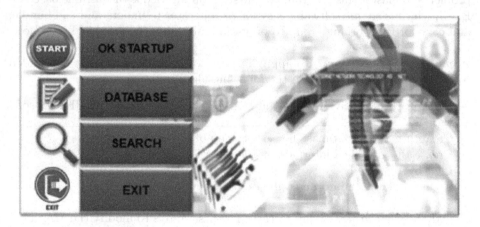

Fig. 3. CRAFTER problems solving framework.

The New OK Startup Standard: After validation of the new automated OK Startup process by the quality department, a new standard was created and implemented by the working group. The reform of the existing standards is important to highlight new improvements and methods to all stakeholders. The new OK Startup standard takes into account the newly digitized version and explains the necessary steps to have a compliant startup of the workstation.

4.5 Tracking of the Main KPIs

After the implementation of these improvements, we have noticed a significant decrease in the number of defects related to the water-proofing at the EOL. The electrical control process stops these defects at 100% after the implementation of all the actions of the quality improvement plan. We have also registered a reduction in customer complaints of approximately 64% as shown in Fig. 4. This is the result of the improved reliability of the poka-yoke operation, and the digitalization of the new OK Startup conditioned by the negative test of the Master harness at the start of every shift.

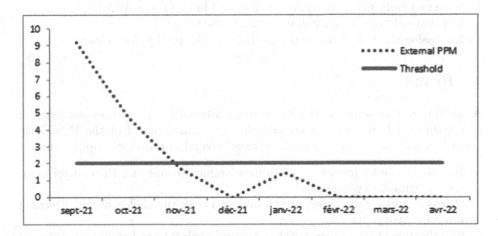

Fig. 4. CRAFTER problems solving framework.

4.6 Effectiveness of the Action Plan

The application created was linked to the local network of the production unit, and then implemented in the process of electrical control of the dashboard harnesses. The working group conducted a training course for the operation of the OK Startup and the real-time data collection. The new procedure was explained to the managers concerned to enable them to master the new standard.

Daily tracking of quality and productivity KPIs confirms the effectiveness of the action plan. No further action is required to confirm this status.

4.7 Reverse Failure Mode and Effect Analysis (Reverse-FMEA)

Reverse FMEA is a relatively new lean tool [25], it's a structured continuous improvement process to update the FMEA analysis. Reverse FMEA is a review of all the failure modes included in the Process FMEA. This analysis is carried out on the shop floor (reality) and is conducted by a multidisciplinary team, aiming to verify that all failure modes have appropriate controls (prevention/detection).

The SNECI website (www.sneci.com) reports in extenso (the Automotive Industry Action Group (AIAG), in collaboration with the German Association of the Automotive Industry (VDA), presented the first international guide on Failure Mode and Effects Analysis (FMEA) in summer 2019. The guide offers orientation and guidance to automotive suppliers, followed by best practices and case studies).

The reverse FMEA Routine was applied Two months after the implementation of the whole action plan, it provides numerous benefits to the company:

- Zero incidents related to water-proofing.
- Reducing the risks and costs of non-quality by 30
- Systematically maintaining, reviewing, and improving FMEAs.
- Continuously improving manufacturing processes.
- Increasing the experience and knowledge of the production teams.

5 Result

After the digitalization of the ok Startup process in the production lines of the dashboard harnesses, we noticed that the daily control of the Poka-Yoke operation with the Master harness revealed several improvement opportunities:

- Improving the frequency of the preventive maintenance for the control modules' pneumatic cylinders.
- Revision and recalculation of the min and max thresholds of the electrical module spare parts.
- Stabilisation of the pressure of the compressed air inlet to the electrical control equipment: installation of pressostats.
- Locking the access to key workstations such as the electrical control equipment: setting up electronic certificates with barcodes to ensure the validity of the operators training during the OK Startup.

5.1 Quantitative Gains of the Research

The reverse FMEA Routine was applied Two months after the implementation of the whole action plan, it provides numerous benefits to the company: - Zero incidents related to water-proofing. - Reducing the risks and costs of non-quality by 30 - Systematically maintaining, reviewing, and improving FMEAs. - Continuously improving manufacturing processes. - Increasing the experience and knowledge of the production teams.

5.2 Quantitative Gains of the Research

To assess the financial benefits of our study, it is necessary to evaluate the time-saving at the end of the production line thanks to the digitalization initiatives.

We used the Makigami approach to evaluate the MOUDAS eliminated through the implementation of our research project. The result of the time measurement conducted at the start of the Shift was significant; a gain of 14 min per shift was achieved, representing an annual gain of 92 K.

We have estimated the gain in Table 2 at 194 Keuros per year for a single production line. This gain has a direct impact on the non-quality costs of this production line, which fall from 1,40% to 0,98%, a reduction of 30%. The roll-out plan will generate at least 4 million euros of profit in addition to customers' satisfaction. This gain has a significant impact on the plant cost rate (PCR), a key performance indicator calculated in euros per hour, and a real competitiveness thermometer for the production units. the more the PCR is low, the more competitive the company is. Our PCR has been improved by about 7%. This percentage of reduction is highly relevant for the companies operating in the manufacturing sector.

Table 2. Saving estimation.

Related costs	Type	Annual gain / investment in euros
OK Startup optimization	Saving	-92000
Spare parts Costs	Investment	+25000
Sorting Costs	Saving	-130000
Other costs	Investment	+3000
Total	Saving	-194000

6   Discussion

6.1   Theoretical Contributions

D. Carnerud and other researchers identified sustainability from two standpoints: one, as the durability of different quality management actions and their long-term impacts, and second, as being equivalent to sustainable development [26].

By combining digitalization with quality tools, the methodology applied in this research has shown its ability to identify new research trends on the interplay between digitalization and quality tools. The target is to propose a sustainable development model to allow the automotive manufacturing companies to be as competitive as the automated ones. This paper contributes to this topic by focusing on:

1) The proposal of the new methodology "CRAFTER" targets the continuous verification of the effectiveness of the quality action plans using the reverse FMEA; and thus ensuring the sustainability of the preventive actions and the continuous improvement of the standards.
2) The highlighting of the digitalization effects on the sustainability of the Poka-Yoke operations within the Manual processes.

6.2 Limitations and Perspectives

We strongly believe that the boundaries of this research are limitless. Indeed, the findings of our study reveal a fertile area to exploit not only in other manual pro-cesses of the automotive sector, but also to expand the application to all manual manufacturing processes for higher competitiveness. The classification and rating by customers, according to the same criteria, of a manual activity with other automated activities has become rational.

7   Conclusion

Our research work presents a new framework to promote creativity, combining several quality tools and digitalization of the poka-yoke operation.

The novelty of this research is to introduce, in the automotive sector, a new framework to enhance competitiveness. CRAFTER gathers several quality tools strength-ened by the reverse FMEA. The combination of this methodology with the digitali-zation of the manual process poka-yoke, used for the first time in this field, proves to be an appropriate way to improve quality performance as well as productivity. The seventh step of our approach, the reverse FMEA routine, is applied every two months after the implementation of the whole action plan, and has provided many benefits to the company:

- Zero waterproofing incidents.
- 64% reduction in customer complaints.
- 30% reduction in non-quality risks and costs.
- 7% improvement in factory cost rate.

This paper highlights the fact that in a continuously developing and growing industry, organizations specializing in manual manufacturing, seeking to differentiate themselves from their competitors, have to ensure a sustainable manufacturing process for customer satisfaction. Therefore, they must safeguard and control the effectiveness of their process output through the digitization of Poka Yoke, continuously review their process and renew standards [27].

Acknowledgments. The authors would like to thank the entire Case of Study team for their support.

References

1. Shivajee, V., Singh, R., Rastogi, S.: Manufacturing conversion cost reduction using quality control tools and digitization of real-time data. J. Cleaner Prod. **237**, 117678 (2019)
2. Pereira, A.C., Romero, F.: A review of the meanings and the implications of the Industry 4.0 concept. Procedia Manuf. **13**, 1206–1214 (2017)
3. Abramowicz, W.: Business Information Systems :18th International Conference, BIS 2015 Poznań, Poland, 24–26 June 2015 Proceedings. In: Lecture Notes in Business Information Processing, vol. 208, pp. 16–27. Springer, Poland (2015). https://doi.org/10.1007/978-3-319-19027-3

4. Buer, S.: The complementary effect of lean manufacturing and digitalisation on operational performance. Int. J. Prod. Res. **59**(7), 1976–1992 (2021)
5. Trento, L.R., Junior, R.S., Habekost, A.F.: Operations Management for Social Good. Springer International Publishing, Location (2020)
6. Monizzaa, G.P., Bendettib, C., Matta, D.T.: Parametric and generative design techniques in mass-production environments as effective enablers of Industry 4.0 approaches in the building industry. Autom. Constr. **92**, 270–285 (2017)
7. Reischauer, G.: Industry 4.0 as policy-driven discourse to institutionalize innovation systems in manufacturing. Technol. Forecast. Soc. Change **132**, 26–33 (2018)
8. El Khatir, N.: The competitive positioning of Moroccan automotive industry?: a diagnosis attempt. Int. J. Innov. Appl. Stud. **33**(2), 9324 (2021)
9. Vijay, S., Prabha, M.G.: Work standardization and line balancing in a windmill gearbox manufacturing cell: a case study. In: Materials Today: Proceedings, pp. 1–2. Elsevier BV. https://doi.org/10.1016/j.matpr.2020.08.584 (2020)
10. Le Groupe Logistique conseil. http://www.logistiqueconseil.org/Articles/Methodes-optimisation/5G. Accessed 2018
11. Parviainen, P., Tihinen, M., Kääriäinen, J., Teppola, S.: Tackling the digitalization challenge: how to benefit from digitalization in practice. Int. J. Inf. Syst. Proj. Manag. **5**(1), 63–77 (2017)
12. Elg, M., Birch-Jensen, A., Gremyr, I., Martin, J., Melin, U.: Digitalisation and quality management: problems and prospects. Prod. Plann. Control **32**(12), 990–1003 (2021)
13. Ponsignon, F., Kleinhans, S., Bressolles, G.: he contribution of quality management to an organisation's digital transformation: a qualitative study. Total Qual. Manag. Bus. Excell. **30**(sup1), S17–S34 (2019)
14. Markovitch, S., Willmott, P.: Accelerating the digitization of business processes. McKinsey & Company, pp. 1–5 (2014)
15. Bajaj, S., Garg, R., Sethi, M.: Total quality management: a critical literature review using Pareto analysis. Int. J. Product. Perform. Manag. **67**(1), 128–154 (2018)
16. Grosfeld-Nir, A., Ronen, B., Kozlovsky, N.: The Pareto managerial principle: when does it apply? Int. J. Prod. Res. **45**(10), 2317–2325 (2017)
17. Nagyova, A., Palko, M., Pacaiova, H.: Analysis and identification of nonconforming products by 5w2h method. In: 9th International Quality Conference, pp. 33–42. http://www.cqm.rs/2015/cd1/pdf/papers/focus_1/006.pdf, Kragujevac (2015)
18. Cao, Y., Zhao, K., Yang, J., Xiong, W.: Constructing the integrated strategic performance indicator system for manufacturing companies. Int. J. Prod. Res. **53**(13), 4102–4116 (2015)
19. Liliana, L.: A new model of Ishikawa diagram for quality assessment. In: IOP Conference Series: Materials Science and Engineering, vol. 161, pp. 012099. (2016). https://doi.org/10.1088/1757-899X/161/1/012099
20. Nagyová, A., Pačaiová, H., Gobanová, A., Turisová, R.: An empirical study of root-cause analysis in automotive supplier organisation. Qual. Innov. Prosperity **23**(2), 34–45 (2019)
21. Lewis, A.C., Sadosky, T.L., Connolly, T.: Effectiveness of group brainstorming in engineering problem solving. IEEE Trans. Eng. Manage. EM-**22**(3), 119–124 (1975)
22. Osbrn, A.F.: Applied Imagination. Scribner's, New York (1953)
23. Haefele, J.W.: The relation of the industrial technical literature to creativity. J. Chem. Docum. **2**(2), 67–72 (1962)

24. Isniah, S., Hardi Purba, H., Debora, F.: Plan do check action (PDCA) method: literature review and research issues. J. Sistem dan Manajemen Industri 4(1), 72–81 (2020)
25. Ebeid, A.A., El-Khouly, I.A., El-Sayed, A.E.: Lean maintenance excellence in the container handling industry: a case study. In: IEEE International Conference on Industrial Engineering and Engineering Management 2016-December, pp. 1646–1650 (2016)
26. Carnerud, D., Mårtensson, A., Ahlin, K., Slumpi, T.P.: Total Quality Management and Business Excellence, 2nd edn. Total Quality Management & Business Excellence, UK (2020)
27. Azzaoui, K., Yousfi, S., Bouamrani, M.L.: Competitiveness improvement of automotive harnesses activity through the integration of digitalisation with the 5G method. In: 2ND Edition Science Week Turkey, pp. 1–2. pre-print, Turkey (2022)

Case Studies and Cyber-Physical Systems 2

Digital Transformation of the Flotation Monitoring Towards an Online Analyzer

Ahmed Bendaouia[1,2]([⊠]), El Hassan Abdelwahed[1], Sara Qassimi[3],
Abdelmalek Boussetta[4], Abderrahmane Benhayoun[4], Intissar Benzakour[4],
Oumkeltoum Amar[3], Yahia Zennayi[3], François Bourzeix[3], Karim Baïna[5],
Salah Baïna[5], Abdessamad Khalil[6], Mouhamed Cherkaoui[6],
and Oussama Hasidi[1,2]

[1] Laboratory of Computer Systems Engineering(LISI), FSSM, Cadi Ayyad
University, Marrakech, Morocco
ahmed.bendaouia@edu.uca.ac.ma
[2] Moroccan Foundation for Advanced Science Innovation and Research MAScIR,
Rabat, Morocco
[3] Laboratory of Computer and Systems Engineering (L2IS), FST, Cadi Ayyad
University, Marrakech, Morocco
[4] Reminex Research and Engineering Center, Managem, Marrakech, Morocco
[5] National School of Computer Science and Systems Analysis (ENSIAS),
Mohammed V University, Rabat, Morocco
[6] National School of Mines of Rabat (ENSMR), Rabat, Morocco

Abstract. Accurate and timely investigation to concentrate grade in
mining industry is a premise of realizing real time and efficient control
in a froth flotation process. This study seeks to use image processing
and artificial intelligence technologies to predict the elemental composition of minerals in the flotation froth. The online analyzer is a flotation
soft sensor solution that predicts the concentrate grade content of the
flotation using froth images and physio-chemical parameters. A froth
image dataset from the lead flotation circuit was collected and prepos-
sessed. Frame selection and data augmentation was used for this dataset.
Feature extraction includes texture and color distribution using image
processing algorithms. Then, several state-of-the-art machine learning
algorithms (Linear regression, Random forest, Decision tree, GR Boost)
are trained to predict the concentrate grades of minerals. A Convolutional neural network architecture is used on the image dataset to predict
the Lead Pb concentrate grade which indicates that the deep learning
has a good industrial performance. The promising results of this study
demonstrate the significant potential of machine vision and deep learning
neural networks in froth image analysis, which is of great importance for
development of the mining industry.

Keywords: Machine vision · Image processing · Mining industry ·
Deep learning · Industry 4.0

© The Author(s), under exclusive license to Springer Nature Switzerland AG 2022
M. Hamlich et al. (Eds.): SADASC 2022, CCIS 1677, pp. 325–338, 2022.
https://doi.org/10.1007/978-3-031-20490-6_26

1   Introduction

Recent studies confirmed the decrease of mineral resources by 28% compared to the last decade [1]. This matter is due to the mineral reserves exhaustion and the unpredictable decreases in raw materials. To encounter these challenges, the industry innovates in mining, exploration, process, logistics, and marketing. The fourth industrial Revolution has occurred since the middle of the last century. The "Industry 4.0", a term coined by Klaus Schwab [2], blurs the lines between the digital domains and offline reality incorporating innovative technologies. Industry 4.0 aims to increase the productivity of smart factories characterized by a range of emerging technologies. It involves disruptive technologies like the Internet of Things (IoT), cloud computing, big data, and Cyber-Physical Systems (CPS). Our study takes place within the context of the digital transformation of the mining industry. We aim to investigate the disruptive technologies and innovation in the mining industry [4] to optimize mineral processing productivity and efficiency. The production chain of the mining industry is made up of different stages ranging from drilling, blasting, extraction, processing and saling. processing begins with crushing, grinding , classification, ore processing by physical separation techniques such as gravimetry, flotation... the concentrates produced are then recovered by solid-liquid separation techniques, filtration, decantation, Etc. Fig. 1. Minerals liberation can be achieved physically by grinders helping to reduce the ore to the desired grain size. Then, based on the characterizations of minerals sought, physical separation techniques are chosen such as gravimetry, flotation or any other suitable separation technique to separate the valuable minerals from the gangue minerals.

Each one of these steps needs continuous monitoring and supervision based on distributed control systems DCS and Programmable Logic Controller PLC. One of the most essential steps in the mining process is flotation Fig. 2. Its ability to rapidly separate complex or low-quality ores with small particle sizes makes it an engaging process compared to gravity, density, or other separation methods. However, the flotation separation technique uses a complex physiochemical process. The flotation needs to be maintained and supervised in real-time, to ensure stability and quality of the minerals separation. This article aims to use machine vision and artificial intelligence in the flotation monitoring towards an online analyzer for the determination of mineral compositions. It is organized as follows: Sect. 2 introduces the context of this research topic; Sect. 3 exhibits a literature review providing a wild range of similar applications in mining industry; Sect. 4 provides data investigation, usage framework and the primary results of the online analyzer; Sect. 5 delivers the conclusion and perspective.

2   Context and Challenges

Recently, we are getting into an era of massive transformation. A huge development in technology and powerful new markets will be driven from resource

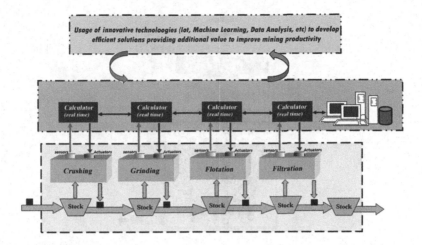

Fig. 1. Process of the flotation in the mine production chain.

dependence to resource efficiency. Disruptive mining technologies are changing the fundamentals of our economy. These technologies affect the standard definition of "Resource efficiency" that means the efficient use of resources like water, gas, oil and metals, by highlighting the efficiency of human resources [3].

The mining industry has shifted its focus to the use of Disruptive mining technologies to improve productivity and efficiency toward a smart mine safer, environment friendly and more competitive. This article takes part in a project named **Smart Connected Mine**, where a number of academic institutions and industrial companies in Morocco are collaborating to develop innovative solutions in mining industry based on artificial intelligence. This consortium aims to achieve process optimisation, guarantee safety of the operators, increase energy efficiency and innovate with efficient solutions through the mining production chain.

Online Analyzer Based on Machine Vision. One of the main research topics of the Smart Connected Mine project is the online determination of minerals grade in the flotation units based on artificial intelligence and machine vision. The identification of the chemical compositions using image-based methods is a cheaper and faster alternative than techniques based on chemical analysis. Considerable attention has been paid to develop efficient and accurate machine vision algorithms and AI solutions for getting control on the flotation performance. The online analyzer contribution aims to respond to real challenges of manual sampling and standard Online Control Systems by developing a real time online analyzer.

Mineral Processing Based on the Flotation. In brief, froth flotation exploits hydrophilic and hydrophobic properties of collectors and minerals within

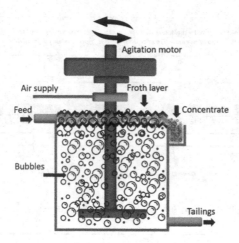

Fig. 2. The flotation froth separation technique.

an ore to induce/stimulate separation. Within a flotation cell, the ground ore particles are mixed with water, air, and adequate reagents to form pulp on the top of the flotation unit to form the froth layer at the surface. This layer is collected as the concentrate in the case of direct flotation, whereas particles that are remaining completely wet stay in the liquid phase to form tailing. Chemicals are added in precise degrees according to elemental composition, mineral concentration and chemical characterisation of the valued minerals. Some of the added chemicals are surface active organic reagents called collectors that impart hydrophobicity to minerals when they adsorb at mineral surfaces. The function of all other reagents is to attain optimal conditions for selective separation of the minerals in an ore. Activators are chemicals that enhance collector adsorption onto a specific mineral, whereas depressants are reagents that prevent collector adsorption or prevent bubble attachment to unwanted mineral surfaces. Modifiers constitute a broad range of inorganic and organic compounds that modulate the flotation environment Fig. 2.

The current study is elaborated on a differential flotation at CMG site in Morocco. This flotation seeks to produce the three base metal concentrates Pb, Cu, Zn separately, through roughers, cleaners and scavengers. The complexity of the differential flotation presents several challenges including the separation of the three metals, the optimization of the recovery of each metal in its own circuit and the production quality of merchant concentrates that meet customer requirements and environmental regulations in terms of quality. The flotation process must act in a specific physio-chemical conditions, e.g., within a fixed range of the pulp pH value, proper slurry agitation, ore-particle size-grade distribution (granularity) and other parameters as mentioned in the Table 3. These parameters affect directly the concentrate grade of the froth flotation. The online analyzer enables real time elemental compositions of the froth based on the physio-chemical parameters and the visual inspection of bubbles.

3   Related Work

Artificial intelligence became a primordial tool to enhance safety and efficiency of the production chain in the mining industry. Nowadays, industrials maintain the process automation based on machine learning models [6]. AI can be applied from the beginning of mining operation to the end of the mine life-cycle, from the exploration and mapping [8], to safety evaluation [9] by finding patterns in events leading to accidents or fatalities, or by controlling undesirable effects of blasting operations on the surrounding environment [10]. AI can be applied also in predicting activities in real-time that can become bottlenecks as presented by [11] that demonstrated the effectiveness of the artificial neural network over empirical models and conventional statistical techniques for predicting the blast performance for the gold mining operation. Artificial neural network techniques is used also in finding patterns in productivity variance, which can help in operations planning and time management since it highlights areas where improvement is immediately possible as proposed recently by [12]. Predictive maintenance also is impacted by machine learning to recognize damage at mining and processing equipment to reduce unplanned down times and avoid fatal breakdowns [13].

The greatest portion of AI applications are in machine vision [5], likely due to the drive to find methods to measure parameters, such as sizing and sorting of particles. In the mineral processing industry, edge detectors and segmentation can be applied to detect the boundaries of particles or bubbles in the flotation froth. Machine vision can be also applied for optical sorting, monitoring electrostatic separation or other separation techniques presented in Table 1. The alternative approach involves feature extraction, which is a range of techniques to extract lower dimensional, abstract features from the high-dimensional images; these features may be correlated with parameters of interest (such as particle size or chemical composition), but do not directly measure these parameters. Feature extraction techniques are closely linked with dimensionality reduction methods, such as principal component analysis. Also, deep learning algorithms, including convolutional neural networks, has proven exceptional accuracy in terms of image recognition [15]. Such techniques can be implemented for mineral resource mapping and exploration using the surface and sub-surface image data. Images from drones or structured data from infrared spectroscopy, can be processed by machine learning algorithms. This technique is used to automate the surface feature detection to classify a complete detailed geological model in mining areas [16]. Automatic classification and recognition of the froth behavior are vital aspects in the monitoring of the flotation. The authors of [18] proposed a solution for automatic identification of the working conditions of froth flotation based on statistical modeling in different working conditions. Such solutions may allow appropriate control and operational guidelines to maintain the optimal production conditions of the flotation. An other promising tool in machine vision is the hyper-spectral imaging. This type of visual data acquisition allows exploring beyond the range of human visibility. Spectral data identifies disrupting phenomena such as the white mica composition, white mica crystallinity, and chlorite composition [17]. Otherwise, the use of machine vision in the flotation monitoring was limited to the monitoring of the froth flotation descriptors, such as color, texture and bubble size. In our proposition, we aim to extend the machine vision capabilities to the prediction of mineral grades based on artificial intelligence.

Table 1. The separation techniques in mining industry.

Difference in hardness	Crushing and screening
Density differences	Gravimetry
Magnetic properties	Magnetic separation
Electrostatic properties	Electrostatic separation
Surface properties	Flotation

4   Proposed Approach: Online Analyzer Based on Computer Vision and Machine Learning

4.1   Human-Eye Visual Control

During the last century, the flotation was an art controlled by the human eye based on the experience of employees. An employee can qualify the performance of the flotation, based on the naked eye observation. The texture, color and bubble size distribution represents directly the underlying probabilities of collision, adhesion. This technique of monitoring is an instant indicator to the flotation state. However, many problems exist in the naked-eye observation based flotation process operation and control such as:

– Human-eye based monitoring stills labor-intensive, experience-dependent and easily influenced by subjective factors of human.
– The accuracy of the results generally depends on the experience of the observers which may lead to a large error
– Human observation is qualitative and lacking in quantitative measurement of the froth surface.
– The evaluation criteria of the froth surface appearance vary significantly. Even for the same froth flotation production status observed at the same time, different operators might report quite different perceptional results.
– Operators cannot monitor the whole flotation circuit effectively because the whole flotation circuit is a long and continuous process including dozens of flotation cells and employees cannot provide a long-term or uninterrupted monitoring of a whole flotation factory
– It demands highly experienced workers that sometimes might not be available

In general, the online analyzer highlights the skills of the human eye visual inspection of the flotation froth as presented in the Table 2. The texture, color, viscosity and bubble size distribution are inspected using Machine Vision techniques and image data.

Table 2. The effect of chemical conditions on froth, recovery and minerals grade.

Condition	Froth state	Results
Collector and adjustment reagents are properly added	Bubbles with clear shapes where most froth bubbles are elliptical	Concentrate grade is generally high, and the contents of valuable ores in the tailing are relatively low
Shortage of collectors	Froth bubbles mostly present polygonal shapes	Bubble loading and recovery of valuable ores are low
Over-dosage of collectors	Froth usually runs slowly with mudding bubbles	The recovery of valuable ores is high, but the concentrate grade is low
Excessive pH adjustment reagent addition	Froth bubbles are generally large and run slowly without loading valuable ores	Verry low recoverry and output grade
Low pH	Froth composed with tiny bubbles	The recovery of ores is low, but the concentrate grade is relatively high
The overload of particles	Froth bubbles load too many mineral particles, causing the bubbles to heavily burst and collapse	The flotation recovery is generally high, but the concentrate grade is low

The online analyzer presents an ideal solution to overcome the real time challenge. The identification of the chemical compositions using image-based methods is a cheaper and fast alternative than techniques based on chemical analysis. The online analyser has no limitation of space or number of analysing point in the flotation factory.

4.2   Data Variety and Challenges

Image Data. are the result of measuring a specific physical phenomenon, such as light, heat, distance or energy. Based on the experts human-eye visual control, physical phenomenon like texture, bubble size and viscosity are the main features that describes the flotation performance Fig. 3. These physical phenomenons are extracted in a numerical form. Deep learning is a recent advance in machine learning that extracts high-level features from image data [19]. The froth surface color involves essential information of the mineral composition in the flotation froth. We can distinguish the mineral type based on the observed highlighted color in the froth. Hence, froth surface color is an important factor to qualify the flotation performance and evaluate the operation instructions based on image data Fig. 4.

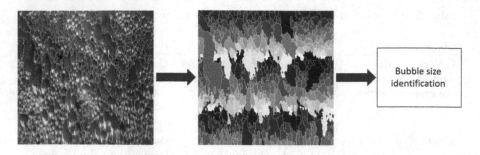

Fig. 3. Detection of bubble size of the froth flotation using segmentation algorithms.

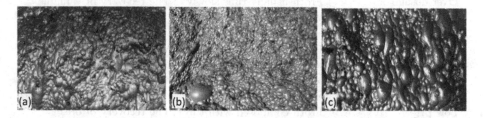

Fig. 4. Froth flotation of the valuable minerals; (a) Copper sulphide (Chalcopyrite) CuFeS2, (b) Zinc sulphide (Sphalerite) ZnS, (c) Plomb sulphide (Galena) PbS, from CMG site in Morocco.

The image details are preserved by deblurring methods, improving the brightness and contrast, or applying the mean filtering to eliminate noise [20]. Dimension reduction processing is effective and economical for feature storage, processing, and successive froth condition clustering [18]. Furthermore, another non negligible adverse factor is the complex mixing blurs, including motion blurs and fog blurs, in the acquired froth images. Motion blurs result from the fast object motion and the relative shifts between the froth surface and the image-acquisition device [21].

Sensor-Based Data. The mineral flotation process must act in a specific physio-chemical condition, e.g., within a fixed range of the pulp pH value, proper slurry agitation, ore-particle size-grade distribution (granularity) and other parameters mentioned in Table 3. All these chemicals and physical parameters need to be supervised to ensure the quality the minerals separation procedure. The identification of the important physical and chemical parameters that impact the flotation quality, leads to a deep understanding of the process complexity. Understanding the process may transfer the flotation control from an art state to machine knowledge. The automatic real time control and decision making with advanced technology improve the flotation productivity.

Table 3. The physiochemical parameters in the flotation unit.

Physical parameters	Chemical parameters
Granularity	The oxidation rate of minerals
Pulp density	The dosage of reagents
Cell characteristics	The pH of the pulp
Pulp's level	The electrochemical potential of the pulp
Pulp flow	Residence time
The slurry agitation rate	Temperature
The air injection rate	The quality of water

4.3   Usage Framework of the Online Analyzer

4.4   Data Acquisition

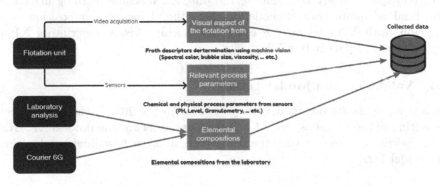

Fig. 5. The data acquisition framework of the online analyzer.

Our main objective is to determine the mineral composition. The data set is composed of visual aspect parameters and the elemental composition of Pb, Cu, Zn and Fe Fig. 5. On the practical side, a sample from the flotation froth is collected and analyzed in the laboratory using the atomic absorption. The Courier 6G provides additional observations of the last cleaners. A video of the flotation froth is recorded using an RGB camera under stable luminosity.

4.5 Building the Model

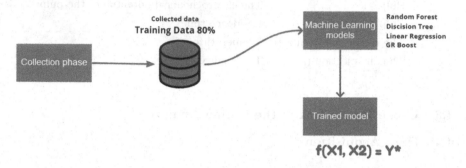

X1 : Froth descriptors dertermination using machine vision (Spectral color, bubble size, viscosity, ... etc.)
X2 : Chemical and physical process parameters from sensors (PH, Level, Granulometry, ... etc.)
Y* : Predicted elemental compositions from the laboratory

Fig. 6. Modeling phase using Machine Learning algorithms.

The Fig. 6 presents the process of building the model. We use 80% of the collected data to explore, study and analyze the different machine learning algorithms. The final adequate trained model predicts the elemental composition of the flotation froth Y based on the extracted machine vision descriptors X1 and physio-chemical parameters X2.

4.6 Validation and Model Tuning

To test and validate our model, we proceed with the 20% of the data collected consisting of the visual aspect X1 and the parameters of the process X2. Evaluation metrics are used to tune the parameters in order to validate and optimize the model Fig. 7.

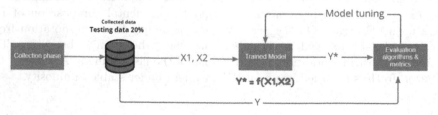

X1 : Froth descriptors dertermination using machine vision (Spectral color, bubble size, viscosity, ... etc.)
X2 : Chemical and physical process parameters from sensors (PH, Level, Granulometry, ... etc.)
Y : Elemental compositions from the laboratory
Y* : Predicted elemental compositions

Fig. 7. Validation and tuning of the model.

4.7 Primary Results

Image data were captured by a mobile machine vision system from an industrial Pb flotation circuit in CMG Managem flotation plant in Morocco. A video camera was mounted at a distance of 35 cm from the froth surface while the illumination of the image was provided by a LED lamp. The video data were recorded at a rate of 25 frames per second. The industrial tests were conducted under different operating conditions (reagent dosage, slurry solid concentration, froth depth and air flow rate).

Videos are labeled with the results of the laboratory analysis. Each label contains the elemental composition of Pb, Fe, Cu and Zn. We augment data to gain more observation from each analysis. Data augmentation consists of selecting the most representative frames from the flotation froth video. Then, each frame is associated with a mineral grade under a tolerable random value ($\pm 0.5\%$) defined by the experts of the mineralogical analysis. The training and validation process includes 10630 observations after data augmentation. Feature extraction consisted mainly on texture and color distribution. Then 600 new testing samples were fed into the trained and validated model to predict the concentrate grades. The Table 4 presents the real and predicted grades of Lead (Pb) in the third cleaner of the lead flotation circuit, and Zinc (Zn) in the fifth cleaner of the Zinc flotation circuit. The model predicts the four elemental compositions Pb, Zn, Cu and Fe for each image of the video test. The quarterly average of the images prediction eliminates the outliers and presents the predicted grades of the video

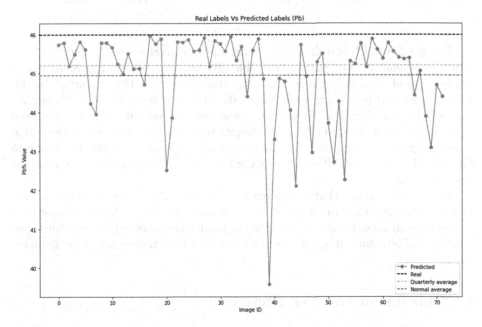

Fig. 8. Predicted Pb concentrate grades in third cleaner of the Pb circuit using Machine Learning and flotation froth visual inspection.

source. We trained our model using programmable neural networks, specifically Convolutional neural networks CNN, to extract height level features from images data. Thus, Convolutional neural networks are regarded as a promising way for flotation soft sensors based on froth images. The CNN architecture is directly inputted by image data with the 400 height, 400 width and 3 depth channels, and this is followed by several stages of convolution and pooling through multiple hidden layers. The entire dataset used in CNN was randomly split into the training (76% of data), the validation (12% of data) and the testing (12% of data) sets. The training set is used to fit the network parameters. During training, the weights are adjusted to minimize the difference between the target and the predicted values. The validation set is used to provide an unbiased estimation of the network performance during training. The network performance after training and validation is evaluated using the testing set. The Table 4 presents the results of Lead (Pb) in the third cleaner of the lead flotation circuit, and Zinc (Zn) in the fifth cleaner of the Zinc flotation circuit.

Table 4. Supervised and unsupervised learning results.

	Third cleaner Pb			Fifth cleaner Zn		
	Observed grades	Supervised	Unsupervised	Observed grades	Supervised	Unsupervised
Pb%	45.99	45.20	32.84	0.34	9.30	2.06
Zn%	3.62	3.73	4.25	49.5	17.54	39.70

The predicted Pb and Zn grades were compared to the actual values from the laboratory analysis to evaluate the reliability our proposition Fig. 8. After the application of several Machine Learning algorithms and Deep Learning architectures, we had promising results regarding the two base minerals Pb and Zn presented in the Table 4. To validate these results, the data test was collected from real world industrial site (CMG flotation site in Morocco), while the actual observed grades are enabled by the laboratory analysis of Reminex Managem Group. The data was collected following the same collection instructions as the training data set.

The results shows that the predicted Pb and Zn grades are close to the actual value, and the online analyzer can accurately detect the changes of high concentrate grades. However, the solution must have more accurate predictions, which could be achieved by an effective Machine Vision inspection of the flotation froth.

5   Conclusion and Perspective

In this article, we have explored the state of artificial intelligence and machine vision applications in mineral processing. We propose the online analyzer as an innovative solution that can achieve real time detection of the concentration grades in the flotation units. The online analyzer is based on the visual inspection of color, texture, viscosity and bubble size. This solution will ensure efficiency and instant monitoring of the flotation circuit. The performance of our proposition is tested on new industrial data from the CMG flotation site in Morocco. Accurately inspecting the flotation froth is a key feature for optimizing and controlling the flotation process. Our proposed solution is less expensive with low maintenance requirements and it enables the mineral grades in real time, which is the added value compared to the existing monitoring techniques.

The online analyzer once deployed on lead circuit will be tested for the three base metals Lead, Copper and Zinc of the CMG differential flotation circuit. The combination of froth features, physio-chemical sensors and the intelligent control techniques can be considered as an alternative and potential flotation monitoring system. Feature extraction of the froth surface properties will be extended to bubble size, viscosity and hyperspectral imaging in future work. Spectral imaging can identify minerals that are present in relatively low quantities. Also, the mineralogical composition at the surface of a sample can be quantified. The texture of samples, such as grain sizes and cross-cutting vein structures, can be characterized [17]. However, it is necessary, for on-site inspection purposes, to use adapted prepossessing algorithmic methods. Pre-processing includes reducing the impact of all the factors affecting the spectral data. The use of a hyper-spectral camera is dedicated to a specific mineralogical phase under specific wavelength range, according to the particles response. Other perspectives consist on using the online analyzer for process optimization through the interaction with the flotation digital twin. Data augmentation, bubble size detection, viscosity, frame selection and the deployment of the online analyzer on the industrial site are the challenges of future work.

Acknowledgment. This research is conducted within the framework of the "Smart Connected Mine" project, which has been supported by the Moroccan Ministry of Higher Education, Scientific Research and Innovation, the Digital Development Agency (DDA), the National Center for Scientific and Technical Research of Morocco (CNRST) through the Al-Khawarizmi program. This article is part of the work undertaken by different partners composed of MASCIR (Moroccan Foundation for Advanced Science, Innovation and Research), REMINEX R&D and Engineering subsidiary of MANAGEM group, UCA (University Cadi Ayyad), ENSMR (National School of Mines of Rabat), and ENSIAS (National School of Computer Science and Systems Analysis). We would like to thank MANAGEM Group and its subsidiary CMG for allowing to conduct research and data collection on site as an industrial partner in this project.

References

1. Peroni, F.R.: Mining haul roads: theory and practice. Chemical Rubber Company 2019
2. Mărgulescu, F.S., Moagăr-Poladian, S.S.: GLOBAL ECONOMIC OBSERVER (2017). http://www.globeco.ro/

3. McKinsey, F.: Report on Economic Impact of disruptive technologies. McKinsey (2015)
4. Qassimi, S., Abdelwahed, E.H.: Disruptive Innovation in Mining Industry 4.0, Distributed Sensing and Intelligent Systems (2022). https://doi.org/10.1007/978-3-030-64258-7_28
5. McCoy, J.T., Auret, F.L.: Machine learning applications in minerals processing: a review. J. Minerals Eng. **132**, 95–109 (2019)
6. Danish, A., Frimpong, S.F.: Identification of digital technologies and digitalisation trends in the mining industry. Artificial Intelligence Review Springer (2020)
7. Barnewold, L., Lottermoser, B.G.: Identification of digital technologies and digitalisation trends in the mining. Int. J. Mining Sci. Technol. **30**, 747–757 (2020)
8. Tabaei, M., Esfahani, M.M., Rasekh, P., Esna-ashari, A.: Mineral prospectivity mapping in GIS using fuzzy logic integration in Khondab area, western Markazi province Iran. J. Tethys (2017)
9. Iphar, M., Cukurluoz, A.K.: Fuzzy risk assessment for mechanized underground coal mines in Turkey. Int. J. Occup. Safety Ergonom. (2020)
10. Bui, X-N., Nguyen, H., Le, H.-A., Bui, H.-B., Do, N.-H.: Prediction of blast-induced air over-pressure in open-pit mine: assessment of different artificial intelligence techniques. J. Nat. Resour. Res. (2020). https://doi.org/10.1007/s11053-019-09461-0
11. Tiile, R.N.: Artificial neural network approach to predict blast-induced ground vibration, airblast and rock fragmentation, Thesis at Missouri University of Science and Technology (2016)
12. Takbiri-Borujeni, A., Fathi, E., Sun, T., Rahmani, R., Khazaeli, F.: Drilling performance monitoring and optimization: a data-driven approach, air blast and rock fragmentation. J. Petroleum Explor. Prod. Technol. (2019)
13. Gohel, H.A., Upadhyay, H., Lagos, L., Cooper, K., Sanzetenea, A.: Predictive maintenance architecture development for nuclear infrastructure using machine learning. J. Nuclear Eng. Technol. (2020)
14. Dusan, P., Fleming-Muñoz, D.: Automation and robotics in mining: jobs, income and inequality implications. J. Extract. Ind. Soc. **8**, 189–193 (2021)
15. Zhiping, W., Changkui, Z., Jinhe, P., Tiancheng, N., Changchun, Z., Zhaolin, L.: Deep learning-based ash content prediction of coal flotation concentrate using convolutional neural network. J. Minerals Eng. (2021)
16. Walker, C.J.: Fourier Transform Infrared Spectroscopy and Machine Learning Techniques for the Sensitive Identification of Organics in Rocks, Thesis in Delaware State University (2020)
17. Dalm, M., Buxton, M., van Ruitenbeek, F.: Discriminating ore and waste in a porphyry copper deposit using short-wavelength infrared (SWIR) hyperspectral imagery. J. Minerals Eng. (2017)
18. Jin, Z., Zhaohui, T., Jinping, L., Zhen, T., Pengfei, X.: Recognition of flotation working conditions through froth image statistical modeling for performance monitoring. J. Minerals Eng. (2016)
19. Zarie, M., Jahedsaravani, A., Massinaei, M.: Flotation froth image classification using convolutional neural networks. J. Minerals Eng. (2016)
20. Mengcheng, T., Changchun, Z., Ningning, Z., Cheng, L., Jinhe, P., Shanshan, C.: Prediction of the ash content of flotation concentrate based on froth image processing and BP neural network modeling. Int. J. Coal Preparation Utilization (2021)
21. Jinping, L., et al.: Online monitoring of flotation froth bubble-size distributions via multiscale deblurring and multistage jumping feature-fused full convolutional networks. J. Trans. Instrum. Meas. (2020)

Air Quality Remote Monitoring Module: I4.0 Application in Smart Poultry Farm

K. A. Ibrahima[1](✉) and Abdoulaye Cissé[2]

[1] Department of Electromechanical Engineering, Ecole Polytechnique Thiès, Thiès, Senegal
ika@ept.sn
[2] Baamtu Technologies, Dakar, Senegal

Abstract. Industrial Internet of Things—IIoT—is being more and more applied to every production field as technology evolves. Poultry farms take advantage of that trend to increase productivity and ease day-to-day management. Chicken meat production is economically feasible if environmental parameters such as temperature humidity and ammonia rate are monitored and controlled in order to lower broiler mortality. This paper presents a remote monitoring solution applied to chicken poultry farms. Temperature, humidity and ammonia rate are obtained using DHT22 and MQ137 sensors. The main hardware component is a custom-designed PCB where an Arduino nano IoT 33 microcontroller is embedded to collect and send data to the cloud. AWS cloud services, CDAP pipeline and PostgreSQL database are then used to store, process and display relevant data on a dashboard. The first part of the paper presents the hardware design process. The second part shows the data workflow. Prototype onsite deployment and test results are discussed in the third part. Finally, future developments of the module are proposed.

Keywords: Industrial Internet of Things · Smart Poultry Farm · AWS cloud · DHT22 · MQ137

1 Introduction

Driven by IoT and connectivity, Industrial Internet of Things (IIoT) or Industry 4.0 (I4.0) revolutionizes the approach of work and eases human efforts towards production of goods and services. All aspects of human life, including meat production, are improved thanks to IIOT systems deployed to increase productivity and quality. Animal welfare is a critical economic issue in the poultry industry where environmental parameters such as temperature, humidity and ammonia rate need to be monitored and controlled. In [1], Kristensen et al. suggest that exposure to ammonia causes irritation to the mucous membranes in the eyes and the respiratory system. According to Corkery et al., there is a close relationship between NH3 rate and relative humidity; both of then affecting bird performance and energy consumption in broiler production farms [2]. Those parameters are considered to be significant factors for mortality, especially in the first week of placement [3].

This paper proposes a module for remote monitoring of environmental parameters (Temperature, humidity and ammonia rate) in a chicken poultry farm. A cloud-based platform for storage and processing of gathered data is developed using AWS cloud services. A mobile application and a web interface are available for users to interact with the system. The first part of the paper presents the hardware design process of the module. The second part shows the data workflow from sensors to a dashboard. Prototype onsite deployment and test results are discussed in the third part. Finally, future developments of the module are proposed.

2   Hardware Design

Environmental data collection requires the development of an electronic board. A microcontroller and sensors are embedded on a custom-designed PCB. The temperature and humidity monitoring are done using AM2302 sensor and the NH3 rate is obtained with a MQ137 gas sensor.

The block diagram in Fig. 1 shows the interconnection between the functional units. Three voltage levels (12 V, 5 V and 3.3 V) are distributed from the power supply unit to the microcontroller and the sensors. A voltage adapter and a level shifter are necessary to adjust the inputs to the Nano IoT 33 board. It is worth noting that the nano IoT 33 board is chosen to design the first prototype. It is indeed a low-cost modular microcontroller. Next versions of the board will be based on a fully integrated microprocessor. Module status is displayed through an RGB led. The module incorporates terminal connectors used to wire the sensors and RGB led. Up to 5 measurement points can be connected to the module.

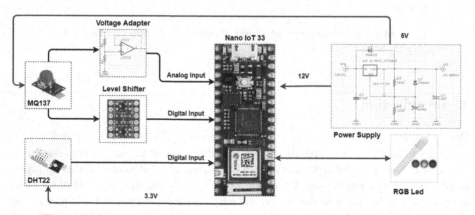

Fig. 1. Wiring of Temperature Humidity and Ammonia rate Monitoring Module.

2.1   Temperature and Humidity Monitoring

AM2302—or DHT22 sensor uses a capacitive humidity sensor and a thermistor to measure the surrounding air and delivers a digital signal on the data pin via a single bus.

An internal chip processes the sensor measurements and generates 40-bit data. The sensing period is approximately 2 s. Technical specifications are shown in Table 1 and experimental setup in Fig. 2.

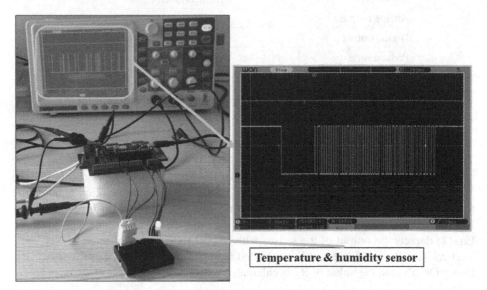

Temperature & humidity sensor

Fig. 2. Experimental setup to test the DHT sensor—signal on the 1-wire bus is observed with a logic level of 3.3 V.

Table 1. Technical specifications AM2302 sensor

Power supply	3.3–6 V
Output signal	Digital signal via single bus
Temperature range	$-40\ °C/80\ °C$
Humidity range	0–100% RH
Temperature accuracy	$< +/-0.5\ °C$
Humidity accuracy	$+/-2\%$ RH
Sensing period	2s
Current	1 mA–1.5 mA

2.2 Ammonia Rate Monitoring

Ammonia gas sensor MQ137 uses SnO_2 sensing element, which has lower conductivity in clean air and high sensitivity to NH3 gas [4]. NH3 presence increases the sensor conductivity which can then be converted to an analog output signal in the range of

Table 2. Technical specifications AM2302 sensor.

Power supply	5V
Sensor type	Semiconductor
Analog output	0–5 V
Digital output	0 V or 5 V (TTL Logic)
Preheat time	Over 48 hours
Detecting concentration scope	5–500 ppm NH$_3$
Sensing resistance	900–4900 KΩ (air)

0–5 V. A digital trigger output is also available, but not used in the scope of this work. Table 2 shows technical specifications of the MQ137 ammonia gas sensor.

Figure 3 shows the standard test circuit of the MQ137 sensor. A heating voltage V_H and a circuit voltage V_C are necessary to respectively supply working temperature to the sensor and detect voltage to the load resistor R_L. The built-in variable resistor R_S, sensitive to NH$_3$, is connected in series with R_L. The load voltage V_{RL} given by Eq. (1) depicts the output of the sensor with respect to the concentration of NH$_3$. The load resistor R_L is 47 kΩ and is connected in series with the variable resistance R_S. Using Ohm's law, the value of R_S is calculated with Eq. (2).

$$V_{RL} = \frac{V_C}{R_S + R_L} \tag{1}$$

$$R_S = \left(\frac{V_C}{V_{RL}} - 1 \right) R_L \tag{2}$$

$$R_0 = \left(\frac{V_C}{V_{RL}^{air}} - 1 \right) R_L \tag{3}$$

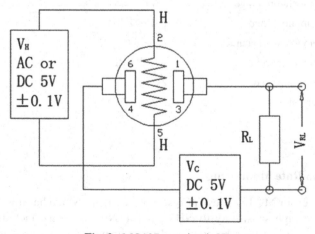

Fig. 3. MQ137 test circuit [5].

$$\frac{R_S}{R_0} = \alpha * ppm + \beta \tag{4}$$

The supplier of the gas sensor provides a log-log scale graph of the sensitivity to NH$_3$ in parts per million (ppm) shown in Fig. 4. The ratio of the resistors $\frac{R_S}{R_0}$ is used as y-axis with R_0 being the resistance of the variable resistor in clean air.

The log-log graph of ratio $\frac{R_S}{R_0}$ and the concentration ppm is linear. Equation (4) illustrates the relationship with calibration parameters α and β given in Fig. 4. A is the slope and β is the y-axis intercept. Practically, the output voltage V$_{RL}$ is measured and the value of the variable resistor is deducted from Eq. (2). Taking into account the constant values of R_0, α and β, the log concentration is calculated with Eq. (4).

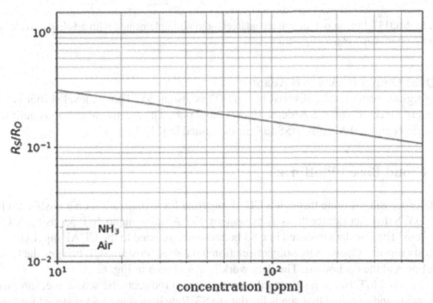

Fig. 4. Typical sensitivity curve—The ordinate is resistance ratio of the sensor (Rs/R0), the abscissa is concentration of gas. Rs means resistance in target gas with different concentration, R0 means resistance of sensor in clean air. All tests are finished under standard test conditions [6].

MQ137 Output Analog Voltage Adapter

The load voltage V$_{RL}$ delivered by the sensing circuit with MQ137 varies between 0 and 5 V. A voltage adapter is required to connect to the Arduino input which requires a maximum voltage of 3.3 V. As shown in Fig. 5, a voltage divider is used on each channel to maintain the output voltage range between 0 and 3.3 V while V$_{RL}$ varies between 0 and 5 V. A follower circuit is built with a LM358 operational amplifier to interface the board input and the voltage divider. It is worth noting that a linear function is theoretical defined with parameters ($\alpha = 0.66$ and $\beta = 5000$) to retrieve the actual voltage level delivered by the sensor.

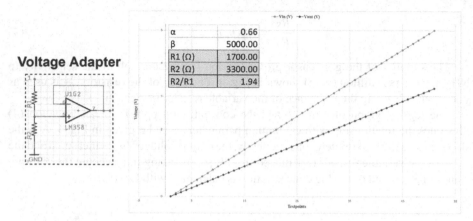

Fig. 5. MQ137 Analog output voltage adapter—circuit implemented with a voltage divider and an amp op in following configuration.

MQ137 Output Logic Level Adapter

The digital output level delivered by MQ137 is also at 5V. Thus, a level shifter is used to interconnect it with the Arduino digital input port. The electronic circuit is built with a single N channel Mosfet (BSS138) as explained in [7].

3   Cloud Based Platform

Data processing is done through a CDAP pipeline for visualization on a dashboard [8]. The AWS IoT service collects data sent by the Arduino nano IoT 33 using MQTT protocol. The raw data is stored in a S3 bucket and streamed to the CDAP pipeline using Kinesis service. Open-source object-relational database PostgreSQL bridges the CDAP pipeline and the dashboard. The data workflow is shown in Fig. 6.

On AWS IoT, two rules are configured. One that redirects the sensor measurements to Kinesis and a second that sends the data to S3. Raw data sent to S3 is stored for future use cases.

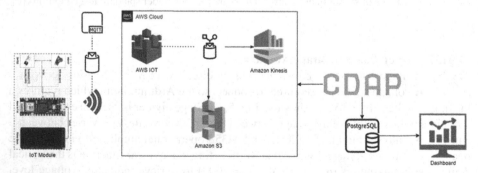

Fig. 6. Data workflow using AWS cloud services, CDAP and PostgreSQL database.

The data sent from Kinesis are collected in real time thanks to the Kinesis streaming plugin available on CDAP. The data is received in byte format, much more resilient to transmission errors. Subsequently, thanks to the different directives of the Wrangler (a plugin of CDAP), which provides fairly simple means to transform, harmonize and enrich the data, necessary transformations are done.

The received bytes are converted into a string and JSON block is then extracted. Subsequently, the different columns are extracted from this JSON and re-named to: date, 'sensor_id', 'temperature', 'humidity', 'nh3_rate', 'heat_index', to match the table schematic in the database. Then we tackle the different conversions of types (integer, decimal value), which are simplified thanks to the directives of the Wrangler. The date is also converted by specifying the appropriate format ("yyyy-MM-dd'T'HH:mm:ss'Z'").

Now that the transformed data is consistent with the corresponding table schema, they are stored in the database. From there, the BI tool retrieves them and displays them on the dashboard.

The JSON payload shown in Fig. 7 is sent every minute with a timestamp, an ID of the module, values of temperature, humidity, heat index and ammonia rate.

```
▼ baamtu

{
    "Date": "2021-12-23T16:12:12Z",
    "sensorId": "Module2_Dht1",
    "temperature": 27.8,
    "humidity": 55,
    "heat_index": 28.66896,
    "NH3_rate": 0.000139
}
```

Fig. 7. JSON payload sent to cloud every minute with environmental parameters.

4   Prototype Deployment and Test Results

The prototype is deployed in a chicken poultry farm in Dakar as shown in Fig. 8. A waterproof and dust free packaging of the main board and the sensors helps secure the prototype in the harsh environment of the poultry. Five measurement locations are possible, one is used for the prototype test.

The data collected for one week are displayed in the dashboard as shown in Fig. 9. It can be seen that the temperature ranges from 26 °C to 17 °C, the humidity from 27% up to 90% at night. The ammonia rate stays below 0.4 ppm.

Fig. 8. Onsite deployment of the prototype in a chicken poultry farm.

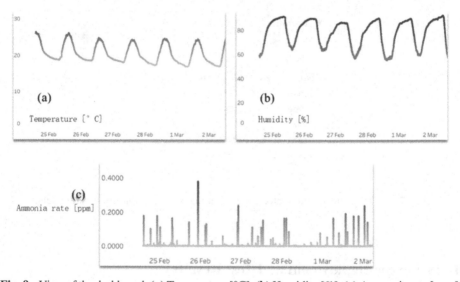

Fig. 9. View of the dashboard: (**a**) Temperature [°C], (**b**) Humidity [%], (**c**) Ammonia rate [ppm].

5 Conclusion

In this paper, a system dedicated to the monitoring of environmental parameters (Temperature, humidity and ammonia rate) of a poultry farm is presented. The module is built with an Arduino nano IoT 33 and two sensors in a custom-designed PCB. It uses AWS cloud services, a CDAP pipeline and a PostgreSQL database to process, analyze and store data sent through WIFI. A visual dashboard is developed to display the data for users.

The device was deployed and tested onsite in a chicken poultry farm. Future work will focus on the usage of collected data to manage the farm thanks to Artificial Intelligence, Machine Learning and Big Data. Behavioral analysis could be applied to automate the management of the farm. It is worth noting that the concept could be associated with other units such as a weight estimation module and CCTV footage in order to fully automate the farm management.

Acknowledgements. This work was funded by Baamtu Technologies under the scope of the SCPF (Smart Chicken Poultry Farm) project.

References

1. Kristensen, H., Wathes, C.: Ammonia and poultry welfare: A review. Worlds Poult. Sci. J. **56**(3), 235–245 (2000). https://doi.org/10.1079/WPS20000018
2. Corkery, G., Ward, S., Kenny, C., Hemmingway, P.: Monitoring environmental parameters in poultry production facilities. Presented at the Computer Aided Process Engineering—CAPE Forum 2013, April 2013 [Online]. Available: https://researchrepository.ucd.ie/handle/10197/4257. Accessed 16 Nov 2021
3. Basset, A.: A Greener World Technical Advice Fact Sheet No. 8, Mortality in Poultry (2011)
4. Barsan, N., Weimar, U.: Understanding the fundamental principles of metal oxide-based gas sensors; the example of CO sensing with SnO2 sensors in the presence of humidity. J. Phys.: Condens. Mat. **15**, R813 (2003)
5. Winsen Ammonia Gas Sensor Manual, Version 1.4, 2015, available here
6. Marko, P., Filip, D., Mateo, T., Lucija, R., Petar, M., Ivana, G.: Ammonia concentration monitoring using Arduino. Environ. Eng. **6**, 21–26 (2019). https://doi.org/10.37023/ee.6.1.4
7. Application note, Bi-directional level shifter for I^2C-bus and other systems, AN97055, http://cdn.sparkfun.com/tutorialimages/BD-LogicLevelConverter/an97055.pdf
8. A. Ndiaye, Pipeline creation with CDAP, https://blog.baamtu.com/en/creation-de-pipeline-avec-cdap/

Smart Greasing System in Mining Facilities: Proactive and Predictive Maintenance Case Study

Mariya Guerroum$^{(\boxtimes)}$ [iD], Mourad Zegrari [iD], and AbdelHafid Ait Elmahjoub [iD]

Laboratory of Complex Cyber Physical Systems (CCPS)—The National Higher School of Arts and Crafts (ENSAM)—Sciences Faculty Ben M'Sik, Hassan II University, Mers Sultan BP 916, Casablanca, Morocco
mariya.guerroum1@gmail.com

Abstract. Maintenance has attracted lately research attention. Interesting advances were brought to the process industry to boost Digital transformation. Specifically, Predictive maintenance has a big role in enhancing productivity and machine reliability. Machines lubrication is a systematic Maintenance activity preventing later parts degradation. Promoting this activity should be taken more seriously as more than 50% of roller bearing in mining industry defects are due to inadequate lubrication. Additionally, actual industrial lubrication practices lack assistance and efficiency. To improve lubrication and generally maintenance in the digitalization context, the process industry requires an upgrade of operations automation and the integration of a certain degree of intelligence. This smart level must be reached in components lubrication, leverage decision-making, and keep up with the mining industry challenges. This study proposes a smart greasing system to achieve proactivity in the ore mining industry lubrication activity as a Proof-of-Concept. A fuzzy logic controller is used to compute input parameters vibrations, temperature, and humidity, collected from smart sensors implemented in a crusher machine. The Controller calculates the dosage correction coefficient to change the grease output on the centralized greasing test bench. This Proof-of-Concept is destined to reduce bearing defects related to the lubrication problem. Last, the Authors present the vision of combining the smart greasing concept and the previously developed predictive maintenance system for a better mining process maintenance real-time monitoring.

Keywords: Smart lubrication · Proactive maintenance · Digital transformation · Fuzzy logic · Roller bearing

1 Introduction

In the last years, research have addressed the predictive maintenance paradigm trying to diagnose occurring defaults or predict machines remaining useful life (RUL). Indeed, it is stated that Roller bearing, the most widespread machines parts in the process industry, could fail for many causes like fatigue, deformation, inappropriate lubrication, mishandling and improper installation [1]. For 90% of rolling bearing lubrication, greases have always been the best choice. The quantity of the necessary grease for the proper functioning of the bearing must occupy a volume equal to approximately 30% of the internal free volume of the latter. A larger or less amount of grease has negative influence on the operation [2]. Thus the bearing RUL depends on the lubrication condition [1]. Lubrication technics are mainly two types: manual lubrication and automatic lubrication.

Efficient greasing would prevent catastrophic breakdowns and unpredictable maintenance. To ensure an efficient greasing, it is necessary to use the right grease with the right quantity and method into the specific point at the optimal intervals [3]. Manual greasing involves safety risks and human errors in addition to bad lubrication [4] especially for continuous production processes.

Random greasing, hard-to-reach points and both manual and automatic lubrication actions lack information induce poor lubrication. This issue has always been pointed at as a roller bearing defect reason. However solutions to this problem haven't been addressed by research. Also, the conventional lubrication actions actually do not meet the digital transformation demand. Furthermore, only 5% of the points to be greased at the ore mining fixed installations are covered by automatic lubrication systems. In this situation, reliable real-time information on the greasing operation progress of are not available on the company's information system.

This work motivation is to develop a smart greasing system as a proof of concept applied to fit the ore mining fixed installation crusher machine. The system is composed of the centralized greasing test bench to be implemented in the mining environment and the simulation environment. Fuzzy Logic (FL) controller is used to compute the grease dose correction coefficient by inferring membership functions of vibration, temperature, and humidity variables. The data are collected by the crusher smart sensors. It is used to evaluate the functionalities of intelligent lubrication on an electromechanical system. The cycles are simulated based on the actual working conditions of a given period of two bearings of the central axis of the crusher. Further, the results are discussed to evaluate for the integration of intelligent greasing at mining industry Fixed Installations and on the implementing an action plan for the deployment of the proposed solution. The tests formalized by this present work aim to: Prove the concept on the bench before testing on industrial production equipment, use data from the field to bring the results and interpretations as close as possible to reality and the conditions under which the system is intended, and empirically identify the causes behind lubrication problems.

2 Literature Review

It is commonly known, lubrication practice is vital for bearings [3]. This activity quality influences directly the bearing and the machinery health state on life cycle [5]. By re-greasing the bearing it would not be necessary to immediately replace with a new one [6].

The foundations of FL were established in 1965 by Professor Lotfi A. Zadeh [7]. At that time, the theory of FL was not taken seriously. As early as 1974, the first industrial applications were found, particularly in the field of robotics. FL by its main characteristic of simulation of human reasoning, it is classified among the techniques of artificial intelligence. This technique makes it possible to model and then replace the monitoring and process control expertise coming from the designer or the user. FL is asserting itself as an operational technique. Used alongside other advanced control techniques, it makes a discreet but appreciated entry into industrial control automation. Its advantages come from its ability to formalize and simulate the expertise of an operator or designer in the conduct and calculation of a process. This technique makes it possible to give a simple answer for processes whose modeling is difficult. FL considers cases or exceptions of different natures without interruption and integrates them gradually into the expertise. Finally, consider several variables and perform "weighted fusion" of the influence quantities.

In classical or Boolean logic, any element of a set admits only one value 1 or 0, but in FL, a set A of the universe of discourse $U = \{x\}$ is defined as a distribution by which each value of x is assigned any number in the interval [0, 1], indicating the degree to which x belongs to set A [8], i.e.:

$$A = \{x = U, \mu A(x) \in [0, 1]\} \tag{1}$$

Thus, a fuzzy concept only makes sense if it can be specified:

- The universe U of discourse of the considered elements x.
- The membership functions $\mu_A(x)$ of the elements $x \in U$ of the fuzzy set A [9].

In general, the physical system can be broken down into three interrelated elements: the input variable, the mathematical model, and the output variable. In addition, there are three essential steps in the implementation of a fuzzy model. The first step is the definition of linguistic variables and their membership functions. The second step is the establishment of inference rules in the form: If… Then. The last step, the defuzzification, is the determination of the output variable by calculating the center of gravity, or by the maximum value. The calculation procedure is called induction [8] while there are.

FL basic models use different types of outputs. Sugeno FL method features linear output and Subtractive Clustering technic enables the fuzzy rules extraction controlled by the clustering radius, which values interval is [0,1] [10]. Besides, Mamdani FL method uses fuzzy implications based on the 'Min' operation. Moreover, Fuzzy C-Means clustering method is used to set the inference rules [11]. In this study, The Mamdani technic is privileged to extract the nonlinear output in order to handle the correction coefficient which is uncertain.

FL has been used for MPPT control to deal with nonlinearity issues in photovoltaic systems [8]. In the agile production domain, since the end of the 20th century, FL has been widely implemented to take care of the evaluation and selection of cutting conditions, control of machine tools, non-destructive inspection, selecting machine procedures, monitoring of turning processes, automatic control, tool wear sensing and detecting and decision making for identification of vibration onset [12]. Mamdani FL technique was adopted to simulate sequential wastewater treatment process by [13]. Also, FL has been adopted to control Energy storage systems [14, 15].

Diagnosis is carried out only when the machine is working as the acquired data is more significant. FL controller helped determine the temperature in the cutting zone while processing machine plastic [16].

FL systems were also used to develop expert systems to make decision to provide intelligence to machine as human beings [17].

Table 1 presents Maintenance applications of the FL control system. In maintenance application, Risk-based Maintenance Analysis was performed by FL controller to overcome the risk of potential failures by choosing the optimal maintenance intervals [18]. FL controller was also used in fault detection in pumping system [19], renewable energy maintenance [14, 20] and on IoT based solutions [21]. No further research works were found on lubrication management to serve maintenance proactivity matters for roller bearing. In the following, the FL technique is applied to determine the grease amount according to the bearing conditions and needs.

Table 1. Fuzzy logic controller maintenance applications

Authors	FL application domain	Publication Year	Reference
Wang	Agile production	2001	[12]
Ratnayake and Antosz	optimal maintenance intervals choosing	2017	[18]
Dutta et al	fault detection in pumping system	2022	[19]
En-nay et al	Improved crowbar strategy for DFIG wind turbine	2022	[20]
Mahrouch et al	Hybrid Autonomous Microgrid	2022	[22]
Han et al	Energy storage system degradation information	2022	[14]
Mihigo et al	On-Device IoT-Based Predictive Maintenance Analytics Model	2022	[21]

3 Methodology

A smart greasing system is proposed as a Proof of Concept. The system is mainly composed by the centralized greasing test bench and the simulation environment. The simulation and the test data are gathered from the real crusher located at the mining fixed installations through a cloud-based service. Authors have used the same use case presented in previous work on defaults diagnosis Machine learning (ML) models [23].

3.1 Materials

In this case study, the same jaw crusher operating in the phosphate mining industry's screening process is studied. This equipment treats waste by reducing the sterile blocks from 90 mm to less than 250 mm. To carry out the tests, we took into consideration the actual operating conditions of the two identical central axis bearings of the crusher in the Benguerir mine destoning unit as presented in Fig. 1. These two components are referenced 231/560CAK/C3 W33 Spherical bearing on 2 rows of rollers.

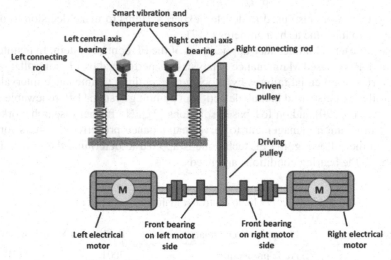

Fig. 1. Kinematic diagram of the jaw crusher

The smart greasing system is used to represent the intelligent centralized lubrication system mode of operation to be implemented in the mining environment. This system is made up of a progressive centralized lubrication test bench equipped with an end-of-cycle sensor, Open Platform Communications (OPC) Server and the FL controller simulation unit for smart greasing. It is used to test the functionalities of intelligent lubrication on the previously presented system. The selected input parameters on which the lubrication tests will be carried out are the Fixed Installations crusher data (e. g. temperature, humidity, and vibration). The vibratory displacement in mm/s, acceleration in g and, temperature in °C, are the wireless sensors data recorded every 4 hours over 20 months. The cycles are simulated based on the actual working conditions of a given period of two bearings of the central axis of the crusher.

The architecture is represented by a hierarchical organization of the decision-making layers in Table 2.

Table 2. Decision-making layers of the smart greasing system

Level	Decision layer	Objective
2	Decision making	Make lubrication intelligent by imposing a running time and cycles adapted to the needs of the bearing
1	Automation and monitoring	Control and command of centralized lubrication system through automation
0	Field	Execute the cycles and collect the data for carrying out the lubrication operations

The proposed solution architecture is shown in Fig. 2.

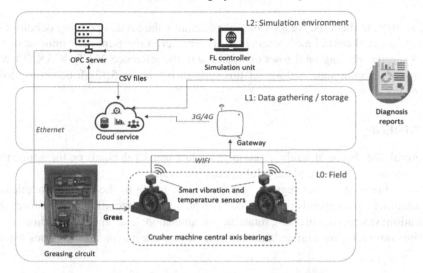

Fig. 2. Smart greasing system architecture

Greasing frequency, grease quantity, on time, off time and number of cycles are outputs issued from the smart lubrication control application. The FL controller makes it possible to determine the test bench greasing pump running time (Tm), pause time (Tp) and number of cycles (N). These parameters are written at the OPC server level to administer them to the PLC for execution insuring the smooth running of intelligent lubrication system. As a result, any changes made at the application level are instantly modified on the test bench.

Figure 3 illustrates the test bench components located in the level 0.

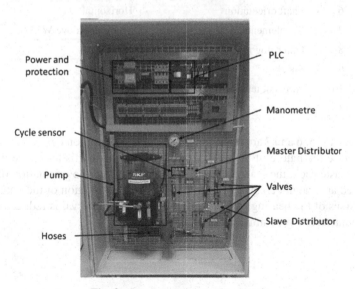

Fig. 3. Smart greasing testing bench

To carry out the tests, we took into consideration the actual operating conditions of the two identical central axis bearings of the crusher in the Benguerir mine destoning unit. Spherical bearing on 2 rows of rollers with the reference 231/560CAK/C3 W33. The average recommended dose for this type of bearing is 5.15g/h according to the bearing constructor.

3.2   Method

In general, the choice of a relubrication procedure usually depends on the application, the operating conditions and the relubrication interval.

The adjustment of the regreasing interval, according to the recommendations of the manufacturers, depends on the following parameters: operating temperature; shaft orientation; vibrations; outer ring rotation; contamination; load; and bearing dimensions.

The constructor recommendations are based on working conditions values listed in Table 3.

Table 3. Standard operating conditions for manufacturers' recommendation of lubrication cycles

No	Parameter	Value
1	Rotation speed (r/min)	340
2	Daily operation	24h
3	Bearing operating temperature	Average
4	Pollution/humidity	Moderate
5	Load	Heavy
6	Shaft orientation	Horizontal
7	Supplements	Through groove W33
8	Outer ring rotation	No
9	Shocks	Yes
10	Ambient temperature	Average

Conditions 2, 5, 6 and 7 are fixed and taken into consideration beforehand modelization. And since the nature of the main function of the crusher is to reduce the particle size of the waste rock, the load is classified as high. Indeed the orientation of the shaft is predefined and cannot change over time, as well as the rotation of the outer ring and the dimensions of the bearing. As a result, the regreasing interval is reduced compared to the manufacturer's recommendation.

Since vibration, temperature and humidity data are acquired through wireless sensors, the following adjustments should be observed:

- Temperature:

  o Every 15 °C exceeding 70 °C, the interval must be reduced the grease undergoes accelerated aging at high temperatures (chemical alteration)
  o Every 15 °C below 70 °C, the interval must be doubled a maximum of 2 times: the risk of aging of the grease is reduced at low temperature

- Vibrations: for high levels of vibration and shock loads, the interval must be reduced to avoid compaction of the grease which causes it to knead. Vibration levels are classified in ISO 10816-6 into three categories normal condition A/B, requireing intervention C and the dangerous state D.
- Contamination: by fluids (moisture) the greasing interval must be reduced.

Next, to achieve the proactivity in the greasing operation, the FL system controller was developed in MATLAB's environment to regulate the grease dosage cycles. The controller has three inputs and one output membership function. The use of FL in this study consists in determining the product of the correction coefficients (Tt.Ta.Te) already presented in the previous paragraph. This coefficient must be applied to the base period (Fb) in order to calculate the corrected period (Fc). For this, we used Matlab's FL toolbox. In Fig. 4, The mamdani FL technic features ANFIS system with three inputs and one output membership function. The input functions are trapezoidal whilst the output function is triangular. 27 Inference rules were set for this case study.

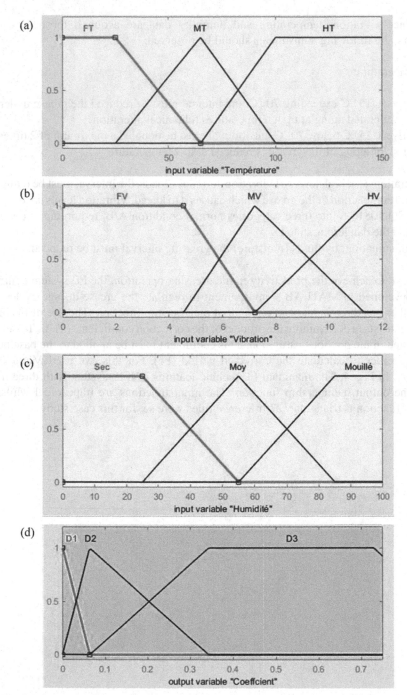

Fig. 4. Membership functions: (**a**) input variable temperature; (**b**) input variable Vibration; (**c**) input variable humidity; (**d**) output variable correction coefficient

4 Results

During the online tests, the connectivity between the software program and the PLC was successfully achieved.

The operating conditions with 72 records for each roller bearing were acquired in the range of twelve days. It is remarkable that during the same day, the relative humidity value fluctuates considerably. The environment is dry in the middle of the day, while the weather becomes very humid during the night and dawn. When examining the acceleration spectrum at the measurement point, the analysis showed a lack of lubrication fault. The mechanical maintenance team was asked if an intervention was carried out to remedy the problem of lack of grease on the ninth day of recording. Indeed, a manual lubrication was carried out with a control of the lubrication circuit.

At the right bearing, records 50 and 52 corresponding respectively to the dates 09/11/2020 at 08:41 and 09/11/2020 at 12:30, represent a displacement of the maximum vibration values in mm/s according to the Standard ISO 10816.

It should be noted that the cycles applied only when the system is running. It is for this reason that when calculating the intelligent lubrication cycle, only the values corresponding to an activated operating state of the equipment influence the results. In the record history, 31 out of 72 values are suitable for the working state. The results of the bearing which presented an anomaly and a large fluctuation show an adaptation to the need in terms of lubrication to tackle the deficit during operation and thus ensure the continuity of the process.

The working conditions of the left bearing are shown in Fig. 5 and 6.

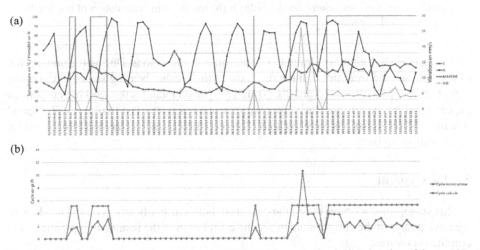

Fig. 5. (a) Representation of the working conditions of the central axis right bearing of the crusher (On time, temperature, vibrations, and humidity); (b) results of the calculation of the intelligent lubrication control application

The intelligent lubrication control program results in cycles with an average frequency of 1.31 gr/h against 5.15 gr/h recommended by the manufacturer. The working conditions of the left bearing are shown in Fig. 6.

A lack of fat is noticed during the results calculated on 02/11/2020 from 00:51:23 and remained visible on the spectral analysis of the vibrations throughout this day. We take for example the sampling of the analysis of the spectrum of accelerations of date 02/11/2020 at 15:26:14 clearly indicating a lubrication defect. After detecting the problem of lack of lubrication through inspection rounds, manual lubrication is carried out to fill the bearing and then restart the crusher.

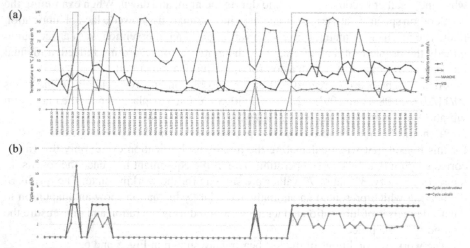

Fig. 6. (**a**) Representation of the working conditions of the central axis right bearing of the crusher (On time, temperature, vibrations, and humidity); (**b**) results of the calculation of the intelligent lubrication control application

To test the algorithm, we simulated all possible combinations. During the preparation of the data set, we went through the database of the crusher bearing stages in the range from October 1, 2019, until April 30, 2021. This period includes the working conditions experienced by the crusher during the various seasons of the last two years. We found that only 12 combinations were verified. The rest of the data is entered to allow all valid combinations to be tried.

5   Discussion

At this stage, since we have tested the data from both crusher bearings on the test bench, we have analyzed the current state to see the correlation of the results with practices and conditions on site.

5.1   Current Practices for Addressing Lubrication Problems

The lubrication intelligence module must operate based on a correctly dimensioned automatic centralized system:

- Adapted and non-failing circuits.

- Sufficient reservoir for system autonomy in terms of grease.
- A grease suitable for the types of bearings and the working environment of the equipment.
- A safe filling mode through an orifice equipped with a non-return valve to avoid contamination.

The service flow rates of the bearings are set at 2.6 g/min, equivalent to 156 g/h. By comparing the doses prescribed by the lubrication application and the doses set on the current system, it is found that the crusher is permanently over-greased. However, inspection rounds and processed vibration signals show that grease shortages are frequently detected. This means that the excessive quantities of grease are not injected by the lubrication circuit into the bearings for which they are intended. A waste of grease results without efficiently greasing the bearings.

5.2 Impact and Correlation of Smart Lubrication on Maintenance Activities

If there is a lack of grease on a crusher bearing, the mechanical atelier team performs manual greasing and then checks the grease circuit before restarting the crusher. This smart greasing approach provides, in the case of grease lack, for the system to compensate for the lack of grease in the bearing automatically by acting on the frequency without interfering with the crusher running state. In addition, to the tank filling mode is performed by entirely opening the tank. This practice is not immune to contamination that can reach the grease before serving the bearing, thus seriously affecting its performance. Bearing manufacturers recommend adopting a "clean" reservoir filling method. Therefore, even if the smart greasing system effectively manages the doses, still this practice influences the grease and the lubrication operation quality. At the crusher level, generally, the most occurring faults are structure defects, misalignments, lubrication lacks, bearing problems, and fixation issues. The crusher's various component's fault classes are extracted from sensors Data and diagnosis reports jointure.

The use of manual or electric pumps allows the grease to be extracted from the sealed barrel or barrel having a single exit mode directly and injected through a one-way port of the circuit pump reservoir.

These observations cited below are among the major causes of lubrication problems at the level of the crusher bearings, in addition to fatigue due to the loads applied to other defects on the kinematic chain and to the various maintenance interventions.

The majority of the vibration values recorded to carry out this test are classified in zone C of the ISO 10816-6 standard. Machines with vibrations in this zone are normally considered unsatisfactory for long continuous service. Typically, the machine can operate under these conditions for a limited time until the opportunity arises to take corrective action. During this period, it is interesting to integrate the intelligent lubrication system at the equipment level to extend the period before correction. And even after the maintenance intervention, such a system will make it possible to preserve the proper functioning of the equipment by minimizing as much as possible the problems linked to unsuitable lubrication.

The crusher dataset includes 5656 downtime hours, where 1877 hours were diagnosed to be due to greasing problem. Figure 7 illustrates the types of crusher machine downtime distribution. The greasing issues represent 33% of the crusher downtime.

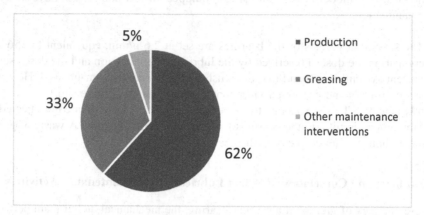

Fig. 7. Types of the crusher machine downtime distribution

The maintenance proactivity could eliminate problems related directly to the lubrication by 73% and indirectly by 40% according to the crusher maintenance reports. This system could be combined with the PdMSys to link action to global decision making when it comes to maintenance [24]. In addition, both systems real-time operating will assure the demanded proactivity and support the digital transformation in the industrial mining environment. The estimated return on investment is 20 times the originally invested amount in Generalizing smart greasing systems to the fixed installations over 20 other machines.

6   Conclusion

In this study, lubrication activity has been presented as a crucial maintenance action to prevent drastic breakdowns and repetitive production shutdowns. To ameliorate the greasing practice in the mining continuous process, upgrading a centralized progressive greasing system to a smarter level. The crusher case study is used to develop the smart greasing system. The proposed system is composed by a centralized greasing test bench and a FL controller simulation unit. The FL method has demonstrated the ability to treat nonlinear problem while simulating the human thinking process. The intelligent lubrication control program has demonstrated its ability to detect the lack of grease as the calculated dosage is higher than the manufacturer's recommendations thanks to the FL technique. This work results demonstrate that intelligent greasing is first and foremost proactive greasing. The solution was designed using all technologies to meet this need. Across the 8486 data lines over a span of 20 months, 1601 times, the lubrication problem was reported, according to the inspection rounds carried out by the operator. Authors claim that smart lubrication could help preventing up to 73% of bearing lubrication issues specially when combined with the Predictive maintenance system operating on real-time basis. The Fixed Installations will therefore be equipped with intelligent greasing systems serving the critical points of the equipment without interfering with the normal operation of the various units. This smart practice would be a step towards the digital transformation in the ore mining industry. Since the FL controller performance depend on sensors, authors recommend the use of a large dataset. Authors aim to combine FL technic alongside other ML models to improve the machine RUL for proactive maintenance practice promotion.

References

1. Motahari-Nezhad, M., Jafari, S.M.: Bearing remaining useful life prediction under starved lubricating condition using time domain acoustic emission signal processing. Exp. Syst. Appl. **168**(November 2020), 114391 (2021). https://doi.org/10.1016/j.eswa.2020.114391
2. Chatra, K.R.S, Lugt, P.M.: Channeling behavior of lubricating greases in rolling bearings: identification and characterization. Tribol. Int. **143**, 106061 (2020). https://doi.org/10.1016/j.triboint.2019.106061
3. Burge, P.: Lubes spread further than PM compacts. Met. Powder Rep. **66**(6), 9 (2011). https://doi.org/10.1016/S0026-0657(12)70013-9
4. Manigandan, N., NaveenPrabhu, V., Devakumar, M.: Design and fabrication of mechanical device for effective degreasing in roller bearing. Procedia Eng. **97**, 134–140 (2014). https://doi.org/10.1016/j.proeng.2014.12.234
5. Akchurin, A., van den Ende, D., Lugt, P.M.: Modeling impact of grease mechanical ageing on bleed and permeability in rolling bearings. Tribol. Int. **170**(January), 107507 (2022). https://doi.org/10.1016/j.triboint.2022.107507
6. Miettinen, J., Andersson, P.: Acoustic emission of rolling bearings lubricated with contaminated grease. Tribol. Int. **33**(11), 777–787 (2000). https://doi.org/10.1016/S0301-679X(00)00124-9
7. Zadeh, L.A.: Fuzzy sets. Inf. Control **8**(3), 338–353 (1965). https://doi.org/10.1016/S0019-9958(65)90241-X
8. Kamal, N.A., Ibrahim, A.M.: *Conventional, intelligent, and fractional-order control method for maximum power point tracking of a photovoltaic system: A review*, no. 2014. Elsevier Inc. (2018)
9. Khettab, K., Bensafia, Y., Bourouba, B., Azar, A.T.: *Enhanced fractional order indirect fuzzy adaptive synchronization of uncertain fractional chaotic systems based on the variable structure control : robust H ∞ design approach*. Elsevier Inc. (2018)
10. Sugeno, M.: An introductory survey of fuzzy control. Inf. Sci. (NY) **36**(1–2), 59–83 (1985)
11. Mamdani, E.H.: Application of fuzzy logic to approximate reasoning using linguistic synthesis. IEEE Trans. Comput. **C–26**(12), 1182–1191 (1977). https://doi.org/10.1109/TC.1977.1674779
12. Wang, K.: *Computational intelligence in agile manufacturing engineering*. Elsevier Science Ltd. (2001)
13. Mazhar, S., Ditta, A., Bulgariu, L., Ahmad, I., Ahmed, M., Nadiri, A.A.: Sequential treatment of paper and pulp industrial wastewater: Prediction of water quality parameters by Mamdani Fuzzy Logic model and phytotoxicity assessment. Chemosphere **227**, 256–268 (2019). https://doi.org/10.1016/j.chemosphere.2019.04.022
14. Han, D., Kwon, S., Kim, J., Yoo, K., Lee, S.E.: Integration of long-short term memory network and fuzzy logic for high-safety in a FR-ESS with degradation and failure. Sustain. Energy Technol. Assess. **49**(July 2021), 101790 (2022). https://doi.org/10.1016/j.seta.2021.101790

15. Yang, X., Yue, H., Ren, J.: Fuzzy empirical mode decomposition for smoothing wind power with battery energy storage system. IFAC-PapersOnLine **50**(1), 8769–8774 (2017). https:// doi.org/10.1016/j.ifacol.2017.08.1735

16. Prvulovic, S., Mosorinski, P., Radosav, D., Tolmac, J., Josimovic, M., Sinik, V.: Determination of the temperature in the cutting zone while processing machine plastic using fuzzy-logic controller (FLC). Ain Shams Eng. J. **13**(3), 101624 (2022). https://doi.org/10.1016/j.asej. 2021.10.019.

17. Kumar, N., Goyal, P., Kapil, G., Agrawal, A., Ahmad Khan, R.: Flood risk finder for IoT based mechanism using fuzzy logic. Mater. Today Proc. (2020). https://doi.org/10.1016/j. matpr.2020.09.698

18. Ratnayake, R.M.C., Antosz, K.: Development of a risk matrix and extending the risk-based maintenance analysis with fuzzy logic. Procedia Eng **182**(1877), 602–610 (2017). https://doi. org/10.1016/j.proeng.2017.03.163

19. Dutta, N., Kaliannan, P., Shanmugam, P.: Application of machine learning for inter turn fault detection in pumping system. Sci. Rep., 1–18 (2022). https://doi.org/10.1038/s41598-022-16987-6

20. En-nay, Z., Moufid, I., El Makrini, A., & El Markhi, H.: Improved crowbar protection technique for DFIG using fuzzy logic. Int. J. Power Electron. Drive Syst. (IJPEDS) **13**(3), 1779–1790 (2022). https://doi.org/10.11591/ijpeds.v13.i3.pp1779-1790

21. Mihigo, I.N., Zennaro, M., Uwitonze, A., Rwigema, J., Rovai, M.: On-device IoT-based predictive maintenance analytics model: comparing TinyLSTM and TinyModel from Edge Impulse, 1–20 (2022)

22. Mahrouch, A., Ouassaid, M.: Primary frequency regulation based on deloaded control, ANN, and 3D-fuzzy logic controller for hybrid autonomous microgrid. Technol. Econ. Smart Grids Sustain. Energy **7**(1) (2022). https://doi.org/10.1007/s40866-022-00125-2

23. Guerroum, M., Zegrari, M., Elmahjoub, A.A., Berquedich, M., Masmoudi, M.: Machine learning for the predictive maintenance of a Jaw Crusher in the mining industry. In: 2021 IEEE International Conference on Technology Management, Operations and Decisions (ICTMOD), 2021, pp. 1–6. https://doi.org/10.1109/ICTMOD52902.2021.9739338

24. Guerroum, M., Zegrari, M., Amalik, H., Elmahjoub, A.A.: Integration of MBSE into mining industry: predictive maintenance system, **12**(4), 170–180 (2022). https://doi.org/10.46338/ije tae0422

Risk Management Based on Hybridized TOPSIS Method Using Genetic Algorithm

Adil Waguaf(✉), Rajaa Benabbou(✉), and Jamal Benhra(✉)

Optimization of Logistic and Industrial Team, Advanced Research Laboratory in Industrial Engineering and Logistics 'LARILE', National Higher School of Electricity and Mechanics, Hassan II University of Casablanca, Casablanca, Morocco
{Adil.waguaf,r.benabbou,jbenhra}@ensem.ac.ma

Abstract. Risk management decision-making is essentially based on the choice of context, this context mainly depends on the criteria chosen and the weightings allocated or calculated for each criterion. Traditional "multicriteria decision-making methods" are generally subjective and depend to a large extent on the weightings expressed by the decision-maker. Our work consists of the proposal of a methodology based on the use of genetic algorithms for the calibration of the weighting coefficients necessary in the process of using the multi-criteria decision method TOPSIS. The aim is to automate the risk management decision-making process and to compare the results obtained with genetic algorithms with the results obtained using conventional multi-criteria decision-making methods. Indeed, the results obtained by using the genetic algorithms to the data in the TOPSIS matrix without the usual intervention of the decision maker in the choice of the weighting of the coefficients are satisfactory. Hence the efficiency of our approach in comparison with the conventional TOPSIS method.

Keywords: TOPSIS · MCDM · Genetic algorithm · Risk management · Weighting coefficients

1 Introduction

Managing risk is both complex and subjective. This includes the identification of risk factors, the establishment of risk thresholds, and the identification of appropriate risk mitigation measures [1]. Risk management is the discipline that seeks to identify, assess and prioritize risks related to the activities of an organization. Whatever the origin of these risks, to process them methodically, to reduce and control the probability of feared events, to minimize the time to detectability and to reduce the possible impact of these events [2]. This risk assessment process is a critical step to a successful risk management system. In addition, the standard gives guidelines for estimating risks by integrating the development of decision criteria or decision support to assess the estimated risks and facilitate the assessment of these risks according to the following Fig. 1 process:

Choosing the decision support method is important for achieving reliable results. TOPSIS is one of the numerical methods of multi-criteria decision-making that was first

M. Hamlich et al. (Eds.): SADASC 2022, CCIS 1677, pp. 363–375, 2022.
https://doi.org/10.1007/978-3-031-20490-6_29

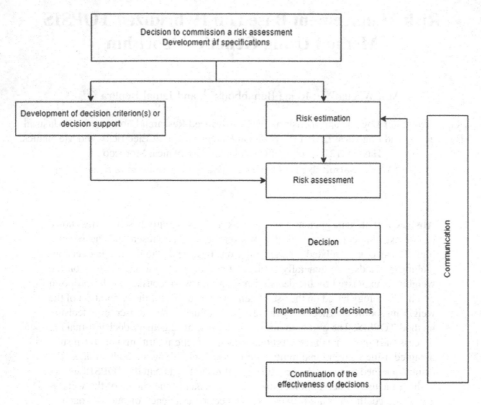

Fig. 1. Risk assessment process according to the standard FD X 50-252

developed in 1981 by Yoon and Hwang. Its basic concept is that the chosen alternative should have the shortest distance from the ideal solution and the farthest from the
negative-ideal solution. Indeed, the integration of Artificial Intelligence in Risk Management will reduce the decision-maker's subjectivity and automate the process to make
it stand-alone and reliable in any unpredictable situation [4, 5].

Our work proposes to optimize the decision support by optimally calculating the
weighting coefficients of the criteria chosen for integration in the calculation of the
TOPSIS method. This optimization will be through an efficient tool in the literature to
find out about genetic algorithms. The use of genetic algorithms automates the decision-
making process without human involvement or by the decision-maker.

The GA is one of the oldest of the best-known optimization techniques, based on
natural selection translated by Darwinian Theory. In GA, we have a population of individuals; each, called a chromosome, represents a potential solution to the problem. The
problem to be solved is defined by the objective function. Depending on the degree of
accuracy an individual is suited to the objective function by the value that represents
the quality attributed to him. This value is referred to as the aptitude of the individual
which is an assessment factor. The highly regarded people have a better chance of being
selected from the new generation of the population. In GA, we have three operators:

selection (the new population of individuals is created according to the aptitude values of individuals of the previous generation), crossing (generally parts of individuals are exchanged between two individuals selected for the crossing), and mutation (the values of certain genes are changed at random) [6–10].

The objectives of our study are:

- Hybridize the tool of genetic algorithms and MCDM methods, especially TOPSIS.
- Evaluate the effectiveness of the results obtained.
- Compare the results of our process with that using classical MCDM methods.

2 State of Art

Our work will allow to hybridize the TOPSIS decision method and genetic algorithms in the field of risk management.

2.1 Genetic Algorithm in Risk Management

Kılıç used GA to provide a fast and effective solution approach to the risk mitigation problem in project planning is formulated as a two-objective optimization problem, expected duration and total cost expected should both be minimized [7]. Wang in his work realized a Risk interaction modifies the probability of occurrence of a risk as well as the impact of the risk, which requires new approaches to make a risk response decision (RRD). In this work, a network model based on the abstraction simulation of risk interactions is built to evaluate the RRDs. Meanwhile, the genetic algorithm (GA) is adapted and improved to optimize RRD, whose crossover operator is designed and improved by social network analysis (SNA) [11]. Pfeifer in his work was able to solve the optimization problem is developed to maximize the project delay under stochastic disturbances of the tasks, and a genetic algorithm is introduced to identify the critical tasks that lead to the maximum risk of project delay [12]. Nezamoddini sets up a new genetic algorithm associated with the artificial neural network that presents previous plans and seeks better ones by reducing any mismatch between supply and demand and compares between classical methods and the model [13]. Bi used a GA to control the risk of scheduling IT Outsourcing (ITO) projects can result in huge economic losses for a business [6]. Srinivasan also proposes a multiple objective genetic algorithm (MOGA) for the analysis of financial data for risk analysis and forecasting. The algorithm is applied to benchmark data sets to predict credit card decision and credit applications [14].

2.2 The Hybrid Use of GA and the TOPSIS Method

Several works address the subject of GA and the TOPSIS method. Azadeh created a hybrid genetic algorithm and TOPSIS simulation (HGTS) to determine the most efficient number of operators and division of labor in cell manufacturing systems [15]. The entropy method was used to estimate the weight of the attributes. The authors concluded for the superiority and advantages of the proposed HGTS over TOPSIS, Data Envelopment Analysis (DEA) and Principal Component Analysis (PCA). Azzam's work was the application of a combination of a genetic algorithm and the concept of e-dominance to solve the multiple-objective reactive power compensation problem and used TOPSIS to evaluate the best solution. From a set of alternatives. The results demonstrate the capabilities of the proposed one-pass technique [16]. Cheng presented a general framework for the multicriteria parameter calibration problem by combining a genetic algorithm with TOPSIS for a rainfall-runoff model for flood prediction in China. TOPSIS gave the order of classification of the alternatives (chromosomes) and the attributes of several criteria are the characteristics of the flood. They concluded that the hybrid method is easier compared to previous studies and feasible and robust to apply in practice [17]. Taleizadeh in used a hybrid Pareto method, TOPSIS and a genetic algorithm to solve multi-period inventory control problems [18]. DALMO Marchetti studies the extreme performance of the Brazilian BRCS rail freight system through a new hybrid model that combines TOPSIS with a genetic algorithm for estimating weights in optimized scenarios [19]. Mehrdad has addressed the subject of genetic algorithms for the calibration of weighting coefficients used in TOPSIS method to define the Sociability Centrality based on topological features of nodes and a representation of their psychological and sociological features that is calculable for large size networks [20].

3   Our Approach

The proposed methodology uses a genetic algorithm to calculate the weights of the criteria from the table of data collected by optimizing the objective function and weighting the coefficients. Then, we use the TOPSIS method for ranking and risk assessment. Then we compare the current hybrid method (GA and TOPSIS) with TOPSIS method.

3.1   Genetic Algorithm

Genetic Algorithms (GAs) were first proposed by John Holland. GA searches the extensive and complex solution space based on guided random procedures to detect "good", but not necessarily optimum solutions, in each timeframe [20].

GA is part of evolutionary computing, which is rapidly developing in the field of artificial intelligence (AI) [21]. In addition, it draws on Darwin's theory of evolution. Simply put, problems are resolved through an evolutionary process resulting in the best (most suitable) (survivor) solution. In GA, the solution evolves several times until the best solution is fixed. To use GA, the solution must be represented as a genome (or chromosome). GA then creates a population of solutions and applies genetic operators such as mutation and crossover to evolve the solutions to find the best one (s) [22].

We use GA to calibrate the weighting coefficients and subsequently use them as weights for the TOPSIS method.

For this we will follow the following steps:

1. Generate a random population with n chromosomes using an appropriate symbolic representation [23].

2. Evaluate the fitness function of each x chromosome in the population using the objective function [24, 25].
3. create a new population by iterating through the following steps until you get the right population.

   a. Select two parent chromosomes in a population according to their suitability for the fitness function
   b. With a predefined cross probability, the crossover will work on the selected parents to form a new offspring (children) [26].
   c. With a predefined mutation probability, the mutation will work on the new off-spring with each gene. The chosen genes are exchanged to make a mutation [25].
   d. Place the new offspring in the new population.

4. Provide the best solution to the current population. If yes, stop
5. If the process does not provide the best solution, go to step 2.

3.2 TOPSIS Method

Multi Criteria Decision Methods problems are Some problems which deal with the evaluation of some choices made based on some criteria consisting of m choices and n criteria. Some solutions methods are AHP [27], VIKOR (Multicriteria Optimization and Compromise Solution, with Pronunciation) [28] and ANP (Analytic network process) [29].

TOPSIS is a technical muti-criterial decision method (MCDM) proposed by Hwang and Yoon [30] based on the concept that the chosen alternative should simultaneously have the shortest distance to an ideal (positive) solution (a^*) and the distance furthest from a negative ideal solution (a_*). The ideal solution maximizes the benefit and minimizes the total cost while the negative ideal solution minimizes the benefit and also maximizes the total cost. The TOPSIS method measures weighted Euclidean distances. This method is used in many applications in various fields such as social network analysis, supply chain management, HSE management and project management.

So, TOPSIS has a reasonable procedure for evaluating some choices (m) based on some criteria (n) with different levels of relative importance. The relative importance of criteria in the evaluation process is shown by weights. It should be noted that in a certain (Multi Criteria Decision Methods) MCDM problem, the final score of each choice will be modified by making some changes in weights of criteria.

The Basic principle of TOPSIS requires the chosen alternative to have the shortest distance from the positive ideal choice and the farthest distance from the negative ideal solution, as shown in Fig.3. To obtain that we follow the steps:

- 1st Step: Normalize performance as follows:

$$E' = \left[e'_{ij} = \frac{g_j(a_i)}{\sqrt{\sum_{i=1}^{m} [g_j(a_i)]^2}} \right]; i = 1, 2, \ldots, met \, j = 1, 2, \ldots, n \qquad (1)$$

- 2nd Step: Calculate the product of the normalized performance by the relative importance coefficients of the attributes using the criteria weighting estimated by the genetic algorithms:

$$e''_{ij} = \pi_j.e'_{ij}; i = 1, 2, \ldots, met \, j = 1, 2, \ldots, n \qquad (2)$$

- 3rd Step: Determine the ideal (a*) and anti-ideal (a$*$) profiles.

$$a^* = \left\{ Max_i e''_{ij}, i = 1, \ldots, met \, j = 1, \ldots, n \right\}$$

$$a^* = \left\{ e^*_j, j = 1, \ldots, n \right\} = \{ e^*_1, e^*_2, \ldots, e^*_n \}; e^*_j = Max_i \left\{ e''_{ij} \right\} \qquad (3)$$

$$a_* = \left\{ Min_i e''_{ij}, i = 1, \ldots, met \, j = 1, \ldots, n \right\}$$

$$a_* = \{ a_{j*}, j = 1, \ldots, n \} = \{ e_{1*}, e_{2*}, \ldots, e_{n*} \}; e_{j*} = Min_i \left\{ e''_{ij} \right\} \qquad (4)$$

- 4th Step: Calculate the Euclidean distance from the profiles a* and a$*$.

$$D^*_i = \sqrt{\sum_{j=1}^{n} \left(e''_{ij} - e^*_j \right)^2}, i = 1, 2, \ldots, m \qquad (5)$$

$$D_{i*} = \sqrt{\sum_{j=1}^{n} \left(e''_{ij} - e_{j*} \right)^2}, i = 1, 2, \ldots, m \qquad (6)$$

- 5th Step: Calculate a coefficient of measurement of the approximation to the ideal profile:

$$C^*_i = D_{i*}/(D_{i*} + D^*_i), i = 1, 2, \ldots, m \qquad (7)$$

- 6th Step: Rank the actions according to decreasing values of C$_i$*.

4 Our Industrial Case Study

Our study will be projected on an industrial case of a high-stakes company, to allow us to assess the effectiveness of this approach compared to traditional methods. We choose large company in the food industry for our study.

4.1 Proposed Procedure

The main objective of the present research is to automatize the process of decision with a performed tool (GA) in a case of risk management. To introduce this method, the following procedure is proposed to evaluate the risks. The proposed procedure is based on TOPSIS and GA with the following steps:

1. Select used data in the Table 1,

   The Ri represent the occupational risks
   R1: Risk of fire and explosion
   R2: Chemical hazard
   R3: Biological risk
   R4: Internal circulation risk
   R5: MSD risk
   R6: noise
   R7: Mechanical risk
   R8: Single storey risk
   R9: Risk of falling from a height
   R10: Risk of falling object
   and the Ci are the criteria chosen to assess these risks [31]: C1: Gravity; C2: Exposure; C3: Protection level; C4: Working environment; C5: Employee skills

Table 1. Ponderation risk/criteria

Risk	C1	C2	C3	C4	C5
R1	4	1	4	2	1
R2	3	3	1	2	1
R3	2	1	1	1	2
R4	4	2	1	1	1
R5	2	3	2	2	1
R6	2	3	2	2	1
R7	3	3	1	2	1
R8	2	2	3	2	1
R9	4	1	3	1	1
R10	3	2	1	1	1

2. Establishment of a value table produced by the manager on the basis of feedback data from last year or according to a mapping pre-established by the company

3. Use GA as an optimization routine to find the best weights for TOPSIS criteria. The main challenge here is to obtain best weights for the criteria, and determination of these weights could thus be considered an optimization problem. Sum of these weights should be equal to 1 and they should be tuned in such away that scores of selected nodes obtained based on TOPSIS exhibit the greatest possible correlation with the scores of Table 1. These weights can be determined by Genetic Algorithms (GA) as tools for approximation of the solution within reasonable time.

4. Perform an additional TOPSIS in which all the risk are considered alternatives, and the calculated values of C1, C2, C3, C4 and C5 are considered the criteria, and the resulting weights from GA in step (c) are considered weights of the criteria. Scores obtained based on the latest TOPSIS show the assessment of each node.

5. Use the TOPSIS method using the weight coefficient of NRSI. The latter will be used for the calculation of the weighting coefficients. This approach is the best known in the literature.

6. Compare the hybrid method (GA-TOPSIS) and the TOPSIS method

4.2 Parameter Tuning of GA

To detect the best weight and to obtain the maximum correlation coefficient of the scores calculated on the basis of TOPSIS [20]. The general diagram of the considered GA is the following:

A) Representations
The putative chromosome in each population consists of 5 genes which represent the weights of various measures of centrality in the TOPSIS method [20]. The constraint on the weights is as follows:

$$Wj \in [0, 1] \, and \, \sum_{j=1}^{5} Wj = 1 \tag{8}$$

B) Fitness Function
Our fitness Function is Function TOPSIS to choose the optimum chromosome respecting the fitness Function and the values of Table 1. This Function is in Eq. 7.

C) Population
In this work, each population is made up of 50 chromosomes, that is pop size $= 50$.

D) Burns
We choose the low burns and upper burns equal respectively to [0.3 0.1 0.1 0.1 0.05] and [0.5 0.3 0.2 0.2 0.15].

E) Crossover and Mutation
In this paper, mutated chromosomes are generated by gaussian mutation method with a coefficient of 0.2 and single point crossover method with 0.8.

4.3 Results

To find the best relative weights of criteria, the proposed genetic algorithm is run in MATLAB (R2021b). The resulting optimum solution is shown in Table 2.

The resulting optimized weights acquired in the previous step are applied as weights of criteria in the second TOPSIS in which all nodes in the studied risk and decision matrix consist of ten alternatives and five criteria. The proposed TOPSIS for developing rank of risks in the dataset is summarized in Table 3 (Table 4).

Table 2. Results of the GA

Criteria	C1	C2	C3	C4	C5
Weight (X)	X1	X2	X3	X4	X5
Value	0.36	0.18	0.19	0.16	0.11

The risk prioritization ranking corresponds to the ranking of the score obtained, the greater risk is the one with the highest score.

For comparing the two hybridized methods (GA-TOPSIS) and TOPSIS, the advantage of this hybridization (GA-TOPSIS) allowed the automation of the decision-making process for use in a purely autonomous system, also the objectivity of the method used unlike conventional MDCMs where the weighting of the weights of the coefficients is subjective and depends on the choice of the decision's maker. The GA uses an interval limited by the lower limit and the upper limit, which gives more fields to the GA to choose the most optimum solution while respecting the fitness function and the constraint function. The advantage of the TOPSIS method is the use of other MCDMs for the calculation of the weights of the weighting coefficients or the use of weights from a reference system such as NRSI or other. Also, its process of use is simple compared to other methods.

The results obtained by the two methods are similar; the risk classifications R1, R3, R9 and R10 are the same for the two compared methods, the risks R5 and R6 are always equal and other risks R2, R4, R7 and R8 have a slight difference of 0.06.

Finally, we retain as result that the most advantageous method is the hybridization of the GA and TOPSIS method, also a categorization of the risks can be done in three different categories according to the two methods for the prioritization of the risks namely: Class 1: R1 and R9; Class 2: R2, R4, R5, R6, R7 and R8; Class 3: R3 and R10.

Table 3. The results of the TOPSIS method with the weights calculated by GA

	C1	C2	C3	C4	C5	Normalization (E')					Weighting (e_ij'')					D^*_i	D_{i*}	C^*_i Scoring	Rang
	0,36	0,18	0,19	0,16	0,11														
R1	4	1	4	2	1	1,438446	0,523411	2,433457	1,319508	0,933033	0,517841	0,094214	0,462357	0,211121	0,102634	0,21	0,45	0,67	1
R2	3	3	1	2	1	1,078835	1,570232	0,608364	1,319508	0,933033	0,38838	0,282642	0,115589	0,211121	0,102634	0,38	0,25	0,40	8
R3	2	1	1	1	2	0,719223	0,523411	0,608364	0,659754	1,866066	0,25892	0,094214	0,115589	0,105561	0,205267	0,48	0,10	0,18	10
R4	4	2	1	1	1	1,438446	1,046821	0,608364	0,659754	0,933033	0,517841	0,188428	0,115589	0,105561	0,102634	0,39	0,28	0,42	4
R5	2	3	2	2	1	0,719223	1,570232	1,216729	1,319508	0,933033	0,25892	0,282642	0,231178	0,211121	0,102634	0,36	0,24	0,40	5
R6	2	3	2	2	1	0,719223	1,570232	1,216729	1,319508	0,933033	0,25892	0,282642	0,231178	0,211121	0,102634	0,36	0,24	0,40	6
R7	3	3	1	2	1	1,078835	1,570232	0,608364	1,319508	0,933033	0,38838	0,282642	0,115589	0,211121	0,102634	0,38	0,25	0,40	7
R8	2	2	3	2	1	0,719223	1,046821	1,825093	1,319508	0,933033	0,25892	0,188428	0,346768	0,211121	0,102634	0,32	0,27	0,46	3
R9	4	1	3	1	1	1,438446	0,523411	1,825093	0,659754	0,933033	0,517841	0,094214	0,346768	0,105561	0,102634	0,27	0,35	0,57	2
R10	3	2	1	1	1	1,078835	1,046821	0,608364	0,659754	0,933033	0,38838	0,188428	0,115589	0,105561	0,102634	0,41	0,16	0,28	9
						1	1	1	1	1	a*	0,517841	0,282642	0,462357	0,211121	0,205267	0,00	0,49	
											a*	0,25892	0,094214	0,115589	0,105561	0,102634	0,49	0,00	
Moy géo	2,780778	1,910546	1,643752	1,515717	1,071773														

Table 4. The processes and results of the TOPSIS method with the weights of NRSI [31]

	C1	C2	C3	C4	C5	Normalization (E')					Weighting (e_{ij}'')					D_i'	D_{i*}	C_i^* scoring	Rang
	0,40	0,20	0,15	0,15	0,10														
R1	4	1	4	2	1	1,438446	0,523411	2,433457	1,319508	0,933033	0,575378	0,104682	0,365019	0,197926	0,093303	0,23	0,41	0,64	1
R2	3	3	1	2	1	1,078835	1,570232	0,608364	1,319508	0,933033	0,431534	0,314046	0,091255	0,197926	0,093303	0,32	0,27	0,46	5
R3	2	1	1	1	2	0,719223	0,523411	0,608364	0,659754	1,866066	0,287689	0,104682	0,091255	0,098963	0,186607	0,46	0,09	0,17	10
R4	4	2	1	1	1	1,438446	1,046821	0,608364	0,659754	0,933033	0,575378	0,209364	0,091255	0,098963	0,093303	0,32	0,31	0,49	3
R5	2	3	2	2	1	0,719223	1,570232	1,216729	1,319508	0,933033	0,287689	0,314046	0,182509	0,197926	0,093303	0,35	0,25	0,41	6
R6	2	3	2	2	1	0,719223	1,570232	1,216729	1,319508	0,933033	0,287689	0,314046	0,182509	0,197926	0,093303	0,35	0,25	0,41	7
R7	3	3	1	2	1	1,078835	1,570232	0,608364	1,319508	0,933033	0,431534	0,314046	0,091255	0,197926	0,093303	0,32	0,27	0,46	4
R8	2	2	3	2	1	0,719223	1,046821	1,825093	1,319508	0,933033	0,287689	0,209364	0,273764	0,197926	0,093303	0,33	0,23	0,41	8
R9	4	1	3	1	1	1,438446	0,523411	1,825093	0,659754	0,933033	0,575378	0,10‹682	0,273764	0,098963	0,093303	0,27	0,34	0,56	2
R10	3	2	1	1	1	1,078835	1,046821	0,608364	0,659754	0,933033	0,431534	0,209364	0,091255	0,098963	0,093303	0,35	0,18	0,33	9
Moy géo	2,780778	1,910546	1,643752	1,515717	1,0‹1773	1	1	1	1	1	a* 0,575378	0,314046	0,365019	0,197926	0,197926	0,00	0,47	1,00	
											a* 0,287689	0,10‹682	0,091255	0,098963	0,098963	0,47	0,00	0,00	

5 Conclusion

The field of decision support is a field where human intervention is almost present to define criteria or to weight them. In a discipline such as risk management, decisions are crucial and decisive and do not admit of subjectivity especially on processes where the decision is instantaneous, the automation of this process has proved to be an inevitable priority. Our study was able to use an effective tool in the literature which is genetic algorithms to automate the decision-making process with an intervention of the decision maker optimized in the weighting of the coefficients for the determination of the weights of the criteria in a short time, then used in the risk assessment and assessment process according to the TOPSIS method. Indeed, classical methods for defining criteria weights are very subjective and prove ineffective in cases where decision making is rapid. The hybridization of Genetic algorithms and TOPSIS method is efficient for efficient and effective decision-making. The results obtained support our choice.

Our research perspectives will focus on the use of other artificial intelligence tools for risk prediction and subsequently to create a framework bringing together the various published works.

References

1. Bernstein, P. L.: The portable MBA in investment. John Wiley & Sons Incorporated 22 (1995)
2. Rubinson, T.C., Geotsi, G.: Risk management using fuzzy logic and genetic algorithms: In: The ordered weighted averaging operators, pp. 155–166. Springer, Boston, MA (1997)
3. AFNOR.: FD X 50-252, Guidelines for risk estimation (2007)
4. Waguaf, A., Benabbou, R., Benhra, J.: Decision support for the control of risks in explosive atmospheres by hybridization of the multicriteria decision methods AHP, TOPSIS and EVAMIX. Int. Sci. J. Manag. Syst. Eng., 28–46 (2019)
5. Waguaf, A., Benabbou, R., Benhra, J.: New ERM framework with multicriterial decision method and multiple linear regression based on ISO 31000. Int. J. Adv. Sci. Technol. **29**(7), 2649–2662 (2020)
6. Bi, H., Lu, F., Duan, S., Huang, M., Zhu, J., Liu, M.: Two-level principal–agent model for schedule risk control of IT outsourcing project based on genetic algorithm. Eng. Appl. Artif. Intell. **91**, 103584 (2020)
7. Kılıç, M., Ulusoy, G., Şerifoğlu, F.S.: A bi-objective genetic algorithm approach to risk mitigation in project scheduling. Int. J. Prod. Econ. **112**(1), 202–216 (2008)
8. Yaohua, H., Chiwai, H.: A binary coding genetic algorithm for multi-purpose process schedule: a case study. Chem. Eng. Sci. **65**(16), 4816–4828 (2010)
9. Yang, X., Yang, Z., Yin, X., Li, J.: Chaos gray-coded genetic algorithm and its application for pollution source identifications in convection–diffusion equation. Commun. Nonlinear Sci. Numer. Simul. **13**(8), 1676–1688 (2008)
10. Tamjidyamcholo, A., Al-Dabbagh, R.D.: Genetic algorithm approach for risk reduction of information security. Int. J. Cyber-Secur. Digit. Forensics (IJCSDF) **1**(1), 59–66 (2012)
11. Wang, L., Sun, T., Qian, C., Goh, M., Mishra, V.K.: Applying social network analysis to genetic algorithm in optimizing project risk response decisions. Inf. Sci. **512**, 1024–1042 (2020)
12. Pfeifer, J., Barker, K., Ramirez-Marquez, J.E., Morshedlou, N.: Quantifying the risk of project delays with a genetic algorithm. Int. J. Prod. Econ. **170**, 34–44 (2015)

13. Nezamoddini, N., Gholami, A., Aqlan, F.: A risk-based optimization framework for integrated supply chains using genetic algorithm and artificial neural networks. Int. J. Prod. Econ. **225**, 107569 (2020)
14. Srinivasan, S., Kamalakannan, T.: Multi criteria decision making in financial risk management with a multi-objective genetic algorithm. Comput. Econ. **52**(2), 443–457 (2018)
15. Azadeh, A., Kor, H., Hatefi, S.M.: A hybrid genetic algorithm-TOPSIS-computer simulation approach for optimum operator assignment in cellular manufacturing systems. J. Chin. Inst. Eng. **34**(1), 57–74 (2011)
16. Azzam, M., Mousa, A.A.: Using genetic algorithm and TOPSIS technique for multiobjective reactive power compensation. Electr. Power Syst. Res. **80**(6), 675–681 (2010)
17. Cheng, C.T., Zhao, M.Y., Chau, K.W., Wu, X.Y.: Using genetic algorithm and TOPSIS for Xinanjiang model calibration with a single procedure. J. Hydrol. **316**(1–4), 129–140 (2006)
18. Taleizadeh, A.A., Niaki, S.T.A., Aryanezhad, M.B.: A hybrid method of Pareto, TOPSIS and genetic algorithm to optimize multi-product multi-constraint inventory control systems with random fuzzy replenishments. Math. Comput. Model. **49**(5–6), 1044–1057 (2009)
19. Marchetti, D., Wanke, P.: Efficiency of the rail sections in Brazilian railway system, using TOPSIS and a genetic algorithm to analyse optimized scenarios. Transp. Res. Part E: Logist. Transp. Rev. **135**, 101858 (2020)
20. Kermani, M.A.M.A., Badiee, A., Aliahmadi, A., Ghazanfari, M., Kalantari, H.: 'Introducing a procedure for developing a novel centrality measure (Sociability Centrality) for social networks using TOPSIS method and genetic algorithm. Comput. Hum. Behav. **56**, 295–305 (2016)
21. Holland, J.H.: Adaptation in natural and artificial systems. MIT Press, Cambridge (1975)
22. Rutkowski, L.: Computational intelligence: methods and techniques. Springer, Berlin (2008)
23. Deep, K., Thakur, M.: A new crossover operator for real coded genetic algorithms. Appl. Math. Comput. **188**(1), 895–911 (2007)
24. Compare, M., Martini, F., Zio, E.: Genetic algorithms for condition-based maintenance optimization under uncertainty. Eur. J. Oper. Res. **244**(2), 611–623 (2015)
25. Yuan, S., Skinner, B., Huang, S., Liu, D.: A new crossover approach for solving the multiple travelling salesmen problem using genetic algorithms. Eur. J. Oper. Res. **228**(1), 72–82 (2013)
26. Toledo, C.F.M., de Oliveira, L., de Freitas Pereira, R., Franca, P.M., Morabito, R.: A genetic algorithm/mathematical programming approach to solve a two-level soft drink production problem. Comput. Oper. Res. **48**, 40–52 (2014)
27. Saaty, T.L.: The analytic hierarchy process: planning, priority setting, resource allocation (1990)
28. Duckstein, L., Opricovic, S.: Multiobjective optimization in river basin development. Water Resour. Res. **16**(1), 14–20 (1980)
29. Saaty, T.L.: Theory and applications of the analytic network process: decision making with benefits, opportunities, costs, and risks. RWS publications (2005)
30. Hwang, C.L., Yoon, K.: Methods for multiple attribute decision making, pp. 58–191. Springer, Berlin, Heidelberg (1981)
31. National Research and Safety Institute.: Basic reference in occupational health and safety prevention (2010)

Case Studies and Cyber-Physical Systems 3

Blockchain Application Methodology for Improving Trust in the Collaborative Supply Chain

Koffi Augustin Kotongo[1]([⊠]) and Idriss Bennis[2]

[1] CERIM, HESTIM, Casablanca, Morocco
`kotongokoffiaugustin@gmail.com`
[2] M2S2I – SID, ENSET, Mohammedia, Morocco
`idriss.bennis@enset-media.ac.ma`

Abstract. The globalization of the economy, the major disruptions due to the COVID-19 crisis, customer requirements as well as the current context of war, are straining global supply chains, which must demonstrate resilience and constantly seek to improve their performance. Performance. Among the essential approaches to achieve these objectives, collaboration between logistics partners through methods and tools that have proven themselves but also have shown limits, particularly in terms of trust. Blockchain technology, which appeared in 2008, now offers an opportunity to improve collaboration by providing answers to concerns about trust. However, its application is not generalized, indeed a large part of the companies do not apply the technology because of its shared database character because the companies have sensitive and confidential data. After an analysis of the literature to highlight the obstacles to the generalization of the use of the blockchain in the supply chain, a methodology of adoption and application of the Blockchain following eight steps is proposed with an emphasis on the smart contract.

Keywords: Collaboration · Supply chain · Blockchain · Smart contract · Trust

1 Introduction

Supply chain management is an approach which consists in making a global analysis of the value chain going from the first supplier to the last customer by making a global optimization of flows and not local [1]. The advent of this approach is due to the complexity and challenges of globalization which has forced companies to group together in order to create strong partnerships with their suppliers and their direct and indirect customers. Faced with this complexity of the logistics chain, companies are faced with the problems of product and information exchange. The effectiveness and efficiency of the supply chain (LC) is the major concern of the actors, it was underlined in the work of the peers that it all started with the finding of irrationality of the behavior of the actors of the CL made by Forrester in 1958 and thereafter other authors continued studies on the same subject but with different points of view. Among them we have Cachon and Fisher who worked on the sharing of information seeking to bring an improvement and

© The Author(s), under exclusive license to Springer Nature Switzerland AG 2022
M. Hamlich et al. (Eds.): SADASC 2022, CCIS 1677, pp. 379–387, 2022.
https://doi.org/10.1007/978-3-031-20490-6_30

coordination to the CL, Chen et al. as for them propose that the concept of risk between customer and supplier is contractualized to improve the profile list of CL actors [2].

Collaboration is a process by which actors who are different in their problems and others agree to explore their differences in a constructive way in order to come up with effective and efficient solutions that go beyond their own vision and expectations, this is what underpins the vastness of the concept of business collaboration [3]. The success of the application of collaboration in the industrial sphere requires the fluidification of business structures, but the exponential instantaneous changes that the world is currently going through presents many agility constraints for the implementation of the concept of collaboration [4]..

Based on previous studies, we want to analyze the impact of Blockchain technology on trust in the Collaborative Supply Chain. The objective in this document is to improve trust in business from a model based on Blockchain technology.

2   Literature Review

Collaborative Supply Chain and Blockchain Technology

[5] raise the hypothesis that it will take a level of commitment from the partners to achieve a successful SCC and [6] will propose rules for decisions. In the same logic, [7] proposes a framework. According to [3] and in business, the evolution of trust is increasing in relation to the evolution of trade. But before that, the company must take the risk for the first exchanges.

The first application of Blockchain technology is Bitcoin created by Satoshi Nakamoto in 2008. Each time we have Bitcoin transactions from one node to another, the transaction is secured and certified by sending a cryptographic key whose decryption confirms the transaction. It takes a large number of confirmations of the transaction before it is validated; This is what makes it safe [8]. According to [9], Blockchain technology today is classified into three categories: Blockchain 1.0 (financial field), Blockchain 2.0 (Smart contracts) and Blockchain 3.0 (Any other business sector including the public sector). Each block constitutes a transaction and is composed of data, a hash and the previous hash. A block can consist of one or more transactions, it all depends on the rules of the block.

According to the explanations of [10] and [11], the technology ensures a change of orientation of the SCC, the actors of the chain would only have to trust the technology itself. Its application in the supply chain can provide answers to several issues:

- **Transparency**: Transparency in the supply chain is not easy because of the number of actors involved in production both upstream and downstream [12]. Blockchain has been proposed as a solution for traceability in the supply chain [13].
- **Traceability**: The reliability and traceability of information can be difficult to ensure due to the high presence of fraud and confidentiality between partners. Today, the demands of customers and consumers on the authentication and transparency of the products they buy are essential [14].

- **Accessibility of information**: The inaccessibility of data by everyone due to centralized databases complicates the collaboration of actors in the chain. Blockchain technology's distributed ledger ensures better collaboration of supply chain platforms by facilitating data accessibility [15].
- **Networking**: The large number of actors involved in Supply Chain networks makes their treatment non-transparent and irresponsible [16]; [17] presents the way in which supply chains are very fragmented and the disadvantage that this has on the collaboration between the actors of the chain by mentioning the harmful effect of intermediation on the transparency and the quality of the information exchanged [5], Blockchain is the proposed solution [18].

Despite these issues, the adoption and application of the Blockchain remains quite limited, companies are still reluctant for various reasons, and among the most important there is the character of a shared database [5].

- **Confidentiality of certain sensitive data**: Blockchain is a decentralized database technology that records all exchanges and all data between network players in a large shared register. So everyone has an encrypted copy of all the trades that have been made.
- **Cost of setting up the technology**: Financially, the development of the technology is expensive and requires a lot of investment. Only a few large multinationals like MAERSK, Carrefour who have been able to develop it.
- **Heterogeneity of the language of information**: since companies use different information systems by their language, it is difficult to exchange information or data
- **Involvement:** A Blockchain development project does not happen alone, to succeed it must have the involvement of the majority of the PPs in the chain. We can see the example of TradeLens [19].
- **Level of development of the technology**: Other companies, having seen that the Blockchain is very recent, they have decided to wait until it is well developed and there are facilitations of its application before embarking on it. Beyond these barriers to the adoption of the technology we also have the interoperability between two or more Blockchain technologies [14] and [5].

In view of these dysfunctions, what is the appropriate solution for an optimal application of Blockchain technology in order to improve trust in the collaborative supply chain ?

We then propose a methodology for applying Blockchain technology (for the SCC). It is a question of adopting the technology in a progressive way compared to the evolution of the exchanges and the relations between partners because the adoption and the absolute application of the technology is function of the level of confidence in the chain.

3 Analysis and Interpretation

Blockchain Technology: Smart Contracts

The smart contract is a Blockchain-based technology that allows the establishment of a large number of digital files between people who do not know each other and who may not trust each other. According to [20], the smart contract is a computer protocol capable of self-executing, autonomous and which facilitates, executes and enforces commercial agreements between two or more parties. In addition to being operational 24 h a day, 7 days a week, it reduces the cost of transactions and ultimately makes business more efficient in the long term. In terms of confidentiality, the smart contract reinforces it by allowing the actors to have the choice on the data to be shared on the distributed database. According to [21]. The construction of a smart contract system requires the identification of the elements, namely:

- **The Builders**: Businessmen, lawyers, designers and digitizers.
- **Users:** the (human) users of both the process (digital contract) and its result (human-readable contract), business users (managers and corporate lawyers), computers: Users of the output machine readable.
- **Information Layers:** This is a back-end repository of codified contract templates, clauses, visualization libraries, and big data libraries of searchable past contracts.
- **Procurement life cycle:** This involves needs assessment, negotiation, re-engagement and terms, implementation, adjustment or dispute resolution.

One can develop thanks to Smart contracts libraries of clauses in a clear, coherent and simple language, libraries of updating of the documents of the contract in real time as well as libraries of visual design models which will be useful in other contracts [21]. So, the smart contract may hold the solution because we will no longer need to share all the data and we have some control over the information we share. However, it also has negative points and shortcomings.

- **Information Hacking easy**
  It is much easier to hack information in a decentralized database than that of a centralized database because with the centralized database, you must first have access to the server before having access to the encrypted data but for the decentralized one, we already have access to encrypted data.
- **The non-possibility of updating or modifying**
  In classic or traditional contracts, it happens that there are changes in the socio-economic, political, or legal environment of the PPs or that there is a crisis, they will seek to bring updates to the contract. This is not possible with the smart contract.
- **Diversity in legal, technological and level of internet access**
  Jurisdictionally, business and commerce differ from country to country. On the technological level, we are witnessing different computer languages in relation to the geographical situation. (There is an inequality of access to the Internet in the world) hence the weakening of the verification of transactions.

Based on the above, here is a suggested solution. It is a technology application methodology that is suitable for the Supply Chain.

4   The Results

In order to overcome the criticisms, we propose an application methodology (See Fig. 1) integrating an AI to automate the activities and the operation of the technology, a security system to reinforce the level of confidentiality and security. It will first go through the application of the smart contract to the absolute Blockchain once trust is established. **The proposed methodology is divided into 8 steps:**

1. Global chain analysis; the project sponsor should perform a comprehensive analysis of the value chain and identify common issues.
2. Involvement plan for value chain actors; after the first step, it is then necessary to prove that the Blockchain is the optimal solution.
3. Theoretical design of the general model of technology and smart contract; after convincing all the PPs.
4. Theoretical design and the first smart contracts, it is a question here of defining the clauses of the contract, the obligations and the commitments of each one as well as the rules
5. Define the graphical interface; the PPs, the contract specialists or the lawyers and the IT specialists will together define the graphic interface in relation to the PPs. Together, they must provide a backup or rescue system that will minimize the damage in the event of hacking.
6. Define the data library; the team must agree on the known of the library, it can contain the exchanges of goods and services, the financial transactions, the exchanges of information and it will feed the automatic updates of the system and the latter will propose to the PP information and optimization practices.
7. Define additional activities and exchanges; Since the idea is to migrate to an absolute Blockchain, the PPs will offer other activities or functionalities if possible that the system will be able to perform or accept.
8. Technology development; once everything is validated, the developer team or the IT specialist will start by developing the technology without forgetting to add a security system based on artificial intelligence (AI) to limit the risk of hacking.

Indeed, smart contracts bring the same advantages as those brought by absolute Blockchain technology with the only difference that only the information (clauses, obligations, etc.) mentioned in the smart contract will be executed and shared on one side; this will allow PPs to have a shared database (Blockchain) and a non-shared one. Here is a **technical design** of the system that will show the tools to strengthen the security of the system (see Fig. 2). Here are a few in the following lines:

The user server made up of the commerce server, everything relating to commercial activities and the application server. This comes from the work of IBM and MAERSK (TradeLens - Solution Brief)
The Library, Inspired by the work of (Marcelo Corrales et al., 2020).
AI (Artificial Intelligence), This last part will allow the system to self-manage, self-regulate and act in case of emergency, danger, following this the AI will trigger the alert system that will automatically block the system,

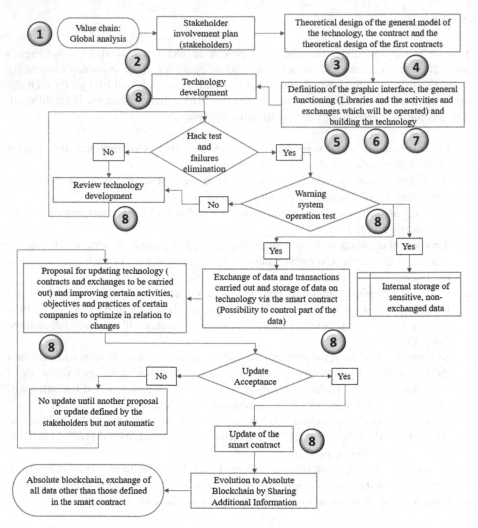

Fig. 1. Method of application of the Blockchain in the collaborative supply chain

The firewall which will contribute to the respect of the network security policy and will monitor and control the different types of network activities, the azure data brick which has the role of triggering the alarm in the event of detection of a hacking attempt and machine learning which aims to bring the system to self-learn on the environment of the PPs of the network.

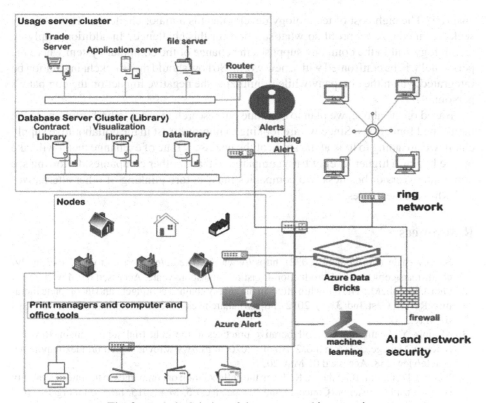

Fig. 2. Technical design of the system and its operation

5 Conclusion

Our work focused on the treatment of the spirit of trust and collaboration in the supply chain by trying to analyze the contribution and the limits that Blockchain technology could bring. Several limitations have been observed in relation to its use, in particular of smart contracts, and this was mainly due to the lack of trust in relation to the sharing of information. We have proposed a methodology which consists of moving from the second version of the Blockchain to the third in order to promote the sharing and exchange of data and transactions in the supply chain by improving confidentiality through the mastery and control of part of the data of the PPs by the PPs and for the PPs. Behind this technology we are adding an artificial intelligence and an alert system that will allow companies in this ecosystem to be more flexible and agile in relation to changes in the ecosystem and to block the operation and access of the system in the event of threat detection. The system's automatic updates system will lead companies to Blockchain 3.0 where they can exchange everything with each other as they see fit. What will be the consequences after the implementation of our solution? will it be effective and efficient? Or will it give us new avenues of research?

The problem of interoperability between two Blockchain technologies is a size limit of when companies from different supply chains can also exchange, so how should it be ensured? The high cost of technology development is a major challenge. The company seeks to maximize its profit so what solution for this challenge? In addition, applying technology within the company supposes the change of the computer system where the personnel will be confronted with a new world. So how should the Blockchain solution be integrated within the company while minimizing the negative impact on the company's personnel?

Based on the above, we plan to continue our research in order to find solutions to the mentioned limitations. Since we are looking to improve trust in the collaborative supply chain, we are going to look at the study of the necessary time of exchange that it will take before having a higher level of trust compared to that of other companies, following see how many years of business two companies make before thinking of other alternatives and what are the causes.

References

1. Supply chain management (2022). https://www.dunod.com/entreprise-et-economie/supply-chain-management-achat-production-logistique-transport-vente. Accessed 02 May 2022
2. Giard, V., Sali, M.: The bullwhip effect in the supply chain: a contingent and incomplete literature. Rev. Fr. Gest. Ind. **31**(2) (2012). https://hal.archives-ouvertes.fr/hal-01508406. Accessed 01 May 2022
3. Mounir, Y., Gouiferda, F.: Collaborative practices in the industrial supply chain. Rev. Int. Science. Manage. **3**(2), Art. no. 2, August 2020. https://www.revue-isg.com/index.php/home/article/view/258. Accessed 01 May 2022
4. Najima, D., Faqihi, B., Ajhoun, R.: From the collaboration of companies to the interoperability of information systems (Concepts and Perspectives) **5**, Mar 2015. https://doi.org/10.7763/IJIET
5. Petersson, E., Baur, K.: Impacts of blockchain technology on supply chain collaboration: a study on the use of blockchain technology in supply chains and how it influences supply chain collaboration (2018)
6. Ganesh, M., Raghunathan, S., Rajendran, C.: The value of information sharing in a multi-product supply chain with product substitution. IIE Trans. **40**, 1124–1140 (2008). https://doi.org/10.1080/07408170701745360
7. Simatupang, T.M., Sridharan, R.: An integrative framework for supply chain collaboration. Int. J. Logistics. Manag. **16**(2), 257–274 (2005). https://doi.org/10.1108/09574090510634548
8. 'Research: Blockchain - ScholarVox University'. http://univ.scholarvox.com.ezproxy.univ-littoral.fr/catalog/search/searchterm/Blockchain%20?searchtype=all. Accessed 02 May 2022
9. Swan, M.: Blockchain: Blueprint for a New Economy, 1st edn. O'Reilly Media, Beijing (2015)
10. Wang, J., Wu, P., Wang, X., Shou, W.: The outlook of blockchain technology for construction engineering management (2017). https://doi.org/10.15302/J-FEM-2017006
11. Weber, I., Xu, X., Riveret, R., Governatori, G., Ponomarev, A., Mendling, J.: Untrusted business process monitoring and execution using blockchain. In: La Rosa, M., Loos, P., Pastor, O. (eds.) BPM 2016. LNS, vol. 9850, pp. 329–347. Springer, Cham (2016). https://doi.org/10.1007/978-3-319-45348-4_19
12. Astill, J., et al.: Transparency in food supply chains: A review of enabling technology solutions. Trends Food Sci. Technol. (2019). https://dx.doi.org/10.1016/j.tifs.2019.07.024. Accessed 02 May 2022
13. O'Marah, K.: Blockchain for supply chain: enormous potential down the road. Forbes. https://www.forbes.com/sites/kevinomarah/2017/03/09/blockchain-for-supply-chain-enormous-potential-down-the-road/. Accessed 02 May 2022

14. Laforet, L., Bilek, G.: Blockchain: an inter-organisational innovation likely to transform supply chain. Supply Chain Forum Int. J. **22**(3), 240–249 (2021). https://doi.org/10.1080/162 58312.2021.1953931
15. Chang, S.E., Chen, Y.-C., Lu, M.-F.: Supply chain re-engineering using blockchain technology: a case of smart contract based tracking process. Technol. Forecast. Soc. Change , **144**(C), 1–11 (2019)
16. Casey, M.J., Wong, P.: Global supply chains are about to get better, thanks to blockchain. Harvard Bus. Rev. (2017). https://hbr.org/2017/03/global-supply-chains-are-about-to-get-better-thanks-to-blockchain. Accessed 02 May 2022
17. Popp, A.: "Swamped in information but starved of data": information and intermediaries in clothing supply chains. Supply Chain Manag. Int. J. **5**(3), 151–161 (2000). https://doi.org/10.1108/13598540010338910
18. McConaghy, M., McMullen, G., Parry, G., McConaghy, T., Holtzman, D.: Visibility and digital art: blockchain as an ownership layer on the Internet. Strateg. Change **26**, 461–470 (2017). https://doi.org/10.1002/jsc.2146
19. A new paradigm in supply chain: TradeLens is unleashing the potential of collaborative digitization in logistics. https://www.maersk.com/news/articles/2021/07/20/tradelens-is-unl eashing-the-potential-of-collaborative-digitization. Accessed 02 May 2022
20. 'The blockchain revolution, smart contracts and financial transactions | Insights | DLA Piper Global Law Firm. DLA Piper. https://www.dlapiper.com/en/uk/insights/publications/2016/04/the-blockchain-revolution/. Accessed 13 Oct 2021
21. Corrales, M., Fenwick, M., Haapio, H. (eds.): Legal Tech, Smart Contracts and Blockchain. PLBI, Springer, Singapore (2019). https://doi.org/10.1007/978-981-13-6086-2

MaroBERTa: Multilabel Classification Language Model for Darija Newspaper

Lotf Hamza[✉][iD] and Ramdani Mohammed[iD]

LIM Laboratory, FSTM, Hassan II University of Casablanca, Mohammedia, Morocco
lotf.hamza@gmail.com, ramdani@fstm.ac.ma

Abstract. A large amount of valuable digital text, audio and video data is available on the web. Thus, a large application of machine learning based on Natural Language Processing (NLP) has taken advantage of these opportunities. Transformers, especially Bidirectional Encoder Representation from Transformers (BERT) based models, have become the state-of-the-art for downstream NLP tasks. Non-normalized languages such as Moroccan Arabic, also known as Darija, increases the complexity of natural language processing. Furthermore, Text written in Darija does not have a standard spelling, and there is a lack of resources, especially for multilabel classification. In this paper, we introduced a multilabel classification model for Moroccan Arabic (Darija) newspapers. Firstly, we created a dataset from 400.000 collected newspaper articles with their titles, written in darija and pre-trained our model: MaroBERTa. Secondly, we implemented a crowd-sourcing platform to help create a novel corpus called Darija Multilabel Dataset for News classification (DMDNews). This dataset contains 28 different classes representing the most frequent topics in Moroccan newspapers. Finally, we fine-tune MaroBERTa and two multilingual models (AraBERT and CAMelBert) for the multilabel classification task using the DMDNews. Experiments shows that our dedicated pretrained Darija model -MaroBERTa- outperforms the existing multilingual models despite of the large amount of data they have been trained on.

Keywords: Morrocan Arabic (Darija) · BERT · NLP · Multilabel classification · RoBERTa · DMDNews

1 Introduction

In the era of big data, digital media is growing at an exploding speed, which consists of a big amount of valuable information available for consumption. However, manually extracting useful knowledge from it, is impractical and a challenging task. The use of machine learning tends to overcome this challenge. Bag of Words representation such as TF-IDF -term frequency-inverse document- was among the widely used techniques [4]. This gives each word a score based on statistical representation on document, without taking into account the semantics of the text. Word embedding models such as word2vec [17] and GloVe [18] try to learn the meaning of words taking semantics into consideration. In such models, the context in which a word appears is not incorporated and the model returns the same embedding for the word regardless of its context. However, contextual word embeddings like ELMo [19] or models based on transformers such as BERT [8] or RoBERTa [14] are context-sensitive. They generate different embedding vectors depending on the context on which the word appears. These models are able to understand most of the language rules and meaning. Recently, research has been focused on the application of transfer learning for downstream NLP tasks. Fine tuning large pretrained language models (ex. BERT, RoBERTa, etc.) results in interesting performance and quality improvement even with limited training dataset. These models have been pre-trained mostly on official languages which resources are available with abundance. Pretraining such a model is expensive in terms of computational cost [21], thus multilingual models have been trained on several languages to overcome this challenge, and permit different similar languages to benefit from the shared structure [7]. Moroccan dialect (Darija) is the mother tongue and the most spoken language in Morocco. It is the language of communication in the private and informal spheres and also in the Moroccan artistic creation (e.g. films, music, theater, etc.). Darija is a mixture between Modern Standard Arabic (MSA), the Amazigh language known as Tamazight and other languages. However, the lack of data and structured resources makes Darija a language that receives less attention in NLP research. In this paper, we propose the first multilabel classification model for Moroccan Arabic (Darija) newspapers. Our model is a transformer, based on RoBERTa architecture. We train the model named MaroBERTa to perform the masked language Model (MLM) task using our private collected newspaper data. The second step consists of implementing a crowdsourcing platform which aims to create the first Multilabel Darija Newspaper classification Dataset (MDND). Our dataset contains the most frequent topics in Moroccan newspapers. Lastly, we fine-tune the model to perform multilabel classification tasks. Experiments show that MaroBERTa achieves a state-of-the-art result on multilabel classification compared to pretrained multilingual models such as AraBERT and CAMeLBERT.

2   Related Work

Before word embeddings, Bag of words methods such as TF-IDF were used in the early text representation. This statistical method ignores the semantic of the words. However, for the past decade, word embeddings have become the state of the art for text representation. The Word2vec model introduced by [17], FastText [13] created by facebook and GloVe [18] achieved good performance but still lacked contextual representation due to using a fixed embedding for each word regardless of the context. Natural Language Processing experienced an inflection point in 2018 with the appearance of new models with more capacity in words and sentences representation. Instead of using a unique embedding for each word like previous models, ELMO [19] based on bidirectional LSTM [10] is a context-sensitive method. It assigns different embedding for a word depending on the entire sentence. ULM-FIT [11] introduced a language model not just an embedding of words and came up with methods to effectively benefit from a pretrained model and fine tune it for other tasks. ULM-FIT finally nails down transfer learning on NLP. Generative Pre-Training approach (GPT) [20], introduced a general task-agnostic model with transformer-based architecture. Transformers have performed well on various NLP tasks, and have been seen as the replacement of LSTMs due to their ability to deal better with long-term dependencies. BERT [8] which stands for Bidirectional Encoder Representations from Transformers, is conditioned on both left and right context in all layers. GPT, XLNet [23] and BERT have brought significant performance gains to understand and capture underlying meanings and relationships in languages. However, the training of those models is computationally expensive, which makes finding the best combination of hyperparameters a challenging task. RoBERTa [14] which stands for Robustly optimized BERT approach, is an improved recipe of training BERT that leads to better downstream task performance. ARABERT [3], ARBERT and MARBERT [2] are multilingual models based on BERT trained on large standard Arabic language datasets. Regarding Arabic dialects, models such as QARiB [1] and CamelBERT [12] are trained on a large amount of standard, Classical and dialectical Arabic dataset. After that a BERT-like model is pretrained and its layers have been tuned to correctly handle language, it can be fine-tuned for downstream tasks such as Sequence Classification, Named Entity Recognition or Question Answering. Multi-label classification as a downstream task on low-resource languages, especially Moroccan Arabic, is a challenging task due to the lack of multilabel dataset. AraCOVID19-MFH [9] is an Arabic COVID-19 Multi-label fake news and hate Speech dataset which contains text in standard Arabic, North african and middle east dialects. In this work we collect and create our multilabel Moroccan Arabic (DARIJA) dataset which we use to fine-tune our proposed MaroBERTa model to perform multilabel classification for news over 28 classes.

3 Framework

Our training procedure consists of two stages. The first stage is pre-training a RoBERTa-like language model on our collected dataset of Moroccan Arabic (Darija) news. This is followed by a fine-tuning stage, where we adapt the model to a discriminative task with our private multi-label dataset.

3.1 Pre-training of MaroBERTa

Authors in [14] demonstrate that BERT could give better results by adjusting and tuning hyperparameters, and propose an improved recipe for training BERT models, which is called RoBERTa. Authors of RoBERTa demonstrate that masked language model (MLM) pretraining, under the right design choices, is competitive with all other recently published methods. Our model called MaroBERTa follows the same architecture of RoBERTa and uses our novel datasets for the training and fine-tuning stages.

A-Pre-training Dataset. Training of a BERT-like model requires a large amount of data. It has been reported that increasing training data size can improve the model quality and performance. However, [16] demonstrate that their model trained on a sample dataset of 4GB performs similarly with the one trained on a much bigger dataset. Unfortunately, few public resources for Moroccan Arabic (Darija) are available. We collected more than 400.000 news articles in Darija with their titles. The average number of words in each article is 117 words. The longest article contains 4761 words. Our dataset contains articles that cover different topics from the year 2011 until the end of 2021. Word average in Titles is 13 words and the longest title contains 69 words. We proceeded to clean the data. Cleaning consists of removing all non-Arabic words, symbols, numbers and emojis. Our dataset contains only Moroccan Darija. It can be used on training BERT-like models for Darija in addition to generating titles from texte.

Vocabulary. Our model needs a vocabulary that contains all the common understandable elements of a language. The process of generating tokens from raw text is known as tokenization. Byte-Pair Encoding (BPE) [5] is a subword segmentation algorithm that breaks down words to sequences of subword units. BPE is used at the level of characters. However, In this paper, we focus on byte-level Byte-Pair Encoding BPE (BBPE) [22] that is used to tokenize text into variable-length byte n-grams. Byte level representation makes the segmentation agnostic to languages and more compact (256 possible values). We created a BBPE tokenizer and we constructed a vocabulary of sizes 35.522. This tokenizer is used in all the steps covered in this work.

Pre-training Procedure. MaroBERTa is trained using the same architecture as RoBERTa with 12 attention heads, 12 hidden layers and the hidden size of 768. Our language model is then pre-trained using the Masked Language Modeling (MLM) task. MLM consists of a technique that randomly masks a sample of tokens in the input sequence and replaces them with the special token <mask>. The objective of the MLM task is to predict the masked tokens using a cross-entropy loss. 15% of the input tokens are selected randomly to be masked. In this process 80% of those selected tokens are replaced by the token <mask>, 10% are replaced by a random token from vocabulary and the other 10% are left unchanged. We used whole word masking and a maximum sequence length of 512. For model training, we use a Google Cloud GPU NVIDIA Tesla T4 with 16 GB of RAM. We choose AdamW [15] as optimizer with a learning rate of 1e−5. In total, we pre-trained our models for 143 epochs for approximately 10 days.

3.2   Fine-Tuning on Multilabel Classification

MaroBERTa is ready to be fine-tuned for downstream tasks such as Sequence Classification, Named Entity Recognition or Question Answering. We studie in this section the multi-label classification as a downstream task. We collect and create a multilabel dataset for Moroccan Arabic (DARIJA), and fine-tune MaroBERTa to classify news over 28 classes. Finally we compared our model with ARABIC-BERT which is a pretrained multilingual model.

Multi-label Dataset. The very few labeled Moroccan Arabic (Darija) datasets publicly available contain just two classes, and are designed for binary classification. Real-world scenarios for such datasets are limited. In this work we are interested in multilabel classification of news. A news article can cover multiple topics at the same time. Since no multilabel darija dataset for news classification is publicly available, we decided to create one from scratch. We collected additional news articles written in Darija and we created a web platform to allow a community of volunteers to perform data-annotation. Back-end of the web platform is written in python using flask restful API and deployed in Heroku. While the front-end is a react application. Data is stored on a MongoDB database. Annotators have to choose multiple labels from 28 different topics for every news. We only required each text to be annotated by one annotator due to the high cost of the task (see Fig. 1).

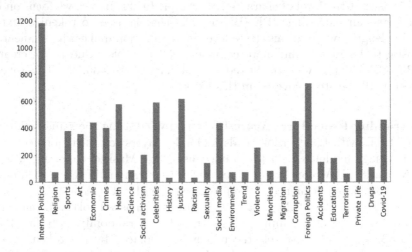

Fig. 1. Distribution of labels

Fine-Tuning Procedure. To best evaluate our model we have to fine-tune it on multilabel classification tasks using our multilabel dataset. Thus, we insert on the top of MaroBERTa a hidden layer that takes all the outputs of the tokens and gives an average before feeding this output to a classification layer. We choose AdamW [15] as optimizer with a learning rate of 1.5e−6. We create a schedule with a learning rate that decreases following a cosine function decreases following the values of the cosine function between the initial learning rate set in the optimizer to 0, after a warm up period during which it increases linearly between 0 and the initial learning rate set in the optimizer.

For such an imbalanced dataset, using accuracy to evaluate the model is not the best choice. However, we evaluate our model using AUC ROC [6] which is a good metric to understand how well the model performs.

4   Experiments

We split our data into 60% for training, 20% for validation and 20% for testing. We fine-tuned MaroBERTa using GPU Tesla P100-PCIE provided by google cloud, and 25 GB of system RAM. We trained the model for 15 epochs with a batch size of 8. The learning rate is set to 1.5e−6 and the warm up parameter is 0.2 with decay set to 0.001. Figure 2 shows training loss and Fig. 3 shows the validation loss during the fine-tuning process of MaroBERTa. The final validation loss is 0.163. Table 1 gives a summary of final training and validating losses for the MaroBERTa, CAMeLBERT and AraBERT models. Results shows that MaroBERTa has the best training loss while it has a validation loss slightly greater than AraBERT.

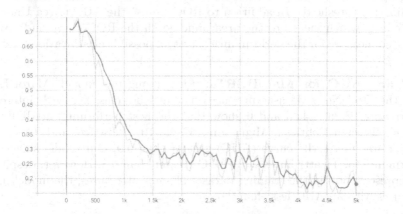

Fig. 2. MaroBERTa training loss.

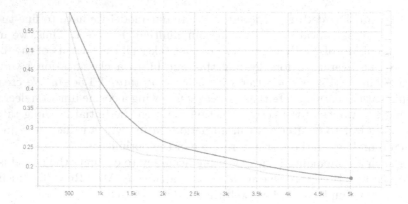

Fig. 3. MaroBERTa validation loss.

Table 1. Final result of training and validating loss for the models.

Model	Training loss	Validation loss
MaroBERTa (our model)	**0.1443**	0.163
CAMelBERT	0.2513	0.1847
AraBERT	0.179	**0.1517**

4.1   Performances of the Models

In this step we use ROC curve (receiver operating characteristic curve) which is a graph showing the performance of the multilabel classifier models at all classification thresholds. In addition to ROC we use the AUC (Area Under the ROC curve) which measures the area underneath the ROC curve and gives an agregated measure for the performance across all possible classification tresholds.

ROC and AUC for MaroBERTa. Fine-tuning our model -MaroBERTa- using the DMDNews dataset produces a multilabel classifier with interesting performance. Figures 4, 5 and 6 show that the best performing attributes are 'Sports', 'Foreign Politics', 'Migration', 'Covid-19 ', 'Justice' and 'Celebrities' with an area under the curve (AUC) greater than 0.9. Our model shows good performance for 18 attributes with AUC greater than 0.8. However, despite the low representation in the training dataset of some attributes, the model has no attributes with an AUC less than 0.6.

ROC and AUC for AraBERT. Figures 7, 8 and 9 show the performance of AraBERT. This model has 19 attributes with AUC greater than 0.8. However, two attributes shows an AUC less than 0.6. The 'History' attribute with 0.27 and 'Racism' with 0.59.

Table 2. Example of MaroBERTa predictions

News	Predicted Labels
المثلة ولات مواضبة على الانستكرّام واخا مكتشاركش فيه يومياتها ولكن حاضرة فيه وكتفاعل مع المتابعين مرات المثل سعد التسولي فرحانة حيث عدد المتابعين وصل للميون .	Celebrities, Social media, Art, Trend
اليوم غادية تعقد لجنة فمجلس النواب لانتخاب رئيسه الامر محسوم مادام احزاب الاغلبية الحكومية حسمت الامر وقررت ترشيح . فنفس النهار غادي يعقد محلس المستشارين جلسة عمومية على الساعة الرابعة بعد الظهر تخصص لانتخاب رئيس المجلس حتى هاد المنصب محسوم غادي الكاتب العام للاتحاد العام للشغالين .	Internal Politics, Social activism

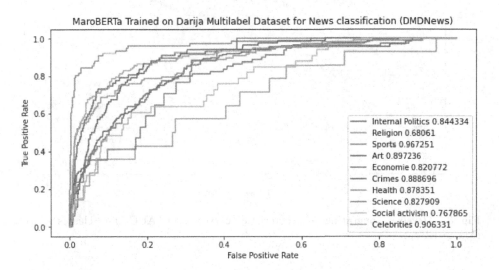

Fig. 4. Receiver operating characteristic curves and AUC for classes part1 (MaroBERTa).

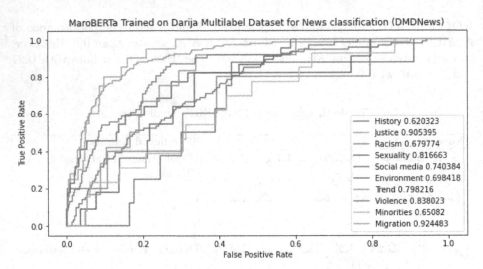

Fig. 5. Receiver operating characteristic curves and AUC for classes part2 (MaroBERTa).

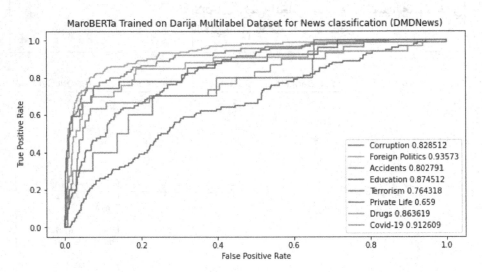

Fig. 6. Receiver operating characteristic curves and AUC for classes part3 (MaroBERTa).

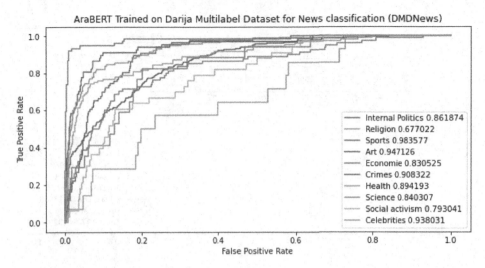

Fig. 7. Receiver operating characteristic curves and AUC for classes part1 (AraBERT).

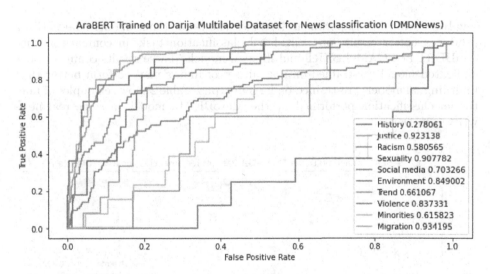

Fig. 8. Receiver operating characteristic curves and AUC for classes part2 (AraBERT).

ROC and AUC for CAMelBERT. Performance of CAMelBERT is shown in Figs. 10, 11 and 12. This model has only 14 attributes with AUC greater than 0.8, and it has 4 attributes with values of AUC less than 0.6.

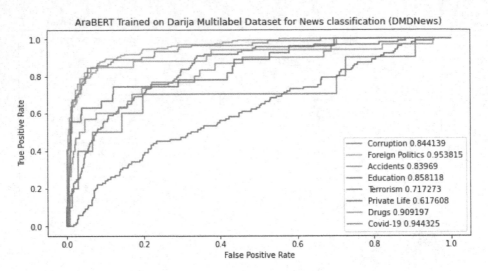

Fig. 9. Receiver operating characteristic curves and AUC for classes part3 (AraBERT).

Evaluation. The Experimental results shows that our model MaroBERTa produces better results on multi-label classification task, in comparison with AraBERT and CAMeLBERT multilingual models. These results confirm that a dedicated model pre-trained on a small set of inputs may perform better than multilingual models pre-trained on larger corpus. Table 2 shows examples of multilabel classification performed by the MaroBERTa model on some real news written in Darija.

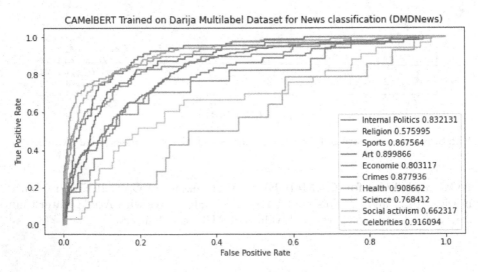

Fig. 10. Receiver operating characteristic curves and AUC for classes part1 (CAMelBERT).

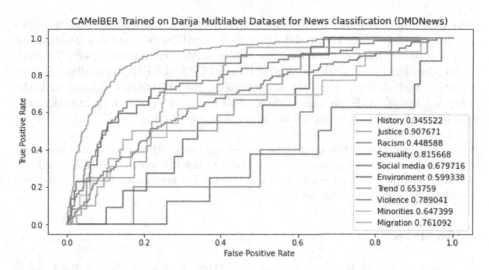

Fig. 11. Receiver operating characteristic curves and AUC for classes part2 (CAMel-BERT).

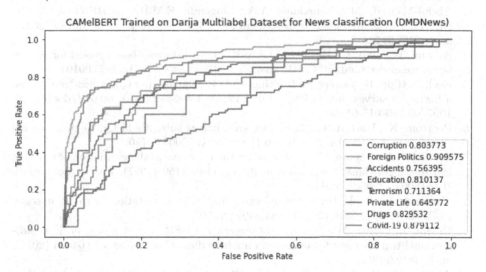

Fig. 12. Receiver operating characteristic curves and AUC for classes part3 (CAMel-BERT).

5 Conclusion

We introduced two new corpus of news articles written in Arabic Morrocan Darija, and we trained a new model to perform multilabel classification for Darija news over 28 different classes. Firstly, we collected, processed and cleaned dataset with more than 400.000 news, which we use to train our model called MaroBERTa that follows the same architecture of RoBERTa. Secondly, we implemented a crowd-sourcing platform whose objective is the manual annotation of articles by users. The result dataset called (DMDNews) contains 28 different classes representing the most frequent topics in Moroccan newspapers. We evaluated MaroBERTa against the AraBERT and CAMeLBERT on multilabel classification task. We fine-tune the models using the DMDNews dataset with the same configuration. Experiments shows that our model performs better than the multilingual models pre-trained on larger amount of data.

Acknowledgements. We would like to express our gratitude to all of those with whom we have had the pleasure to cooperate during this project. Special thanks to Mr. Lotf Mohammed, for the effort he had done in the annotation process. This work wouldn't be possible without his help.

References

1. Abdelali, A., Hassan, S., Mubarak, H., Darwish, K., Samih, Y.: Pre-training BERT on Arabic tweets: practical considerations. CoRR abs/2102.10684 (2021). arxiv:2102.10684
2. Abdul-Mageed, M., Elmadany, A.A., Nagoudi, E.M.B.: ARBERT & MARBERT: deep bidirectional transformers for arabic. CoRR abs/2101.01785 (2021). arxiv:2101.01785
3. Antoun, W., Baly, F., Hajj, H.M.: AraBERT: transformer-based model for Arabic language understanding. CoRR abs/2003.00104 (2020). arxiv:2003.00104
4. Beel, J., Gipp, B., Langer, S., Breitinger, C.: Research-paper recommender systems: a literature survey. Int. J. Digit. Libr. **17**(4), 305–338 (2015). https://doi.org/10.1007/s00799-015-0156-0
5. Bostrom, K., Durrett, G.: Byte pair encoding is suboptimal for language model pretraining. CoRR abs/2004.03720 (2020). arxiv:2004.03720
6. Bradley, A.P.: The use of the area under the roc curve in the evaluation of machine learning algorithms. Patt. Recogn. **30**(7), 1145–1159 (1997). https://doi.org/10.1016/S0031-3203(96)00142-2
7. Conneau, A., et al.: Unsupervised cross-lingual representation learning at scale. CoRR abs/1911.02116 (2019). arxiv:1911.02116
8. Devlin, J., Chang, M., Lee, K., Toutanova, K.: BERT: pre-training of deep bidirectional transformers for language understanding. CoRR abs/1810.04805 (2018). arxiv:1810.04805
9. Ameur, M.S.H., Aliane, H.: Aracovid19-mfh: Arabic covid-19 multi-label fake news & hate speech detection dataset. Procedia Comput. Sci. **189**, 232–241 (2021). https://doi.org/10.1016/j.procs.2021.05.086, https://www.sciencedirect.com/science/article/pii/S1877050921012059, aI in Computational Linguistics
10. Hochreiter, S., Schmidhuber, J.: Long short-term memory. Neural Comput. **9**, 1735–1780 (1997). https://doi.org/10.1162/neco.1997.9.8.1735
11. Howard, J., Ruder, S.: Fine-tuned language models for text classification. CoRR abs/1801.06146 (2018). arxiv:1801.06146
12. Inoue, G., Alhafni, B., Baimukan, N., Bouamor, H., Habash, N.: The interplay of variant, size, and task type in Arabic pre-trained language models. In: Proceedings of the Sixth Arabic Natural Language Processing Workshop. Association for Computational Linguistics, Kyiv, Ukraine (Online), April 2021

13. Joulin, A., Grave, E., Bojanowski, P., Mikolov, T.: Bag of tricks for efficient text classification. CoRR abs/1607.01759 (2016). arxiv:1607.01759
14. Liu, Y., et al.: RoBERTa: a robustly optimized BERT pretraining approach. CoRR abs/1907.11692 (2019). arxiv:1907.11692
15. Loshchilov, I., Hutter, F.: Fixing weight decay regularization in adam. CoRR abs/1711.05101 (2017). arxiv:1711.05101
16. Martin, L., et al.: CamemBERT: a tasty French language model. In: Proceedings of the 58th Annual Meeting of the Association for Computational Linguistics, pp. 7203–7219. Association for Computational Linguistics, Online, July 2020. https://doi.org/10.18653/v1/2020.acl-main.645, https://aclanthology.org/2020.acl-main.645
17. Mikolov, T., Sutskever, I., Chen, K., Corrado, G.S., Dean, J.: Distributed representations of words and phrases and their compositionality. In: Burges, C., Bottou, L., Welling, M., Ghahramani, Z., Weinberger, K. (eds.) Advances in Neural Information Processing Systems, vol. 26. Curran Associates, Inc. (2013). https://proceedings.neurips.cc/paper/2013/file/9aa42b31882ec039965f3c4923ce901b-Paper.pdf
18. Pennington, J., Socher, R., Manning, C.: Glove: global vectors for word representation, vol. 14, pp. 1532–1543 (2014). https://doi.org/10.3115/v1/D14-1162
19. Peters, M.E., et al.: Deep contextualized word representations. CoRR abs/1802.05365 (2018). arxiv:1802.05365
20. Radford, A., Narasimhan, K., Salimans, T., Sutskever, I.: Improving language understanding by generative pre-training (2018)
21. Raffel, C., et al.: Exploring the limits of transfer learning with a unified text-to-text transformer. CoRR abs/1910.10683 (2019). arxiv:1910.10683
22. Wei, J., Liu, Q., Guo, Y., Jiang, X.: Training multilingual pre-trained language model with byte-level subwords. CoRR abs/2101.09469 (2021). arxiv:2101.09469
23. Yang, Z., Dai, Z., Yang, Y., Carbonell, J., Salakhutdinov, R., Le, Q.V.: XLNet: generalized autoregressive pretraining for language understanding (2019). http://arxiv.org/abs/1906.08237, cite arxiv:1906.08237 Comment: Pretrained models and code are available at https://github.com/zihangdai/xlnet

MBSE Grid: Operational Analysis for the Implementation of Hydroelectric Group Health Monitoring and Management Unit

Mohammed Bouaicha[1]($\boxtimes$) (iD), Nadia Machkour[1], Imad El Adraoui[2] (iD),
and Mourad Zegrari[1]

[1] Laboratory of Complex Cyber Physical Systems (LCCPS), ENSAM, Hassan II University,
Mers Sultan BP 9167, Casablanca, Morocco
bouaicha.med@gmail.com
[2] Laboratory of Engineering, Industrial Management and Innovation (IMII),
The Faculty of Sciences and Technology, Hassan 1St University, PO Box 577, Settat, Morocco

Abstract. Any study or project within the framework of system design has chosen to start the modeling phase with the model-based systems engineering approach (MBSE), it will encounter decision-making difficulties with the approach. to adopt. During the last two decades, many MBSE methodologies have been developed, but the majority of them present an incomplete or abstract architectural framework for organizing the modeling work. The MBSE Grid-based Systems Modeling Language (SysML) approach has made the modeling task easier for system engineers. Indeed, SysML constitutes a powerful tool, using its diagrams, to model the points of view according to the principle of development of requirement, behavior, or structure of the system. This paper summarizes the MBSE methodologies most used in research work and development projects. In the context of our study, the MBSE Grid approach is adopted with slight modifications concerning the names of the domains of the grid. By combining with Bombardier Transport SysMM's MBSE methodology, which consists of three main phases, the proposed MBSE grid presents a modeling approach by analysis: the operational, functional, and technical of the system. The purpose of this work is to conduct an operational analysis, for the implementation of a Health Monitoring and Management Unit (HMMU) of a hydropower group.

Keywords: System Engineering · MBSE · MBSE Grid · Operational Analysis · SysML · Hydroelectric group

1 Introduction

Systems Engineering (SE) is an interdisciplinary methodological approach to mastering the design of complex systems and products. The practices of this approach are now listed in standards, carried out using methods, and supported by tools. Systems Engineering Methods provide technical approaches based on Model-Based Systems

M. Hamlich et al. (Eds.): SADASC 2022, CCIS 1677, pp. 402–410, 2022.
https://doi.org/10.1007/978-3-031-20490-6_32

Engineering (MBSE) to carry out these general activities. Language and modeling tools now computerized assist the implementation of processes and methods.

Any MBSE approach promises to facilitate communication between different engineering disciplines [1]. Therefore, it should support different architecture views for a single model, offering guidance on how to start modeling the system, how to create the model structure, which views to create, and in what order [2, 3]. To meet this challenge, the approach is obliged to implement the appropriate framework and process, the language, as well as the specific software tool. To ensure a successful implementation of MBSE, the modeling language must be combined with the methodology to become useful [4]. Recent MBSE approaches adopt the Systems Modeling Language (SysML), but it does not provide guidelines or recommendations on the modeling process [5, 6].

The systems engineering community has recognized and used many MBSE methodologies over the past two decades. The most popular among them are IBM Harmony, OSEM, Vitech, SYSMOD, and Enterprise Architecture Frameworks (EAF) for systems engineering, such as DoDAF / MODAF, TOGAF, NAF. A new approach called MBSE Grid was proposed in 2015 by [2]. It is a grid organized in a Zachman-style matrix [7], where rows represent viewpoints, columns represent pillars of systems engineering, and cells represent different views of the system model. The MBSE Grid offers a simplified approach and gives unambiguous guidelines for the modeling process using SysML.

The number of methods available for the MBSE is not large and not significant. Most of them provide an incomplete or abstract architectural framework for organizing the modeling work. In this paper, the MBSE Grid approach is adopted, the objective of which is to focus our study on the operational analysis of the process for the implementation of a health monitoring and management unit (HMMU). Through a vibratory signature of a hydroelectric group installed in the 90s, and today has cracks. The precise definition of the mission of the HMMU unit, the services it offers, and the relationships (requirements) with its environment (Hydroelectric group, User, control room, etc.) are one of the most important phases and critiques of the design of complex systems [3, 8]. More than 80% of the faults in a system or product come from the requirements definition stage [9].

We start our article in section II with a presentation of the work modeled by the different MBSE methodologies. Section III is devoted to the operational analysis by the MBSE Grid approach, for the implementation of the unit for monitoring and managing the state of health of a hydroelectric group. In section IV, conclusions are drawn, and future goals are revealed.

2   MBSE Approaches

The review of the different MBSE methodologies has been presented in [2], and this section describes and analyzes the most used.

2.1   MBSE Methodologies

- *IBM Rational Harmony for SE.* The process of system development is represented by the classic "V" waterfall diagram, where the flow is iterative for several cycles. The left branch describes the design from top to bottom, while the right side shows the implementation and testing phases from the bottom up to system acceptance [10].

- *Object-Oriented Systems Engineering Methodology (OOSEM).* It is a design approach based on systems engineering models with object-oriented techniques. OOSEM developed in 2010 by INCOSE, aims to reconcile the processes practiced by any project or organization for the development of a system [4].
- *Vitech MBSE Methodology.* Vitech's MBSE methodology comprises four main systems engineering activities: requirements analysis, behavioral analysis, architecture, and verification and validation [11]. SE activities are linked to four areas: Requirements, Behavior, Architecture, and Verification and Validation [12]. The four domains are all executed at a given level of detail before a transition to the next layer takes place.
- *JPL State Analysis (SA).* The methodology was developed within the California Institute of Technology by the Jet Propulsion Laboratory (JPL). It provides activities for modeling the behavior of the system as a function of state variables. Models show how the state evolves [13].
- *Systems Modeling Toolbox (SYSMOD).* Based on the SysML language, it begins the modeling with the description of the context of the project, to reach the end of the internal structure of the system and these parameters, simultaneously performing the steps of elaboration of requirements; definition of the context of the system; specification of use cases and process modeling [14].

The MBSE methodologies described above solve different missions of the systems engineering process [15, 16]. They use step-by-step iterations for data collection. However, this does not provide considerable support for identifying levels of abstraction, which can become an obstacle in assigning responsibilities to stakeholders.

2.2 Enterprise Architecture Frameworks

The process of analyzing a system by iterations, from viewpoints (layers of abstraction), also has its origins in several Enterprise Architecture Frameworks (EAF). We can distinguish two categories of FAEs: those oriented toward defense and those oriented toward the industry.

The Ministry of Defense Architecture Frameworks (DoDAF/MODAF) and the NATO Architecture Framework (NAF) are standardized frameworks for defense architectures, that allow modeling in different levels of abstraction. These frameworks are similar and use the same modeling language, developed by the OMG, called Unified Profile for DoDAF and MODAF (UPDM) [17].

The TOGAF, FEAF, and Zachman architectural frameworks are particularly used in scientific research work and considered more oriented towards industrial architectures [18, 19]. They are based on UML languages.

Other architectural frameworks exist in the world of transportation and defense industries such as BT SysMM. This framework consists of three phases to analyze and model the system of interest (Fig. 1). The operational analysis phase aims to specify the relationships between the system and its environment, the second functional analysis phase aims to explain the functioning of the system, while the technical analysis phase defines how the physical components are organized. (Hardware, Software) to implement the system [20].

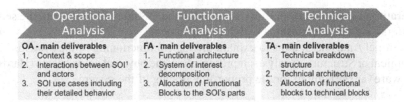

Operational Analysis	Functional Analysis	Technical Analysis
OA - main deliverables	**FA - main deliverables**	**TA - main deliverables**
1. Context & scope	1. Functional architecture	1. Technical breakdown structure
2. Interactions between SOI[1] and actors	2. System of interest decomposition	2. Technical architecture
3. SOI use cases including their detailed behavior	3. Allocation of Functional Blocks to the SOI's parts	3. Allocation of functional blocks to technical blocks

Fig. 1. BT System Modeling Method

EAFs methodologies present several problems which are summed up in the complexity of the model and the less clear relationships between the different layers (Specification, Design, and Structure). EAFs are very powerful for building the framework of enterprise architectures, but not quite suitable for systems, they are relatively complex for systems engineers. It is, for this reason, a new MBSE approach based on the strengths of existing methodologies, which should be oriented to the modeling of systems.

2.3 MBSE Grid

The initial MBSE Grid approach applied in 2015 by [2] briefly describes the cells composing the matrix. Adjustments have been applied by [21, 22] where the initial MBSE grid is kept.

For this paper, the MBSE Grid approach updated by [22] is adopted with slight modifications concerning the domain names of the grid. Combining with Bombardier Transport SysMM's MBSE methodology which takes place in three main phases by analysis: operational, functional, and technical. In our modeling approach, we also use these three main analysis approaches (Fig. 2).

		Pillar			
		Requirements	Behavior	Structure	Parametrics
Layer of Abstraction	Operational Analysis	Stakeholder Needs	Use Cases	System context	Measurements of Effectiveness
	Functional Analysis	System Requirements	Functional Analysis	Logical Subsystems Communication	MoEs for Subsystems
	Technical Analysis	Component Requirements	Component Behavior	Component Assembly	Component Parameters

Fig. 2. MBSE Grid framework adopted

- Operational Analysis: its purpose is to define the mission of the system, the services it offers, and the relationships with its environment.
- Functional Analysis: it aims to explain the logical functioning of the system.
- Technical or Structural Analysis: it presents how the physical components (Hardware, Software) are structured for the proper functioning of the system.

The purpose of the study is to conduct an operational analysis of the MBSE Grid approach adopted, to implement a Health Monitoring and Management Unit (HMMU) of a hydroelectric group.

3 Operational Analysis of the HMMU

3.1 Description of the Hydroelectric Group

The 80 MW hydroelectric group, installed for three decades, today presents cracks in certain welds of its braces. To assess this defect, two studies were conducted by [23, 24] in partnership with a service provider specializing in the condition-based maintenance of rotating machinery by vibration analysis, the objective of which is to find out whether vibrations are the cause of these cracks.

The diagnosis was carried out by performing tests in several operating modes to determine the types of faults that the group shaft may have. The identified faults are unbalanced, angular misalignment of the upper alternator bearing, and high displacements of the centers of the turbine and upper alternator bearings, the values of which place them in critical areas. The summary that emerged during the study [24] provides for permanent monitoring of the bearing clearances, the objective of which is to predict the horizon for exceeding the thresholds of the standardized global vibration levels and the bearing clearance limits recommended by the manufacturer. A unit, of great importance, that deals with the monitoring and management of the state of health (HMMU) of the hydraulic unit will have to be installed.

3.2 Operational Analysis of the HMMU

The first step in the operational analysis phase is to define Stakeholder needs, including guidelines related to regulations, standards, etc. The SysML requirements diagram (req) is best suited to express the needs. Each specified need is manifested by a requirement. All the needs can be expressed in a diagram view.

In the case of the HMMU unit, two needs are analyzed in-depth:

- SN1: Unit Management Modes - The unit must be able to monitor the machine in modes: Offline or Online.
- SN2: Data Type - The unit collects and analyzes vibration signals and displacement measurements of the bearing pins.

These needs are expressed and represented in the SysML requirements diagram (Fig. 3). These requirements are then refined by use cases in a "use case" (uc) diagram. These express the actions or tasks carried out by the actors and the unit.

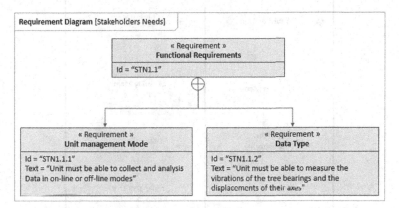

Fig. 3. Stakeholder needs expressed in requirements diagram

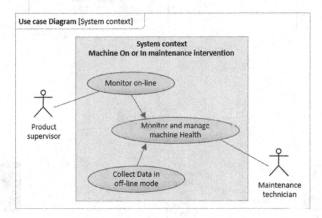

Fig. 4. Diagram unit use cases

Thus Fig. 4 details the use case "Monitor and Manage Machine Heath" in the context "Machine On or In Maintenance Intervention".

A use case is clarified by a flow of actions in the form of a scenario of exchanges between the actors and the system. This scenario is represented by the SysML activity diagram, where the actors and the system are modeled by channels. Figure 5 details the "Monitor and manage machine Heath" use case scenario, where unit activities are considered top-level functions. The user can be the supervisor or the technician.

Subsequently, the definition of the context of the system is necessary to show how the HMMU unit interacts with its external environment (User, Machine, D.B Storage, etc.). The SysML internal block diagram (Fig. 6) is used as well, to manifest these interactions in the context of "Machine On or In Maintenance Intervention".

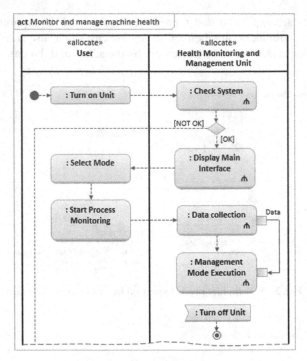

Fig. 5. Use case scenario

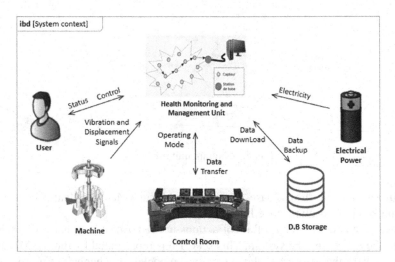

Fig. 6. Unit system context

The final step of the analysis is the specification of the non-functional objectives of the stakeholders submitted digitally. This step is called "measures of effectiveness".

A separate block will be created to manifest these operational parameters of the HMMU unit, shown in the SysML block definition diagram (Fig. 7).

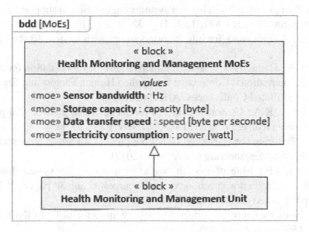

Fig. 7. Measurements of effectiveness

4   Conclusion

Many systems modeling approaches have been proposed and used in case studies or real projects. Most of them are difficult to implement and do not rely on a model-based modeling language.

The most recent and comprehensive approach based on models is the "MBSE Grid" methodology. The successful implementation of this approach on real projects has prompted us to use it in our modeling approach for the implementation of a Hydropower Group Health Monitoring and Management Unit (HMMU). The operational analysis process deployed in this paper has proven its effectiveness in modeling the system. Our short-term objective is to continue our integration project of the HMMU unit by proposing the following modeling by the two phases of functional and technical analyzes allowing respectively to explain the functioning of the system and how it will be its future structure.

References

1. Delp, C., Lam, D., Fosse, E., Cin-Young, L.: Model-based document and report generation for systems engineering. In: Aerospace Conference, IEEE (2013)
2. Morkevicius, A., Bisikirskiene, L., Jankevicius, N.: We choose MBSE: what's next? In: Proceedings of the Sixth International Conference on Complex Systems Design & Management, CSD&M, p. 313 (2015)
3. Morkevicius, A., Jankevicius, N.: An approach: SysML-based automated requirements verification. In: Systems Engineering (ISSE), IEEE International Symposium, pp. 28–30 (2015)

4. Pearce, P., Hause, M.: ISO-15288: OOSEM and Model-Based Submarine Design (2008)
5. Estefan, J.A.: Survey of Model-Based Systems Engineering (MBSE) Methodologies. INCOSE MBSE Initiative (2008)
6. Topper, J.S., Horner, N.C.: Model-based systems engineering in support of complex systems development. Johns Hopkins APL Tech. Dig. **32**(1) (2013)
7. Zachman, J.A.: A framework for information systems architecture. IBM Syst. J. **26**(3), 276–292 (1987)
8. Gregoriadesa, A., Hadjicostia, J., et al.: Human requirements validation for complex systems design. In: 6th International Conference on Applied Human Factors and Ergonomics (AHFE 2015) and the Affiliated Conferences, AHFE (2015)
9. Hooks, I.F., Farry, K.A.: Customer-centered products: creating successful products through smart requirements management. AMACOM, New York (2001)
10. Chadburn, F.: Tailoring the Harmony/SE MBSE process for automotive sector. In: INCOSE UK Annual Systems Engineering Conference (2017)
11. JR, L.B., Long, J.E.: Role of system engineering across the system life cycle. Vienna, Virginia (2007). http://www.vitechcorp.com/resources/technical_papers/200701031632040.baker_long.pdf (visited on 09/01/2020)
12. Stuart, T.B.: Network centric architectures: are we up to the task? In INCOSE International Symposium **15**(1), 600–609 (2005)
13. Ingham, M.D., Rasmussen, R.D., Bennett, M.B., Moncada, A.C.: Generating requirements for complex embedded systems using state analysis. Acta Astronaut. **58**(12), 648–661 (2006)
14. Weilkiens, T.: Systems engineering profile—SYSMOD. In: Systems Engineering with SysML/UML, pp. 271–284. Elsevier (2007). https://doi.org/10.1016/B978-0-12-374274-2.00005-5
15. Dickerson, C.E., Mavris, D.N.: Architecture and principles of systems engineering. CRC Press Auerbach Publications, Boca Raton, FL, USA (2009)
16. Friedenthal, S., Griego, R., Sampson, M.: INCOSE model-based systems engineering (MBSE) initiative. INCOSE International Symposium, USA (2007)
17. OMG: Unified profile for the DoDAF and MODAF. Needham, MA (2009)
18. The Open Group: TOGAF Version 9. Van Haren Publishing, Zaltbommel (2009)
19. Lankhorst, M.: Enterprise architecture at work. Springer, Berlin (2009)
20. Naas, O., Chami, M., Oggier, P., Heinz, M.: Real world application of MBSE at bombardier transportation. SWISSED (2015)
21. Mazeika, D., Morkevicius, A., Aleksandraviciene, A.: MBSE driven approach for defining problem domain. In: 11th Systems of Systems Engineering Conference, SoSE this link is disabled (2016)
22. Morkevicius, A., Aleksandraviciene, A., Mazeika, D., Bisikirskiene, L., Strolia, Z.: MBSE grid: a simplified SysML-based approach for modeling complex systems. In: 27th Annual INCOSE International Symposium (2017)
23. El Adraoui, I., Bouaicha, M., Gziri, H., Zegrari, M.: Implementation of a diagnostic approach based on vibration analysis: case study of a hydroelectric group. Int. J. Eng. Trends Technol. **69**(9), 97–106 (2021)
24. Bouaicha, M., Guerroum, M., El Adraoui, I., Zegrari, M., Gziri, H., Ait Elmahjoub, A.: Diagnosis of mechanical faults affecting a hydroelectric group by vibration analysis. Int. J. Emerg. Technol. Adv. Eng. **11**(11), 86–100 (2021)

Digital Twins-Based Smart Monitoring and Optimisation of Mineral Processing Industry

Oussama Hasidi[1,3]([✉]), El Hassan Abdelwahed[1], Aimad Qazdar[1],
Abdellah Boulaamail[2], Mohamed Krafi[2], Intissar Benzakour[2],
François Bourzeix[3], Salah Baïna[4], Karim Baïna[4], Mohamed Cherkaoui[5],
and Ahmed Bendaouia[1,3]

[1] Computer Systems Engineering Laboratory (LISI), Computer Science Department,
Faculty of Sciences Semlalia, Cadi Ayyad University (UCA), Marrakech, Morocco
Oussama.hasidi@ced.uca.ma, abdelwahed@uca.ac.ma
[2] R&D and Engineering Center, Reminex, Marrakech, Morocco
[3] Moroccan Foundation for Advanced Science Innovation and Research (MAScIR),
Rabat, Morocco
[4] National School of Computer Science and Systems Analysis (ENSIAS), Mohammed
V University, Rabat, Morocco
[5] National School of Mines of Rabat (ENSMR), Rabat, Morocco

Abstract. Beside all the challenges regarding climate change, resources
scarcity and quality degradation of deposits, the mining industry is
becoming an environment that is constantly under pressure and restric-
tive. The increasing of raw materials prices, the unstable and high volatile
commodity prices, the decreasing ore grades and the rising energy cost
have shown a clinical impact on the mining sector. One way to mitigate
the variability caused by these external forces is to take advantage of the
latest advanced information technologies and set up an innovative strategy to optimise the processing cost. A key enabler for the optimisation
of the mineral processing value chain and for the digital disruption of the
mining sector is the Digital Twin. Digital Twin encompasses digital models of the production models enabling a virtual representation of a physical system and ensuring a continuous real time interaction, correction,
control and optimisation. Consequently, the Digital Twin could afford an
alleviation of the mineral processing variability in terms of mineralogy,
final product's grades, mechanical setting and processing configuration.
This topic is a part of the Moroccan national project "Smart Connected
Mine" that arose after the consortium of industrials and researchers for
the digital transformation of the mining industry. In this paper, the background of the Digital Twin, its types and the major misconceptions about
it are presented. The values, challenges of the implementation of such
concept and its key enablers technologies are highlighted. Also an architectural framework for the Digital Twin implementation in a mineral
processing plant is proposed and the modeling approaches are discussed.

© The Author(s), under exclusive license to Springer Nature Switzerland AG 2022
M. Hamlich et al. (Eds.): SADASC 2022, CCIS 1677, pp. 411–424, 2022.
https://doi.org/10.1007/978-3-031-20490-6_33

Keywords: Digital twin · Disruptive technology · Smart control and supervision · Digital transformation · Mineral processing · Innovation · Industry 4.0

1   Introduction

While the mining industry remains one of the world's largest industrial sectors, there are a number of concerns regarding its long-term viability. Exhaustion of mineral reserve, low grade minerals, scarcity of resources, rising energy cost, and commodity market imbalances are the trends that challenge the future of the mining industry. These changes imply volatile, uncertain, complex, and ambiguous environments for firms and affect them across their strategic environment [1]. Various initiatives emphasized the urgency for advanced innovative strategies to tackle those challenges and to support the economic growth and the competitiveness of mining companies on the market.

Along with the adoption of the new generation information technologies in the industry, the term "Digital Twin" has experienced a growth in popularity, and is now recognised as a key enabler for the digital disruption of the industrial operational activity. Digital Twin is defined as the virtual and computerized counterpart of a physical asset, process or system [2]. Digital Twin mirrors the physical systems and the processes that are articulated alongside the system in question, and across its life-cycle, mimicking its operation in real-time. Digital twins consists of several components such as models, data streams coming from the Internet of Things (IoT), sensors, data models, artificial intelligence and machine learning-enabled analytics and algorithms [3]. When combined with information and communication technologies and powerful data analytic algorithms such as artificial intelligence, Digital Twins allow industrials to perform advanced diagnostic, predictive analyses and control during operations [4].

This paper aims to provide the basis for further work in the field of the Digital Twin for the mine value chain optimization. This topic is a part of the Moroccan national project "Smart Connected Mine" that arose after the consortium of industrials and researchers for the digital transformation of the mining industry. The content of this paper addresses Background, definitions, challenges, key enabling technologies and values of Digital Twins, as well as an architecture for the implementation of such concept to smartly control mineral processing is proposed. This paper is structured as follows: In Sect. 2, Digital Twin background, definitions, types and misconceptions are presented. In Sect. 3, the values of a process Digital Twin in a mineral processing plant are listed. In Sect. 4, a generic architecture of the integration of Digital Twins in mineral processing plant is proposed, as well as the different approaches of developing a process Digital Model are detailed. Section 5 and 6 present the challenges and key enabling technologies of process Digital Twin adoption. A conclusion and work perspective are given, by the end, in Sect. 7.

2 Digital Twin: Background, Definitions and Types

2.1 Background and Definitions of Digital Twins

The use of "Twins" dates back to NASA's Apollo program, when two identical spacecraft were developed to allow for mirroring of the spacecraft's conditions during the voyage. A Digital Twin can be used to mirror the behavior of an asset for various purposes, exploiting a real time synchronization of the sensed data originating from the field-level and is able to decide between a set of actions with the focus to arrange and execute the whole production system in an optimal way [4,5]. At first, though, this idea was named the Mirrored Spaces Model, before it was later referred to as the concept of a Digital Twins [6,7].

Digital Twin is not a completely new concept [8]. It is rooted in some existing technologies [9], such as 3D modeling, system simulation, digital prototyping (including geometric, functional, and behavioral prototyping).

Various definitions of Digital Twins appeared over time. These definitions are reviewed by [10] and [11]. At present, the two most widely accepted definitions were given by Grieves and NASA. NASA defined a Digital Twin for a space vehicle as "an integrated multi-physics, multiscale, probabilistic simulation of an as-built vehicle or system that uses the best available physical models, sensor updates, fleet history and other tools to mirror the life of its corresponding flying twin" [12].

Digital twin extends the concept of twin in Apollo project to virtual space, and creates a virtual product which is similar to the physical entity in external appearance and internal nature by digital means [13]. The relationship between virtual space and physical space is established, so that data and information can be exchanged between them. The concept of virtual instead of real, interaction between virtual and real and controlling reality with virtual are visually and intuitively reflected. With the help of this concept, from a small product to a large workshop, even to a factory and a complex system can establish a corresponding Digital Twin, thus building a "living" virtual space [13].

Similar to a digital model (DM), a Digital Twin is a digital representation of a physical object, but features bi-directional and automatic data flow of operational data and feedback between them [14]. Digital Twins have the potential to improve a manufacturing system by predicting future events, such as machine faults or production bottlenecks, based on its current status and expected behavior and then implementing the appropriate responses to optimize performance in near real-time [15,16].

2.2 Digital Twin: Types and Nominations

As the Digital Twin concept has attracted strong interests from researchers in the late years, several definitions of Digital Twin has taken place as well as multiple lexical nominations of the concept appeared. The given definitions and nominations of Digital twin differ based the level of data integration between the physical and digital counterpart [14].

- Digital Model (Fig 1-a): A Digital Model is a digital representation of an existing or planned physical object that does not use any form of automated data exchange between the physical object and the digital object. Simulation softwares are good examples of Digital Models. Simulation softwares contain model-based equations that describes the behavior of a physical system and enable offline simulation with manually integrated data.
- Digital Shadow (Fig 1-b): A digital shadow is a digital representation of an object that has a one-way flow between the physical and digital object. A change in the state of the physical object leads to a change in the digital object and not vice versa. As the Digital Model receives automatically real time data, it behaves as realistically as the Physical Object and one might refer to such a combination as Digital Shadow.
- Digital Twin (Fig 1-c): If further, the data flows between an existing physical object and a digital object are fully integrated in both directions, one might refer to it as Digital Twin. A change made to the physical object automatically leads to a change in the digital object and vice versa.

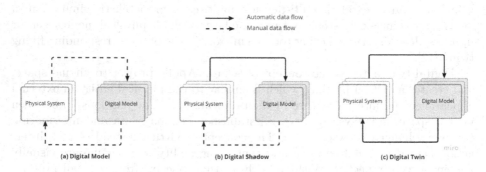

Fig. 1. Digital Twin nominations according to its degree of automation.

These three definitions are only to be taken into consideration and not always reliable. One might consider a Digital Shadow as a complete Digital Twin as it already twins the behavior of the physical object associated to. Also this identify the common misconceptions seen in the literature about Digital Twin. Amongst the misconceptions are the misconception that Digital Twins have to be an exact 3D model or just a 3D model of a physical thing [17]. Not to forget the misconceptions and confusions between Digital Twin and Simulation.

2.3 Simulation vs. Digital Twin: What's the Difference Between Them ?

There are different views on the relationship between Digital Twin and other concepts such as Simulation [18]. Simulation is a digital model that is commonly used during the design phase and often uses computer-aided design software applications. Digital twins, on the other hand, are virtual models created to accurately represent existing physical objects. The physical object is fitted with sensors that produce real time data about different aspects of the object's performance. This data is then relayed to a processing system and applied to the models encapsulated in the Digital Twin [19]. These digital models are used to run simulations, study current performance and generate potential improvements to be applied back in real time to the actual physical object.

While simulations and Digital Twins each use digital model to replicate products and processes, there are a few key variations among the two. The most important difference to be noted is that a Digital Twin creates a virtual environment able to study several simulations, backed up with real-time data and a two-way flow of information between the physical and digital counterparts [18]. Moreover, Simulation only focuses on what could happen in the real world (What-if scenarios), in other hand Digital Twin focuses more on what is currently happening by giving a high-fidelity representation of the operational dynamics of its physical counterpart [19]. An other difference is that Digital Twin is considered as active compared to simulation which is static. A Digital Twin will begin much the same as a simulation model, however the introduction of real-time data means that the twin can change and develop to provide a more active simulation.

3   Digital Twin in Mineral Processing: Values and Benefits

The last thirty years have seen a dynamic shift in mineral processing. After years of extraction and exploitation, new deposits nowadays have lower grades, are more difficult to process, and have more complicated mineralogy than older deposits. Moreover, lower grades require greater tonnages to be treated to deliver the same amount of product, which means higher chemical reagents, energy and water consumption. The following section will showcase how Digital Twins, throughout advanced process monitoring, fault diagnosis, self-control, intelligent soft sensing, decision making and value-chain optimisation could stand face to the complexity and variability of the industry and optimise the operational activity of mineral processing.

Real-Time Remote Monitoring, Optimisation and Control. Digital Twins by to their very own nature provide a real time mirroring, prediction and optimisation as a smart control strategy. Throughout sensors and actuators, Digital Twins enable the remote processes monitoring without having to physically be present at specific locations within the plant. The remote monitoring generally involves viewing the operations through a screen or dashboard showcasing the Digital Twins, getting predictions and visualisations of the overall operations performance and sending back actions to be done to the physical process in terms of optimisation and redress. Digital Twins will thus enable the process monitoring taking into account all variations that impact performances and that could harm or vary the outcomes in terms of yield, quality and cost.

Scenario and Risk Assessment. Not to perturb the system, Digital Twins enable what-if analysis by performing and studying in the virtual world what we can't do, or takes a lot of efforts, time or is very costly and risky, in the physical world. Which is helpful to synthesize unexpected scenarios and study the response of the system as well as the corresponding mitigation strategies.

Predictive Maintenance and Scheduling. Through data captured from sensors and a smart analysis, faults in the system can be detected much in advance. Beyond testing the viability of a component, Digital Twins help with maintenance operations as well. The ability to monitor a whole process using Digital Twins brings additional advantages in terms of planning operational events and improving maintenance strategies. In a situation in which an equipment is expected to fail soon, Digital Twins can assess how this will affect the efficiency of the process and what it will cost.

More Efficient from Operators and Informed Decision Support System. Availability of quantitative data and advanced analytics in real-time will assist in more informed and faster decision makings. The power of the Digital Twin in manufacturing is to facilitate the decision-making process and to enable decision automation through pre-simulation [20]. With easy to use and understandable interfaces, operators and engineers are more likely to monitor remotely the systems, and teams can better utilize their time in improving synergies and collaborations leading to greater productivity. Moreover, being able to explore across the multiple disciplines and fields; e.g., process control, maintenance and R&D, the Digital Twins adoption paves the way to discover a new strategy for operational excellency towards better performances in terms of costs, energy and reagents consumption, recovery, quality and environment impact.

4   Generic Multi-layered Architecture of Digital Twin in Industrial Field: Use Case Mineral Processing

4.1   Data Circulation Between the Physical and Digital Counterparts

One thing that binds most definitions of Digital Twin on literature, other than being a virtual representation, is the bidirectional transmission of data between the physical and digital counterparts. The data to be circulated between the two twins includes quantitative and qualitative data connected to materials, production, process, environmental data, sensors data [21], as well as model's output data. The journey of interactivity between the physical and digital worlds underscores the profound potential of the digital twin. Thousands of sensors taking continuous measurements that are streamed to a digital platform, which, in turn, performs near-real-time analysis to optimize a business process in a transparent manner.

The data-centric model in Fig. 2 illustrates the enabling components (sensors and actuators from the physical process, data, and analytics) as well as the phases of the continuously updated digital twin application. By using sensors

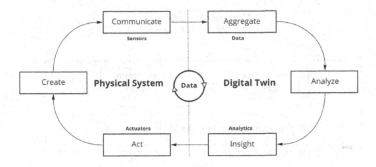

Fig. 2. Manufacturing Process Digital Twin model.

to measure the physical process, scientists and engineers are allowed to collect a wealth of data that can be mapped into virtual models after aggregation. This data-charged model perform analysis and provide insights about how the physical thing will respond to the real world. The Digital Twin then sends back actions to be warranted in the real world, by the way of actuators, in terms of refinement and improvement. A Digital Twin helps understand not only how a product or system is currently performing, but also how it may perform in its futuristic behaviors [17,22].

4.2 Proposed Multi-layered Architecture for the Implementation

There is not a unique comprehensive framework for a Digital Twin for manufacturing. The most global comprehensive model, presented in [23], consists of five layers covering all requirements to represent the physical space in the virtual space. The cyber-physical store data layer, the primary processing layer, the models and algorithms layer, the analysis layer, and the visualization and user interface layer.

Every other published architectural framework of Digital Twins implementation for manufacturing operations comprises 4 main components (data gathering component, data pre-processing and analysis component, models and algorithms component and user interface component). Based on this, we shaped a generic layered architecture adaptive to process Digital Twin of mineral processing value chain in 4 levels (Control, Monitoring, Knowledge and Management). The Fig. 4 represents the proposed architecture and illustrates the levels in question and conceptualizes the data flow circulation between the different layers. In this architecture, the models and algorithms component, from other published frameworks, is divided into predictive and optimisation layers. As shown in the Fig. 4, the shaped architecture comprises a layer for physical systems, a Control Layer, 3 core layers of the Digital Twin (Supervision and Monitoring, Predictive and Optimisation) and a Management layer. Each layer of the architecture packs a specific service and exchanges data with its neighbor layer. Compared to other ones, This shaped architecture handles the data workflow more efficiently and ensures the overall scalability and interoperability of the Digital Twin.

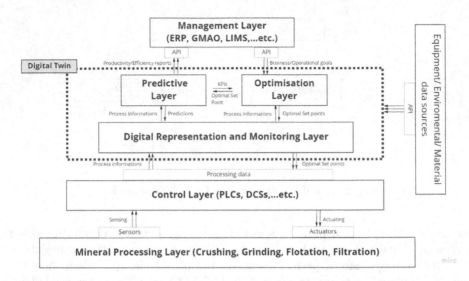

Fig. 3. Digital Twin for Mineral Processing: visualized architecture and data flow circulation.

The Control Layer bridges the physical world and their digital counterparts. Controllers and calculators (PLCs, DCSs) are often deployed for the automatic control and are directly linked to sensors and actuators making it possible to know and ensure the continued operation of the production in stable conditions. Besides regulation purpose, controllers transmit information the upper Monitoring Layer. The Monitoring Layer consists of the virtual representation (mostly 3D) of the gathered process information for advanced supervision. The Monitoring Layer, in turn, sends process information to the Knowledge Layers (Predictive and Optimisation Layers) to perform predictive analytics and run optimisation algorithms based on the actual state of the process. The Predictive Layer performs futuristic predictions of the actual operations and forwards them back to the Monitoring Layer for supervision and to the Optimisation Layer. The input data fed to the Predictive Layer are mostly the fusion of processing data from sensors and other information from external data sources such as environmental data and equipment sizing. The Optimisation Layer, in other hand, represents the core of actuating and decision making. With the aid of the neighbor Predictive Layer, the Optimisation Layer evaluates the KPIs and predictions, compares it with the business goals set by the upper Management Layer and runs optimisations algorithms. Optimisation algorithms return the optimal set points to be applied to the operations in order to redress it and to meet the final pre-set plant's objectives.

Following this conceptual architecture not only allows an efficient orchestration of the services and data workflow after implementation, but also helps in the development phase. By setting apart the Digital Twin into units, it becomes convenient to emphasize a component over an other to start the development journey with. Moreover, this architecture is quite generic as it can be implemented at any fields with data provenance from physical systems and can be extended to other manufacturing operations as well.

4.3 Predictive Layer: Modeling Approaches

The Predictive Layer in the Digital Twin proposed architecture (Fig. 4) encapsulates digital models that are interrogated by the Control Layer. These digital models might be developed through different paradigms and approaches; data-driven approach, model-driven approach or a hybrid modeling approach.

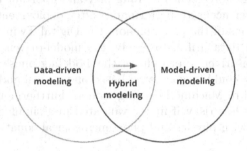

Fig. 4. Modeling approaches of Digital Twin's Predictive layer.

Data-Driven Approach and Model-Driven Approach. Data-driven methods rely on the previously observed data, making it a paradigm that focuses more on data and variable's correlation rather than the phenomenon's physical causation [24]. This includes unsupervised statistical methods or cluster techniques, as well as supervised classification or regression techniques. By analysing the historical operational data of previous performances, Machine learning algorithms can spot connections and patterns that may not even know to suspect, discover features with the most impact and learn how an operation or a system behaves. However, aside its ability of modeling and describing the behavior of a system, the data-driven approach is data hungry and requires a good bit of data to get decent results.

The Model-driven approach, in other side, is actually starting with a solid idea of how the physical system works and re-modeling the system by relying mainly on the physical and phenomenological equations. This way of modeling, as it depends on a deep understanding of systems and processes, demand the collaboration of operators and engineers that understand the physical, mechanical, electronic and all appropriate details of the complex system [25].

Hybrid Approach. Each approach (data-driven and model-driven) shows advantages and limitations, and one way to get the most of benefits from the both approaches is to combine them towards a hybrid modelling approach [26]. The combination of data-based and knowledge-based modelling is motivated by applications that are partly based on causal relationships, while other effects result from hidden dependencies that are represented in huge amounts of data [27].

The data-driven approach could assist the model-driven approach in various ways. Tiny Machine Learning-based algorithms could be advantageous for the inference of complex measurements that are hard to measure or that are not bound to be directly measured. Statistical methods could also play a major role in studying and investigating hidden parameters dependencies. Moreover, Data assimilation and Reinforcement Learning play an important role in guarantying the Predictive Layer accurate performance after deployment. By continuously injecting observations of the phenomenon, the Digital Twin stays updated preventing itself from data drifts. Inversely, the model-driven approach could as well assist the data-driven approach. In the modeling phase for instance, additional training data could be generated based on physical and phenomenological equations to be fed to Machine Learning models. Furthermore, testing Machine Learning models is less risky if firstly validated in a simulation-based environment that is built with physics and phenomenological equations.

5   Digital Twin in Mineral Processing; Challenges of Adoption

In order to make a Digital Twin completely indistinguishable from its physical counterparts and to ensure the fidelity of the data-centric strategy, many challenges have to be addressed [17].

Mutual Understanding and Integration of Different Domains for the Predictive Layer Modeling

The main objective of adopting Digital Twins in mineral processing is to simulate as realistically as possible the processes and to cover the whole process's life cycle. The toughest challenges is to own a deep understanding and knowledge across the different domains involved in that process and to encapsulate this knowledge into virtual models. Process Digital Twins must be including all scenarios and changes occurring to products, the key parameters resulting these changes and the complexity of the concerned system. Effectively asset knowledge must include information about the whole production. The abilities and scope of actions must also be clarified by experts in order to come closer to a common optimum.

Data Variety, Security and Connectivity

The amount of data collected from the numerous endpoints existing in a mineral processing plant is massive and various. Such a large variety of data raises the data integration, data cleansing, data fusion and data storage issues [29]. Also, each of the endpoints represents a potential area of security vulnerability. Therefor, manufacturer must be careful not to rush into the adoption of Digital Twins without assessing and updating their current security protocols and access privileges. Moreover, the concept of twinning requires a near zero low latency for the information circulating. It is necessary then to take into account the connectivity and the various data flow control challenges, ensuring that it can be organized and used efficiently to maintain promising, fast and secure delivery.

User Friendly Interfaces for Information Exchange
Human actions and interactions with machines in the production environment are prone to accidents. Human-Machine interaction is a key aspect in adopting Digital Twins for smart manufacturing, which primarily focuses on the issues of communication, interaction, and cooperation between engineers and machines to furnish a remote mode of visualisation and control. Therefore, the efficiency and safety of a Digital Twin relies mostly on how the information will be displayed to the operators in the simplest way allowing an accurate readability, providing understandable decisions and enabling easy remote monitoring.

6   Digital Twin in Mineral Processing: Underpinning Technologies

Internet of Things
The first enabler of the Digital Twin concept is the internet of things (IoT), and specifically industrial internet of things (IIoT) for manufacturing environment. IoT/IIoT devices are made up of sensors, actuators, controllers and Networks. IoT/IIoT have a huge impact on improving manufacturing processes, allowing for tasks to be evaluated with greater knowledge and providing the remote supervision and control through connected devices. From Digital Twin perspective, IoT/IIoT bridges the physical world with its virtual twin. The online data collected by the sensors will eventually serve the virtual twin as an entryway for algorithms to be processed, then control signals are generated for the actuators according to the actions needed to perform.

Machine Learning
The vast majority of target systems have multiple variables and multiple streams of data. Machine learning (ML) algorithm can be trained to recognize process behavior by feeding it thousands of historic observations that have been linked to the process performance. After training and testing, the ML algorithm can then be put to work monitoring the system and alerting when it observes suspected abnormal behavior or deviation. Furthermore, Digital Twin's consistent efficiency after deployment requires an active monitoring of its performance. Therefore, Reinforcement Learning comes to automate this process by continuously feeding observations for active learning and accuracy regulating.

Heuristic Optimisation
Given their ability to process large datasets based on user-defined objectives, heuristic algorithms can perform complex optimisation using heuristic methods [28]. With a pre-set objectives, system's behavior equations and the current process state, heuristic algorithms are used to automatically compute optimal

values of control variables that might drive the system from its current state to the pre-set objective. These optimal values are systematically sent afterwards to the actuators to act in the physical process in terms of optimisation.

Big Data Technologies
Sensors certainly generates a huge amount of information, which must be stored, treated and analysed for the benefice of the digital twin. The infrastructure for storing and processing high volume data has been advanced considerably over the last decades. And many available platforms are available to handle big data projects in terms of integration, storage, centralized management, interactive analysis, visualization, accessibility and security.

Cloud Computing and Networks
Collecting and transmitting information and ensuring a real time communication and latency represent a big challenge. Cloud and Edge computing, 5G networks and Data encryption techniques are certainly expected to play a major role pushing towards facing these challenges and guaranteeing the efficient interactive aspect of the Digital Twin.

Encryption - Data Protection Techniques
Information and data security are a continuous critical concern for every industrial business. Digital Twin creates valuable information that needs to be protected. Today, different methods and techniques are developed to ensure data safety and protect its availability only for authorized persons and systems.

7   Conclusion and Perspective

Materials and minerals processing Industries are bound to increasingly adopt digital technologies in order to ensure product safety and quality, minimize costs in the face of low profit margins, shorten lead times and guarantee timely delivery of an increasing number of products despite production dead times and uncertainties. The concept of a digital twin put forward in the context of Industry 4.0 encompasses digital models of the production model that imitate the physical system, perform prediction and interacts with it in terms of optimisation.

The Digital Twin concept transforms data in real time into operational information allowing an advanced real time supervision and control. The implementation framework of a process Digital Twin for mineral processing follows a layered architecture; Control Layer bridging between the physical process and its digital counterpart, Monitoring Layer for the supervision, Predictive Layer encapsulating data-driven and model-driven equations, Optimisation Layer encapsulating optimisation algorithms and Management Layer providing goals and objectives to meet.

As part of the Moroccan National Project "Smart Connected Mine", this topic is an applied research and development axe that aims to provide a Digital Twin prototype to digital disrupt the mineral processing control system. This paper addressed the background, challenges and potential benefits of implementing Digital Twin for minerals processing units, as well as an architecture of the implementation is proposed. The further work will mainly be focused on the development of a flotation process Digital Twin as prototype. The model development and validation of the Digital Twin and the challenges encountered will be tackled in next papers.

Acknowledgement. This work is supported by the Ministry of Higher Education, Scientific Research and Innovation, the Digital Development Agency (DDA) and the CNRST of Morocco through Al-Khawarizmi program. This publication is part of the work undertaken by the consortium of partners which is composed of MAScIR (Moroccan Foundation for Advanced Science, Innovation and Research), Reminex; the R&D and Engineering subsidiary of Managem group, UCA, ENSIAS and ENSMR. We would like to thank the Managem Group and its subsidiary CMG for allowing the conduction of this research on its operational site as an industrial partner of this project.

References

1. Qassimi, S., Abdelwahed, E.: Disruptive Innovation in Mining Industry 4.0. Distributed Sensing and Intelligent Systems, pp. 313–325 (2022)
2. Bergs, T., Gierlings, S., Auerbach, T., Klink, A., Schraknepper, D., Augspurger, T.: The concept of digital twin and digital shadow in manufacturing. Proc. CIRP **101**, 81–84 (2021)
3. Rudrappa, S.: Architecture To Bridge Physical world to Virtual Digital World. Medium, November 2019
4. Grieves, M., Vickers, J.: Digital Twin: Mitigating Unpredictable, Undesirable Emergent Behavior in Complex Systems, 1 August 2017
5. Grieves, M.: Digital Twin: Manufacturing Excellence through Virtual Factory Replication (2015)
6. Grieves, M.: Origins of the Digital Twin Concept, 31 August 2016
7. Grieves, M.: Product lifecycle management: the new paradigm for enterprises. Int. J. Prod. Dev. **1/2**, 71–84 (2005)
8. Qi, Q., et al.: Enabling technologies and tools for digital twin. J. Manuf. Syst. **58**, 3–21 (2021)
9. Boschert, S., Rosen, R.: Digital Twin-The Simulation Aspect. Mechatronic Futures: Challenges and Solutions for Mechatronic Systems and their Designers, pp. 59–74 (2016)
10. Tao, F., Zhang, H., Liu, A., Nee, A.: Digital Twin in Industry: State-of-the-Art. IEEE Trans. Ind. Inf. **15**, 2405–2415 (2019)
11. Negri, E., Fumagalli, L., Macchi, M.: A review of the roles of digital twin in CPS-based production systems. Procedia Manuf. **11**, 939–948 (2017)
12. Shafto, M., Rich, M., Doyle, G., Kris, K., Jacqueline, L., Lui, W.: Modeling, SiMulation, InforMation Technology & ProceSSing RoadMaP (2012)
13. Li, L., Lei, B., Mao, C.: Digital twin in smart manufacturing. J. Ind. Inf. Integr., 100289 (2022)
14. Kritzinger, W., Karner, M., Traar, G., Henjes, J., Sihn, W.: Digital twin in manufacturing: a categorical literature review and classification. IFAC-PapersOnLine, pp. 1016–1022 (2018)
15. Zhuang, C., Liu, J., Xiong, H.: Digital twin-based smart production management and control framework for the complex product assembly shop-floor. Int. J. Adv. Manuf. Technol. **96**, 1149–1163 (2018)

16. Shao, G., Helu, M.: Framework for a digital twin in manufacturing: scope and requirements. Manuf. Lett. **24**, 105–107 (2020)
17. Rasheed, A., et al.: Digital Twin: Values, Challenges and Enablers From a Modeling Perspective (2020)
18. Lu, Y., Liu, C., Wang, K., Huang, H., Xu, X.: Digital Twin-driven smart manufacturing: connotation, reference model, applications and research issues. Robot. Comput.-Integr. Manuf. **61**, 101837 (2020)
19. Wright, L., Davidson, S.: How to tell the difference between a model and a digital twin. Adv. Model. Simul. Eng. Sci. **1**, 13 (2020)
20. Kunath, M., Winkler, H: Integrating the digital twin of the manufacturing system into a decision support system for improving the order management process (2018)
21. Singh, M., Fuenmayor, E., Hinchy, E., Qiao, Y., Murray, N., Devine, D.: Digital twin: origin to future. Appl. Syst. Innov. **36** (2021)
22. Negri, E., et al.: A review of the roles of digital twin in CPS-based production systems (2017)
23. Bazaz, S., Lohtander, M., Varis, J.: 5-dimensional definition for a manufacturing digital twin. Proc. Manuf. **38**, 1705–1712 (2019)
24. Wang, X., et al.: New Paradigm of Data-Driven Smart Customisation through Digital Twin (2021)
25. Ritto, T., et al.: Digital twin, physics-based model, and machine learning applied to damage detection in structures (2021)
26. Liao, L., Köttig, F.: A hybrid framework combining data-driven and model-based methods for system remaining useful life prediction. Appl. Soft Comput. **44**, 191–199 (2016)
27. Rueden, L., Mayer, S., Sifa, R., Bauckhage, C., Garcke, J.: Combining machine learning and simulation to a hybrid modelling approach: current and future directions. Adv. Intell. Data Anal. **XVIII**, 548–560 (2020)
28. Christopher, R., Benjamin, S., Mansour, E., Carl, H.: Computational Algorithms for Digital Twin Support in Construction (2020)
29. Tao, F., Zhang, M.: Digital twin shop-floor: a new shop-floor paradigm towards smart manufacturing. IEEE Access, 20418–20427 (2017)

Optimization of Collaborative Transport and Distribution Strategies: Trends and Research Opportunities

Yousra Chabba[✉], Ali El Oualidi, and Mustapha Ahlaqqach

Laboratory of Advanced Research in Industrial and Logistic Engineering, ENSEM, Hassan II University, Casablanca, Morocco
yousra.chabba@ensem.ac.ma

Abstract. During the last two decades, global market competitiveness has reached higher levels between companies operating worldwide. A situation that results from the new growing trends of globalization, the effects of the COVID19 pandemic on the whole world, and sustainability challenges. So, to maintain a sustainable supply chain in the current context, many enterprises choose to invest in logistic collaborations with presumed partners. Hence, logistic collaboration seems to be an efficient solution for companies willing to share their resources in order to reduce transport costs, CO_2 emissions, congestion along with traffic accidents. 73 scientific articles have been collected and studied as part of a systematic literature review about optimization of collaborative transport and distribution strategies. So, this study aims to analyze the existing literature on this topic to find gaps and opportunities for future research. The results highlight the most to the less studied types of collaboration and trending resolution techniques used.

Keywords: Logistic collaboration · Optimization · Sustainable supply chain · Logistic strategy · Transport · Distribution

1 Introduction

In the last years, globalization is enhancing the development of new technologies, which both, have a huge impact on the worldwide economy. The transport and logistics sectors, playing an important role in the economic growth, are also affected. Since both enhance national and international trading, moreover uphold the economy's recovery specifically during and after global economic crises such as the one caused by COVID19 pandemic. In addition to struggles related to globalization and digitalization, sustainability challenges are becoming more and more intense to be unignorable due to the establishment of laws, by many countries, concerning, environmentally, the reduction of carbon prints and the reduction of greenhouse gases, to prevent more of the global warming consequences on the planet. Many solutions were advanced by multiple firms along with research of the field, solutions that aimed to increase a firm's profitability and its competitiveness, moreover sustain its development. As one of the solutions, many companies, particularly, choose to commit into collaborations.

Whether concerning freight transportation or passengers' transportation in normal daily life or in case of emergencies, many organizations choose to combine their efforts in order to gain advantages they struggled to achieve alone. These alliances that concern particularly the transport of goods and people, are technically referred to as logistic collaborations or logistic pooling.

Since the existing review articles aimed to find research gaps and most studied research topics based on a categorization decision making levels, this paper aims to examine recent studies conducted on the optimization of collaborative transport and distribution strategies in the last decade, to establish the existing state of the art of the subject and find the emerging trends used in solving issues related to collaboration between organizations under sustainability challenges, also to identify research gaps and future research opportunities.

The remainder of this paper shall be organized into 5 sections. **Research methodology**, Sect. 2, explains the methodology used while elaborating this review. Section 3 shows the **Results** of the systematic review conducted. As Sect. 4, **Discussion,** is dedicated to discuss the findings of this study. Finally, the last section summarizes the whole work.

2   Research Methodology

Since this work concerns a state of the art on the subject of the optimization of collaborative transport and distribution strategies, a Systematic Literature Review is conducted. It includes 5 major steps. The first step revolves about the formulation of the search question then fixing the appropriate keywords for the review. The second step concerns the definition of both inclusion and exclusion criteria. The third step is a search step applied upon eligible databases. Whereas, papers are selected in the fourth step, discussed then the results are analyzed. Finally, reporting the results comes as in the last step. [1].

2.1   Aim of the Research and Keywords

The aim of this research, as mentioned above, is to examine the existing literature on the logistics and transport field concerning the optimization of collaborative strategies of transport and distribution. Thus, this review article answers the following questions: What are the trending technological solutions used among collaborating organizations nowadays? And what are the issues related to logistic coalitions that are yet to be studied?

After formulating the search questions of the systematic review, the choice of the keywords remains the second most crucial step, since they enable to focus, localize and limit the study. In this case, two categories of keywords were established. The first category, referred to as the main category which is related to the field of the search, includes: "optimization", "logistics", "supply chain", "transport" and "distribution". And the second category contains the vocabulary related to collaboration, it includes: "collaborative", "cooperative", "coalition", "pooling" and "alliance".

2.2 Inclusion and Exclusion Criteria

In order to select the most appropriate articles related to the search questions, a list of inclusion and exclusion criteria is established. The following table, Table 1, identify those criteria distinctively for the purpose of limiting the literature search.

Table 1. Inclusion and exclusion criteria of the study

Inclusion criteria	Exclusion criteria
Article written in English	Non-English written article
Article published between 2012 and first trimester of 2022	Article published before 2012
Article dealing with logistic optimization and collaborative logistics	Article dealing with types of collaborations between organizations other than logistic collaboration

2.3 Databases

Before selecting papers for the study, it is important to identify the source databases that are selected for the search. So, in this paper, many electronic resources are chosen, including: Web of Science, ScienceDirect, Scopus, Emerald Insight, Taylor & Francis, Wiley Online Library, IEEE Xplore, Google Scholar and Springer.

2.4 Papers' Selection

The selection of papers for this review shall be done through the application of filters using inclusion and exclusion criteria after entering keywords of the search in the selected databases. Once the results are shown, it is important to identify the most relevant of the papers to focus on.

2.5 Results' Reporting

Once the papers for the study are selected, the next step is to read them thoroughly, analyze them, then discuss their results. Above all, a descriptive analysis should be conducted, papers need to be classified, and studies are yet to be categorized according to the research methodology used. After that, an in-depth conclusion is to be made about the conducted analysis of the literature identified. This conclusion will help in determining the current trends in the topic, identifying research gaps along with future research opportunities.

3 Results

First, in the preselection phase, a number of 122 articles were selected, including articles that mainly discussed urban traffic, public transport, in addition to vehicle rooting problems. The first-hand chosen articles were analyzed to know about research advancements on those subjects and make comparison between collaborative and non-collaborative scenarios. These articles were eliminated from through the selection process, resulting in a total of 73 selected articles that are appropriate to the research theme.

3.1 Selected Papers

The Table 2 below contains research papers that were selected according to the research methodology described in the previous section. Information on the papers as per their title, their type, and the year of publishing are collected and presented.

Table 2. Informations about the selected papers for the review

Paper title	Year	Paper type	Resolution method category
An Integrated Fuzzy Approach for Strategic Alliance Partner Selection in Third-Party Logistics [18]	2012	Research article	Fuzzy AHP technique
An Intelligent Scheduling Strategy of Collaborative Logistics for Mass Customization [69]	2012	Research article	PSO heuristic algorithm & Simulation
How to anticipate the level of activity of a sustainable collaborative network: the case of urban freight delivery through logistics platforms [21]	2013	Conference paper	Modeling & Game theory
A Multi-Agent Distributed Framework for Collaborative Transportation Planning [44]	2013	Conference paper	Multi-Agent Modeling
Combined demand and capacity sharing with best matching decisions in enterprise collaboration [45]	2013	Research article	Fuzzy MIP model
Collaborative Logistics from the Perspective of Road Transportation Companies [63]	2013	Review article	Systematic Literature Review

(*continued*)

Table 2. (*continued*)

Paper title	Year	Paper type	Resolution method category
A Collaborative Supply Chain Management System for a Maritime Port Logistics Chain [5]	2014	Research article	Modeling & Simulation
A Performance Evaluation Research on Collaborative Operation between Logistics Enterprise and Manufacturing Enterprise [12]	2014	Research article	Modeling based on AHP and fuzzy comprehensive analysis
Supply Chain Collaboration, Integration, and Relational Technology: How Complex Operant Resources Increase Performance Outcomes [23]	2014	Research article	Empirical Survey & Data Analysis
Collaborative Urban Logistics – Synchronizing the Last Mile [71]	2014	Research article	Modeling
Developing a Collaborative Planning Framework for Sustainable Transportation [72]	2014	Research article	Modified K-means clustering approach
Advanced predictive-analysis-based decision support for collaborative logistics networks [32]	2015	Research article	Modeling
Collaborative relationships between logistics service providers and humanitarian organizations during disaster relief operations [8]	2016	Research article	Survey & Data analysis
Effective logistics alliance design and management [9]	2016	Review article	Systematic Literature Review
Definition of a Collaborative Working Model to the Logistics Area using Design for Six Sigma [10]	2016	Research article	DMADV methodology
Determining collaborative profits in coalitions formed by two partners with varying characteristics [14]	2016	Research article	Simulation & Data Analysis

(*continued*)

Table 2. (*continued*)

Paper title	Year	Paper type	Resolution method category
An Intelligent Multi-Agent Based Model for Collaborative Logistics Systems [37]	2016	Research article	Game Theory & LP & MOLP
Enterprises' Readiness to Establish and Develop Collaboration in the Area of Logistics [60]	2016	Research article	Data Analysis
Are People the Key to Enabling Collaborative Smart Logistics? [7]	2017	Conference paper	Data analysis
GoodsPooling: An Intelligent Approach for Urban Logistics [22]	2017	Conference paper	Modeling (UML)
Collaborative vehicle routing: a survey [25]	2017	Review article	Systematic Literature Review
Enabling sustainable energy futures: factors influencing green supply chain collaboration [33]	2017	Research article	Literature Review & Modeling
Collaborative shipping under different cost-sharing agreements [51]	2017	Research article	Modeling
Economies of Product Diversity in Collaborative Logistics [59]	2017	Research article	Integer Linear Program
Design optimization of resource combination for collaborative logistics network under uncertainty [67]	2017	Research article	Modeling & Simulation
Collaborative urban transportation: Recent advances in theory and practice [11]	2018	Review article	Narrative Literature Review
Centralized bundle generation in auction-based collaborative transportation [24]	2018	Research article	GA Heuristic Algorithm
Disagreement on the Gain Sharing Method in Supply Chain Collaborations [36]	2018	Research article	Quantitative Case Study Approach

(*continued*)

Table 2. (*continued*)

Paper title	Year	Paper type	Resolution method category
Horizontal collaboration in logistics: decision framework and typology [43]	2018	Research article	Modeling
Centralised horizontal cooperation and profit sharing in a shipping pool [65]	2018	Research article	Game theory
Optimization of tuna fishing logistic routes through information sharing policies: A game theory-based approach [27]	2019	Research article	Game theory
Collaborative distribution: strategies to generate efficiencies in urban distribution - Results of two pilot tests in the city of Bogotá [30]	2019	Research article	Pilot tests
Cooperation of customers in traveling salesman problems with profits [49]	2019	Research article	Game Theory
Cooperative game-theoretic features of cost sharing in location-routing [50]	2019	Research article	Game Theory
A triple-win scenario for horizontal collaboration in logistics: Determining enabling and key success factors [52]	2019	Research article	Case study methodology
Horizontal collaborative transport: survey of solutions and practical implementation issues [53]	2019	Review article	Systematic Literature Review
Effect of strategic alliance based on port characteristic and integrated global supply chain for enhancing industrial port performance [58]	2019	Research article	Survey & Structural Equation Modeling
A GRASPxILS for the Shared Customer Collaboration Vehicle Routing Problem [62]	2019	Conference paper	Hybridized GRASPxILS metaheuristic

(*continued*)

Table 2. (*continued*)

Paper title	Year	Paper type	Resolution method category
Environmental impact assessment in the case of pooling Moroccan Hydrocarbon supply chain resources [17]	2020	Conference paper	Simulation
City logistics: Towards a blockchain decision framework for collaborative parcel deliveries in micro-hubs [31]	2020	Research article	Modeling
Collaborative profit allocation schemes for logistics enterprise coalitions with incomplete information [34]	2020	Research article	Game Theory & Quadratic Programming Model
Allocating Cost to Freight Carriers in Horizontal Logistic Collaborative Transportation Planning on Leading Company Perspective [41]	2020	Research article	Modeling
The quality-driven vehicle routing problem: Model and application to a case of cooperative logistics [42]	2020	Research article	Modeling
A green lateral collaborative problem under different transportation strategies and profit allocation methods [55]	2020	Research article	Mathematical modeling
Collaboration of sustainability and digital supply chain management of achieving a successful company [56]	2020	Review article	Literature Review
A Multi-Layer Collaboration Framework for Industrial Parks with 5G Vehicle-to-Everything Networks [57]	2020	Research article	Modeling
A decision-making support system in logistics cooperation using a modified VIKOR method under an intuituinistic Fuzzy environment [61]	2020	Research article	Multi-criteria decision making & intuitionistic fuzzy set

(*continued*)

Table 2. (*continued*)

Paper title	Year	Paper type	Resolution method category
Closed loop location routing supply chain network design in the end-of-life pharmaceutical products [73]	2020	Research article	MILP
Hybridization of game theory and ridesharing to optimize reverse logistics of healthcare textiles [74]	2020	Conference Paper	Game Theory
Towards a collaborative and integrated optimization approach in sustainable freight transportation [4]	2021	Conference paper	MILP
Systematic literature review on collaborative sustainable transportation: overview, analysis and perspectives [6]	2021	Review article	Systematic Literature Review
An investigation on the effect of inter-organizational collaboration on reverse logistics [13]	2021	Research article	Data Analysis
An algorithmic approach for sustainable and collaborative logistics: A case study in Greece [15]	2021	Research article	TONN heuristic algorithm
Public-private collaborations in emergency logistics: A framework based on logistical and game-theoretical concepts [16]	2021	Research article	Game theory
Leadership strategies, management decisions and safety culture in road transport organizations [26]	2021	Research article	Interviews & Braun & Clarke thematic analysis
Environmental benefits from shared-fleet logistics: lessons from a public-private sector collaboration [28]	2021	Research article	Survey & Data Analysis

(*continued*)

Table 2. (*continued*)

Paper title	Year	Paper type	Resolution method category
Lateral collaboration with cost-sharing in sustainable supply chain optimisation: A combinatorial framework [29]	2021	Research article	MILP
Cooperation between Sea Ports and Carriers in the Logistics Chain [38]	2021	Research article	Game Theory
Towards learning behavior modeling of military logistics agent utilizing profit sharing reinforcement learning algorithm [39]	2021	Research article	Multi-agent model & profit-sharing reinforcement learning algorithm
Analysis of an evolutionary game of pallet pooling with participation of third-party platform [40]	2021	Research article	Game Theory
Genetic Algorithm Based on Clark & Wright's Savings Algorithm for Reducing the Transportation Cost in a Pooled Logistic System [47]	2021	Research article	Heuristic algorithm GA and Clark &Wright's algorithm
Impact of operational constraints in city logistics pooling efficiency [48]	2021	Research article	Mathematical model & SA & VNS methods
Blockchain-Empowered Digital Twins Collaboration: Smart Transportation Use Case [54]	2021	Research article	Modeling
A Blockchain-IoT Platform for the Smart Pallet Pooling Management [66]	2021	Research article	Modeling and Case study methodology
Collaborative logistics network: a new business mode in the platform economy [68]	2021	Research article	5W1H method
Collaborative Vehicle Routing Problem in the Urban Ring Logistics Network under the COVID-19 Epidemic [70]	2021	Research article	MILP & metaheuristic VNS algorithm

(*continued*)

Table 2. (*continued*)

Paper title	Year	Paper type	Resolution method category
Demonstration of a blockchain-based framework using smart contracts for supply chain collaboration [2]	2022	Research article	Modeling
The "Lateral Transshipment" is a Cooperative Tool for Optimizing the Profitability of a Distribution System [19]	2022	Book Chapter	Modeling & Simulation
Cooperation and coopetition among retailers third party logistics providers alliances under different risk behaviors, uncertainty demand and environmental considerations [20]	2022	Research article	Non-Linear Program
Design of Supply Chain Transportation Pooling Strategy for Reducing CO_2 Emissions Using a Simulation-Based Methodology: A Case Study [35]	2022	Research article	Discrete-Event Simulation-based methodology
Introducing CRISTAL: A model of collaborative, informed, strategic trade agents with logistics [46]	2022	Research article	Modeling
Towards intelligent public transport systems in Smart Cities; Collaborative decisions to be made [64]	2022	Research article	Modeling

3.2 Statistical Descriptive Analysis

After collecting all necessary data about the selected works for this review, the number of papers, dealing with the subject of the study "Optimization of Shared transport and distribution strategies", is quantified per year in the time frame chosen between 2012 and the first trimester of 2022. This is shown in the Fig. 1 below.

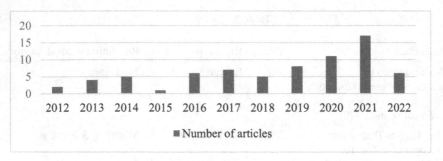

Fig. 1. Number of papers published in the last decade about the study subject

As it is seen, the number of works that deals with Collaboration transport and distribution strategies and their optimization has been growing over the last decade, which proves the importance of the subject between the researchers and the scholars' community. As per the type of the papers selected, it is remarked that a majority of 58 paper works tend to be research articles which is slightly less than 80% of the whole. While more than 20% of the remaining works are divided between: 8 conference papers, 7 review articles and one book chapter.

3.3 Categorization and Content Analysis

Since the statistical data analysis has been done, the next step of the systematic literature review needs to be conducted. It consists of a classification and categorization of the papers selected in Table 1. This categorization mainly distinguishes between papers based on the types of collaborations studied depending on the stakeholders engaging in, and the characteristics of those collaborations. In addition to that, another classification differentiates between these papers depending on the resolution techniques used in these studies.

3.3.1 Types of Collaboration

Business-to-business collaborations
Many researchers got interested in logistic collaborations between firms and collaborative supply chain, whether it being a vertical collaboration, a horizontal or a lateral one. Among those researchers, in this work [4], authors were interested in quantifying the benefits of implementing a collaborative strategy economically, socially and environmentally in integrated inventory, location and routing decisions. While in [67] the problem of selection of the optimal network design scheme for Collaborative Logistic Networks under uncertainty was studied. Others were interested in collaboration between firms operating in the food industry [42], where researchers quantified the effects of multi-stop transportation on food quality while taking in consideration the

unloading time, both internal and external temperature for the transportation vehicles, driving speed and cooling rate.

Public-private collaborations

Some researchers got rather interested in logistic collaboration forms between public and private organizations. This work [16] shed light on this kind of collaborations under an emergency context. Based on game theory and logistical concepts, a framework is developed for public-private emergency collaborations. The developed framework unraveled the constraints of partnership for each of the public organizations and the firms, and its effects on both, especially the reputational ones. While in [8], authors got interested in the collaboration that can be formed during disaster cases, between humanitarian organizations and logistics service providers. It identified the benefits of such collaboration and the challenges that it faces. It also shows how crucial and efficient of a collaboration it is in saving human lives in case of disasters.

City logistics collaborations

The majority of researches done on collaborative logistics focused on city logistic collaborations and last-mile freight transport. Researchers studied Courier, Express and Parcel (CEP) carriers engaging in horizontal collaboration, and developed a blockchain decision framework for last-mile distribution in the context of micro-hubs [31]. Others proposed a new architecture for the management of Cooperative Intelligent public Transport Systems (C-ITS) in Smart cities. An architecture that enhances collaboration between participants to the eco-system' mobility, that is constantly updated and that is sustainable [64].

3.3.2 Trending Resolution Techniques

Blockchain technology

Since its appearance in 2009, blockchain technology has been used in different field others than the environment where it was initially developed, that is cryptocurrency. It showed its benefits in the logistic and transport field for enabling safe tracking of goods and vehicles and many other advantages. It is now mainly used between firms committing in horizontal coalitions, as it keeps transparency of transactions and ensures that the shared informations between different stakeholders remain confidential supporting by then the trust among them. In this work [2], authors modeled a framework used in collaborative resource sharing context based on blockchain. Models were designed through UML diagrams and BPMN models, while smart contracts are to be verified and validated through an algorithm developed simultaneously. In this paper [54], authors explored the combination of Digital Twins and Blockchains as two highly useful technology in the Industry 4.0 era, and they proposed a framework applied for collaborative smart transportation.

Multi-agent-based frameworks

Another highly adopted resolution method consists of adopting multi-agent-based frameworks. In this work [39], researchers explore a new way for simulating combat along with military logistics effectiveness during times of peace. They propose a model for military logistics based on multi-agent model and profit-sharing reinforcement learning algorithm. Both the developed model and the proposed algorithm show their feasibility and validity through simulation experiments. The algorithm gives more accurate results for a high number of simulations, and the simulation results are proved to be highly consistent with actual war experiments according to military experts. Another work investigates the issue related to collaboration planning in logistics and proposes an agent-based approach embettering the management of collaborative logistics [37].

4 Discussion

Hence, after reporting the literature contents on the subject of "Optimization of collaborative transport and distribution strategies", here we state the research gaps and the topics of literature on the subject had remained scarce, and consequently identify. First, we remark that collaboration strategies, in the literature, mainly focus on city logistics and road freight transport. However, a combination of transport means under a collaborative strategy is yet to be addressed. Due to the importance given to the multimodal transport for people and goods, it is necessary to study its effect while combined with a horizontal or lateral collaborative strategy especially in the industrial context. Second, the majority of research articles studying organizations engaging in logistic collaborations opt for optimizing routing planning under constant variables of the environment, making the obtained solutions less accurate to reality. Thus, it is necessary to solve the routing planning related problems in the real context under changing variables related to road conditions and uncertain demand variation. A benchmark realized on the non-cooperative cases in the literature may be helpful since more researches have been elaborated in this context. Third, little the problem of finding the most stable coalition is studied. It is hard to maintain coalitions under nowadays context, which makes it hard for organizations depending on it. Consequently, it is so important to be able to identify the most suitable formation and configuration of collaboration to engage in, whether it is a large one or rather a sub-coalition. Fourth, among the existent forms of logistic collaboration in literature, almost in all of them, partners consider collaborations under their mutual objectives. Nevertheless, the effect of their different strategies and opposite interests on the collaborations formed should be studied thoroughly. Fifth, practically all of the recent research on logistic collaborations propose blockchain frameworks that are supposed to alleviate issues mainly regarding informations' privacy and confidentiality, to support trust among stakeholders. However, the developed framework architectures and models are yet to be technically applied in the industrial context. Sixth, the technological advancements have been proved to be theoretically very useful regarding resolution of issues faced among collaborating organizations, yet the existing literature has poorly explored if investments in acquiring those technologies is profitable on the medium and long terms. Since it is difficult to deal with consequential changes of digitalization, private organizations always prefer to invest on those that allow them the maximum benefits. It is crucial, then, to investigate their profitability on the long run. Lastly, public-private collaborations received less attention in the literature, which make this kind of collaborations a good research opportunity, since this collaboration can be very important in contexts of not only emergencies, but also in context of city logistics management, and others.

5 Conclusion

In this paper, we explored the existing literature dealing with "Optimization of collaborative transport and distribution strategies". Under a systematic literature review, we were able to collect data about the most studied topics and the recent advancements in this research field. Topics of city logistics and last mile urban freight collaborations are the most studied amongst others. Also, horizontal collaboration and lateral collaboration have gained much more attention in the last decade being the new forms of collaboration mitigated to. And while recent applied laws on firms taxed their carbon prints, most of logistic collaboration solutions were addressed under a green or sustainable perspective. Hence, the resolution methods consisted majorly on modeling multi-agent-based frameworks or modeling decision making blockchain frameworks. In the end, it is concluded that blockchain technology should not only be studied theoretically but rather be put into use in real industrial context to better know its effects. Also, logistic collaborations between public and private organizations should be more studied in the future.

Acknowledgments. This work has been supported by CNRST in the form of a Scholarship of Excellence.

References

1. Kembro, J., Wieland, A., Durach, C.F.: A new paradigm for systematic literature reviews in supply chain management. J. Supply Chain. Manag. **53**(4) (2017)
2. Agrawal, T.K., Angelis, J., Khilji, W.A., Kalaiarasan, R., Wiktorsson, M.: Demonstration of a blockchain-based framework using smart contracts for supply chain collaboration. Int. J. Prod. Res. (2022)
3. Allen, J., Bektas, T., Cherrett, T., Friday, A., McLeod, F., Piecyk, M., Piotrowska, M., Austwick, M.Z.: Enabling a freight traffic controller for collaborative multidrop urban logistics practical and theoretical challenges. Transp. Res. Rec.: J. Transp. Res. Board, 77–84 (2017)
4. Aloui, A., Mrabti, N., Hamani, N., Laurent, D.: Towards a collaborative and integrated optimization approach in sustainable freight transportation. IFAC PapersOnLine (2021)
5. Ascencio, L., Gonzalez-Ramirez, R., Bearzotti, L., Smith, N., Camacho-Vallejo, J.: A collaborative supply chain management system for a maritime port logistics Chain. J. Appl. Res. Technol., 444-458 (2014)
6. Aloui, A., Hamani, N., Derrouiche, R., Delahoche, L.: Systematic literature review on collaborative sustainable transportation: overview, analysis and perspectives. Transp. Res. Interdiscip. Perspect. **9** (2021)
7. Bates, O., Knowles, B., Friday, A.: Are people the key to enabling collaborative smart logistics? in *CHI'17* (2017)
8. Bealt, J., Fernandez Barrera, J.C., Mansouri, S.A.: Collaborative relationships between logistics service providers and humanitarian organizations during disaster relief operations. J. Hum. Logist. Supply Chain. Manag., 118–144 (2016)

9. Brekalo, L., Albers, S.: Effective logistics alliance design and management. Int. J. Phys. Distrib. & Logist. Manag. (2016)
10. Carvalho, M.S., souse Magalhaes, D., Varela, M.L., Sa, J.O., Gonçalves, I.: Definition of a collaborative working model to the logistics area using design for six sigma. Int. J. Qual. & Reliab. Manag., 465–475 (2016)
11. Cleophas, C., Cottrill, C., Ehmke, J.F., Tierney, K.: Collaborative urban transportation: recent advances in theory and practice. Eur. J. Oper. Res., 801–8016 (2018)
12. Chen, C., Sun, X., Ding, B.: A performance evaluation research on collaborative operation between logistics enterprise and manufacturing enterprise. Open Cybern. & Syst. J., 468–473 (2014)
13. Cricelli, L., Greco, M., Grimaldi, M.: An investigation on the effect of inter-organizational collaboration on reverse logistics. Int. J. Prod. Econ. (2021)
14. Cuervo, D.P., Vanovermeire, C., Sorensen, K.: Determining collaborative profits in coalitions formed by two partners with varying characteristics. Transp. Res. Part C, 171–184 (2016)
15. Konstantakopoulus, G.D., Gayialis, S.P., Kechagias, E.P., Papadopoulos, G.A., Tatsiopoulus, I.P.: An algorithmic approach for sustainable and collaborative logistics: a case study in Greece. Int. J. Inf. Manag. Data Insights (2021)
16. Diehlmann, F., Lüttenberg, M., Verdonck, L., Wiens, M., Zienau, A., Schultmann, F.: Public-private collaborations in emergency logistics: a framework based on logistical and game-theoretical concepts. Saf. Sci. (2021)
17. El bouazzaoui, Y., Abou elala, M., Kebe, S.A., Mimouni, F.: Environmental impact assessment in the case of pooling Moroccan Hydrocarbon supply chain resources. IEEE (2020)
18. Erkayman, B., Gundogar, E., Yilmaz, A.: An integrated fuzzy approach for strategic alliance partner selection in third-party logistics. Sci. World J. (2012)
19. Fadoi, E.: The "lateral transshipment" is a cooperative tool for optimizing the profitability of a distribution system. In: Innovation, Research and Development and Capital Evaluation (2022)
20. Fallahi, N., Hafezalkotob, A., Raissi, S., Ghezavati, V.: Cooperation and coopetition among retailers-third party logistics providers alliances under different risk behaviors, uncertainty demand and environmental considerations. Environ. Dev. Sustain. (2022)
21. Faure, L., Battaia, G., Guillaume, R., Vega-Mejia, C.A., Montoya-Torres, J.R., Munoz-Villamizar, A., Quintero-Araujo, C.L.: How to anticipate the level of activity of a sustainable collaborative network: the case of urban freight delivery through logistics platforms. IEEE (2013)
22. Ferreira, J.C., Martins, A.L., Pereira, R.: GoodsPooling: an intelligent approach for urban logistics. In: Ambient Intelligence—Software and Applications—8th International Symposium on Ambient Intelligence (2017)
23. Adams, F.G., Glenn Richey Jr., R., Autry, C.W., Morgan, T.R., Gabler, C.B.: Supply chain collaboration, integration, and relational technology: how complex operant resources increase performance outcomes. J. Bus. Logist., 299–317 (2014)
24. Gansterer, M., Hartl, R.F.: Centralized bundle generation in auction-based collaborative transportation. OR Spectrum **40**(3), 613–635 (2018). https://doi.org/10.1007/s00291-018-0516-4
25. Gansterer, M., Hartl, R.F.: Collaborative vehicle routing: a survey. Eur. J. Oper. Res. (2017)
26. Grinerud, K., Aarseth, W.K., Robertsen, R.: Leadership strategies, management decisions and safety culture in road transport organizations. Res. Transp. Bus. & Manag. (2021)
27. Groba, C., Sartal, A., Bergantiño, G.: Optimization of tuna fishing logistic routes through information sharing policies: a game theory-based approach. Marine Policy (2019)
28. Grote, M., Cherrett, T., Whittle, G., Tuck, N.: Environmental benefits from shared-fleet logistics: lessons from a public-private sector collaboration. Int. J. Logist. Res. Appl. (2021)

29. Guo, Y., Yu, J., Allaoui, H., Choudhary, A.: Lateral collaboration with cost-sharing in sustainable supply chain optimisation: a combinatorial framework. Transp. Res. Part E (2021)
30. Gutiérrez-Rubiano, D.F., Hincapié-Montes, J.A., Leon-Villalba, A.F.: Collaborative distribution: strategies to generate efficiencies in urban distribution - Results of two pilot tests in the city of Bogotá. *DYNA*, 42–51 (2019)
31. Hribernik, M., Zero, K., Kummer, S., Herold, D.M.: City logistics: towards a blockchain decision framework for collaborative parcel deliveries in micro-hubs. Transp. Res. Interdiscip. Perspect. (2020)
32. Ilie-Zudor, E., Ekart, A., Kemeny, Z., Buckingham, C., Welch, P., Monostori, L.: Advanced predictive-analysis-based decision support for collaborative logistics networks. Supply Chain. Manag.: Int. J., 369–388 (2015)
33. Irani, Z., Kamal, M.M., Sharif, A., Love, P.E.D.: Enabling sustainable energy futures: factors influencing green supply chain collaboration. Prod. Plan. & Control., 684–705 (2017)
34. Liu, J.C., Sheu, J.B., Li, D.F., Dai, Y.W.: Collaborative profit allocation schemes for logistics enterprise coalitions with incomplete information. Omega (2020)
35. Jerbi, A., Jribi, H., Aljuaid, A.M., Hachicha, W., Masmoudi, F.: Design of supply chain transportation pooling strategy for reducing CO_2 emissions using a simulation based methodology: a case study. Sustainability (2022)
36. Jung, V., Peeters, M., Vredeveld, T.: Disagreement on the gain sharing method in supply chain collaborations. Russ. Manag. J. (2018)
37. Khayyat, M., Awasthi, A.: An intelligent multi-agent based model for collaborative logistics systems. Transp. Res. Procedia, 325–338 (2016)
38. Lezhnina, E.A., Balykina, Y.E.: Cooperation between sea ports and carriers in the logistics chain. J. Mar. Sci. Eng. (2021)
39. Li, X., Pu, W., Zhao, X.: Towards learning behavior modeling of military logistics agent utilizing profit sharing reinforcement learning algorithm, Appl. Soft Comput. (2021)
40. Liu, C., Li, X., Liu, Q.: Analysis of an evolutionary game of pallet pooling with participation of third-party platform. PLoS ONE (2021)
41. Liu, N., Cheng, Y.: Allocating cost to freight carriers in horizontal logistic collaborative transportation planning on leading company perspective. Math. Probl. Eng. (2020)
42. Stellingwerf, H.M., Groeneveld, L.H.C., Laporte, G., Kanellopoulos, A., Bloemhof, J.M., Behdani, B.: The quality-driven vehicle routing problem: Model and application to a case of cooperative logistics. Int. J. Prod. Econ. (2020)
43. Martin, N., Verdonck, L., Caris, A., Depaire, B.: Horizontal collaboration in logistics: decision framework and typology. Oper. Manag. Res. 11(1–2), 32–50 (2018). https://doi.org/10.1007/s12063-018-0131-1
44. Memon, M.A., Archimede, B.: A multi-agent distributed framework for collaborative transportation planning. IFAC (2013)
45. Moghaddam, M., Nof, S.Y.: Combined demand and capacity sharing with best matching decisions in enterprise collaboration. Int. J. Prod. Econ., 93–109 (2013)
46. Monique Stinson, A.M.: Introducing CRISTAL: a model of collaborative, informed, strategic trade agents with logistics. Transp. Res. Interdiscip. Perspect. (2022)
47. Mrad, M., Bamatraf, K., Alkahtani, M., Hidri, L.: Genetic algorithm based on Clark & Wright's savings algorithm for reducing the transportation cost in a pooled logistic system. Int. Conf. Ind. Eng. Oper. Manag. (2021)
48. Neghabadi, P.D., Espinouse, M.-L., Lionet, E.: Impact of operational constraints in city logistics pooling efficiency. Int. J. Logist. Res. Appl. (2021)
49. Osicka, O., Guajardo, M., Jörnsten, K.: Cooperation of customers in traveling salesman problems with profits. Optim. Lett. 14(5), 1219–1233 (2019). https://doi.org/10.1007/s11590-019-01429-6

50. Osicka, O., Guajardo, M., van Oost, T.: Cooperative game-theoretic features of cost sharing in location-routing. Int. Trans. Oper. Res., 1–27 (2019)
51. Padilla Tinoco, S.V., Creemers, S., Boute, R.N.: Collaborative shipping under different cost-sharing agreements. Eur. J. Oper. Res., 827–837 (2017)
52. Palmieri, A., Pomponi, F., Russo, A.: A triple-win scenario for horizontal collaboration in logistics: determining enabling and key success factors. Bus. Strat. Environ. (2019)
53. Pan, S., Trentesaux, D., Ballot, E., Huang, G.Q.: Horizontal collaborative transport: survey of solutions and practical implementation issues. Int. J. Prod. Res. (2019)
54. Sahal, R., Alsamhi, S.H., Brown, K.N., O'Shea, D., McCarthy, C., Guizani, M.: Blockchain-empowered digital twins collaboration: smart transportation use case. Machines (2021)
55. Santos, M.J., Martins, S., Amorim, P., Almada-Lobo, B.: A green lateral collaborative problem under different transportation strategies and profit allocation methods. J. Clean. Prod. (2020)
56. Sembiring, N., Tambunan, M.M., Ginting, E.: Collaboration of sustainability and digital supply chain management of achieving a successful company. In: IOP Conference Series: Materials Science and Engineering (2020)
57. Shi, Y., Han, Q., Shen, W., Wang, X.: A multi-layer collaboration framework for industrial parks with 5G vehicle-to-everything networks. Engineering (2020)
58. Sirajuddin, T. Y. Zagloel and Sunaryo: Effect of strategic alliance based on port character-istic and integrated global supply chain for enhancing industrial port performance. *Cogent Business & Management* (2019)
59. Suzuki, Y., Lu, S.-H.: Economies of product diversity in collaborative logistics. J. Bus. Logist., 1–15 (2017)
60. Switala, M.: Enterprises' readiness to establish and develop collaboration in the area of logistics. LogForum, 215–224 (2016)
61. Tatarczak, A.: A decision making support system in logistics cooperation using a modified VIKOR method under an intuituinistic Fuzzy environment. In: LogForum (2020)
62. Torres-Ramos, A.F., Labadie, N., Velasco, N., Montoya-Torres, J.R.: A GRASPxILS for the shared customer collaboration vehicle routing problem. In: IFAC (2019)
63. Verdonck, L., Caris, A., Ramaekers, K., Janssens, G.K.: Collaborative logistics from the perspective of road transportation companies. Transp. Rev., 700–719 (2013)
64. Visan, M., Negrea, S.L., Mone, F.: Towards intelligent public transport systems in smart cities; collaborative decisions to be made. Procedia Comput. Sci., 1221–1228 (2022)
65. Wen, M., Larsen, R., Ropke, S., Petersen, H.L., Madsen, O.B.G.: Centralised horizontal cooperation and profit sharing in a shipping pool. J. Oper. Res. Soc. (2018)
66. Wu, C.-H., Tsang, Y.-P., Lee, C.K.-m., Ching, W.-k.: A blockchain-IoT platform for the smart pallet pooling management. MDPI (2021)
67. Xu, X.-F., Hao, J., Deng, Y.-R., Wang, Y.: Design optimization of resource combination for collaborative logistics network under uncertainty. Appl. Soft Comput., 684–691 (2017)
68. Xu, X., He, Y., Ji, Q.: Collaborative logistics network: a new business mode in the platform economy. Int. J. Logist. Res. Appl. (2021)
69. Zhang, M.-H., Gao, X.-L., Zhou, X.-Y., Yang, J.: An intelligent scheduling strategy of collaborative logistics for mass customization. Procedia Eng., 2621–2626 (2012)
70. Zheng, W., Wang, Z., Sun, L.: Collaborative vehicle routing problem in the urban ring logistics network under the COVID-19 epidemic. Math. Probl. Eng. (2021)
71. de Souza, R., Goh, M., Lau, H.-C., Ng, W.-S., Tan, P.-S.: Collaborative urban logistics – synchronizing the last mile. Procedia Soc. Behav. Sci., 422–431 (2014)
72. Özener, O.Ö.: Developing a collaborative planning framework for sustainable transportation. Math. Probl. Eng. (2014)
73. Ahlaqqach, M., Benhra, J., Mouatassim, S., Lamrani, S.: Closed loop location routing supply chain network design in the end of life pharmaceutical products. Supply Chain Forum (2020)
74. Ahlaqqach, M., Benhra, J., Moatassim, S., Lamrani, S.: Hybridization of game theory and ridesharing to optimize reverse logistics of healthcare textiles. Mater. Sci. Eng. (2020)

Comparative Analysis of Three-Phase Photovoltaic Inverters Control Techniques

Oussama Id Bouhouch[1,2](✉), Nabila Rabbah[1], Hicham Oufettoul[2,3], Aboubakr Benazzou[2], Ibtihal Ait Abdelmoula[2], and Mourad Zegrari[1]

[1] Laboratory of Complex Cyber Physical Systems (LCCPS),
The National Higher School of Arts and Crafts (ENSAM), Hassan II University, 20000 Casablanca, Morocco
idbouhouch.oussama@ensam-casa.ma
[2] Green Energy Park, Km 2 Route Régionale R206, 43150 Benguerir, Morocco
[3] Mohammadia School of Engineers, Mohammed V University, 10080 Rabat, Morocco

Abstract. The energy management and distribution will be complicated by upgrading the consecutive components in the future electrical grid. Therefore, several mechanisms amongst the inverter achieve the flexible injection of energy. The current framework presents a comparative analysis of the most frequently used industrial inverter controllers. In this context. Specifically, the Sinusoidal Pulse Width Modulation approach (SPWM), Third Harmonic Injection Pulse Width Modulation (THIPWM), and Space Vector Pulse Width Modulation approach (SVPWM) strive to determine the optimum strategy regarding harmonic components, distortion factors, and their effect on power management flow and quality. Furthermore, various inverter control strategies are described in the literature under normal operating circumstances. Therefore, this paper aims to shed new light on the realistic comparison of inverter control under typical and shadow conditions using advanced fuzzy logic Maximum Power Point Tracking (MPPT) and grey wolf optimizer techniques specified in test scenarios. Finally, multiple indicators are combined to conclude that the Space Vector Pulse Width Modulation (SVPWM) technique is a preferable inverter control approach that should be emphasized when designing solar inverters.

Keywords: Photovoltaic array · Grid · MPPT · Inverter · Converter · SPWM · SVPWM · THIPWM · Shadowing effect

1 Introduction

Over the last few decades, renewable energy research and development have emerged as a global trend due to the progressive depletion of fossil fuels and the constant stress of environmental pollution[1, 2]. Therefore, renewable energies, particularly the photovoltaic (PV) system, appear as the alternative and the most appropriate solution to electricity production due to several factors, such as the reduced cost of the photovoltaic modules [3]. The interconnection of photovoltaic systems to the grid has recently developed to satisfy the needs of certain electrical loads supplied solely by AC voltage and the rising usage of clean, carbon-free energy [4]. The power converters have figured out a vital role in power integration into the electrical grid and operating in many applications. Furthermore, power electronics have brought degrees of freedom, allowing the development of more complex control algorithms and improving photovoltaic performance [5]. Single-phase inverters are widely applied in household applications, including PV technology. They may operate alone or in conjunction with the grid. Switching inverters are divided into two major types: square wave and pulse width modulation (PWM) inverters. However, the three-level voltage inverters are increasingly being used for a wide range of high-power applications, including energy injection and high voltage motor drives [6]. In the literature, numerous papers mentioned that the three-phase topologies have a longer lifespan than single-phase inverters. Due to the lack of an electrolytic capacitor and the decreased stress and scaling of semiconductors and magnetic components, single-phase topologies have a longer life, higher efficiency, smaller size, and lower prices [6]. As suggested for this investigation, various research papers have been published on improving inverter controls. However, one of such papers is that of Matale et al. which implements an application-specific integrated circuit for discrete-time current control and SVPWM with a five-segment asymmetric switching scheme for an AC motor control application [7]. Hence the operating findings demonstrate a 33% reduction in inverter switching times and power loss compared to the conventional SVPWM. A similar investigation to the present inquiry has been published, where the comparisons of SPWM, THIPWM, and PDPWM are undertaken. The author discovered that the PDPWM approach exhibits superior power quality and a low THD index as compared to SPWM and THIPWM [8]. Another exciting trend being pursued by current research is the practicality of inverters and converters to improve microgrid management, including coupling renewable energy to the grid and upgrading the system for grid synchronization instead of the conventional phase-locked loop (PLL). In the same context, Shameem Ahmad et al. develop a model for the PV inverter of a grid-connected AC microgrid without a phase-locked loop based on the direct power control approach and fuzzy logic algorithm [5]. Finally, the crucial performance requirements for inverters that link solar modules to the electrical grid include dependability, efficiency, size, and cost. Subsequently, they may significantly impact the yearly electrical energy generation and, consequently, the financial viability of a system. The present paper aims to develop a comparative analysis of several popular inverter control algorithms, in this context. The applied system relies on maximum global power point extraction strategies to preserve the high photovoltaic module efficiency, making the comparative analysis considerably meaningful.

Naturally, the first step is to investigate the effectiveness of each algorithm in which the photovoltaic system operates in typical and mismatched scenarios. The novelty of this research may be considered in terms of the usual operation, and mismatch condition of the three simulated methodologies. Hence, the current paper is briefly organized as follows:

- The second section covers typologies and the three-phase inverter model
- The third section briefly describes the principle of each technique.
- The fourth part delves further into the four control methods before examining the acquired outcomes by modeling the solar array in two different operation scenarios.

Finally, a well-defined conclusion on the strengths and weaknesses of each approach, indicating potential perspectives for further research.

2 Three Phase Inverter Topologies

An inverter is a static power electronics converter that converts directly to alternating current. As inverters control the velocity of alternating current machines, it produces alternating voltages and currents of variable frequency and amplitude, in addition to supplying fixed frequency and amplitude alternating voltages and currents. Throughout the power outage case, the inverter is thus required to maintain the continuity of the emergency power supply. There are several inverter topologies, each of which corresponds to a specific application or allows for a specific level of performance. The inverter topologies may be roughly categorized into types: three-Phase three-wire inverter topology, three-Phase four-wire inverter topologies, three-phase multi-string Inverter, multilevel Inverter, three-phase Inverter with stabilizing, and three-phase parallel Inverter. Figures 1, 2, and 3 depict the aforementioned inverter topologies. Furthermore, the literature includes multiple architectures of three-phase grid-connected inverters for photovoltaic applications, specifically voltage-source inverters, current-source inverters, and Z-source inverters, as outlined in the following ref. Voltage source inverters are frequently applied in uninterruptible power supplies to interconnect photovoltaic generators to the AC power grid. As long as the output voltage is always lower than the input voltage. In the current source inverter, the input maintains a constant current source regardless of the load. While the voltage increases to reach the maximum voltage level, otherwise the inverter is out of control. Regarding dependability, the incapacity of voltage source inverters and current source inverters to operate as buck-boost converters and their susceptibility to electromagnetic interference noise may be circumvented by using a Z-source inverter with two inductors and two capacitors.

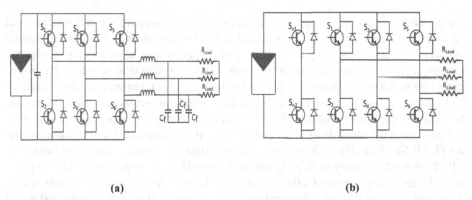

(a)   **(b)**

Fig. 1. (a) Three-phase three-wires inverter topology, and (b) Three phase four legs inverter topology [9]

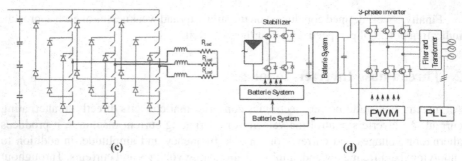

Fig. 2. (c) Three-phase five-level topology of a diode clamped multilevel inverter, (d) Three-phase inverter with stabilizer and transformer topology [9]

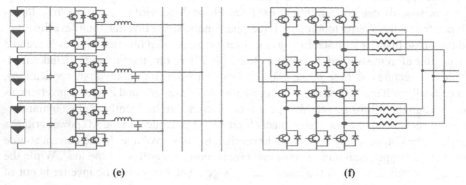

Fig. 3. (e) Three-phase four-wires multi-string inverter topology, (f) Parallel Connection of Two Three-Phase Inverters [9]

3   Inverter Controllers Principle

The primary purpose of inverter control techniques is to improve the performance and the electrical signal quality generated by PV solar farms under normal and abnormal operating conditions such as partial shading effect. Therefore, selecting the appropriate interconnection architecture and inverter type is a critical step in establishing PV power plants. Specifically, the power supply and voltage margin requirements, the variety of PV systems (AC or DC), and the load's category (single-phase, three-phase). Therefore, the simulation test is evaluated under two distinct scenarios previously mentioned (normal and anomaly conditions): The inverter circuit was simulated and designed using MATLAB Simulink. For each situation, the experiment is conducted in three steps. The MPPT approaches (fuzzy logic and Grey wolf optimizer) are implemented [10, 11], followed by the configuration of a three-phase inverter, and then involves the identification of the optimal filter. The fig.4 demonstrates the implementation of the blocks performed on the MATLAB software. In addition, a brief description of the proposed approaches is provided.

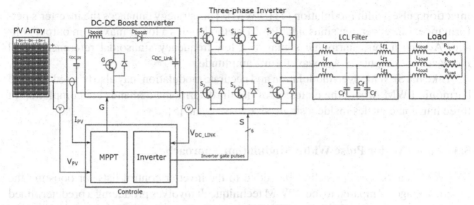

Fig. 4. Synoptic diagram of the PV system stages

3.1 Sinusoidal Pulse Width Modulation Approach

The most common method for operating single-phase inverters, especially three-phase inverters, is sinusoidal pulse width modulation. To calculate the closing and opening timings of switches in real-time, this command relies on the intersections of a sinusoidal modulating wave and a usually triangular carrier wave. The modulating wave frequency is substantially higher than the carrier wave frequency.

The SPWM technique has two features: the modulation index, which is defined as the ratio of the carrier wave and modulating wave frequencies, and the adjustment coefficient, which is defined as the ratio of the triangular carrier wave and modulation wave amplitudes[12]. The SPWM control concept is shown in Fig. 5

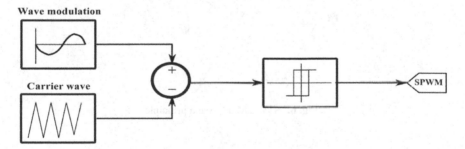

Fig. 5. Block schematic of the inverter control SPWM

3.2 Third Harmonic Injection Pulse Width Modulation Approach

Sinusoidal PWM is simple to comprehend and implement. Nevertheless, it cannot fully utilize the DC bus power source. This issue has led to the creation of a third harmonic injection pulse-width modulation (THIPWM). This strategy enhances the inverter's performance. Moreover, the sinusoidal PWM method yields a lower maximum output voltage. Adding a third harmonic signal to a low-frequency sinusoidal reference signal increases the output voltage waveform's amplitude.

Like the SPWM, over-modulation and accurate modulation may also be used for third harmonic PWM, where the inclusion of the third harmonic demands the completion of three harmonic cycles inside a single sine wave cycle [5].

3.3   Space Vector Pulse Width Modulation Approach

SVPWM is another approach to be added to the inverter control lists for boosting the output voltage, compared to the SPWM technique. It involves producing a predetermined inverter state sequence. Utilizing the fact that a vector may represent the three voltages of a three-phase zero-sum system, the property of this methodology is explored to interface with modern AC machine controllers. Hence the SVPWM principle consists of the reconstruction of the reference voltage vector based on eight voltage vectors. Each vector corresponds to a state combination of the three-phase voltage inverter switches. It examines the three-phase system globally and performs a Concordia transform to return to the (Vi, Vj) plane[13]. The three-phase system of voltages to be formed during the current sampling period may thus be represented as a single vector, as seen in Fig. 6.

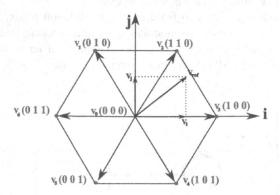

Fig. 6. SVPWM approach principle

3.4   PV Inverter Simulation with MATLAB Software

The photovoltaic field is tested on the first test bench under normal weather conditions, where the I-V curve exhibits a single maximum power point. The second testbed would also address the subjecting of a PV array to a non-uniform irradiance distribution, leading to multiple peaks on the system's I-V curve. In the MPPT block, the approaches adopted in this research are the fuzzy logic for the first test and the grey wolf optimizer for the shading case to efficiently extract the PV GMPPT [1]. Finally, this part includes the simulation results related to the MATLAB model blocks.

3.4.1 PV System Structure Under Normal Conditions

This test bench is mainly composed of a photovoltaic array of six strings, each containing 12 solar panels connected in series, with a total output power of 20 kW, while the current and voltage are equal to 47 A and 432 V, respectively. The Table 1 contains a listing of the panel's properties. The photovoltaic arrays are connected through a boost converter to the inverter and interfaced with an MPPT block operating according to a fuzzy logic approach whose efficiency and resilience have been proven in the literature[10]. The system is then connected to the load through a high-precision LCL filter (see Fig. 7).

Table 1. Characteristics of the PV panel at the STC

Characteristics	Values
Nominal Power P_{max}	285 W
η Efficiency	17.4%
V_{mpp} Voltage At Maximum Power Point	36.25 V
I_{mpp} Current At Maximum Power Point	7.86 A
V_{oc} Open Circuit Voltage	44.5 V
I_{SC} Short circuit current	8.49 A
Number of Cells	36

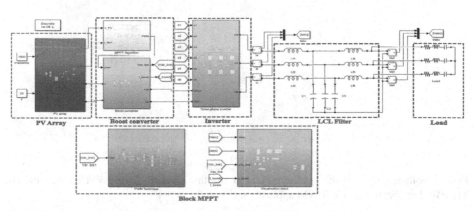

Fig. 7. Photovoltaic system simulation under MATLAB Software for normal operation scenario

3.4.2 PV System Structure Under Partial Shading Conditions

The testbed adopted in this subsection consists of four series of interconnecting solar panels subjected to distinct irradiance levels to mimic the shading presence. The overall power output of the system is 1.1 kW under standard test conditions. The grey wolf optimization approach is applied to the global maximum power point tracking in the following scenario. The GWO approach is well-known for its effectiveness and is based on stochastic search [14]. The remainder of the system description is identical to the previous pattern as shown in Fig. 8.

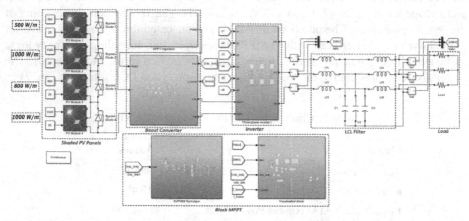

Fig. 8. Photovoltaic system simulation under MATLAB Software for shaded operation scenario

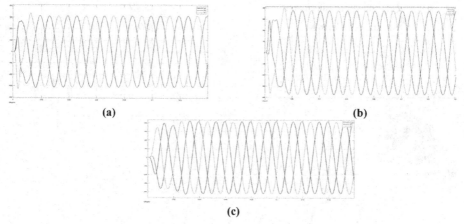

Fig. 9. Voltage curves at the load terminals of the first scenario (a) SPWM application, (b) THIPWM application, (c) SVPWM application

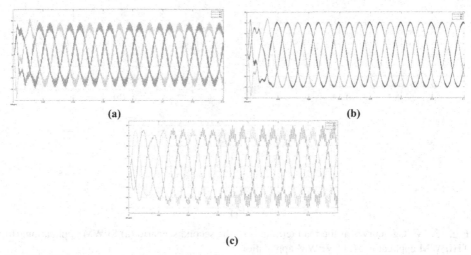

Fig. 10. Current curves at the load terminals of the first scenario (a) SPWM application, (b) THIPWM application, (c) SVPWM application

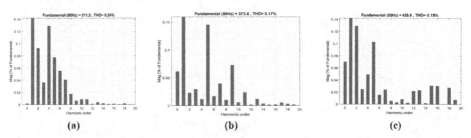

Fig. 11. Voltage harmonic specter of the first scenario (a) SPWM application, (b) THIPWM application, (c) SVPWM application

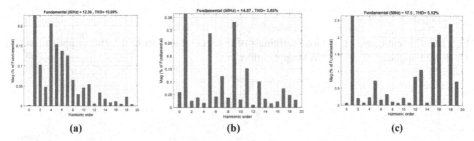

Fig. 12. Current harmonic specter of the first scenario (a) SPWM application, (b) THIPWM application, (c) SVPWM application

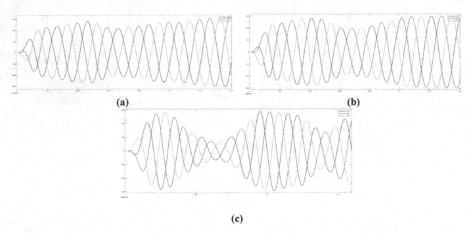

(a)   (b)

(c)

Fig. 13. Voltage curves at the load terminals of the second scenario (a) SPWM application, (b) THIPWM application, (c) SVPWM application

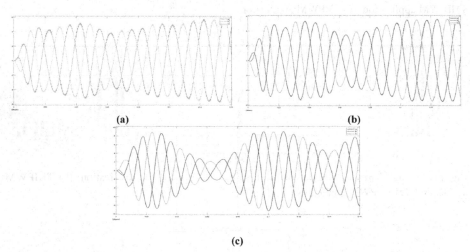

(a)   (b)

(c)

Fig. 14. Current curves at the load terminals of the second scenario (a) SPWM application, (b) THIPWM application, (c) SVPWM application

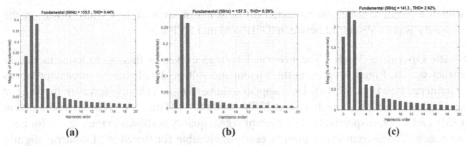

Fig. 15. Voltage harmonic specter of the second scenario (a) SPWM application, (b) THIPWM application, (c) SVPWM application

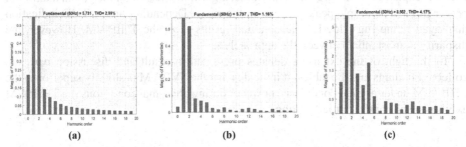

Fig. 16. Current harmonic specter of the second scenario (a) SPWM application, (b) THIPWM application, (c) SVPWM application

4 Result and Discussion

Numerous inverter control approaches have been developed and proven effective in the literature. Thus, the subsequent research focuses on the industry's three most prevalent inverter control approaches. The recommended approach assessed the electrical signal quality while testing both testbed scenarios' output current and voltage, besides using critical performance indicators, particularly THD, a suitable indication for the approach examination. The extensive results of each testing model are further presented, including signal clearness with visualization of the voltage and current curves of each control implementation. Furthermore, the two tables at the end of the section contain numerical values for the performance indicators (as shown in Tables 2–3 in the appendix).

Normal Operating Mode: The voltage curves observed in the Fig. 9, for the three approaches considered, appear to have a smooth shape. However, the voltage level favors SVPWM, which is assessed at 428 V, whereas SPWM and THIPDW are evaluated at 311V and 374V, respectively. The current signal quality is plotted in the Fig. 10 for each approach. The current fluctuation is easily noticeable for the SPWM control, slightly fluctuating for the two techniques, THIPWM and SVPWM. In the early milliseconds, voltage and current signals indicate only a minor disturbance and a delay in stabilizing, which is likely attributed to the MPPT technique involved in maximum power point extraction. According to the THD indication visible in the Figs. 11, 12, that is evaluated after the response time, the collected findings are in favor of THIPWM, however, the disparity is not substantial between THIPWM and SVPWM.

Shade Operating Mode: The observed voltage curves in this operational mode are attractive. The Figures represent the current and voltage details for the three approaches considered (see Figs. 13, 14). They appear to have a smooth shape. However, the voltage level favors THIPWM, evaluated at 157V, while SPWM and SVPWM are estimated at 155V and 141V, respectively. The current signal quality is shown in the Fig. 14 for each approach. The current fluctuation is easily noticeable for the SPWM control, slightly fluctuating for both techniques, THIPWM and SVPWM. Within the first milliseconds, the voltage and current signals exhibit a minor disturbance and a significant time delay, which is explained by the grey wolf optimizer algorithm's search for the global maximum power point, as multiple peaks appear on the curve. Depending on the THD indication displayed in the Figs. 15, 16, the obtained results favor the THIPWM. However, the disparity is substantial between the approaches.

In the light of the extensive debates presented in result and discussion part, the collected findings and the tables, it indicates that the SVPWM is slightly superior to the THIPWM under normal conditions, however during abnormal conditions the THIPWM exhibits a substantial outperforming.

5 Conclusion

In the context of an efficient smart grid, this contribution provides a comprehensive MAT-LAB simulation on the evaluation and performance assessment of several approaches, including SPWM, THIPWM, and SVPWM, involving a three-phase voltage source inverter under normal and mismatch conditions. Furthermore, it considers total harmonic distortion analysis as a critical performance indicator. Finally, a thorough analysis revealed that the THIPWM approach application in abnormal scenarios, while the SVPWM strategy outperformed the further control approaches under normal circumstances. As a result, this paper recommends that scholars adopt the earlier approaches while respecting their application to particular scenarios (standard and mismatch situations). As a perspective of further research, the conventional inverter requires efficient control. Consequently, a novel digital twin inverter will be constructed, as well as an inverter that might switch among several PWM techniques following the special events.

Funding. This framework is part of the Green Energy Park, and EDF funded Smart O&M project. The authors would also like to acknowledge the Green Energy Park research platform for providing excellent working circumstances, as well as access to the use of all needed measuring and testing equipment.

Appendix

Table 2. Performance indicators of the PWM techniques studied under normal conditions.

PWM techniques Indicators	SPWM	THIPWM	SVPWM
THD of Voltage	0.24%	0.17%	0.19%
THD of Current	10.99%	3.85%	5.12%
Voltage amplitude	311 V	373.8 V	428.6 V
Current amplitude	12.39 A	14.87 A	17.5 A

Table 3. Performance indicators of PWM techniques studied under partial shading conditions.

PWM techniques Indicators	SPWM	THIPWM	SVPWM
THD of Voltage	0.44%	0.28%	2.62%
THD of Current	2.99%	1.16%	4.17%
Voltage amplitude	155.5 V	157.5 V	141.3 V
Current amplitude	5.731 A	5.797 A	8.98 A

References

1. Oufettoul, H., Motahhir, S., Aniba, G., Masud, M., AlZain, M.: Improved TCT topology for shaded photovoltaic arrays. Energy Rep. **8**, 5943–5956 (2022). https://doi.org/10.1016/j.egyr.2022.04.042
2. Perera, F.: Pollution from fossil-fuel combustion is the leading environmental threat to global pediatric health and equity: solutions exist. Int. J. Environ. Res. Public Health **15**, 16 (2018). https://doi.org/10.3390/ijerph15010016
3. Cengiz, M.S., Mamiş, M.S.: Price-efficiency relationship for photovoltaic systems on a global basis. Int. J. Photoenergy **2015**, e256101 (2015). https://doi.org/10.1155/2015/256101
4. El Chaar, L.: Chapter 3 - photovoltaic system conversion. In: Rashid, M.H. (ed.) Alternative Energy in Power Electronics, pp. 155–175. Butterworth-Heinemann, Boston (2011)

5. Chaturvedi, L., Yadav, D.K., Pancholi, G.: Comparison of SPWM, THIPWM and PDPWM technique based voltage source inverters for application in renewable energy. J. Green Eng. (2017) https://doi.org/10.13052/JGE1904-4720.7125

6. Gulyaev, A., Fokin, D., Ten, E., Vlasyevsky, V.: PWM algorithms synthesis. Procedia Eng. **165**, 1529–1535 (2016). https://doi.org/10.1016/j.proeng.2016.11.889

7. Matale, N., Thakre, M., Shriwastava, R.: A simplified SVPWM method for cascaded multi-level inverters. J Phys. Conf. Ser. **2062**, 012032 (2021). https://doi.org/10.1088/1742-6596/2062/1/012032

8. Tsai, M.-F., Tseng, C., Cheng, P.: Implementation of an FPGA-based current control and SVPWM ASIC with asymmetric five-segment switching scheme for AC motor drives. Energies (2021). https://doi.org/10.3390/EN14051462

9. Akoro, E., Faye, M.E., Sene, M., Tevi, G., jean, P., Maiga, A.S.: Differents topologies of three-phase grid connected inverter for photovoltaic systems, a review. Sci. Appliquées Ing **2**, 33–41 (2018)

10. Oufettoul, H., Aniba, G., Motahhir, S.: MPPT techniques investigation in photovoltaic system. In: 2021 9th International Renewable and Sustainable Energy Conference (IRSEC), pp. 1–7 (2021)

11. Davoodkhani, F., Nowdeh, S.A., Abdelaziz, A., Mansoori, S., Nasri, S., Alijani, M.: A new hybrid method based on gray wolf optimizer-crow search algorithm for maximum power point tracking of photovoltaic energy system. In: Modern Maximum Power Point Tracking Techniques Photovoltaic Energy Systems. Springer, Cham (2019) https://doi.org/10.1007/978-3-030-05578-3_16

12. Rath, D., Kar, S., Patra, A.K.: Harmonic distortion assessment in the single-phase photovoltaic (PV) system based on SPWM technique. Arab. J. Sci. Eng. **46**(10), 9601–9615 (2021). https://doi.org/10.1007/s13369-021-05437-6

13. Gnanasaravanan, A., Jeyaprakash, A., Gnanachandran, J.J., Annapandi, A., Ravi, A., Selvakumar, S.: Improved series Z source inverter for PV system using SVPWM technique. In: 2021 5th International Conference Trends in Electronics Informatics. ICOEI (2021). https://doi.org/10.1109/ICOEI51242.2021.9453059

14. Keskin, V., Khalejan, S.H.P.R., Çikla, R.: Investigation of the shading effect on the performance of a grid-connected PV Plant in Samsun/Turkey. J. Polytech (2020). https://doi.org/10.2339/politeknik.701525

Author Index

Printed in the United States
by Baker & Taylor Publisher Services

Printed in the United States
by Baker & Taylor Publisher Services